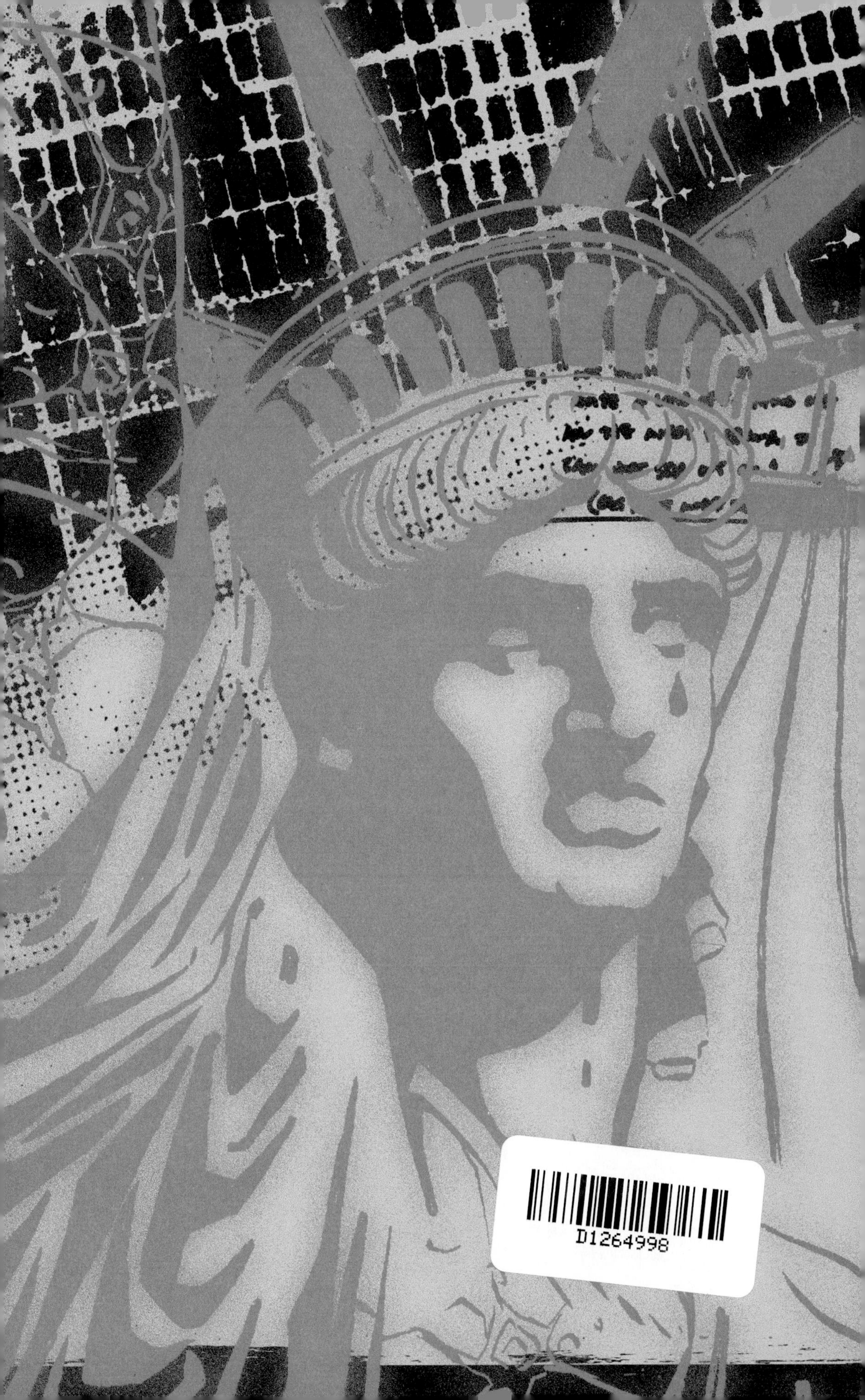

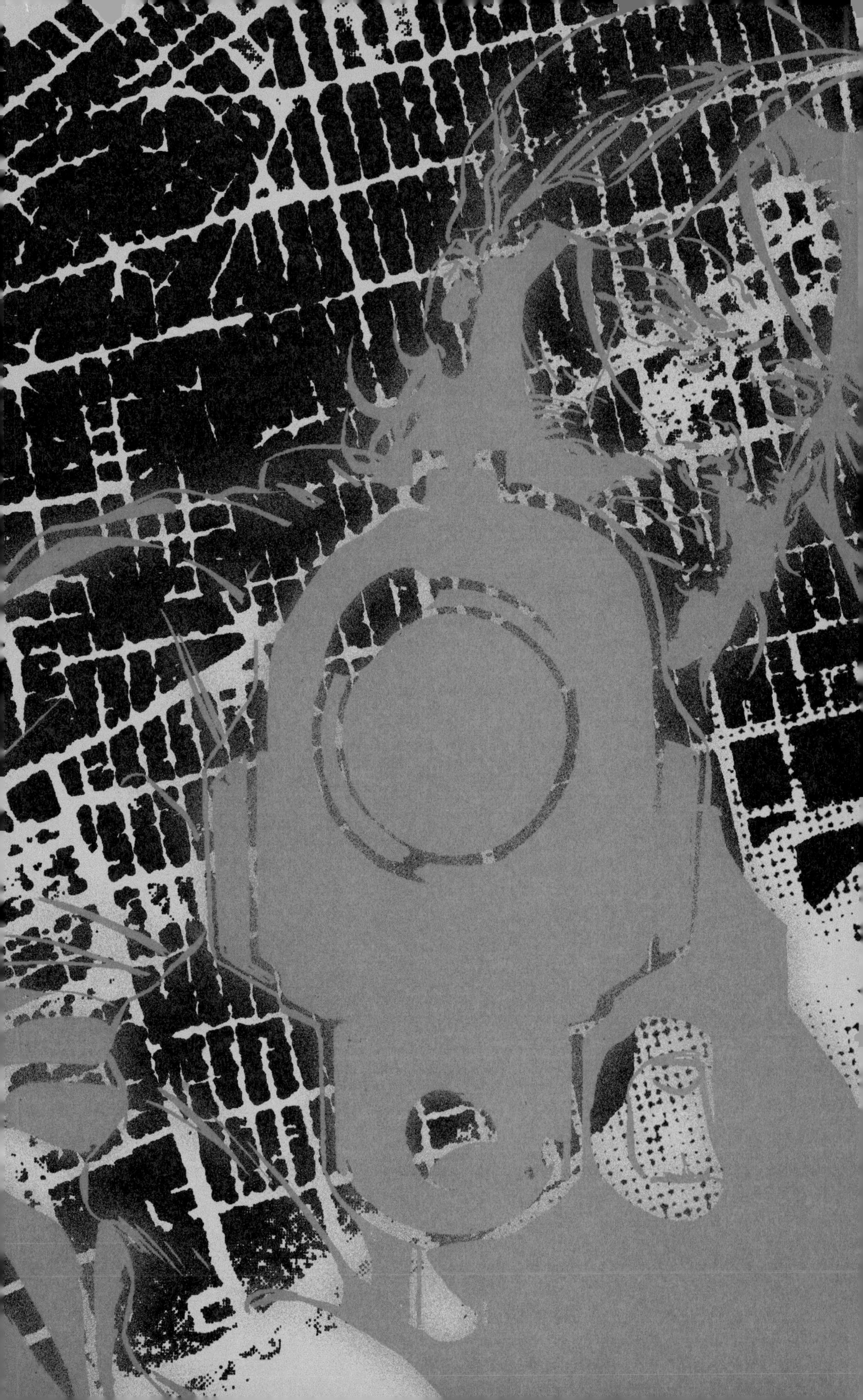

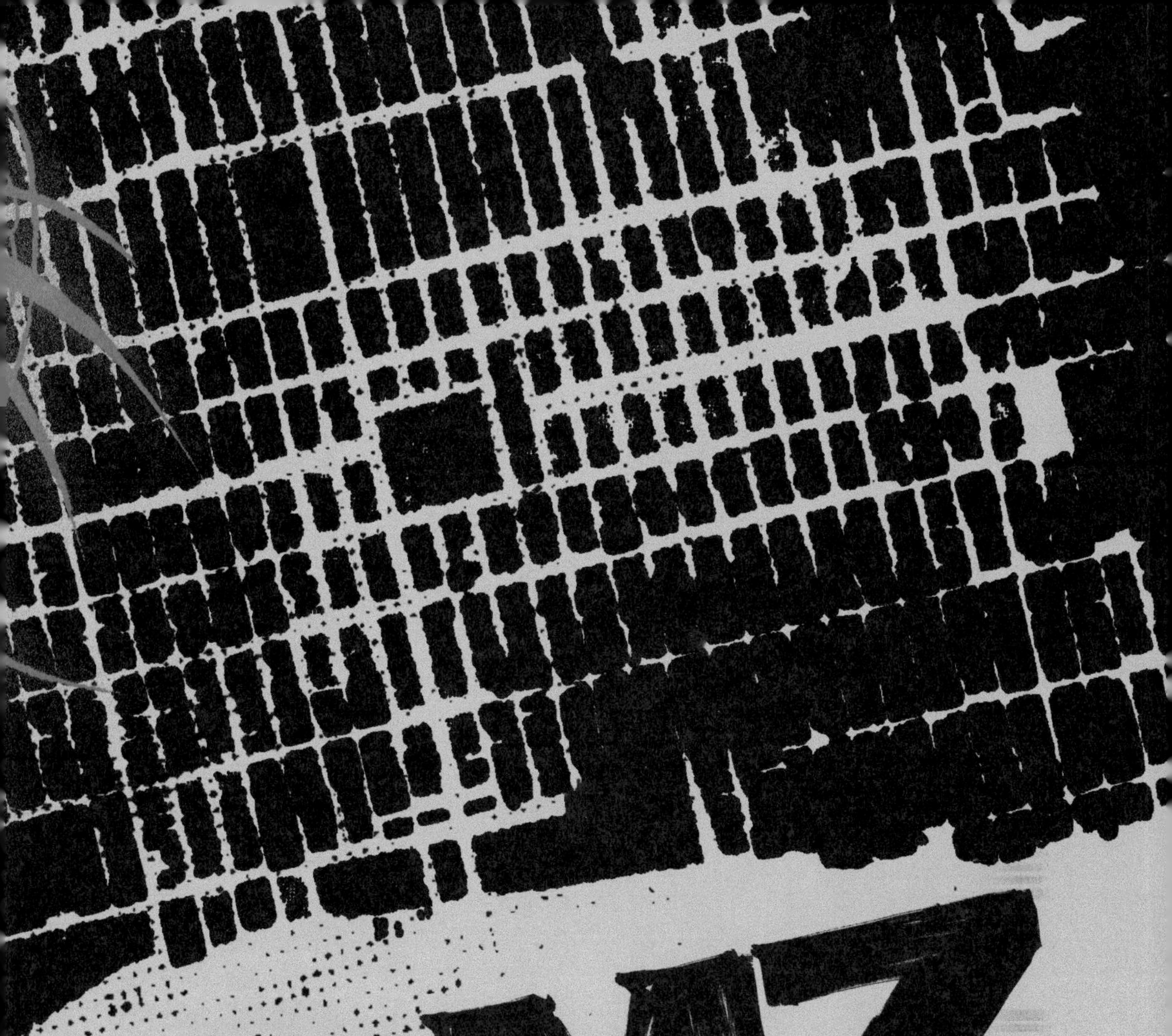

DMZ

BOOK THREE

BRIAN WOOD WRITER

RICCARDO BURCHIELLI KRISTIAN DONALDSON RYAN KELLY NIKKI COOK ARTISTS

JEROMY COX COLORIST

JARED K. FLETCHER LETTERER

BRIAN WOOD COVER ARTIST

DMZ CREATED BY BRIAN WOOD AND RICCARDO BURCHIELLI

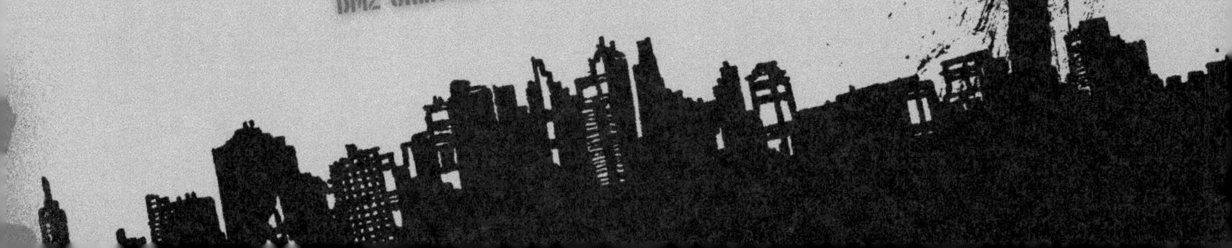

WILL DENNIS Editor – Original Series
MARK DOYLE Associate Editor – Original Series
CASEY SEIJAS Assistant Editor – Original Series
JAMIE RICH Group Editor – Vertigo Comics
JEB WOODARD Group Editor – Collected Editions
STEVE COOK Design Director – Books
LOUIS PRANDI Publication Design

DMZ logo designed by Brian Wood.

DMZ BOOK 3 Published by DC Comics. Compilation and all new material Copyright © 2017 Brian Wood and Riccardo Burchielli. All Rights Reserved. Originally published in single magazine form as DMZ 29-44 © 2008, 2009 Brian Wood and Riccardo Burchielli. All Rights Reserved. All characters, their distinctive likenesses and related elements featured in this publication are trademarks of DC Comics. VERTIGO is a trademark of DC Comics. The stories, characters and incidents featured in this publication are entirely fictional. DC Comics does not read or accept unsolicited ideas, stories or artwork. DC Comics, 2900 West Alameda Ave., Burbank, CA 91505
Printed in the USA. First Printing.
ISBN: 978-1-4012-6843-5

Library of Congress Cataloging-in-Publication Data

Wood, Brian, 1972- author.
  DMZ book three / Brian Wood, writer ; Riccardo Burchielli, Ryan Kelly, artists.
      pages cm
  ISBN 978-1-4012-6843-5
  1. Militia movements—United States—Comic books, strips, etc. 2. New York (N.Y.)—Fiction. 3. Graphic novels. I. Burchielli, Riccardo, illustrator. II. Kelly, Ryan, 1976- illustrator. III. Title.

PN6727.W59D5768 2014
741.5'973--dc23

2014027360

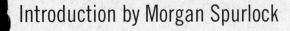

Introduction by Morgan Spurlock

We're lucky here in the United States. There hasn't been a war fought on American soil in more than 145 years. We've been distanced, protected, and made safe from the fear and horrors of war, especially from the possibility of having one in our own backyard.

When you go home tonight, turn on one of our big four TV news networks and see how much coverage is actually dedicated to any of the ongoing struggles happening beyond our borders. In the United States, we have helped support and create a government and a media machine that puts us in a bubble, reinforces a xenophobic view of the world and puts all of our troubles "out of sight and out of mind."

But all that stops in **DMZ** — and I find that to be the bravest and most important part of this revolutionary series.

Insurgencies. Suicide bombers. Nuclear armed states. These are all scary scenarios that could be ripped each day from the world's top stories, but in the hands of Brian Wood and Riccardo Burchielli, they create something much more frightening.

Rogue nations, outspoken dictators, private contractors and heartless mercenaries all find a place in the pages of **DMZ**. They open our eyes and our ears to events that, while fictional in the frames of this groundbreaking creation, are links in the chains of our global existence. Each story, each character and each page is undeniably tied to the world in which we live, and for me — that is **DMZ**'s greatest triumph.

It would be easy to continue to go through life with blinders on to shield us from the ugly truths that, to this day, still send brave men and women to fight overseas. Soldiers who, we're told, are fighting "over there" so we won't have to here. By the time this hits the newsstands, nearly one percent of the current population, more than 3,000,000 Americans, will have fought either in Iraq or Afghanistan … a number that makes the stories of **DMZ** all the more terrifying, all the more plausible and at once all the more realistic.

What these books also do, especially the series that you are about to read, is bring into question the influence and power of hope. **DMZ,** like our own world, has been overshadowed with the beliefs that certain men and women, when given the chance, would reshape the course of human history. They would right the wrongs that had come before them and cut a clear path toward harmony. Citizens put their faith in these outspoken people, and now, as tensions mount both here and on the world's stage, we all stand poised to see if they will rise to the challenge we have given them, or if Icarus will fall to the ground.

When you read "No Future" and "Hearts and Minds," you will unquestionably draw parallels to questions in your own life, but what I hope happens more than anything else is that in some small way, you actually start to find some answers.

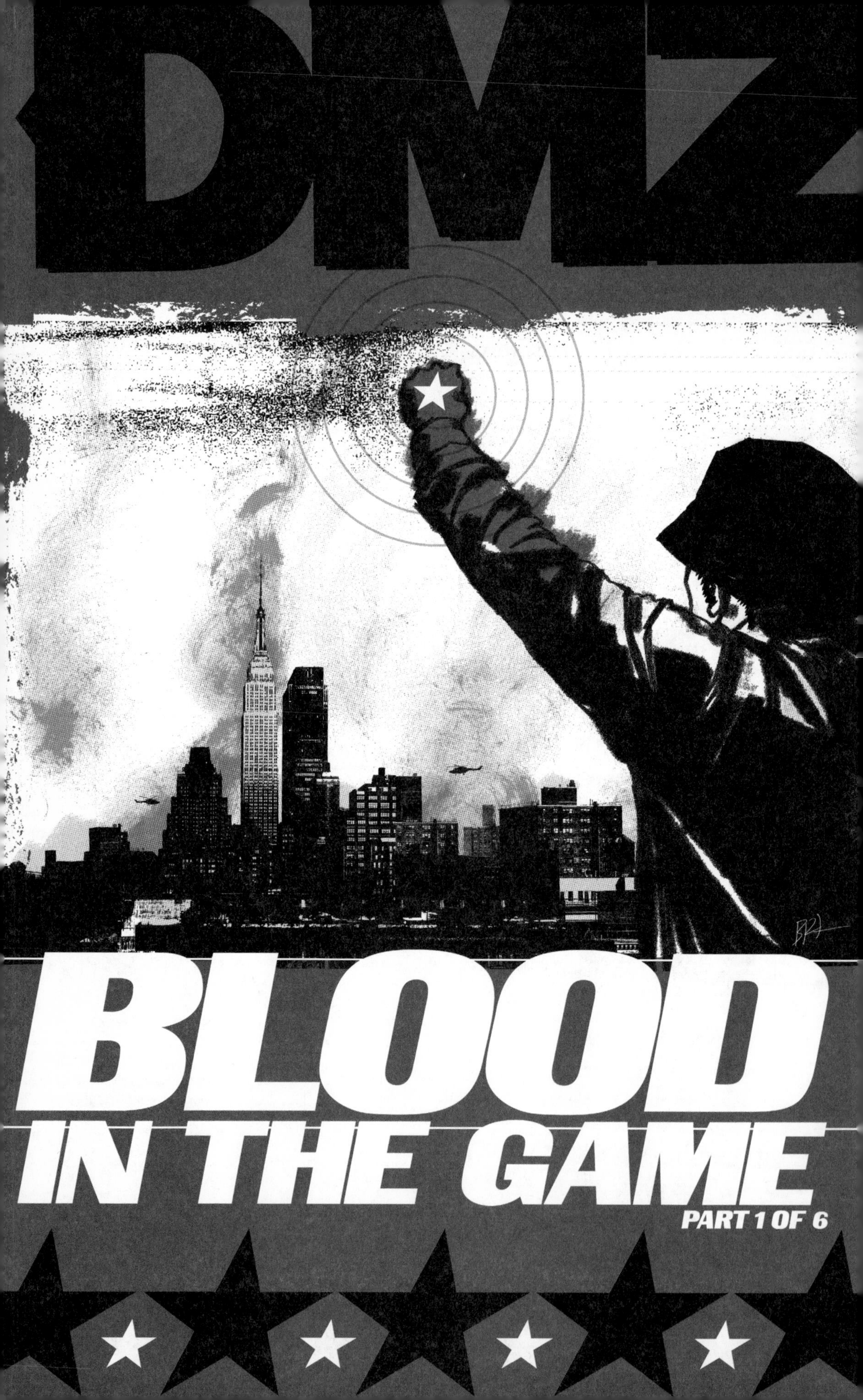
DMZ
BLOOD
IN THE GAME
PART 1 OF 6

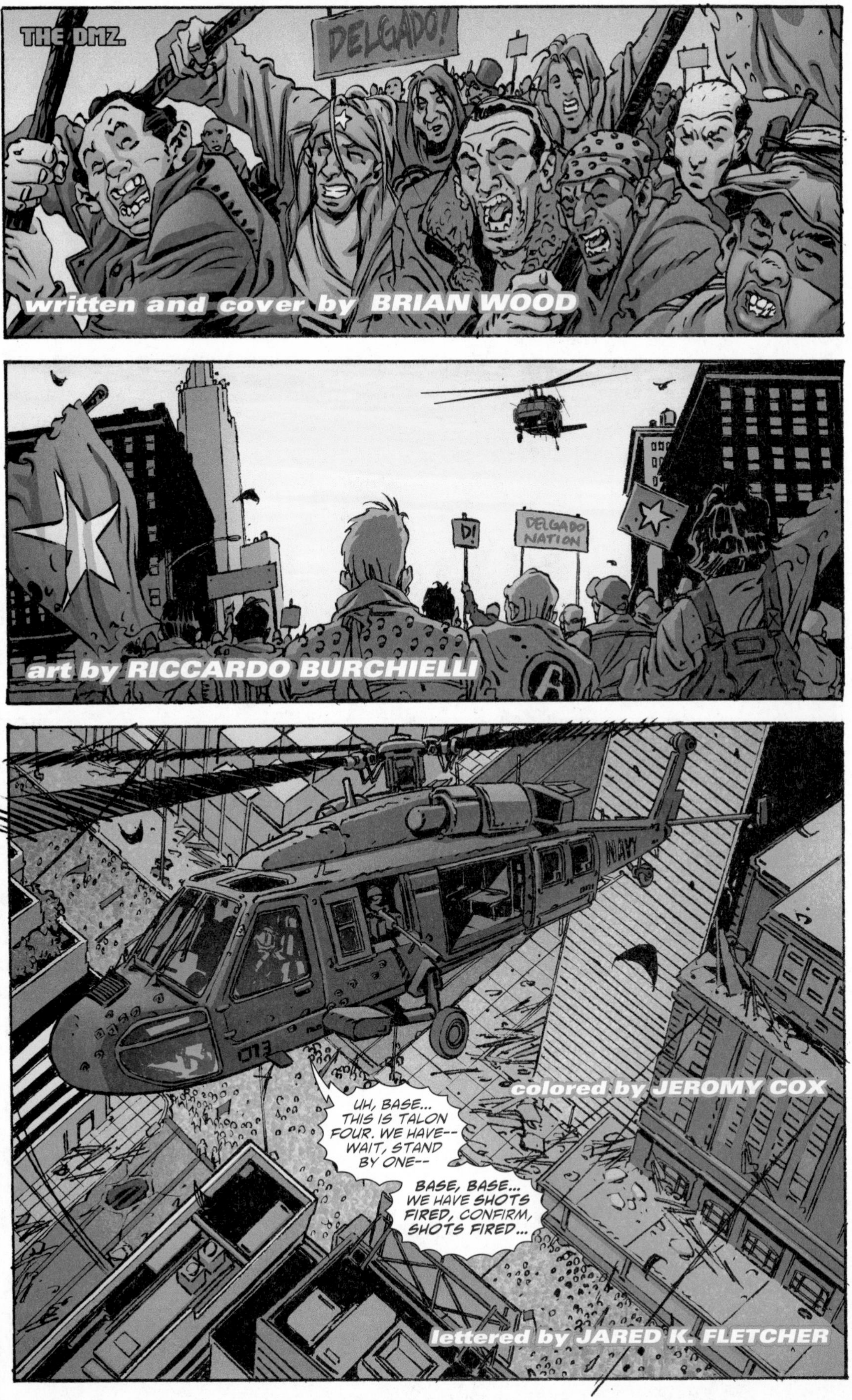
THE DMZ.
DELGADO!
written and cover by BRIAN WOOD
D!
DELGADO NATION
art by RICCARDO BURCHIELLI
NAVY
colored by JEROMY COX
UH, BASE... THIS IS TALON FOUR. WE HAVE-- WAIT, STAND BY ONE--
BASE, BASE... WE HAVE SHOTS FIRED, CONFIRM, SHOTS FIRED...
lettered by JARED K. FLETCHER

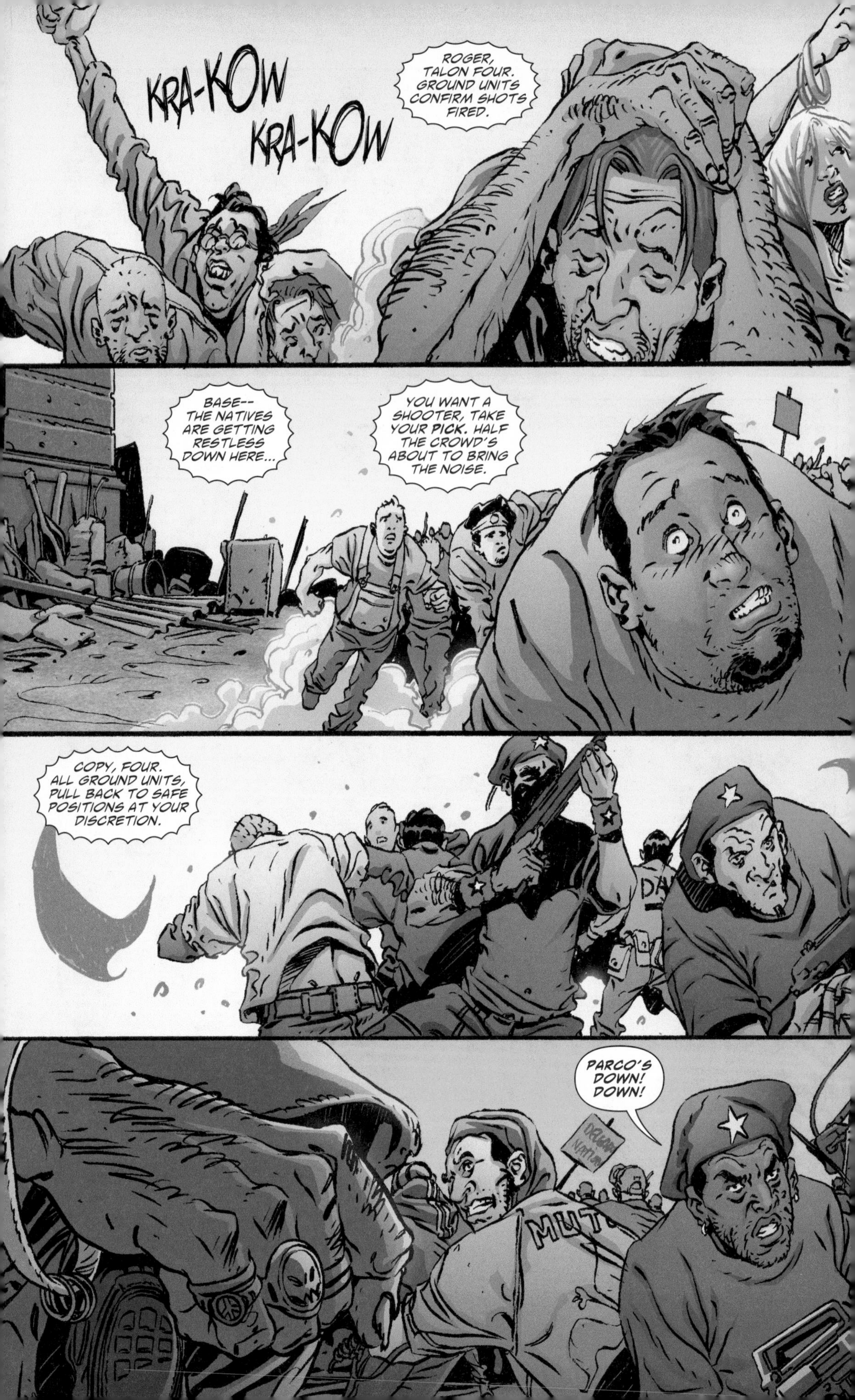
KRA-KOW
KRA-KOW
ROGER, TALON FOUR. GROUND UNITS CONFIRM SHOTS FIRED.
BASE-- THE NATIVES ARE GETTING RESTLESS DOWN HERE...
YOU WANT A SHOOTER, TAKE YOUR PICK. HALF THE CROWD'S ABOUT TO BRING THE NOISE.
COPY, FOUR. ALL GROUND UNITS, PULL BACK TO SAFE POSITIONS AT YOUR DISCRETION.
PARCO'S DOWN! DOWN!

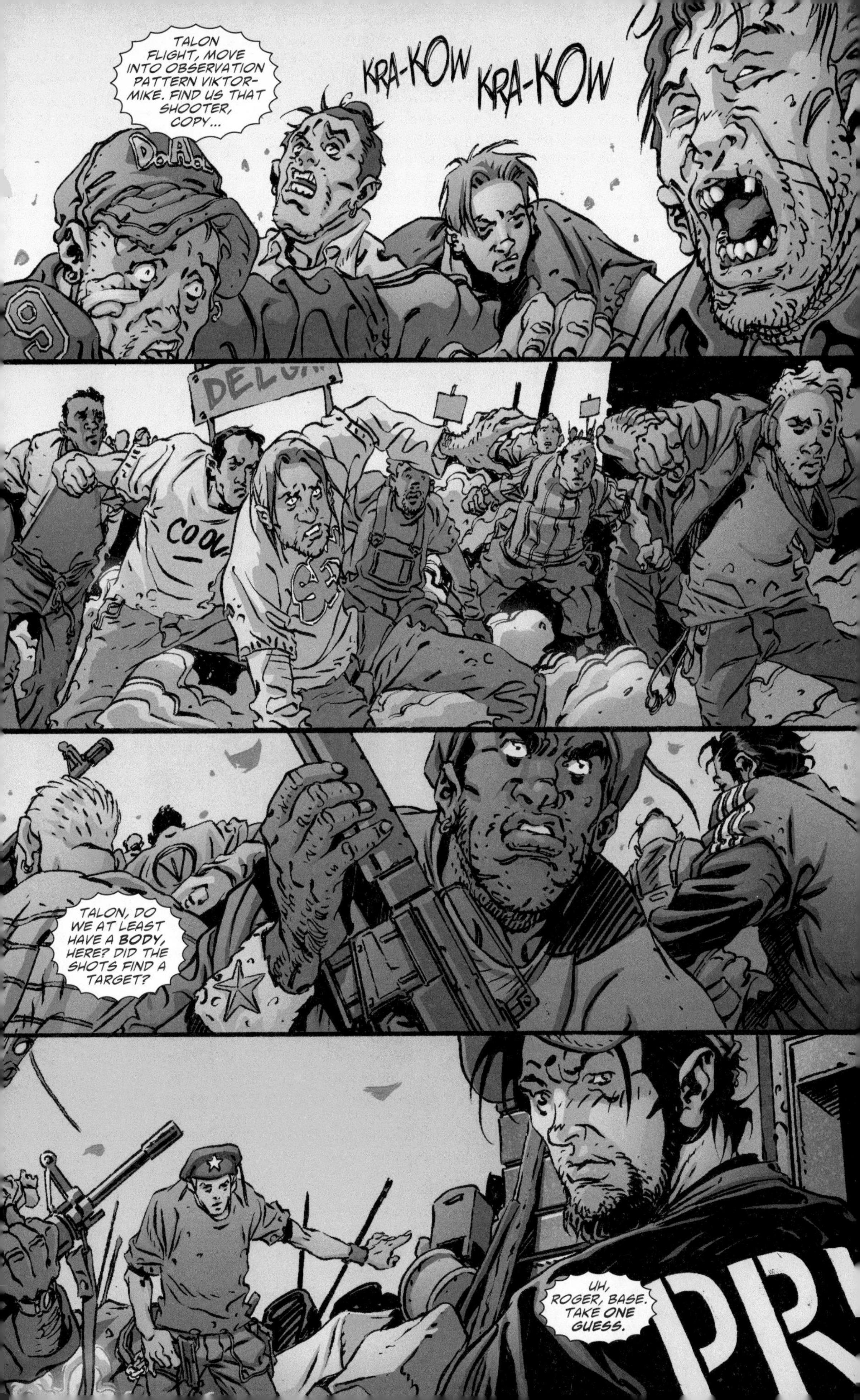
TALON FLIGHT, MOVE INTO OBSERVATION PATTERN VIKTOR-MIKE. FIND US THAT SHOOTER, COPY...
KRA-KOW KRA-KOW
D.A.L
COOL
TALON, DO WE AT LEAST HAVE A BODY, HERE? DID THE SHOTS FIND A TARGET?
UH, ROGER, BASE. TAKE ONE GUESS.

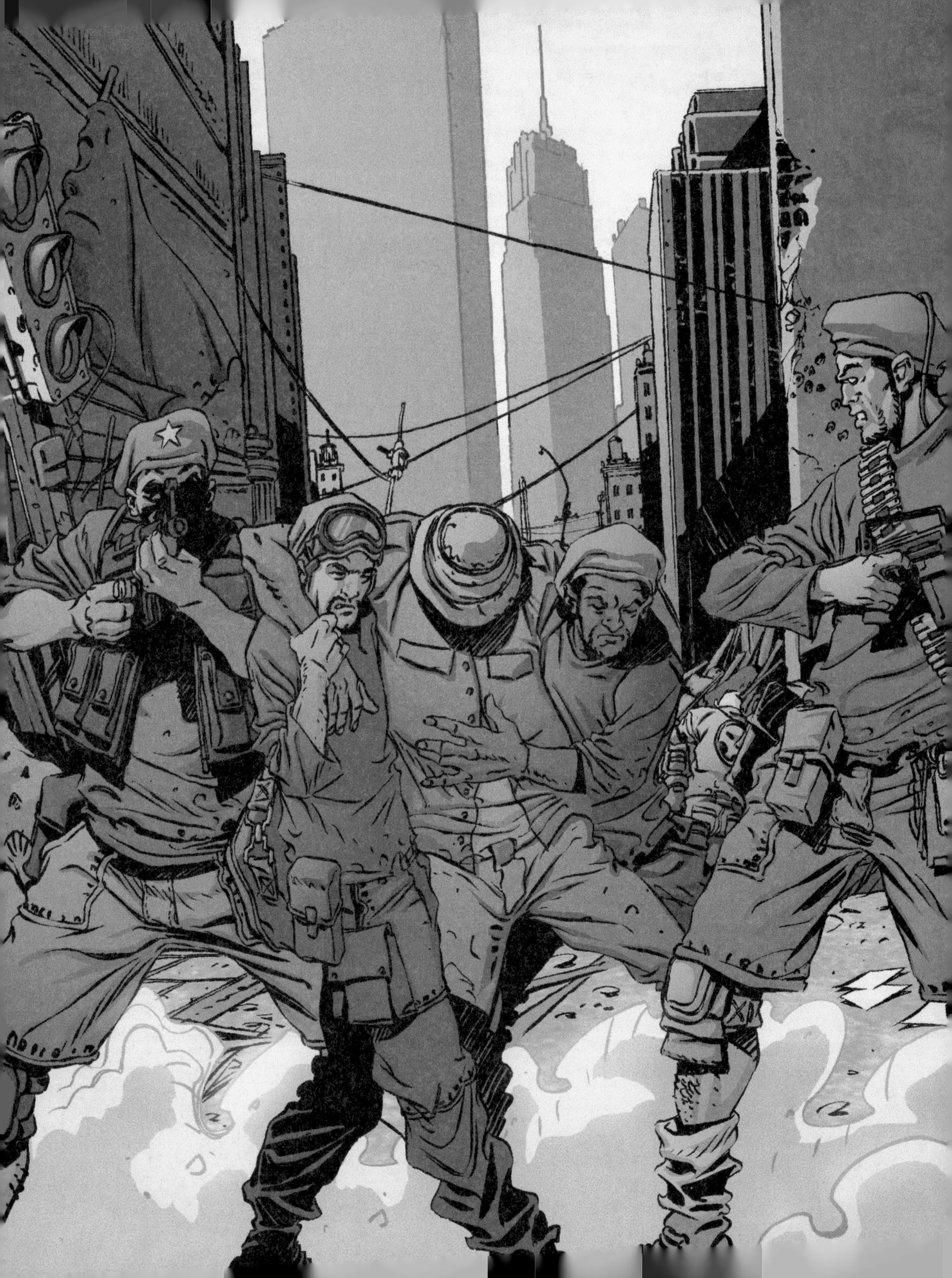

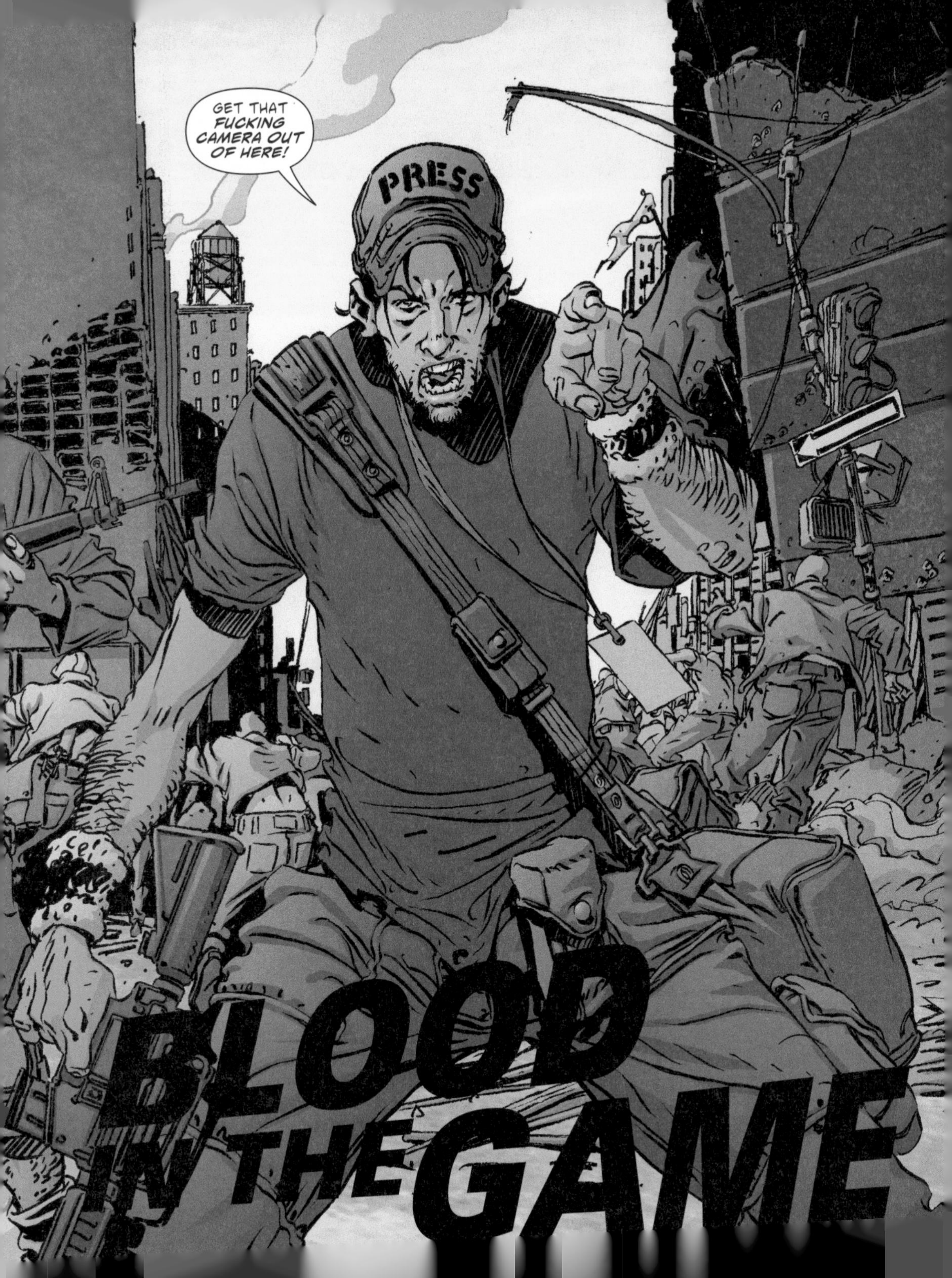
GET THAT FUCKING CAMERA OUT OF HERE!
PRESS
BLOOD IN THE GAME

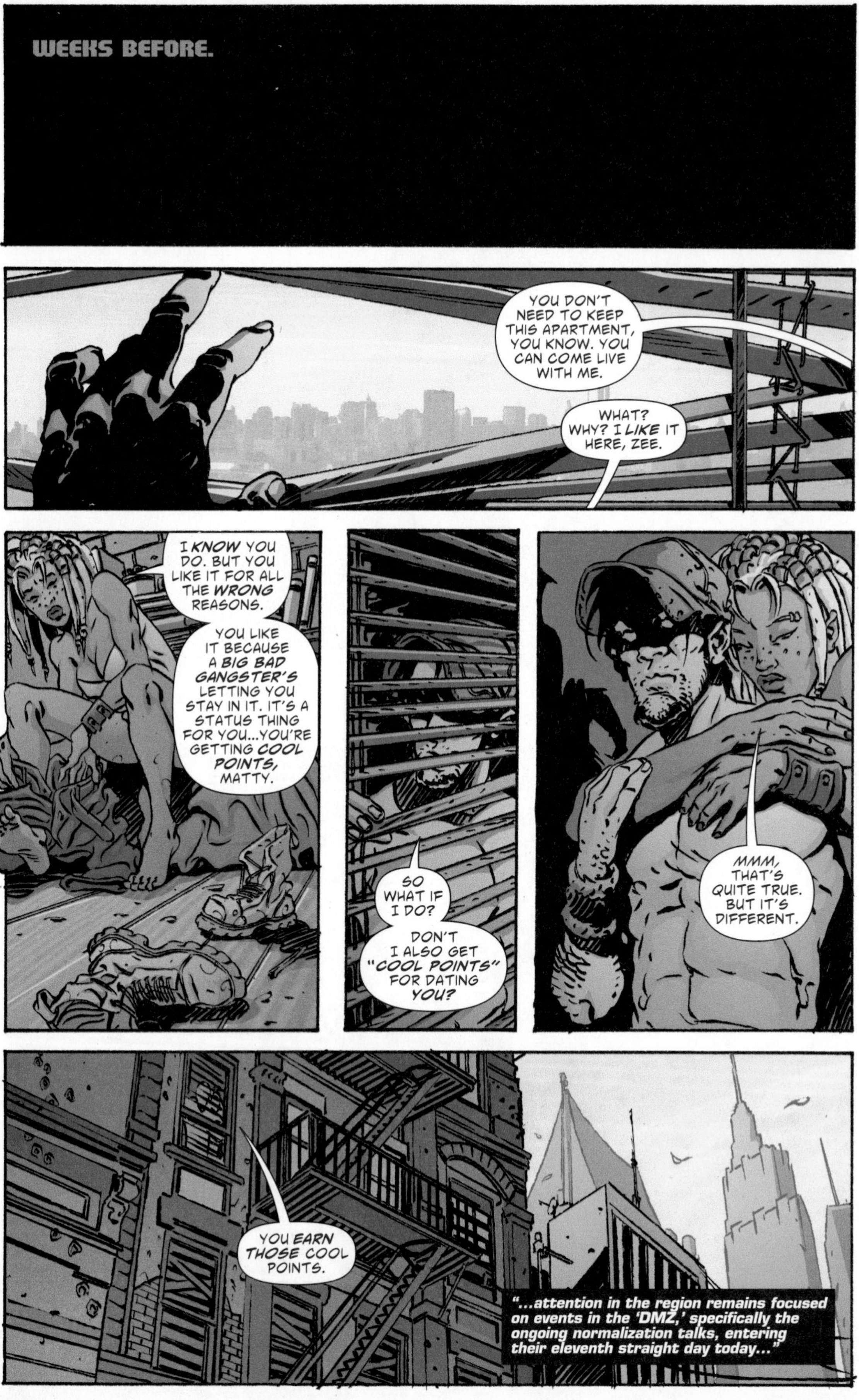
WEEKS BEFORE.
YOU DON'T NEED TO KEEP THIS APARTMENT, YOU KNOW. YOU CAN COME LIVE WITH ME.
WHAT? WHY? I LIKE IT HERE, ZEE.
I KNOW YOU DO. BUT YOU LIKE IT FOR ALL THE WRONG REASONS.
YOU LIKE IT BECAUSE A BIG BAD GANGSTER'S LETTING YOU STAY IN IT. IT'S A STATUS THING FOR YOU...YOU'RE GETTING COOL POINTS, MATTY.
SO WHAT IF I DO?
DON'T I ALSO GET "COOL POINTS" FOR DATING YOU?
MMM, THAT'S QUITE TRUE. BUT IT'S DIFFERENT.
YOU EARN THOSE COOL POINTS.
"...attention in the region remains focused on events in the 'DMZ,' specifically the ongoing normalization talks, entering their eleventh straight day today..."

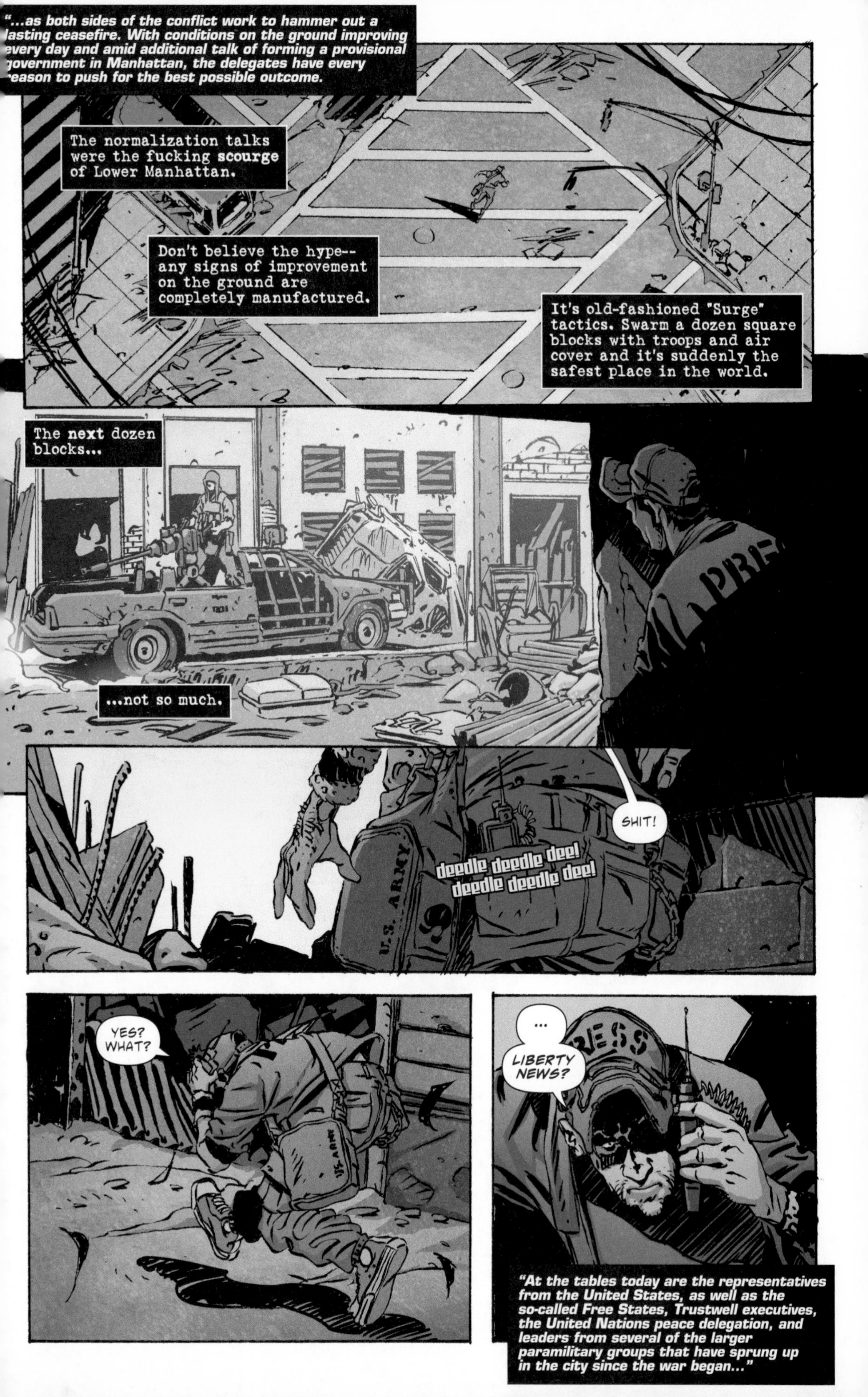
"...as both sides of the conflict work to hammer out a lasting ceasefire. With conditions on the ground improving every day and amid additional talk of forming a provisional government in Manhattan, the delegates have every reason to push for the best possible outcome.
The normalization talks were the fucking scourge of Lower Manhattan.
Don't believe the hype--any signs of improvement on the ground are completely manufactured.
It's old-fashioned "Surge" tactics. Swarm a dozen square blocks with troops and air cover and it's suddenly the safest place in the world.
The next dozen blocks...
...not so much.
SHIT!
deedle deedle dee! deedle deedle dee!
U.S. ARMY
YES? WHAT?
...
LIBERTY NEWS?
"At the tables today are the representatives from the United States, as well as the so-called Free States, Trustwell executives, the United Nations peace delegation, and leaders from several of the larger paramilitary groups that have sprung up in the city since the war began..."

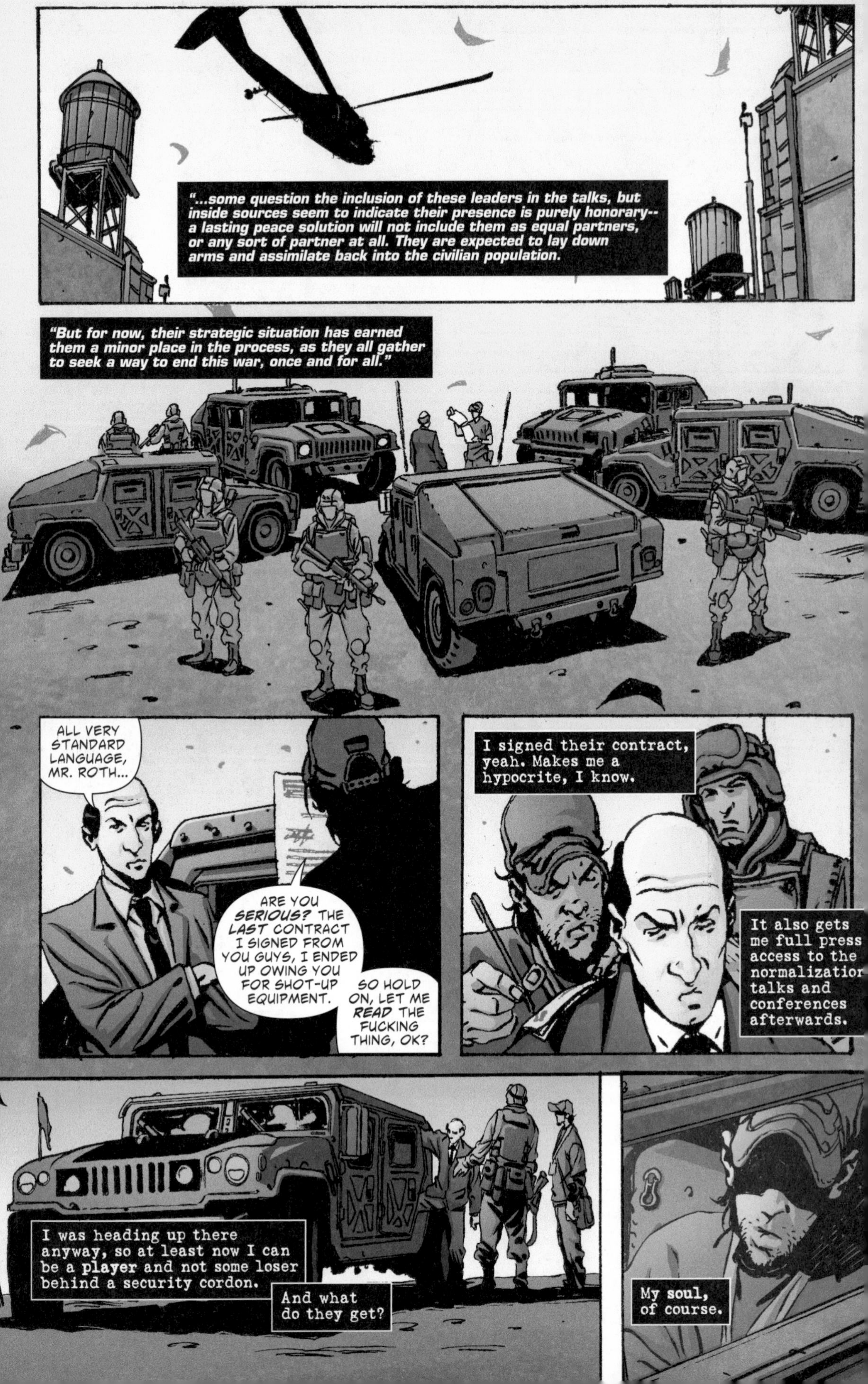
"...some question the inclusion of these leaders in the talks, but inside sources seem to indicate their presence is purely honorary--a lasting peace solution will not include them as equal partners, or any sort of partner at all. They are expected to lay down arms and assimilate back into the civilian population.
"But for now, their strategic situation has earned them a minor place in the process, as they all gather to seek a way to end this war, once and for all."
ALL VERY STANDARD LANGUAGE, MR. ROTH...
ARE YOU SERIOUS? THE LAST CONTRACT I SIGNED FROM YOU GUYS, I ENDED UP OWING YOU FOR SHOT-UP EQUIPMENT.
SO HOLD ON, LET ME READ THE FUCKING THING, OK?
I signed their contract, yeah. Makes me a hypocrite, I know.
It also gets me full press access to the normalization talks and conferences afterwards.
I was heading up there anyway, so at least now I can be a player and not some loser behind a security cordon.
And what do they get?
My soul, of course.

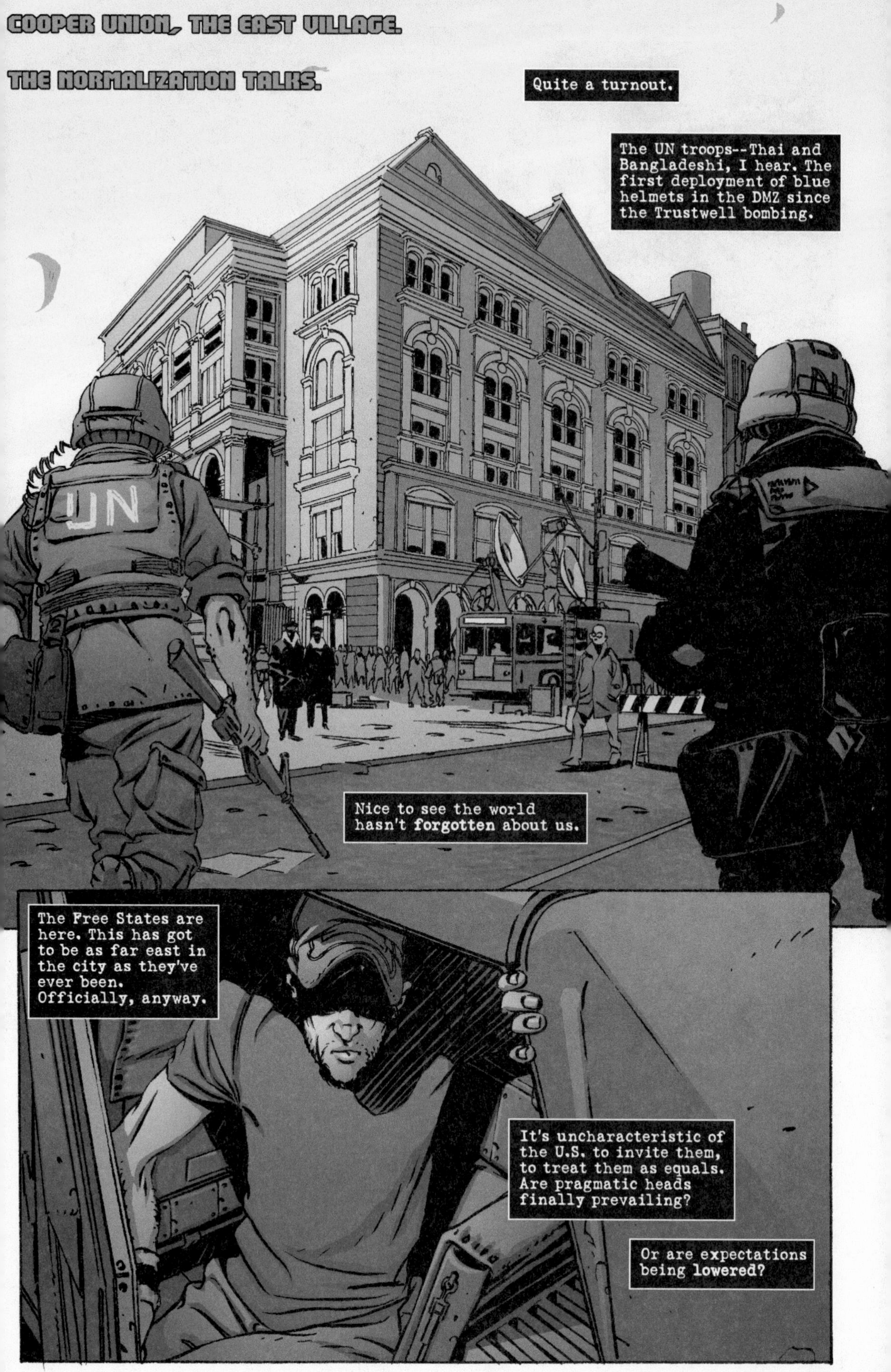

COOPER UNION, THE EAST VILLAGE.
THE NORMALIZATION TALKS.
Quite a turnout.
The UN troops--Thai and Bangladeshi, I hear. The first deployment of blue helmets in the DMZ since the Trustwell bombing.
Nice to see the world hasn't **forgotten** about us.
The Free States are here. This has got to be as far east in the city as they've ever been. Officially, anyway.
It's uncharacteristic of the U.S. to invite them, to treat them as equals. Are pragmatic heads finally prevailing?
Or are expectations being **lowered?**

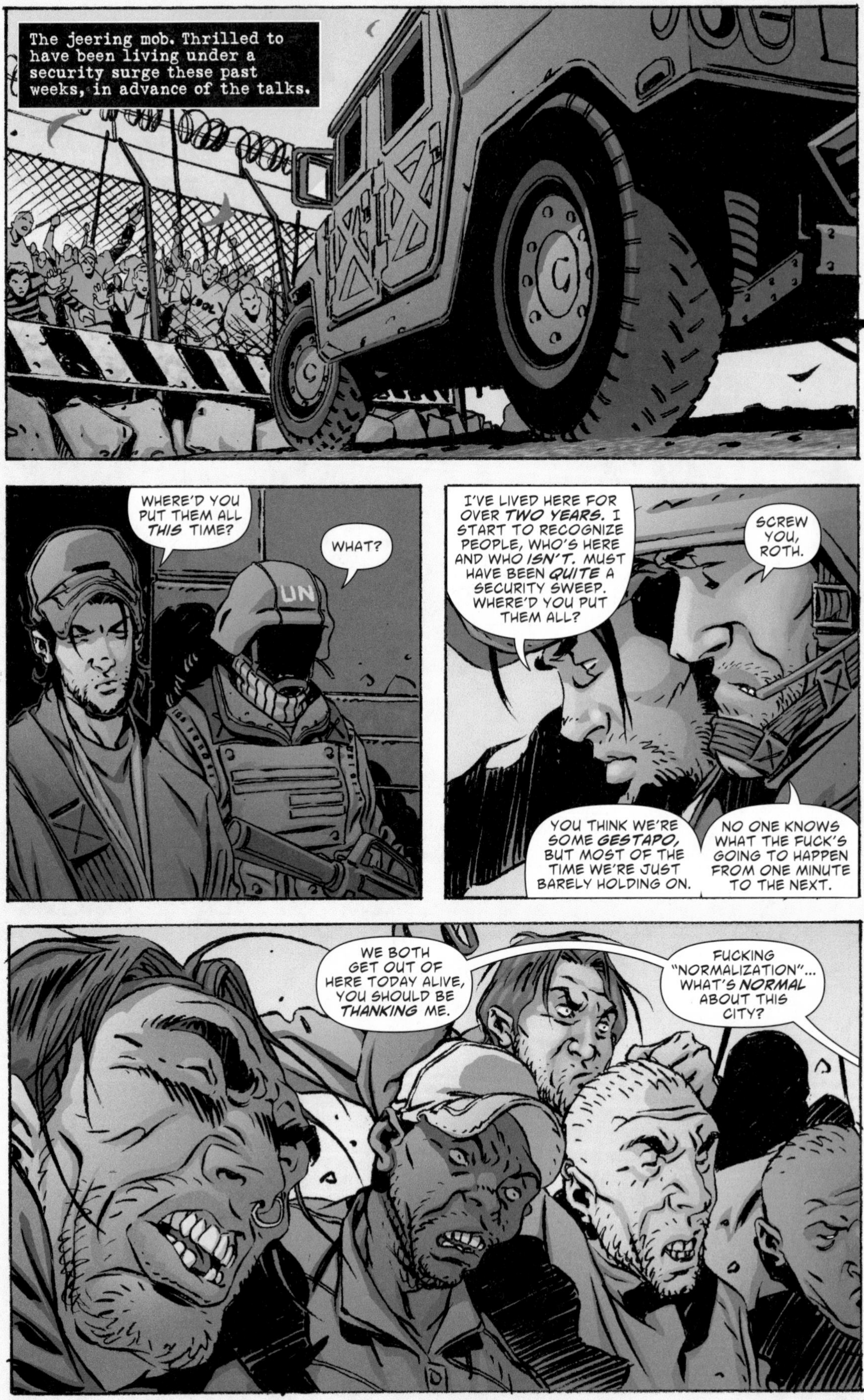
The jeering mob. Thrilled to have been living under a security surge these past weeks, in advance of the talks.
WHERE'D YOU PUT THEM ALL THIS TIME?
WHAT?
I'VE LIVED HERE FOR OVER TWO YEARS. I START TO RECOGNIZE PEOPLE, WHO'S HERE AND WHO ISN'T. MUST HAVE BEEN QUITE A SECURITY SWEEP. WHERE'D YOU PUT THEM ALL?
SCREW YOU, ROTH.
YOU THINK WE'RE SOME GESTAPO, BUT MOST OF THE TIME WE'RE JUST BARELY HOLDING ON.
NO ONE KNOWS WHAT THE FUCK'S GOING TO HAPPEN FROM ONE MINUTE TO THE NEXT.
WE BOTH GET OUT OF HERE TODAY ALIVE, YOU SHOULD BE THANKING ME.
FUCKING "NORMALIZATION"... WHAT'S NORMAL ABOUT THIS CITY?

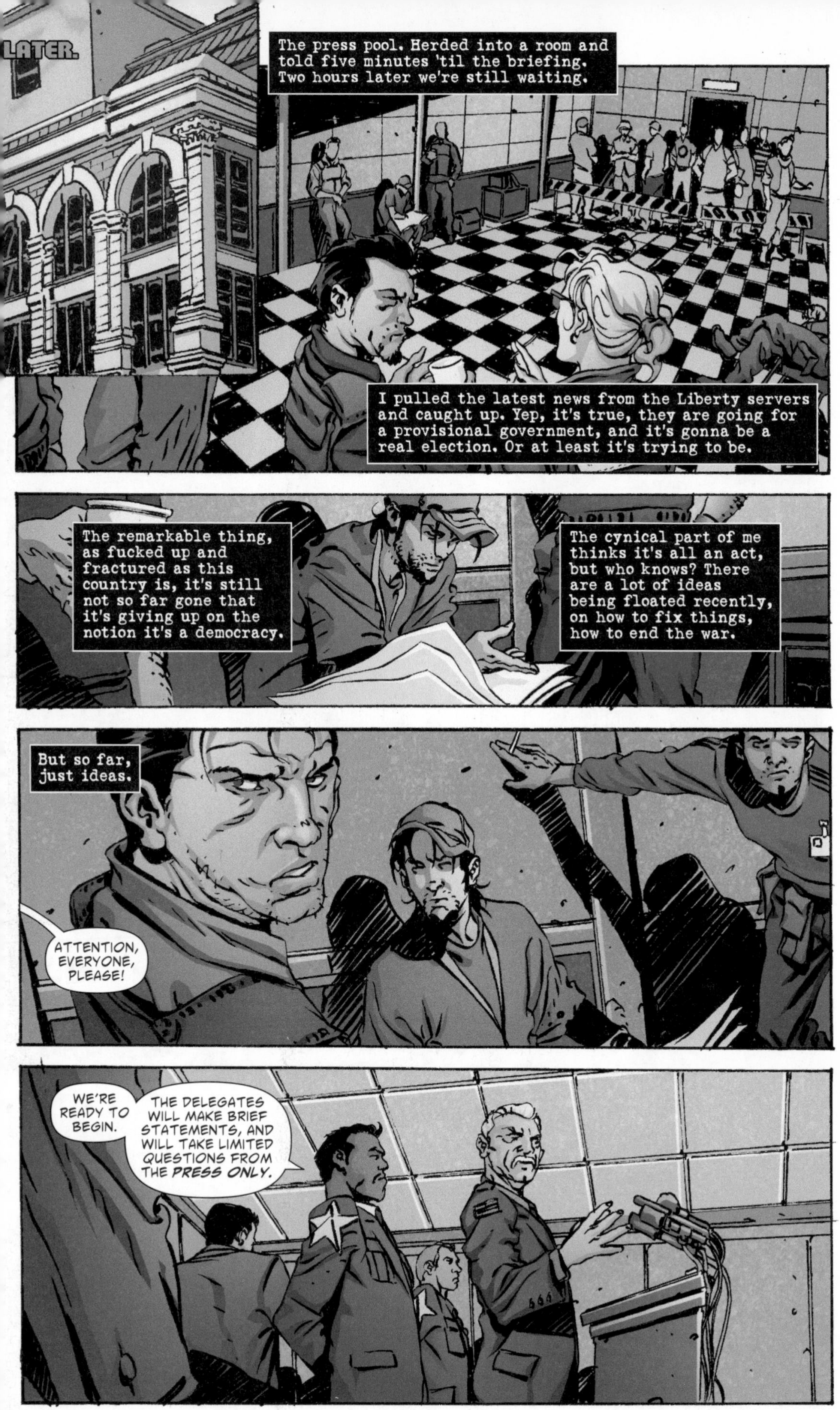
LATER.
The press pool. Herded into a room and told five minutes 'til the briefing. Two hours later we're still waiting.
I pulled the latest news from the Liberty servers and caught up. Yep, it's true, they are going for a provisional government, and it's gonna be a real election. Or at least it's trying to be.
The remarkable thing, as fucked up and fractured as this country is, it's still not so far gone that it's giving up on the notion it's a democracy.
The cynical part of me thinks it's all an act, but who knows? There are a lot of ideas being floated recently, on how to fix things, how to end the war.
But so far, just ideas.
ATTENTION, EVERYONE, PLEASE!
WE'RE READY TO BEGIN.
THE DELEGATES WILL MAKE BRIEF STATEMENTS, AND WILL TAKE LIMITED QUESTIONS FROM THE PRESS ONLY.

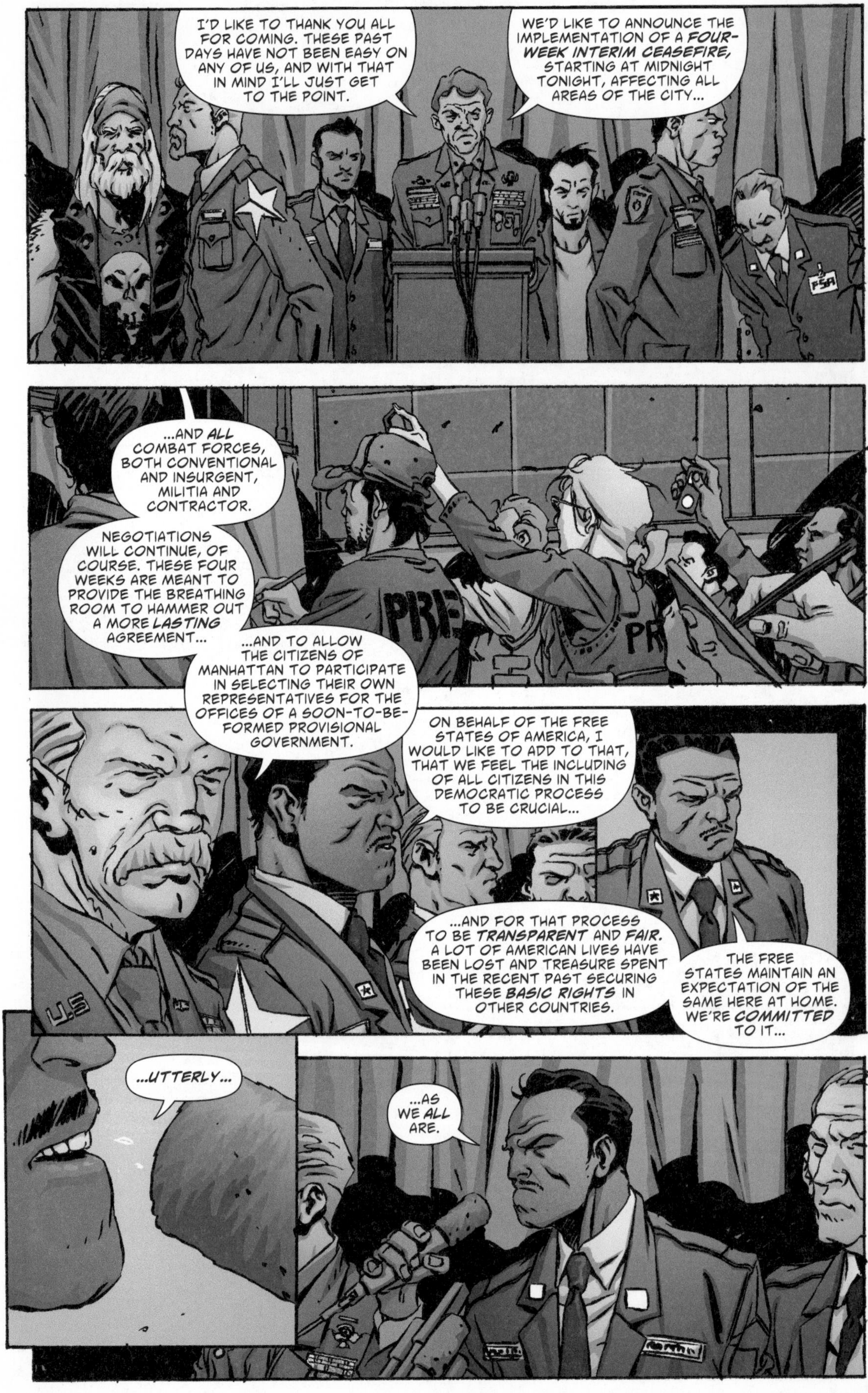
I'D LIKE TO THANK YOU ALL FOR COMING. THESE PAST DAYS HAVE NOT BEEN EASY ON ANY OF US, AND WITH THAT IN MIND I'LL JUST GET TO THE POINT.
WE'D LIKE TO ANNOUNCE THE IMPLEMENTATION OF A FOUR-WEEK INTERIM CEASEFIRE, STARTING AT MIDNIGHT TONIGHT, AFFECTING ALL AREAS OF THE CITY...
...AND ALL COMBAT FORCES, BOTH CONVENTIONAL AND INSURGENT, MILITIA AND CONTRACTOR.
NEGOTIATIONS WILL CONTINUE, OF COURSE. THESE FOUR WEEKS ARE MEANT TO PROVIDE THE BREATHING ROOM TO HAMMER OUT A MORE LASTING AGREEMENT...
...AND TO ALLOW THE CITIZENS OF MANHATTAN TO PARTICIPATE IN SELECTING THEIR OWN REPRESENTATIVES FOR THE OFFICES OF A SOON-TO-BE-FORMED PROVISIONAL GOVERNMENT.
PRE
PR
ON BEHALF OF THE FREE STATES OF AMERICA, I WOULD LIKE TO ADD TO THAT, THAT WE FEEL THE INCLUDING OF ALL CITIZENS IN THIS DEMOCRATIC PROCESS TO BE CRUCIAL...
...AND FOR THAT PROCESS TO BE TRANSPARENT AND FAIR. A LOT OF AMERICAN LIVES HAVE BEEN LOST AND TREASURE SPENT IN THE RECENT PAST SECURING THESE BASIC RIGHTS IN OTHER COUNTRIES.
THE FREE STATES MAINTAIN AN EXPECTATION OF THE SAME HERE AT HOME. WE'RE COMMITTED TO IT...
U.S
...UTTERLY...
...AS WE ALL ARE.

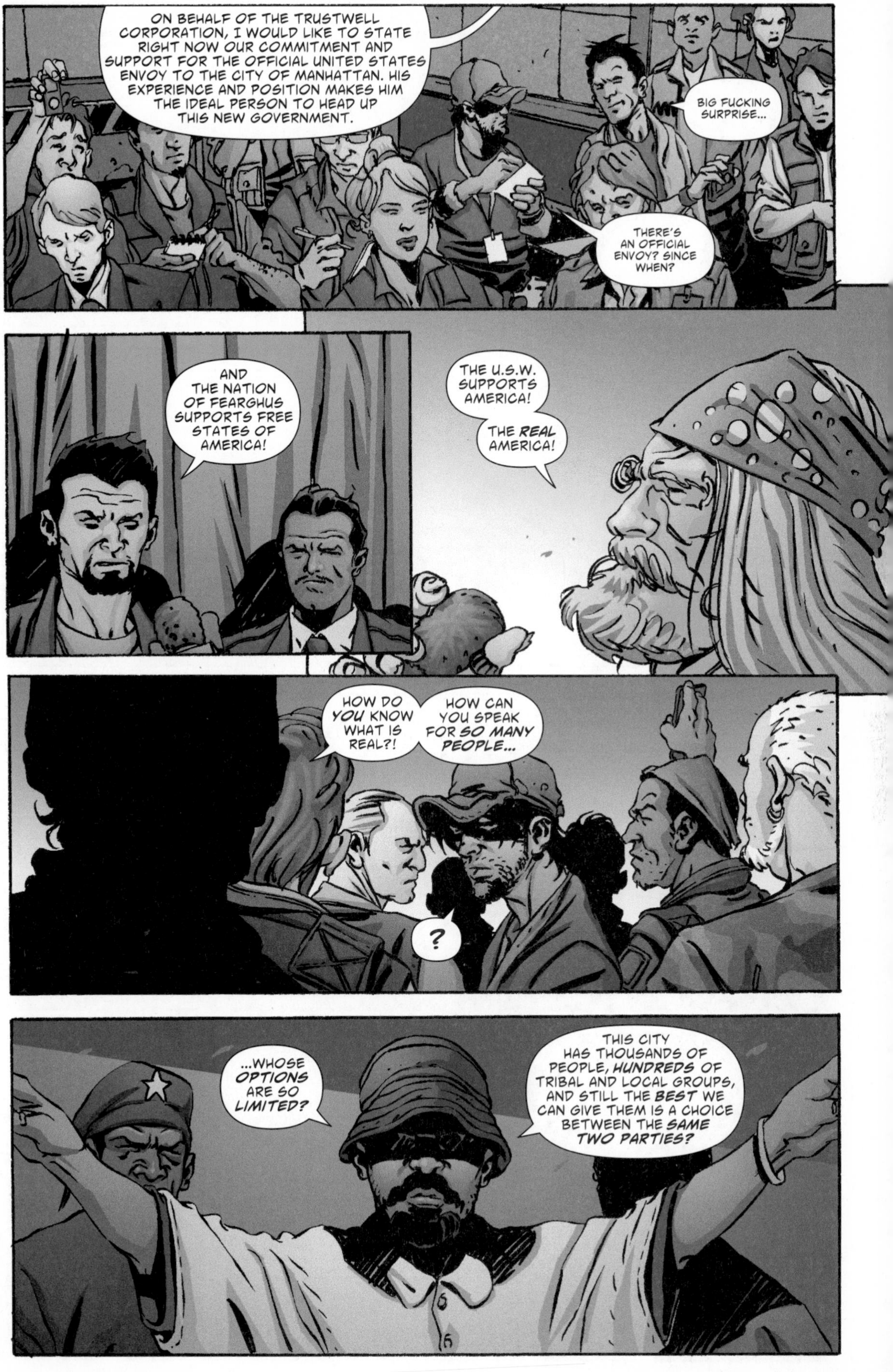
ON BEHALF OF THE TRUSTWELL CORPORATION, I WOULD LIKE TO STATE RIGHT NOW OUR COMMITMENT AND SUPPORT FOR THE OFFICIAL UNITED STATES ENVOY TO THE CITY OF MANHATTAN. HIS EXPERIENCE AND POSITION MAKES HIM THE IDEAL PERSON TO HEAD UP THIS NEW GOVERNMENT.
BIG FUCKING SURPRISE...
THERE'S AN OFFICIAL ENVOY? SINCE WHEN?
AND THE NATION OF FEARGHUS SUPPORTS FREE STATES OF AMERICA!
THE U.S.W. SUPPORTS AMERICA!
THE *REAL* AMERICA!
HOW DO *YOU* KNOW WHAT IS REAL?!
HOW CAN YOU SPEAK FOR *SO MANY PEOPLE...*
?
...WHOSE *OPTIONS* ARE SO *LIMITED?*
THIS CITY HAS THOUSANDS OF PEOPLE, *HUNDREDS* OF TRIBAL AND LOCAL GROUPS, AND STILL THE *BEST* WE CAN GIVE THEM IS A CHOICE BETWEEN THE *SAME TWO PARTIES?*

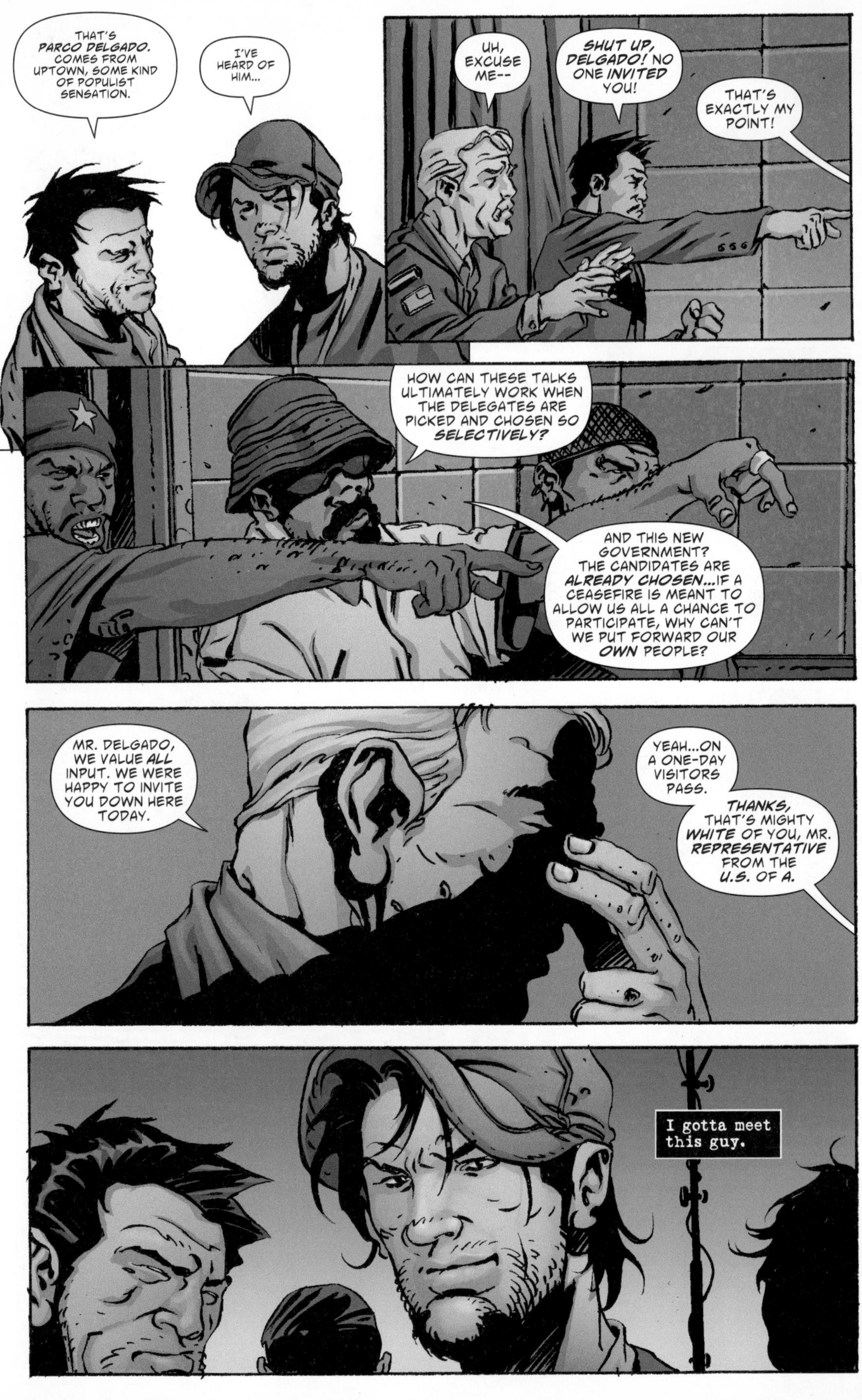
THAT'S PARCO DELGADO. COMES FROM UPTOWN, SOME KIND OF POPULIST SENSATION.
I'VE HEARD OF HIM...
UH, EXCUSE ME--
SHUT UP, DELGADO! NO ONE INVITED YOU!
THAT'S EXACTLY MY POINT!
HOW CAN THESE TALKS ULTIMATELY WORK WHEN THE DELEGATES ARE PICKED AND CHOSEN SO SELECTIVELY?
AND THIS NEW GOVERNMENT? THE CANDIDATES ARE ALREADY CHOSEN...IF A CEASEFIRE IS MEANT TO ALLOW US ALL A CHANCE TO PARTICIPATE, WHY CAN'T WE PUT FORWARD OUR OWN PEOPLE?
MR. DELGADO, WE VALUE ALL INPUT. WE WERE HAPPY TO INVITE YOU DOWN HERE TODAY.
YEAH...ON A ONE-DAY VISITORS PASS.
THANKS, THAT'S MIGHTY WHITE OF YOU, MR. REPRESENTATIVE FROM THE U.S. OF A.
I gotta meet this guy.

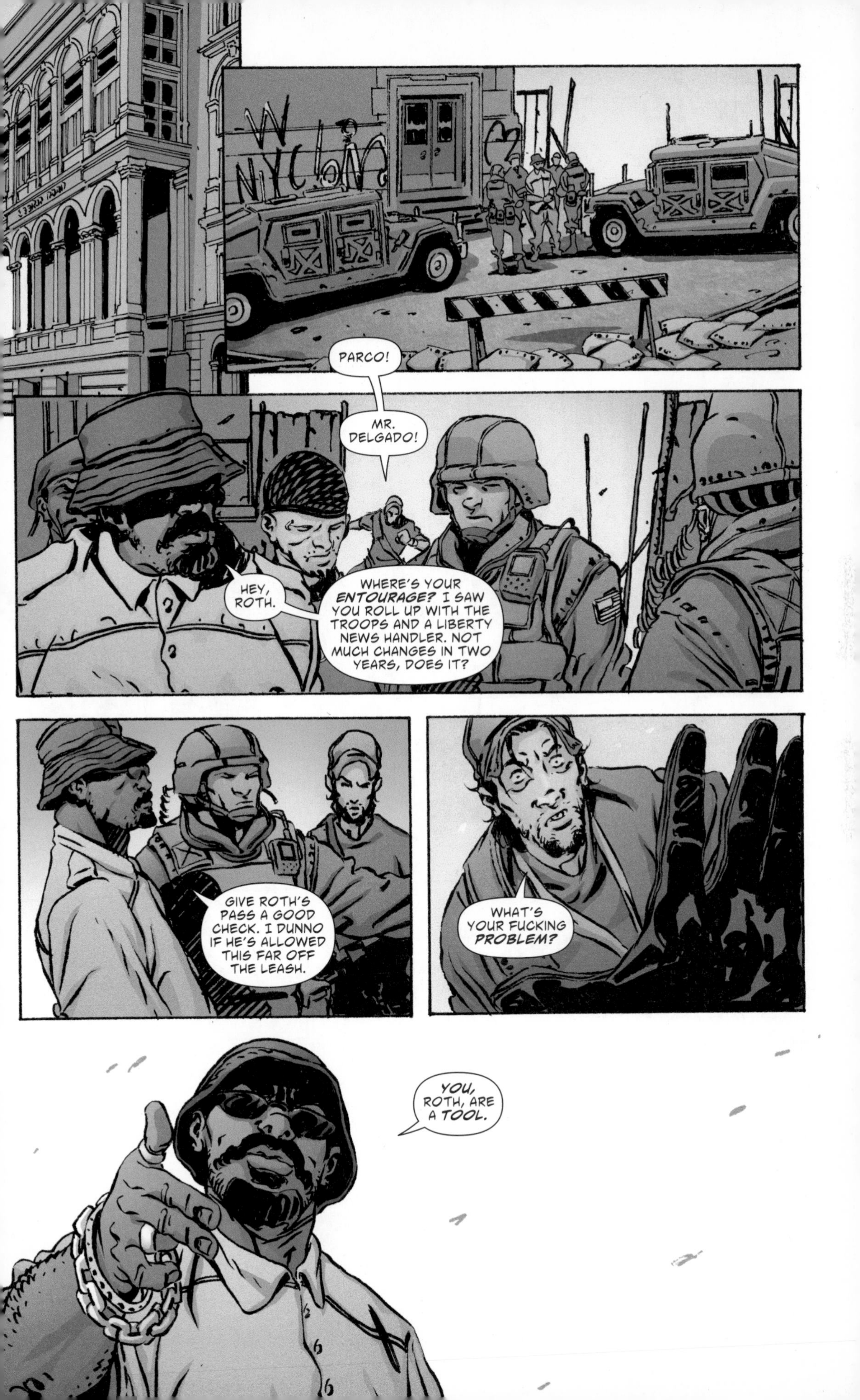
PARCO!
MR. DELGADO!
HEY, ROTH.
WHERE'S YOUR *ENTOURAGE?* I SAW YOU ROLL UP WITH THE TROOPS AND A LIBERTY NEWS HANDLER. NOT MUCH CHANGES IN TWO YEARS, DOES IT?
GIVE ROTH'S PASS A GOOD CHECK. I DUNNO IF HE'S ALLOWED THIS FAR OFF THE LEASH.
WHAT'S YOUR FUCKING *PROBLEM?*
YOU, ROTH, ARE A *TOOL.*

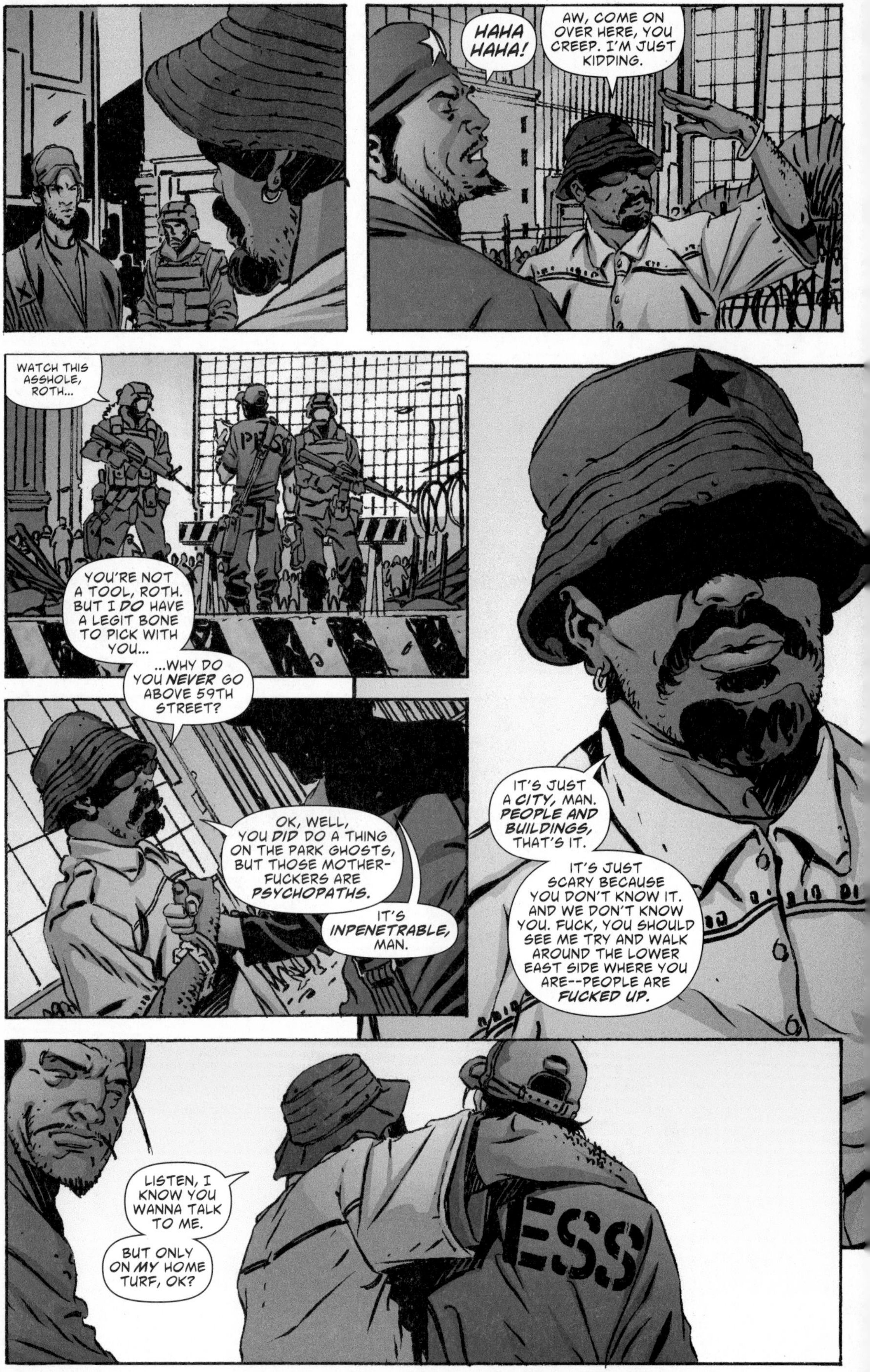
HAHA HAHA!
AW, COME ON OVER HERE, YOU CREEP. I'M JUST KIDDING.
WATCH THIS ASSHOLE, ROTH...
YOU'RE NOT A TOOL, ROTH. BUT I DO HAVE A LEGIT BONE TO PICK WITH YOU...
...WHY DO YOU NEVER GO ABOVE 59TH STREET?
IT'S JUST A CITY, MAN. PEOPLE AND BUILDINGS, THAT'S IT.
IT'S JUST SCARY BECAUSE YOU DON'T KNOW IT. AND WE DON'T KNOW YOU. FUCK, YOU SHOULD SEE ME TRY AND WALK AROUND THE LOWER EAST SIDE WHERE YOU ARE--PEOPLE ARE FUCKED UP.
OK, WELL, YOU DID DO A THING ON THE PARK GHOSTS, BUT THOSE MOTHER-FUCKERS ARE PSYCHOPATHS.
IT'S INPENETRABLE, MAN.
LISTEN, I KNOW YOU WANNA TALK TO ME.
BUT ONLY ON MY HOME TURF, OK?
ESS

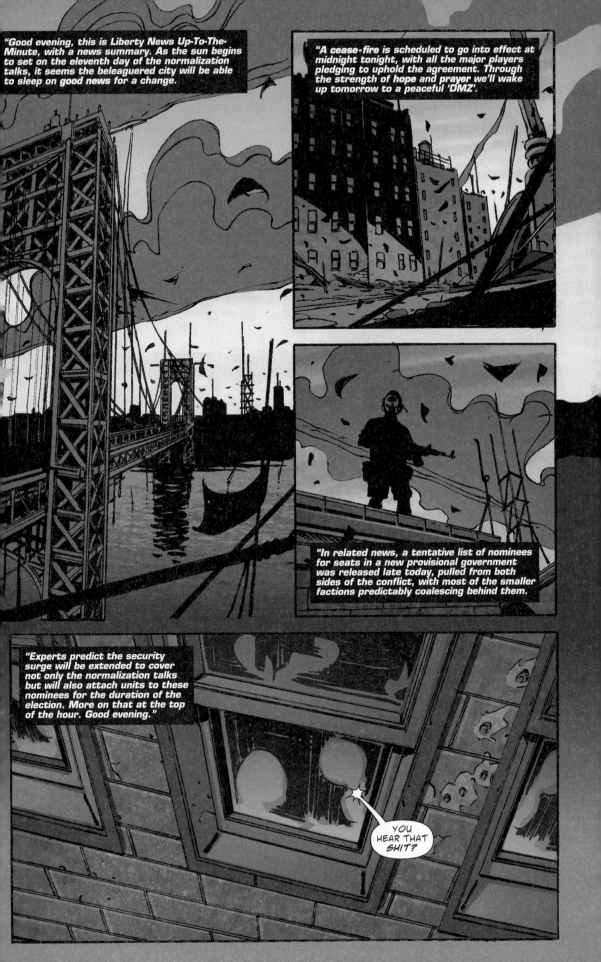

"Good evening, this is Liberty News Up-To-The-Minute, with a news summary. As the sun begins to set on the eleventh day of the normalization talks, it seems the beleaguered city will be able to sleep on good news for a change.

"A cease-fire is scheduled to go into effect at midnight tonight, with all the major players pledging to uphold the agreement. Through the strength of hope and prayer we'll wake up tomorrow to a peaceful 'DMZ'.

"In related news, a tentative list of nominees for seats in a new provisional government was released late today, pulled from both sides of the conflict, with most of the smaller factions predictably coalescing behind them.

"Experts predict the security surge will be extended to cover not only the normalization talks but will also attach units to these nominees for the duration of the election. More on that at the top of the hour. Good evening."

YOU HEAR THAT SHIT?

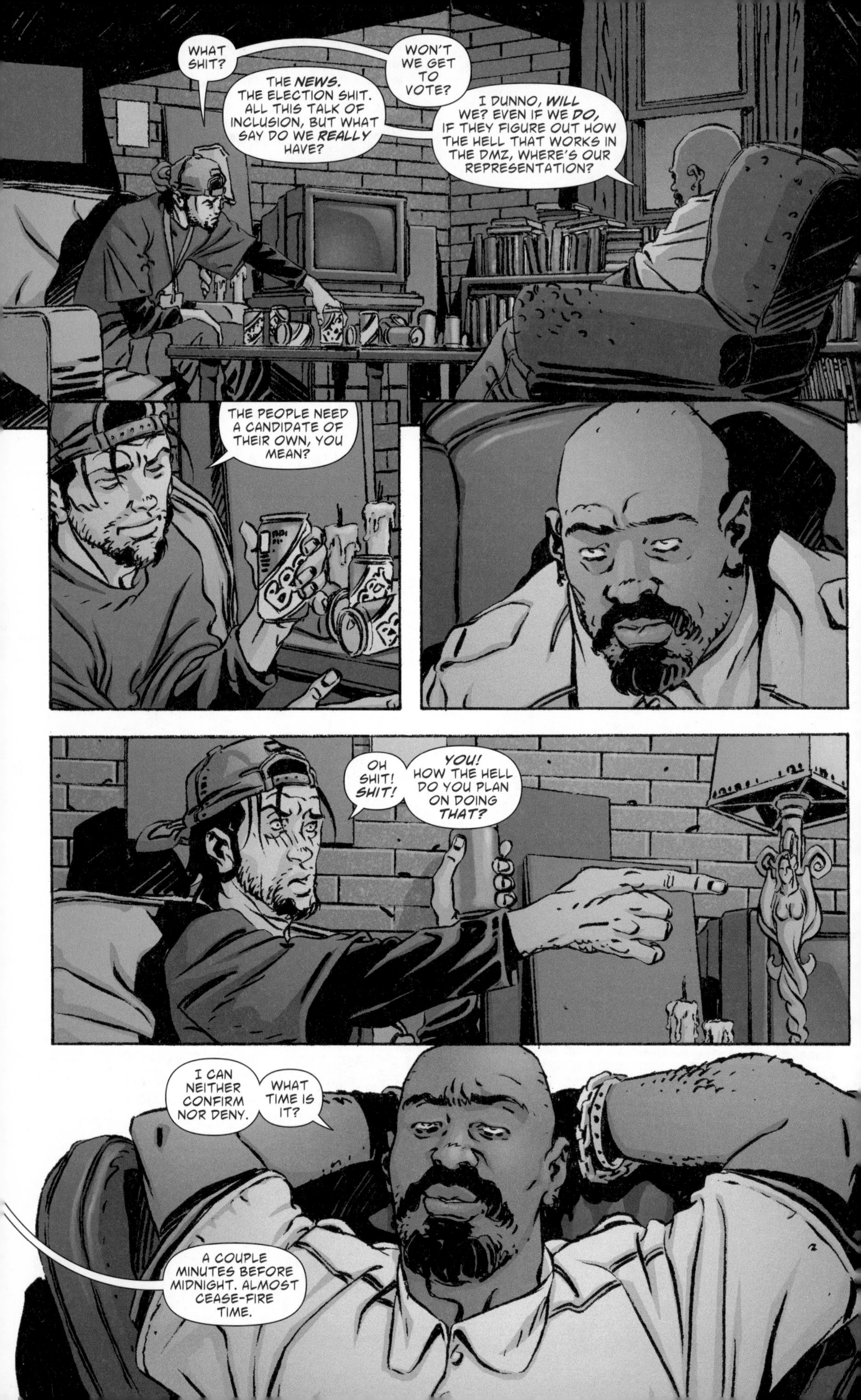
WHAT SHIT?
WON'T WE GET TO VOTE?
THE NEWS. THE ELECTION SHIT. ALL THIS TALK OF INCLUSION, BUT WHAT SAY DO WE REALLY HAVE?
I DUNNO, WILL WE? EVEN IF WE DO, IF THEY FIGURE OUT HOW THE HELL THAT WORKS IN THE DMZ, WHERE'S OUR REPRESENTATION?
THE PEOPLE NEED A CANDIDATE OF THEIR OWN, YOU MEAN?
OH SHIT! SHIT!
YOU! HOW THE HELL DO YOU PLAN ON DOING THAT?
I CAN NEITHER CONFIRM NOR DENY.
WHAT TIME IS IT?
A COUPLE MINUTES BEFORE MIDNIGHT. ALMOST CEASE-FIRE TIME.

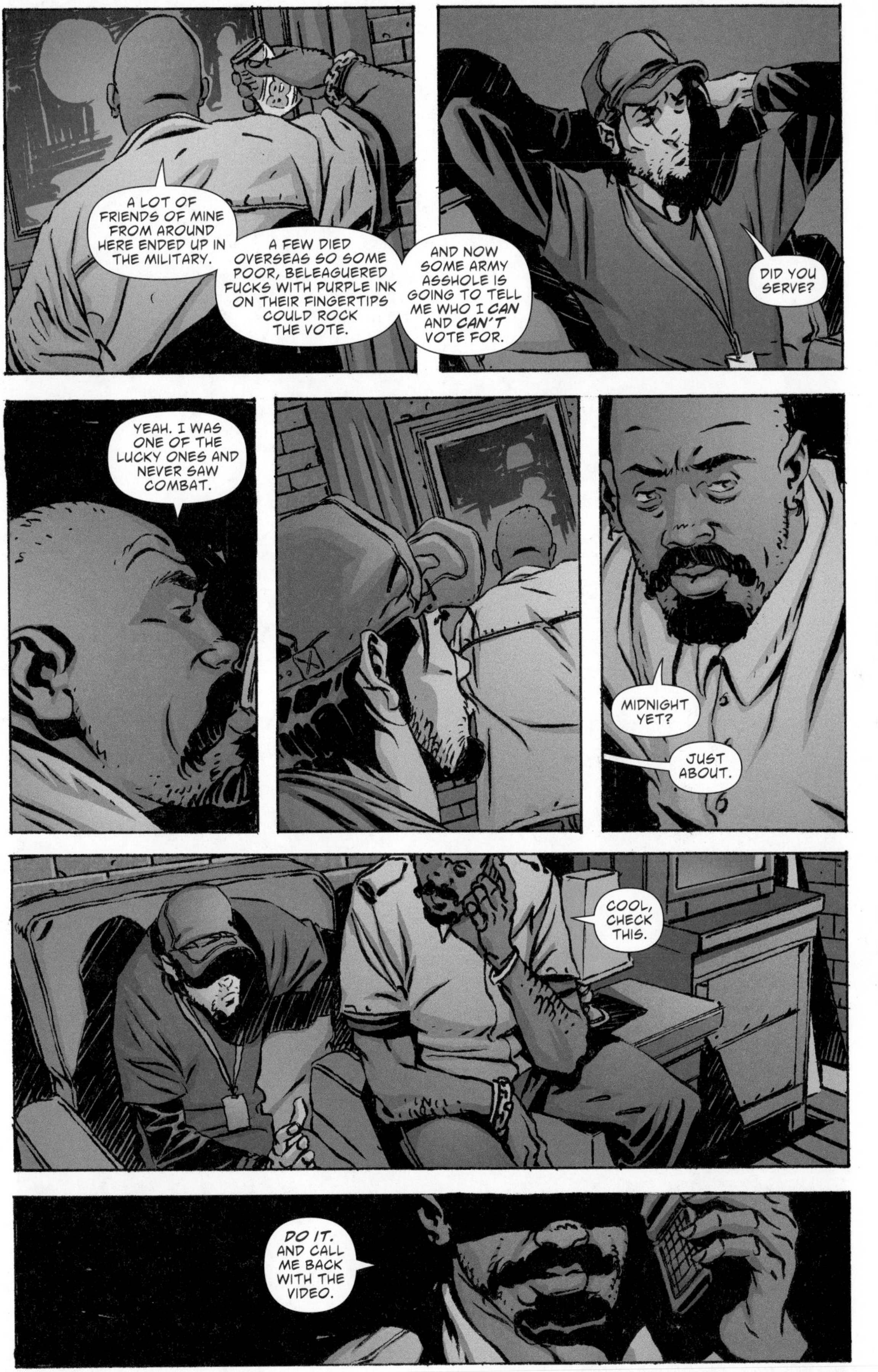
A LOT OF FRIENDS OF MINE FROM AROUND HERE ENDED UP IN THE MILITARY.
A FEW DIED OVERSEAS SO SOME POOR, BELEAGUERED FUCKS WITH PURPLE INK ON THEIR FINGERTIPS COULD ROCK THE VOTE.
AND NOW SOME ARMY ASSHOLE IS GOING TO TELL ME WHO I *CAN* AND *CAN'T* VOTE FOR.
DID YOU SERVE?
YEAH. I WAS ONE OF THE LUCKY ONES AND NEVER SAW COMBAT.
MIDNIGHT YET?
JUST ABOUT.
COOL, CHECK THIS.
DO IT. AND CALL ME BACK WITH THE VIDEO.

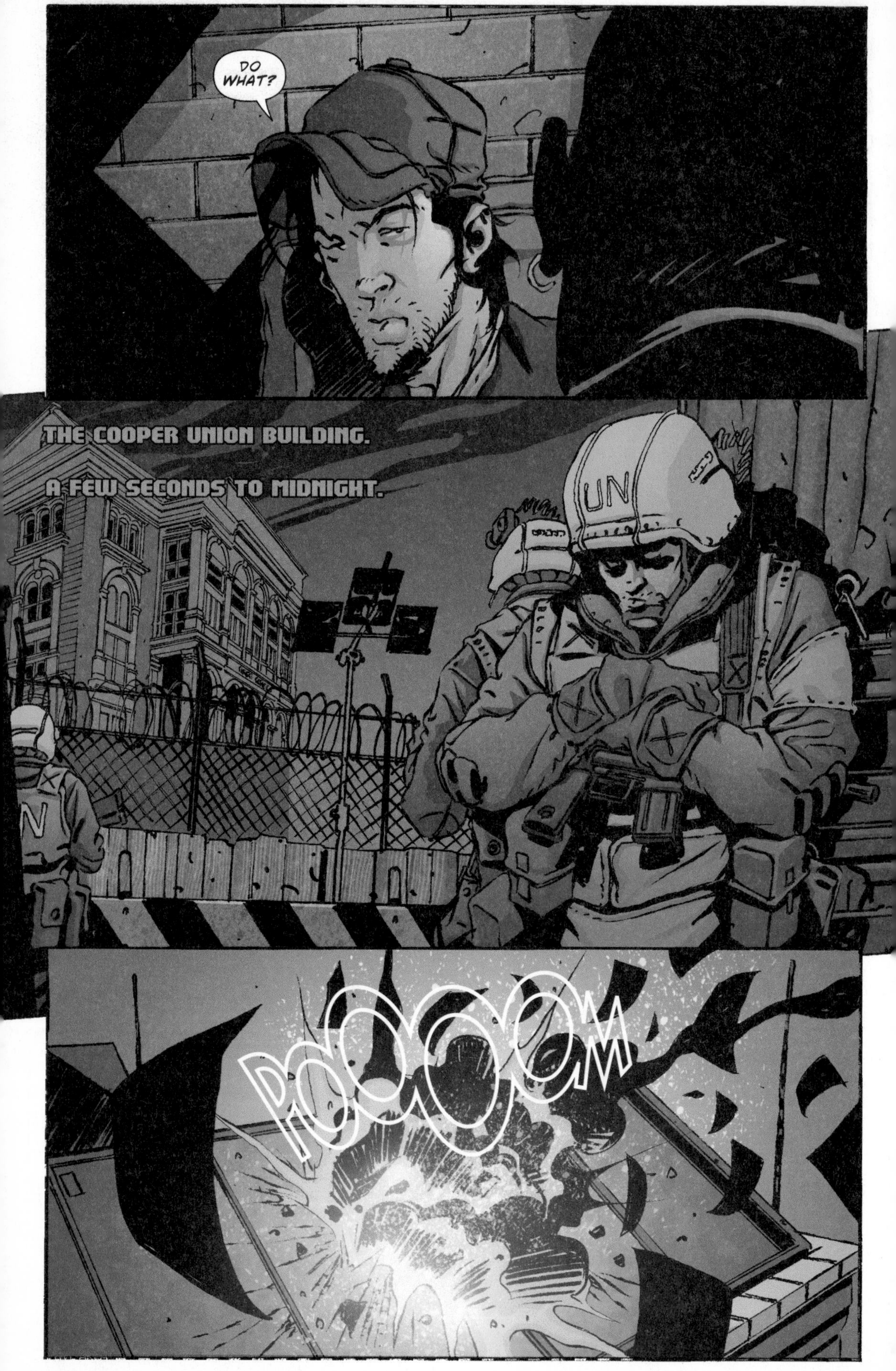
DO WHAT?
THE COOPER UNION BUILDING.
A FEW SECONDS TO MIDNIGHT.
UN
UN
BOOOOOM

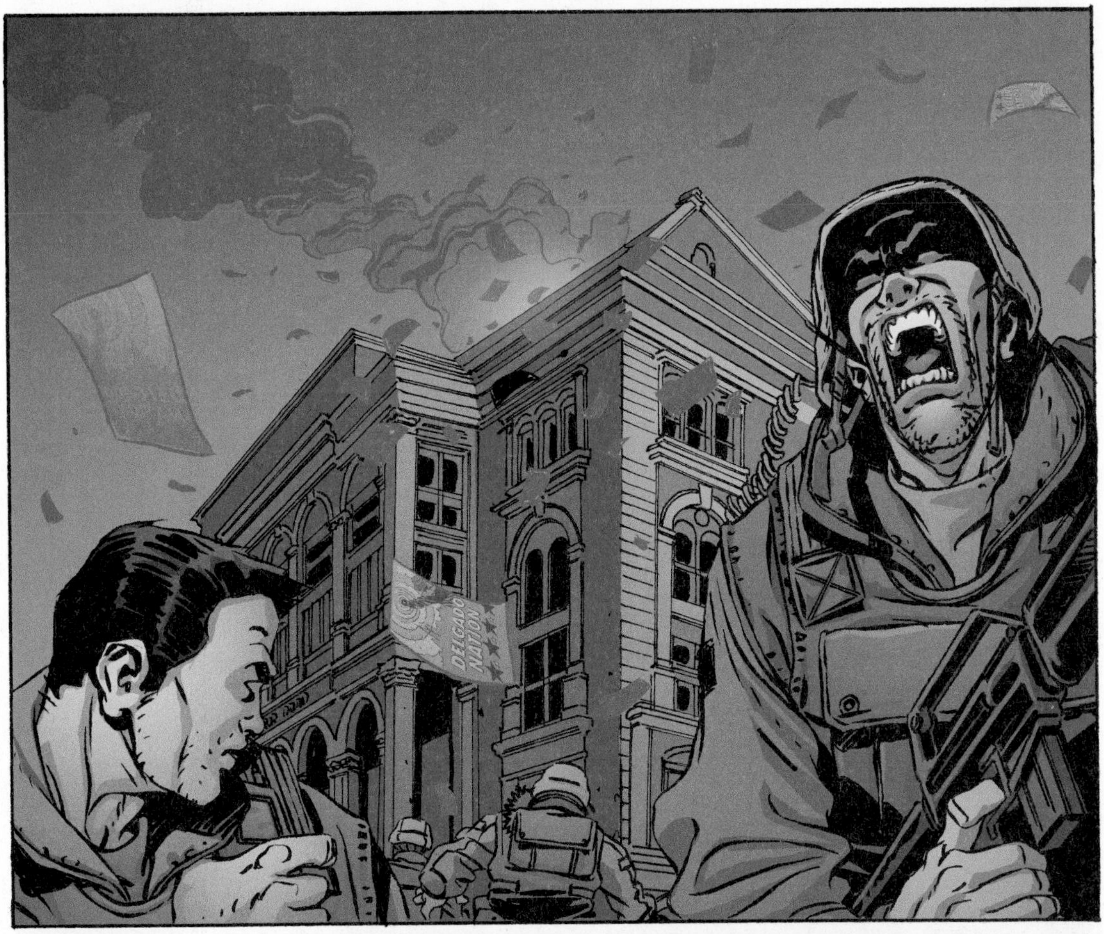
DELGADO NATION

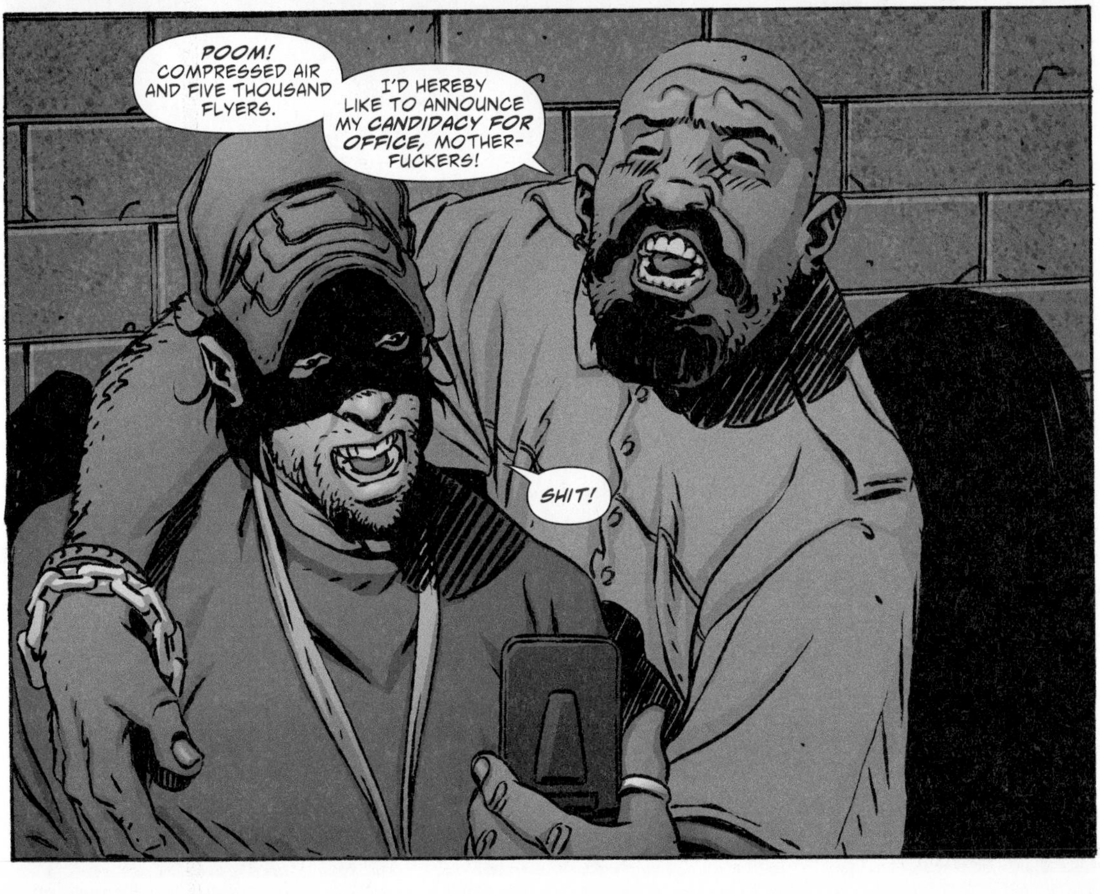
POOM! COMPRESSED AIR AND FIVE THOUSAND FLYERS.
I'D HEREBY LIKE TO ANNOUNCE MY CANDIDACY FOR OFFICE, MOTHER-FUCKERS!
SHIT!

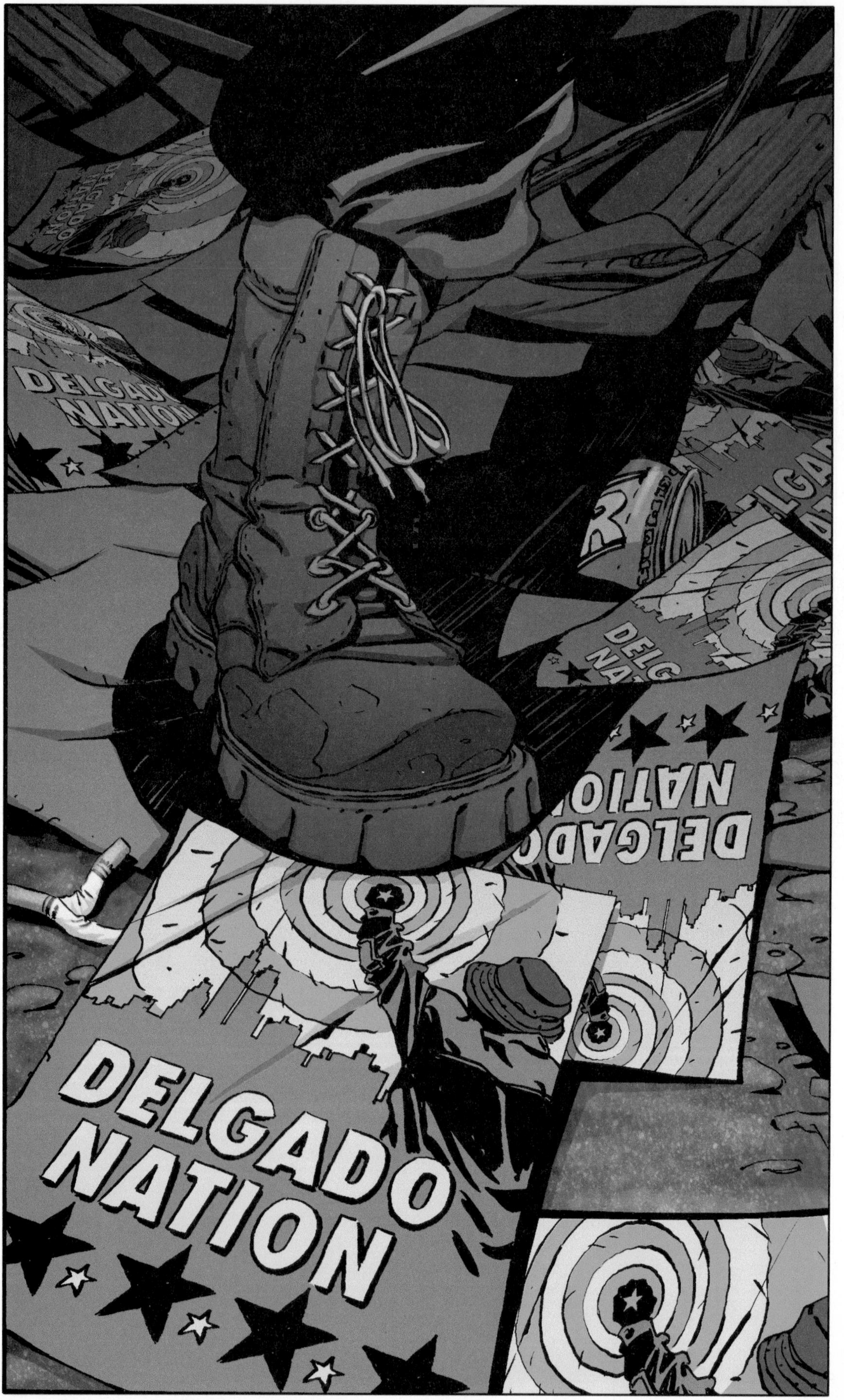
DELGADO NATION
DELGADO NATION
DELGADO NATION

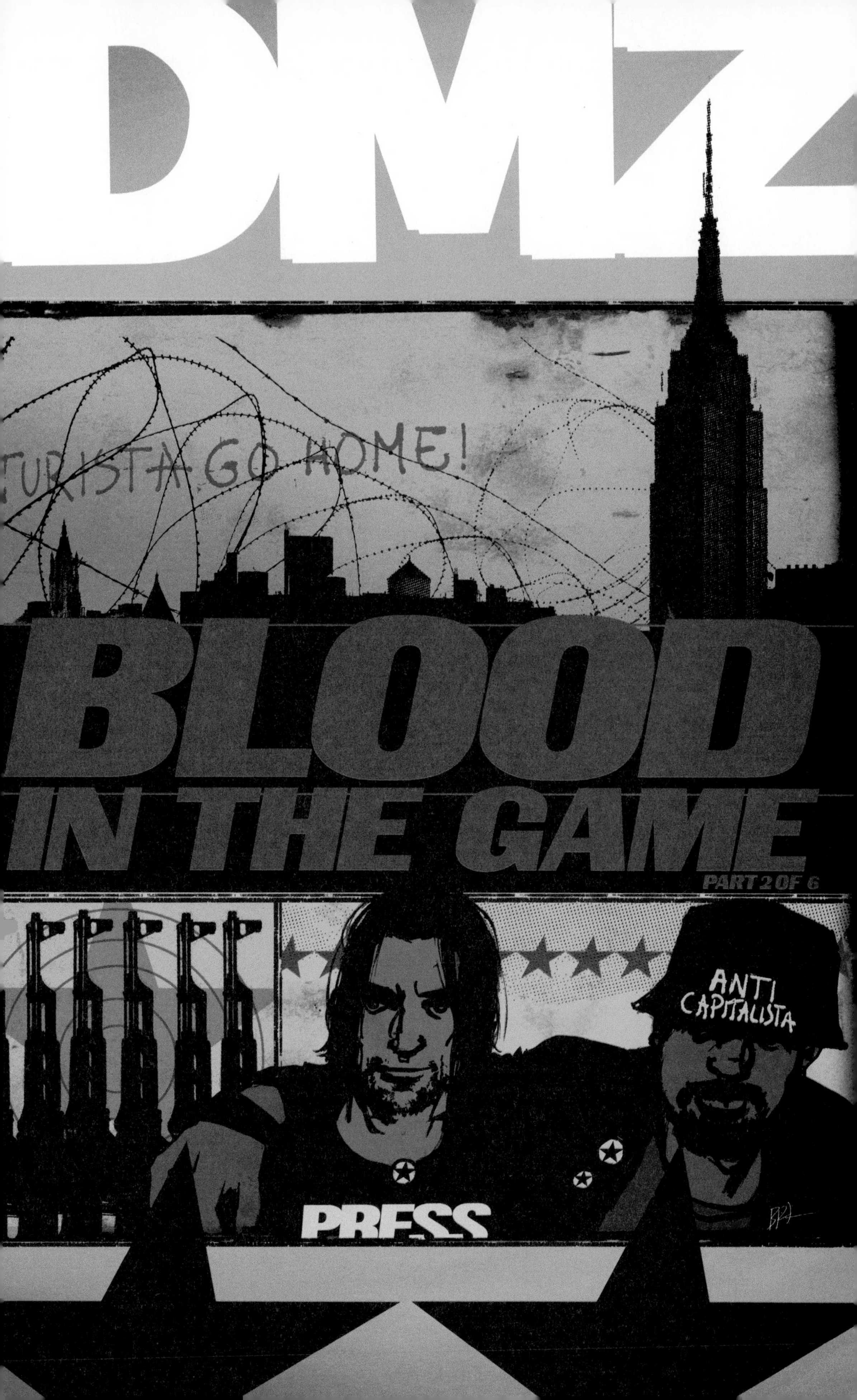
DMZ
TURISTA GO HOME!
BLOOD IN THE GAME
PART 2 OF 6
ANTI CAPITALISTA
PRESS

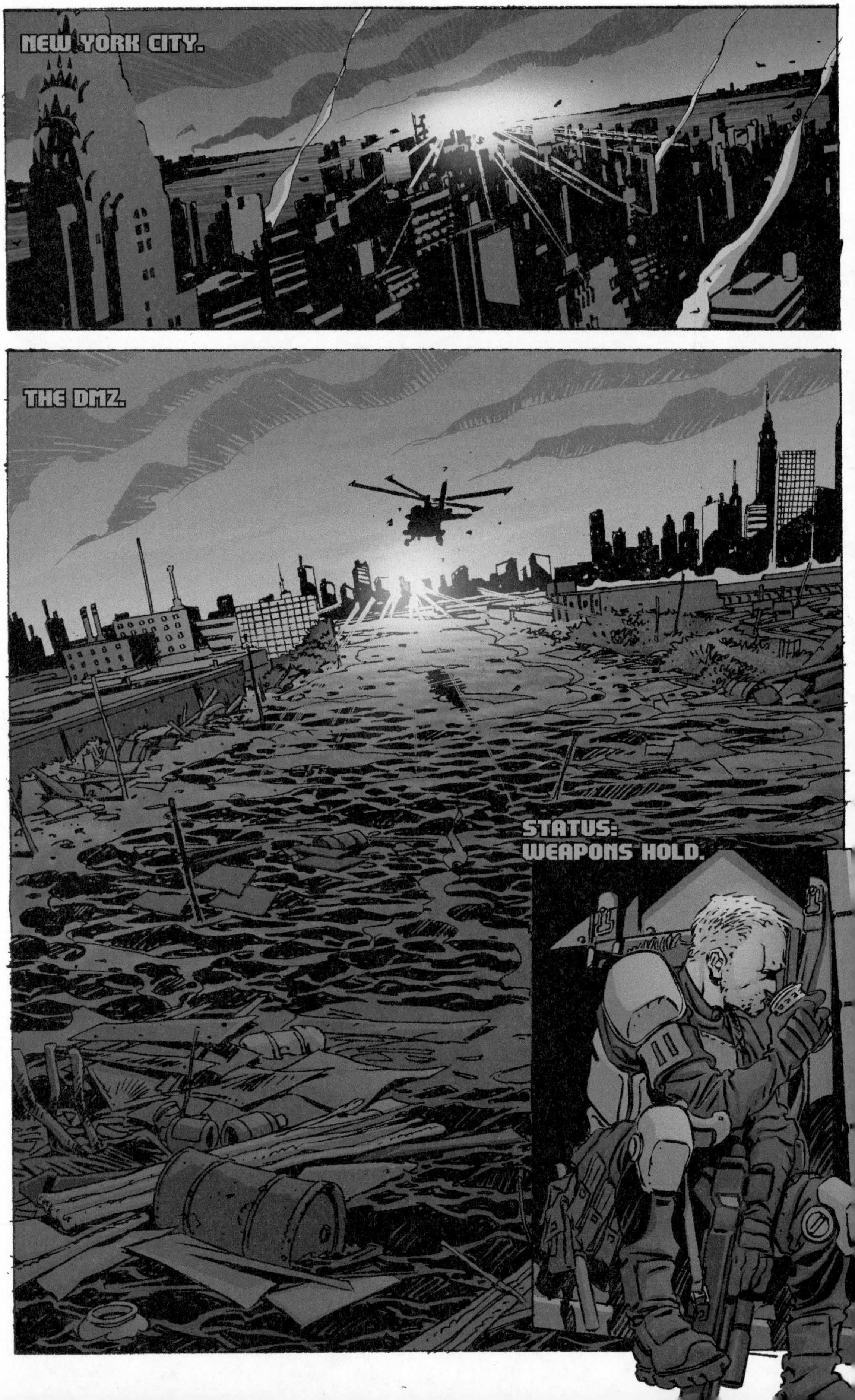
NEW YORK CITY.
THE DMZ.
STATUS:
WEAPONS HOLD.

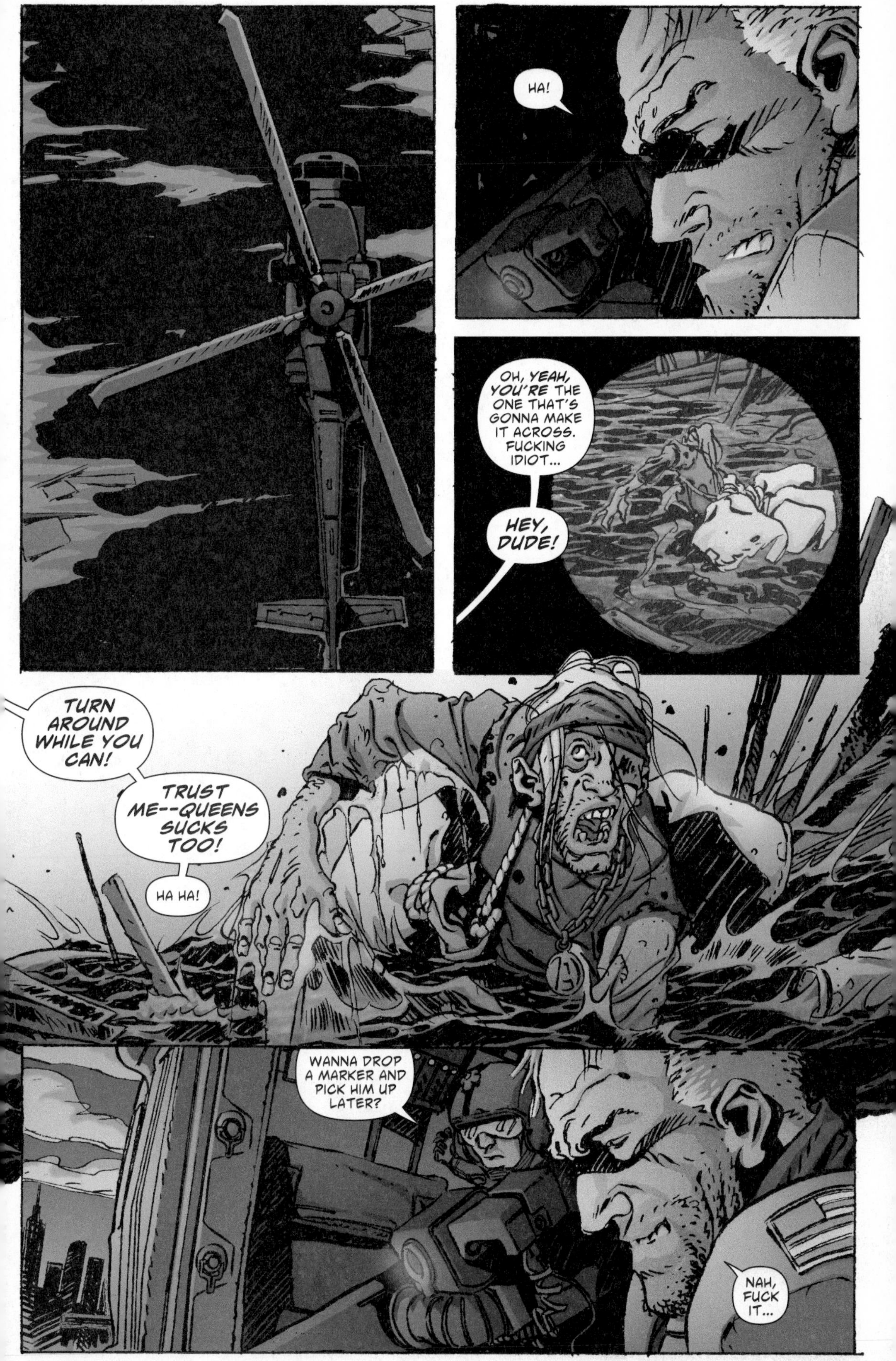
HA!
OH, YEAH, YOU'RE THE ONE THAT'S GONNA MAKE IT ACROSS. FUCKING IDIOT...
HEY, DUDE!
TURN AROUND WHILE YOU CAN!
TRUST ME--QUEENS SUCKS TOO!
HA HA!
WANNA DROP A MARKER AND PICK HIM UP LATER?
NAH, FUCK IT...

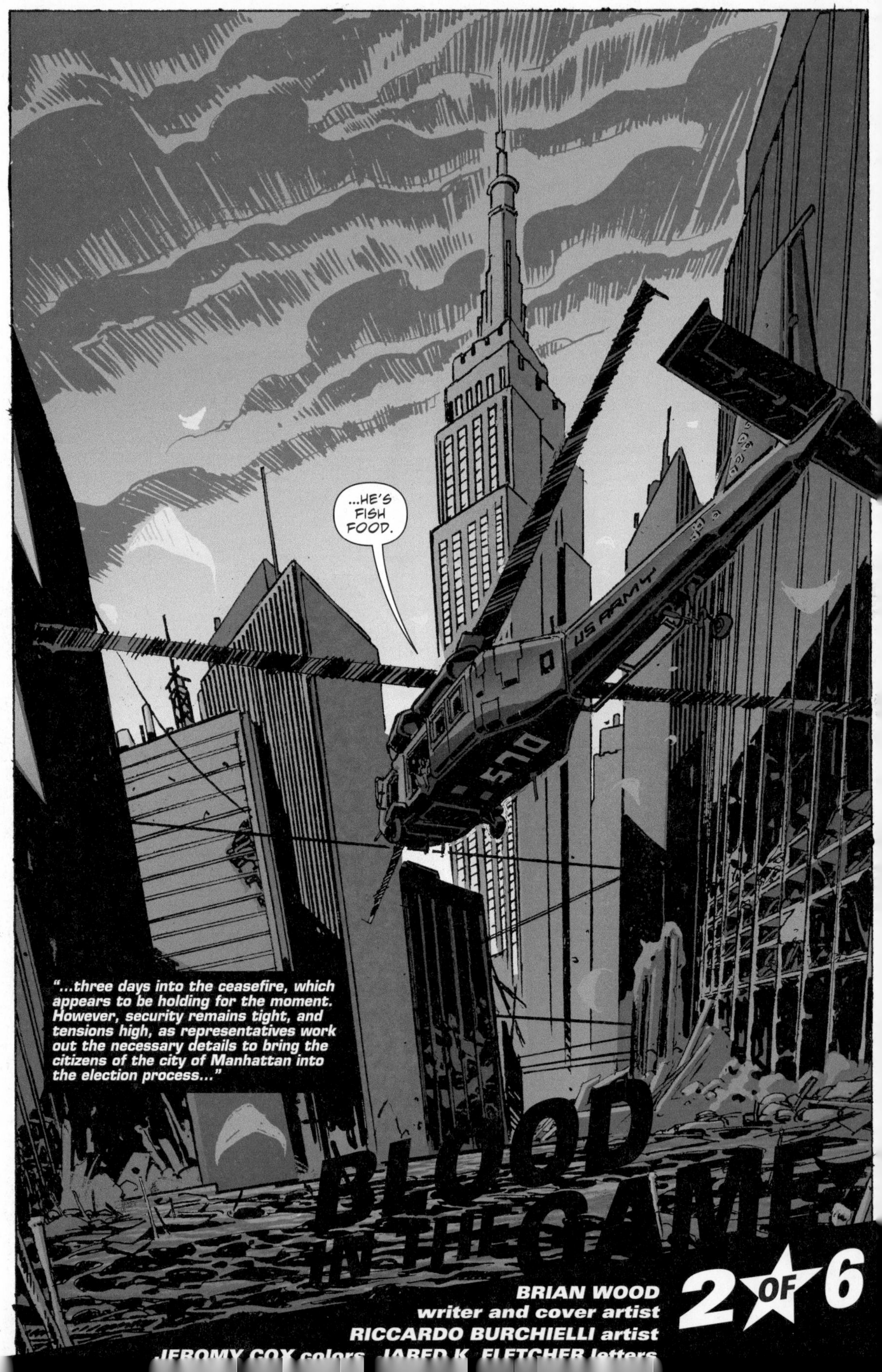
...HE'S FISH FOOD.
"...three days into the ceasefire, which appears to be holding for the moment. However, security remains tight, and tensions high, as representatives work out the necessary details to bring the citizens of the city of Manhattan into the election process..."
BLOOD IN THE GAME
2 OF 6
BRIAN WOOD writer and cover artist
RICCARDO BURCHIELLI artist
JEROMY COX colors JARED K. FLETCHER letters

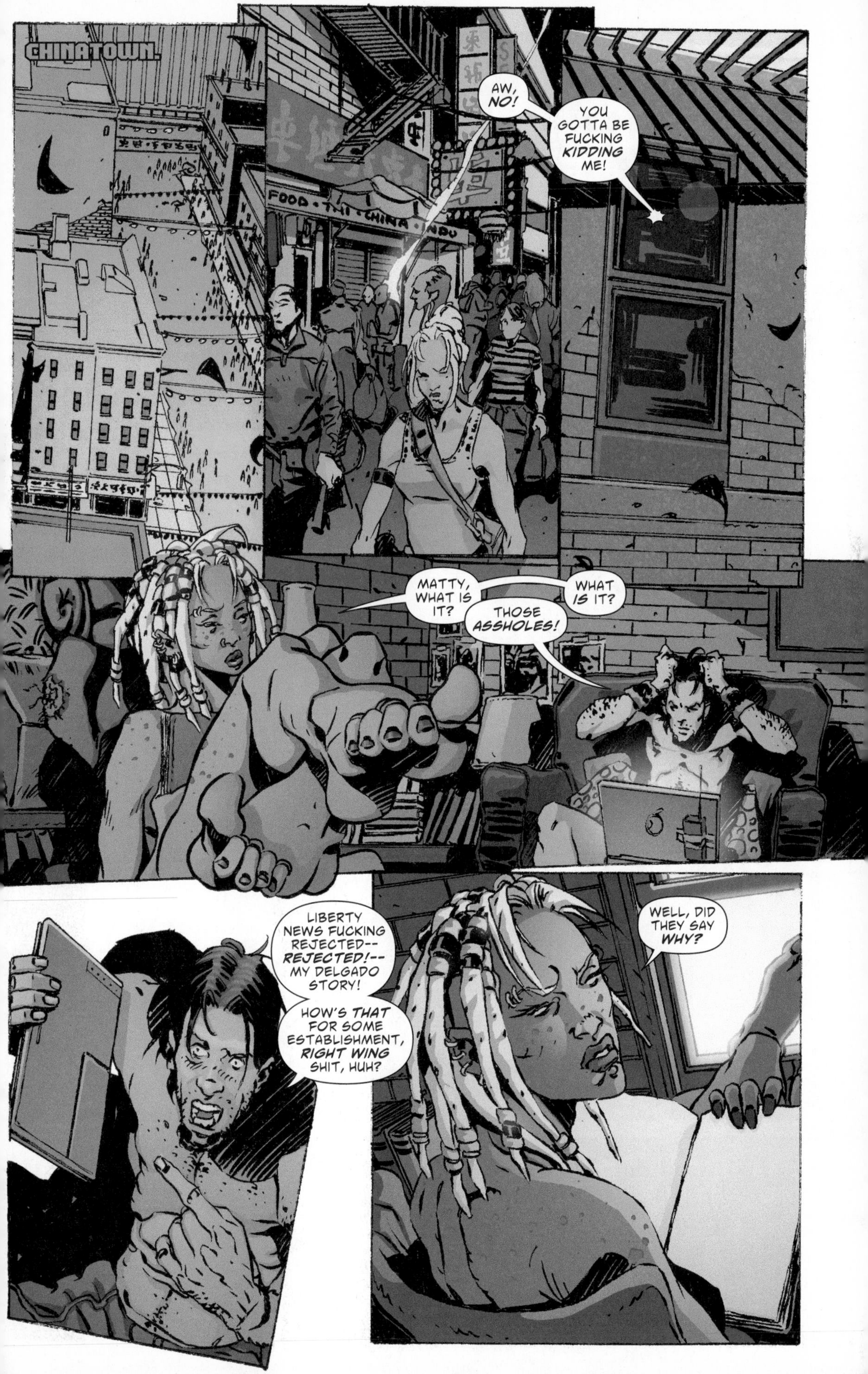

CHINATOWN.
AW, NO!
YOU GOTTA BE FUCKING KIDDING ME!
MATTY, WHAT IS IT?
WHAT IS IT?
THOSE ASSHOLES!
LIBERTY NEWS FUCKING REJECTED-- REJECTED!-- MY DELGADO STORY!
HOW'S THAT FOR SOME ESTABLISHMENT, RIGHT WING SHIT, HUH?
WELL, DID THEY SAY WHY?

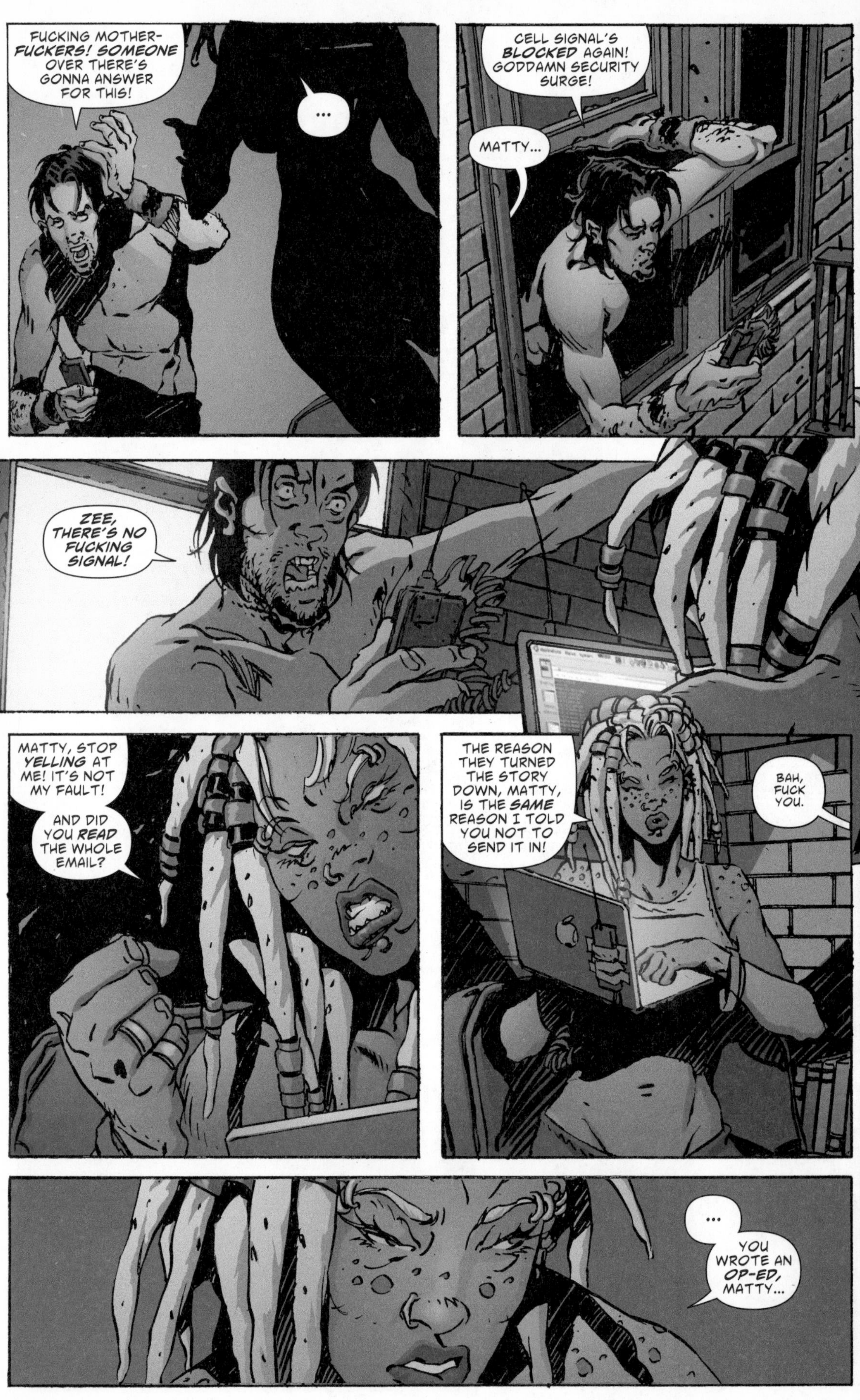
FUCKING MOTHER-FUCKERS! SOMEONE OVER THERE'S GONNA ANSWER FOR THIS!
...
CELL SIGNAL'S BLOCKED AGAIN! GODDAMN SECURITY SURGE!
MATTY...
ZEE, THERE'S NO FUCKING SIGNAL!
MATTY, STOP YELLING AT ME! IT'S NOT MY FAULT!
AND DID YOU READ THE WHOLE EMAIL?
THE REASON THEY TURNED THE STORY DOWN, MATTY, IS THE SAME REASON I TOLD YOU NOT TO SEND IT IN!
BAH, FUCK YOU.
...
YOU WROTE AN OP-ED, MATTY...

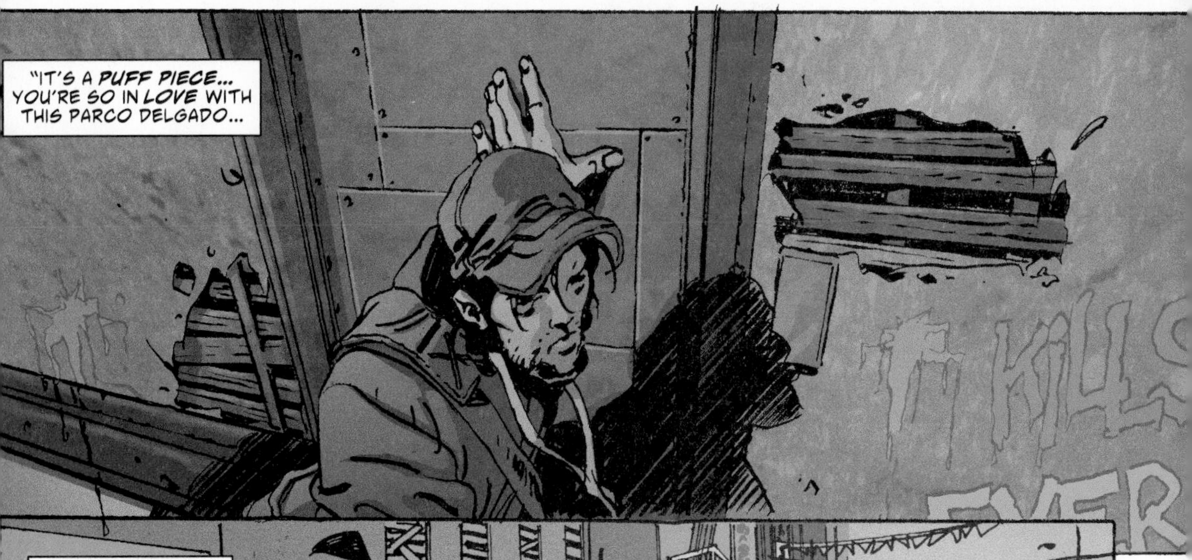
"IT'S A PUFF PIECE... YOU'RE SO IN LOVE WITH THIS PARCO DELGADO...
KILLS
EVER

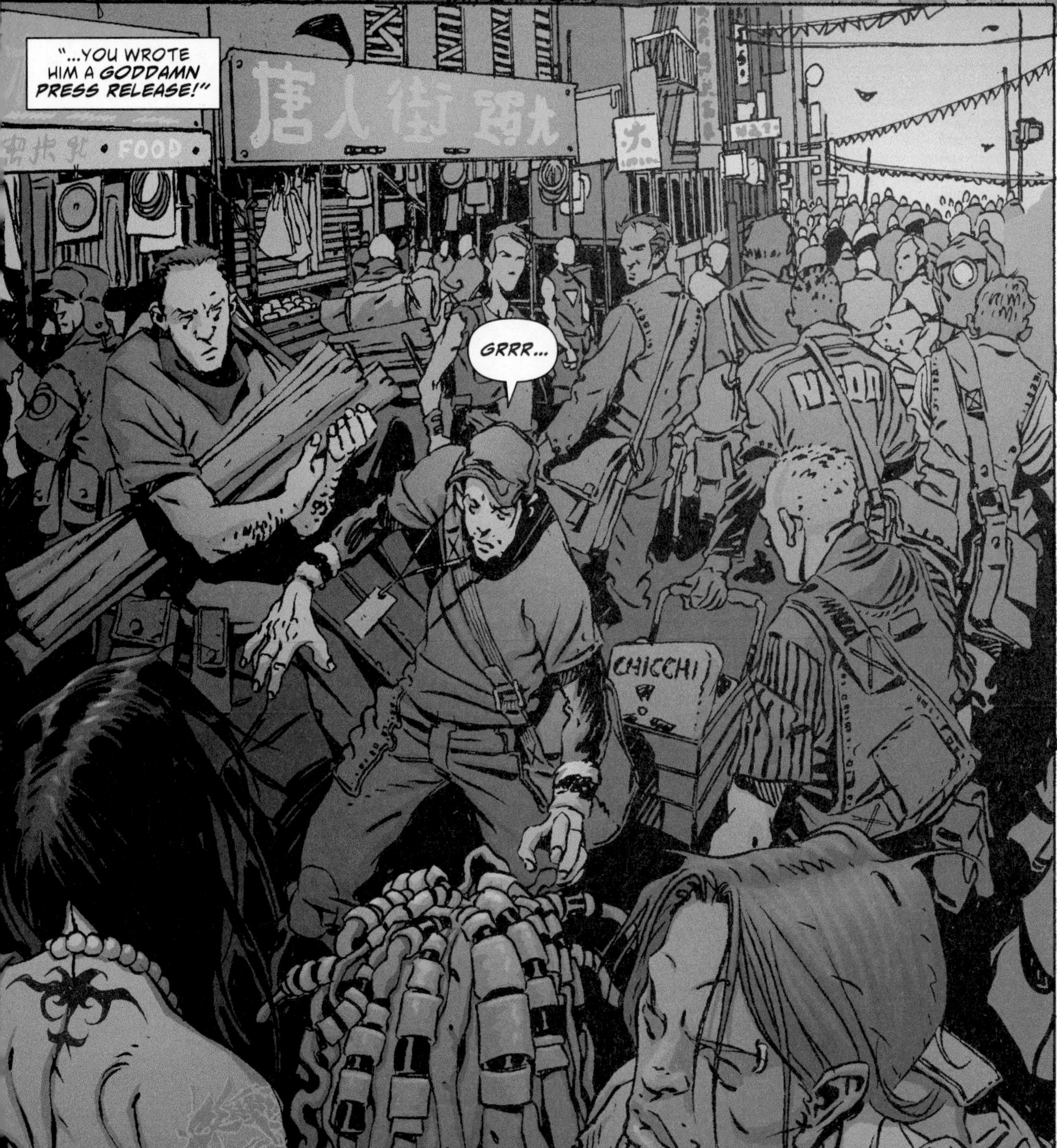
"...YOU WROTE HIM A GODDAMN PRESS RELEASE!"
唐人街
FOOD
GRRR...
CHICCHI

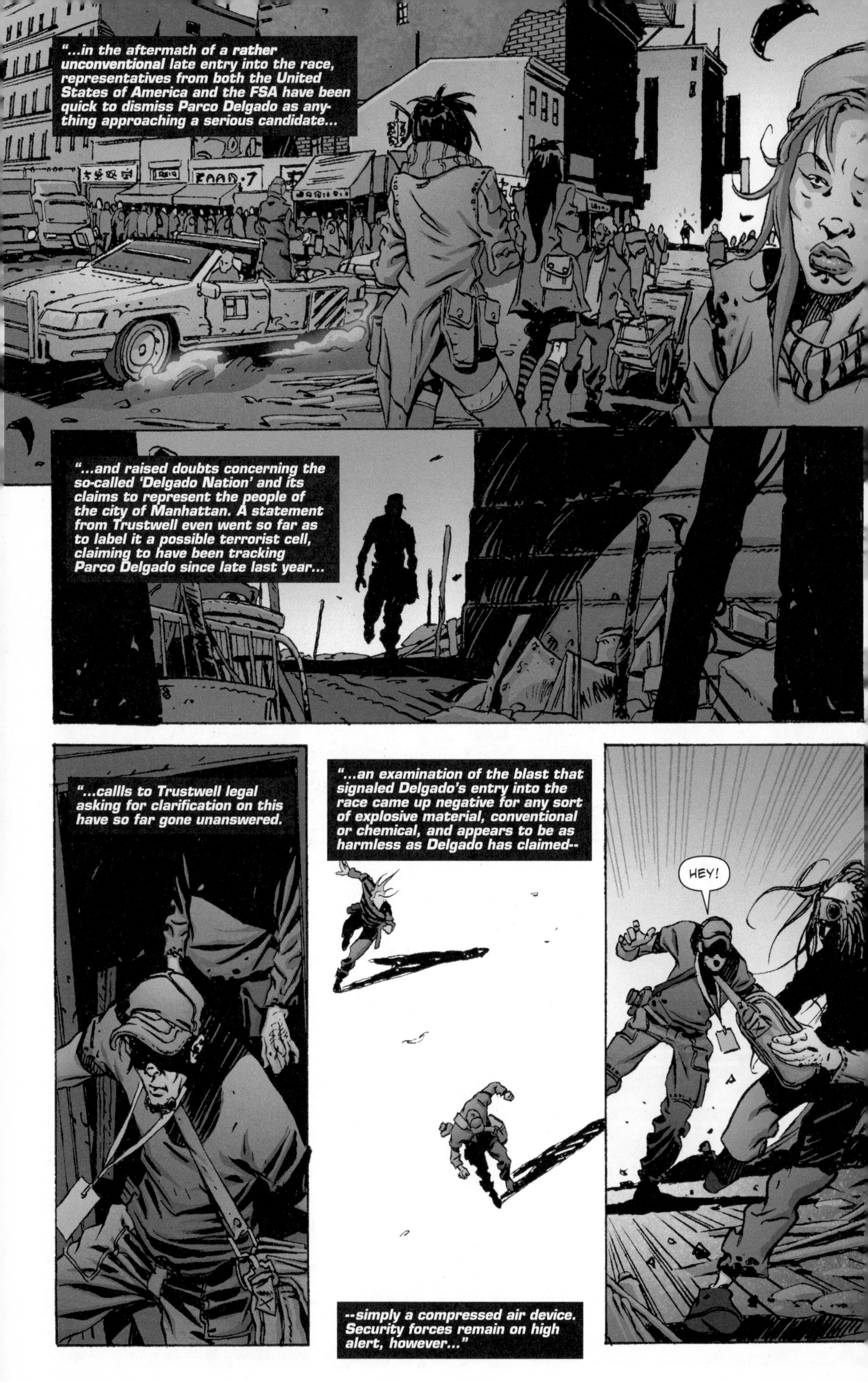
"...in the aftermath of a rather unconventional late entry into the race, representatives from both the United States of America and the FSA have been quick to dismiss Parco Delgado as anything approaching a serious candidate...
"...and raised doubts concerning the so-called 'Delgado Nation' and its claims to represent the people of the city of Manhattan. A statement from Trustwell even went so far as to label it a possible terrorist cell, claiming to have been tracking Parco Delgado since late last year...
"...callls to Trustwell legal asking for clarification on this have so far gone unanswered.
"...an examination of the blast that signaled Delgado's entry into the race came up negative for any sort of explosive material, conventional or chemical, and appears to be as harmless as Delgado has claimed--
--simply a compressed air device. Security forces remain on high alert, however..."
HEY!

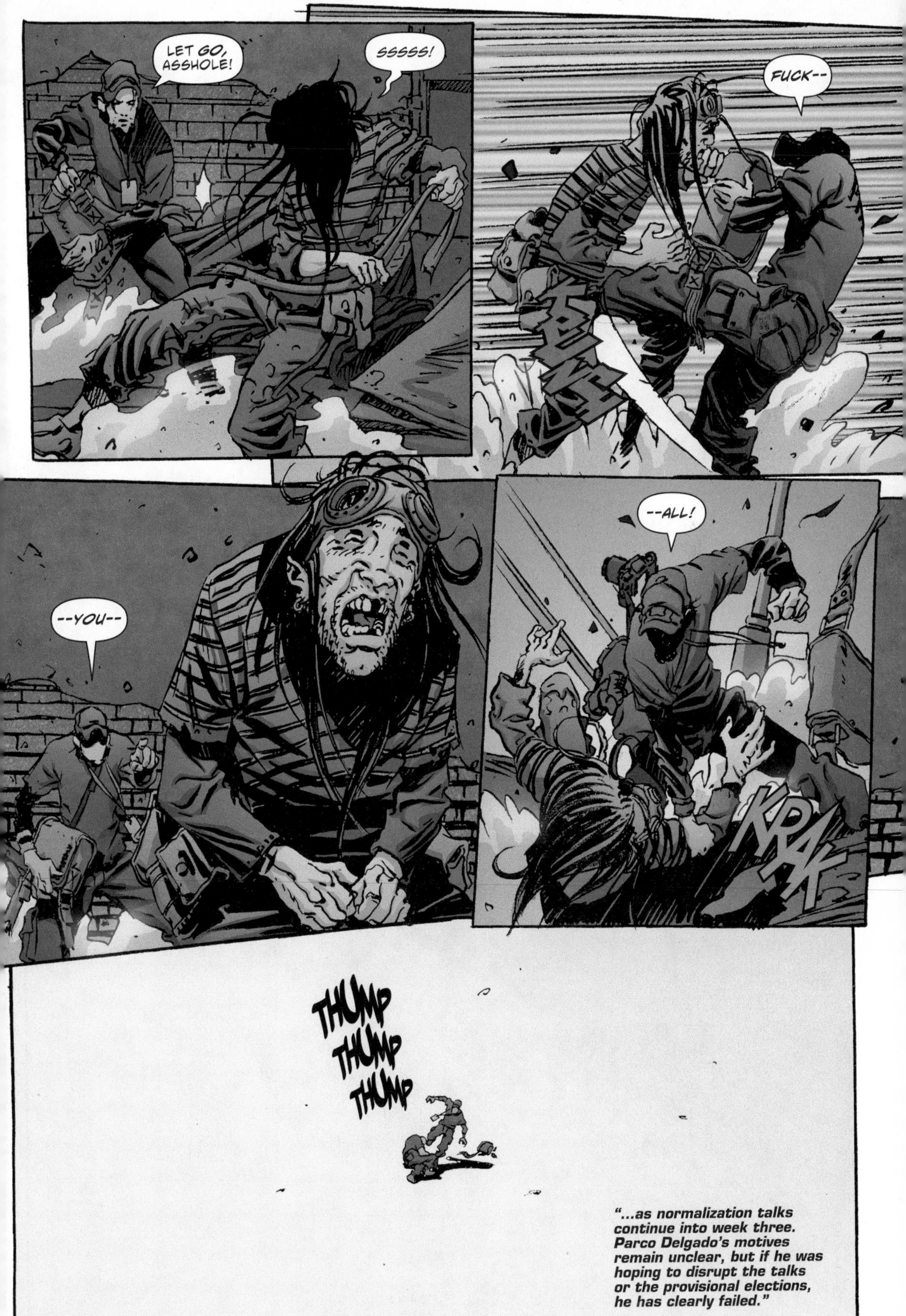
LET GO, ASSHOLE!
SSSSS!
FUCK--
--YOU--
--ALL!
KRAK
THUMP
THUMP
THUMP
"...as normalization talks continue into week three. Parco Delgado's motives remain unclear, but if he was hoping to disrupt the talks or the provisional elections, he has clearly failed."

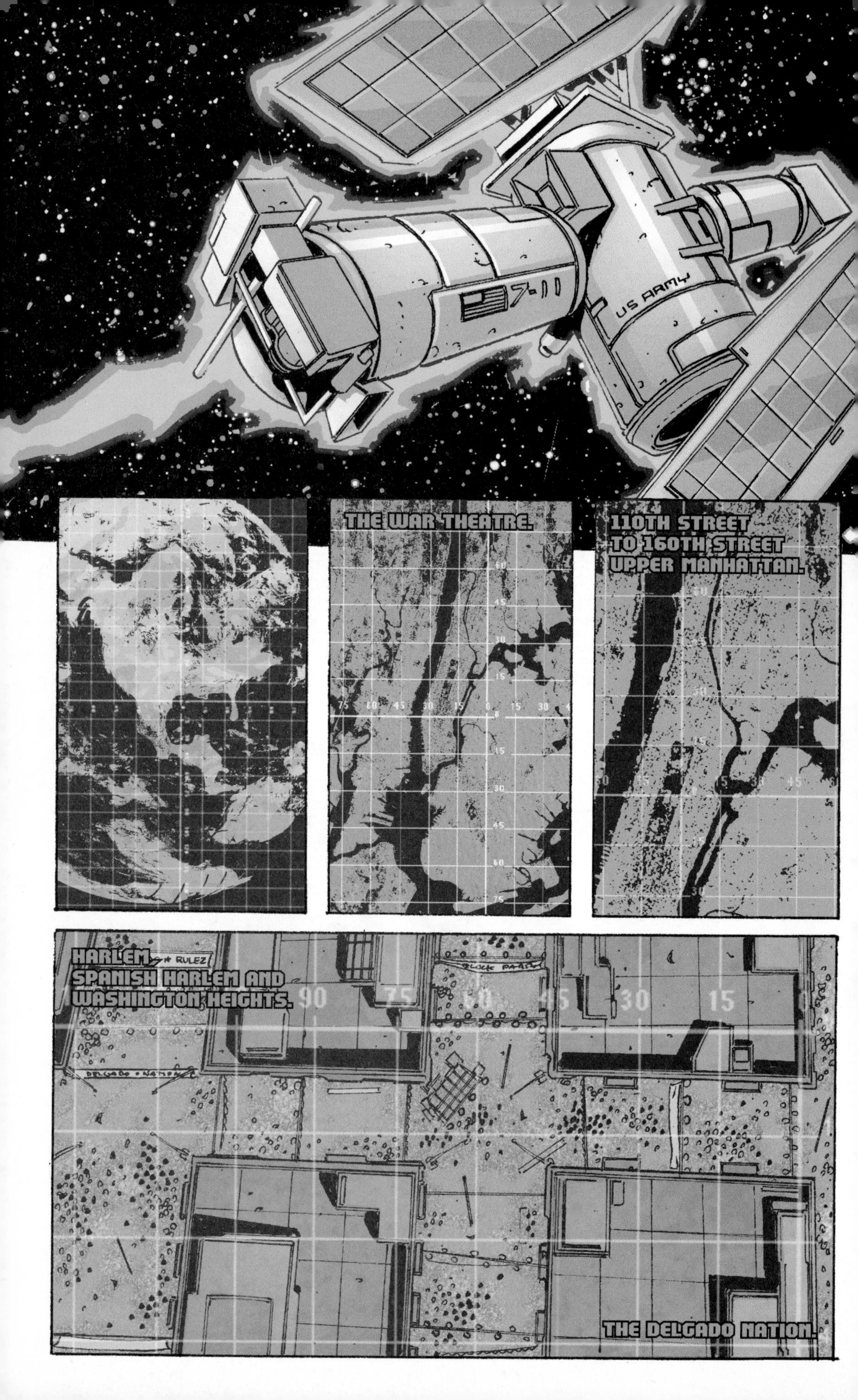
US ARMY
THE WAR THEATRE.
110TH STREET
TO 160TH STREET
UPPER MANHATTAN.
HARLEM
SPANISH HARLEM AND
WASHINGTON HEIGHTS.
THE DELGADO NATION.

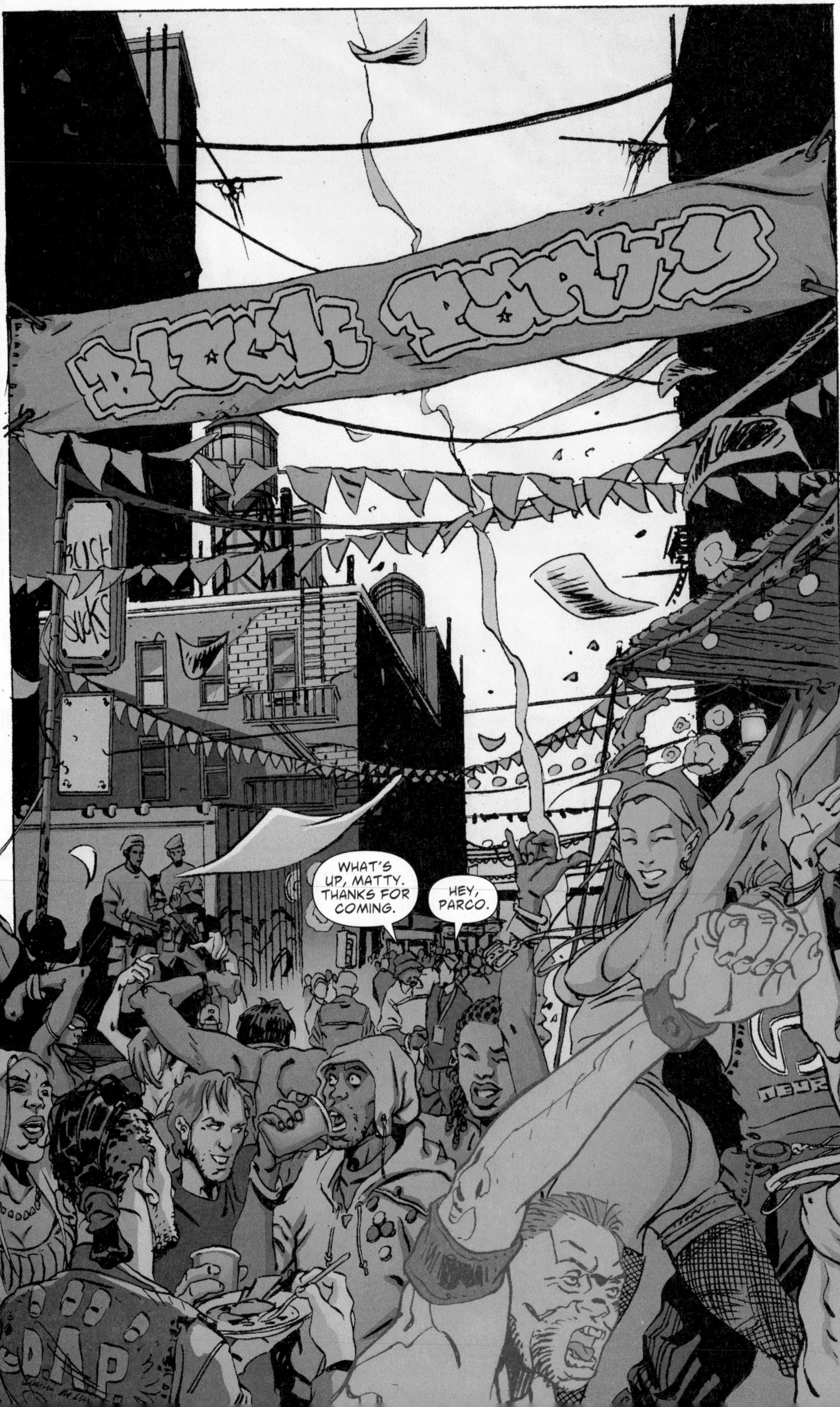
BLOCK PARTY
BUSH SUCKS
WHAT'S UP, MATTY. THANKS FOR COMING.
HEY, PARCO.

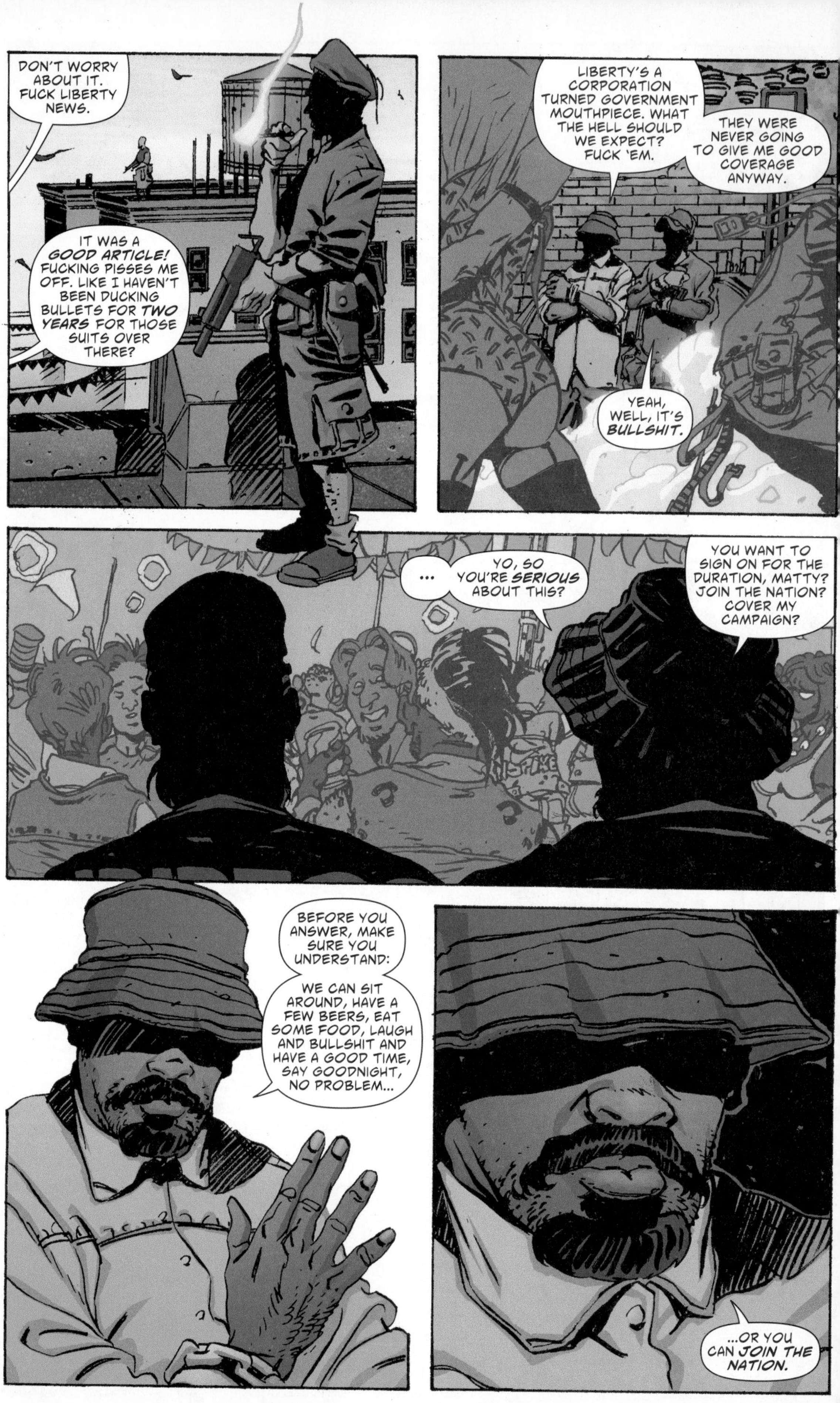
DON'T WORRY ABOUT IT. FUCK LIBERTY NEWS.
IT WAS A *GOOD ARTICLE!* FUCKING PISSES ME OFF. LIKE I HAVEN'T BEEN DUCKING BULLETS FOR *TWO YEARS* FOR THOSE SUITS OVER THERE?
LIBERTY'S A CORPORATION TURNED GOVERNMENT MOUTHPIECE. WHAT THE HELL SHOULD WE EXPECT? FUCK 'EM.
THEY WERE NEVER GOING TO GIVE ME GOOD COVERAGE ANYWAY.
YEAH, WELL, IT'S *BULLSHIT.*
...
YO, SO YOU'RE *SERIOUS* ABOUT THIS?
YOU WANT TO SIGN ON FOR THE DURATION, MATTY? JOIN THE NATION? COVER MY CAMPAIGN?
BEFORE YOU ANSWER, MAKE SURE YOU UNDERSTAND:
WE CAN SIT AROUND, HAVE A FEW BEERS, EAT SOME FOOD, LAUGH AND BULLSHIT AND HAVE A GOOD TIME, SAY GOODNIGHT, NO PROBLEM...
...OR YOU CAN *JOIN THE NATION.*

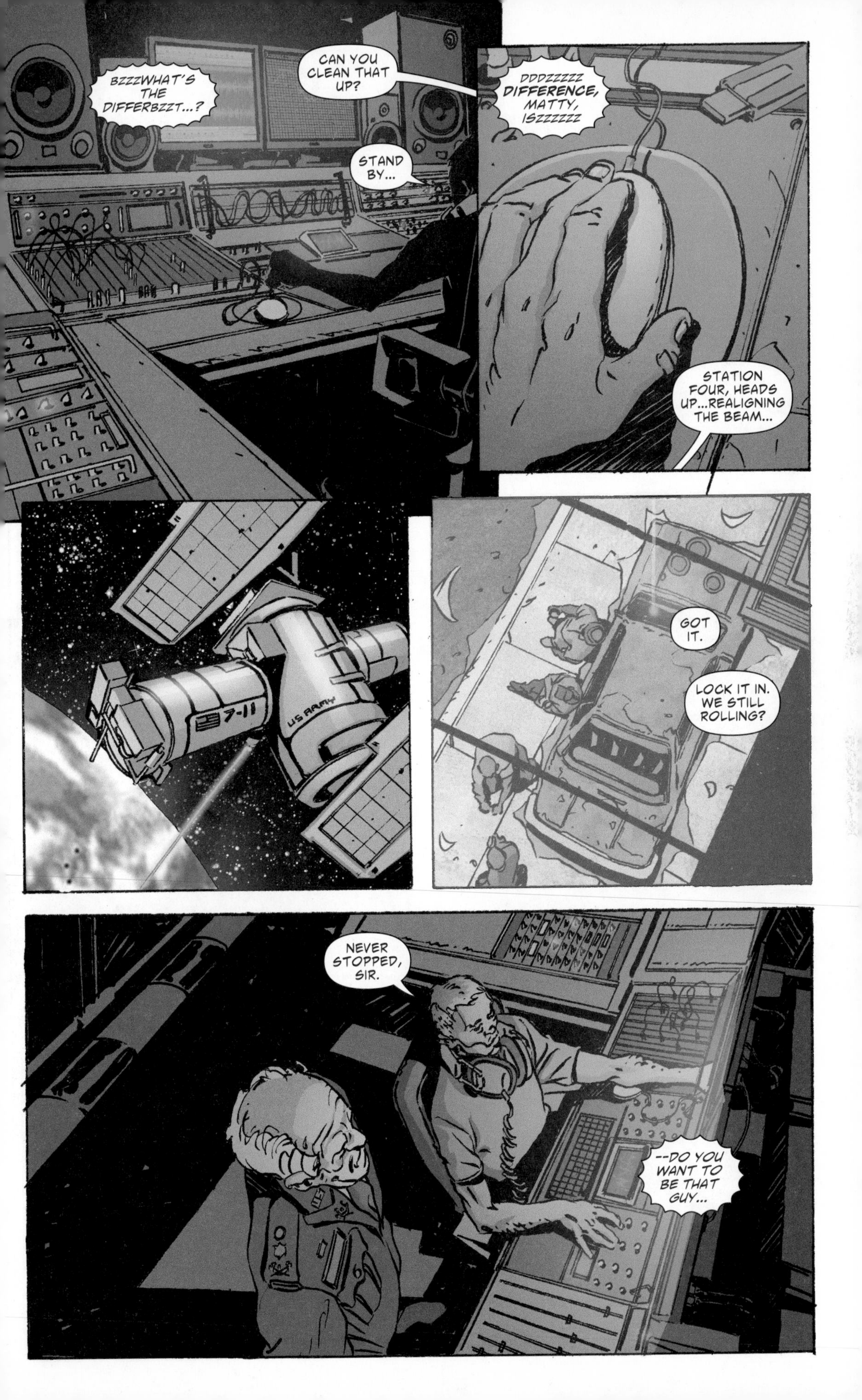
BZZZWHAT'S THE DIFFERBZZT...?
CAN YOU CLEAN THAT UP?
STAND BY...
DDDZZZZZ DIFFERENCE, MATTY, ISZZZZZZ
STATION FOUR, HEADS UP...REALIGNING THE BEAM...
U.S. ARMY
7-11
GOT IT.
LOCK IT IN. WE STILL ROLLING?
NEVER STOPPED, SIR.
--DO YOU WANT TO BE THAT GUY...

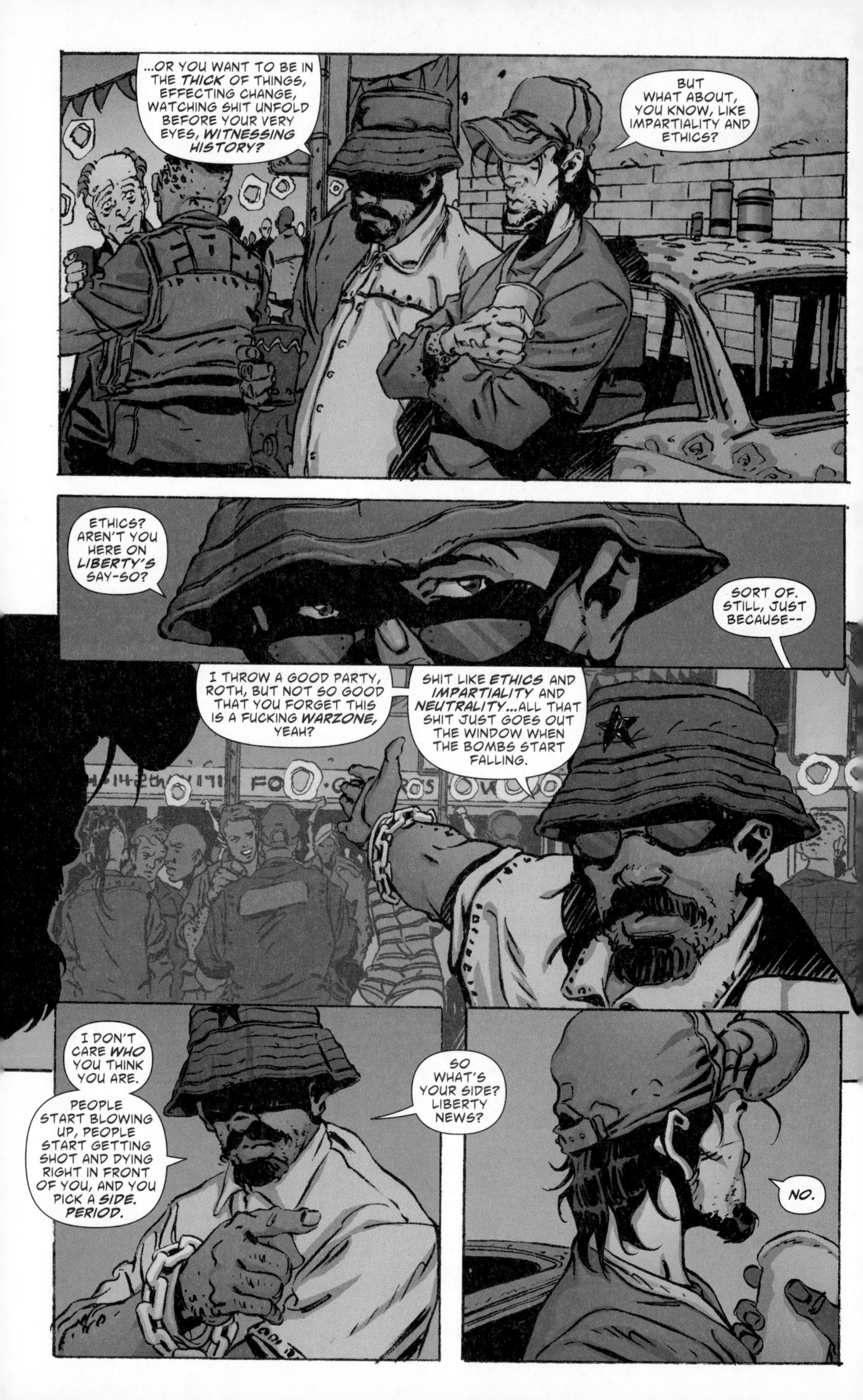
...OR YOU WANT TO BE IN THE *THICK* OF THINGS, EFFECTING CHANGE, WATCHING SHIT UNFOLD BEFORE YOUR VERY EYES, *WITNESSING HISTORY?*
BUT WHAT ABOUT, YOU KNOW, LIKE IMPARTIALITY AND ETHICS?
ETHICS? AREN'T YOU HERE ON *LIBERTY'S* SAY-SO?
SORT OF. STILL, JUST BECAUSE--
I THROW A GOOD PARTY, ROTH, BUT NOT SO GOOD THAT YOU FORGET THIS IS A FUCKING *WARZONE,* YEAH?
SHIT LIKE *ETHICS* AND *IMPARTIALITY* AND *NEUTRALITY*...ALL THAT SHIT JUST GOES OUT THE WINDOW WHEN THE BOMBS START FALLING.
I DON'T CARE *WHO* YOU THINK YOU ARE.
PEOPLE START BLOWING UP, PEOPLE START GETTING SHOT AND DYING RIGHT IN FRONT OF YOU, AND YOU PICK A *SIDE.* *PERIOD.*
SO WHAT'S YOUR SIDE? LIBERTY NEWS?
NO.

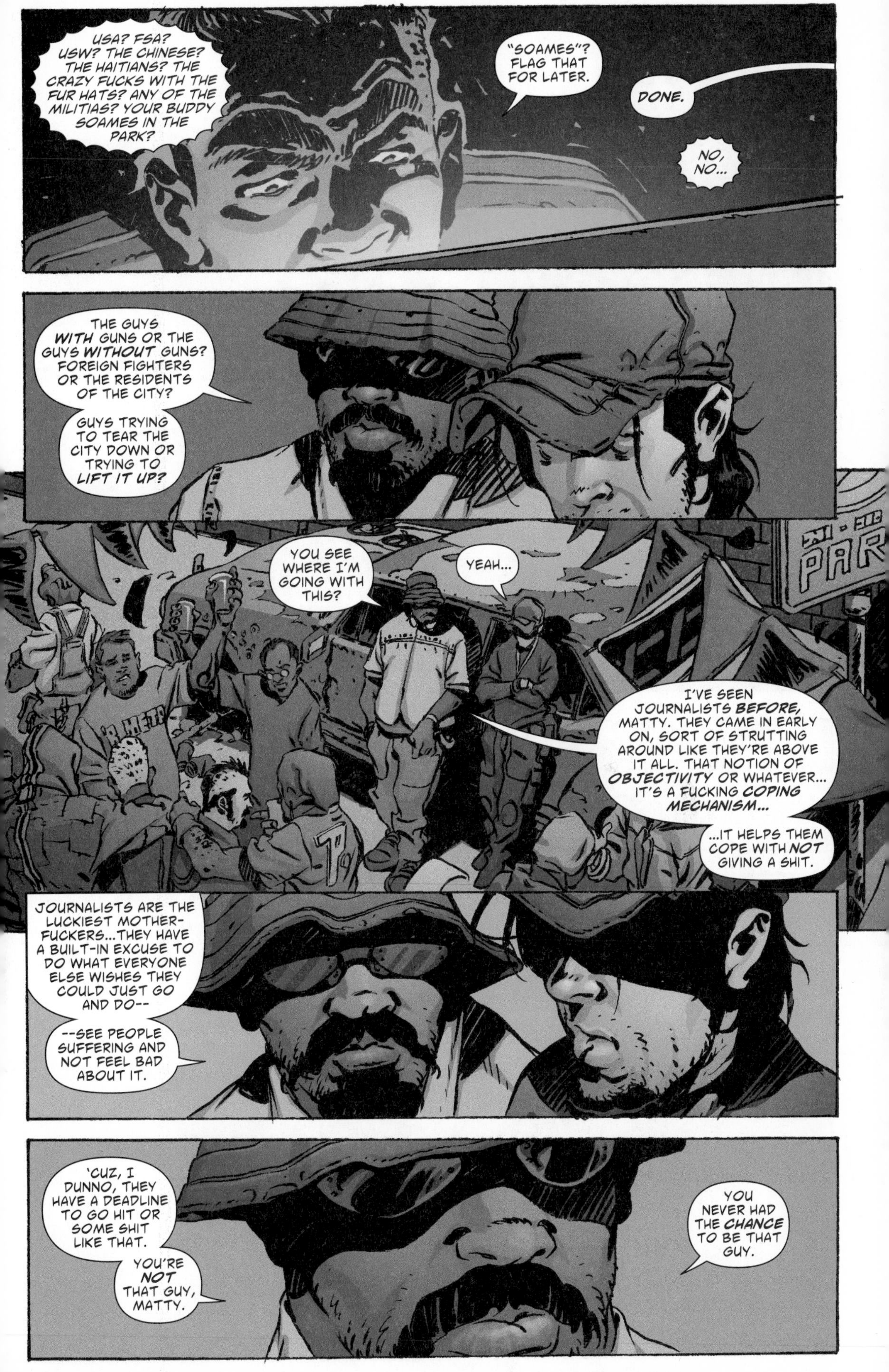
USA? FSA? USW? THE CHINESE? THE HAITIANS? THE CRAZY FUCKS WITH THE FUR HATS? ANY OF THE MILITIAS? YOUR BUDDY SOAMES IN THE PARK?
"SOAMES"? FLAG THAT FOR LATER.
DONE.
NO, NO...
THE GUYS WITH GUNS OR THE GUYS WITHOUT GUNS? FOREIGN FIGHTERS OR THE RESIDENTS OF THE CITY?
GUYS TRYING TO TEAR THE CITY DOWN OR TRYING TO LIFT IT UP?
YOU SEE WHERE I'M GOING WITH THIS?
YEAH...
PAR
I'VE SEEN JOURNALISTS BEFORE, MATTY. THEY CAME IN EARLY ON, SORT OF STRUTTING AROUND LIKE THEY'RE ABOVE IT ALL. THAT NOTION OF OBJECTIVITY OR WHATEVER... IT'S A FUCKING COPING MECHANISM...
...IT HELPS THEM COPE WITH NOT GIVING A SHIT.
JOURNALISTS ARE THE LUCKIEST MOTHER-FUCKERS...THEY HAVE A BUILT-IN EXCUSE TO DO WHAT EVERYONE ELSE WISHES THEY COULD JUST GO AND DO--
--SEE PEOPLE SUFFERING AND NOT FEEL BAD ABOUT IT.
'CUZ, I DUNNO, THEY HAVE A DEADLINE TO GO HIT OR SOME SHIT LIKE THAT.
YOU'RE NOT THAT GUY, MATTY.
YOU NEVER HAD THE CHANCE TO BE THAT GUY.

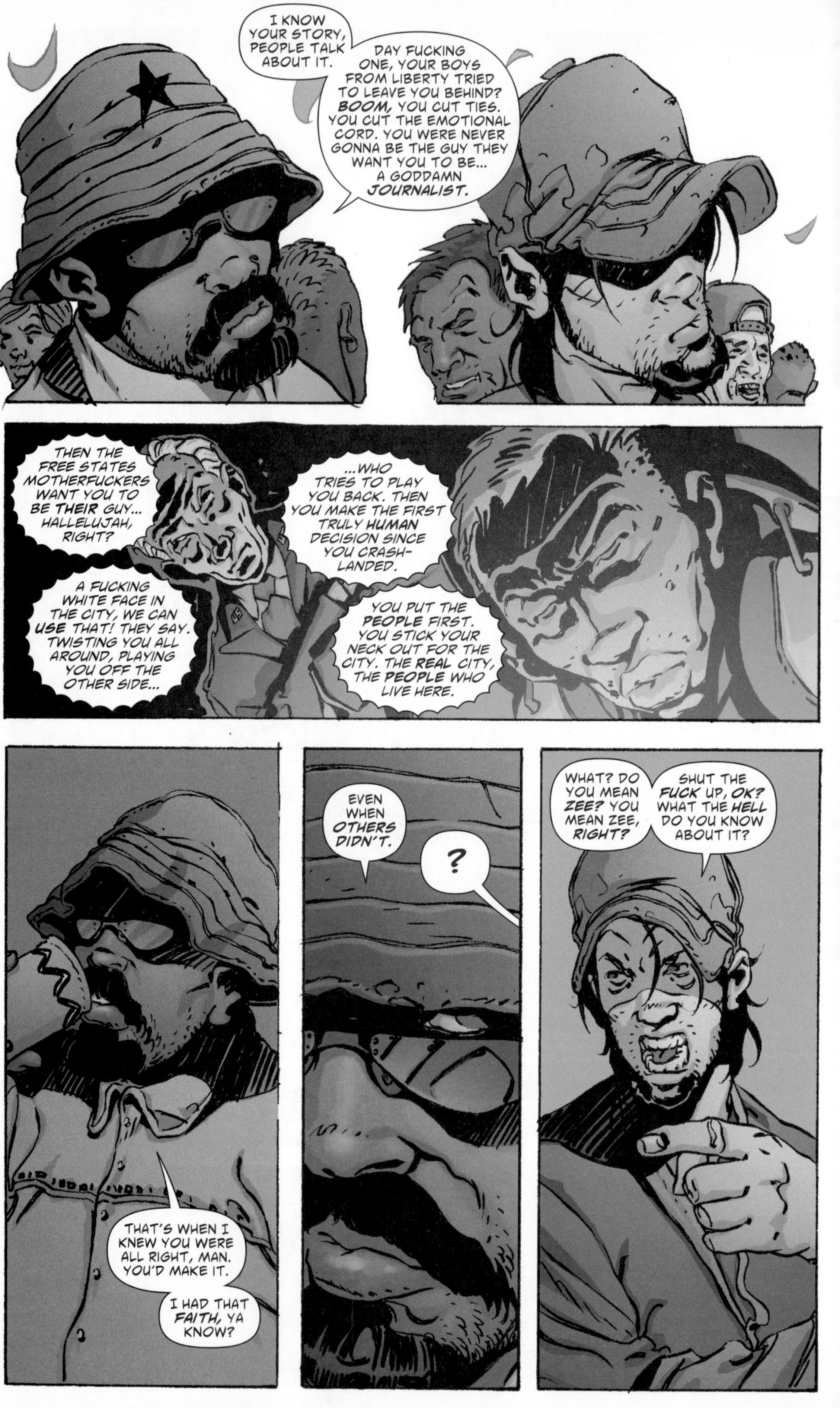
I KNOW YOUR STORY, PEOPLE TALK ABOUT IT.
DAY FUCKING ONE, YOUR BOYS FROM LIBERTY TRIED TO LEAVE YOU BEHIND? BOOM, YOU CUT TIES. YOU CUT THE EMOTIONAL CORD. YOU WERE NEVER GONNA BE THE GUY THEY WANT YOU TO BE... A GODDAMN JOURNALIST.
THEN THE FREE STATES MOTHERFUCKERS WANT YOU TO BE THEIR GUY... HALLELUJAH, RIGHT?
A FUCKING WHITE FACE IN THE CITY, WE CAN USE THAT! THEY SAY. TWISTING YOU ALL AROUND, PLAYING YOU OFF THE OTHER SIDE...
...WHO TRIES TO PLAY YOU BACK. THEN YOU MAKE THE FIRST TRULY HUMAN DECISION SINCE YOU CRASH-LANDED.
YOU PUT THE PEOPLE FIRST. YOU STICK YOUR NECK OUT FOR THE CITY. THE REAL CITY, THE PEOPLE WHO LIVE HERE.
THAT'S WHEN I KNEW YOU WERE ALL RIGHT, MAN. YOU'D MAKE IT.
I HAD THAT FAITH, YA KNOW?
EVEN WHEN OTHERS DIDN'T.
?
WHAT? DO YOU MEAN ZEE? YOU MEAN ZEE, RIGHT?
SHUT THE FUCK UP, OK? WHAT THE HELL DO YOU KNOW ABOUT IT?

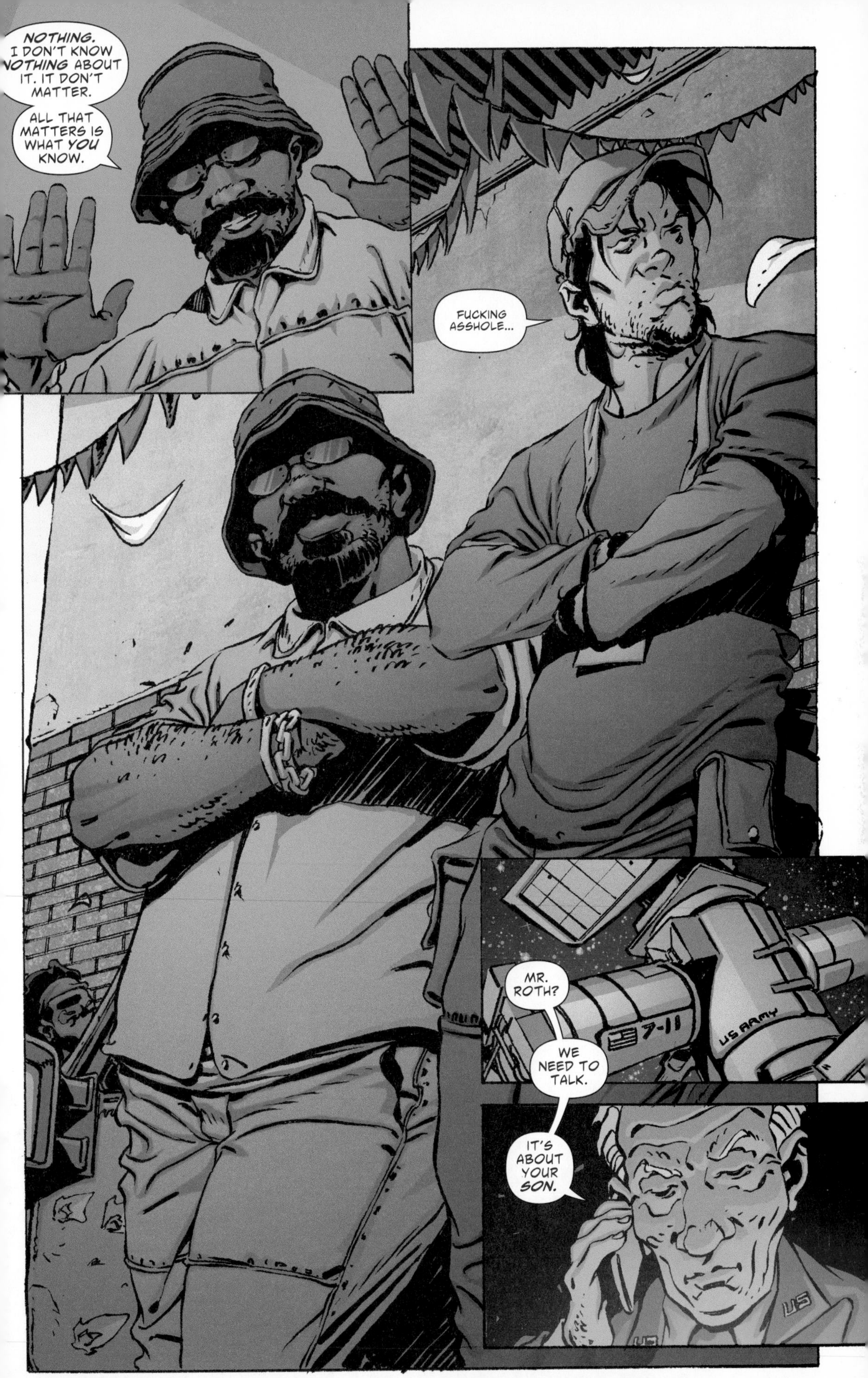
NOTHING. I DON'T KNOW NOTHING ABOUT IT. IT DON'T MATTER.
ALL THAT MATTERS IS WHAT YOU KNOW.
FUCKING ASSHOLE...
MR. ROTH?
WE NEED TO TALK.
IT'S ABOUT YOUR SON.
7-11
US ARMY
US

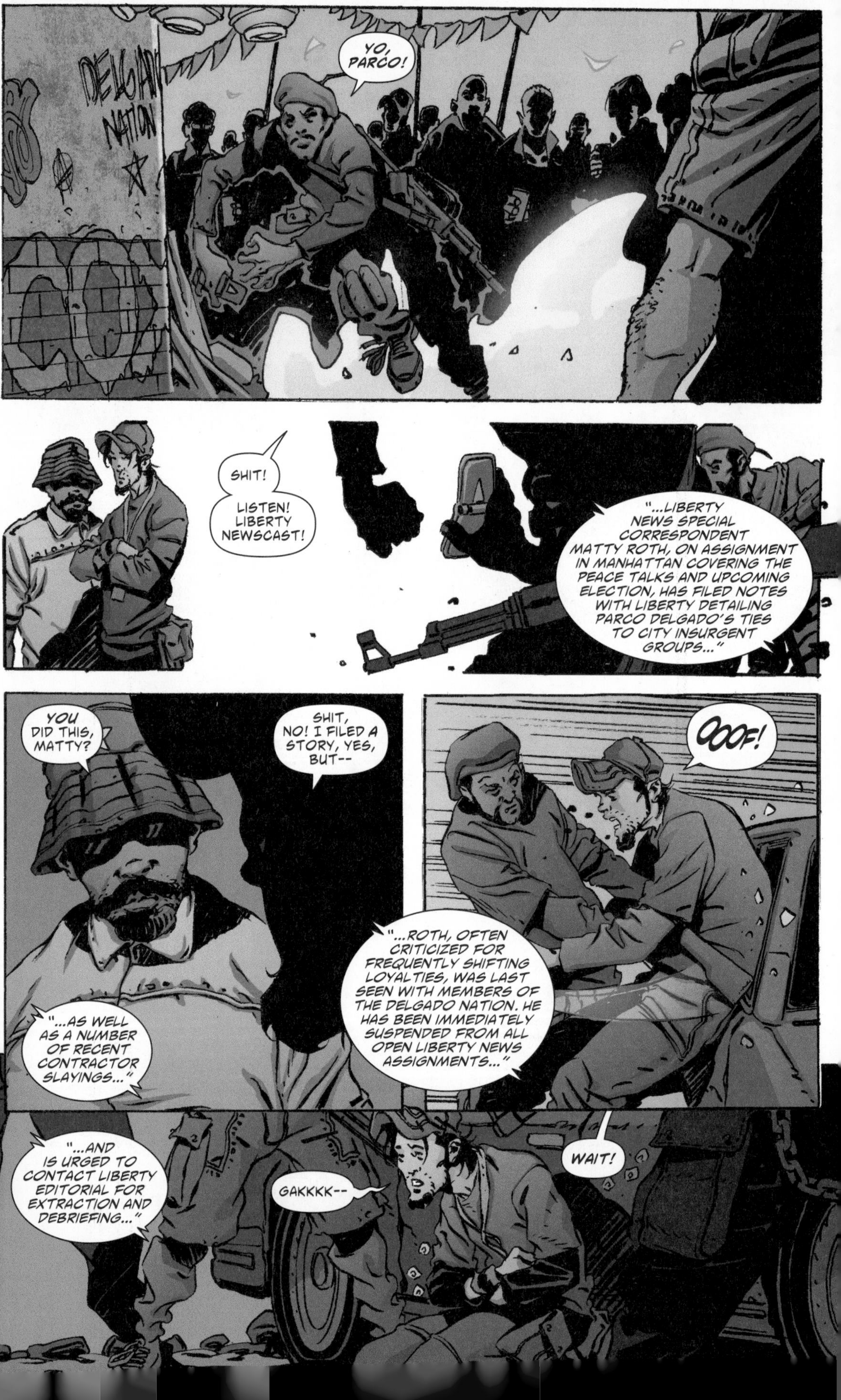
DELGADO NATION
YO, PARCO!
SHIT!
LISTEN! LIBERTY NEWSCAST!
"...LIBERTY NEWS SPECIAL CORRESPONDENT MATTY ROTH, ON ASSIGNMENT IN MANHATTAN COVERING THE PEACE TALKS AND UPCOMING ELECTION, HAS FILED NOTES WITH LIBERTY DETAILING PARCO DELGADO'S TIES TO CITY INSURGENT GROUPS..."
YOU DID THIS, MATTY?
SHIT, NO! I FILED A STORY, YES, BUT--
"...AS WELL AS A NUMBER OF RECENT CONTRACTOR SLAYINGS..."
OOOF!
"...ROTH, OFTEN CRITICIZED FOR FREQUENTLY SHIFTING LOYALTIES, WAS LAST SEEN WITH MEMBERS OF THE DELGADO NATION. HE HAS BEEN IMMEDIATELY SUSPENDED FROM ALL OPEN LIBERTY NEWS ASSIGNMENTS..."
"...AND IS URGED TO CONTACT LIBERTY EDITORIAL FOR EXTRACTION AND DEBRIEFING..."
GAKKKK--
WAIT!

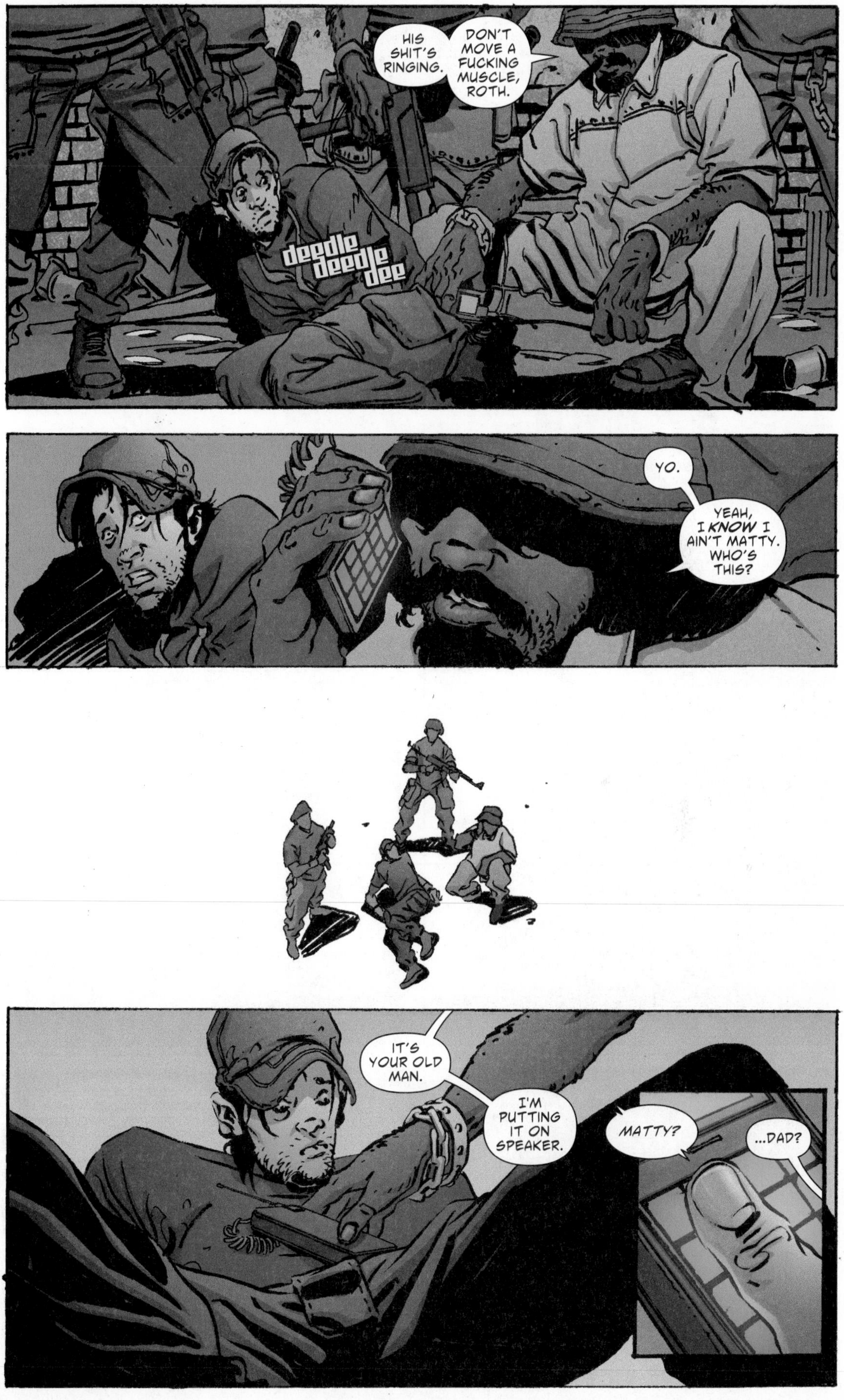
HIS SHIT'S RINGING.
DON'T MOVE A FUCKING MUSCLE, ROTH.
deedle deedle dee
YO.
YEAH, I *KNOW* I AIN'T MATTY. WHO'S THIS?
IT'S YOUR OLD MAN.
I'M PUTTING IT ON SPEAKER.
MATTY?
...DAD?

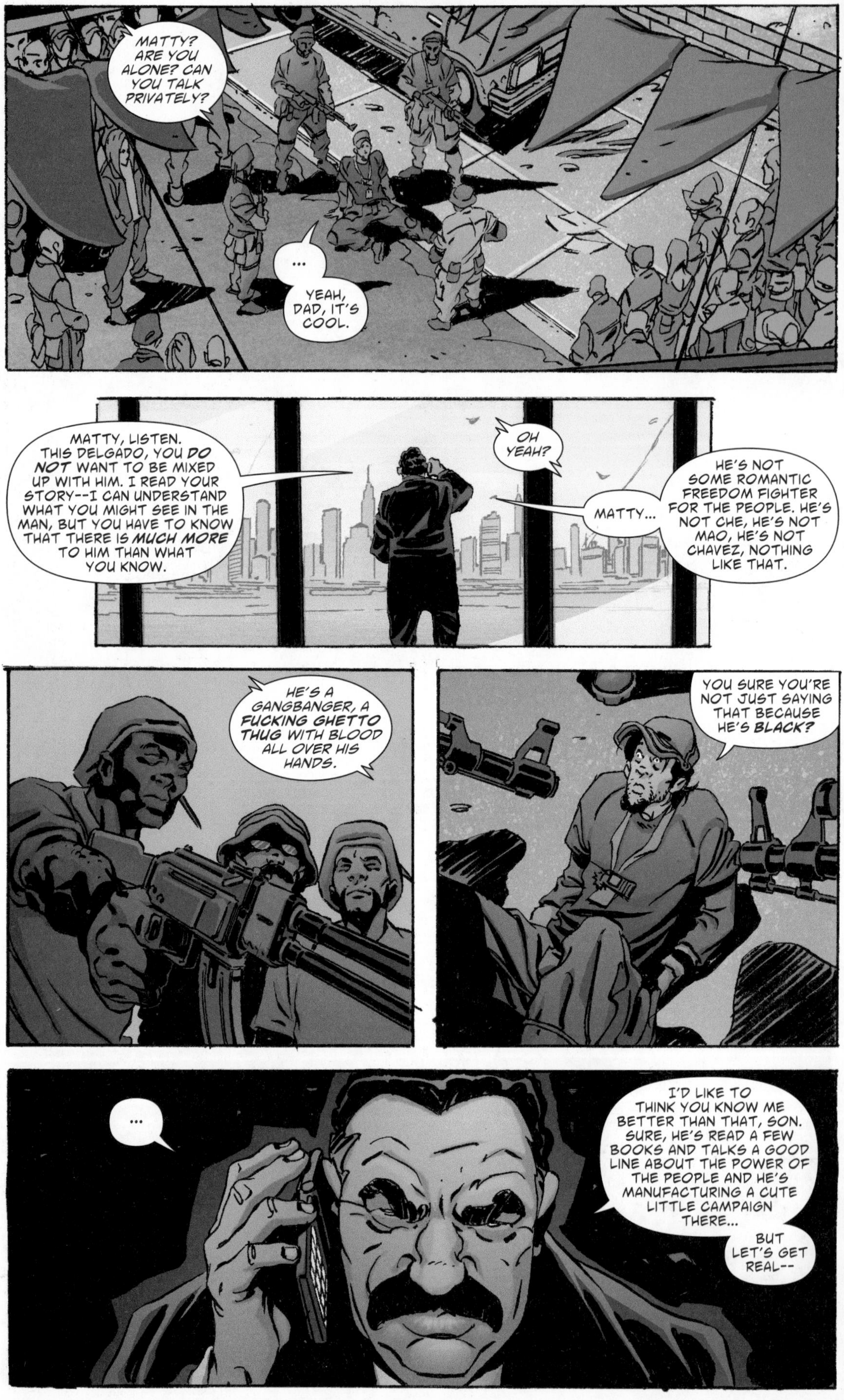
MATTY? ARE YOU ALONE? CAN YOU TALK PRIVATELY?
...
YEAH, DAD, IT'S COOL.
MATTY, LISTEN. THIS DELGADO, YOU DO NOT WANT TO BE MIXED UP WITH HIM. I READ YOUR STORY--I CAN UNDERSTAND WHAT YOU MIGHT SEE IN THE MAN, BUT YOU HAVE TO KNOW THAT THERE IS MUCH MORE TO HIM THAN WHAT YOU KNOW.
OH YEAH?
MATTY...
HE'S NOT SOME ROMANTIC FREEDOM FIGHTER FOR THE PEOPLE. HE'S NOT CHE, HE'S NOT MAO, HE'S NOT CHAVEZ, NOTHING LIKE THAT.
HE'S A GANGBANGER, A FUCKING GHETTO THUG WITH BLOOD ALL OVER HIS HANDS.
YOU SURE YOU'RE NOT JUST SAYING THAT BECAUSE HE'S BLACK?
...
I'D LIKE TO THINK YOU KNOW ME BETTER THAN THAT, SON. SURE, HE'S READ A FEW BOOKS AND TALKS A GOOD LINE ABOUT THE POWER OF THE PEOPLE AND HE'S MANUFACTURING A CUTE LITTLE CAMPAIGN THERE...
BUT LET'S GET REAL--

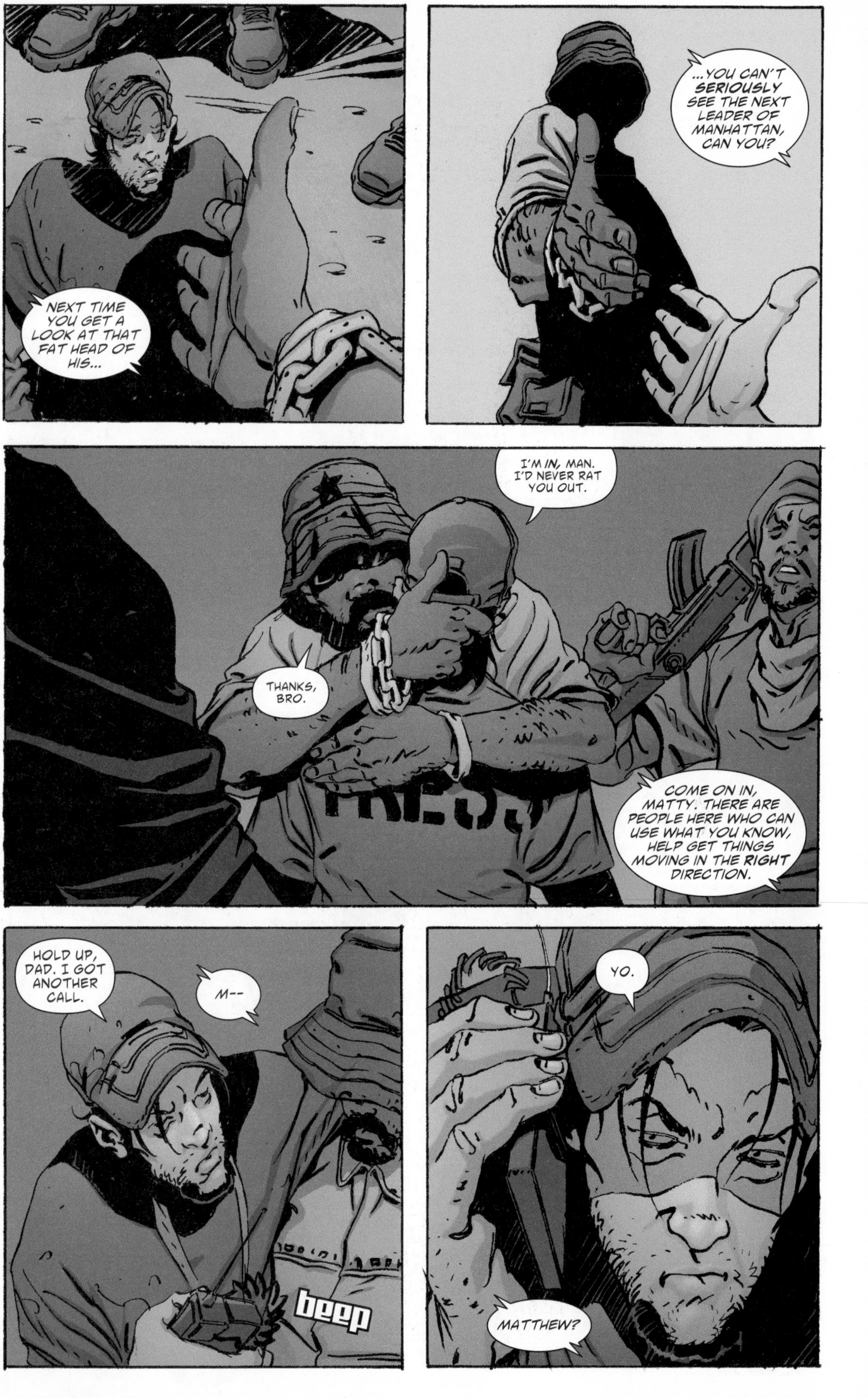
NEXT TIME YOU GET A LOOK AT THAT FAT HEAD OF HIS...
...YOU CAN'T SERIOUSLY SEE THE NEXT LEADER OF MANHATTAN, CAN YOU?
I'M IN, MAN. I'D NEVER RAT YOU OUT.
THANKS, BRO.
COME ON IN, MATTY. THERE ARE PEOPLE HERE WHO CAN USE WHAT YOU KNOW, HELP GET THINGS MOVING IN THE RIGHT DIRECTION.
HOLD UP, DAD. I GOT ANOTHER CALL.
M--
beep
YO.
MATTHEW?

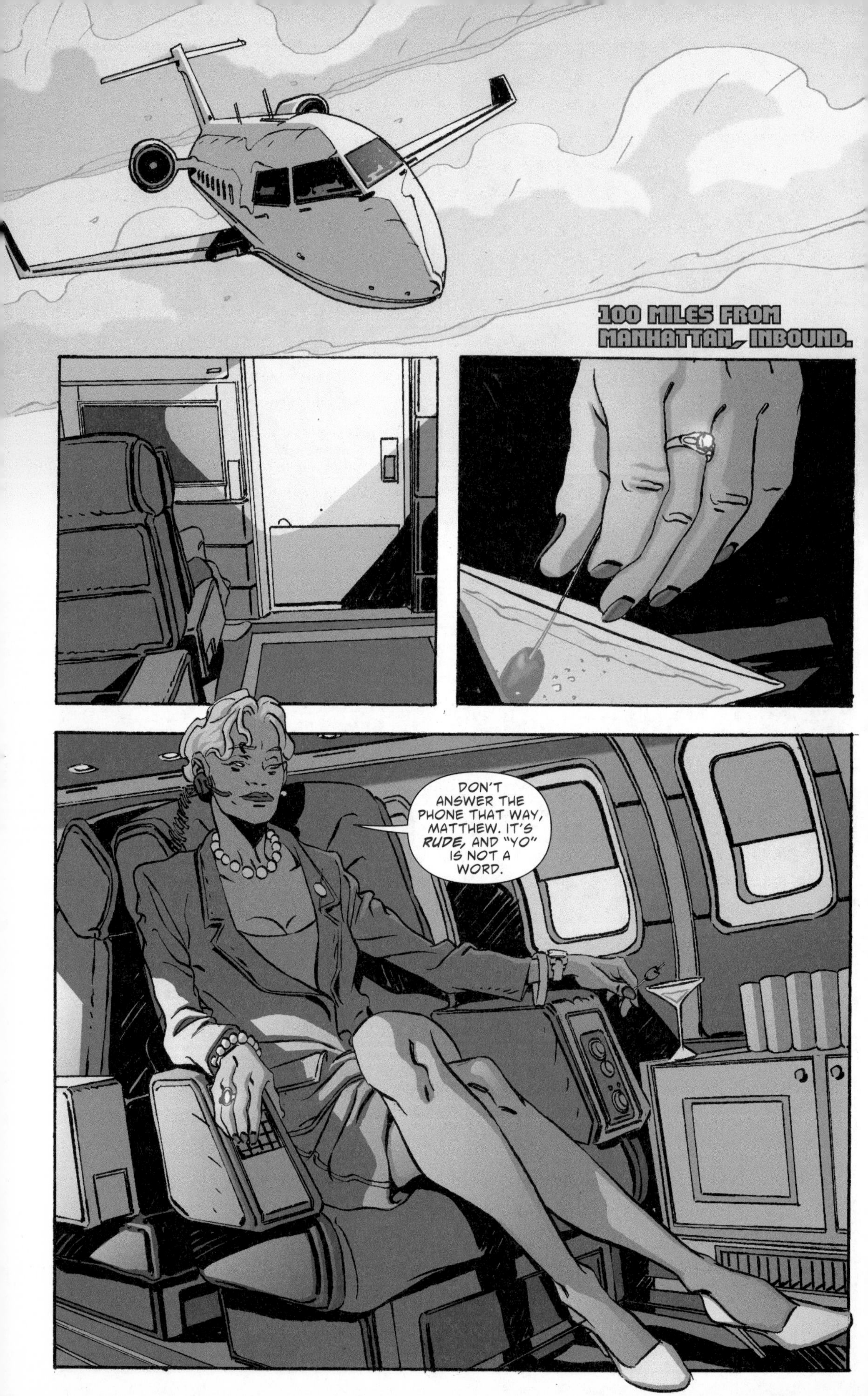
100 MILES FROM MANHATTAN, INBOUND.
DON'T ANSWER THE PHONE THAT WAY, MATTHEW. IT'S *RUDE,* AND "YO" IS NOT A WORD.

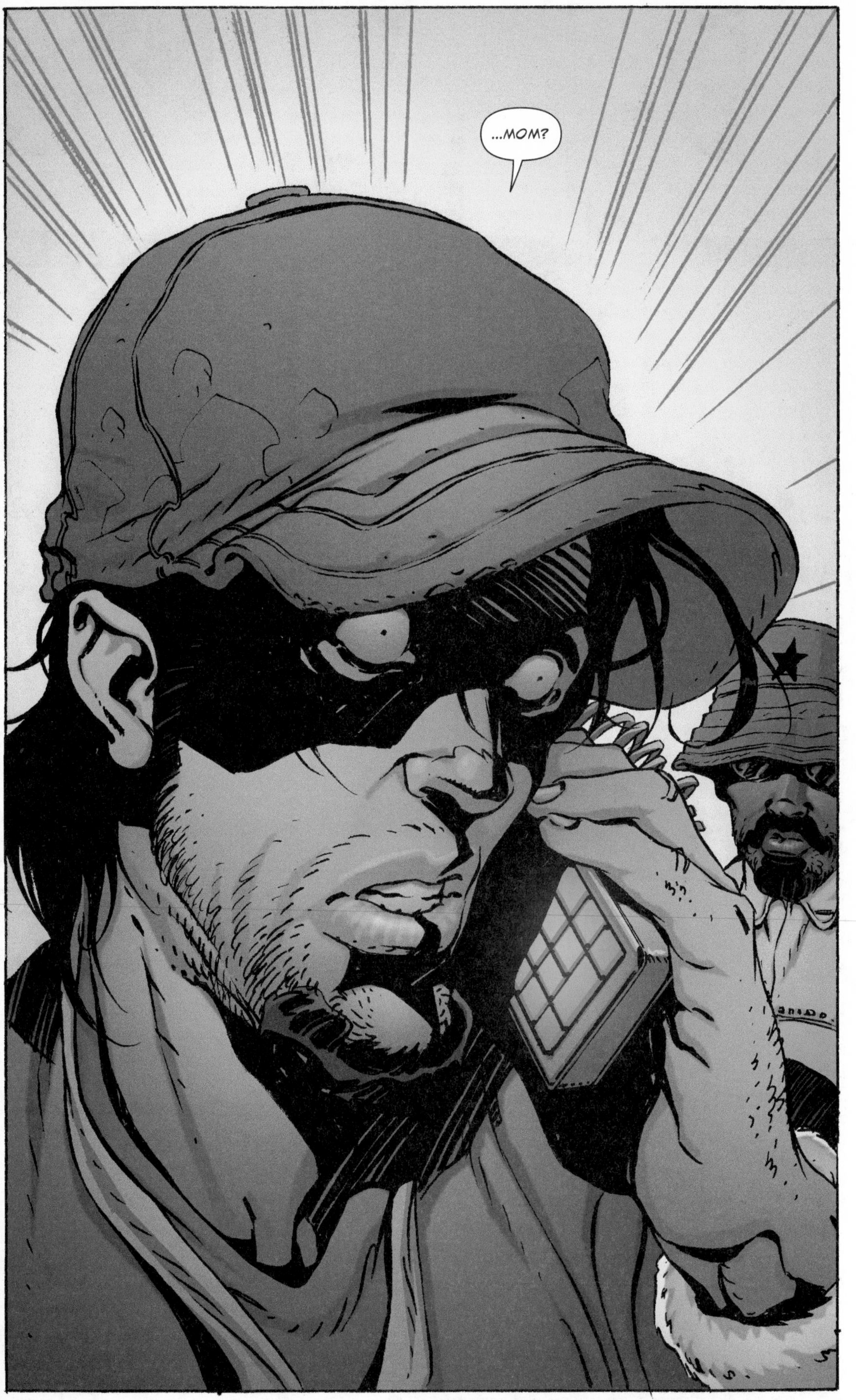
...MOM?

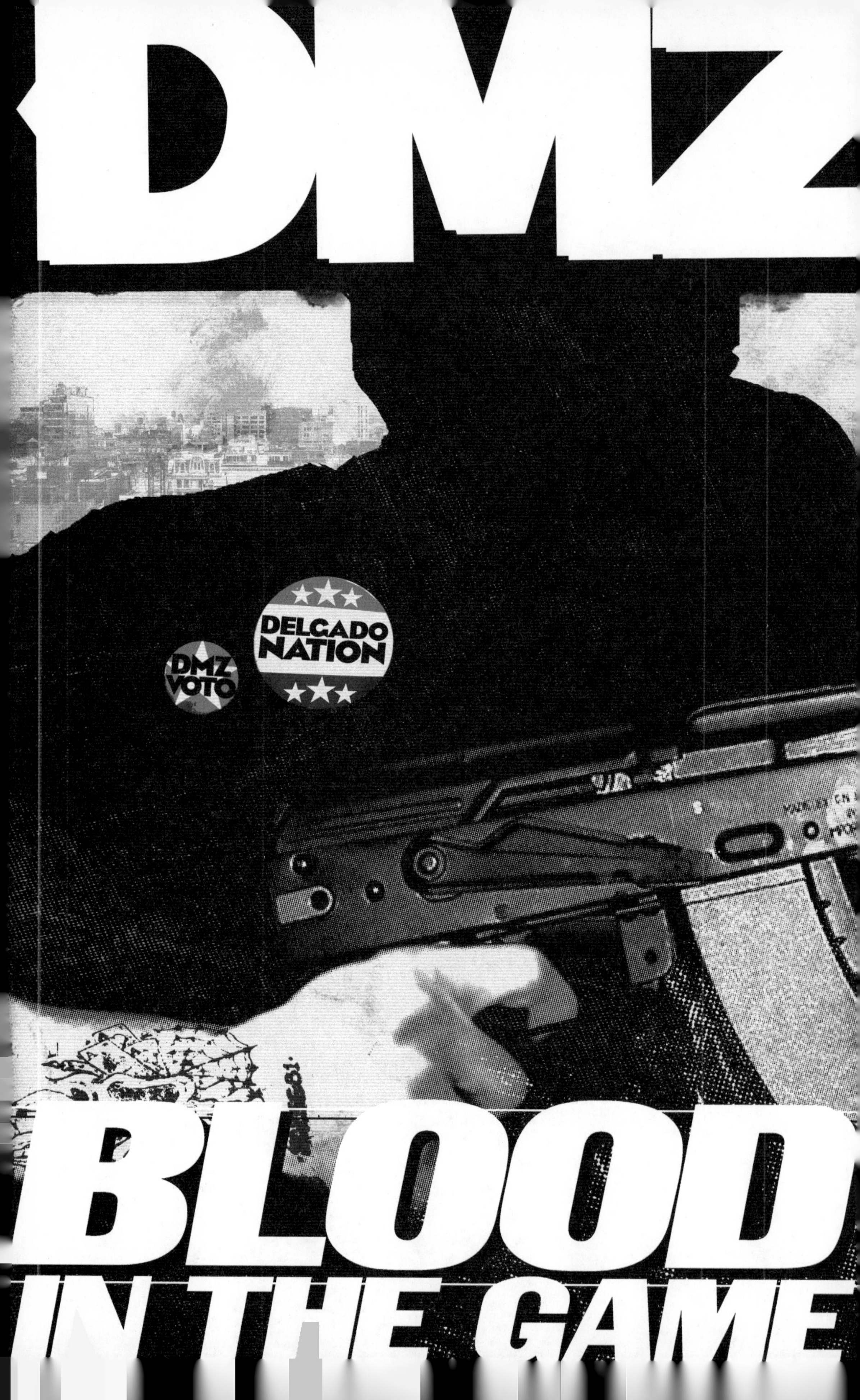
DMZ
DELGADO NATION
DMZ VOTO
BLOOD IN THE GAME

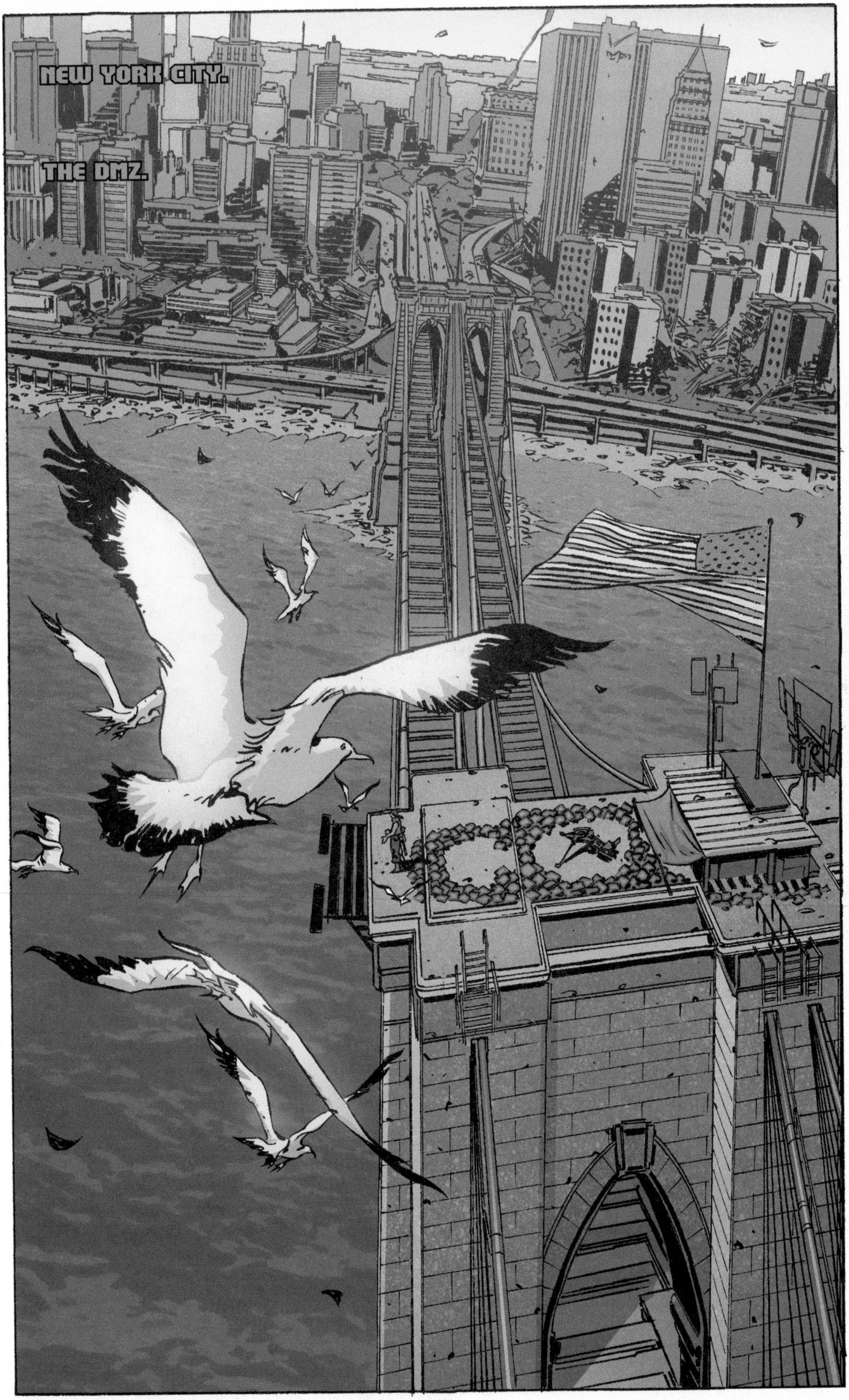
NEW YORK CITY.
THE DMZ.

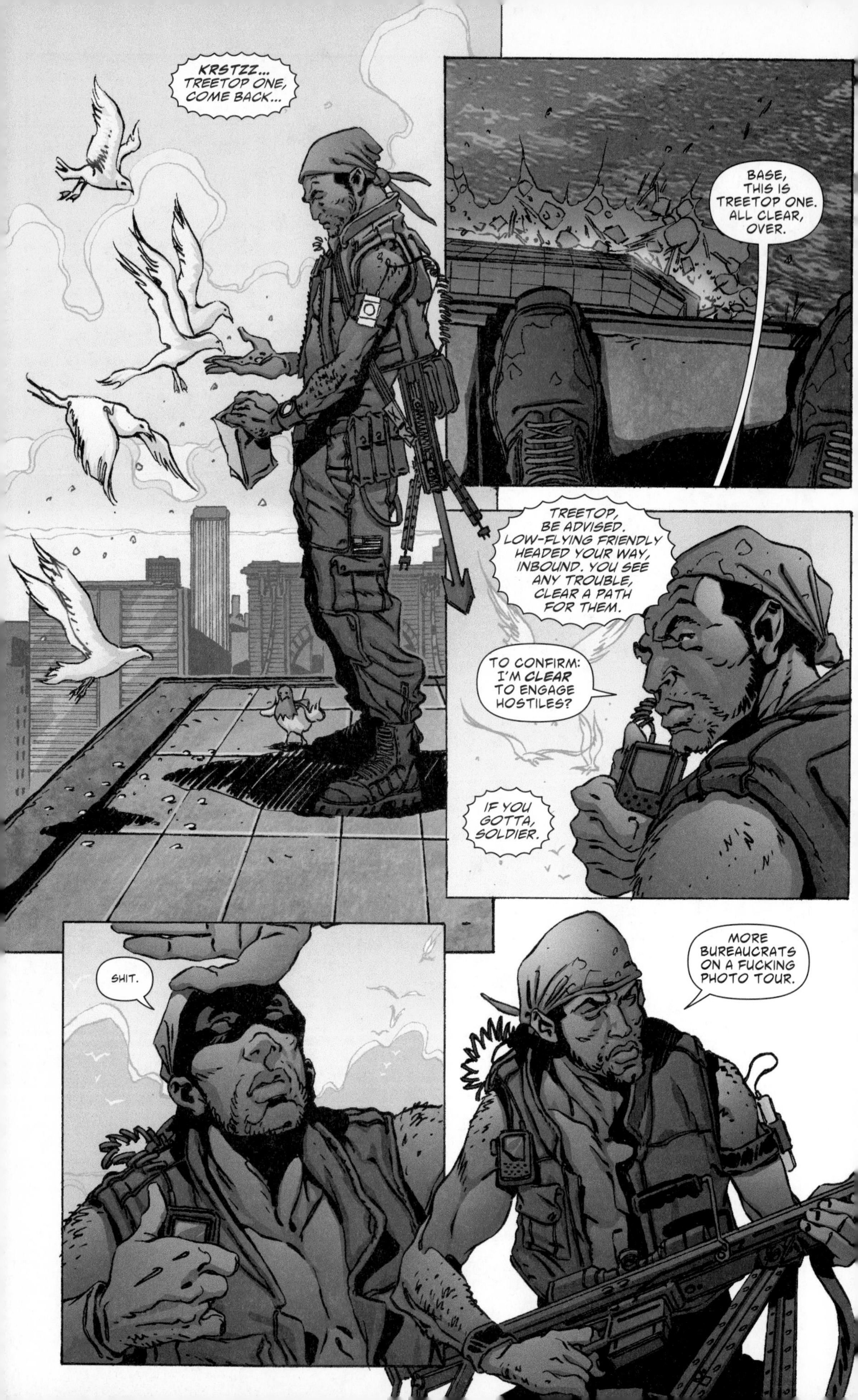
KRSTZZ... TREETOP ONE, COME BACK...
BASE, THIS IS TREETOP ONE. ALL CLEAR, OVER.
TREETOP, BE ADVISED. LOW-FLYING FRIENDLY HEADED YOUR WAY, INBOUND. YOU SEE ANY TROUBLE, CLEAR A PATH FOR THEM.
TO CONFIRM: I'M CLEAR TO ENGAGE HOSTILES?
IF YOU GOTTA, SOLDIER.
SHIT.
MORE BUREAUCRATS ON A FUCKING PHOTO TOUR.

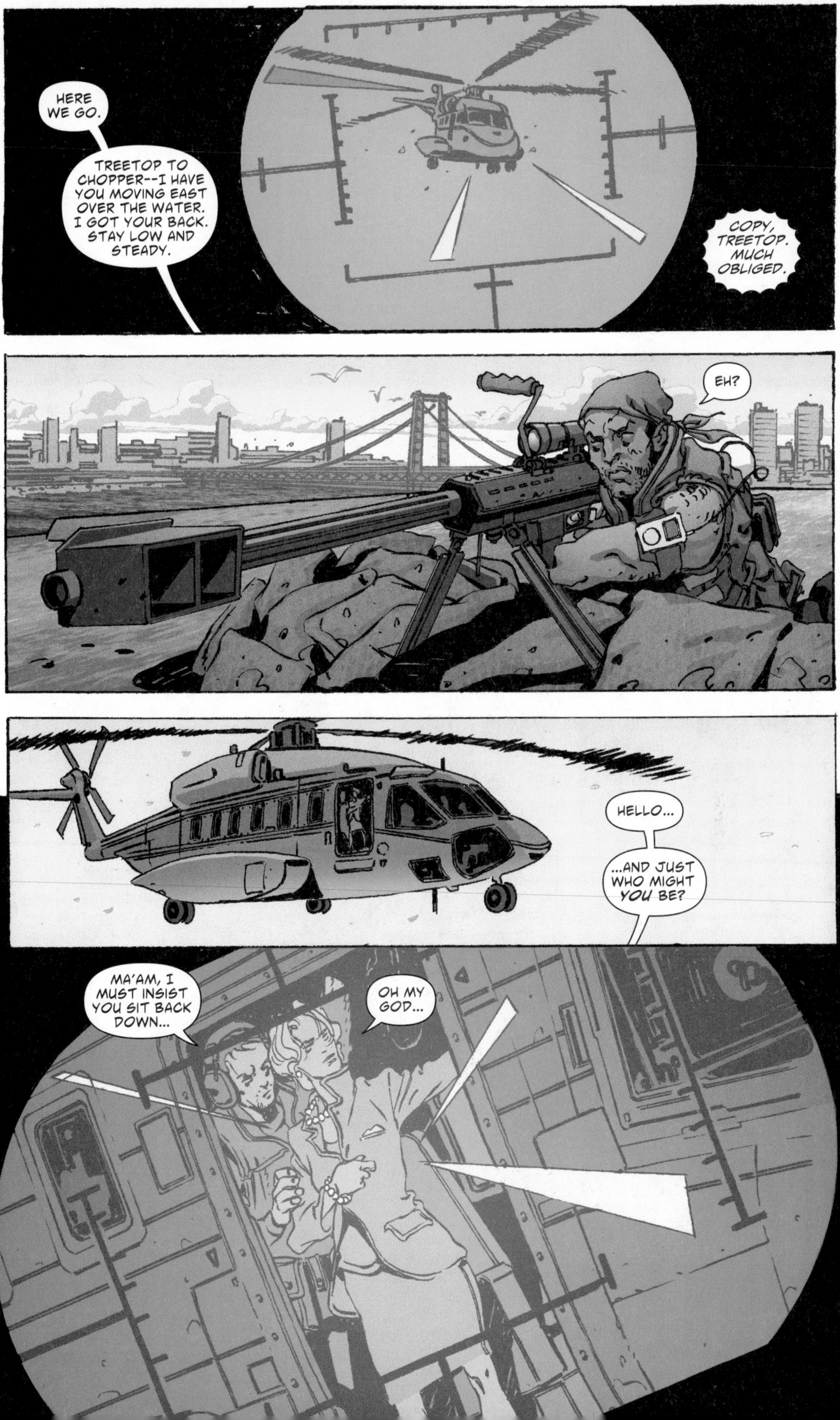
HERE WE GO.
TREETOP TO CHOPPER--I HAVE YOU MOVING EAST OVER THE WATER. I GOT YOUR BACK. STAY LOW AND STEADY.
COPY, TREETOP. MUCH OBLIGED.
EH?
HELLO...
...AND JUST WHO MIGHT YOU BE?
MA'AM, I MUST INSIST YOU SIT BACK DOWN...
OH MY GOD...

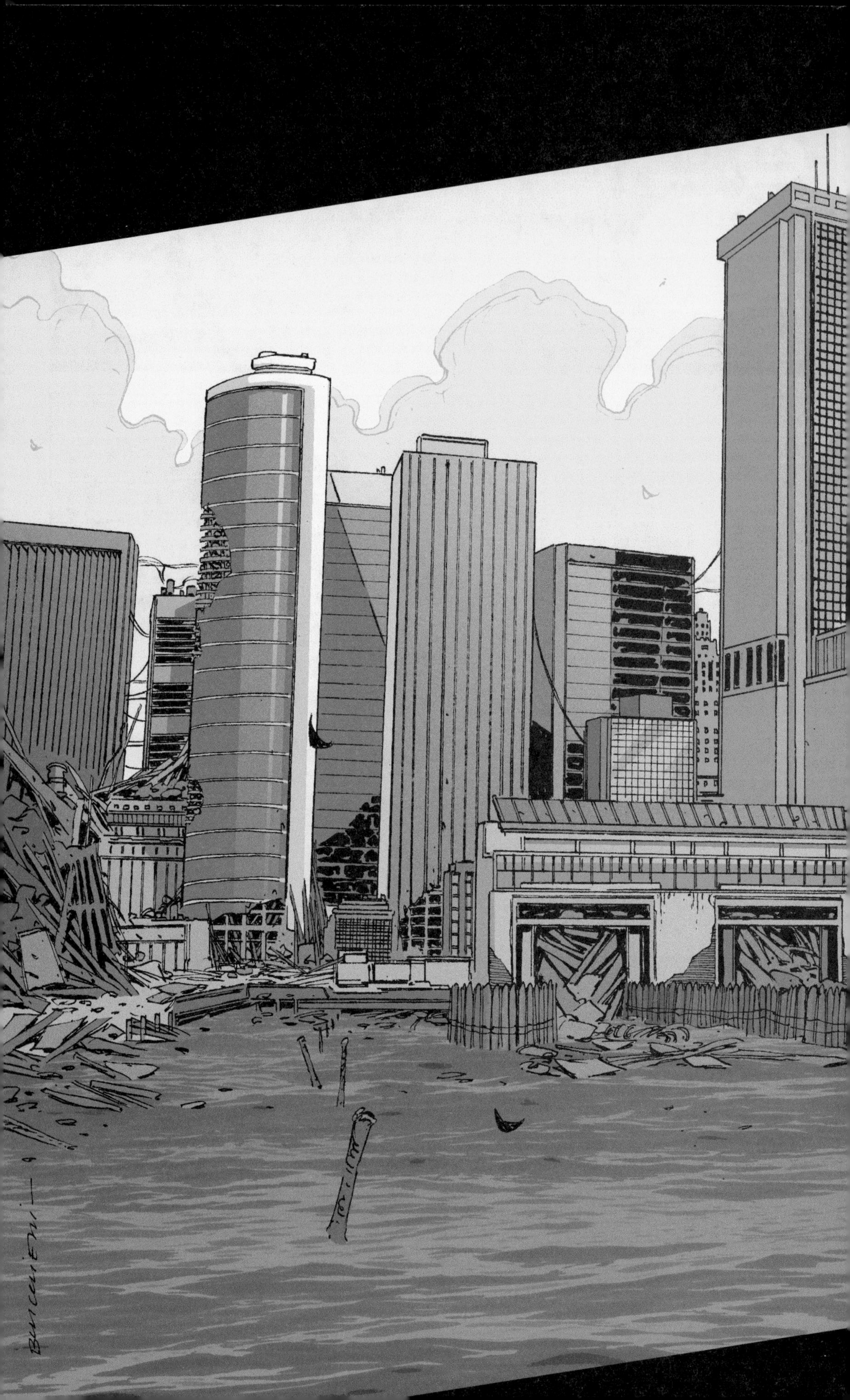

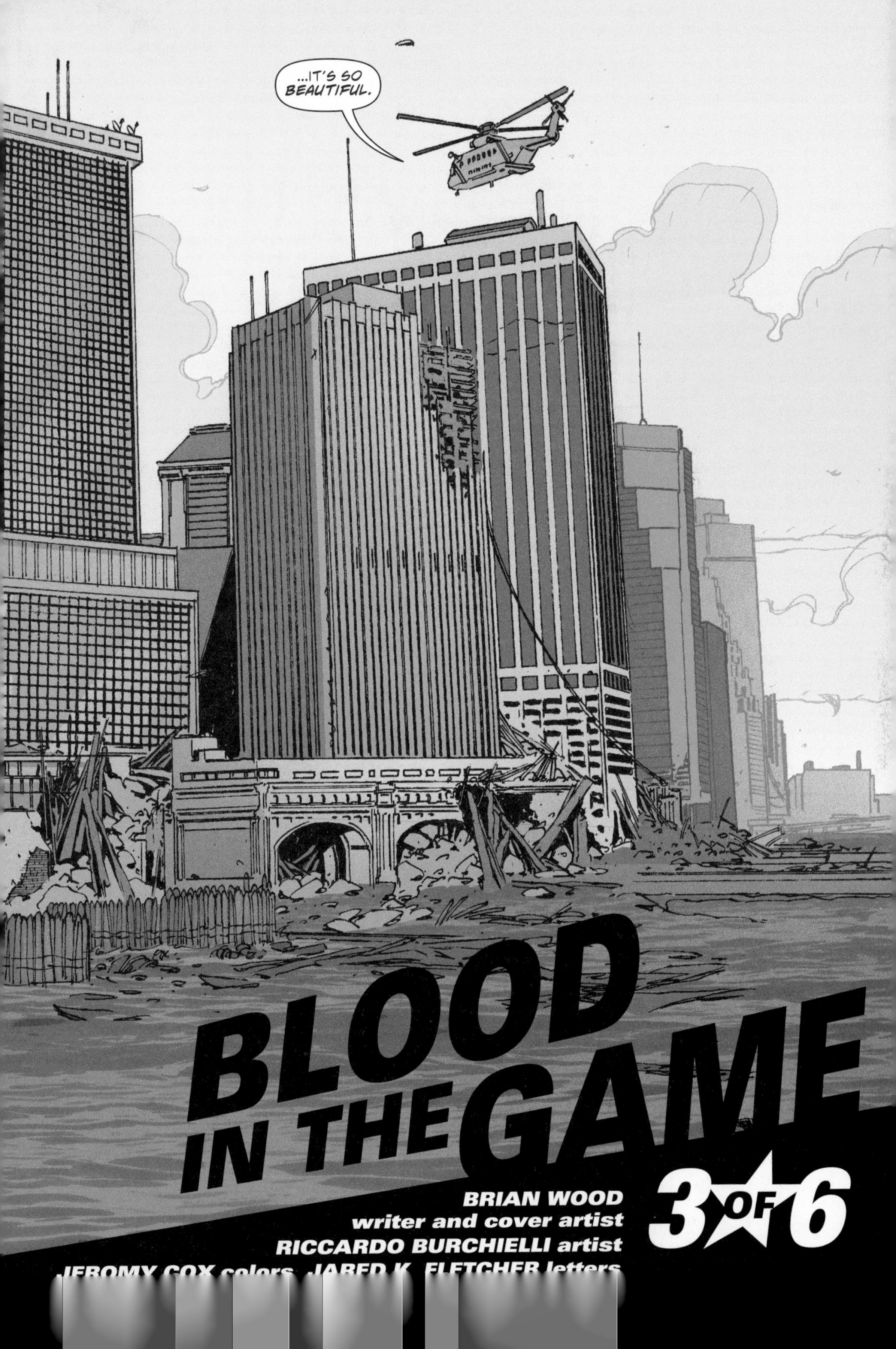

...IT'S SO BEAUTIFUL.
BLOOD IN THE GAME
3 OF 6
BRIAN WOOD
writer and cover artist
RICCARDO BURCHIELLI artist
JEROMY COX colors, JARED K. FLETCHER letters

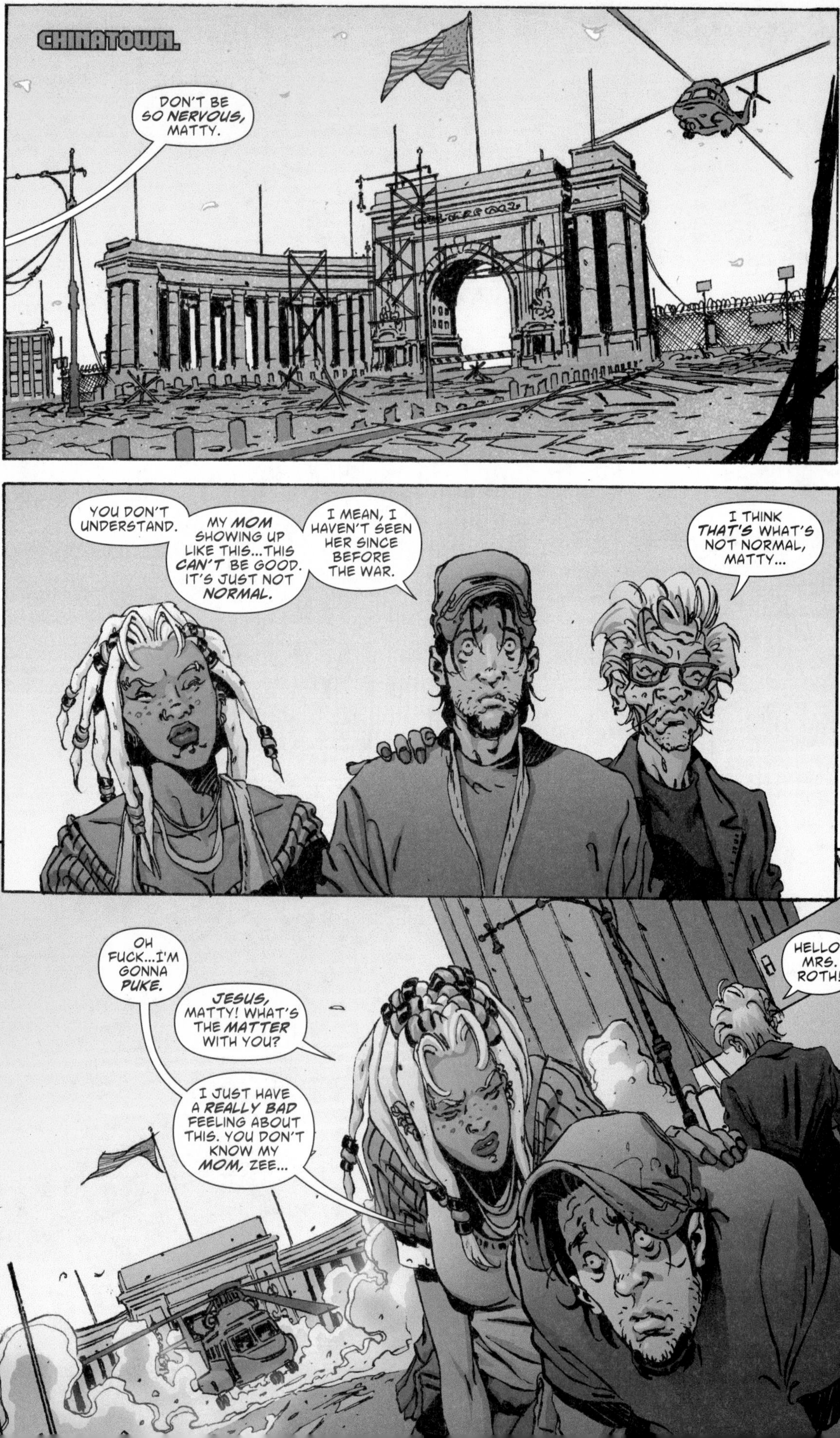
CHINATOWN.
DON'T BE SO NERVOUS, MATTY.
YOU DON'T UNDERSTAND.
MY MOM SHOWING UP LIKE THIS...THIS CAN'T BE GOOD. IT'S JUST NOT NORMAL.
I MEAN, I HAVEN'T SEEN HER SINCE BEFORE THE WAR.
I THINK THAT'S WHAT'S NOT NORMAL, MATTY...
OH FUCK...I'M GONNA PUKE.
JESUS, MATTY! WHAT'S THE MATTER WITH YOU?
I JUST HAVE A REALLY BAD FEELING ABOUT THIS. YOU DON'T KNOW MY MOM, ZEE...
HELLO! MRS. ROTH!

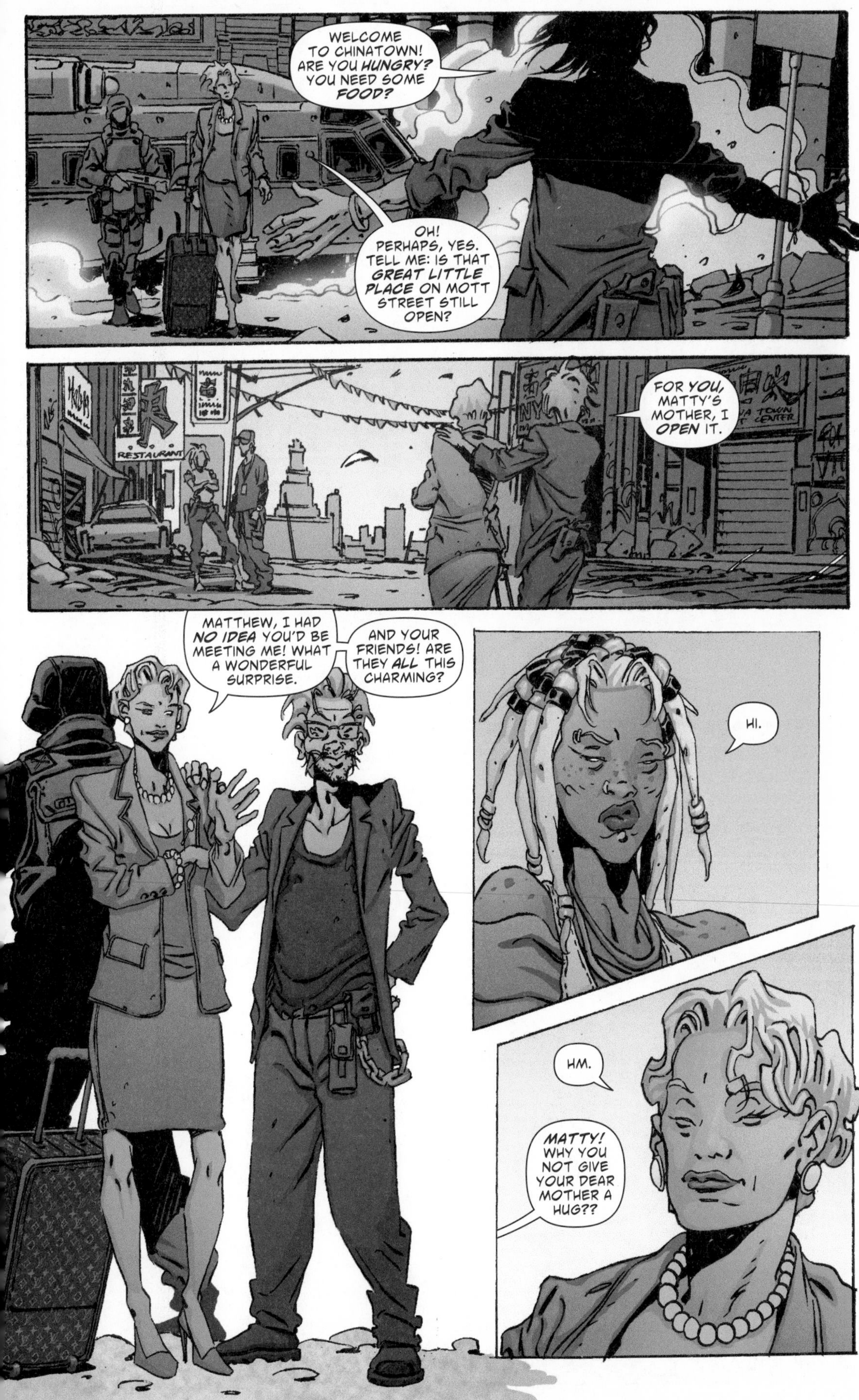
WELCOME TO CHINATOWN! ARE YOU HUNGRY? YOU NEED SOME FOOD?
OH! PERHAPS, YES. TELL ME: IS THAT GREAT LITTLE PLACE ON MOTT STREET STILL OPEN?
RESTAURANT
FOR YOU, MATTY'S MOTHER, I OPEN IT.
MATTHEW, I HAD NO IDEA YOU'D BE MEETING ME! WHAT A WONDERFUL SURPRISE.
AND YOUR FRIENDS! ARE THEY ALL THIS CHARMING?
HI.
HM.
MATTY! WHY YOU NOT GIVE YOUR DEAR MOTHER A HUG??

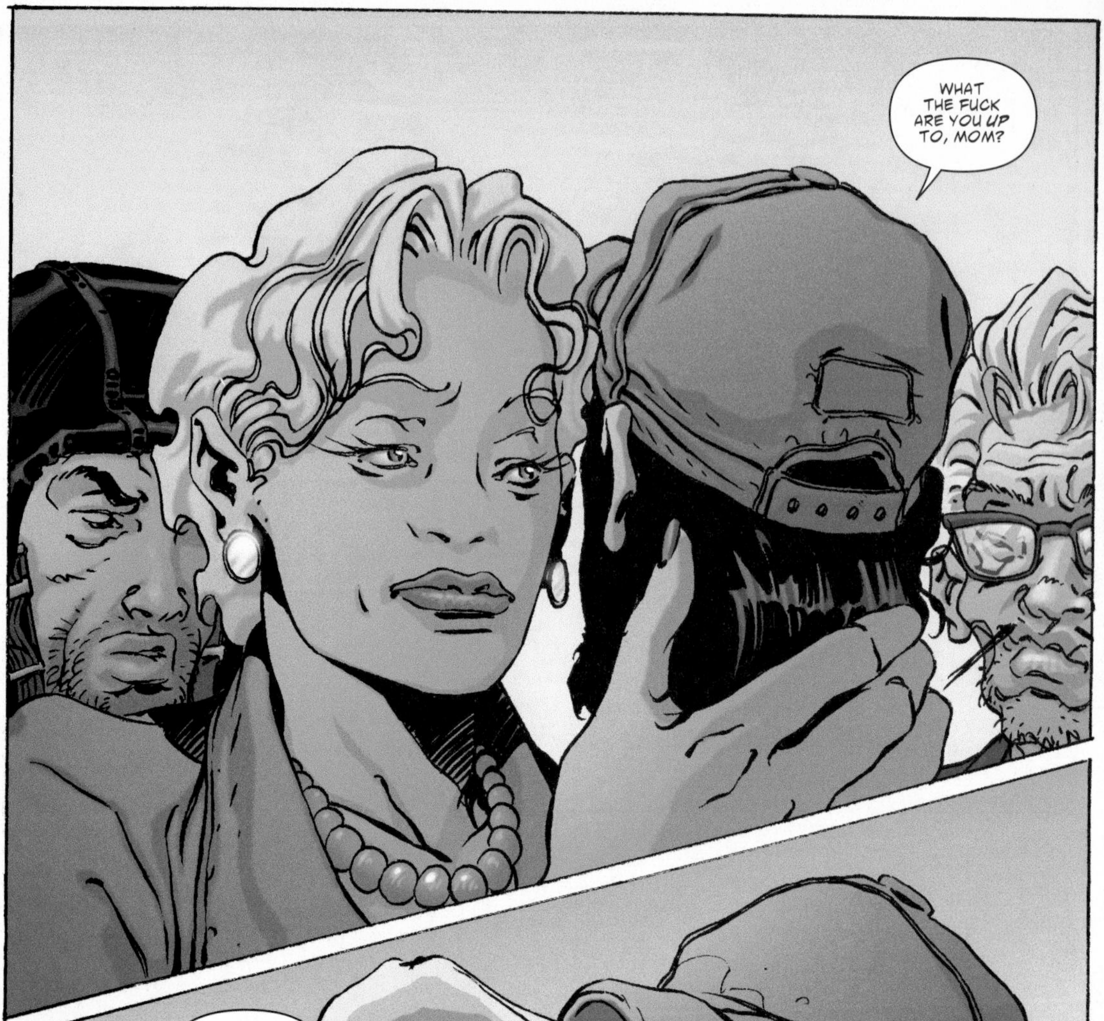
WHAT THE FUCK ARE YOU *UP* TO, MOM?

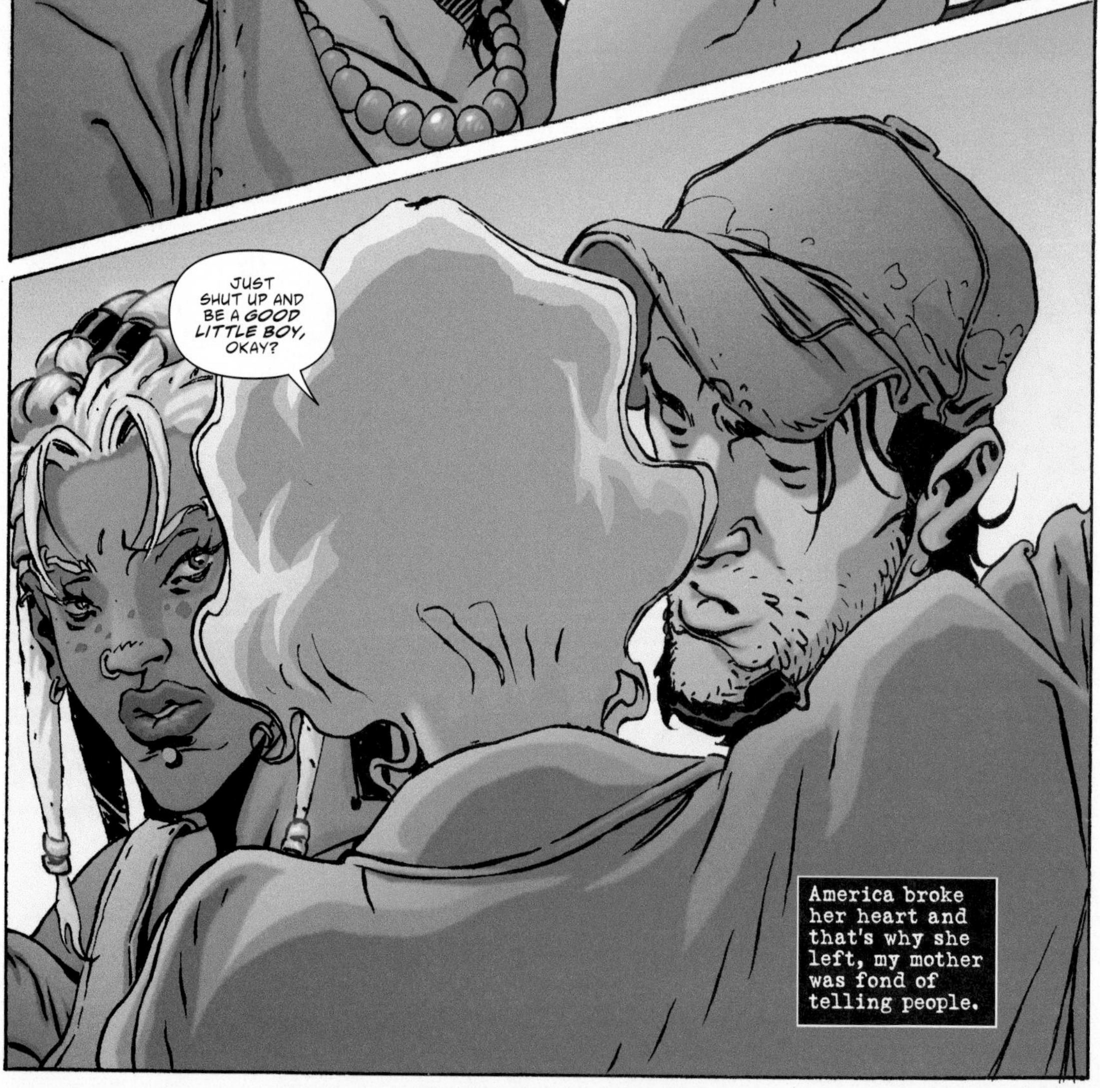
JUST SHUT UP AND BE A *GOOD LITTLE BOY*, OKAY?
America broke her heart and that's why she left, my mother was fond of telling people.

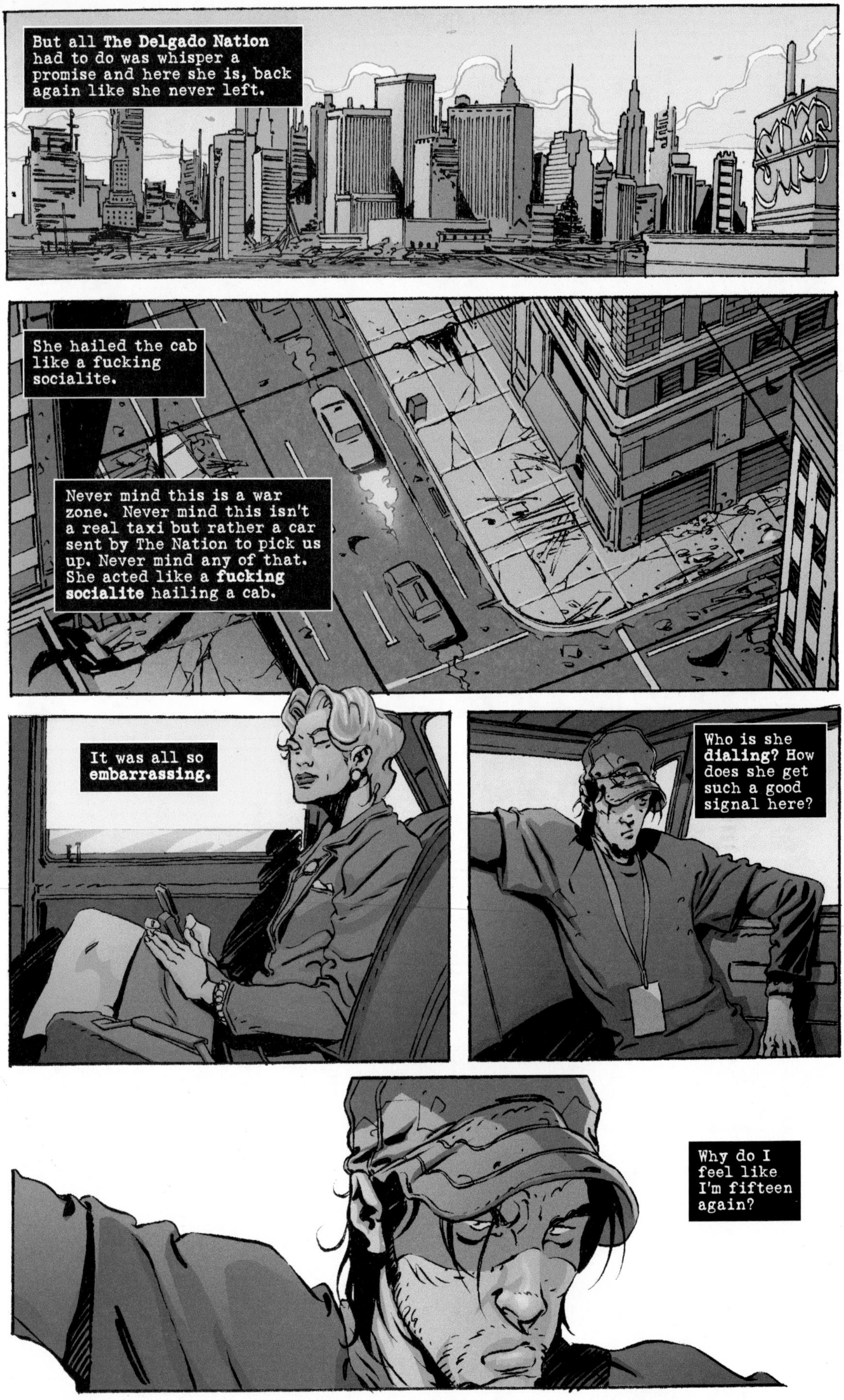
But all The Delgado Nation had to do was whisper a promise and here she is, back again like she never left.
She hailed the cab like a fucking socialite.
Never mind this is a war zone. Never mind this isn't a real taxi but rather a car sent by The Nation to pick us up. Never mind any of that. She acted like a fucking socialite hailing a cab.
It was all so embarrassing.
Who is she dialing? How does she get such a good signal here?
Why do I feel like I'm fifteen again?

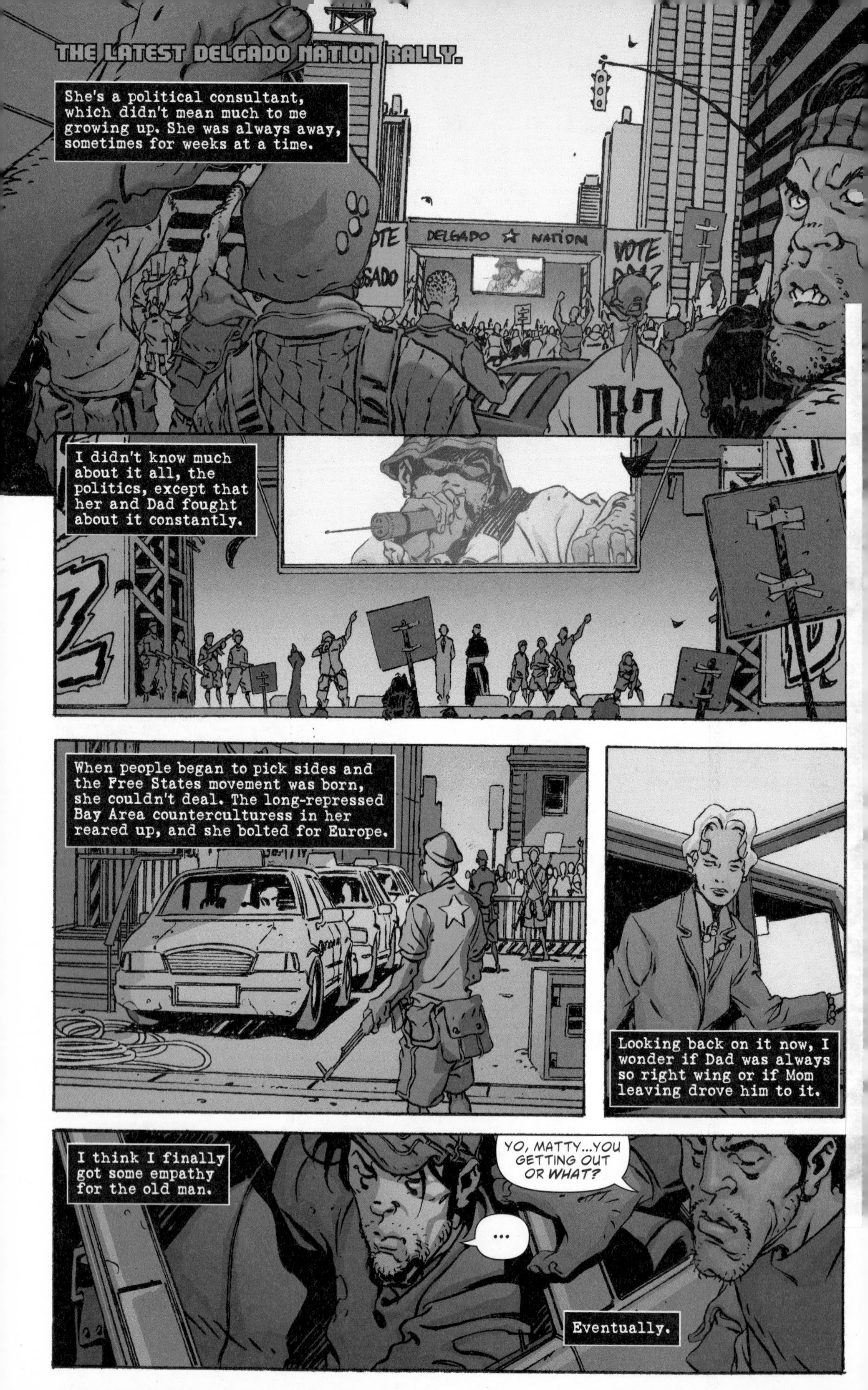
THE LATEST DELGADO NATION RALLY.
She's a political consultant, which didn't mean much to me growing up. She was always away, sometimes for weeks at a time.
DELGADO ☆ NATION
VOTE
I didn't know much about it all, the politics, except that her and Dad fought about it constantly.
When people began to pick sides and the Free States movement was born, she couldn't deal. The long-repressed Bay Area counterculturess in her reared up, and she bolted for Europe.
Looking back on it now, I wonder if Dad was always so right wing or if Mom leaving drove him to it.
I think I finally got some empathy for the old man.
YO, MATTY...YOU GETTING OUT OR WHAT?
...
Eventually.

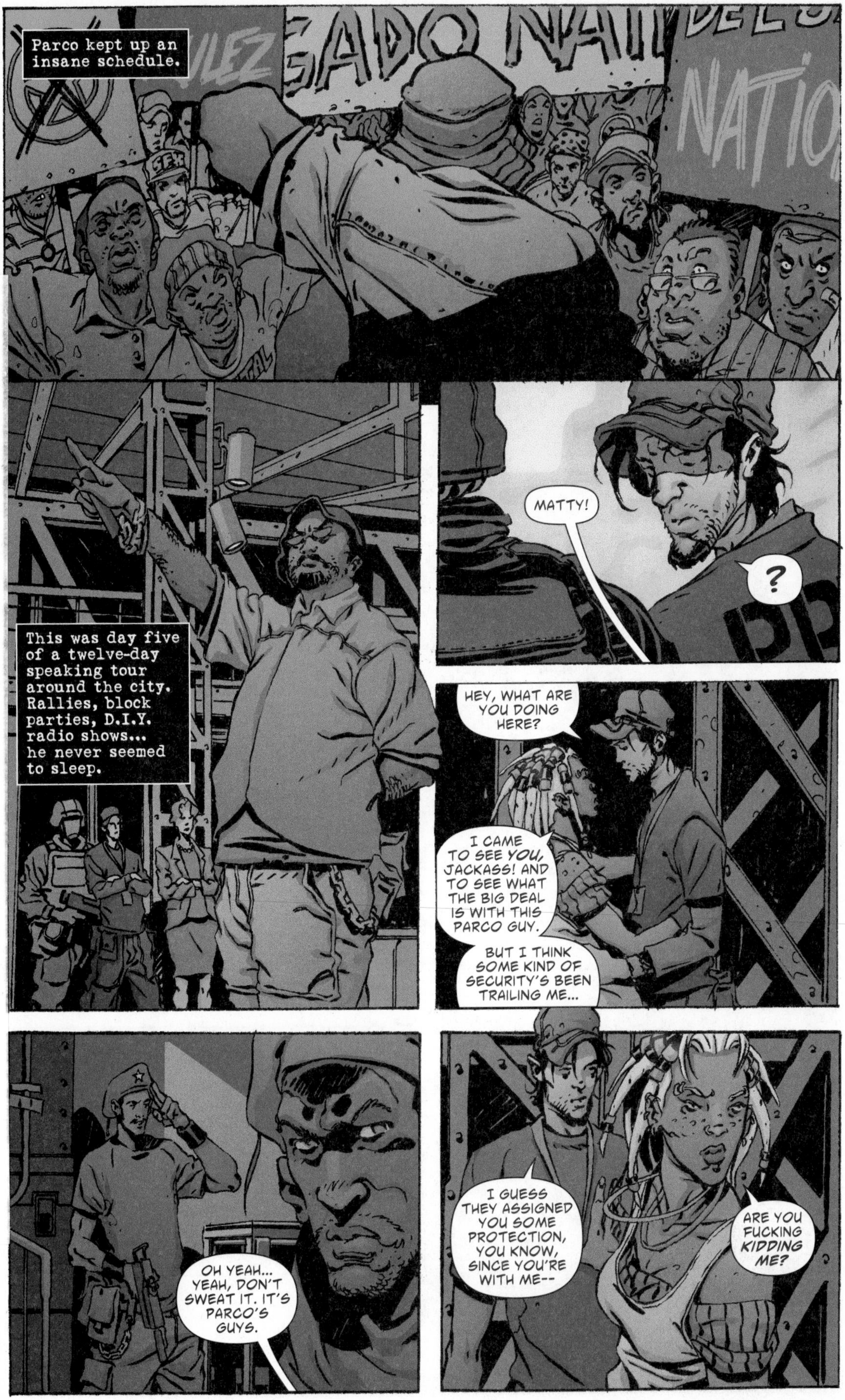
Parco kept up an insane schedule.
ADO NA
NATIO
This was day five of a twelve-day speaking tour around the city. Rallies, block parties, D.I.Y. radio shows... he never seemed to sleep.
MATTY!
?
HEY, WHAT ARE YOU DOING HERE?
I CAME TO SEE YOU, JACKASS! AND TO SEE WHAT THE BIG DEAL IS WITH THIS PARCO GUY.
BUT I THINK SOME KIND OF SECURITY'S BEEN TRAILING ME...
OH YEAH... YEAH, DON'T SWEAT IT. IT'S PARCO'S GUYS.
I GUESS THEY ASSIGNED YOU SOME PROTECTION, YOU KNOW, SINCE YOU'RE WITH ME--
ARE YOU FUCKING KIDDING ME?

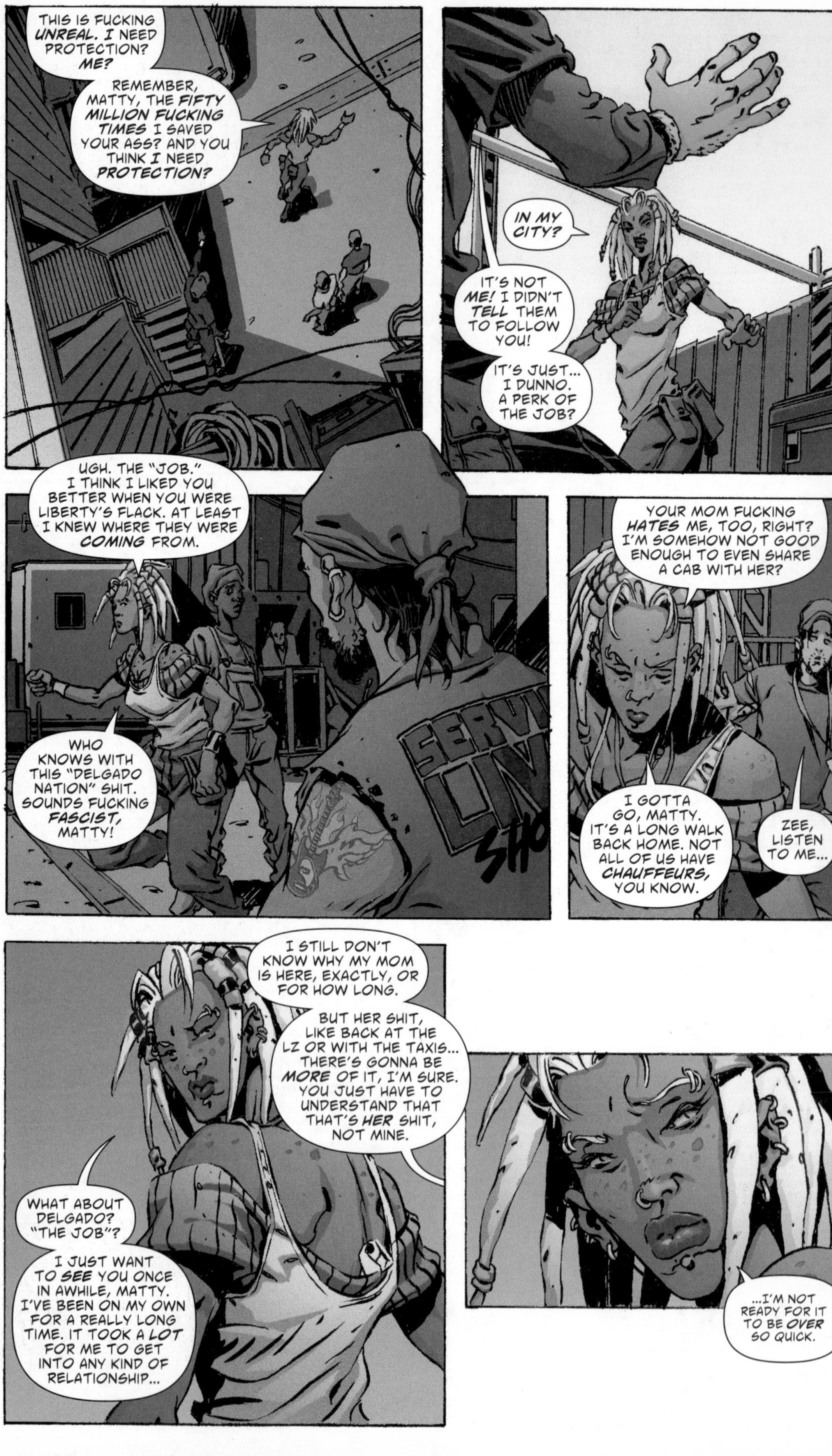
THIS IS FUCKING UNREAL. I NEED PROTECTION? ME?
REMEMBER, MATTY, THE FIFTY MILLION FUCKING TIMES I SAVED YOUR ASS? AND YOU THINK I NEED PROTECTION?
IN MY CITY?
IT'S NOT ME! I DIDN'T TELL THEM TO FOLLOW YOU!
IT'S JUST... I DUNNO. A PERK OF THE JOB?
UGH. THE "JOB." I THINK I LIKED YOU BETTER WHEN YOU WERE LIBERTY'S FLACK. AT LEAST I KNEW WHERE THEY WERE COMING FROM.
WHO KNOWS WITH THIS "DELGADO NATION" SHIT. SOUNDS FUCKING FASCIST, MATTY!
YOUR MOM FUCKING HATES ME, TOO, RIGHT? I'M SOMEHOW NOT GOOD ENOUGH TO EVEN SHARE A CAB WITH HER?
I GOTTA GO, MATTY. IT'S A LONG WALK BACK HOME. NOT ALL OF US HAVE CHAUFFEURS, YOU KNOW.
ZEE, LISTEN TO ME...
I STILL DON'T KNOW WHY MY MOM IS HERE, EXACTLY, OR FOR HOW LONG.
BUT HER SHIT, LIKE BACK AT THE LZ OR WITH THE TAXIS... THERE'S GONNA BE MORE OF IT, I'M SURE. YOU JUST HAVE TO UNDERSTAND THAT THAT'S HER SHIT, NOT MINE.
WHAT ABOUT DELGADO? "THE JOB"?
I JUST WANT TO SEE YOU ONCE IN AWHILE, MATTY. I'VE BEEN ON MY OWN FOR A REALLY LONG TIME. IT TOOK A LOT FOR ME TO GET INTO ANY KIND OF RELATIONSHIP...
...I'M NOT READY FOR IT TO BE OVER SO QUICK.

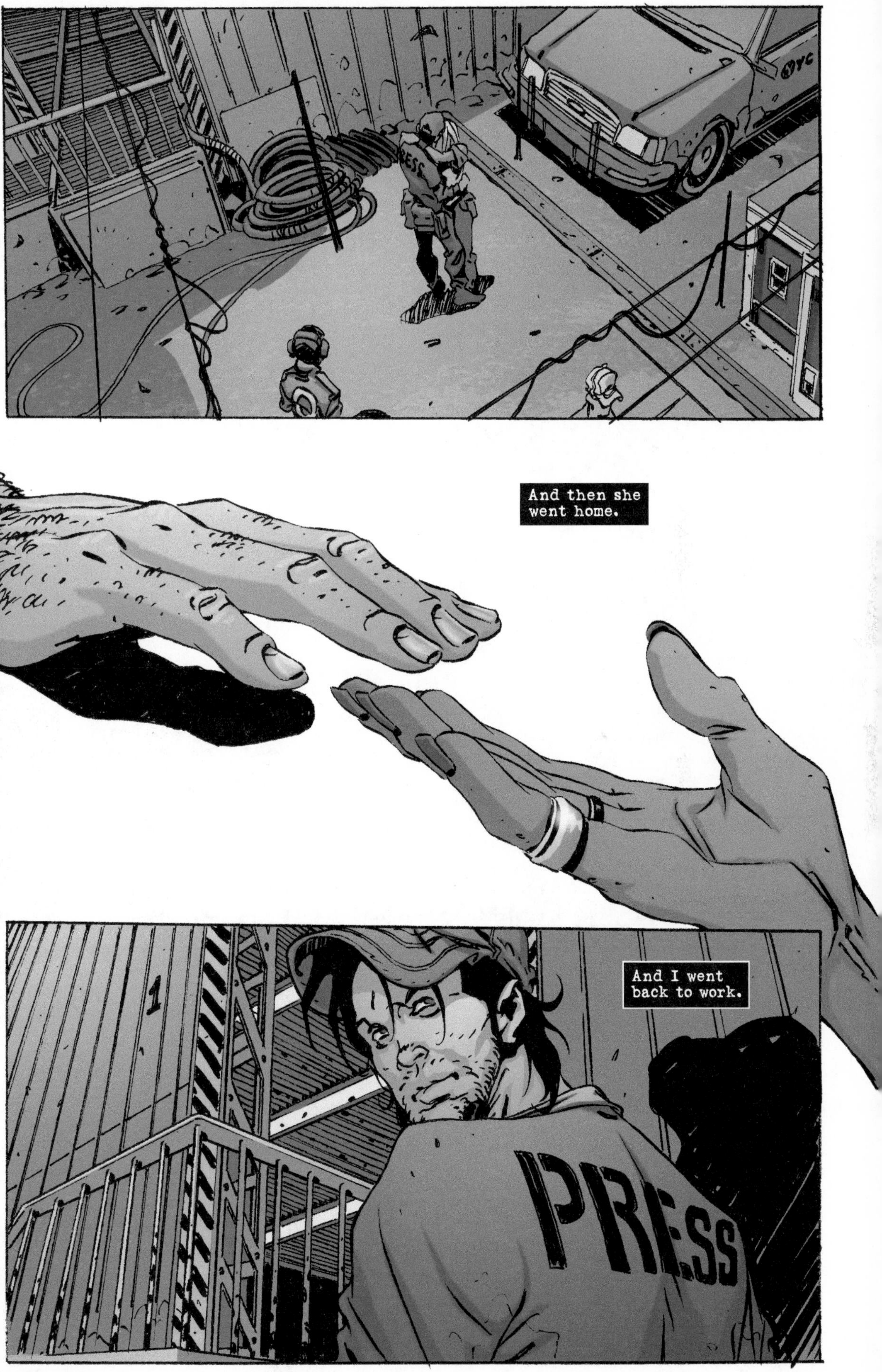
And then she went home.
And I went back to work.
PRESS

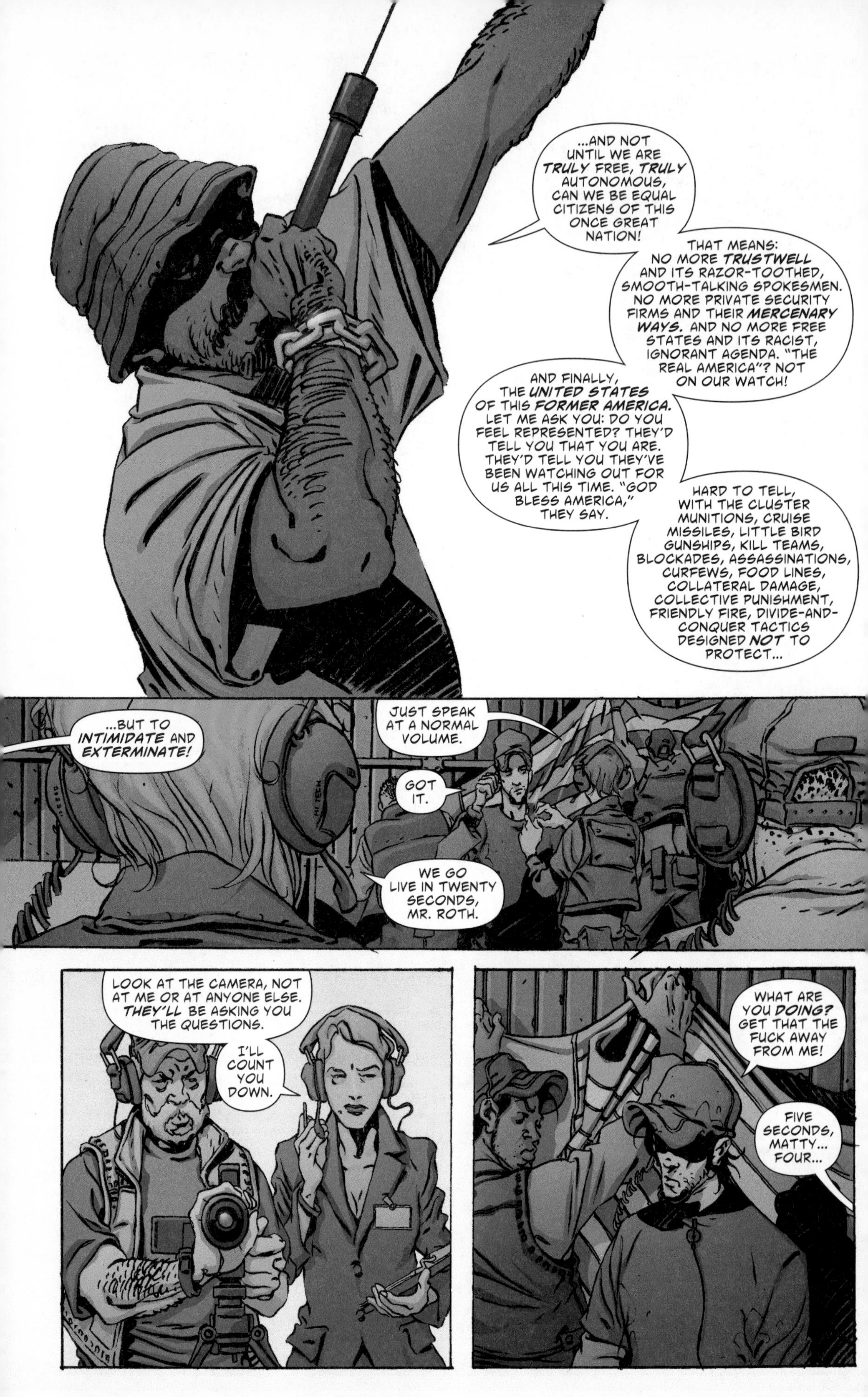
...AND NOT UNTIL WE ARE *TRULY* FREE, *TRULY* AUTONOMOUS, CAN WE BE EQUAL CITIZENS OF THIS ONCE GREAT NATION!
THAT MEANS: NO MORE *TRUSTWELL* AND ITS RAZOR-TOOTHED, SMOOTH-TALKING SPOKESMEN. NO MORE PRIVATE SECURITY FIRMS AND THEIR *MERCENARY WAYS.* AND NO MORE FREE STATES AND ITS RACIST, IGNORANT AGENDA. "THE REAL AMERICA"? NOT ON OUR WATCH!
AND FINALLY, THE *UNITED STATES* OF THIS *FORMER AMERICA.* LET ME ASK YOU: DO YOU FEEL REPRESENTED? THEY'D TELL YOU THAT YOU ARE. THEY'D TELL YOU THEY'VE BEEN WATCHING OUT FOR US ALL THIS TIME. "GOD BLESS AMERICA," THEY SAY.
HARD TO TELL, WITH THE CLUSTER MUNITIONS, CRUISE MISSILES, LITTLE BIRD GUNSHIPS, KILL TEAMS, BLOCKADES, ASSASSINATIONS, CURFEWS, FOOD LINES, COLLATERAL DAMAGE, COLLECTIVE PUNISHMENT, FRIENDLY FIRE, DIVIDE-AND-CONQUER TACTICS DESIGNED *NOT* TO PROTECT...
...BUT TO *INTIMIDATE* AND *EXTERMINATE!*
JUST SPEAK AT A NORMAL VOLUME.
GOT IT.
WE GO LIVE IN TWENTY SECONDS, MR. ROTH.
LOOK AT THE CAMERA, NOT AT ME OR AT ANYONE ELSE. *THEY'LL* BE ASKING YOU THE QUESTIONS.
I'LL COUNT YOU DOWN.
WHAT ARE YOU *DOING?* GET THAT THE FUCK AWAY FROM ME!
FIVE SECONDS, MATTY... FOUR...

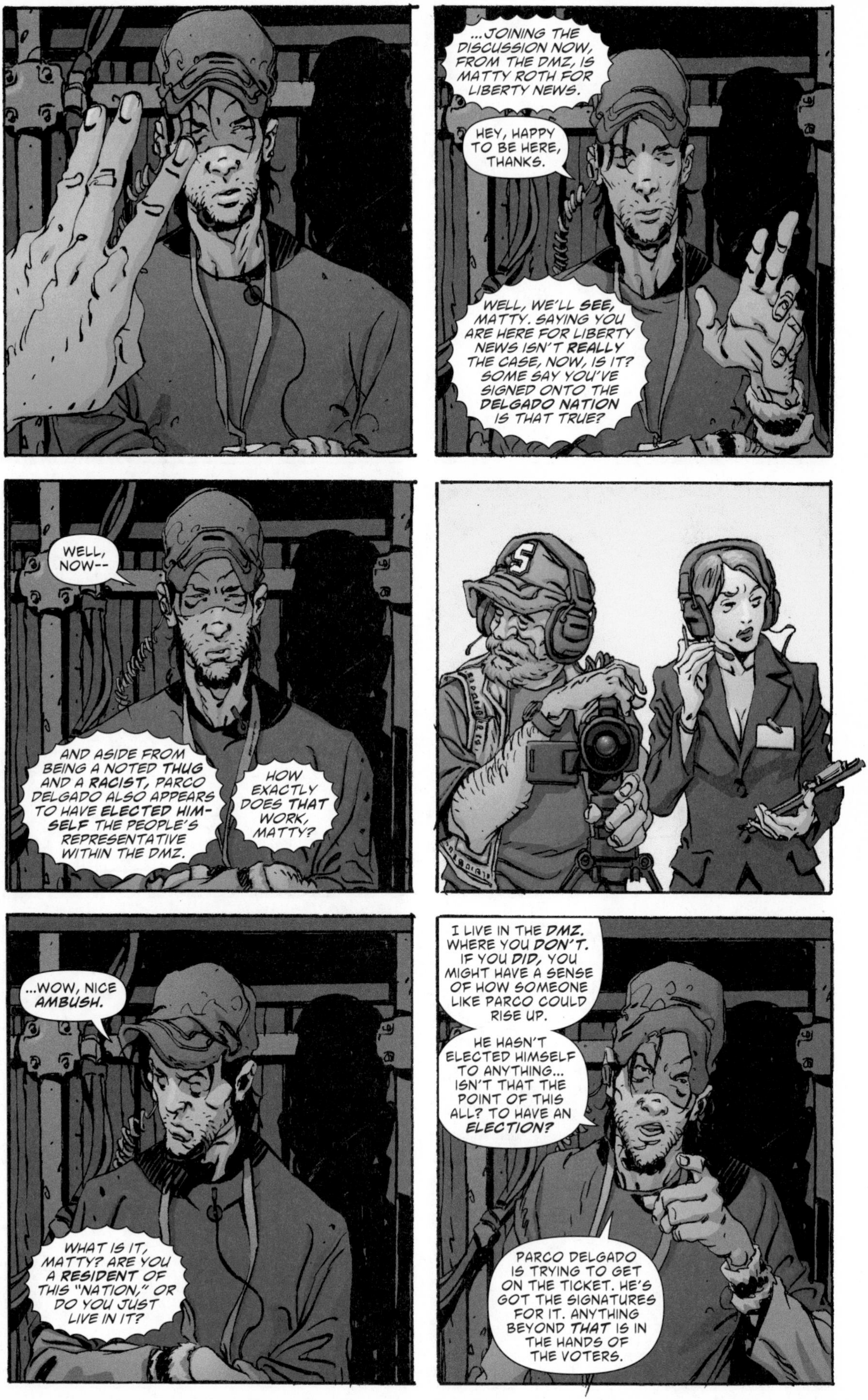

...JOINING THE DISCUSSION NOW, FROM THE DMZ, IS MATTY ROTH FOR LIBERTY NEWS.
HEY, HAPPY TO BE HERE, THANKS.
WELL, WE'LL SEE, MATTY. SAYING YOU ARE HERE FOR LIBERTY NEWS ISN'T REALLY THE CASE, NOW, IS IT? SOME SAY YOU'VE SIGNED ONTO THE DELGADO NATION IS THAT TRUE?
WELL, NOW--
AND ASIDE FROM BEING A NOTED THUG AND A RACIST, PARCO DELGADO ALSO APPEARS TO HAVE ELECTED HIMSELF THE PEOPLE'S REPRESENTATIVE WITHIN THE DMZ.
HOW EXACTLY DOES THAT WORK, MATTY?
...WOW, NICE AMBUSH.
WHAT IS IT, MATTY? ARE YOU A RESIDENT OF THIS "NATION," OR DO YOU JUST LIVE IN IT?
I LIVE IN THE DMZ. WHERE YOU DON'T. IF YOU DID, YOU MIGHT HAVE A SENSE OF HOW SOMEONE LIKE PARCO COULD RISE UP.
HE HASN'T ELECTED HIMSELF TO ANYTHING... ISN'T THAT THE POINT OF THIS ALL? TO HAVE AN ELECTION?
PARCO DELGADO IS TRYING TO GET ON THE TICKET. HE'S GOT THE SIGNATURES FOR IT. ANYTHING BEYOND THAT IS IN THE HANDS OF THE VOTERS.

BUT THIS ELECTION, THIS *PROVISIONAL* ELECTION, IT'S LARGELY *SYMBOLIC*, ISN'T IT?

THE UNITED STATES ALREADY APPOINTED AN ENVOY AND ADMINISTRATOR TO THE BOROUGH OF MANHATTAN AT THE START OF THE WAR.

IT BEGS THE QUESTION: *WHY* IS PARCO DELGADO DOING THIS?

YEAH, THAT'S FUNNY...

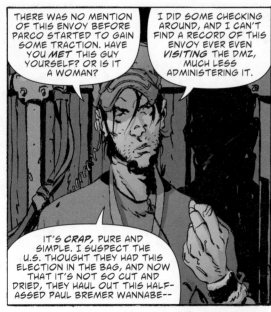

THERE WAS NO MENTION OF THIS ENVOY BEFORE PARCO STARTED TO GAIN SOME TRACTION. HAVE YOU *MET* THIS GUY YOURSELF? OR IS IT A WOMAN?

I DID SOME CHECKING AROUND, AND I CAN'T FIND A RECORD OF THIS ENVOY EVER EVEN *VISITING* THE DMZ, MUCH LESS ADMINISTERING IT.

IT'S *CRAP*, PURE AND SIMPLE. I SUSPECT THE U.S. THOUGHT THEY HAD THIS ELECTION IN THE BAG, AND NOW THAT IT'S NOT SO CUT AND DRIED, THEY HAUL OUT THIS HALF-ASSED PAUL BREMER WANNABE--

--AND SAY "HOLD ON, THE DMZ ALREADY *HAS* A PROVISIONAL LEADER." WHO CARES IF HE'S BEEN *BUNKERED DOWN* SOME-WHERE FOR THE LAST FIVE YEARS. AND THEY START TO DOWNPLAY THE NEED FOR AN ELECTION.

IT'S A TOTAL SLAP IN THE FACE, NOT ONLY TO US, BUT THE FREE STATES AND EVERYONE ELSE INVOLVED.

OK, THE TIMING ON THIS DOES FEEL AWKWARD...BUT THE FACT OF THE MATTER IS, THIS ENVOY *DOES* EXIST, HE IS THE *PRESIDENTIALLY APPOINTED* LEADER OF THE CITY. SO THAT'S NOT VALID ANYMORE?

THE DMZ *NEEDS* AN *ELECTION.* PUT THIS MYSTERY ENVOY ON THE TICKET ALONG WITH EVERYONE ELSE. BUT HE NEEDS TO *EARN* HIS POSITION.

THAT BRINGS US BACK TO MY FIRST POINT: PARCO DELGADO, THE *VOICE OF THE PEOPLE*? WHO IS THIS GUY? WHY IS EVERYONE SO WORRIED ABOUT HIM?

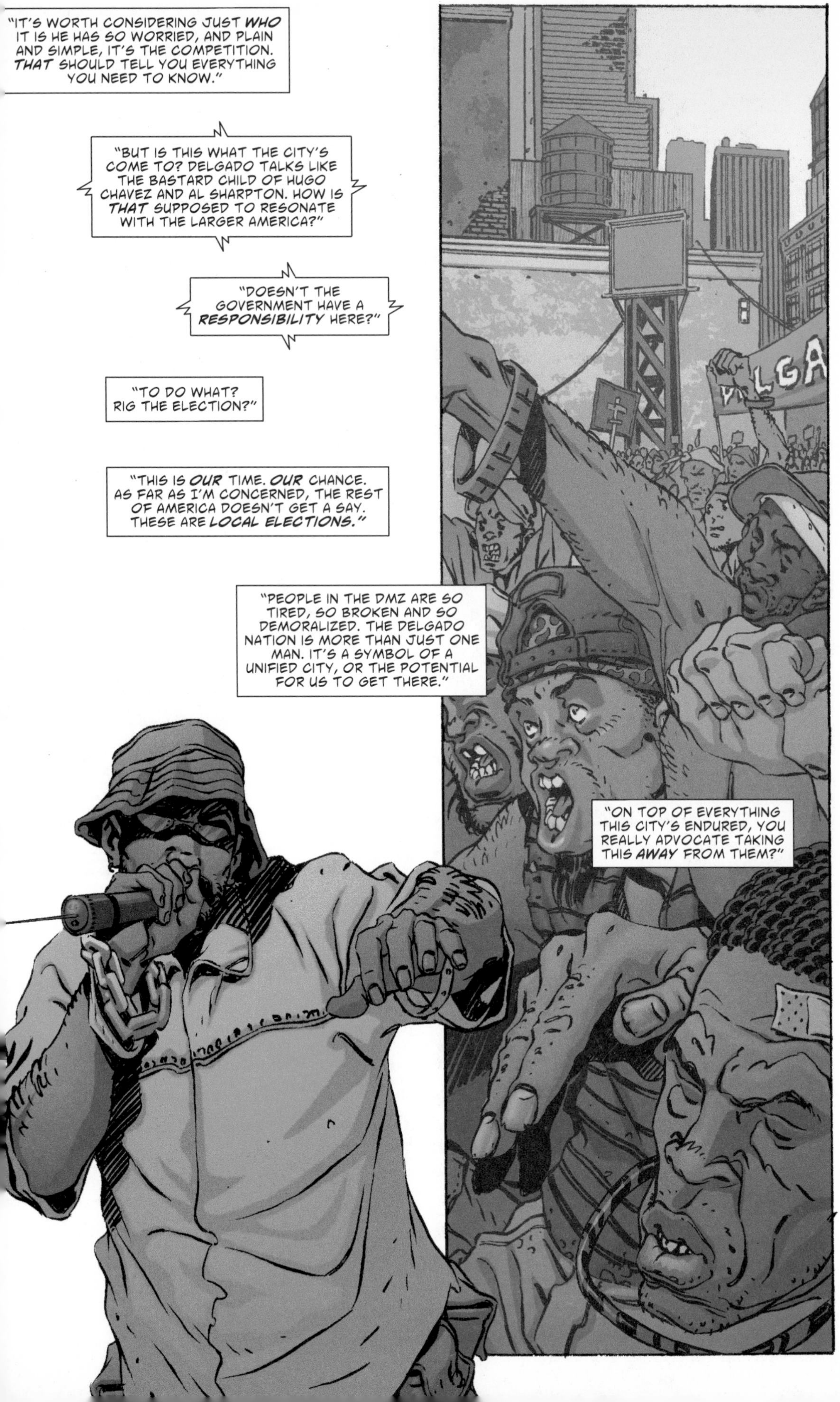
"IT'S WORTH CONSIDERING JUST *WHO* IT IS HE HAS SO WORRIED, AND PLAIN AND SIMPLE, IT'S THE COMPETITION. *THAT* SHOULD TELL YOU EVERYTHING YOU NEED TO KNOW."
"BUT IS THIS WHAT THE CITY'S COME TO? DELGADO TALKS LIKE THE BASTARD CHILD OF HUGO CHAVEZ AND AL SHARPTON. HOW IS *THAT* SUPPOSED TO RESONATE WITH THE LARGER AMERICA?"
"DOESN'T THE GOVERNMENT HAVE A *RESPONSIBILITY* HERE?"
"TO DO WHAT? RIG THE ELECTION?"
"THIS IS *OUR* TIME. *OUR* CHANCE. AS FAR AS I'M CONCERNED, THE REST OF AMERICA DOESN'T GET A SAY. THESE ARE *LOCAL ELECTIONS.*"
"PEOPLE IN THE DMZ ARE SO TIRED, SO BROKEN AND SO DEMORALIZED. THE DELGADO NATION IS MORE THAN JUST ONE MAN. IT'S A SYMBOL OF A UNIFIED CITY, OR THE POTENTIAL FOR US TO GET THERE."
"ON TOP OF EVERYTHING THIS CITY'S ENDURED, YOU REALLY ADVOCATE TAKING THIS *AWAY* FROM THEM?"

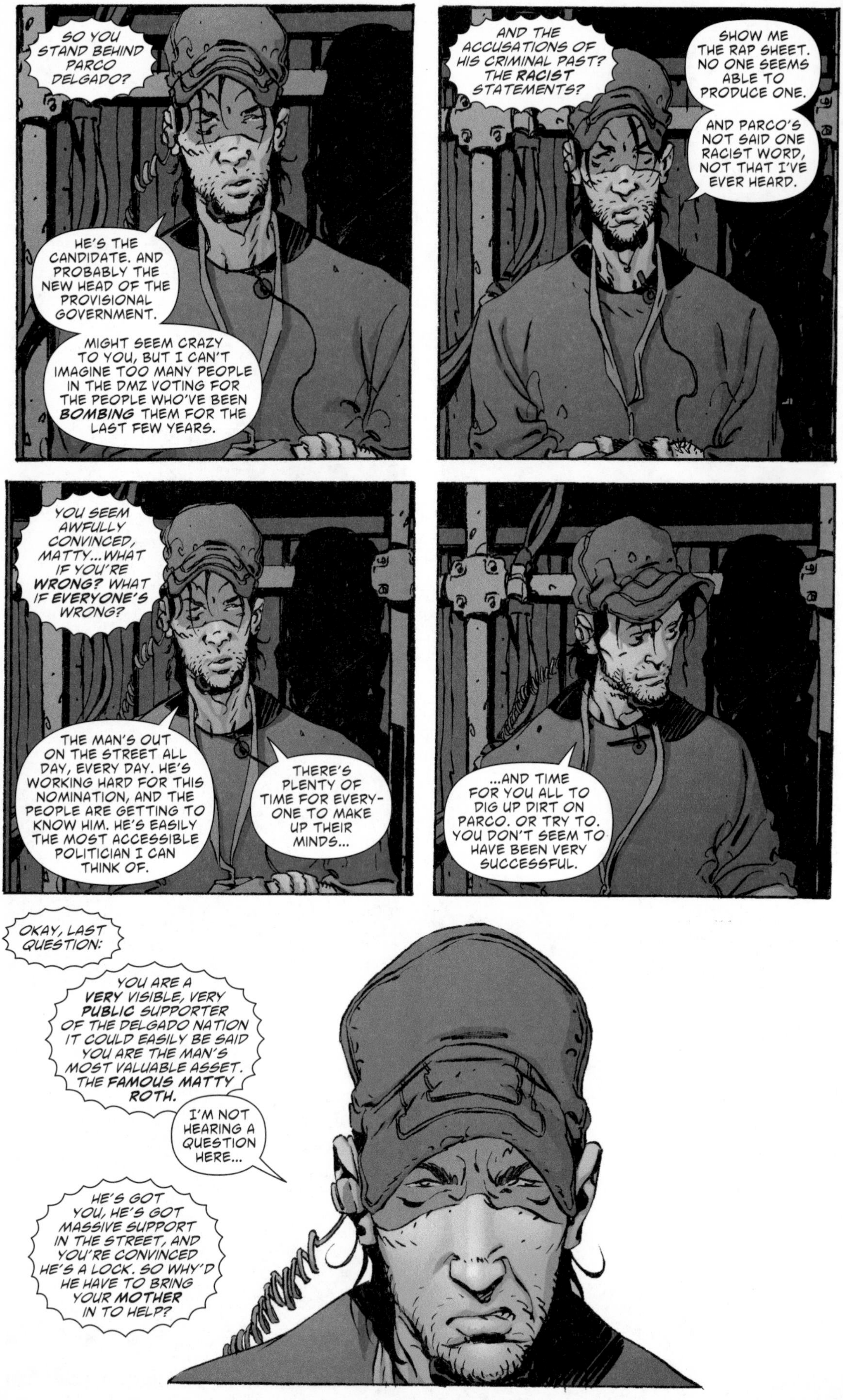
SO YOU STAND BEHIND PARCO DELGADO?
HE'S THE CANDIDATE. AND PROBABLY THE NEW HEAD OF THE PROVISIONAL GOVERNMENT.
MIGHT SEEM CRAZY TO YOU, BUT I CAN'T IMAGINE TOO MANY PEOPLE IN THE DMZ VOTING FOR THE PEOPLE WHO'VE BEEN BOMBING THEM FOR THE LAST FEW YEARS.
AND THE ACCUSATIONS OF HIS CRIMINAL PAST? THE RACIST STATEMENTS?
SHOW ME THE RAP SHEET. NO ONE SEEMS ABLE TO PRODUCE ONE.
AND PARCO'S NOT SAID ONE RACIST WORD, NOT THAT I'VE EVER HEARD.
YOU SEEM AWFULLY CONVINCED, MATTY... WHAT IF YOU'RE WRONG? WHAT IF EVERYONE'S WRONG?
THE MAN'S OUT ON THE STREET ALL DAY, EVERY DAY. HE'S WORKING HARD FOR THIS NOMINATION, AND THE PEOPLE ARE GETTING TO KNOW HIM. HE'S EASILY THE MOST ACCESSIBLE POLITICIAN I CAN THINK OF.
THERE'S PLENTY OF TIME FOR EVERY-ONE TO MAKE UP THEIR MINDS...
...AND TIME FOR YOU ALL TO DIG UP DIRT ON PARCO. OR TRY TO. YOU DON'T SEEM TO HAVE BEEN VERY SUCCESSFUL.
OKAY, LAST QUESTION:
YOU ARE A VERY VISIBLE, VERY PUBLIC SUPPORTER OF THE DELGADO NATION IT COULD EASILY BE SAID YOU ARE THE MAN'S MOST VALUABLE ASSET. THE FAMOUS MATTY ROTH.
I'M NOT HEARING A QUESTION HERE...
HE'S GOT YOU, HE'S GOT MASSIVE SUPPORT IN THE STREET, AND YOU'RE CONVINCED HE'S A LOCK. SO WHY'D HE HAVE TO BRING YOUR MOTHER IN TO HELP?

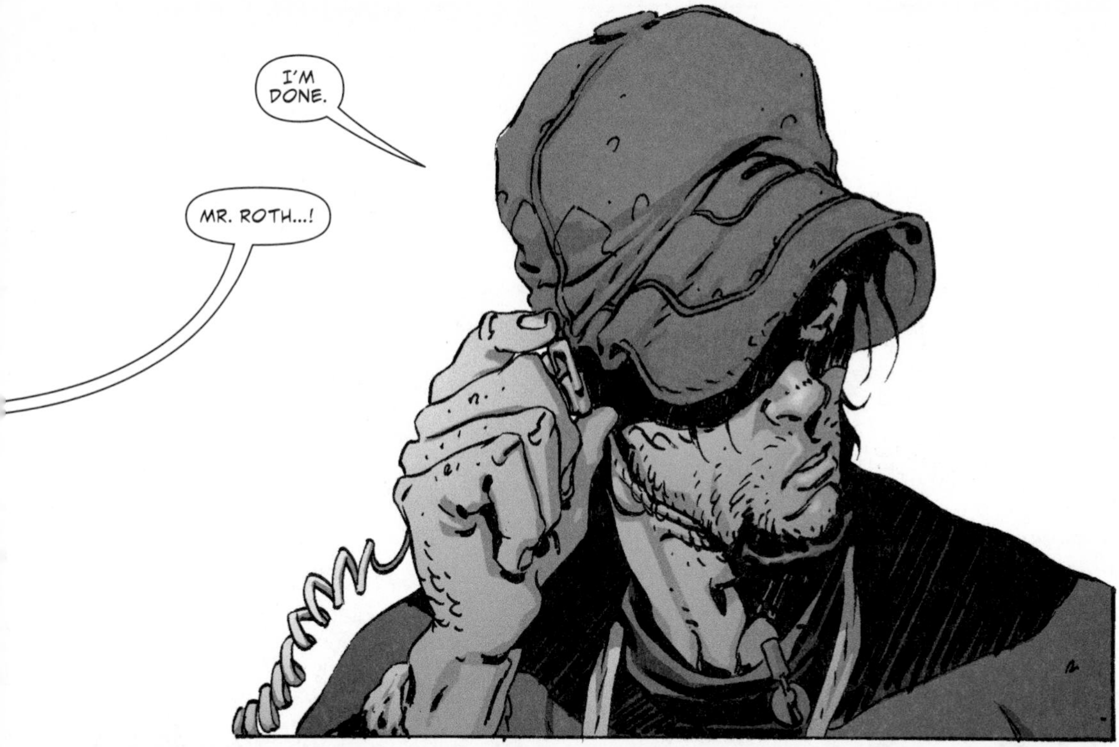
I'M DONE.
MR. ROTH...!

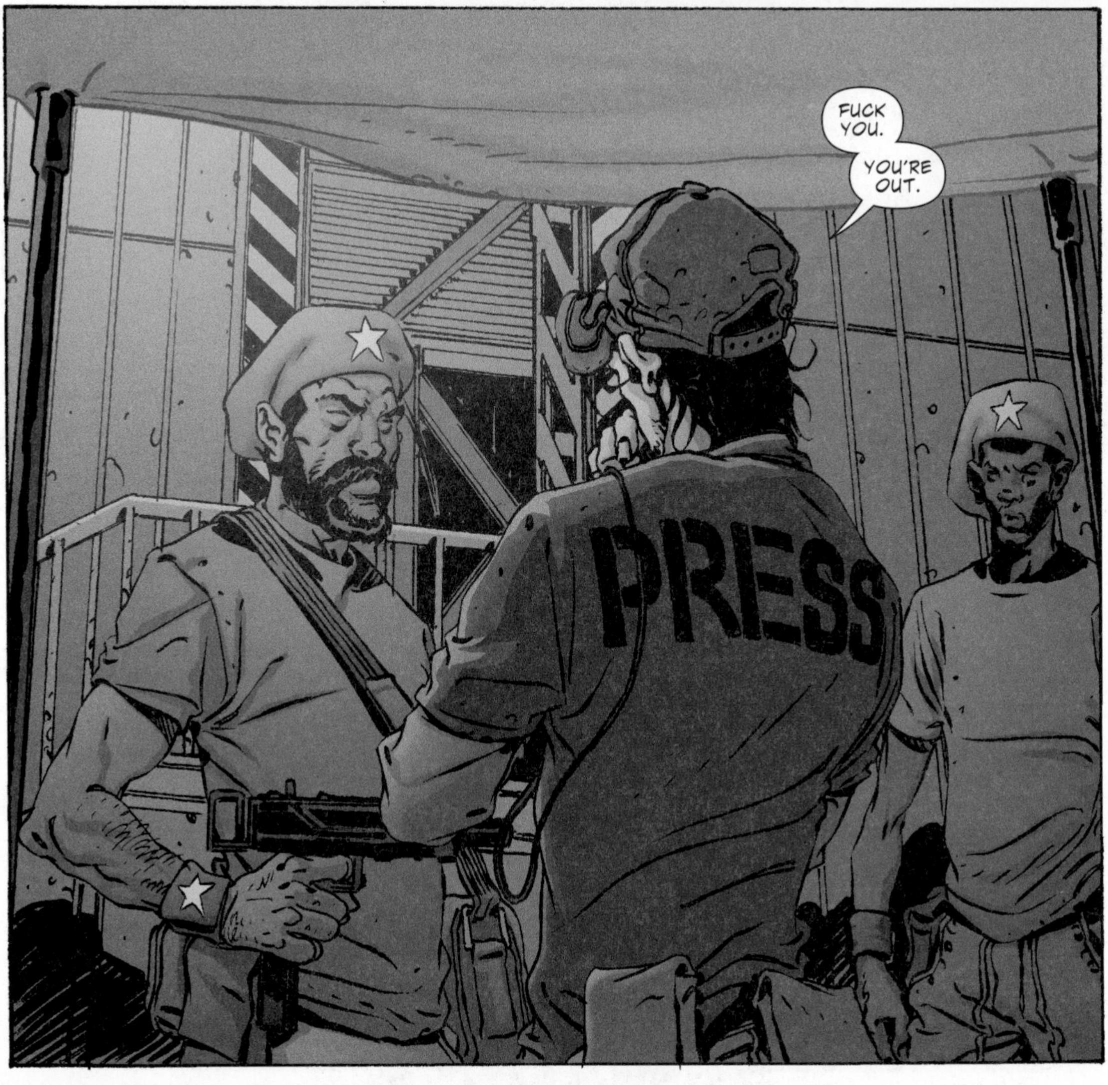
FUCK YOU.
YOU'RE OUT.
PRESS

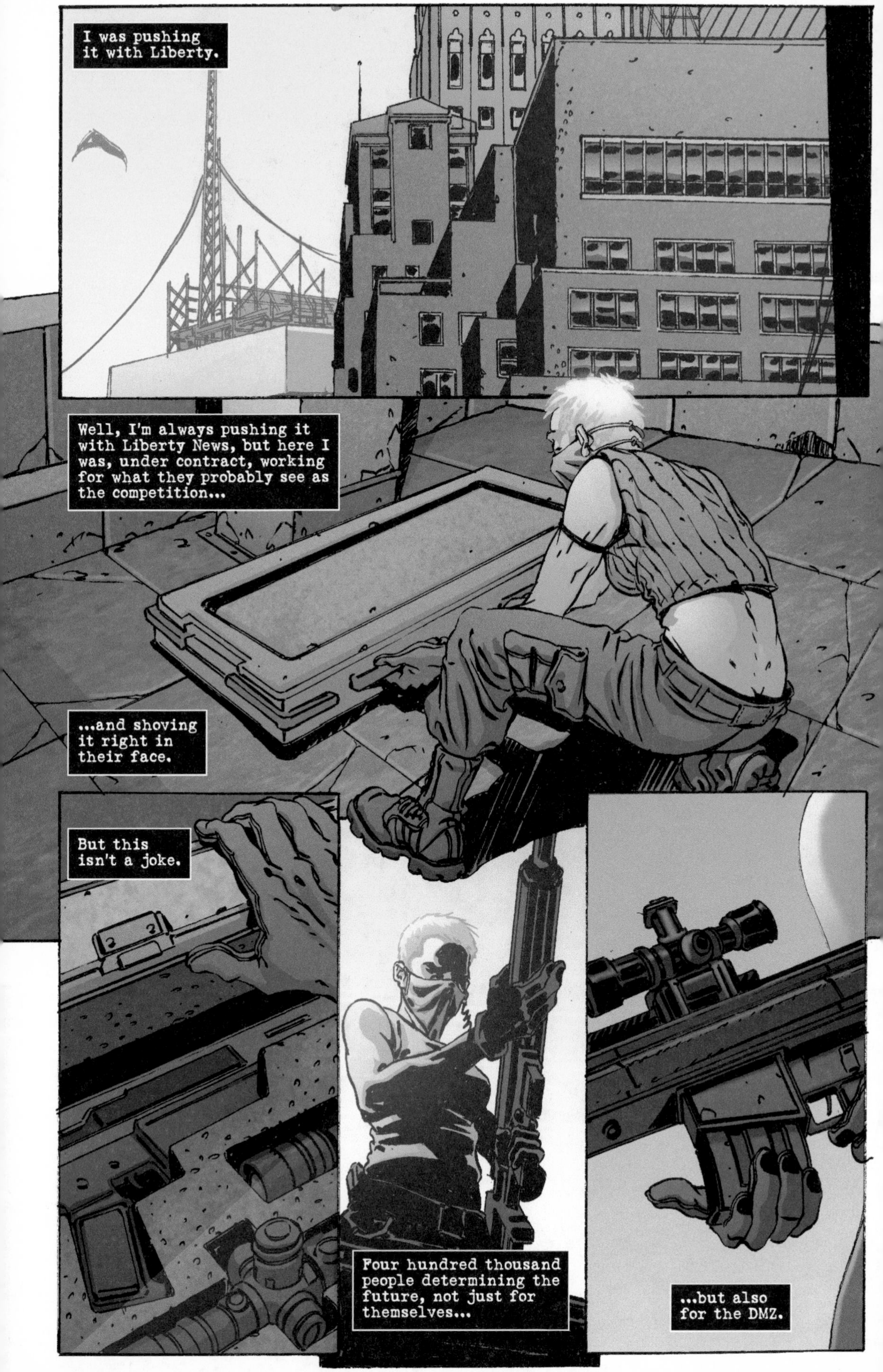

I was pushing it with Liberty.
Well, I'm always pushing it with Liberty News, but here I was, under contract, working for what they probably see as the competition...
...and shoving it right in their face.
But this isn't a joke.
Four hundred thousand people determining the future, not just for themselves...
...but also for the DMZ.

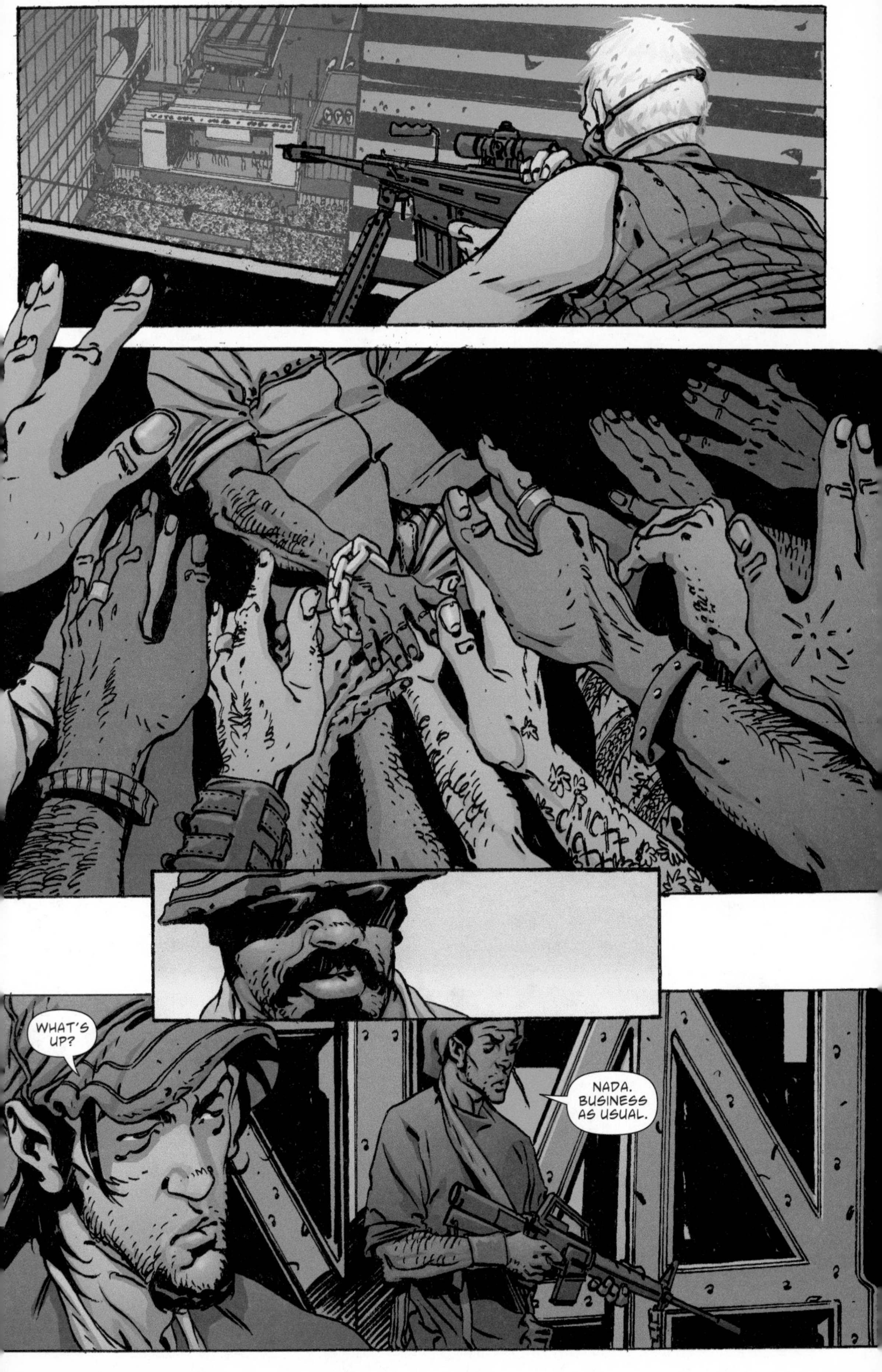
WHAT'S UP?
NADA. BUSINESS AS USUAL.

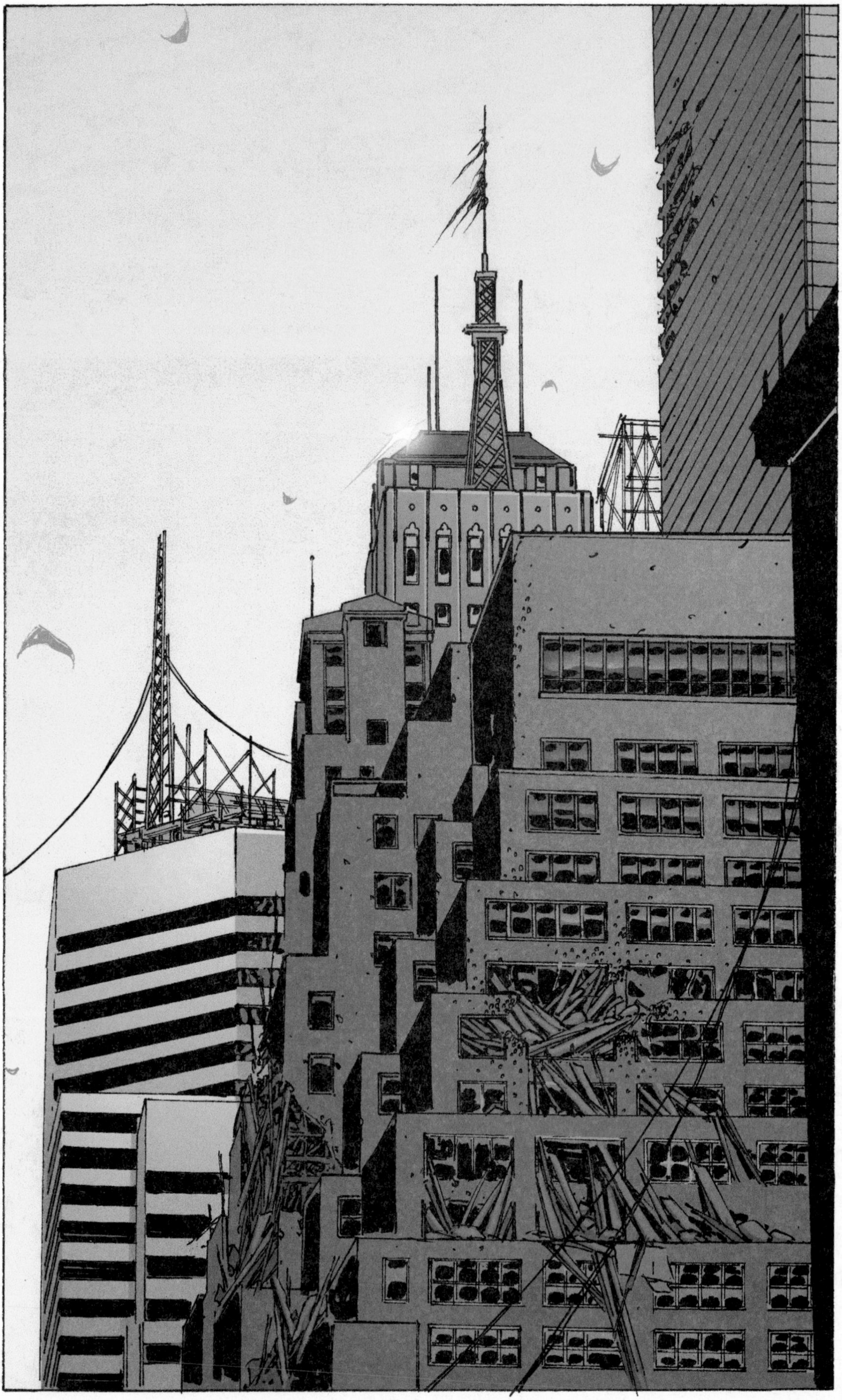

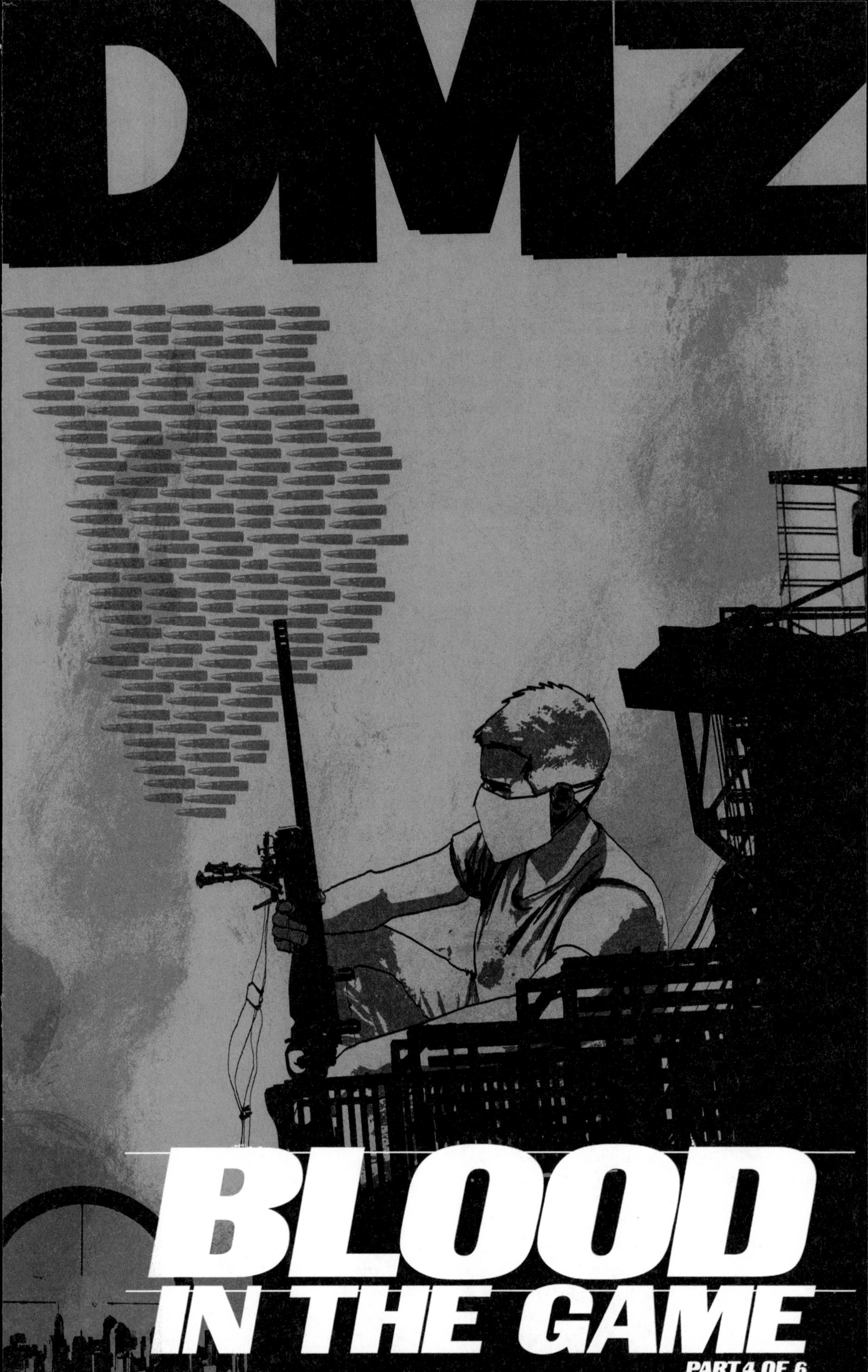

DMZ
BLOOD
IN THE GAME
PART 4 OF 6

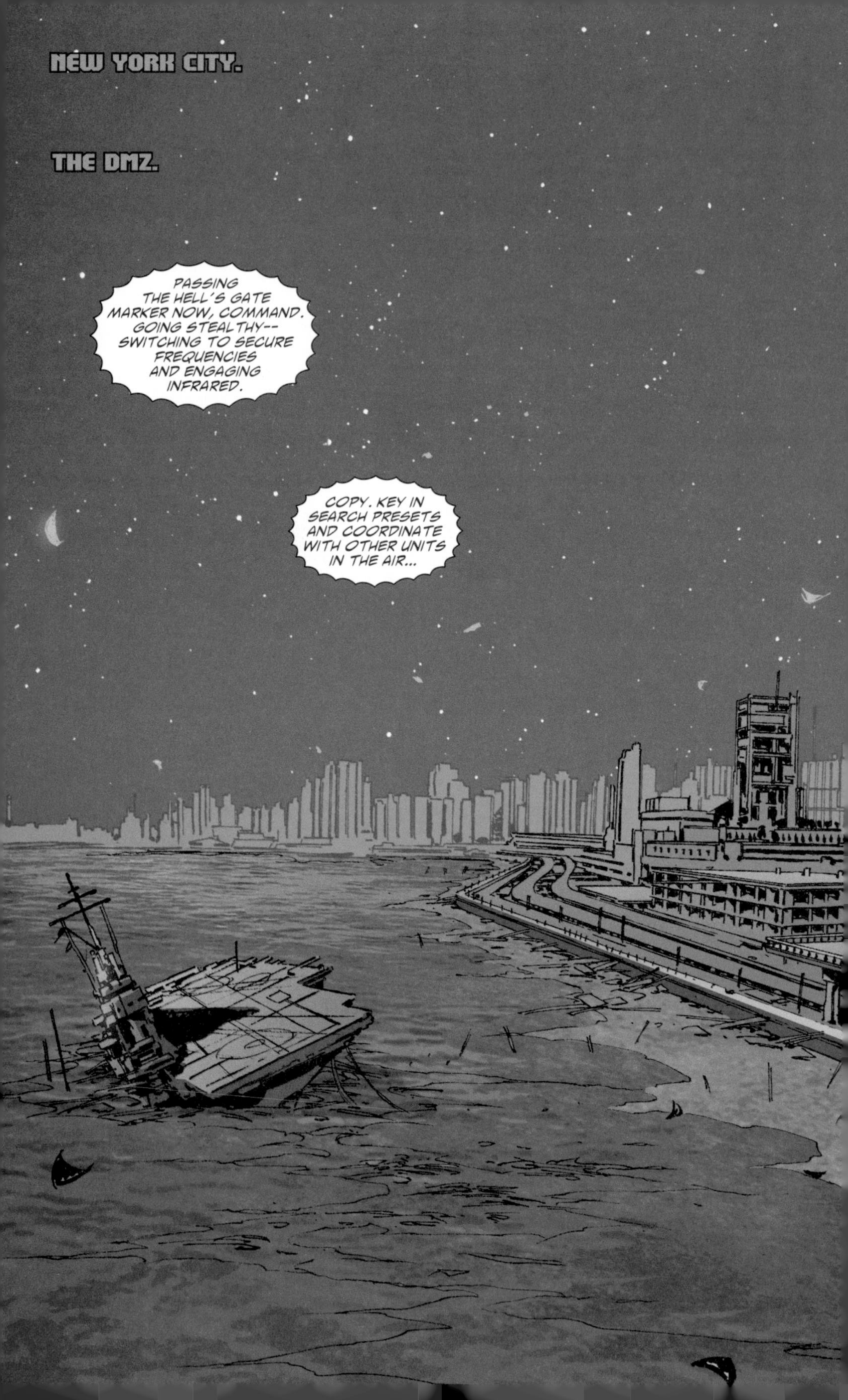
NEW YORK CITY.
THE DMZ.
PASSING THE HELL'S GATE MARKER NOW, COMMAND. GOING STEALTHY-- SWITCHING TO SECURE FREQUENCIES AND ENGAGING INFRARED.
COPY. KEY IN SEARCH PRESETS AND COORDINATE WITH OTHER UNITS IN THE AIR...

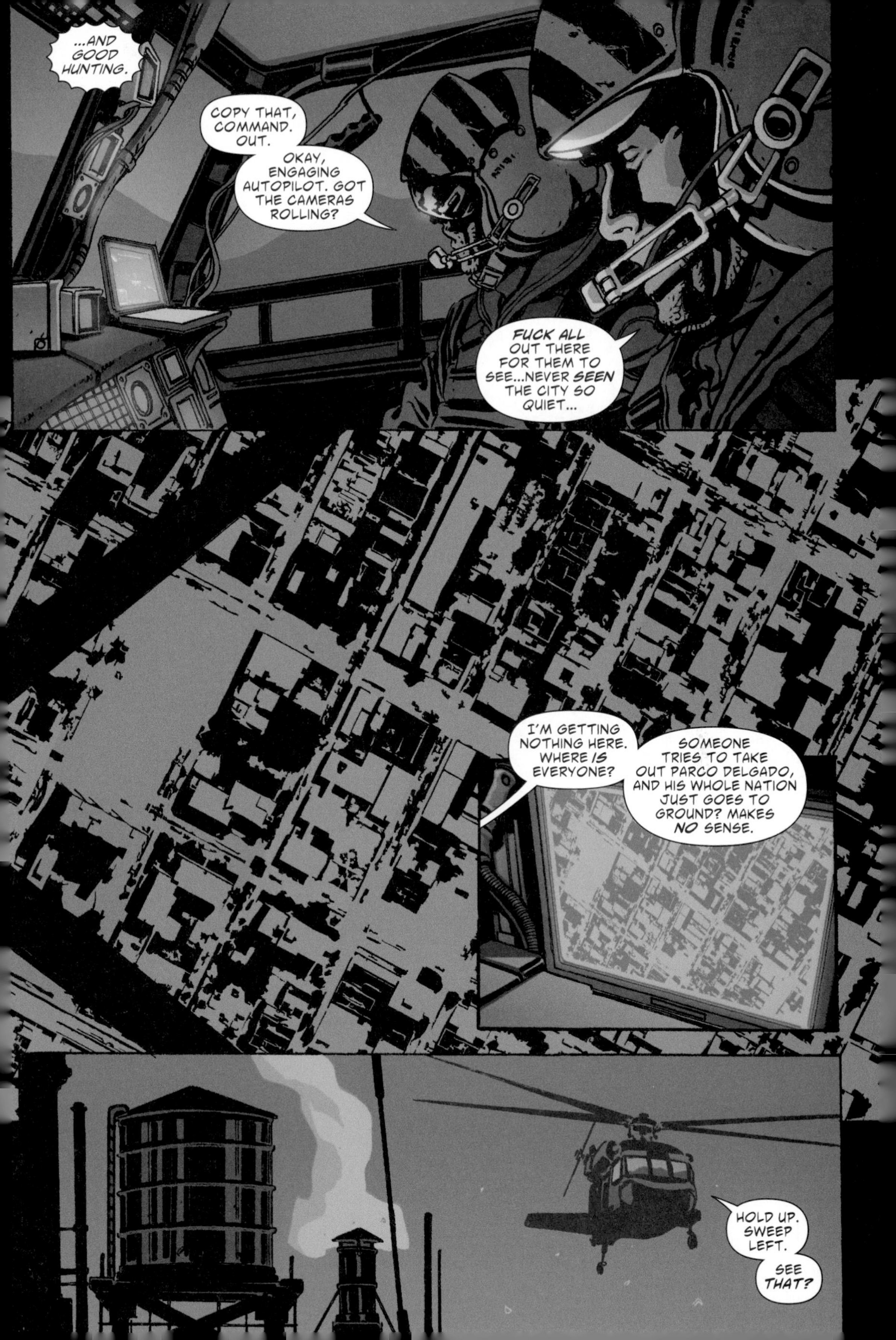
...AND GOOD HUNTING.
COPY THAT, COMMAND. OUT.
OKAY, ENGAGING AUTOPILOT. GOT THE CAMERAS ROLLING?
FUCK ALL OUT THERE FOR THEM TO SEE...NEVER SEEN THE CITY SO QUIET...
I'M GETTING NOTHING HERE. WHERE IS EVERYONE?
SOMEONE TRIES TO TAKE OUT PARCO DELGADO, AND HIS WHOLE NATION JUST GOES TO GROUND? MAKES NO SENSE.
HOLD UP. SWEEP LEFT.
SEE THAT?

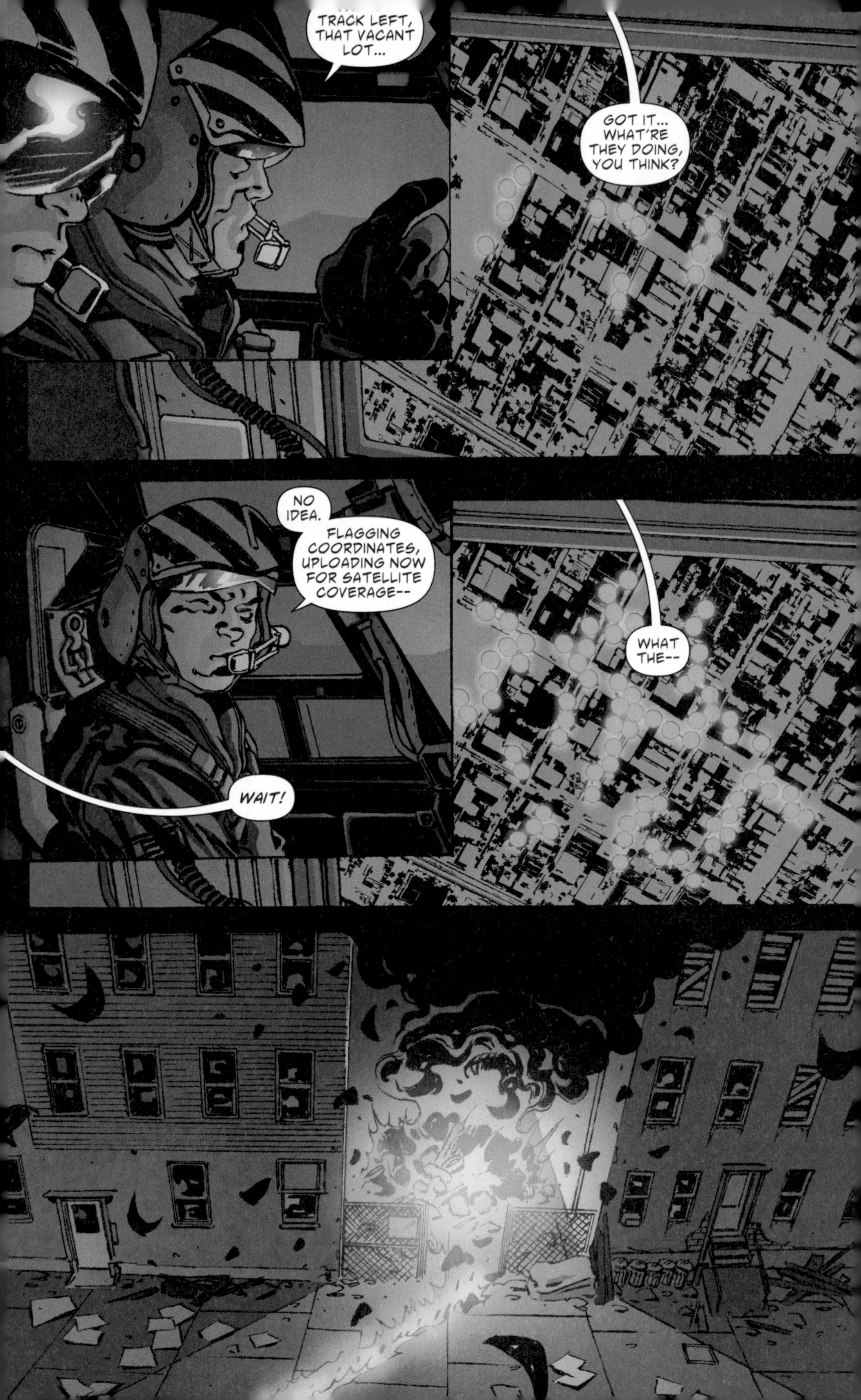
TRACK LEFT, THAT VACANT LOT...
GOT IT... WHAT'RE THEY DOING, YOU THINK?
NO IDEA.
FLAGGING COORDINATES, UPLOADING NOW FOR SATELLITE COVERAGE--
WHAT THE--
WAIT!

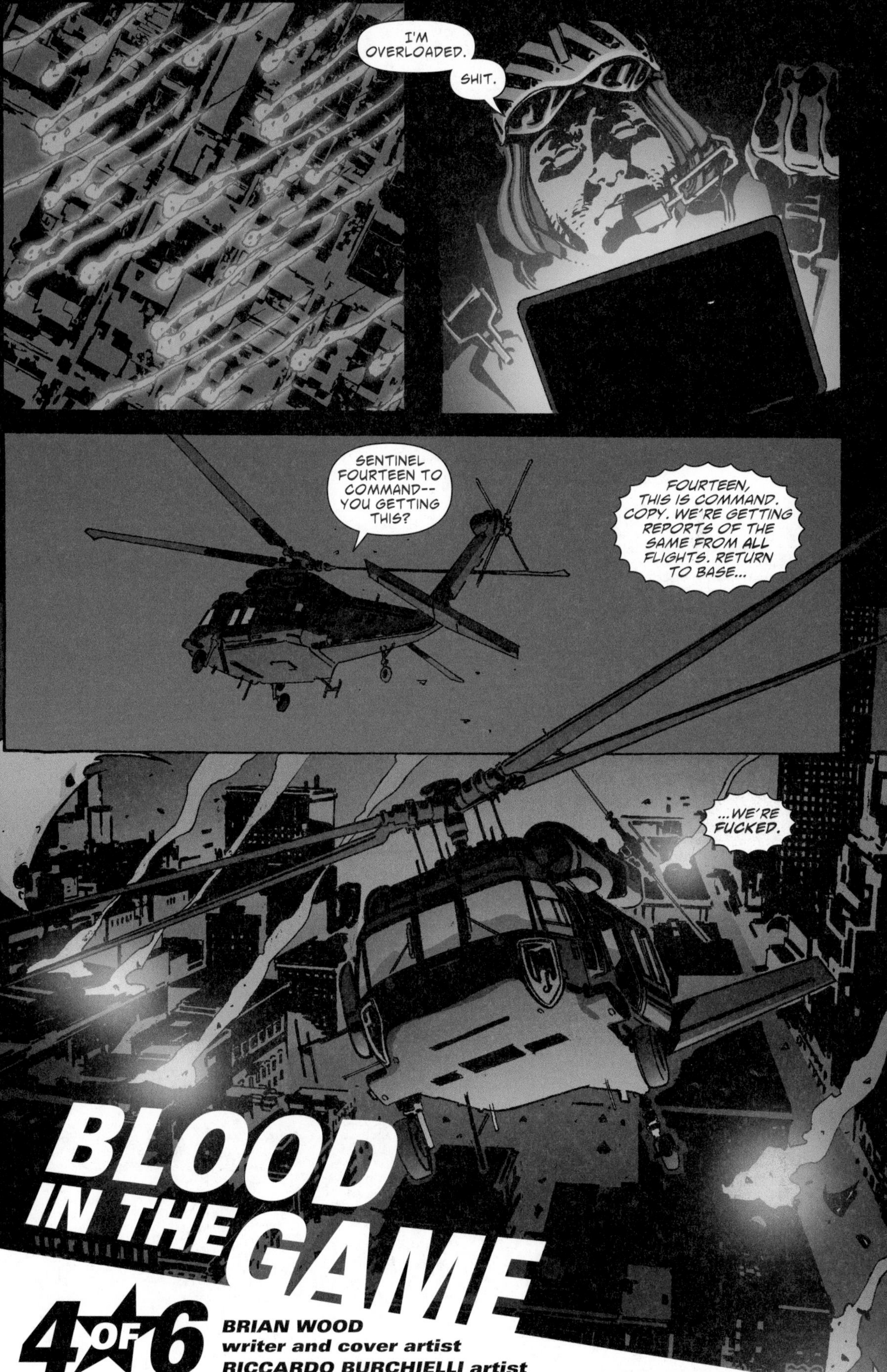
I'M OVERLOADED.
SHIT.
SENTINEL FOURTEEN TO COMMAND-- YOU GETTING THIS?
FOURTEEN, THIS IS COMMAND. COPY. WE'RE GETTING REPORTS OF THE SAME FROM ALL FLIGHTS. RETURN TO BASE...
...WE'RE FUCKED.
BLOOD IN THE GAME
4 OF 6
BRIAN WOOD writer and cover artist
RICCARDO BURCHIELLI artist
JEROMY COX colors JARED K. FLETCHER letters

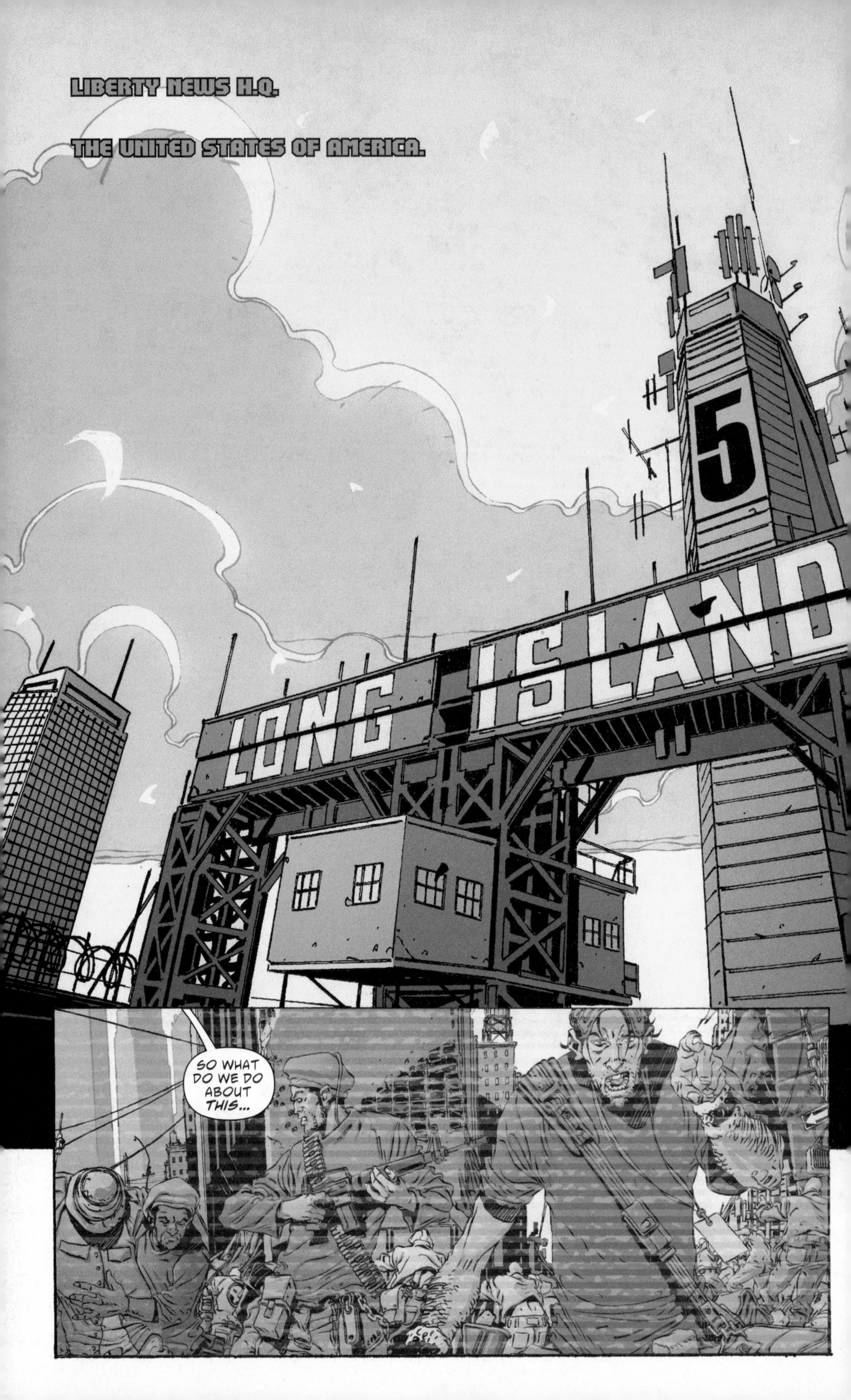
LIBERTY NEWS H.Q.
THE UNITED STATES OF AMERICA.
LONG ISLAND
5
SO WHAT DO WE DO ABOUT THIS...

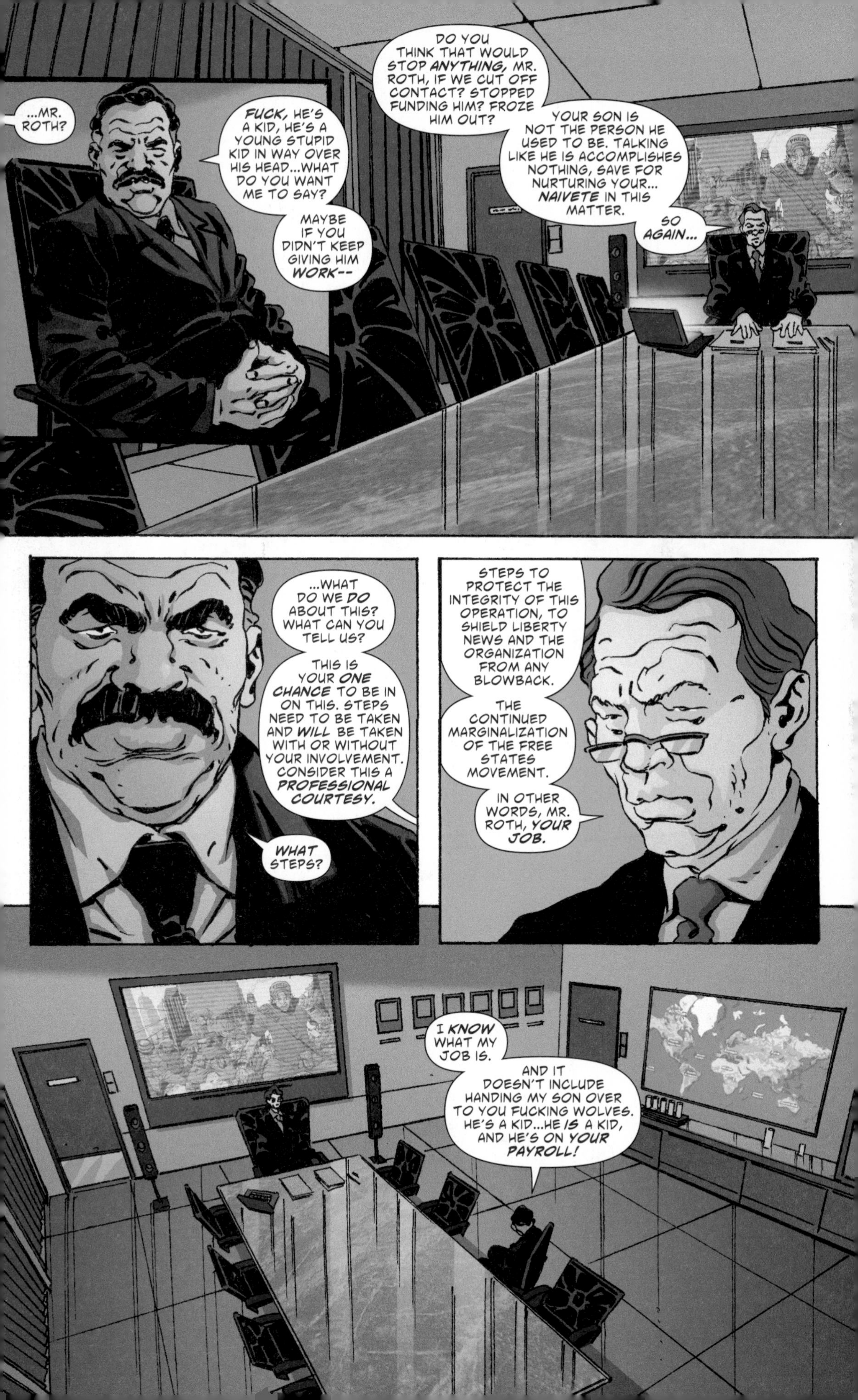
...MR. ROTH?
FUCK, HE'S A KID, HE'S A YOUNG STUPID KID IN WAY OVER HIS HEAD...WHAT DO YOU WANT ME TO SAY?
MAYBE IF YOU DIDN'T KEEP GIVING HIM WORK--
DO YOU THINK THAT WOULD STOP ANYTHING, MR. ROTH, IF WE CUT OFF CONTACT? STOPPED FUNDING HIM? FROZE HIM OUT?
YOUR SON IS NOT THE PERSON HE USED TO BE. TALKING LIKE HE IS ACCOMPLISHES NOTHING, SAVE FOR NURTURING YOUR... NAIVETE IN THIS MATTER.
SO AGAIN...
...WHAT DO WE DO ABOUT THIS? WHAT CAN YOU TELL US?
THIS IS YOUR ONE CHANCE TO BE IN ON THIS. STEPS NEED TO BE TAKEN AND WILL BE TAKEN WITH OR WITHOUT YOUR INVOLVEMENT. CONSIDER THIS A PROFESSIONAL COURTESY.
WHAT STEPS?
STEPS TO PROTECT THE INTEGRITY OF THIS OPERATION, TO SHIELD LIBERTY NEWS AND THE ORGANIZATION FROM ANY BLOWBACK.
THE CONTINUED MARGINALIZATION OF THE FREE STATES MOVEMENT.
IN OTHER WORDS, MR. ROTH, YOUR JOB.
I KNOW WHAT MY JOB IS.
AND IT DOESN'T INCLUDE HANDING MY SON OVER TO YOU FUCKING WOLVES. HE'S A KID...HE IS A KID, AND HE'S ON YOUR PAYROLL!

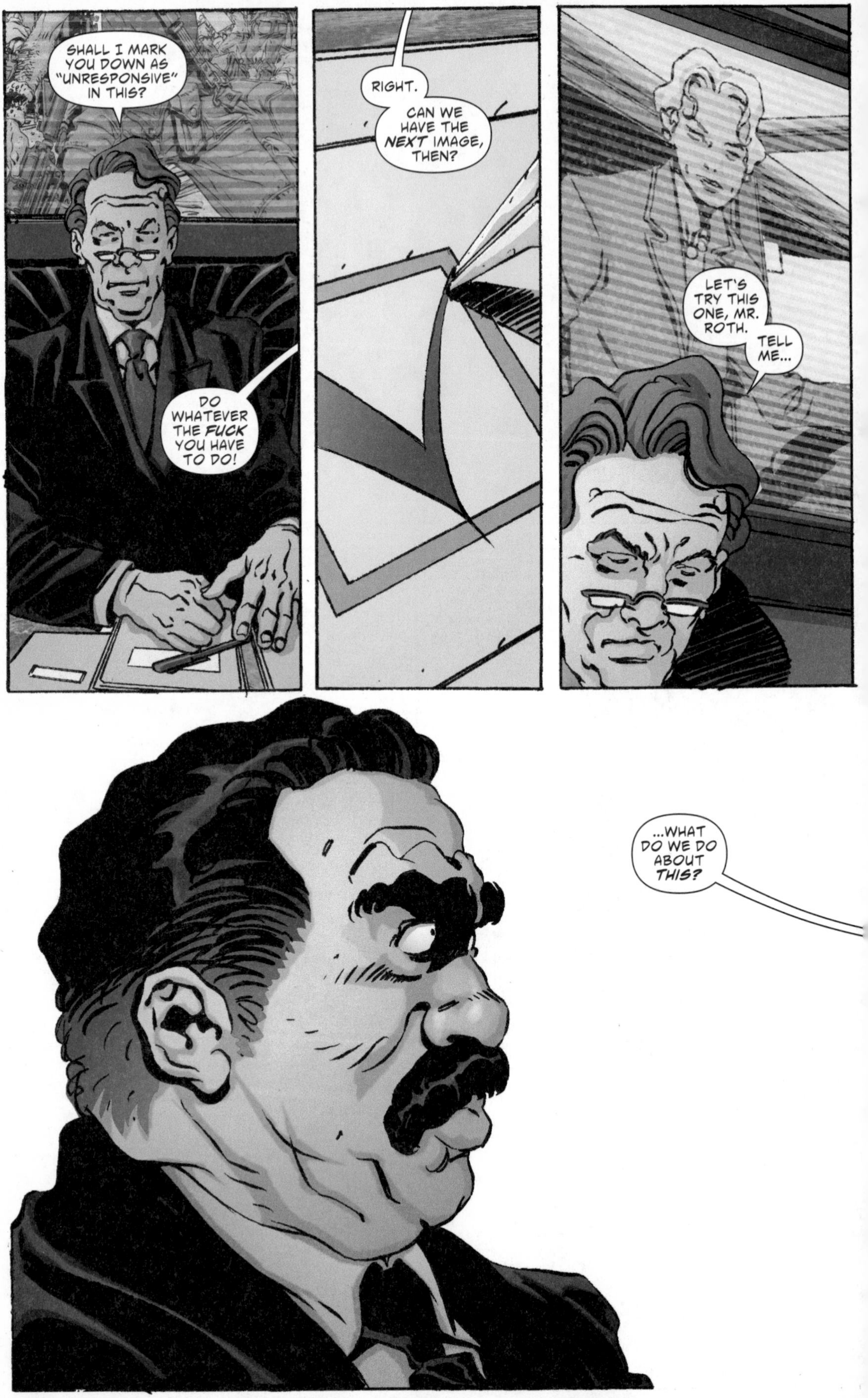
SHALL I MARK YOU DOWN AS "UNRESPONSIVE" IN THIS?
DO WHATEVER THE *FUCK* YOU HAVE TO DO!
RIGHT.
CAN WE HAVE THE *NEXT* IMAGE, THEN?
LET'S TRY THIS ONE, MR. ROTH.
TELL ME...
...WHAT DO WE DO ABOUT *THIS?*

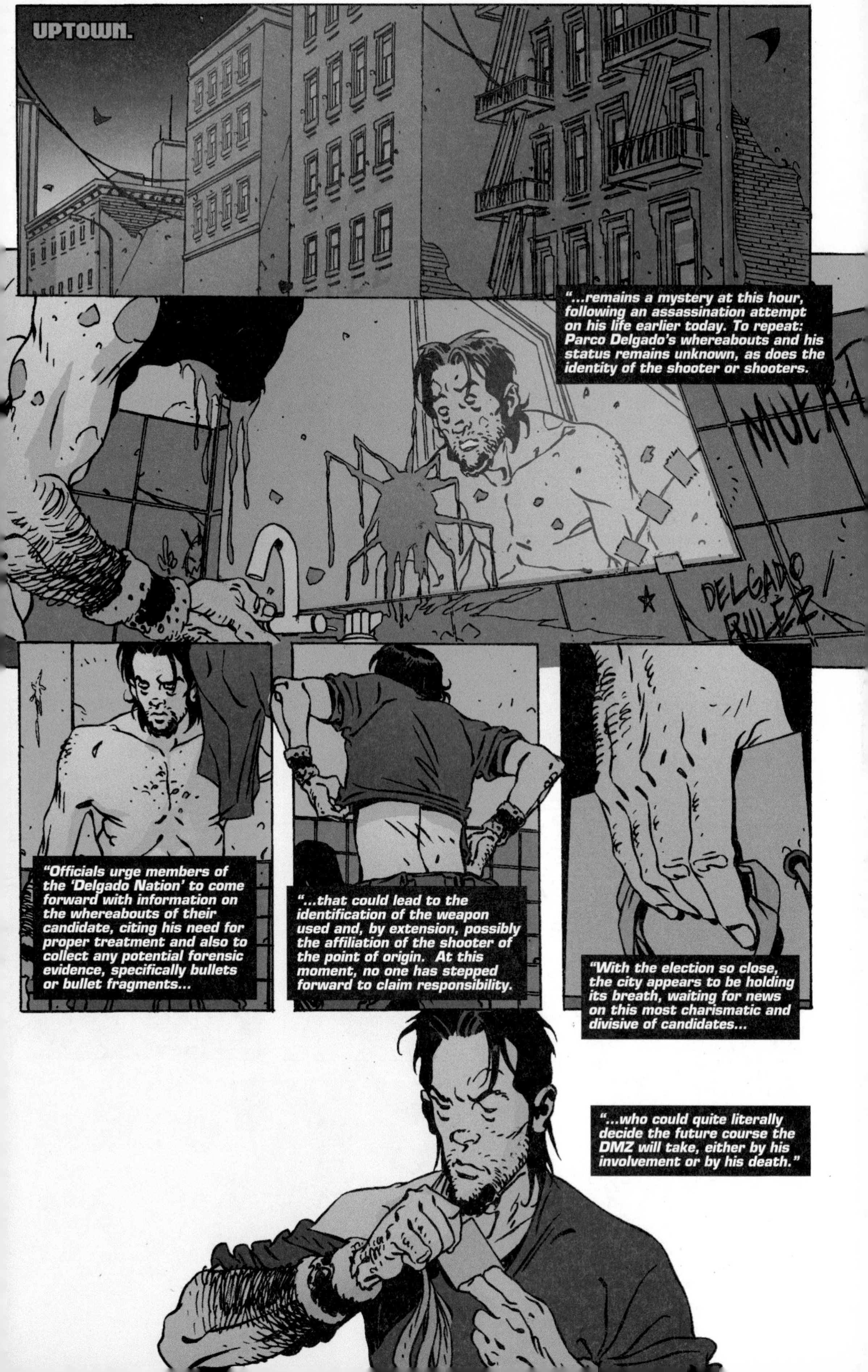
UPTOWN.
"...remains a mystery at this hour, following an assassination attempt on his life earlier today. To repeat: Parco Delgado's whereabouts and his status remains unknown, as does the identity of the shooter or shooters.
DELGADO RULEZ!
"Officials urge members of the 'Delgado Nation' to come forward with information on the whereabouts of their candidate, citing his need for proper treatment and also to collect any potential forensic evidence, specifically bullets or bullet fragments...
"...that could lead to the identification of the weapon used and, by extension, possibly the affiliation of the shooter of the point of origin. At this moment, no one has stepped forward to claim responsibility.
"With the election so close, the city appears to be holding its breath, waiting for news on this most charismatic and divisive of candidates...
"...who could quite literally decide the future course the DMZ will take, either by his involvement or by his death."

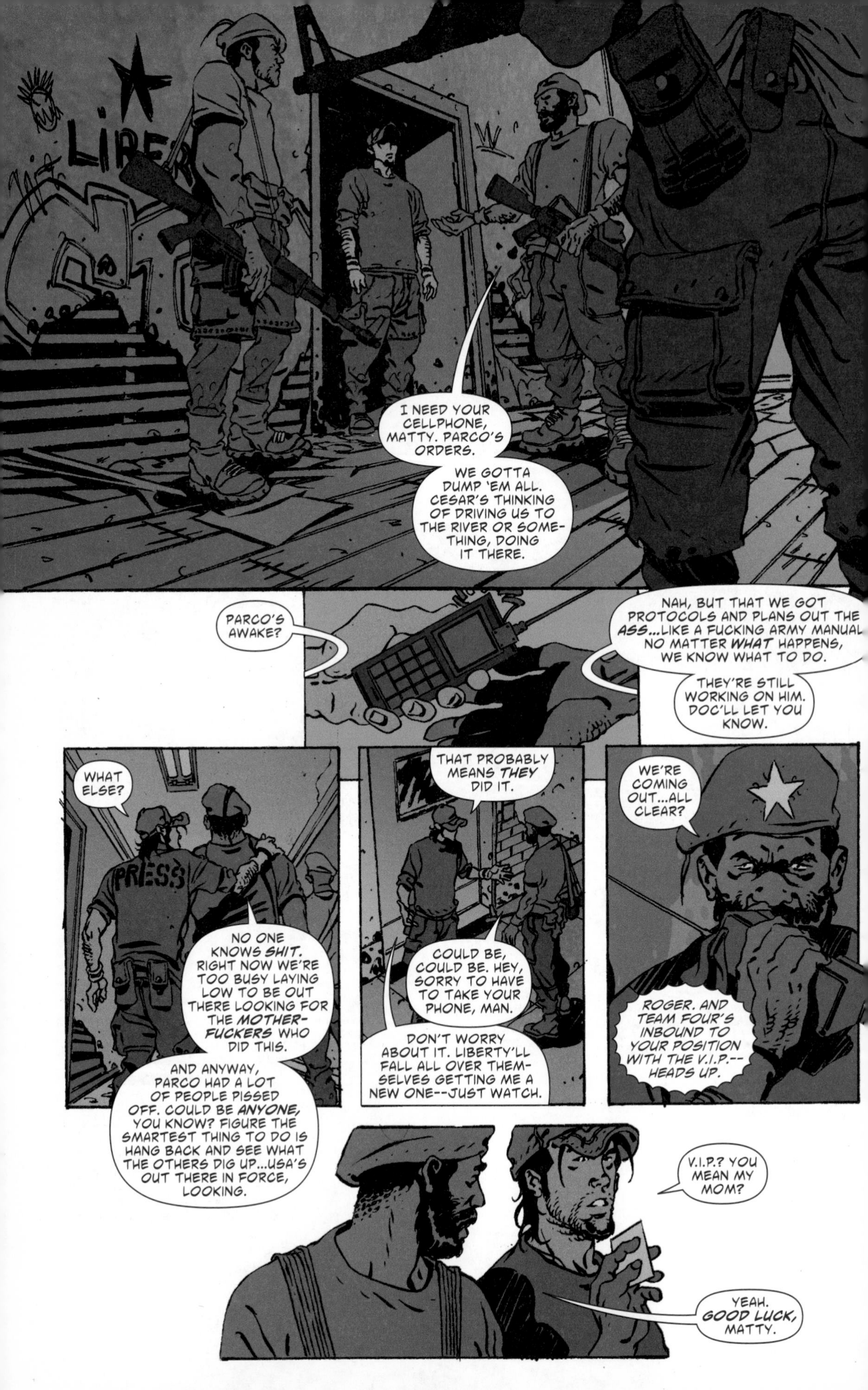

LIBER
I NEED YOUR CELLPHONE, MATTY. PARCO'S ORDERS.
WE GOTTA DUMP 'EM ALL. CESAR'S THINKING OF DRIVING US TO THE RIVER OR SOME-THING, DOING IT THERE.
PARCO'S AWAKE?
NAH, BUT THAT WE GOT PROTOCOLS AND PLANS OUT THE ASS...LIKE A FUCKING ARMY MANUAL. NO MATTER WHAT HAPPENS, WE KNOW WHAT TO DO.
THEY'RE STILL WORKING ON HIM. DOC'LL LET YOU KNOW.
WHAT ELSE?
PRESS
NO ONE KNOWS SHIT. RIGHT NOW WE'RE TOO BUSY LAYING LOW TO BE OUT THERE LOOKING FOR THE MOTHER-FUCKERS WHO DID THIS.
AND ANYWAY, PARCO HAD A LOT OF PEOPLE PISSED OFF. COULD BE ANYONE, YOU KNOW? FIGURE THE SMARTEST THING TO DO IS HANG BACK AND SEE WHAT THE OTHERS DIG UP...USA'S OUT THERE IN FORCE, LOOKING.
THAT PROBABLY MEANS THEY DID IT.
COULD BE, COULD BE. HEY, SORRY TO HAVE TO TAKE YOUR PHONE, MAN.
DON'T WORRY ABOUT IT. LIBERTY'LL FALL ALL OVER THEM-SELVES GETTING ME A NEW ONE--JUST WATCH.
WE'RE COMING OUT...ALL CLEAR?
ROGER. AND TEAM FOUR'S INBOUND TO YOUR POSITION WITH THE V.I.P.--HEADS UP.
V.I.P.? YOU MEAN MY MOM?
YEAH. GOOD LUCK, MATTY.

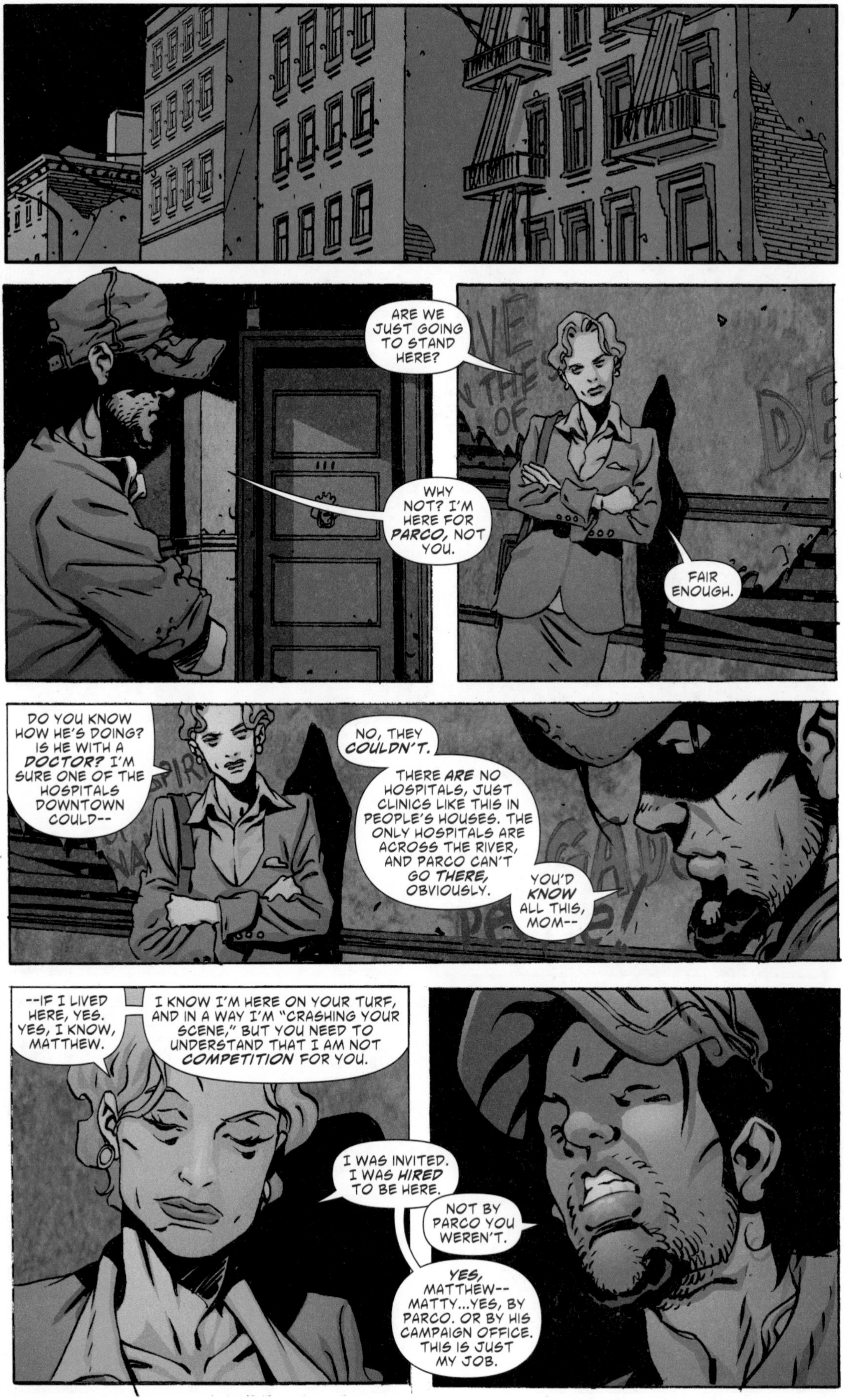
ARE WE JUST GOING TO STAND HERE?
WHY NOT? I'M HERE FOR PARCO, NOT YOU.
FAIR ENOUGH.
DO YOU KNOW HOW HE'S DOING? IS HE WITH A DOCTOR? I'M SURE ONE OF THE HOSPITALS DOWNTOWN COULD--
NO, THEY COULDN'T.
THERE ARE NO HOSPITALS, JUST CLINICS LIKE THIS IN PEOPLE'S HOUSES. THE ONLY HOSPITALS ARE ACROSS THE RIVER, AND PARCO CAN'T GO THERE, OBVIOUSLY.
YOU'D KNOW ALL THIS, MOM--
--IF I LIVED HERE, YES. YES, I KNOW, MATTHEW.
I KNOW I'M HERE ON YOUR TURF, AND IN A WAY I'M "CRASHING YOUR SCENE," BUT YOU NEED TO UNDERSTAND THAT I AM NOT COMPETITION FOR YOU.
I WAS INVITED. I WAS HIRED TO BE HERE.
NOT BY PARCO YOU WEREN'T.
YES, MATTHEW-- MATTY...YES, BY PARCO. OR BY HIS CAMPAIGN OFFICE. THIS IS JUST MY JOB.

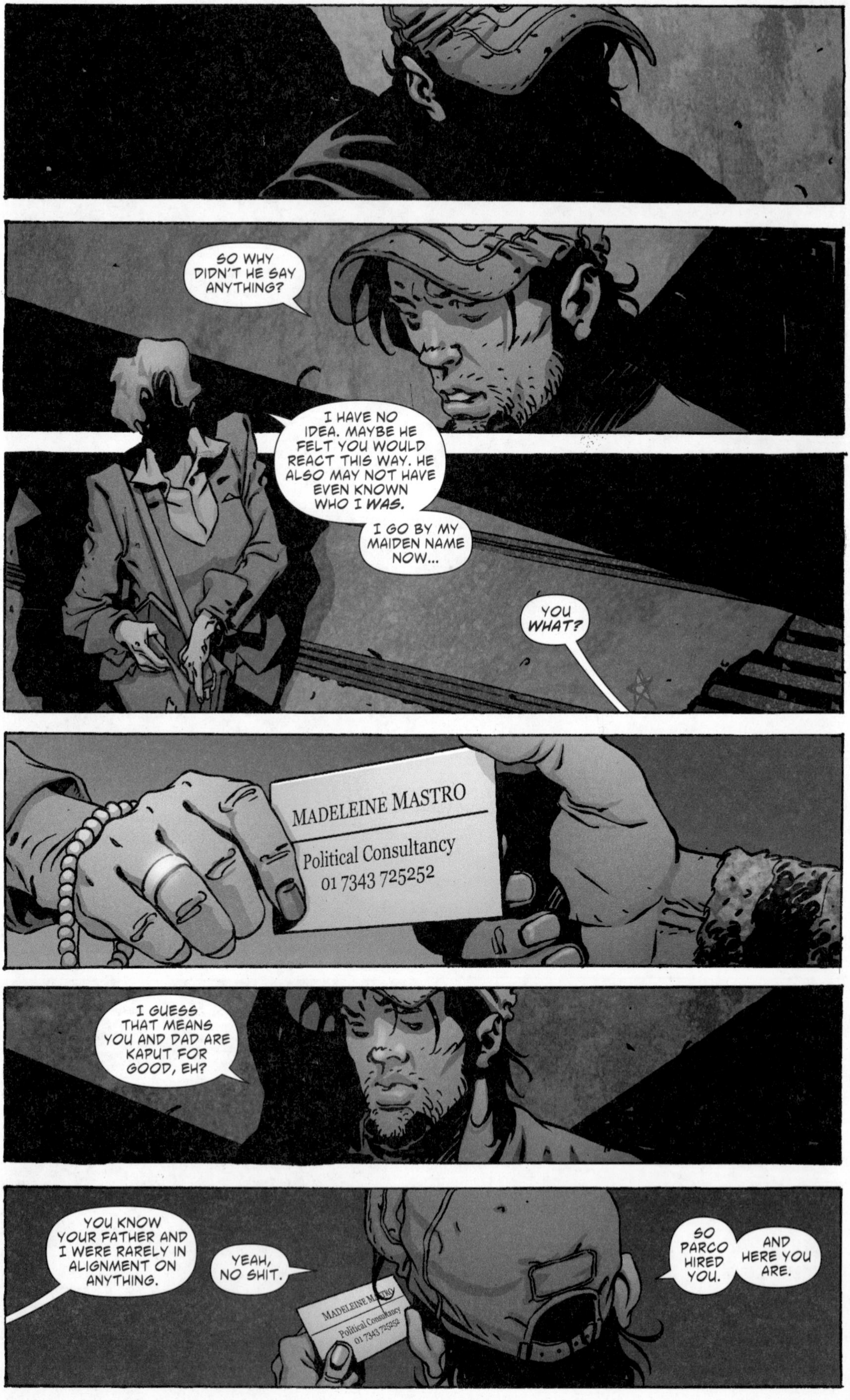
SO WHY DIDN'T HE SAY ANYTHING?
I HAVE NO IDEA. MAYBE HE FELT YOU WOULD REACT THIS WAY. HE ALSO MAY NOT HAVE EVEN KNOWN WHO I *WAS.*
I GO BY MY MAIDEN NAME NOW...
YOU *WHAT?*
MADELEINE MASTRO
Political Consultancy
01 7343 725252
I GUESS THAT MEANS YOU AND DAD ARE KAPUT FOR GOOD, EH?
YOU KNOW YOUR FATHER AND I WERE RARELY IN ALIGNMENT ON ANYTHING.
YEAH, NO SHIT.
SO PARCO HIRED YOU.
AND HERE YOU ARE.
MADELEINE MASTRO
Political Consultancy
01 7343 725252

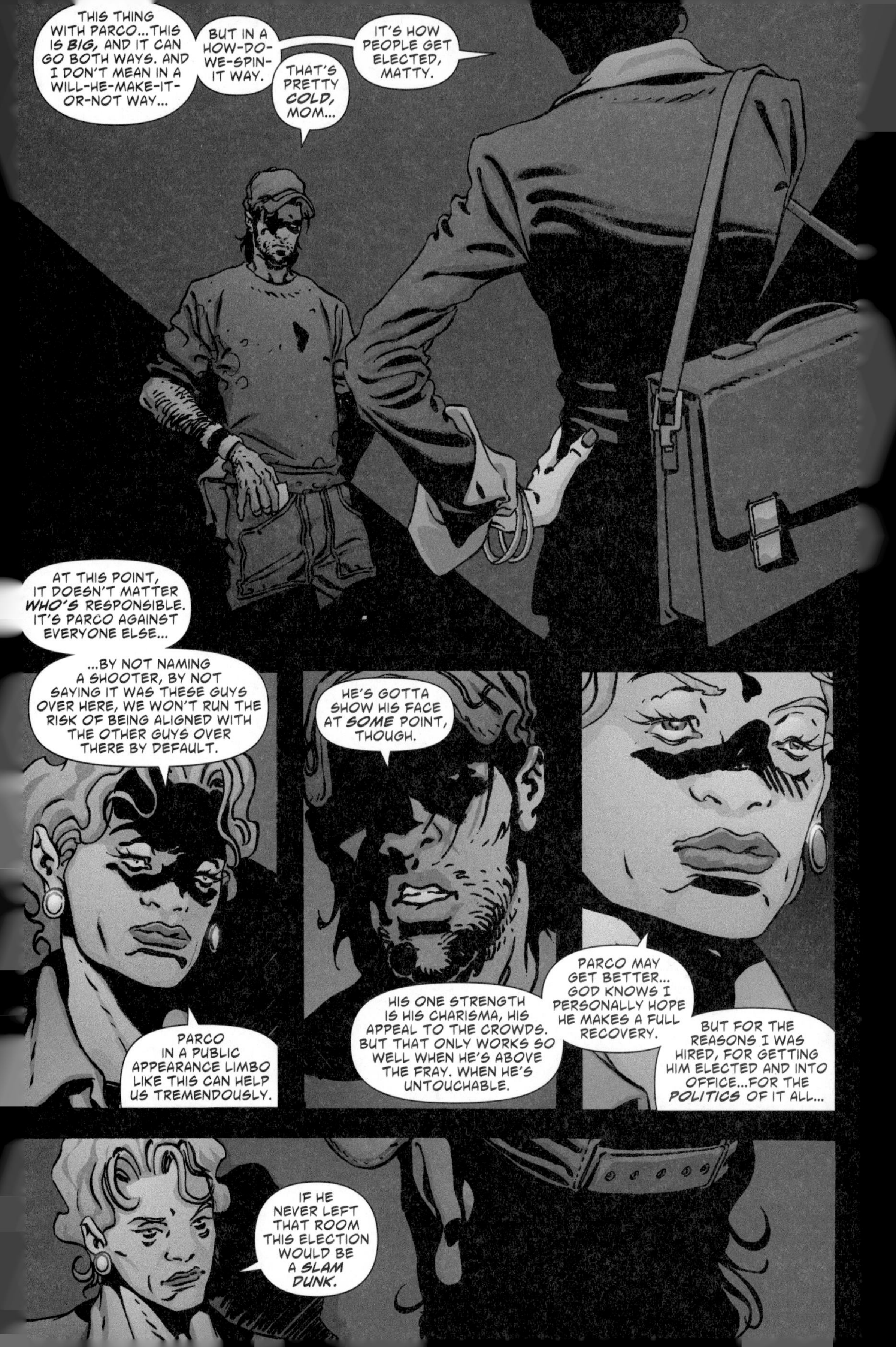

THIS THING WITH PARCO...THIS IS *BIG,* AND IT CAN GO BOTH WAYS. AND I DON'T MEAN IN A WILL-HE-MAKE-IT-OR-NOT WAY...
BUT IN A HOW-DO-WE-SPIN-IT WAY.
THAT'S PRETTY *COLD,* MOM...
IT'S HOW PEOPLE GET ELECTED, MATTY.
AT THIS POINT, IT DOESN'T MATTER *WHO'S* RESPONSIBLE. IT'S PARCO AGAINST EVERYONE ELSE...
...BY NOT NAMING A SHOOTER, BY NOT SAYING IT WAS THESE GUYS OVER HERE, WE WON'T RUN THE RISK OF BEING ALIGNED WITH THE OTHER GUYS OVER THERE BY DEFAULT.
PARCO IN A PUBLIC APPEARANCE LIMBO LIKE THIS CAN HELP US TREMENDOUSLY.
HE'S GOTTA SHOW HIS FACE AT *SOME* POINT, THOUGH.
HIS ONE STRENGTH IS HIS CHARISMA, HIS APPEAL TO THE CROWDS. BUT THAT ONLY WORKS SO WELL WHEN HE'S ABOVE THE FRAY. WHEN HE'S UNTOUCHABLE.
PARCO MAY GET BETTER... GOD KNOWS I PERSONALLY HOPE HE MAKES A FULL RECOVERY.
BUT FOR THE REASONS I WAS HIRED, FOR GETTING HIM ELECTED AND INTO OFFICE...FOR THE *POLITICS* OF IT ALL...
IF HE NEVER LEFT THAT ROOM THIS ELECTION WOULD BE A *SLAM DUNK.*

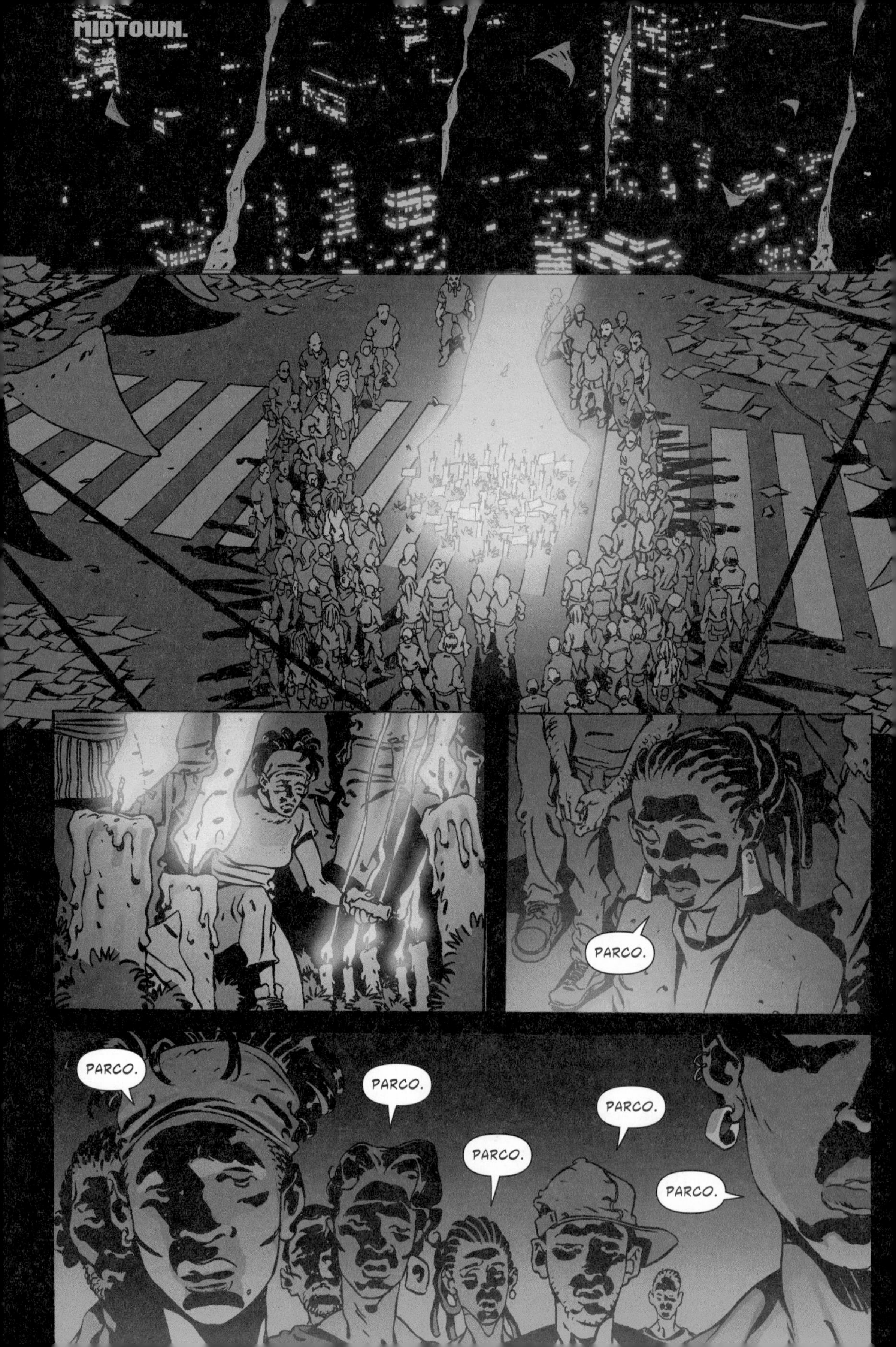
MIDTOWN.
PARCO.
PARCO.
PARCO.
PARCO.
PARCO.
PARCO.

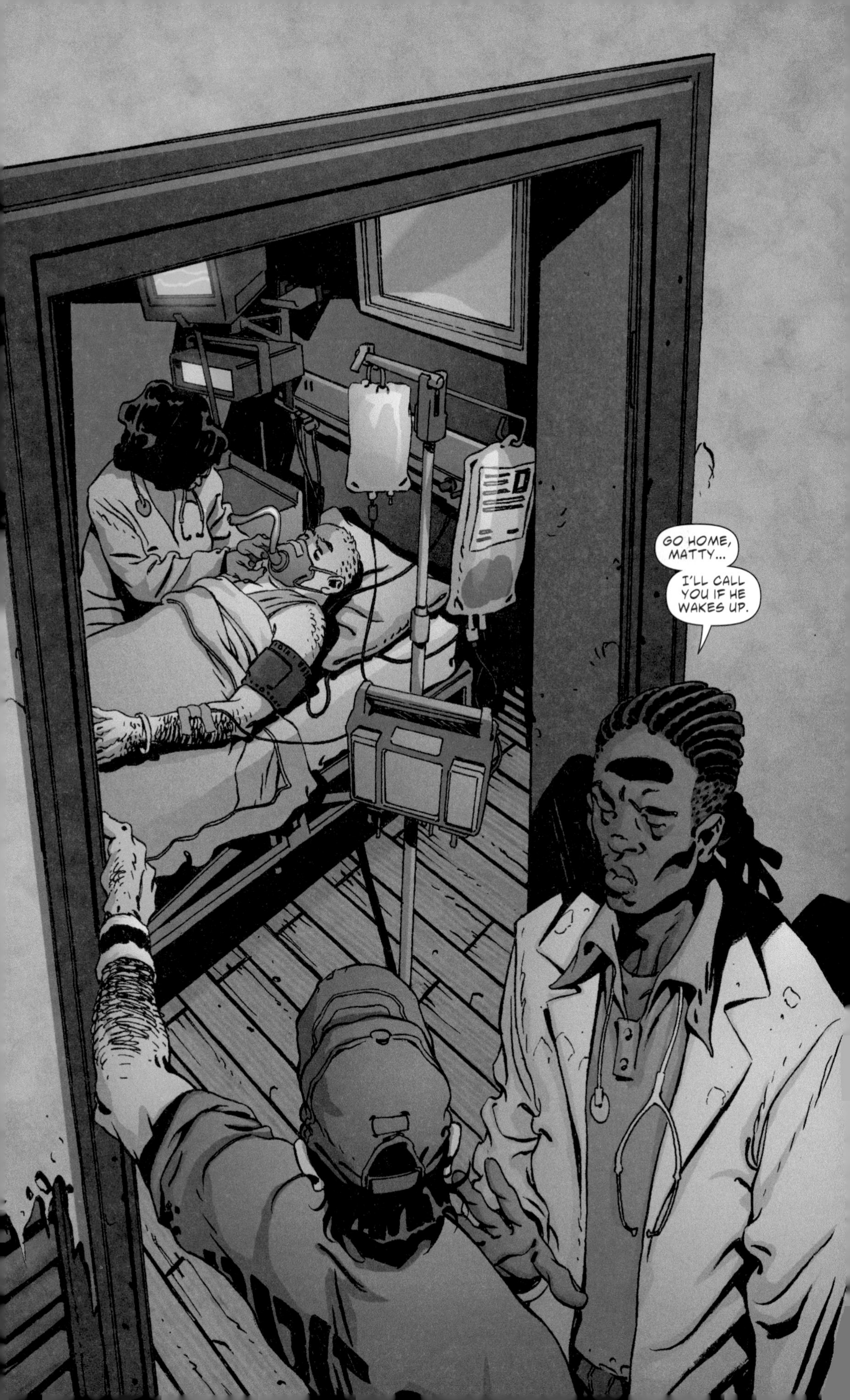
GO HOME, MATTY...
I'LL CALL YOU IF HE WAKES UP.

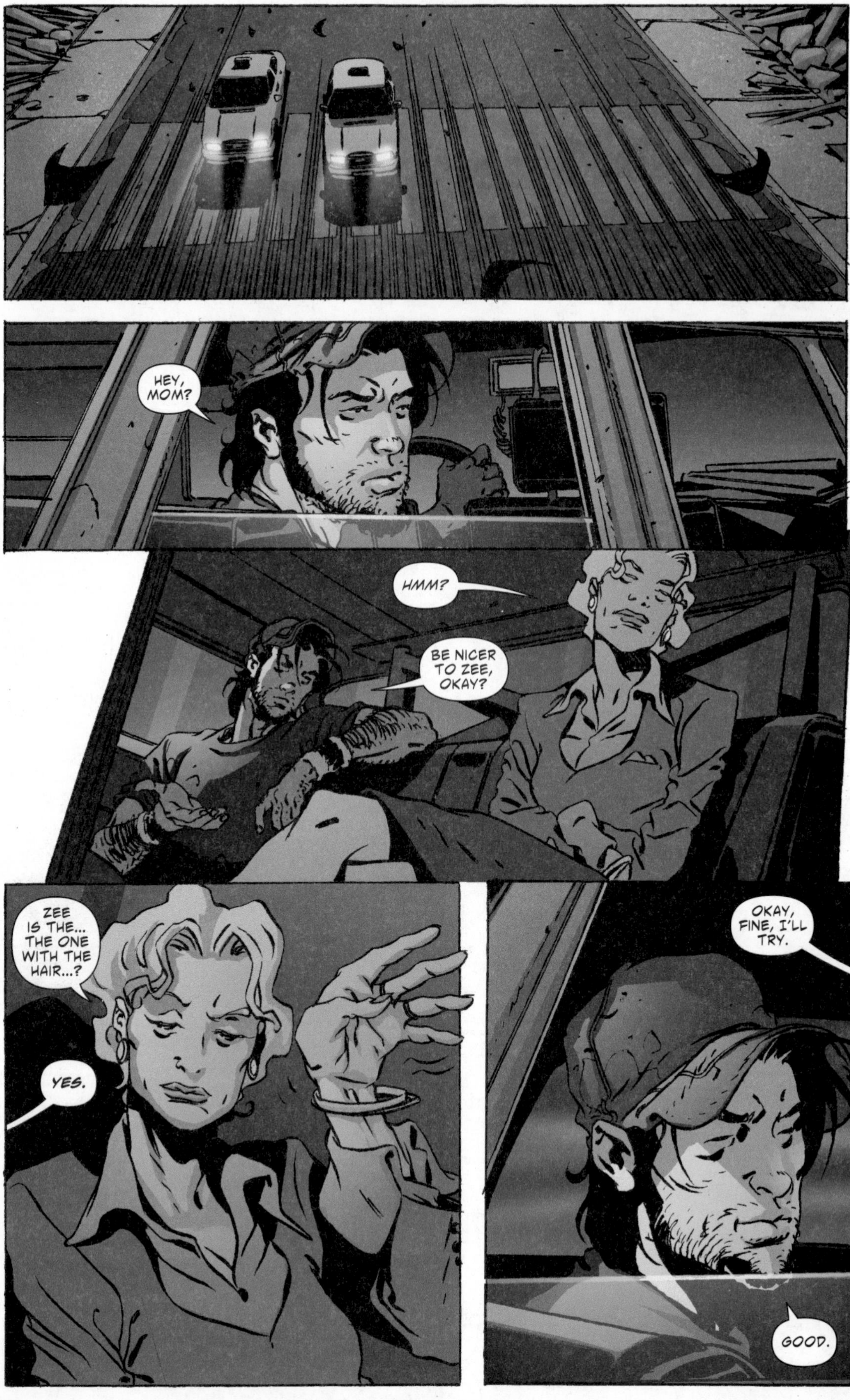
HEY, MOM?
HMM?
BE NICER TO ZEE, OKAY?
ZEE IS THE... THE ONE WITH THE HAIR...?
YES.
OKAY, FINE, I'LL TRY.
GOOD.

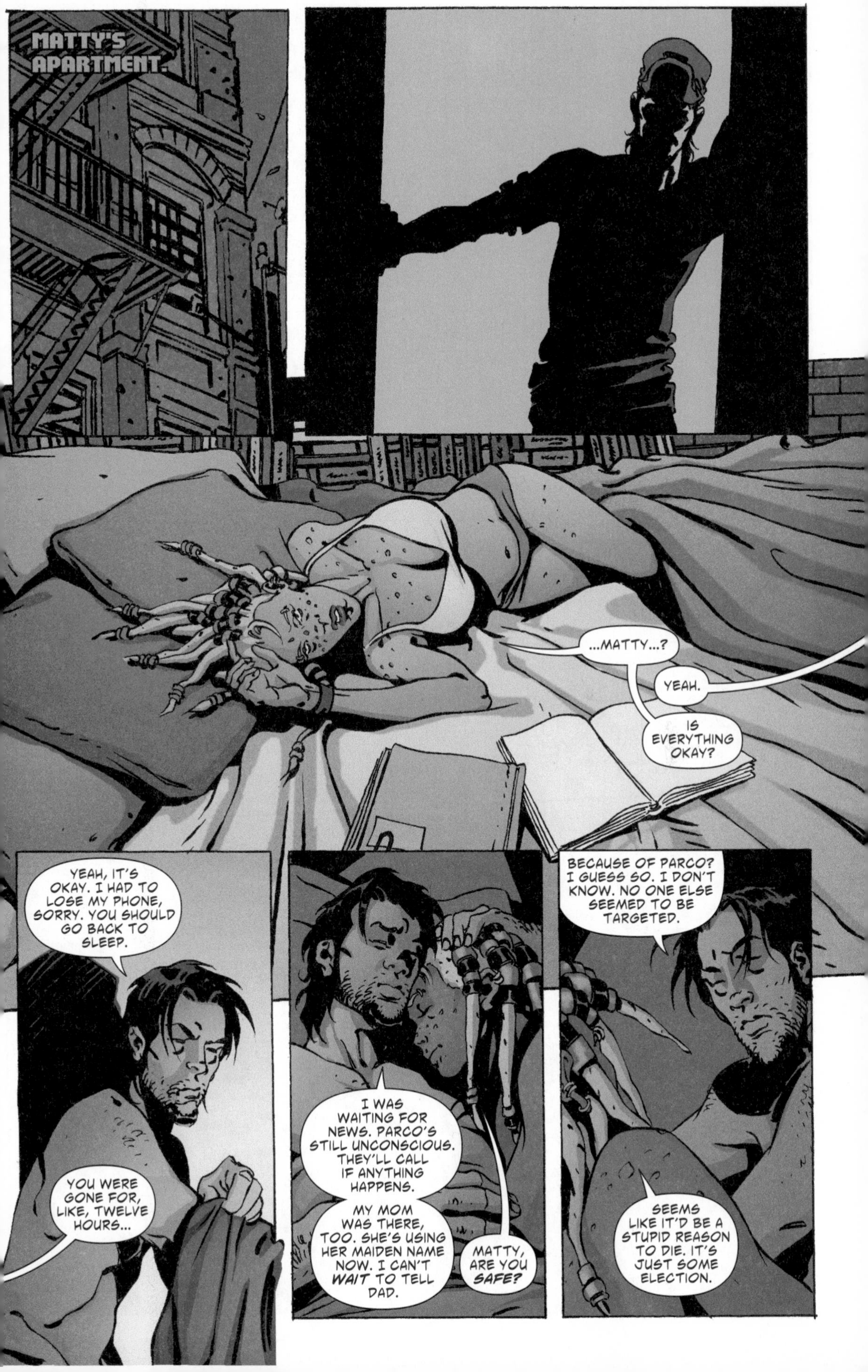
MATTY'S APARTMENT.
...MATTY...?
YEAH.
IS EVERYTHING OKAY?
YEAH, IT'S OKAY. I HAD TO LOSE MY PHONE, SORRY. YOU SHOULD GO BACK TO SLEEP.
YOU WERE GONE FOR, LIKE, TWELVE HOURS...
I WAS WAITING FOR NEWS. PARCO'S STILL UNCONSCIOUS. THEY'LL CALL IF ANYTHING HAPPENS.
MY MOM WAS THERE, TOO. SHE'S USING HER MAIDEN NAME NOW. I CAN'T WAIT TO TELL DAD.
MATTY, ARE YOU SAFE?
BECAUSE OF PARCO? I GUESS SO. I DON'T KNOW. NO ONE ELSE SEEMED TO BE TARGETED.
SEEMS LIKE IT'D BE A STUPID REASON TO DIE. IT'S JUST SOME ELECTION.

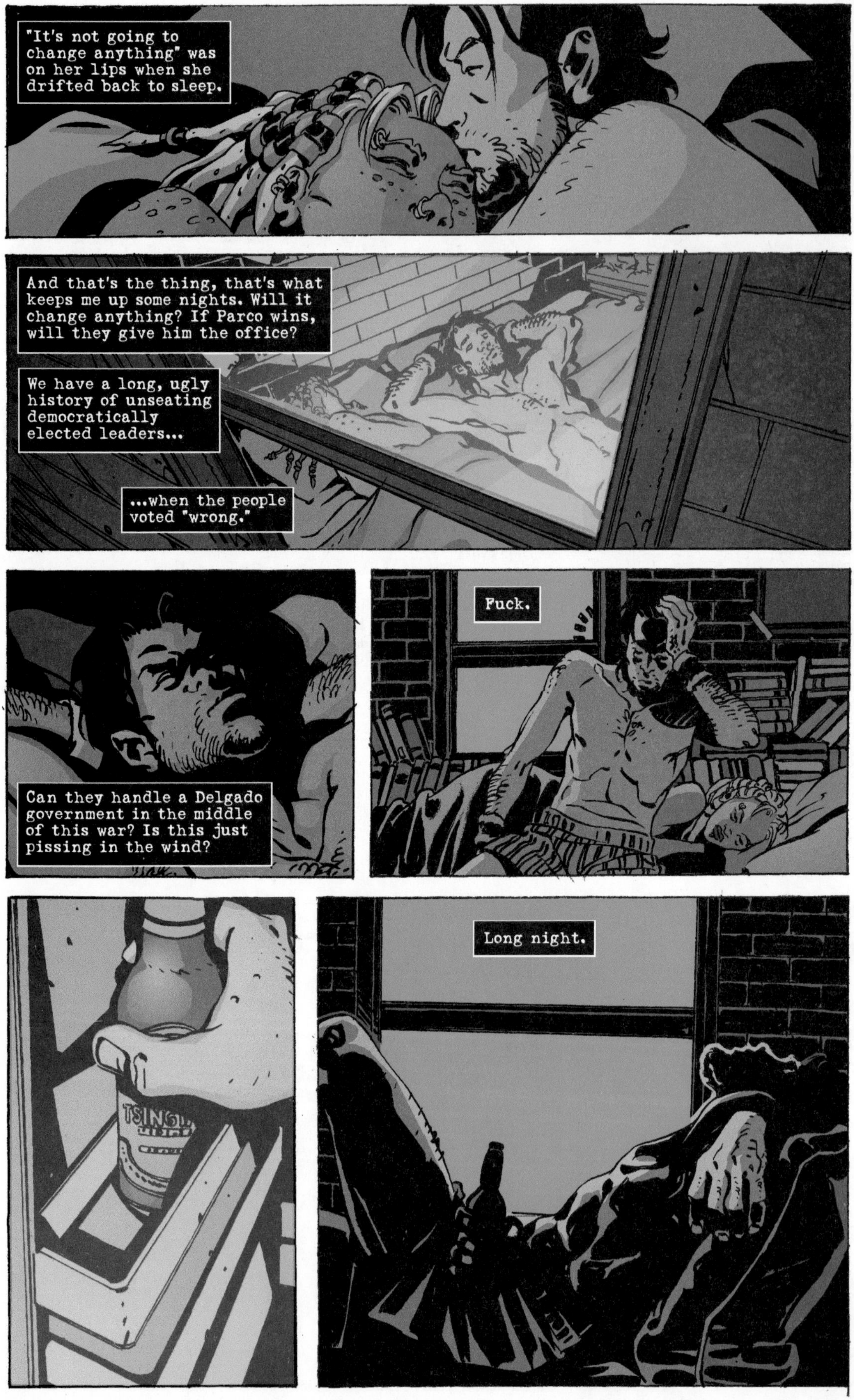
"It's not going to change anything" was on her lips when she drifted back to sleep.
And that's the thing, that's what keeps me up some nights. Will it change anything? If Parco wins, will they give him the office?
We have a long, ugly history of unseating democratically elected leaders...
...when the people voted "wrong."
Can they handle a Delgado government in the middle of this war? Is this just pissing in the wind?
Fuck.
Long night.

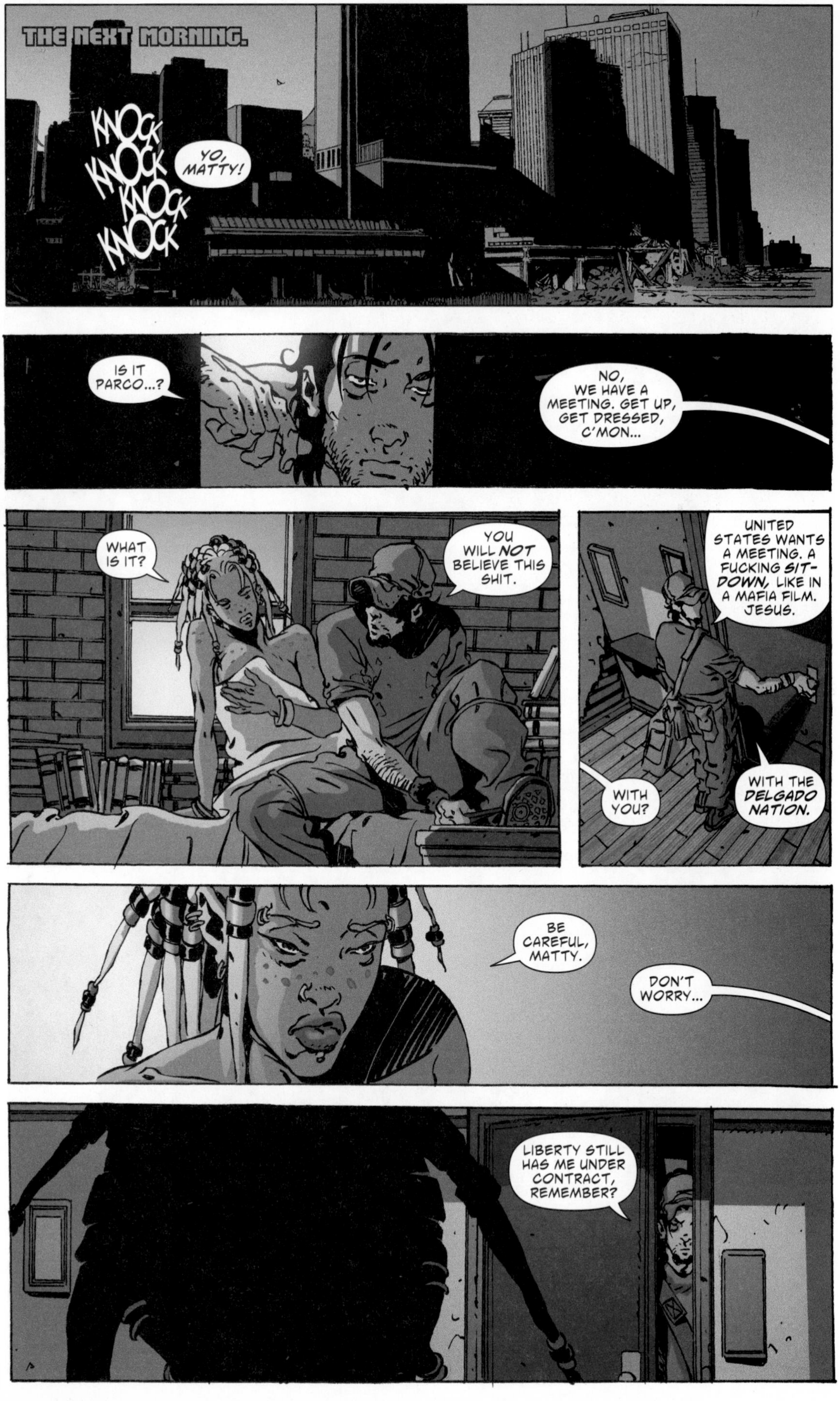
THE NEXT MORNING.
KNOCK KNOCK KNOCK KNOCK
YO, MATTY!
IS IT PARCO...?
NO, WE HAVE A MEETING. GET UP, GET DRESSED, C'MON...
WHAT IS IT?
YOU WILL NOT BELIEVE THIS SHIT.
UNITED STATES WANTS A MEETING. A FUCKING SIT-DOWN, LIKE IN A MAFIA FILM. JESUS.
WITH YOU?
WITH THE DELGADO NATION.
BE CAREFUL, MATTY.
DON'T WORRY...
LIBERTY STILL HAS ME UNDER CONTRACT, REMEMBER?

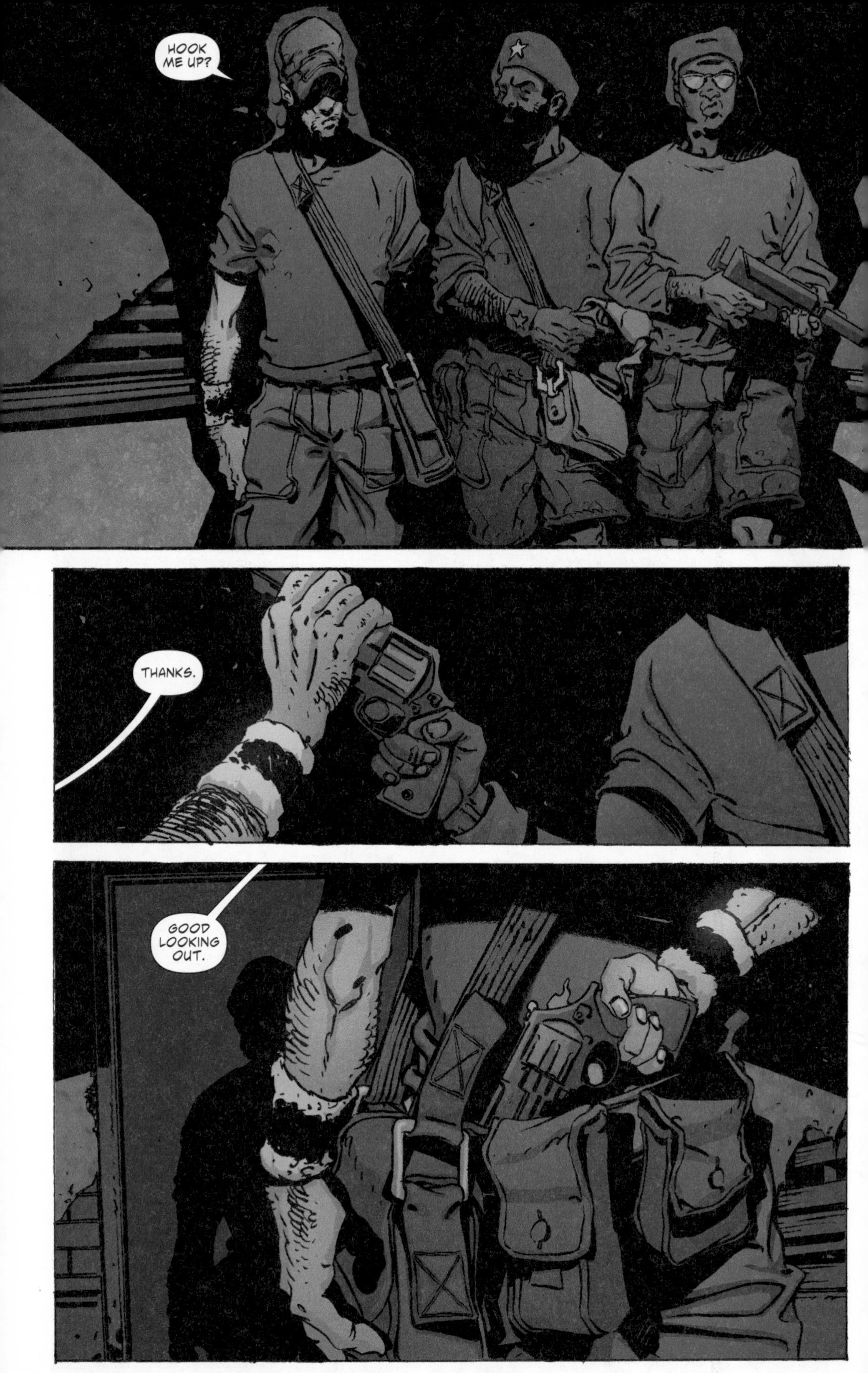
HOOK ME UP?
THANKS.
GOOD LOOKING OUT.

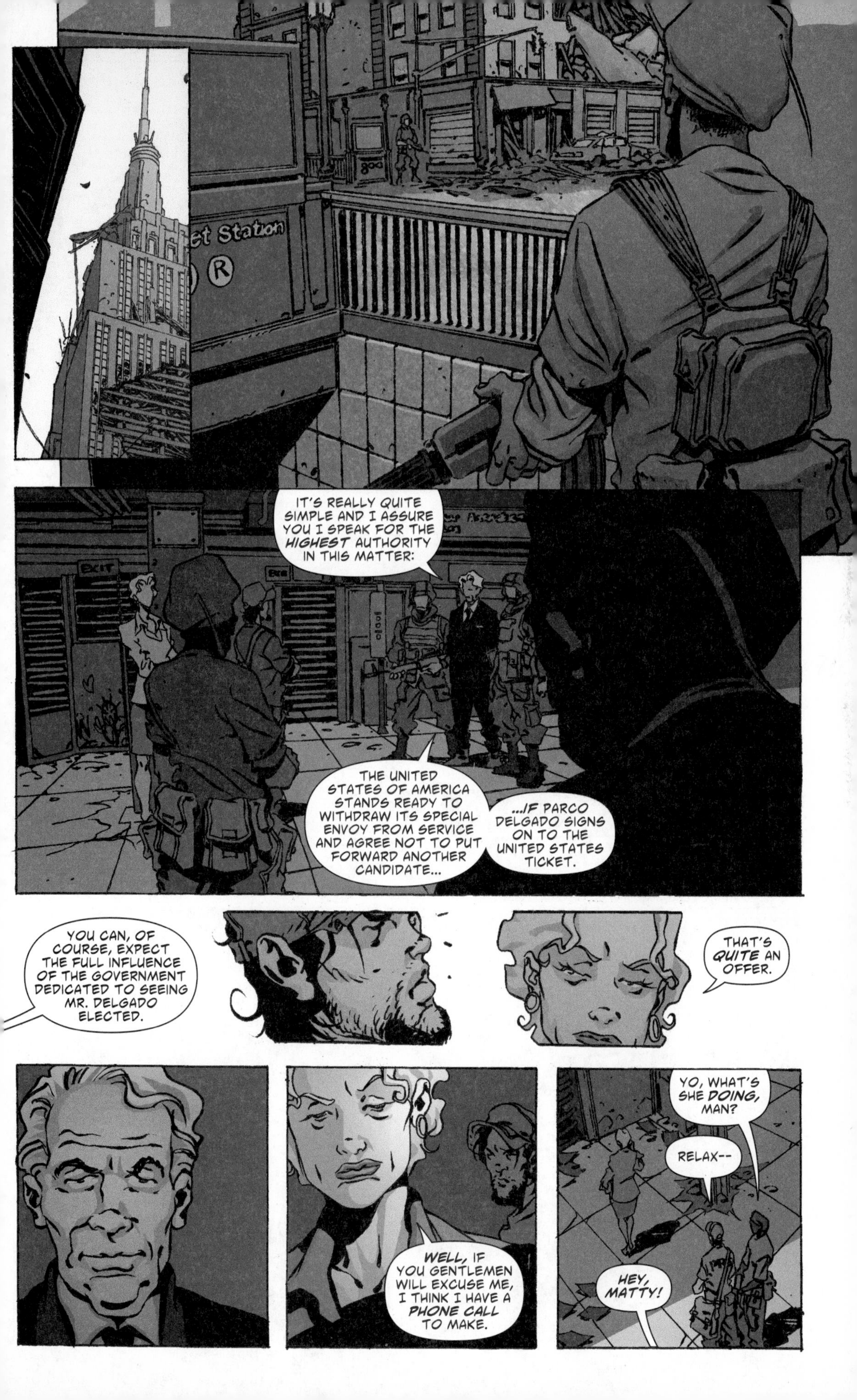

et Station
R
IT'S REALLY QUITE SIMPLE AND I ASSURE YOU I SPEAK FOR THE *HIGHEST* AUTHORITY IN THIS MATTER:
THE UNITED STATES OF AMERICA STANDS READY TO WITHDRAW ITS SPECIAL ENVOY FROM SERVICE AND AGREE NOT TO PUT FORWARD ANOTHER CANDIDATE...
...*IF* PARCO DELGADO SIGNS ON TO THE UNITED STATES TICKET.
YOU CAN, OF COURSE, EXPECT THE FULL INFLUENCE OF THE GOVERNMENT DEDICATED TO SEEING MR. DELGADO ELECTED.
THAT'S *QUITE* AN OFFER.
WELL, IF YOU GENTLEMEN WILL EXCUSE ME, I THINK I HAVE A *PHONE CALL* TO MAKE.
YO, WHAT'S SHE *DOING,* MAN?
RELAX--
HEY, MATTY!

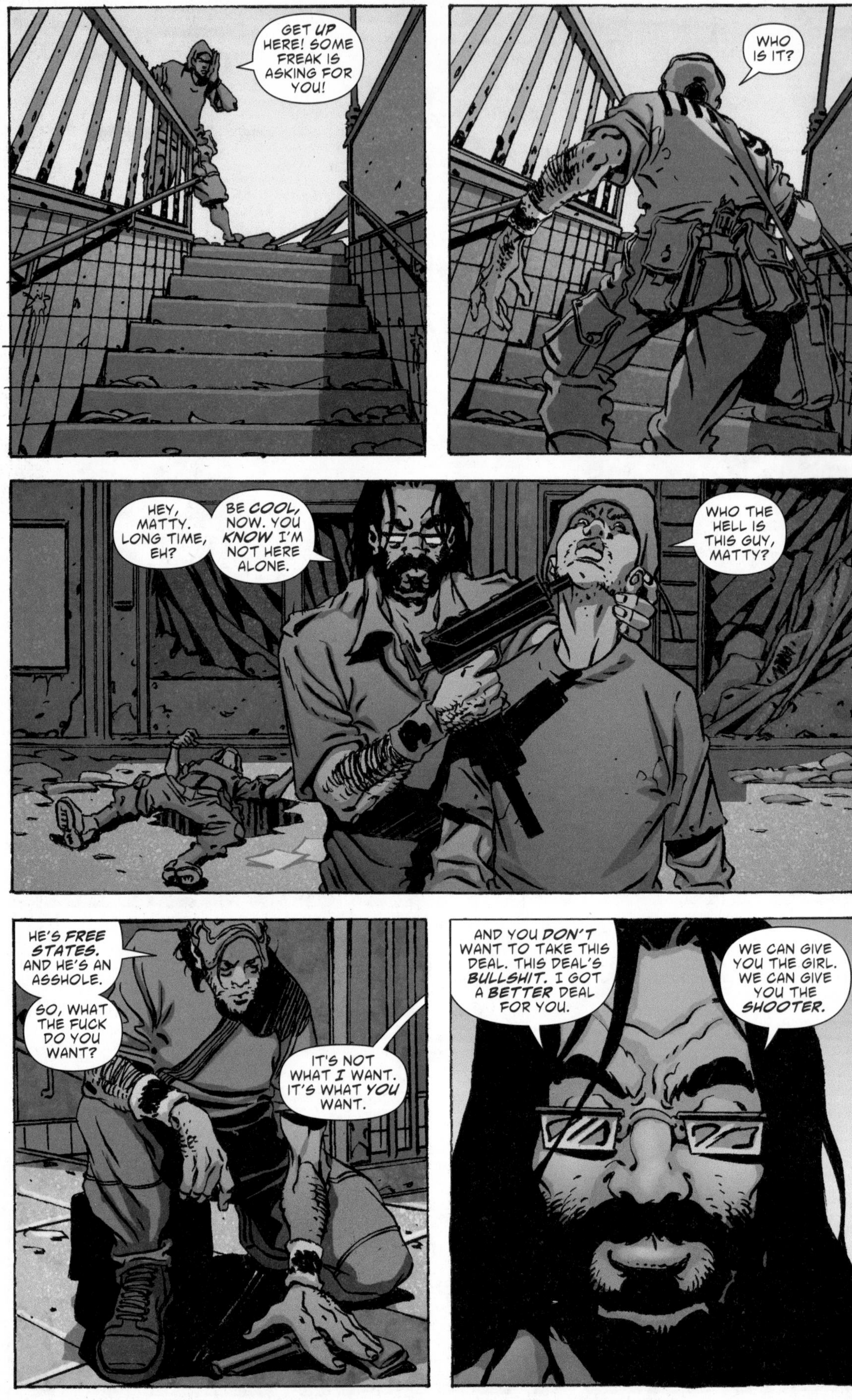
GET UP HERE! SOME FREAK IS ASKING FOR YOU!
WHO IS IT?
HEY, MATTY. LONG TIME, EH?
BE COOL, NOW. YOU KNOW I'M NOT HERE ALONE.
WHO THE HELL IS THIS GUY, MATTY?
HE'S FREE STATES. AND HE'S AN ASSHOLE.
SO, WHAT THE FUCK DO YOU WANT?
IT'S NOT WHAT I WANT. IT'S WHAT YOU WANT.
AND YOU DON'T WANT TO TAKE THIS DEAL. THIS DEAL'S BULLSHIT. I GOT A BETTER DEAL FOR YOU.
WE CAN GIVE YOU THE GIRL. WE CAN GIVE YOU THE SHOOTER.

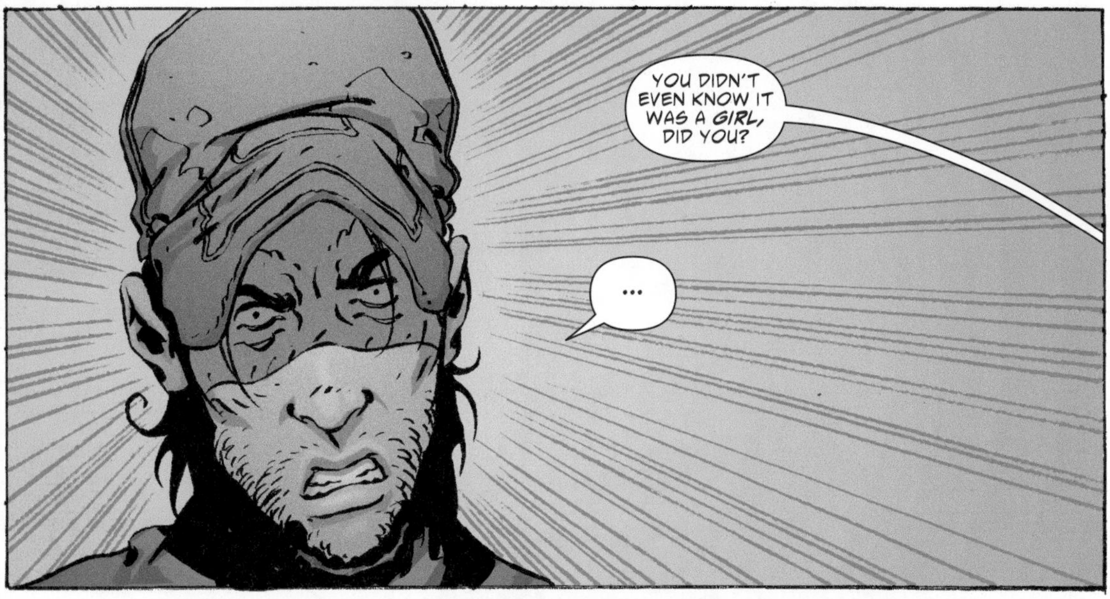
YOU DIDN'T EVEN KNOW IT WAS A *GIRL*, DID YOU?
...

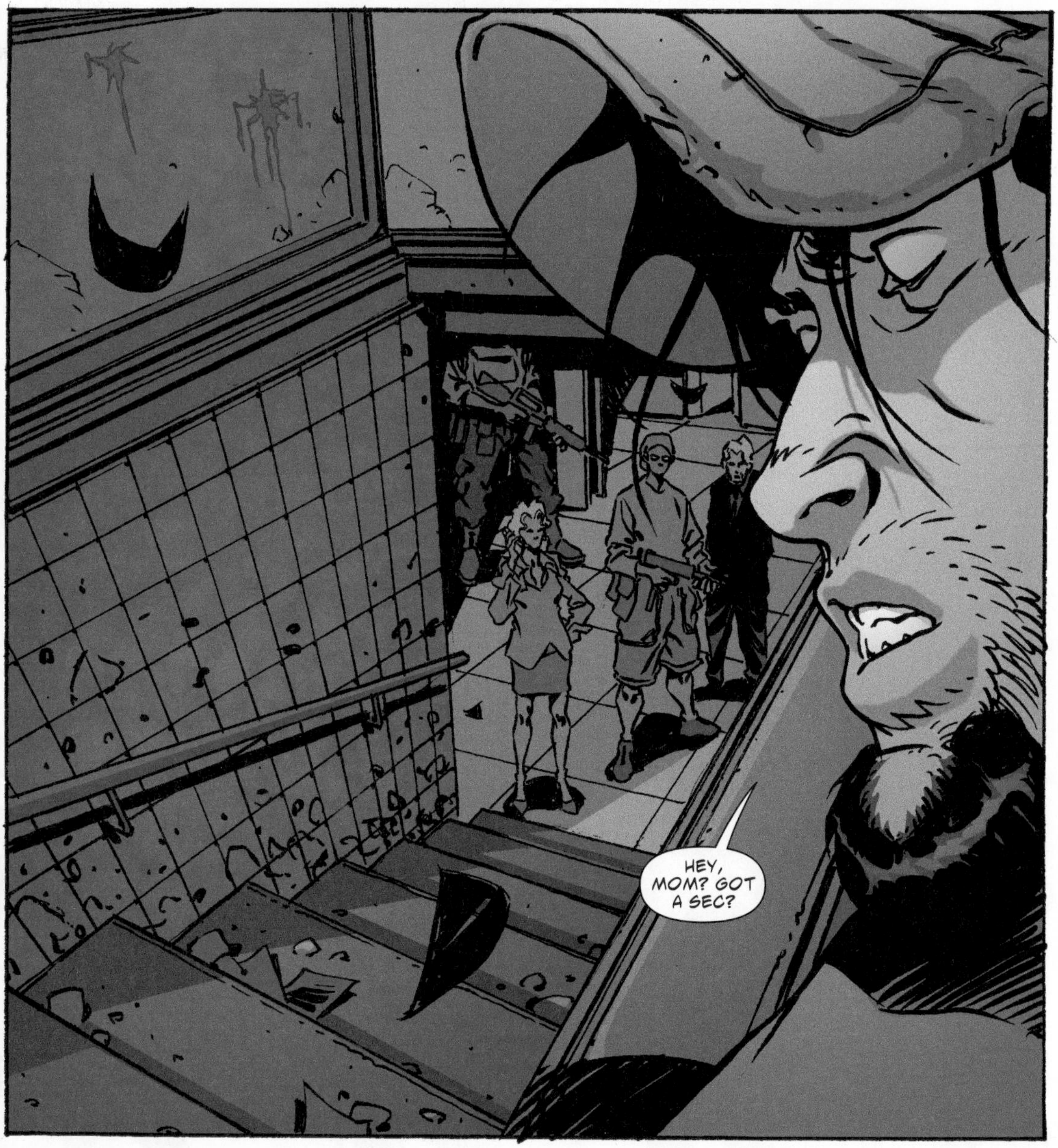
HEY, MOM? GOT A SEC?

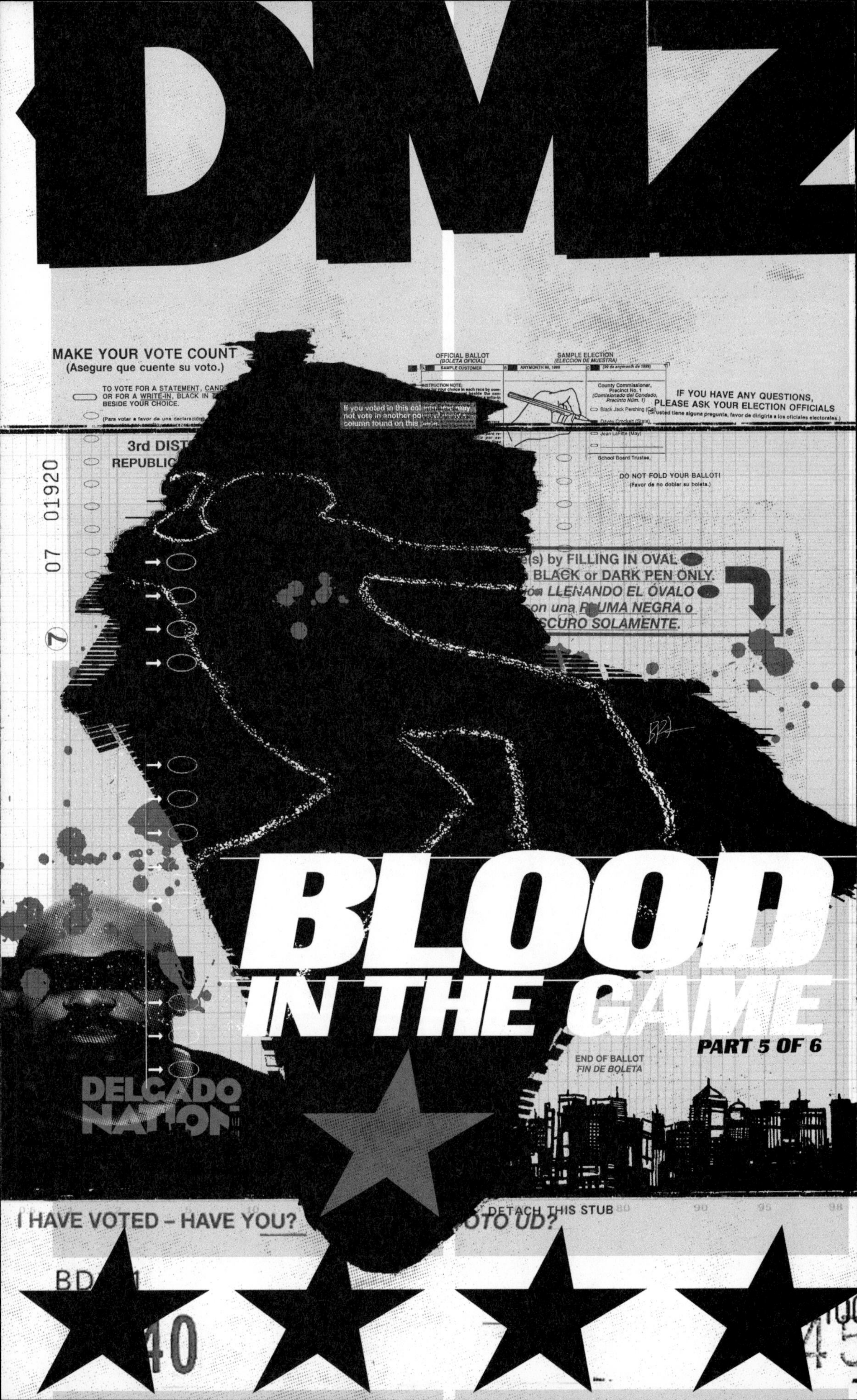

DMZ

MAKE YOUR VOTE COUNT
(Asegure que cuente su voto.)

TO VOTE FOR A STATEMENT, CAND...
OR FOR A WRITE-IN, BLACK IN ...
BESIDE YOUR CHOICE.

(Para votar a favor de una declaración...

OFFICIAL BALLOT
(BOLETA OFICIAL)

SAMPLE CUSTOMER

ANYMONTH 00, 1999

SAMPLE ELECTION
(ELECCIÓN DE MUESTRA)

(00 de anymonth de 1999)

County Commissioner,
Precinct No. 1
(Comisionado del Condado,
Precinto Núm. 1)

Black Jack Pershing (Sit)

Davey Crockett (Dvt)

Jean LaFitte (May)

School Board Trustee,

IF YOU HAVE ANY QUESTIONS,
PLEASE ASK YOUR ELECTION OFFICIALS

(Si usted tiene alguna pregunta, favor de dirigirle a los oficiales electorales.)

3rd DIST...
REPUBLI...

07 01920

07

If you voted in this column, may
not vote in another column
column found on this part...

DO NOT FOLD YOUR BALLOT!
(Favor de no doblar su boleta.)

e(s) by FILLING IN OVAL
BLACK or DARK PEN ONLY.
ón LLENANDO EL ÓVALO
on una PLUMA NEGRA o
SCURO SOLAMENTE.

BLOOD
IN THE GAME

PART 5 OF 6

END OF BALLOT
FIN DE BOLETA

DELCADO
NATION

I HAVE VOTED – HAVE YOU?

...DETACH THIS STUB

OTO UD?

BD

40

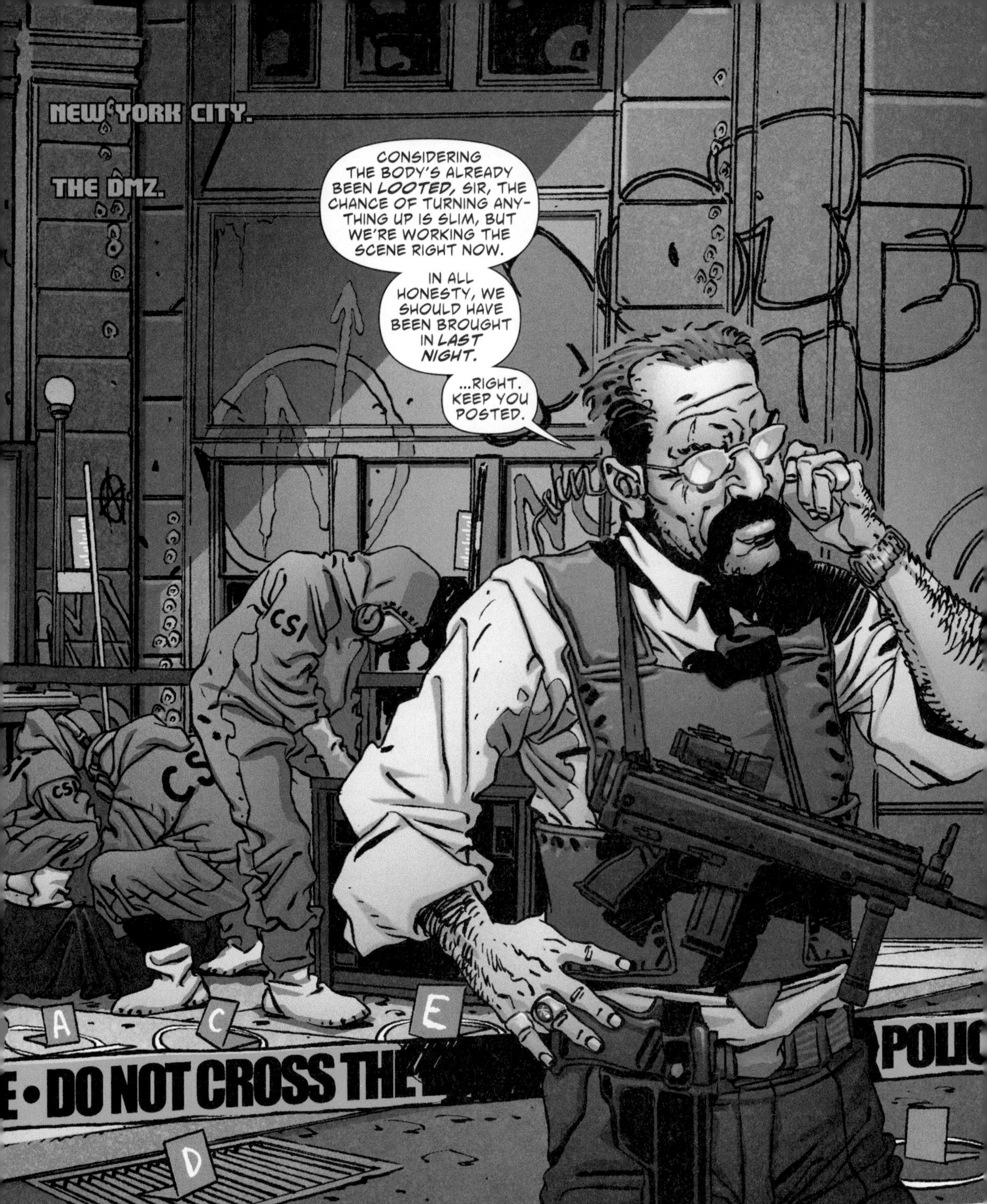
NEW YORK CITY.
THE DMZ.
CONSIDERING THE BODY'S ALREADY BEEN *LOOTED,* SIR, THE CHANCE OF TURNING ANYTHING UP IS SLIM, BUT WE'RE WORKING THE SCENE RIGHT NOW.
IN ALL HONESTY, WE SHOULD HAVE BEEN BROUGHT IN *LAST NIGHT.*
...RIGHT. KEEP YOU POSTED.
E • DO NOT CROSS THE
POLIC
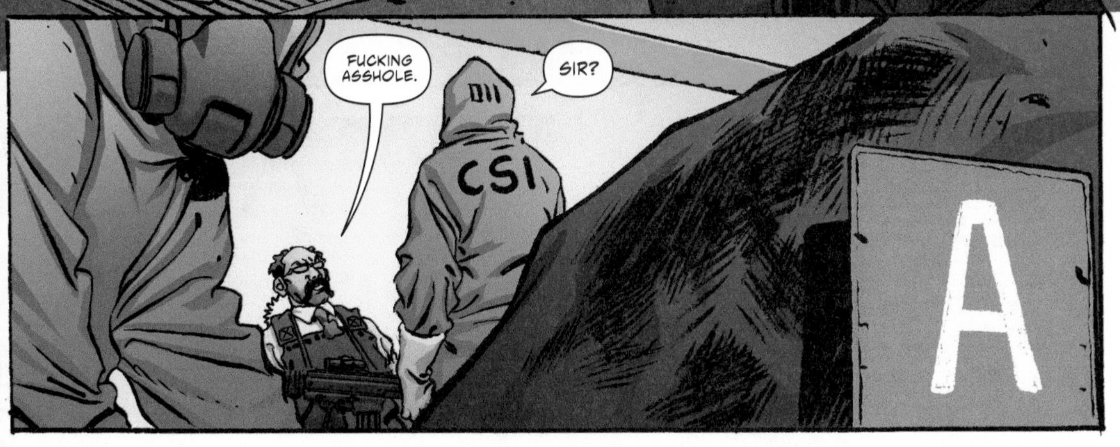
FUCKING ASSHOLE.
SIR?

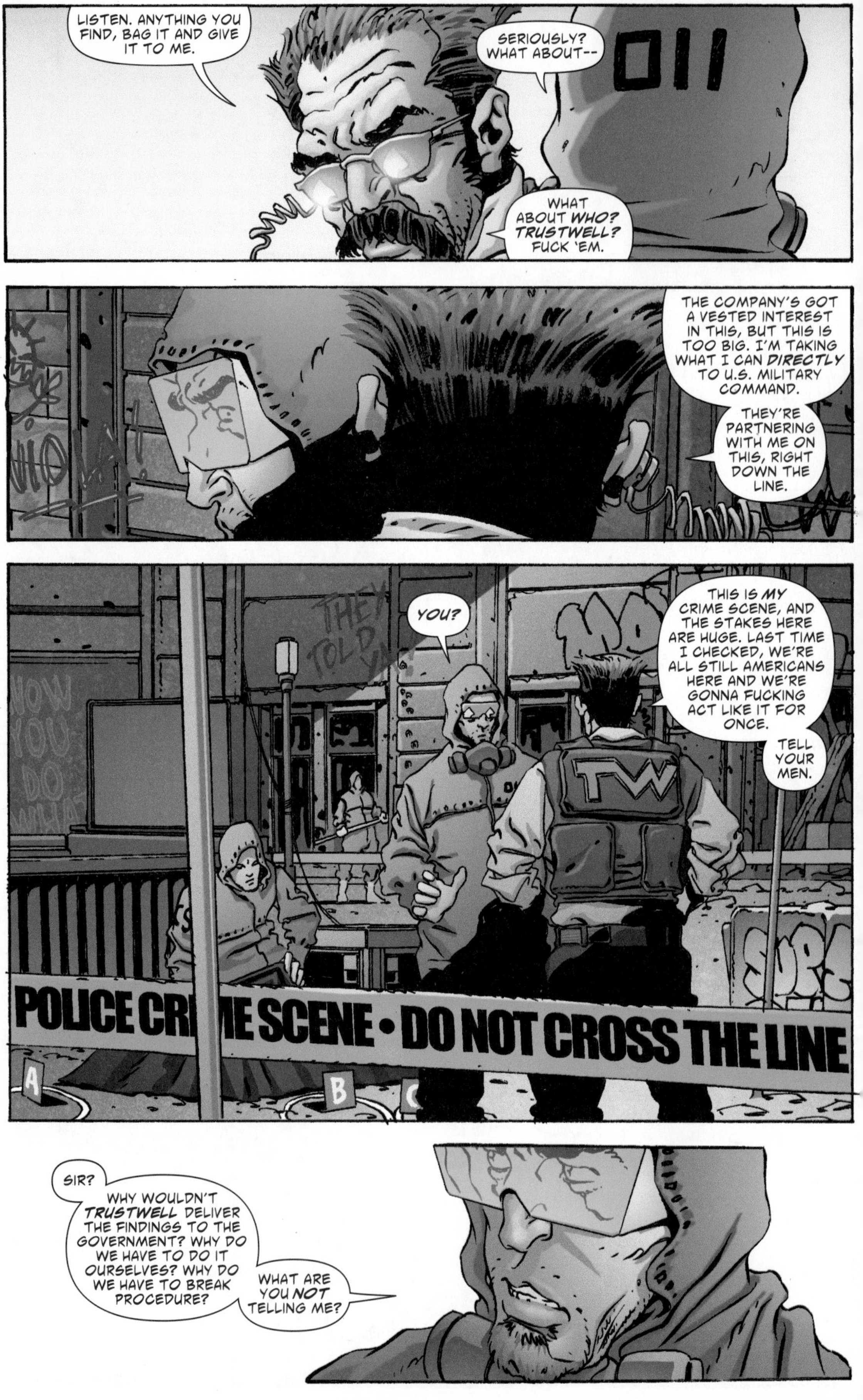
LISTEN. ANYTHING YOU FIND, BAG IT AND GIVE IT TO ME.
SERIOUSLY? WHAT ABOUT--
WHAT ABOUT WHO? TRUSTWELL? FUCK 'EM.
THE COMPANY'S GOT A VESTED INTEREST IN THIS, BUT THIS IS TOO BIG. I'M TAKING WHAT I CAN DIRECTLY TO U.S. MILITARY COMMAND.
THEY'RE PARTNERING WITH ME ON THIS, RIGHT DOWN THE LINE.
YOU?
THIS IS MY CRIME SCENE, AND THE STAKES HERE ARE HUGE. LAST TIME I CHECKED, WE'RE ALL STILL AMERICANS HERE AND WE'RE GONNA FUCKING ACT LIKE IT FOR ONCE.
TELL YOUR MEN.
POLICE CRIME SCENE • DO NOT CROSS THE LINE
SIR?
WHY WOULDN'T TRUSTWELL DELIVER THE FINDINGS TO THE GOVERNMENT? WHY DO WE HAVE TO DO IT OURSELVES? WHY DO WE HAVE TO BREAK PROCEDURE?
WHAT ARE YOU NOT TELLING ME?

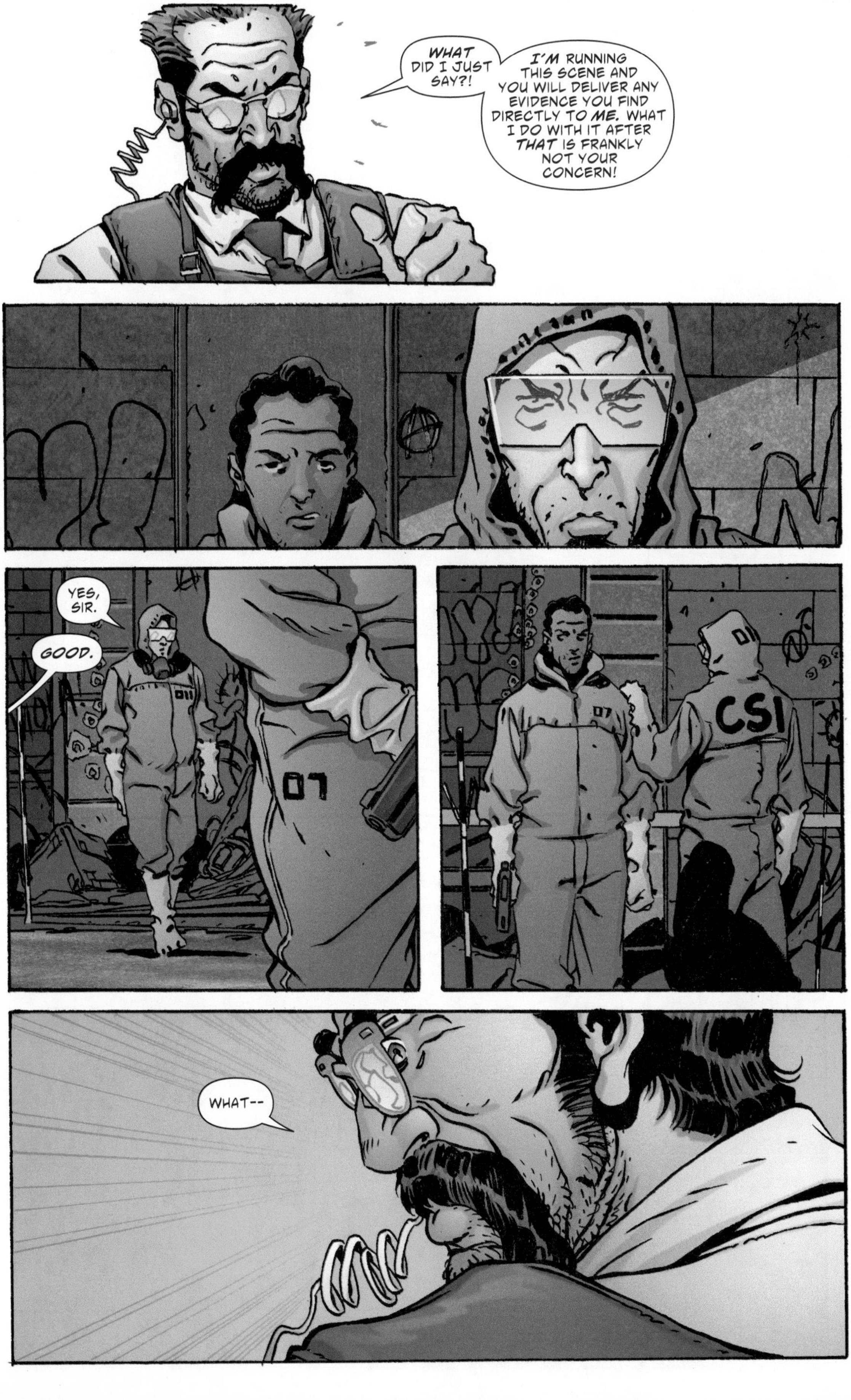
WHAT DID I JUST SAY?!
I'M RUNNING THIS SCENE AND YOU WILL DELIVER ANY EVIDENCE YOU FIND DIRECTLY TO ME. WHAT I DO WITH IT AFTER THAT IS FRANKLY NOT YOUR CONCERN!
YES, SIR.
GOOD.
CSI
WHAT--

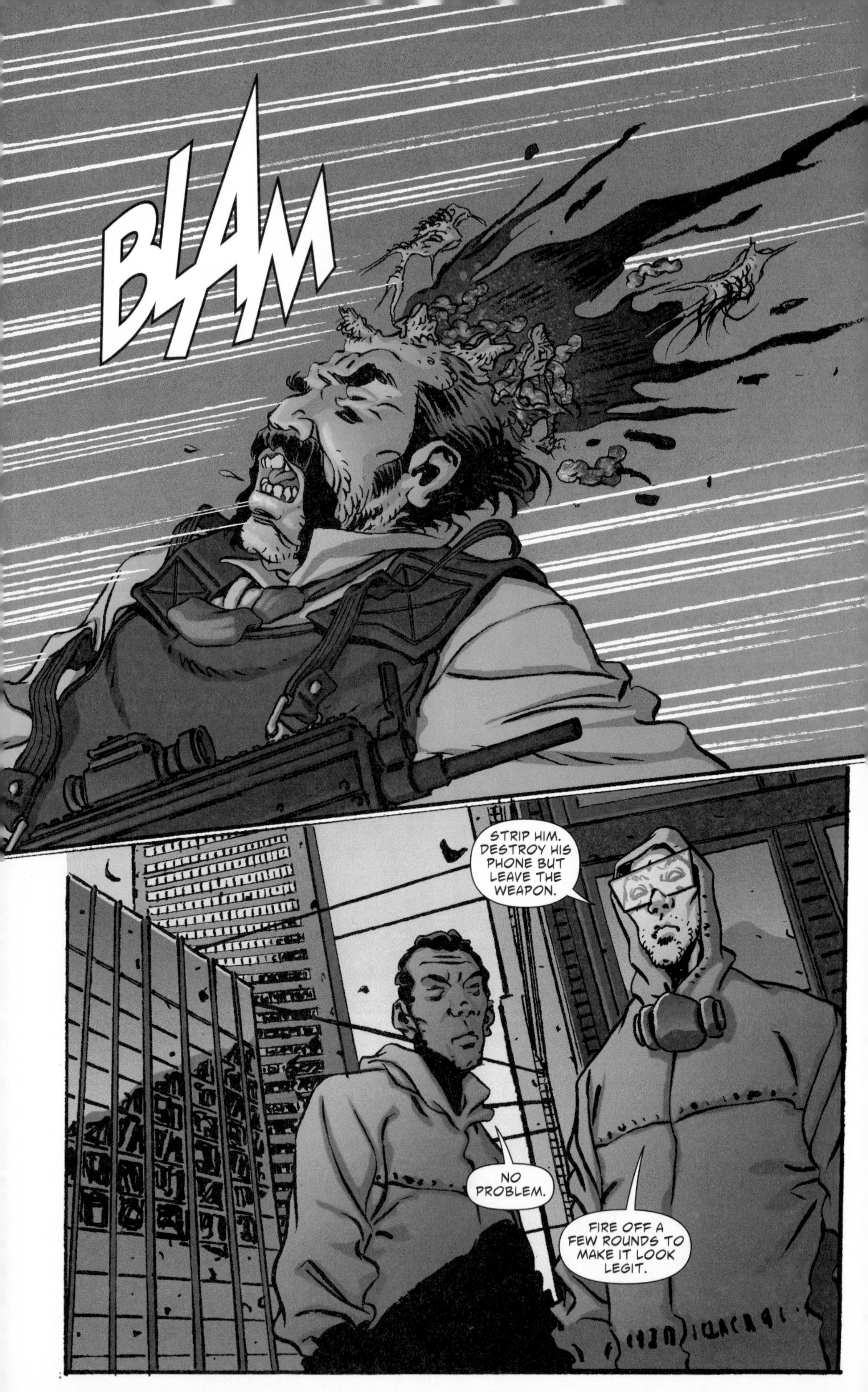
BLAM
STRIP HIM. DESTROY HIS PHONE BUT LEAVE THE WEAPON.
NO PROBLEM.
FIRE OFF A FEW ROUNDS TO MAKE IT LOOK LEGIT.

THE NATIVES DID THIS. THAT'S HOW IT'S GOTTA LOOK--ORDERS FROM UP THE CHAIN.
TRUSTWELL IS TO BE PROTECTED AT ALL COSTS.
CSI
BLOOD IN THE GAME 5 OF 6
BRIAN WOOD writer and cover artist
RICCARDO BURCHIELLI artist
JEROMY COX colors JARED K. FLETCHER letters

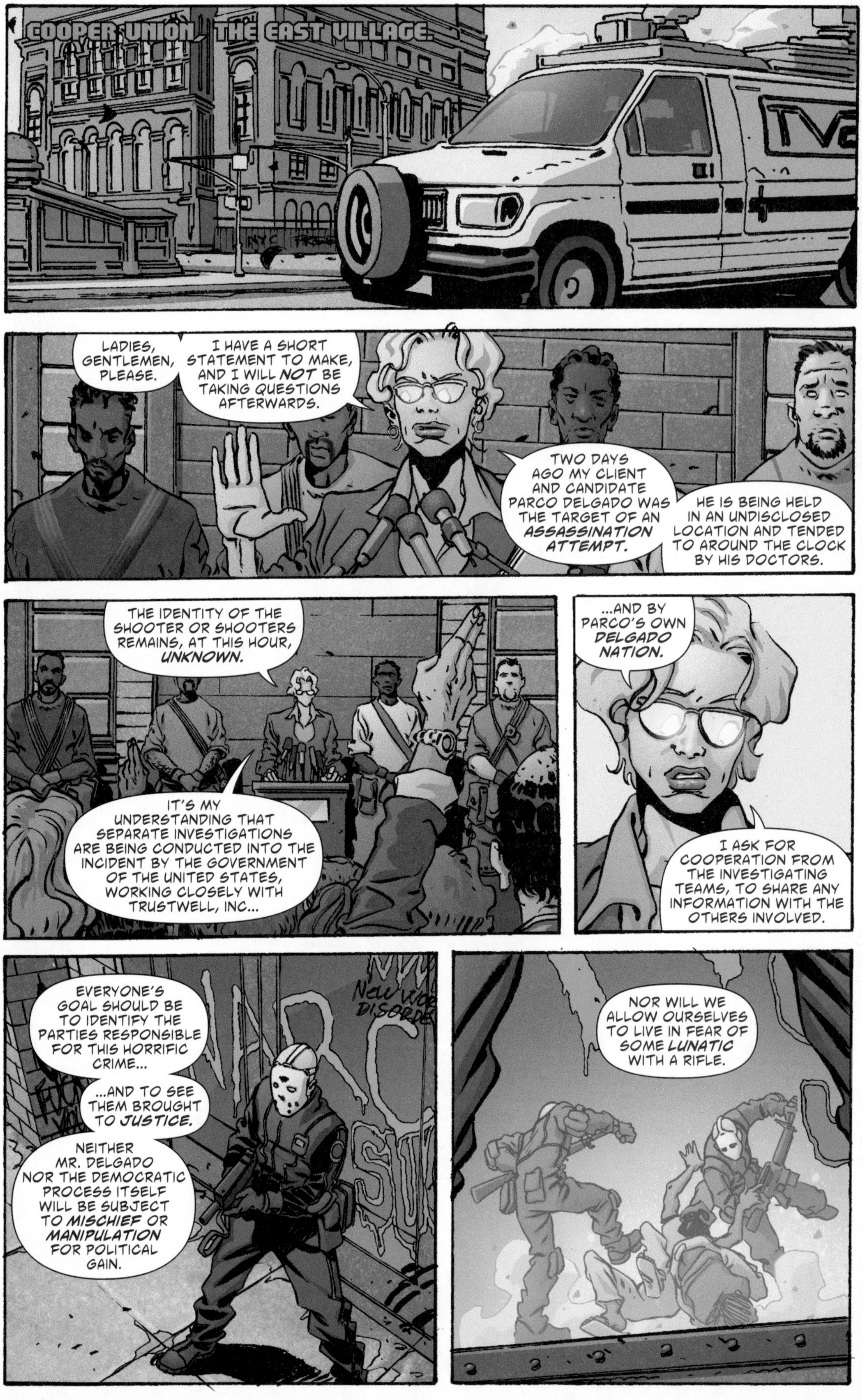
COOPER UNION, THE EAST VILLAGE.
LADIES, GENTLEMEN, PLEASE.
I HAVE A SHORT STATEMENT TO MAKE, AND I WILL NOT BE TAKING QUESTIONS AFTERWARDS.
TWO DAYS AGO MY CLIENT AND CANDIDATE PARCO DELGADO WAS THE TARGET OF AN ASSASSINATION ATTEMPT.
HE IS BEING HELD IN AN UNDISCLOSED LOCATION AND TENDED TO AROUND THE CLOCK BY HIS DOCTORS.
...AND BY PARCO'S OWN DELGADO NATION.
THE IDENTITY OF THE SHOOTER OR SHOOTERS REMAINS, AT THIS HOUR, UNKNOWN.
IT'S MY UNDERSTANDING THAT SEPARATE INVESTIGATIONS ARE BEING CONDUCTED INTO THE INCIDENT BY THE GOVERNMENT OF THE UNITED STATES, WORKING CLOSELY WITH TRUSTWELL, INC...
I ASK FOR COOPERATION FROM THE INVESTIGATING TEAMS, TO SHARE ANY INFORMATION WITH THE OTHERS INVOLVED.
EVERYONE'S GOAL SHOULD BE TO IDENTIFY THE PARTIES RESPONSIBLE FOR THIS HORRIFIC CRIME...
...AND TO SEE THEM BROUGHT TO JUSTICE.
NEITHER MR. DELGADO NOR THE DEMOCRATIC PROCESS ITSELF WILL BE SUBJECT TO MISCHIEF OR MANIPULATION FOR POLITICAL GAIN.
NOR WILL WE ALLOW OURSELVES TO LIVE IN FEAR OF SOME LUNATIC WITH A RIFLE.

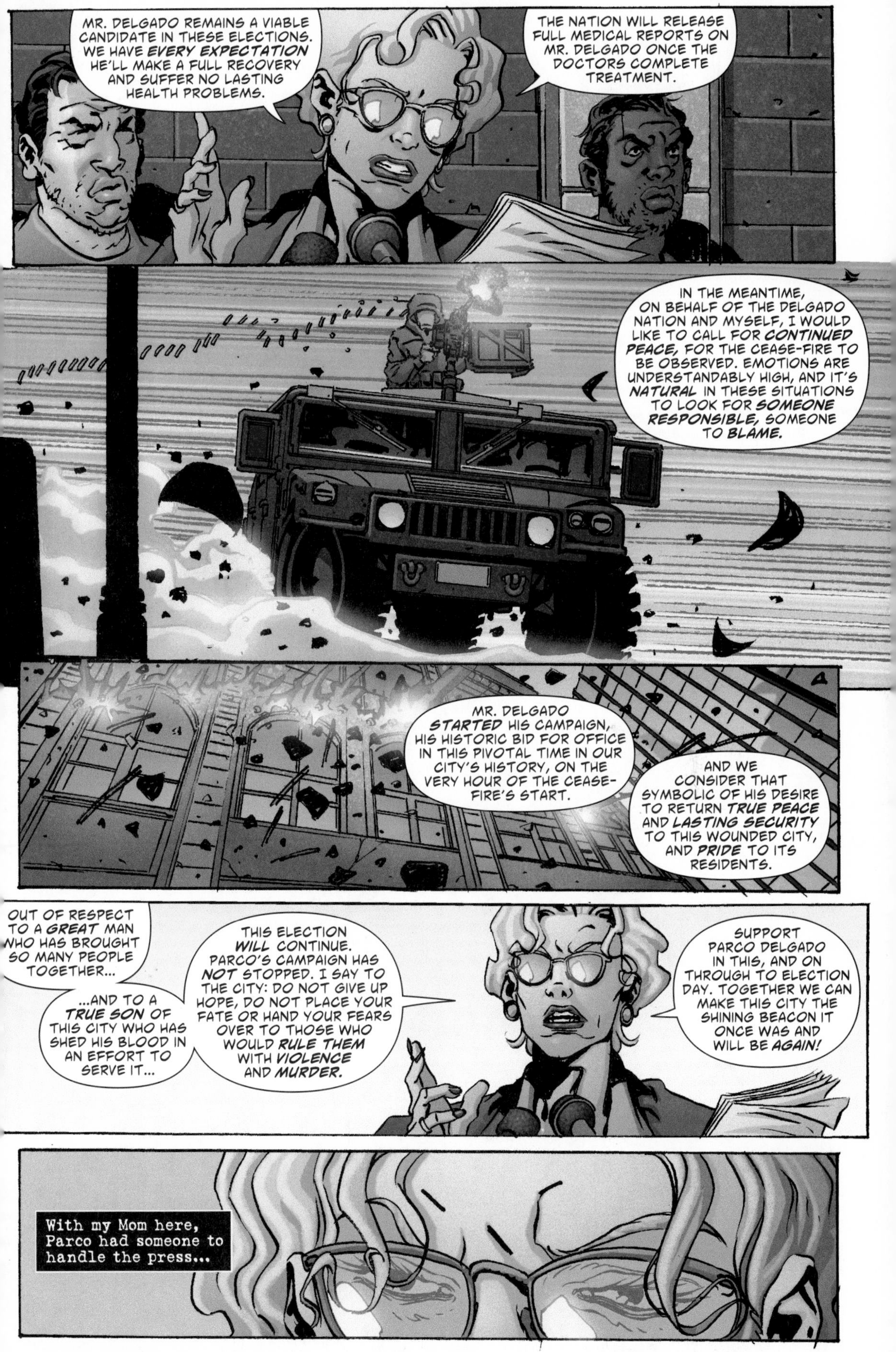
MR. DELGADO REMAINS A VIABLE CANDIDATE IN THESE ELECTIONS. WE HAVE EVERY EXPECTATION HE'LL MAKE A FULL RECOVERY AND SUFFER NO LASTING HEALTH PROBLEMS.
THE NATION WILL RELEASE FULL MEDICAL REPORTS ON MR. DELGADO ONCE THE DOCTORS COMPLETE TREATMENT.
IN THE MEANTIME, ON BEHALF OF THE DELGADO NATION AND MYSELF, I WOULD LIKE TO CALL FOR CONTINUED PEACE, FOR THE CEASE-FIRE TO BE OBSERVED. EMOTIONS ARE UNDERSTANDABLY HIGH, AND IT'S NATURAL IN THESE SITUATIONS TO LOOK FOR SOMEONE RESPONSIBLE, SOMEONE TO BLAME.
MR. DELGADO STARTED HIS CAMPAIGN, HIS HISTORIC BID FOR OFFICE IN THIS PIVOTAL TIME IN OUR CITY'S HISTORY, ON THE VERY HOUR OF THE CEASE-FIRE'S START.
AND WE CONSIDER THAT SYMBOLIC OF HIS DESIRE TO RETURN TRUE PEACE AND LASTING SECURITY TO THIS WOUNDED CITY, AND PRIDE TO ITS RESIDENTS.
OUT OF RESPECT TO A GREAT MAN WHO HAS BROUGHT SO MANY PEOPLE TOGETHER...
...AND TO A TRUE SON OF THIS CITY WHO HAS SHED HIS BLOOD IN AN EFFORT TO SERVE IT...
THIS ELECTION WILL CONTINUE. PARCO'S CAMPAIGN HAS NOT STOPPED. I SAY TO THE CITY: DO NOT GIVE UP HOPE, DO NOT PLACE YOUR FATE OR HAND YOUR FEARS OVER TO THOSE WHO WOULD RULE THEM WITH VIOLENCE AND MURDER.
SUPPORT PARCO DELGADO IN THIS, AND ON THROUGH TO ELECTION DAY. TOGETHER WE CAN MAKE THIS CITY THE SHINING BEACON IT ONCE WAS AND WILL BE AGAIN!
With my Mom here, Parco had someone to handle the press...

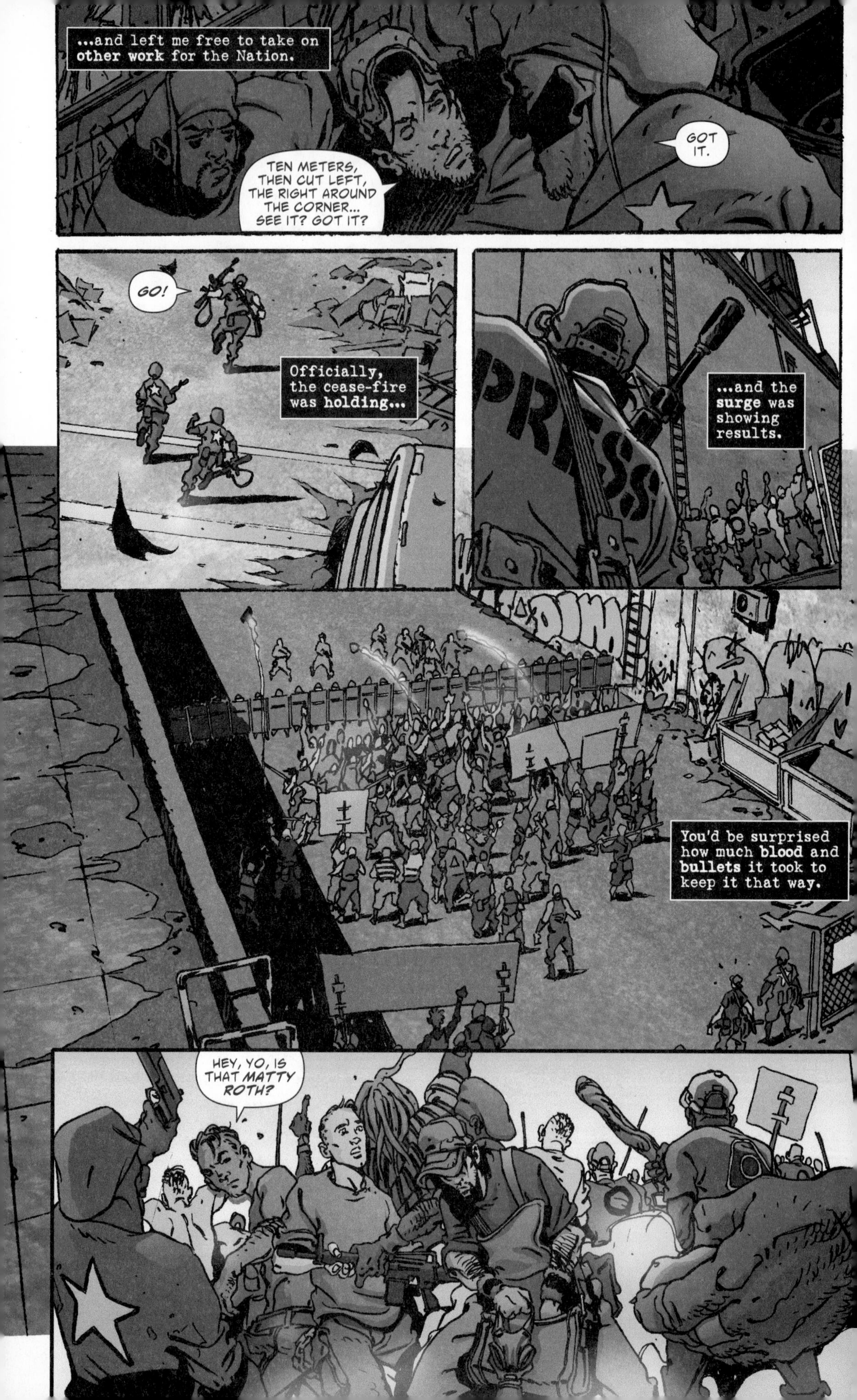
...and left me free to take on other work for the Nation.
TEN METERS, THEN CUT LEFT, THE RIGHT AROUND THE CORNER... SEE IT? GOT IT?
GOT IT.
GO!
Officially, the cease-fire was holding...
...and the surge was showing results.
PRESS
You'd be surprised how much blood and bullets it took to keep it that way.
HEY, YO, IS THAT MATTY ROTH?

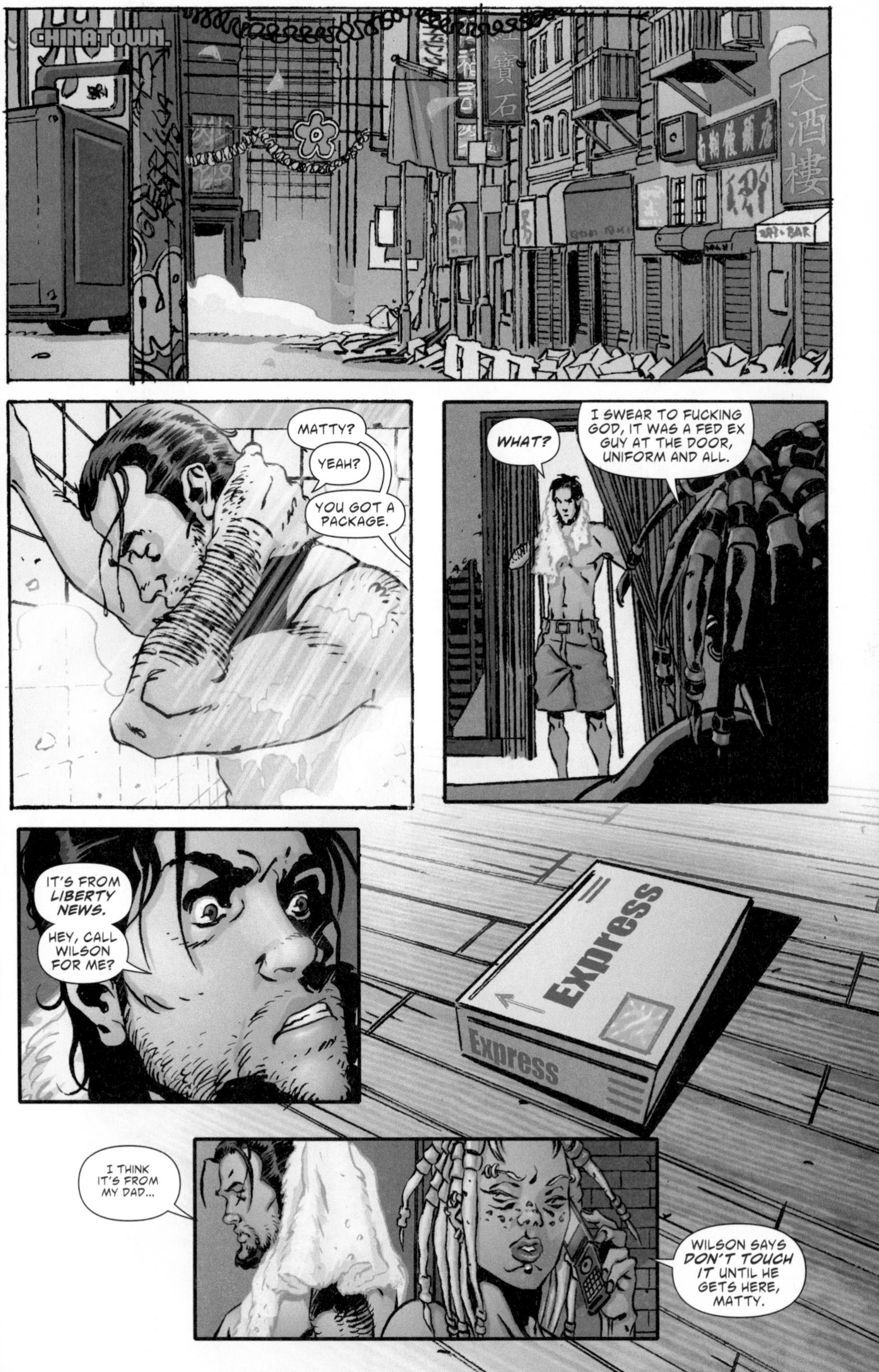
CHINATOWN.
MATTY?
YEAH?
YOU GOT A PACKAGE.
WHAT?
I SWEAR TO FUCKING GOD, IT WAS A FED EX GUY AT THE DOOR, UNIFORM AND ALL.
IT'S FROM LIBERTY NEWS.
HEY, CALL WILSON FOR ME?
Express
Express
I THINK IT'S FROM MY DAD...
WILSON SAYS DON'T TOUCH IT UNTIL HE GETS HERE, MATTY.

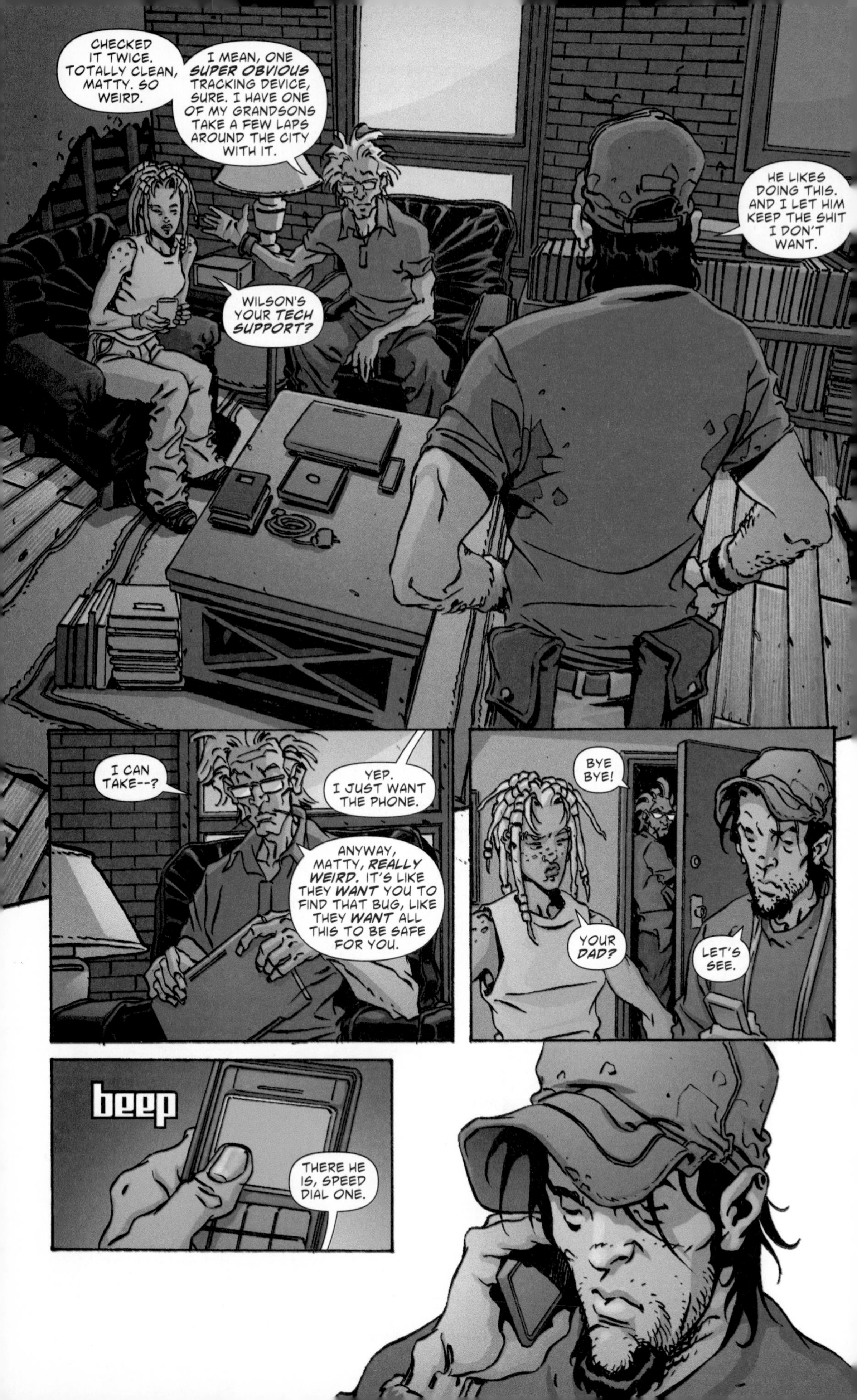
CHECKED IT TWICE. TOTALLY CLEAN, MATTY. SO WEIRD.
I MEAN, ONE **SUPER OBVIOUS** TRACKING DEVICE, SURE. I HAVE ONE OF MY GRANDSONS TAKE A FEW LAPS AROUND THE CITY WITH IT.
HE LIKES DOING THIS. AND I LET HIM KEEP THE SHIT I DON'T WANT.
WILSON'S YOUR *TECH SUPPORT?*
I CAN TAKE--?
YEP. I JUST WANT THE PHONE.
ANYWAY, MATTY, ***REALLY WEIRD.*** IT'S LIKE THEY ***WANT*** YOU TO FIND THAT BUG, LIKE THEY ***WANT*** ALL THIS TO BE SAFE FOR YOU.
BYE BYE!
YOUR *DAD?*
LET'S SEE.
beep
THERE HE IS, SPEED DIAL ONE.

...DAD...DAD, LISTEN.

THEY AREN'T ON THE LEVEL, MATTY. THE DEAL-- THE DEAL IS GARBAGE.

I KNOW, DAD.

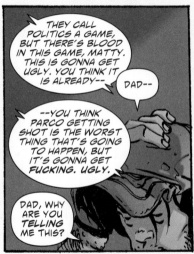

THEY CALL POLITICS A GAME, BUT THERE'S BLOOD IN THIS GAME, MATTY. THIS IS GONNA GET UGLY. YOU THINK IT IS ALREADY--

DAD--

--YOU THINK PARCO GETTING SHOT IS THE WORST THING THAT'S GOING TO HAPPEN, BUT IT'S GONNA GET FUCKING. UGLY.

DAD, WHY ARE YOU TELLING ME THIS?

THEY CAME ROUND TO SEE ME, ASKING ABOUT YOU. AND YOUR MOTHER.

I'M ON FORCED LEAVE. I'M AT HOME, MATTY, AND TO BE HONEST I DON'T THINK I'M MEANT TO LEAVE THE APARTMENT.

SHIT.

LISTEN. DON'T WORRY. JUST DON'T DO ANY- THING.

JUST FIND A DARK HOLE AND CRAWL INTO IT, AND STAY THERE UNTIL AFTER ELECTION DAY.

MAYBE THERE WILL STILL BE A CITY LEFT WHEN YOU DO.

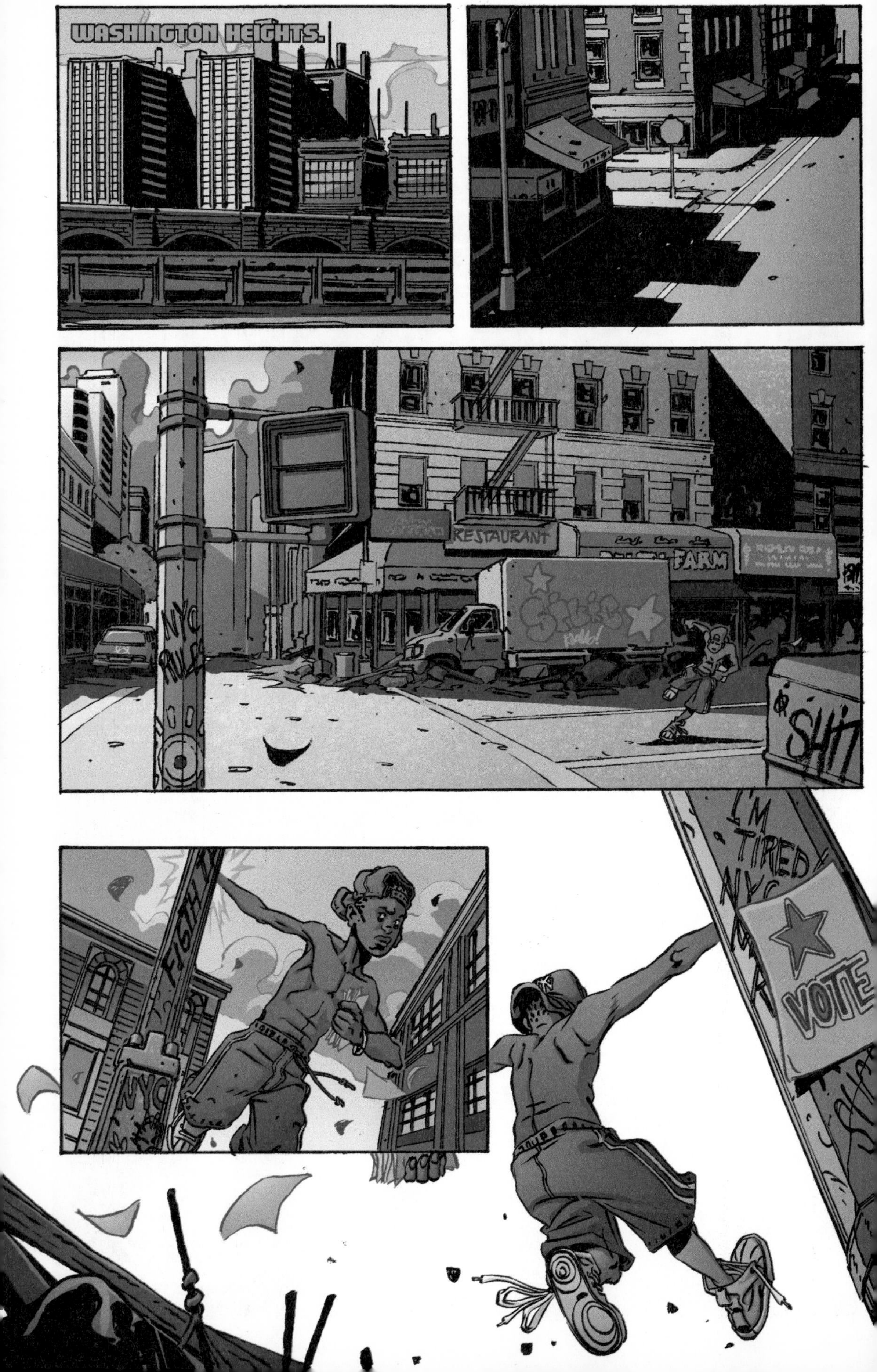
WASHINGTON HEIGHTS.
RESTAURANT
FARM
NYC RULES
SHIT
I'M TIRED
VOTE
NYC

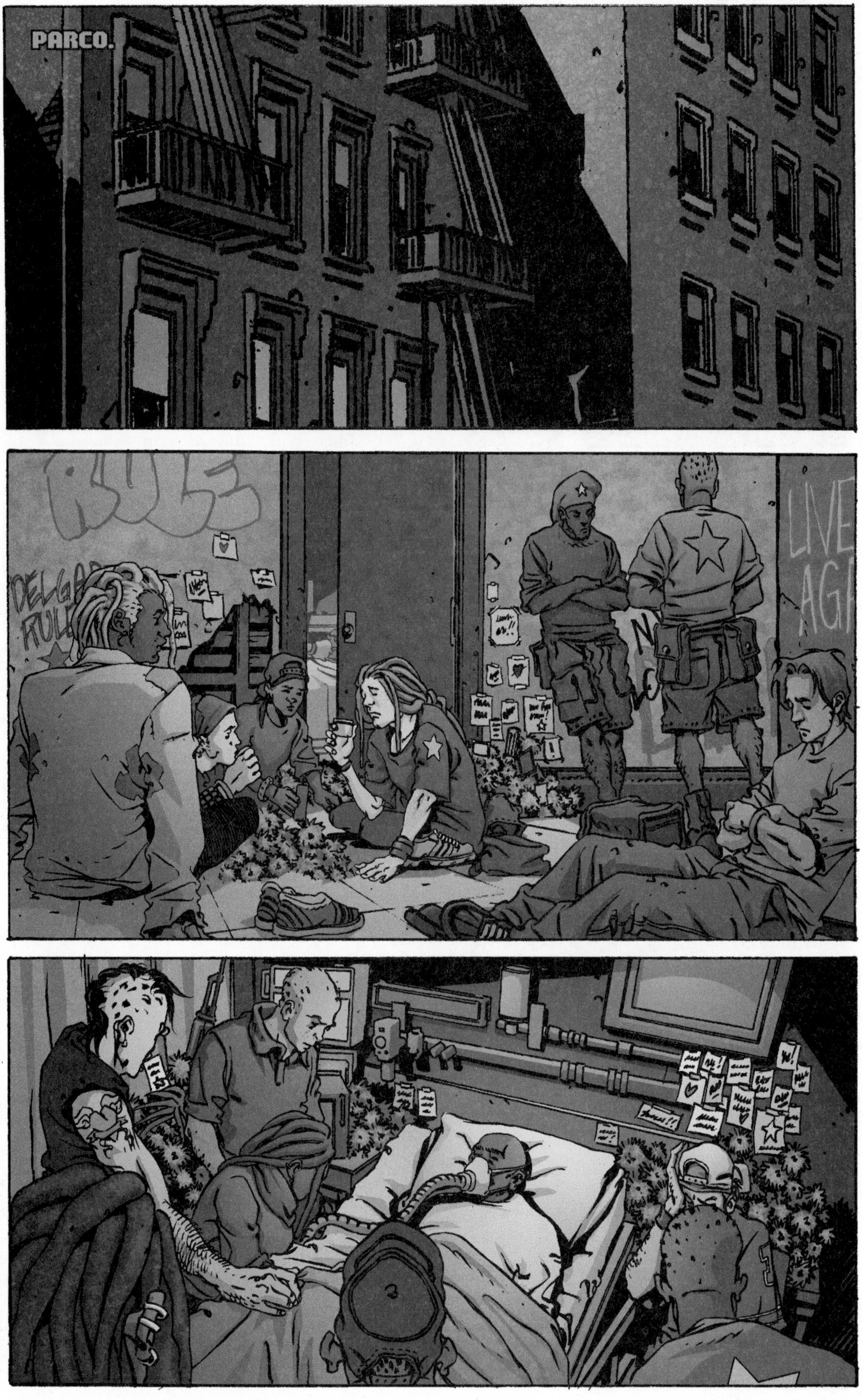
PARCO.

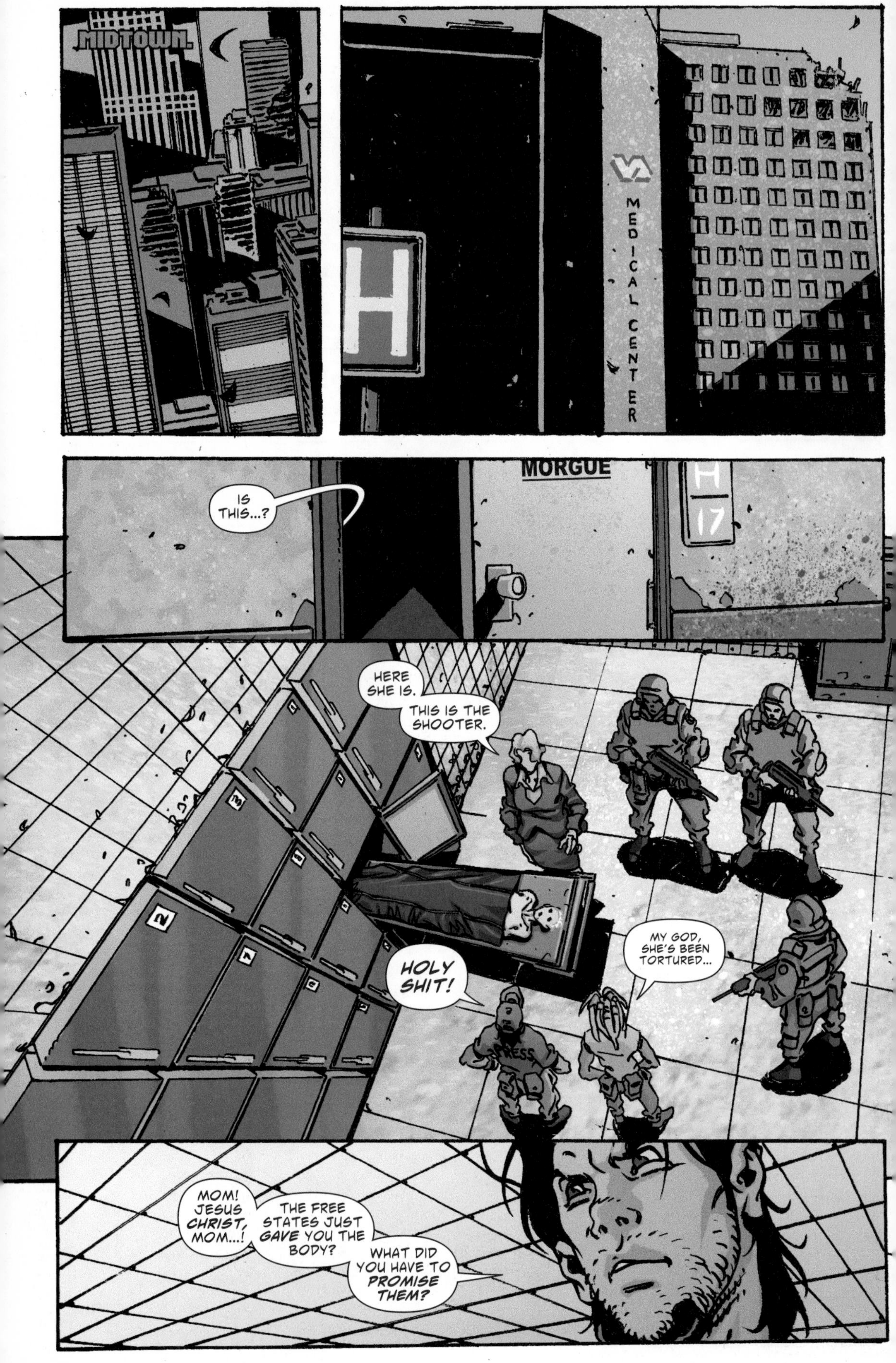

MIDTOWN.
MEDICAL CENTER
H
MORGUE
H 17
IS THIS...?
HERE SHE IS.
THIS IS THE SHOOTER.
HOLY SHIT!
MY GOD, SHE'S BEEN TORTURED...
PRESS
MOM! JESUS CHRIST, MOM...!
THE FREE STATES JUST GAVE YOU THE BODY?
WHAT DID YOU HAVE TO PROMISE THEM?

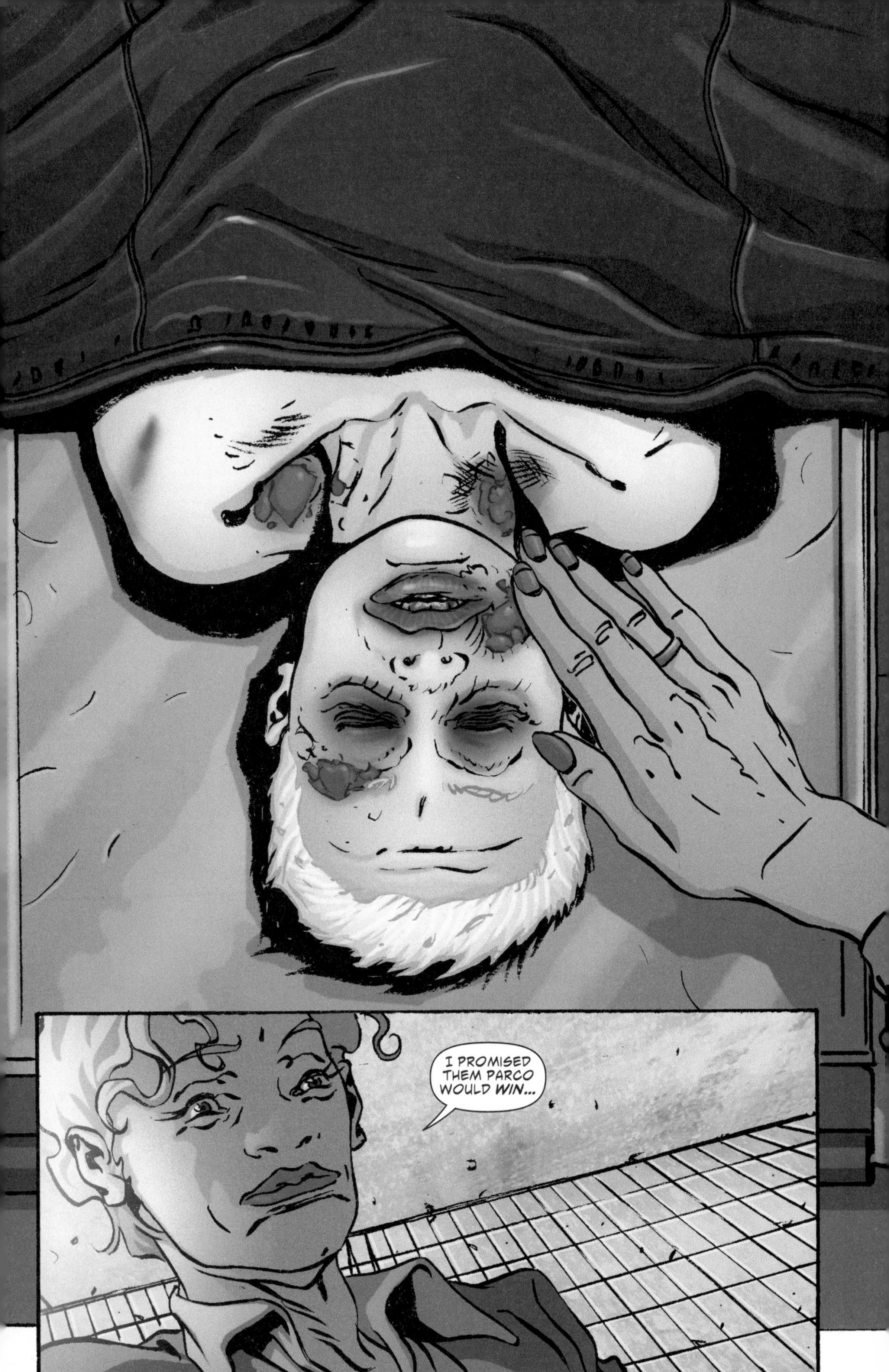
I PROMISED THEM PARCO WOULD WIN...

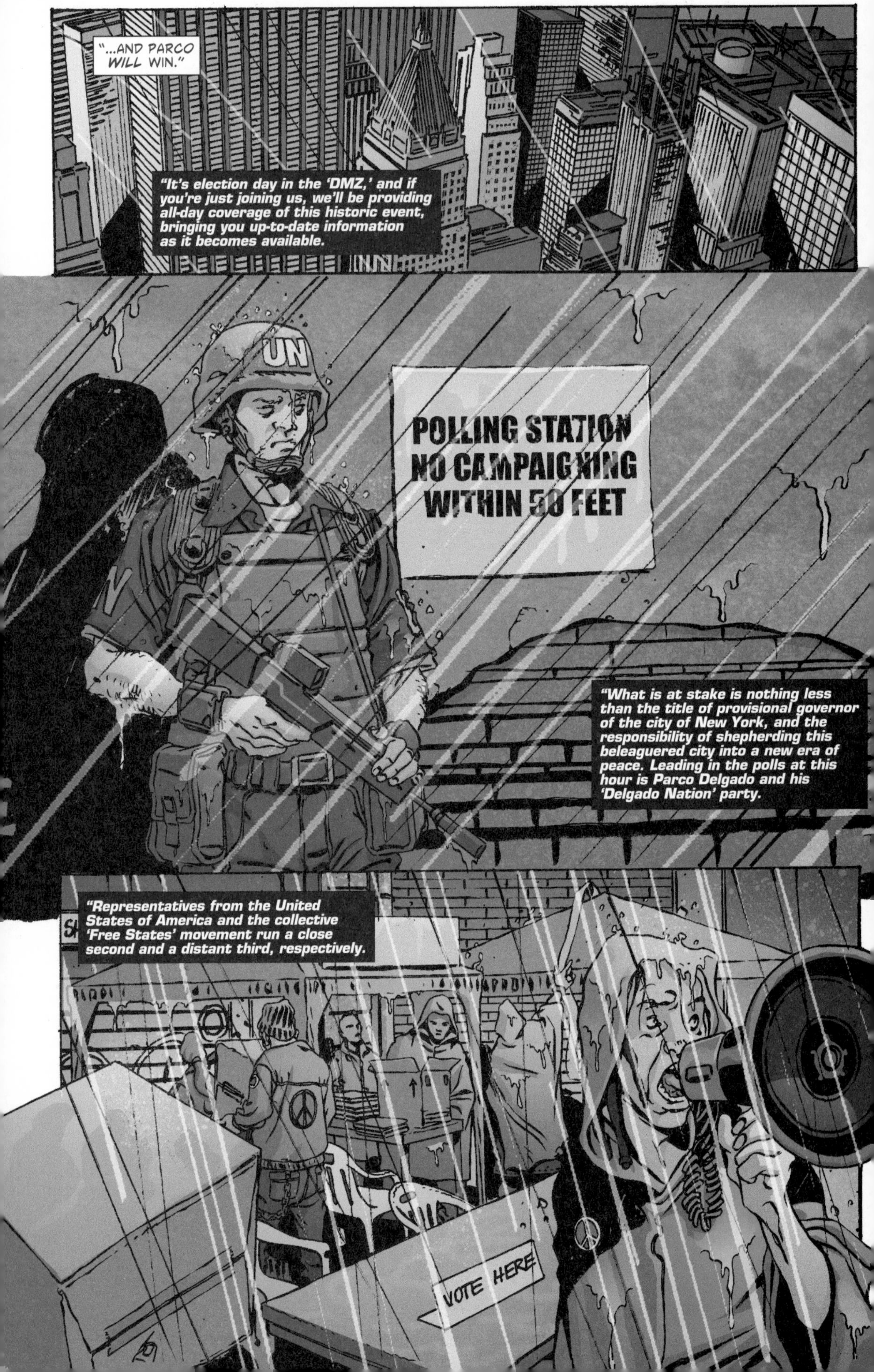
"...AND PARCO WILL WIN."
"It's election day in the 'DMZ,' and if you're just joining us, we'll be providing all-day coverage of this historic event, bringing you up-to-date information as it becomes available.
UN
POLLING STATION NO CAMPAIGNING WITHIN 50 FEET
"What is at stake is nothing less than the title of provisional governor of the city of New York, and the responsibility of shepherding this beleaguered city into a new era of peace. Leading in the polls at this hour is Parco Delgado and his 'Delgado Nation' party.
"Representatives from the United States of America and the collective 'Free States' movement run a close second and a distant third, respectively.
VOTE HERE

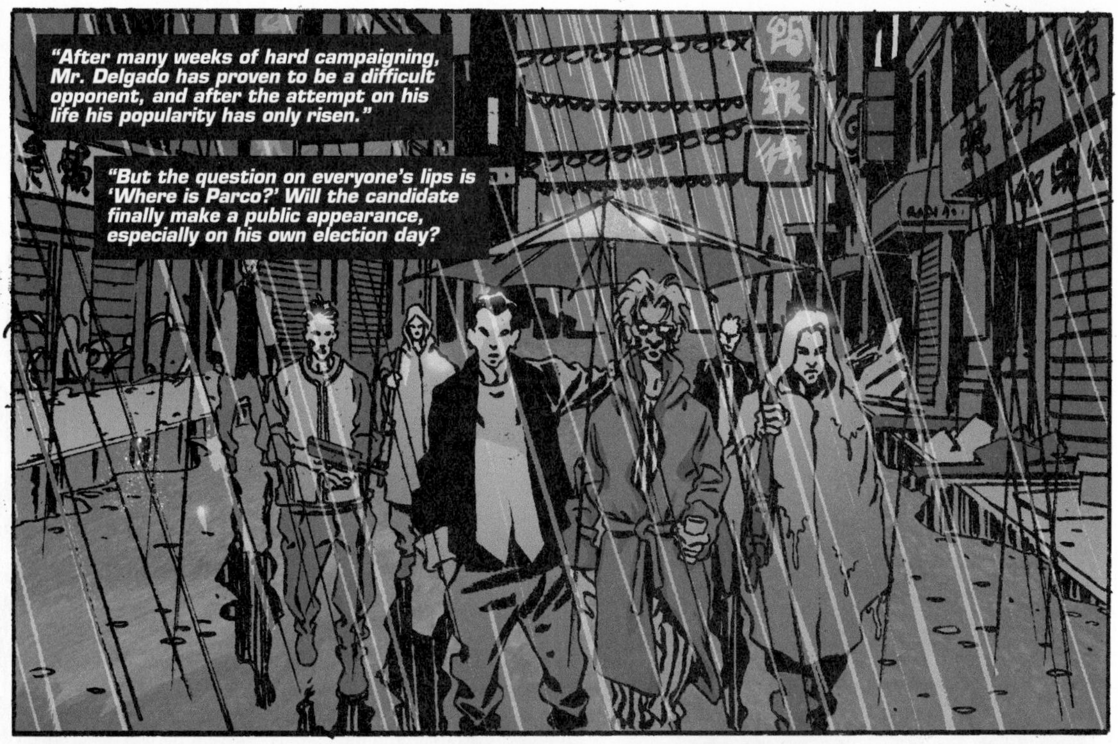
"After many weeks of hard campaigning, Mr. Delgado has proven to be a difficult opponent, and after the attempt on his life his popularity has only risen."
"But the question on everyone's lips is 'Where is Parco?' Will the candidate finally make a public appearance, especially on his own election day?

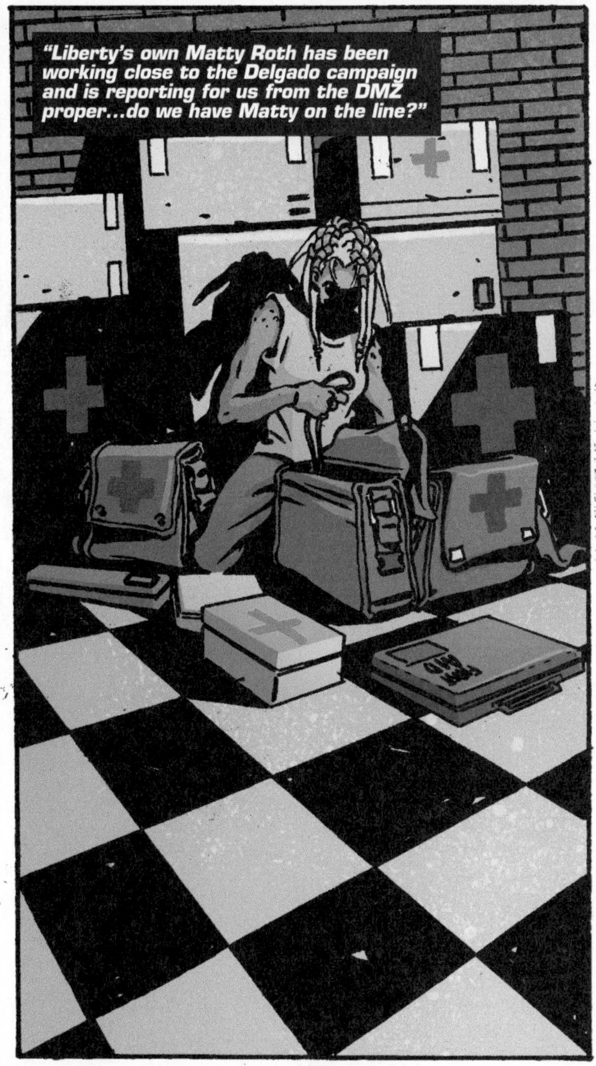
"Liberty's own Matty Roth has been working close to the Delgado campaign and is reporting for us from the DMZ proper...do we have Matty on the line?"

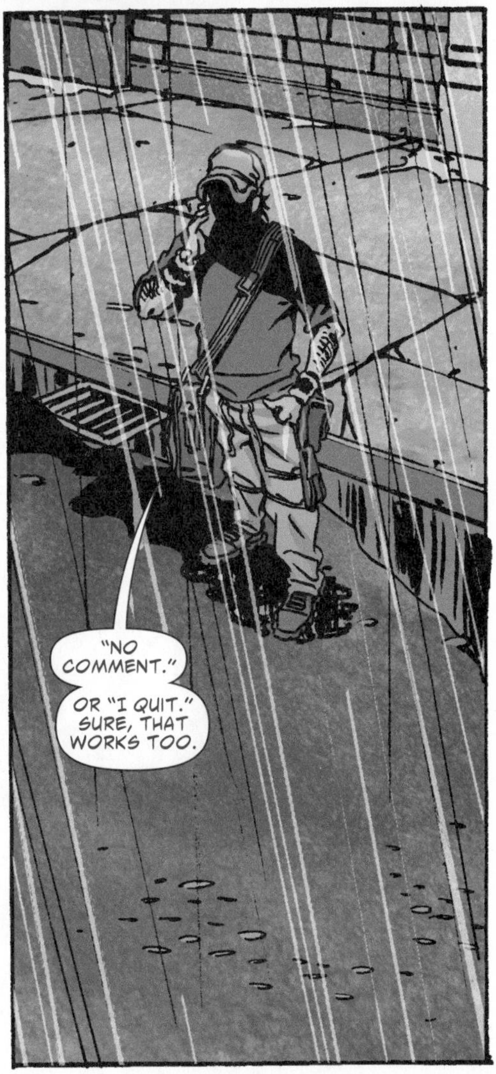
"NO COMMENT."
OR "I QUIT." SURE, THAT WORKS TOO.

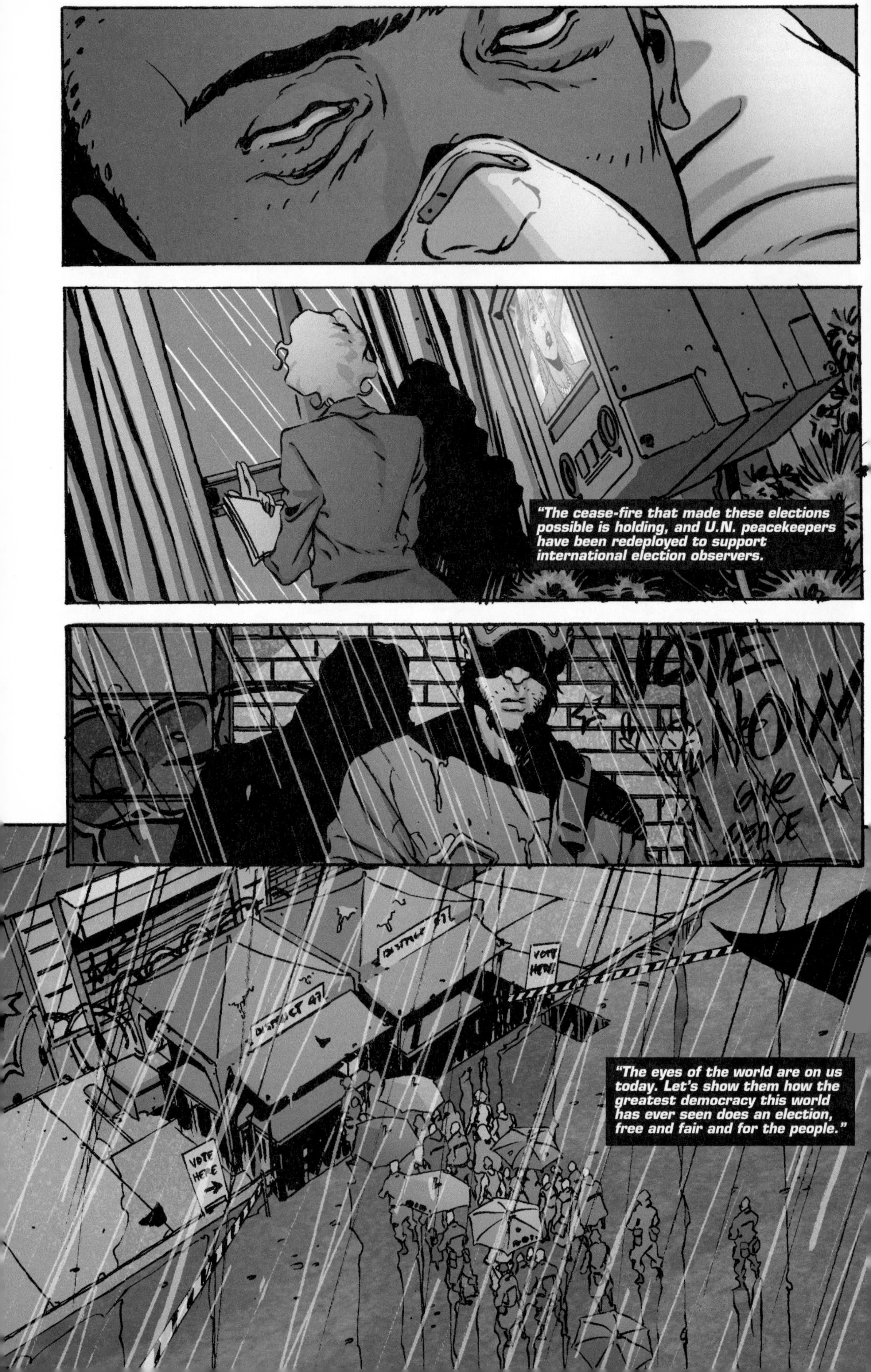
"The cease-fire that made these elections possible is holding, and U.N. peacekeepers have been redeployed to support international election observers.
DISTRICT 47
VOTE HERE
"The eyes of the world are on us today. Let's show them how the greatest democracy this world has ever seen does an election, free and fair and for the people."

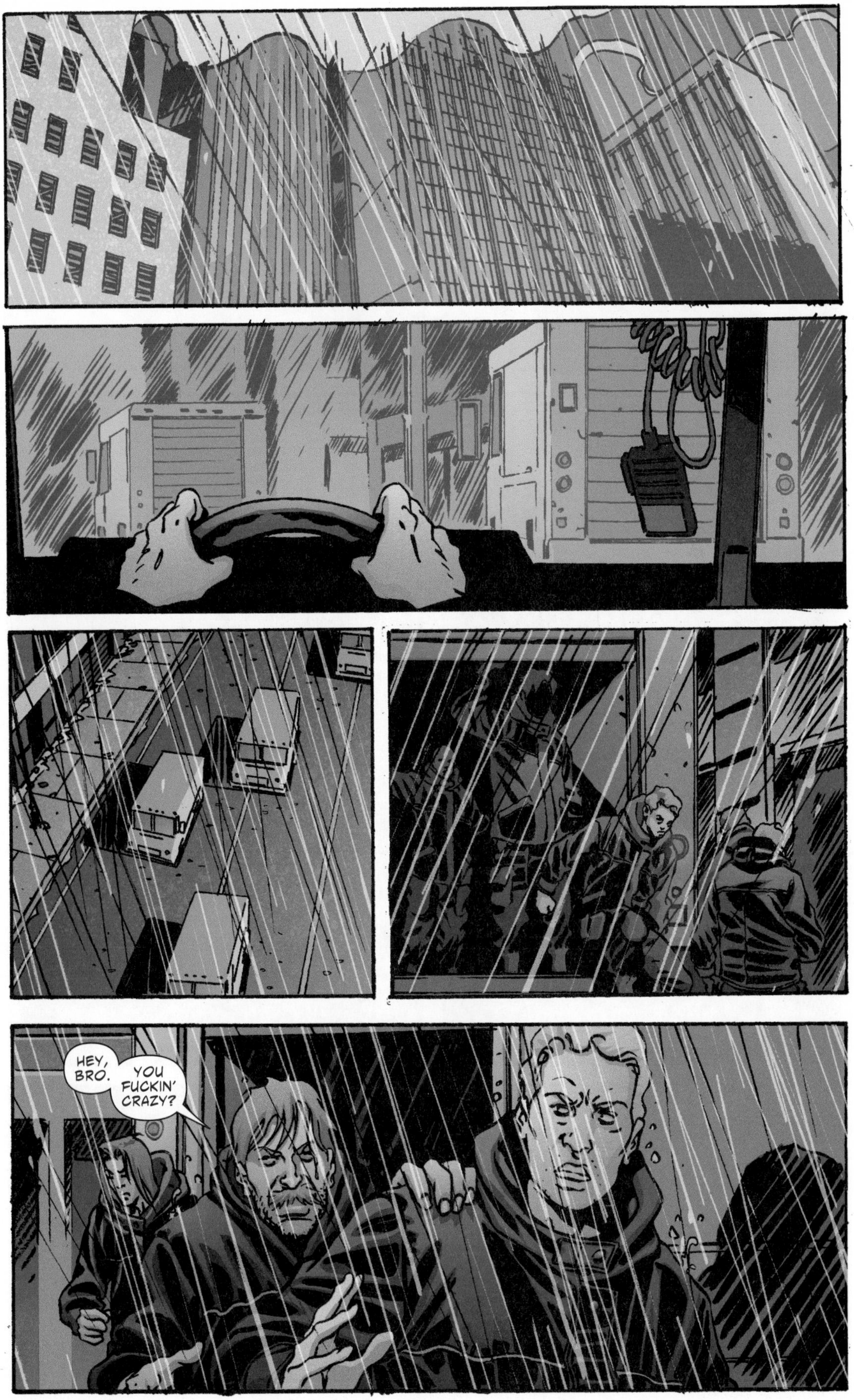
HEY, BRO.
YOU FUCKIN' CRAZY?

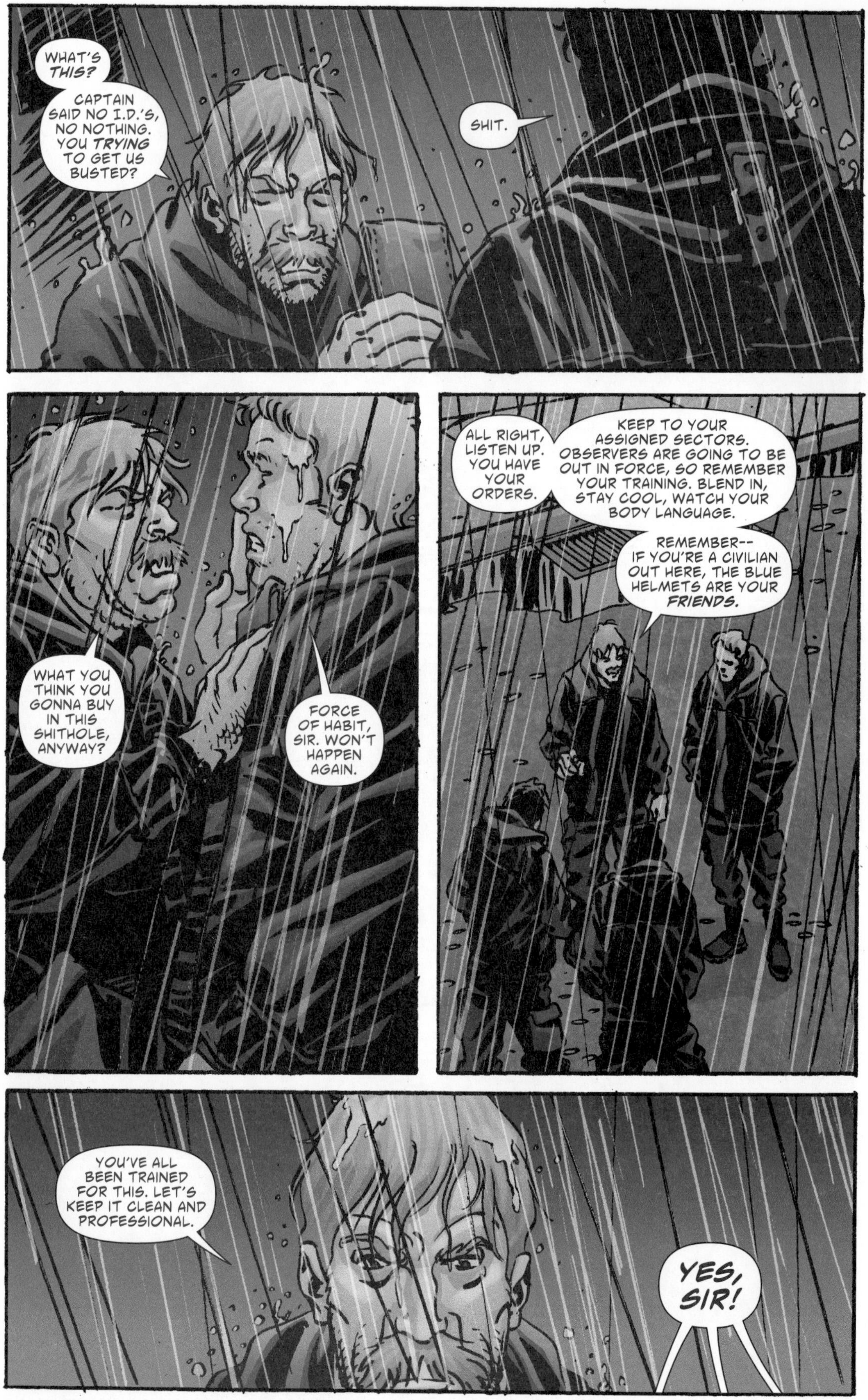
WHAT'S THIS?
CAPTAIN SAID NO I.D.'S, NO NOTHING. YOU TRYING TO GET US BUSTED?
SHIT.
WHAT YOU THINK YOU GONNA BUY IN THIS SHITHOLE, ANYWAY?
FORCE OF HABIT, SIR. WON'T HAPPEN AGAIN.
ALL RIGHT, LISTEN UP. YOU HAVE YOUR ORDERS.
KEEP TO YOUR ASSIGNED SECTORS. OBSERVERS ARE GOING TO BE OUT IN FORCE, SO REMEMBER YOUR TRAINING. BLEND IN, STAY COOL, WATCH YOUR BODY LANGUAGE.
REMEMBER-- IF YOU'RE A CIVILIAN OUT HERE, THE BLUE HELMETS ARE YOUR FRIENDS.
YOU'VE ALL BEEN TRAINED FOR THIS. LET'S KEEP IT CLEAN AND PROFESSIONAL.
YES, SIR!

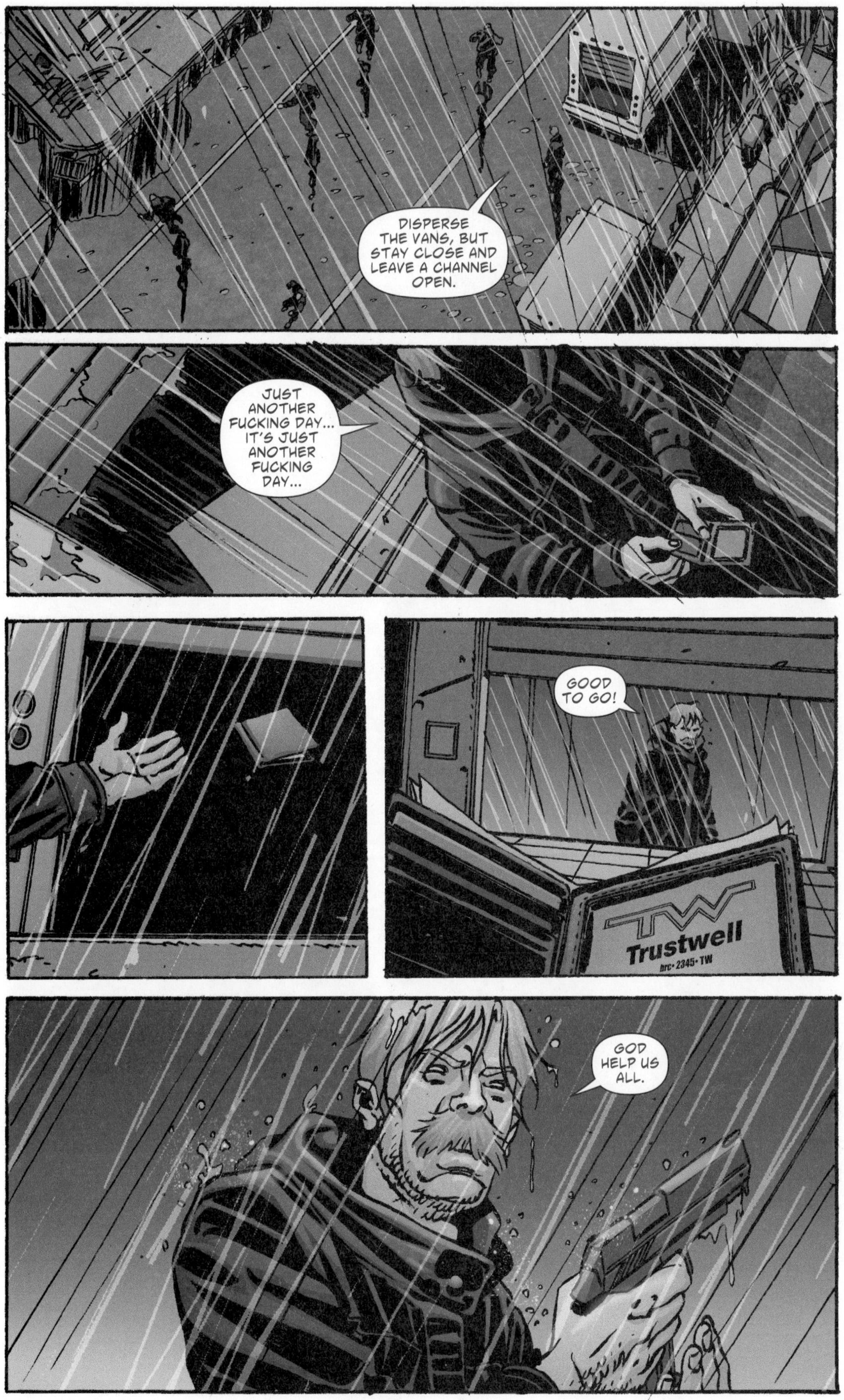
DISPERSE THE VANS, BUT STAY CLOSE AND LEAVE A CHANNEL OPEN.
JUST ANOTHER FUCKING DAY... IT'S JUST ANOTHER FUCKING DAY...
GOOD TO GO!
Trustwell
hrc • 2345 • TW
GOD HELP US ALL.

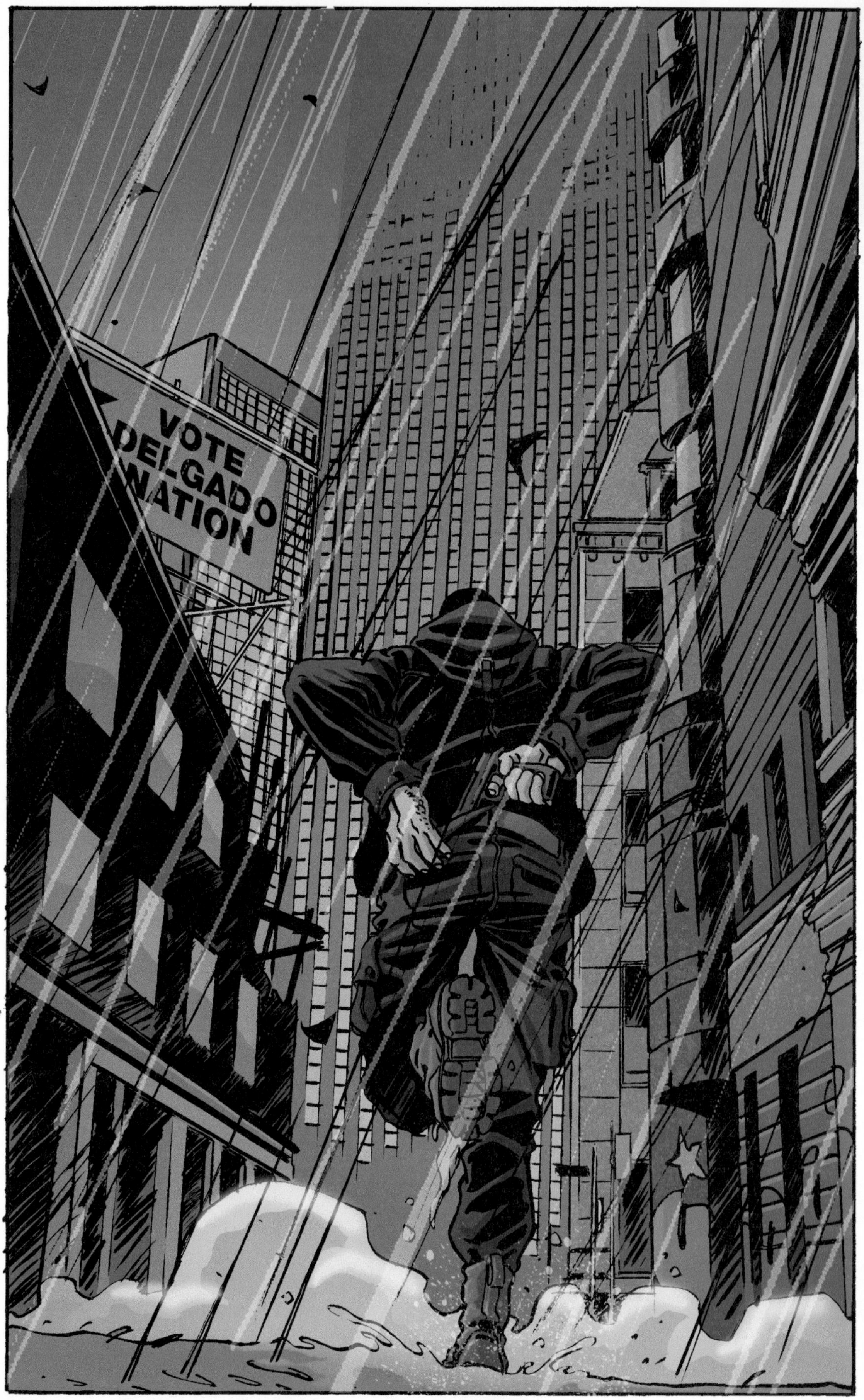
VOTE
DELGADO
NATION

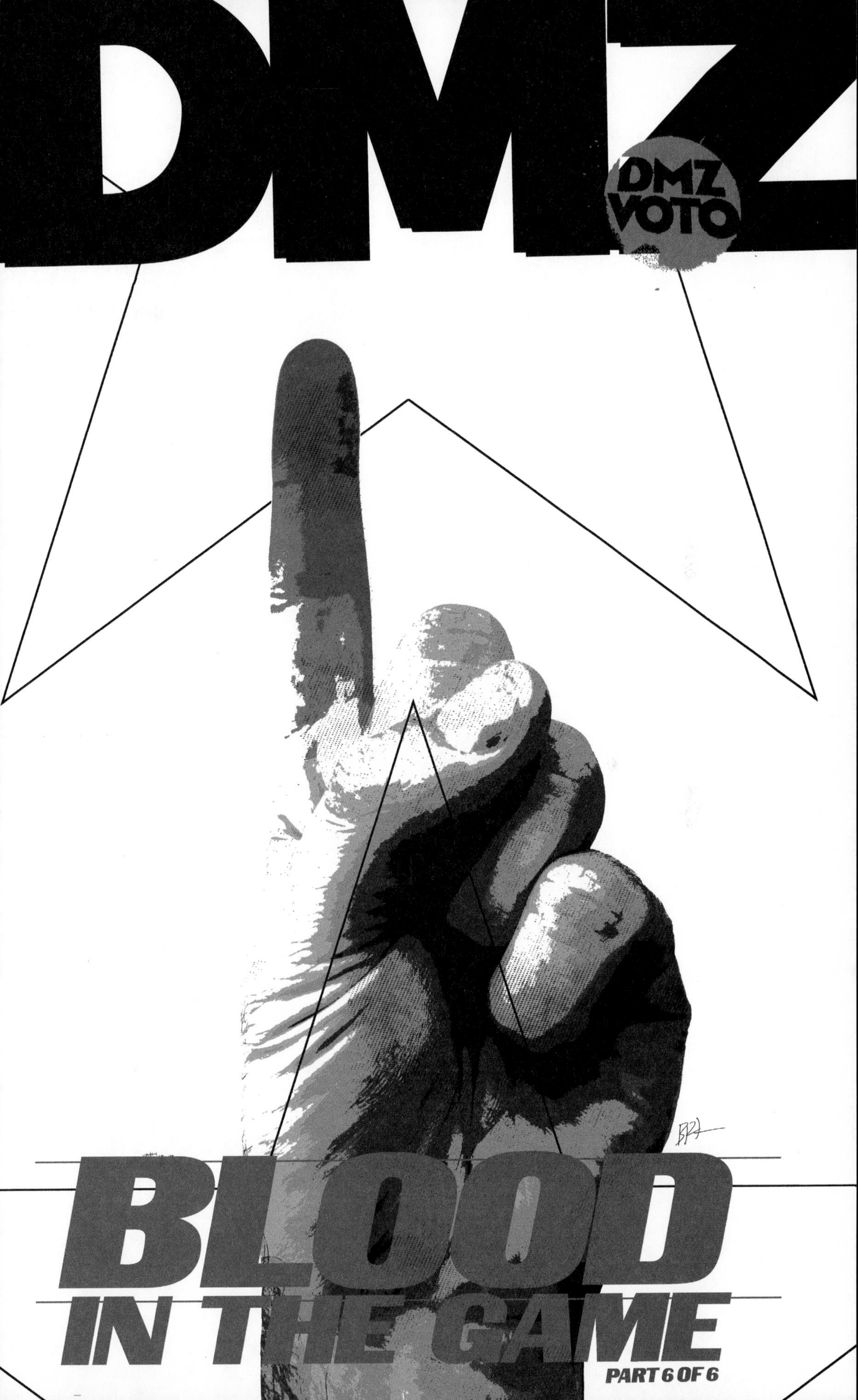
DMZ
DMZ
VOTO
BLOOD
IN THE GAME
PART 6 OF 6

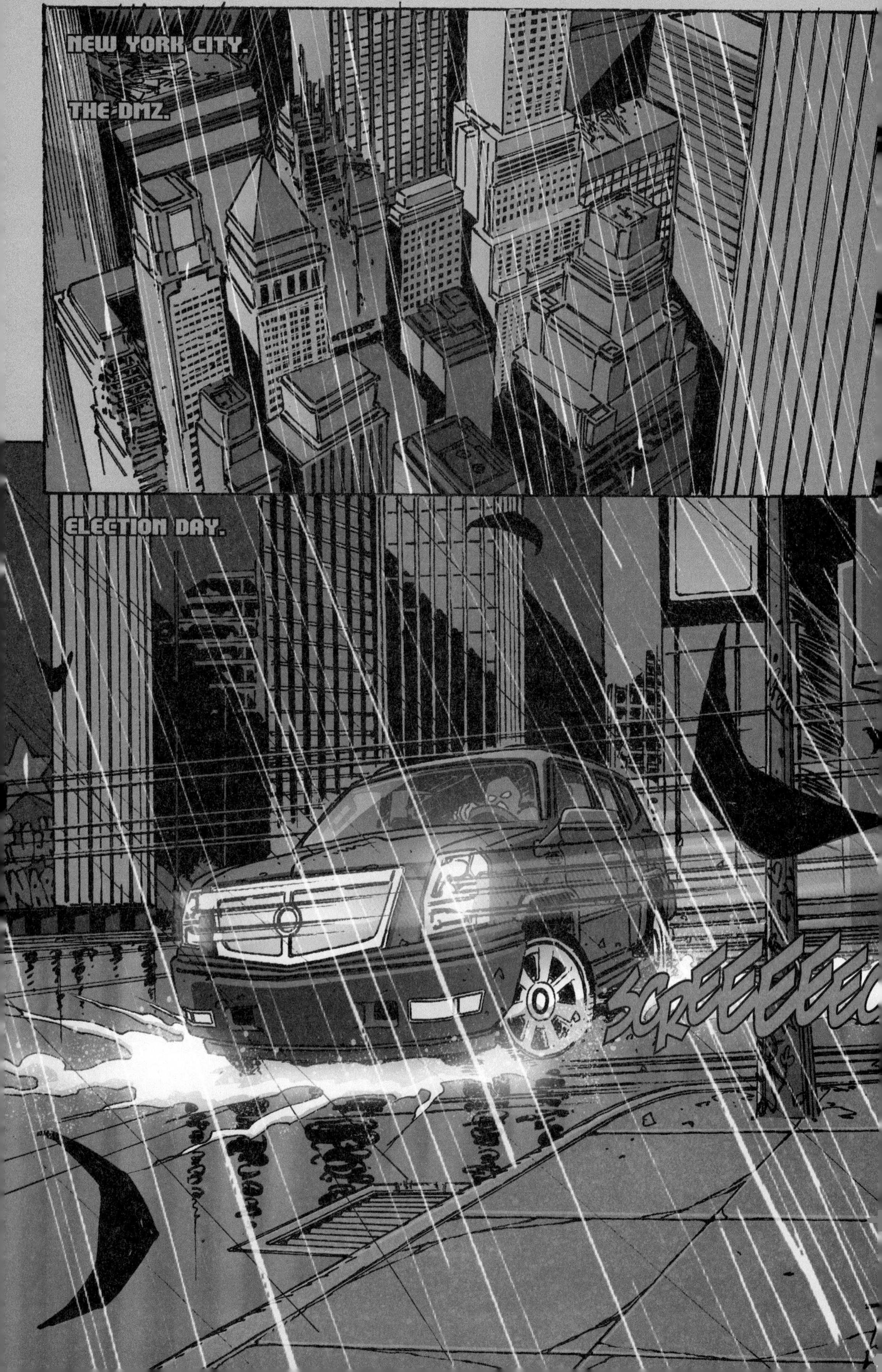
NEW YORK CITY.
THE DMZ.
ELECTION DAY.
SCREEEEEC

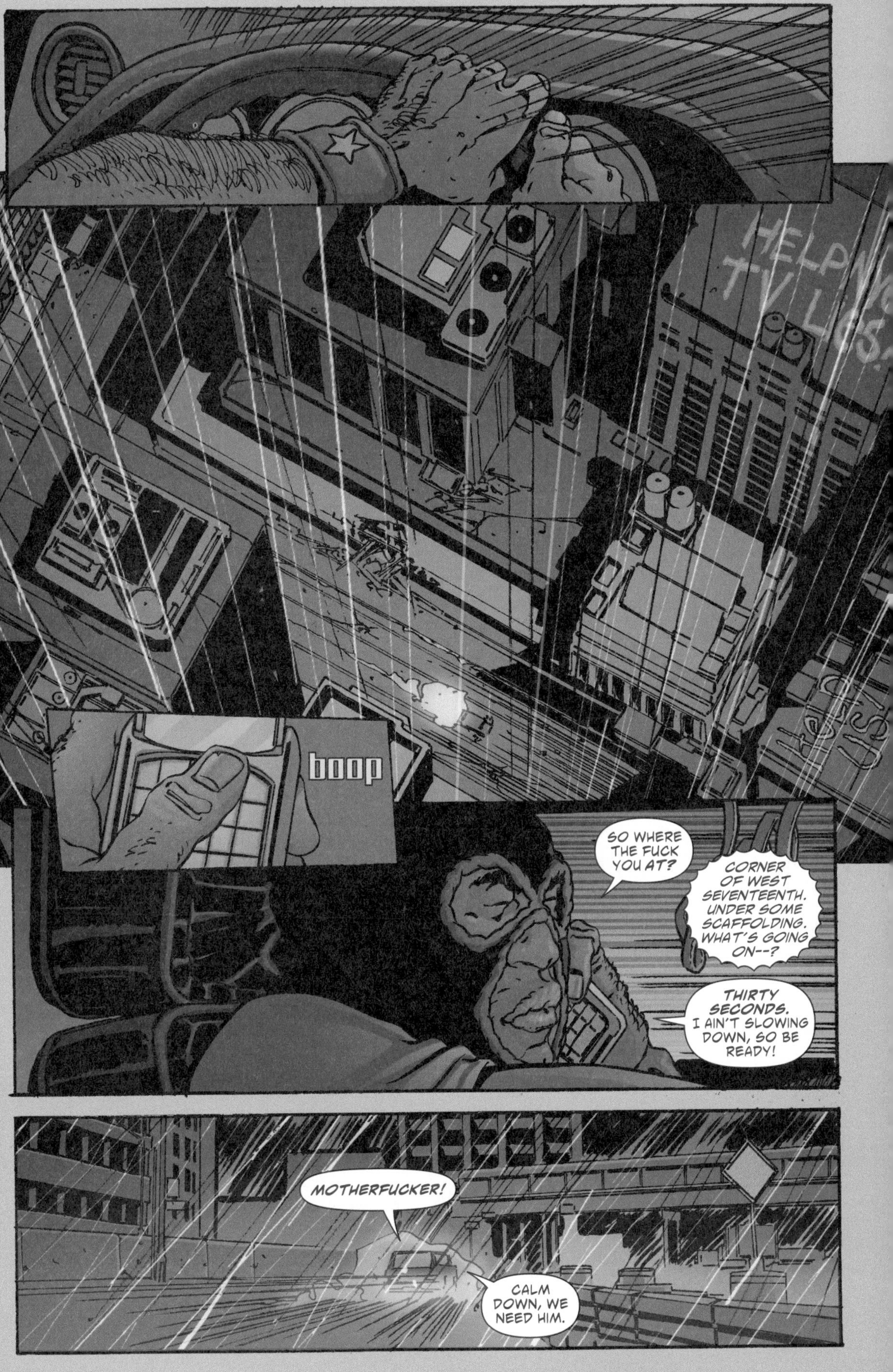
boop
SO WHERE THE FUCK YOU AT?
CORNER OF WEST SEVENTEENTH. UNDER SOME SCAFFOLDING. WHAT'S GOING ON--?
THIRTY SECONDS. I AIN'T SLOWING DOWN, SO BE READY!
MOTHERFUCKER!
CALM DOWN, WE NEED HIM.

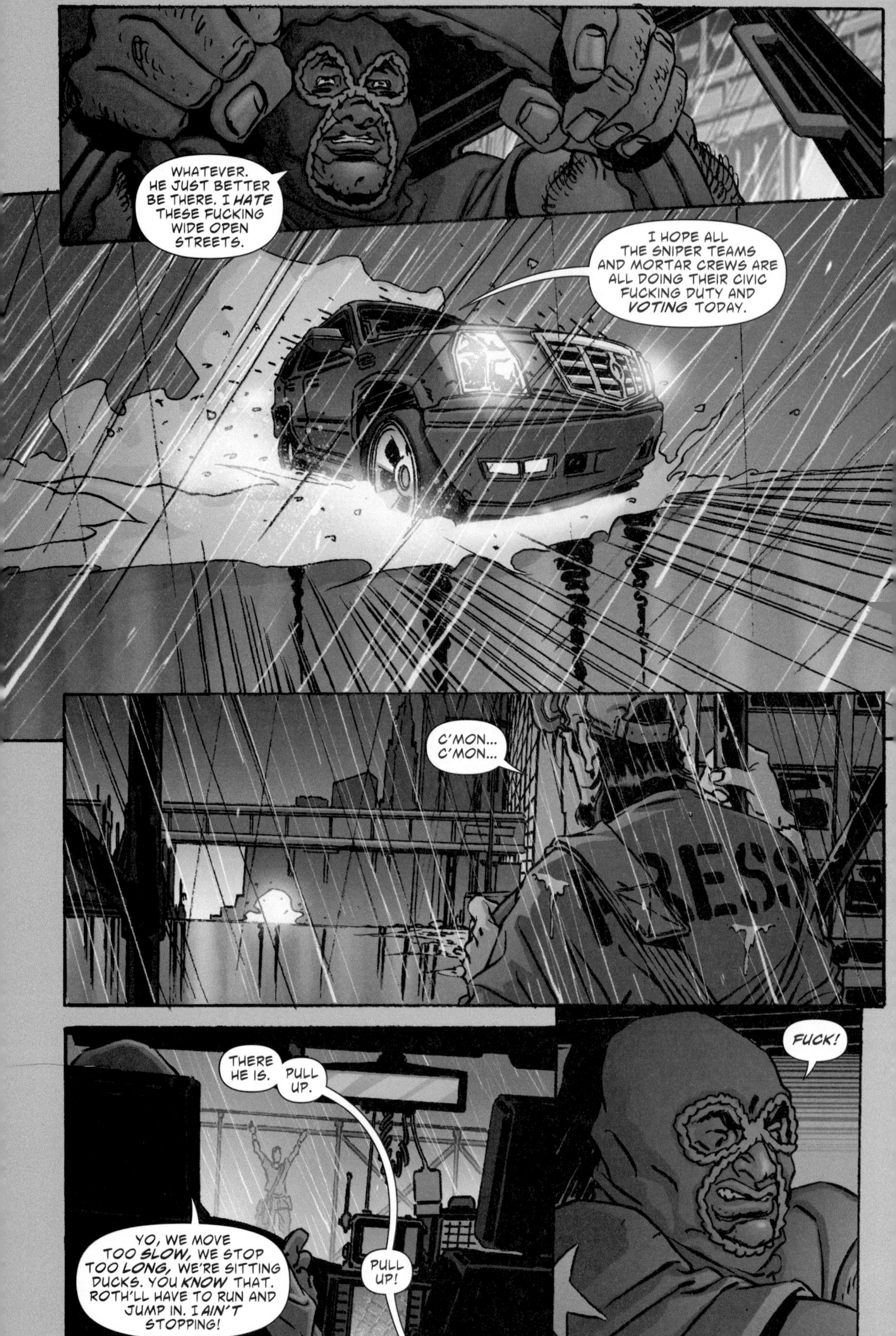
WHATEVER. HE JUST BETTER BE THERE. I HATE THESE FUCKING WIDE OPEN STREETS.
I HOPE ALL THE SNIPER TEAMS AND MORTAR CREWS ARE ALL DOING THEIR CIVIC FUCKING DUTY AND VOTING TODAY.
C'MON... C'MON...
PRESS
THERE HE IS.
PULL UP.
PULL UP!
YO, WE MOVE TOO SLOW, WE STOP TOO LONG, WE'RE SITTING DUCKS. YOU KNOW THAT. ROTH'LL HAVE TO RUN AND JUMP IN. I AIN'T STOPPING!
FUCK!

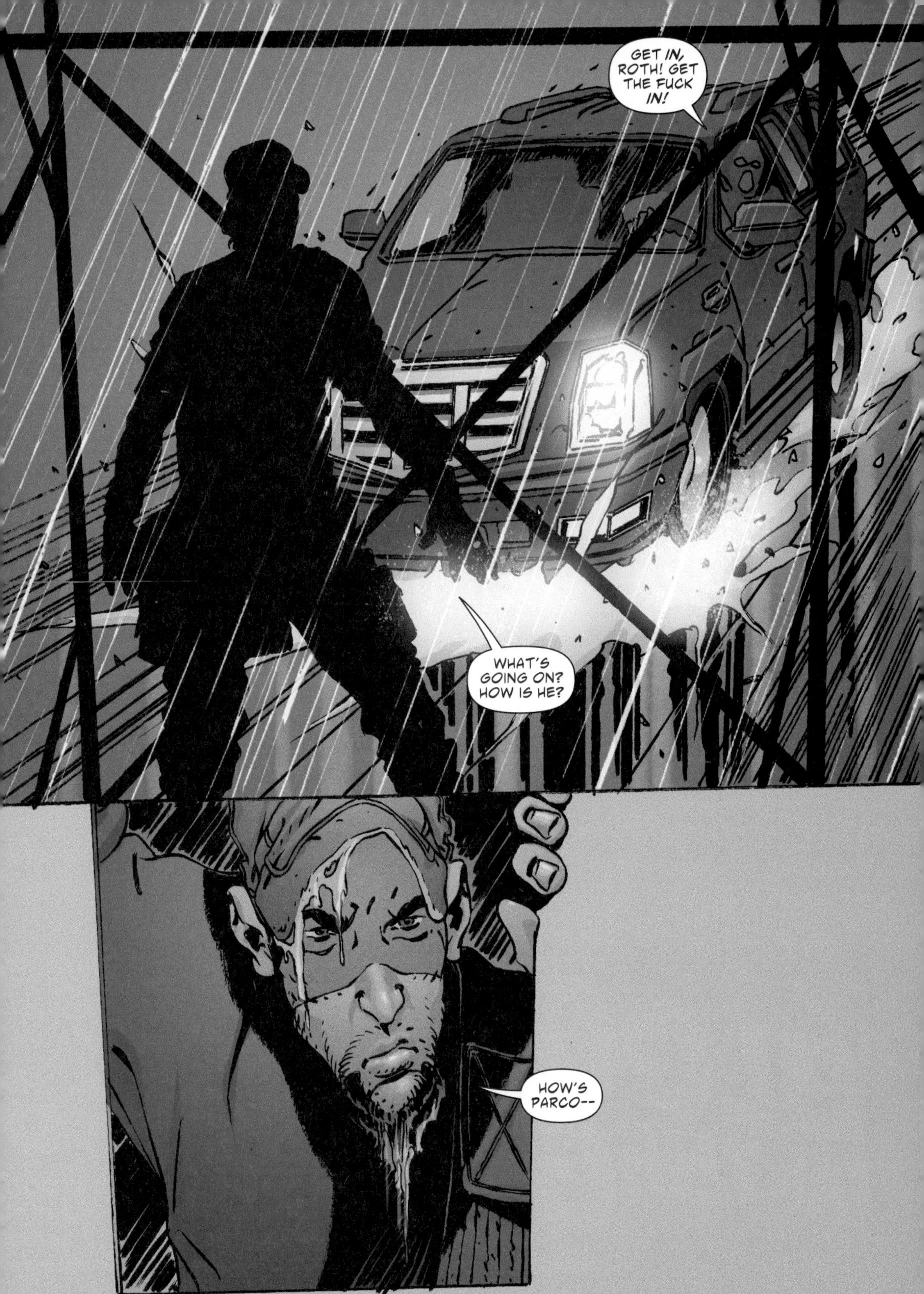
GET IN, ROTH! GET THE FUCK IN!
WHAT'S GOING ON? HOW IS HE?
HOW'S PARCO--

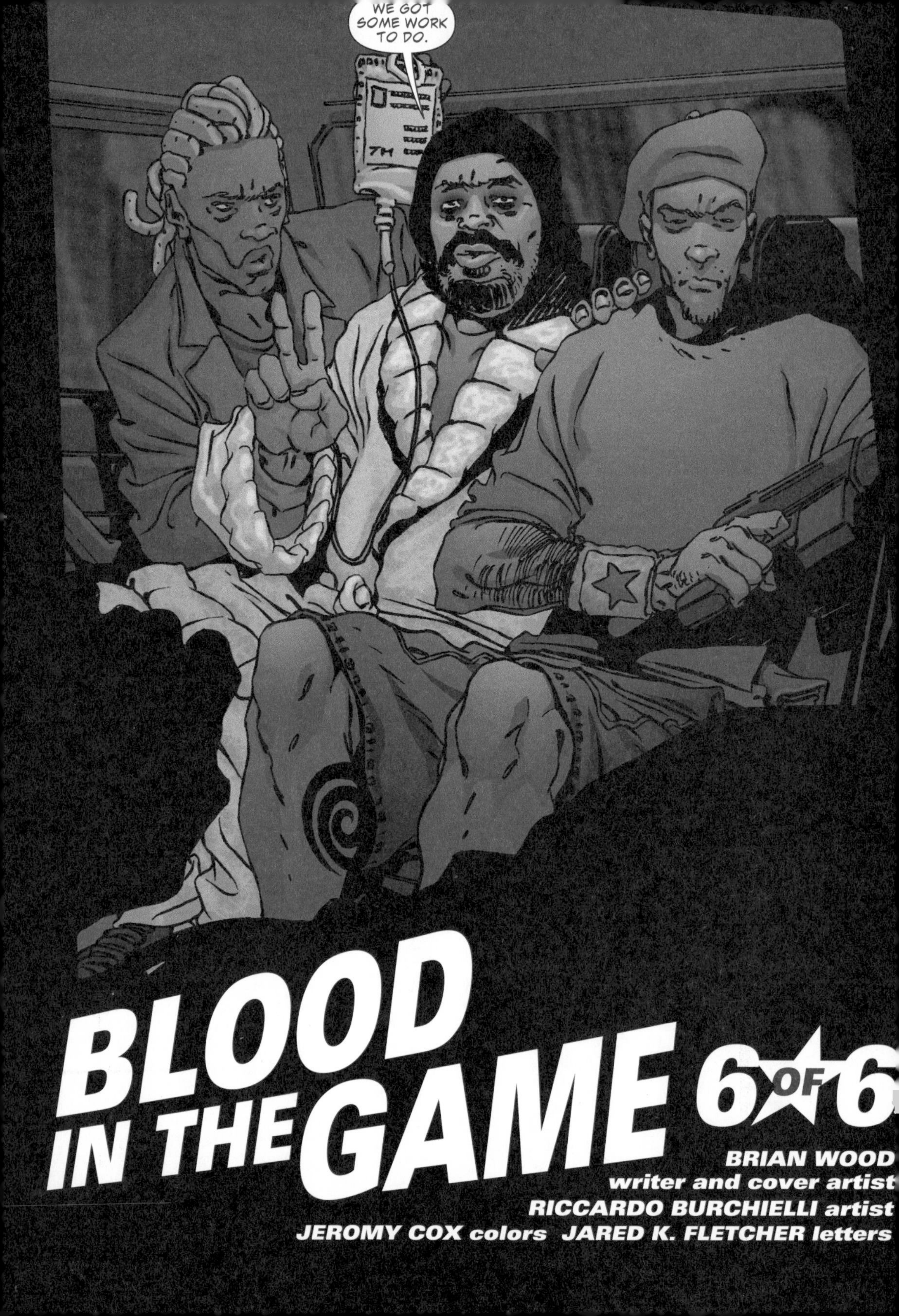
WE GOT SOME WORK TO DO.

BLOOD IN THE GAME 6 OF 6

BRIAN WOOD writer and cover artist
RICCARDO BURCHIELLI artist
JEROMY COX colors JARED K. FLETCHER letters

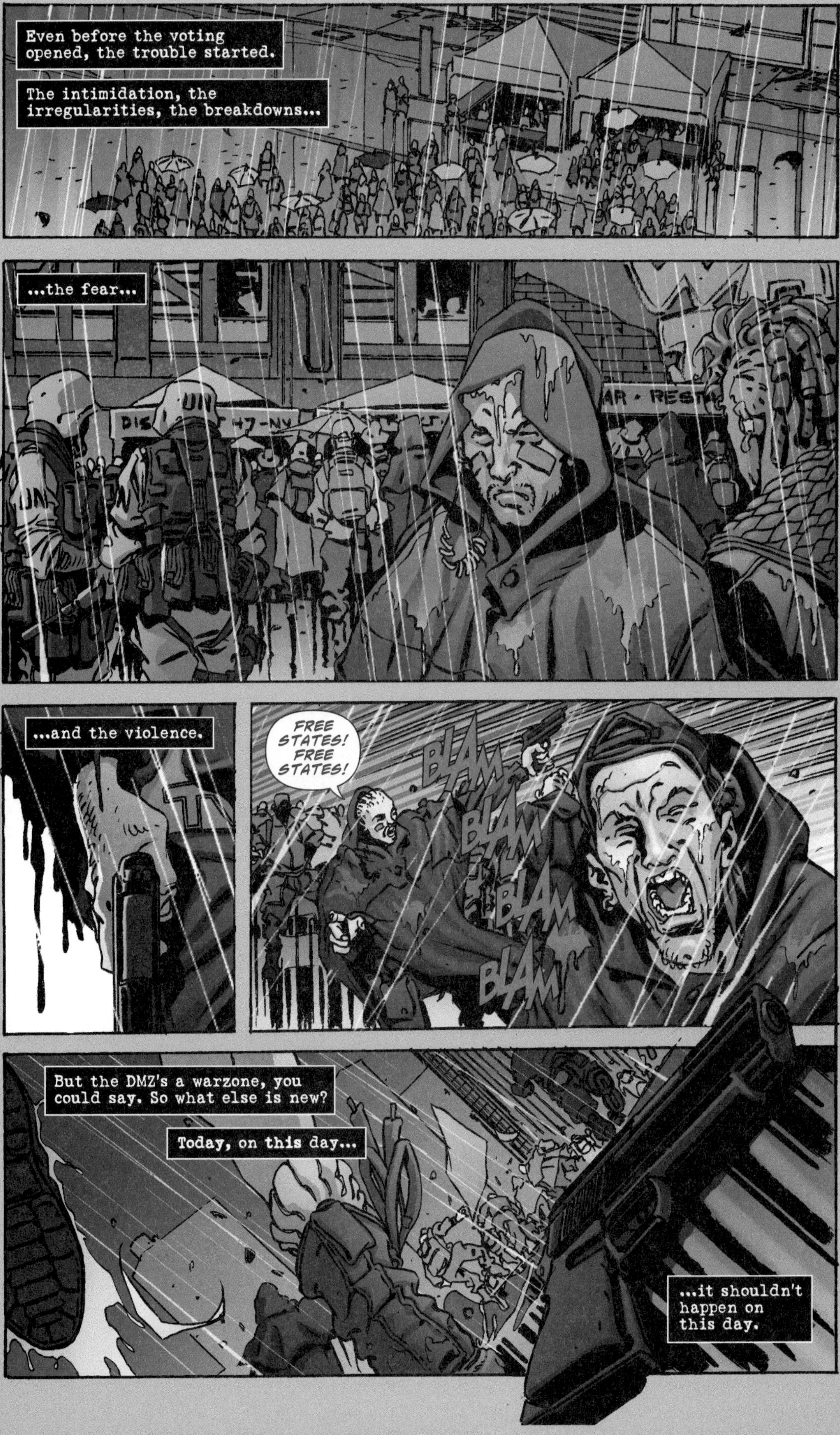
Even before the voting opened, the trouble started.
The intimidation, the irregularities, the breakdowns...
...the fear...
...and the violence.
FREE STATES! FREE STATES!
BLAM
BLAM
BLAM
BLAM
But the DMZ's a warzone, you could say. So what else is new?
Today, on this day...
...it shouldn't happen on this day.

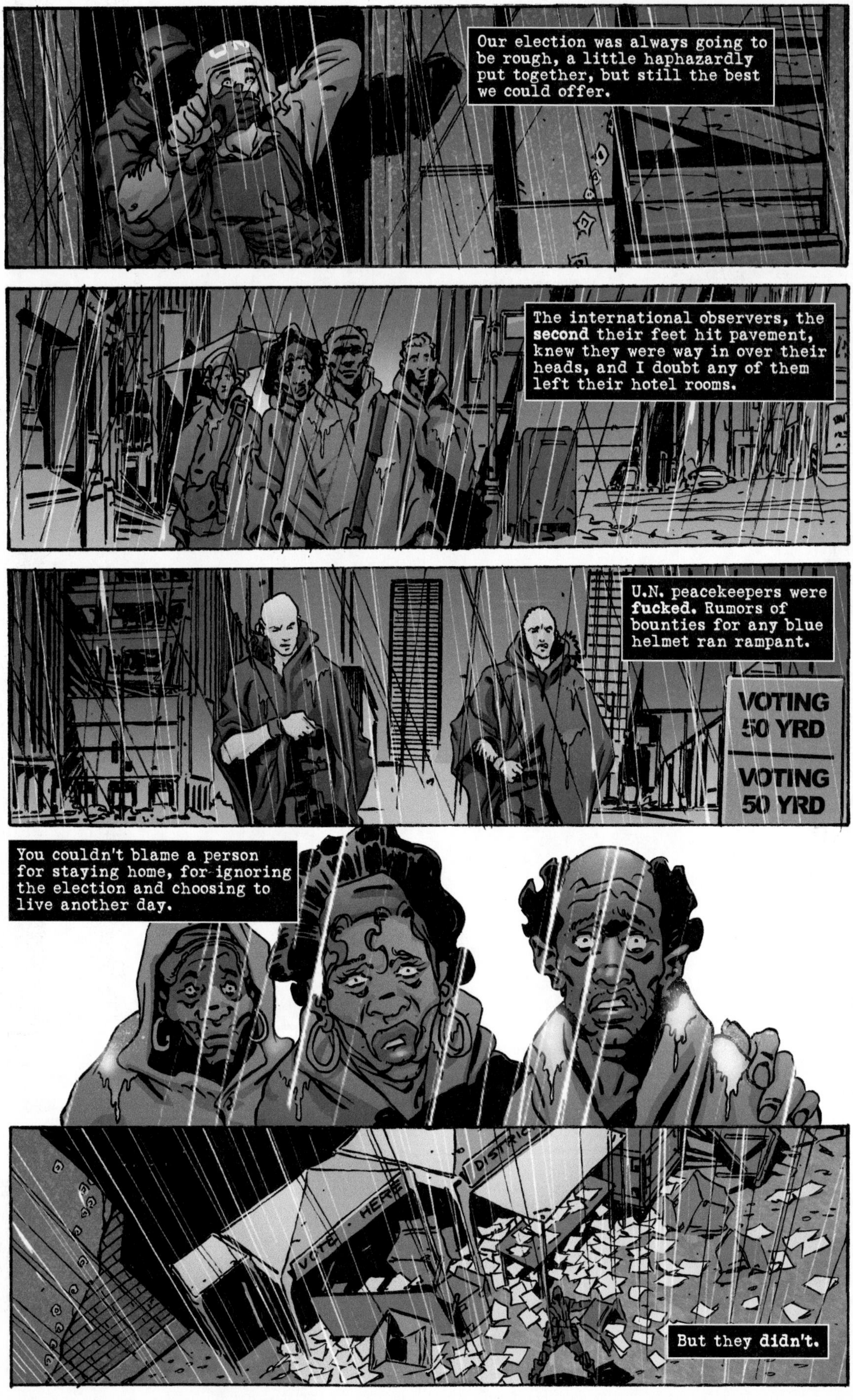
Our election was always going to be rough, a little haphazardly put together, but still the best we could offer.
The international observers, the **second** their feet hit pavement, knew they were way in over their heads, and I doubt any of them left their hotel rooms.
U.N. peacekeepers were **fucked.** Rumors of bounties for any blue helmet ran rampant.
VOTING 50 YRD
VOTING 50 YRD
You couldn't blame a person for staying home, for ignoring the election and choosing to live another day.
DISTRIC
VOTE HERE
But they **didn't.**

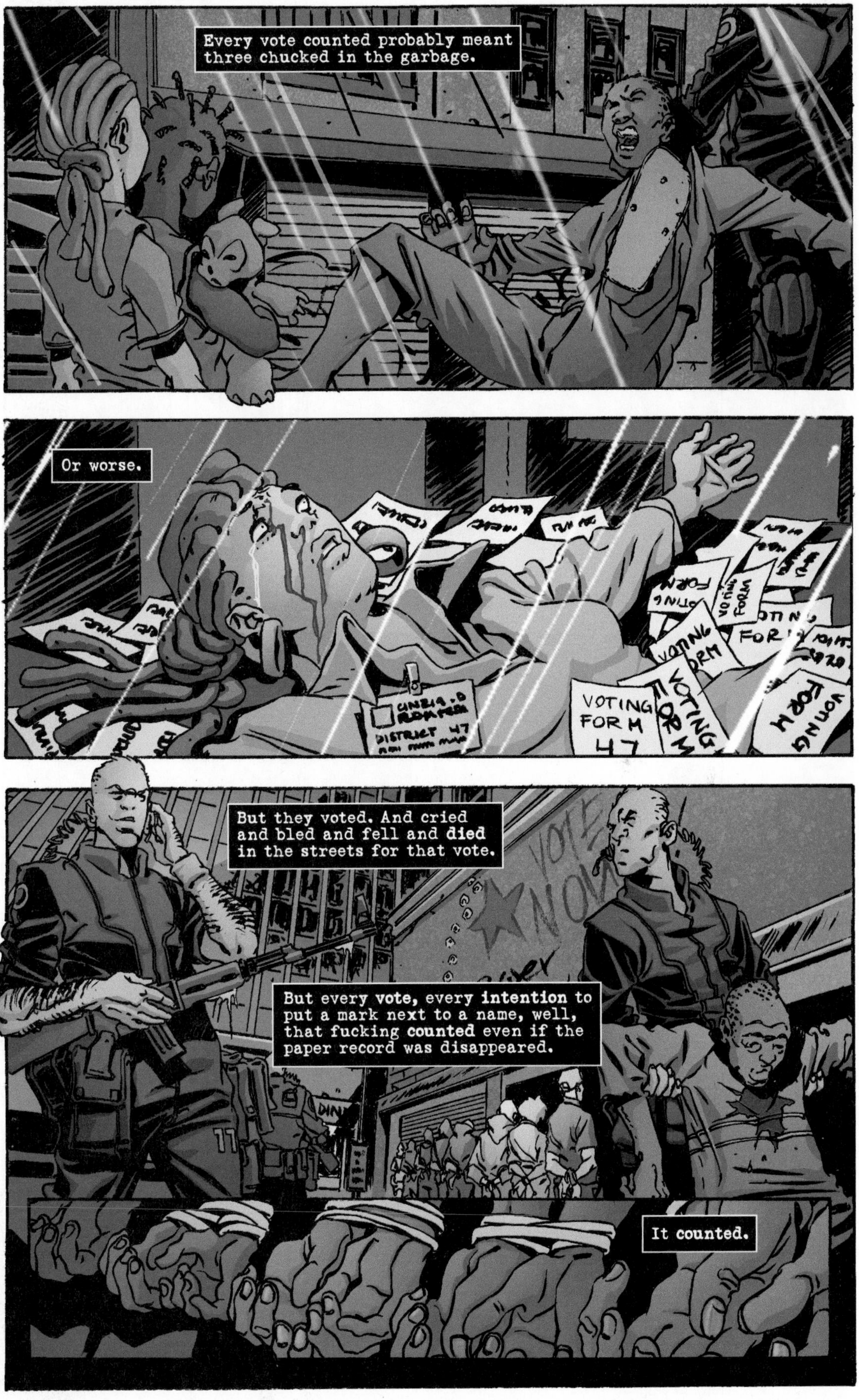
Every vote counted probably meant three chucked in the garbage.
Or worse.
DISTRICT 47
VOTING FORM 47
But they voted. And cried and bled and fell and **died** in the streets for that vote.
But every **vote**, every **intention** to put a mark next to a name, well, that fucking **counted** even if the paper record was disappeared.
It counted.

MADISON SQUARE PARK.
FLATIRON DISTRICT.

DELGADO NATION RALLY POINT.

HOLY SHIT...

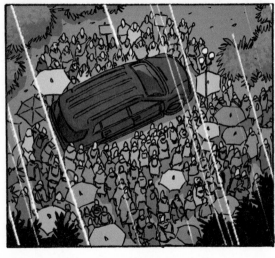

MAKE WAY, PLEASE! MAKE WAY!

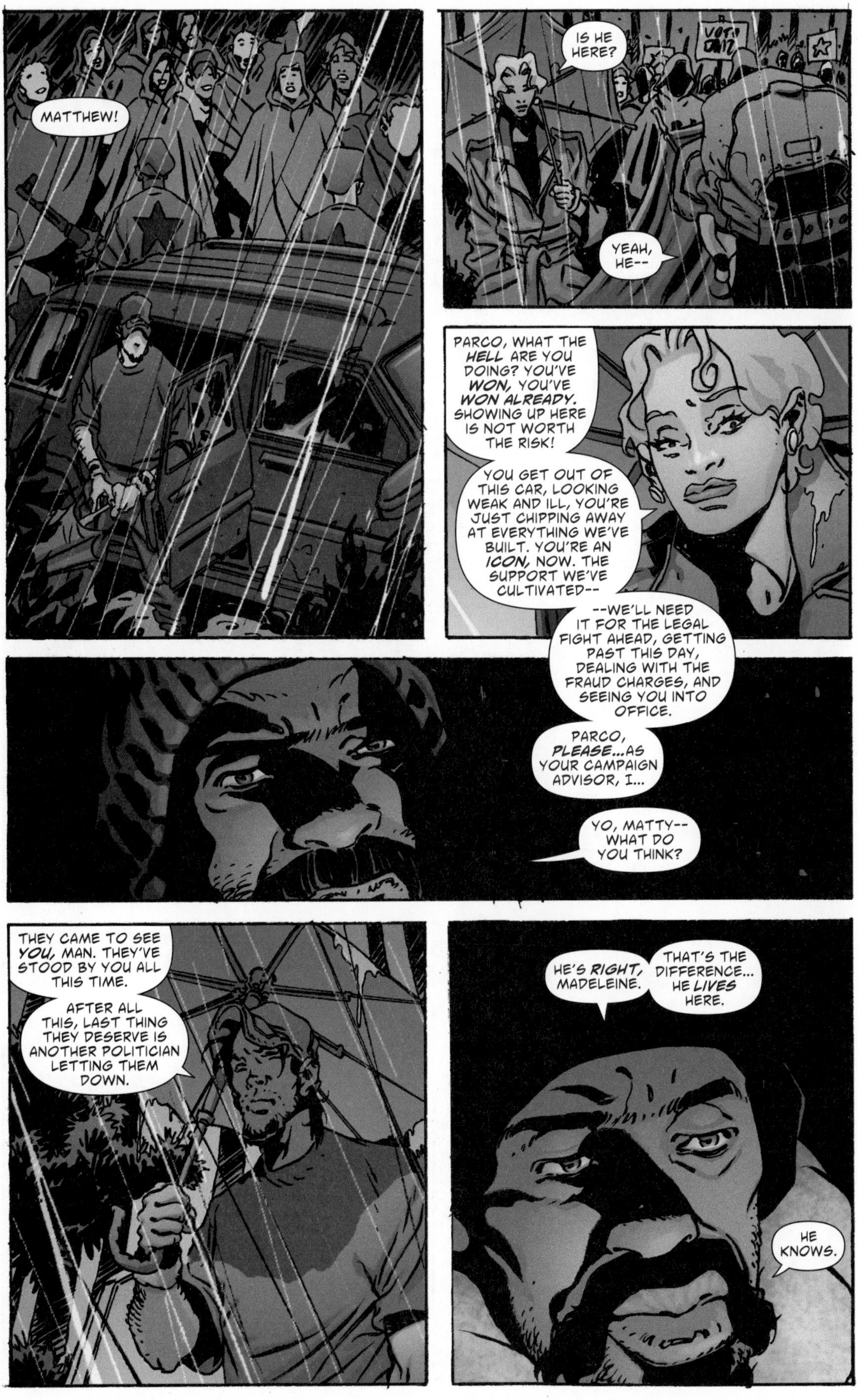
MATTHEW!
IS HE HERE?
YEAH, HE--
PARCO, WHAT THE HELL ARE YOU DOING? YOU'VE WON, YOU'VE WON ALREADY. SHOWING UP HERE IS NOT WORTH THE RISK!
YOU GET OUT OF THIS CAR, LOOKING WEAK AND ILL, YOU'RE JUST CHIPPING AWAY AT EVERYTHING WE'VE BUILT. YOU'RE AN ICON, NOW. THE SUPPORT WE'VE CULTIVATED--
--WE'LL NEED IT FOR THE LEGAL FIGHT AHEAD, GETTING PAST THIS DAY, DEALING WITH THE FRAUD CHARGES, AND SEEING YOU INTO OFFICE.
PARCO, PLEASE...AS YOUR CAMPAIGN ADVISOR, I...
YO, MATTY-- WHAT DO YOU THINK?
THEY CAME TO SEE YOU, MAN. THEY'VE STOOD BY YOU ALL THIS TIME.
AFTER ALL THIS, LAST THING THEY DESERVE IS ANOTHER POLITICIAN LETTING THEM DOWN.
HE'S RIGHT, MADELEINE.
THAT'S THE DIFFERENCE... HE LIVES HERE.
HE KNOWS.

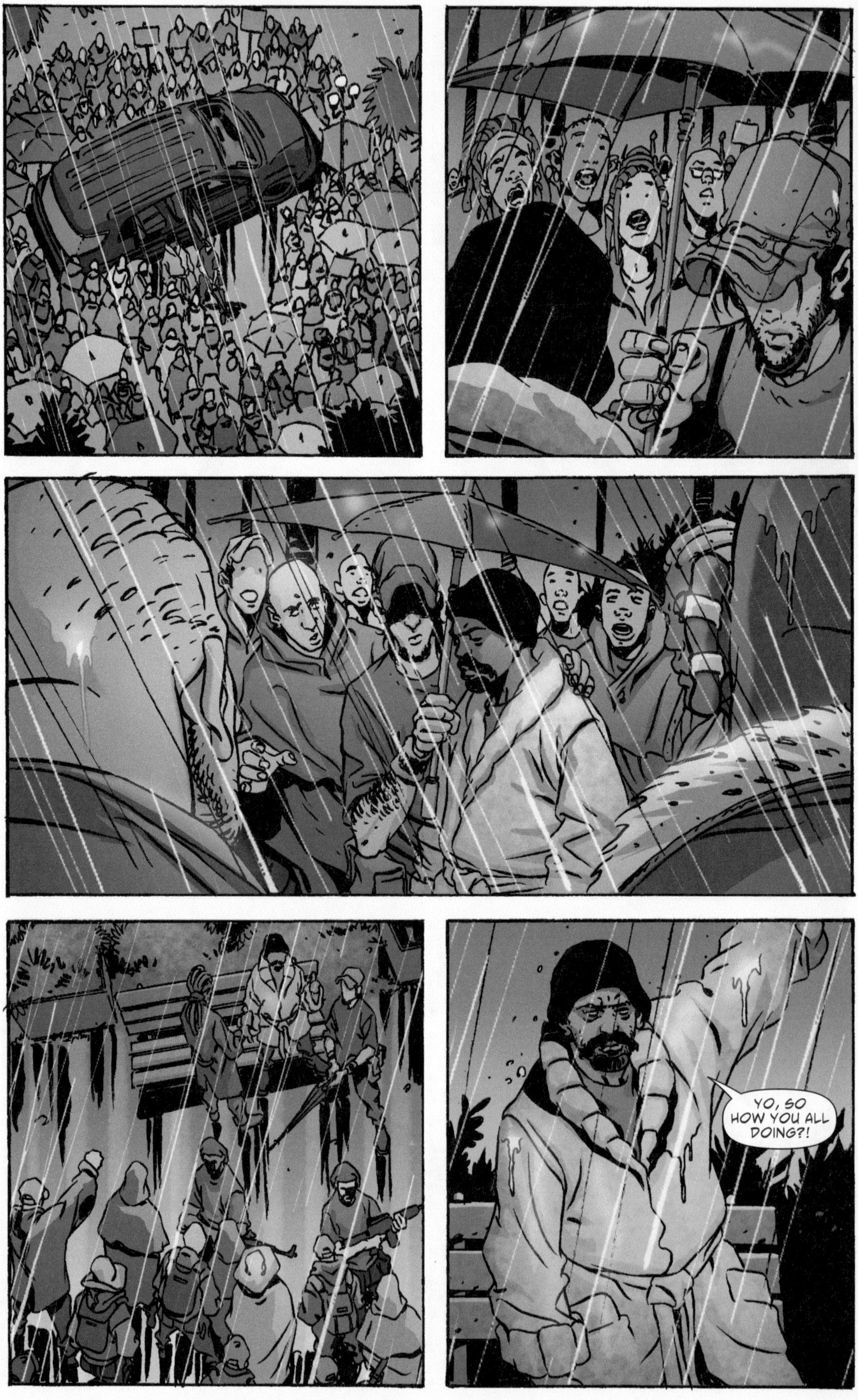
YO, SO
HOW YOU ALL
DOING?!

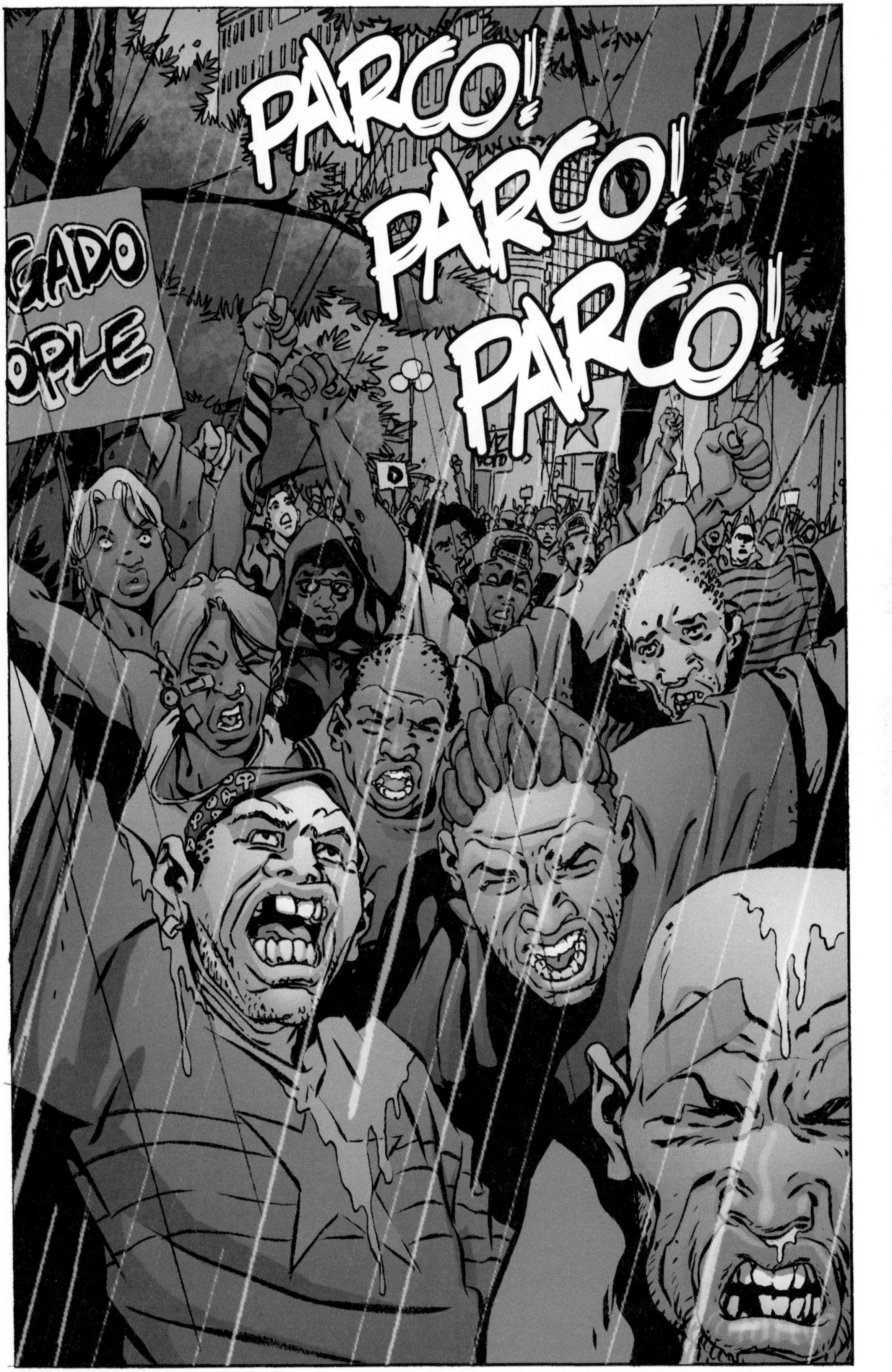
PARCO!
PARCO!
PARCO!

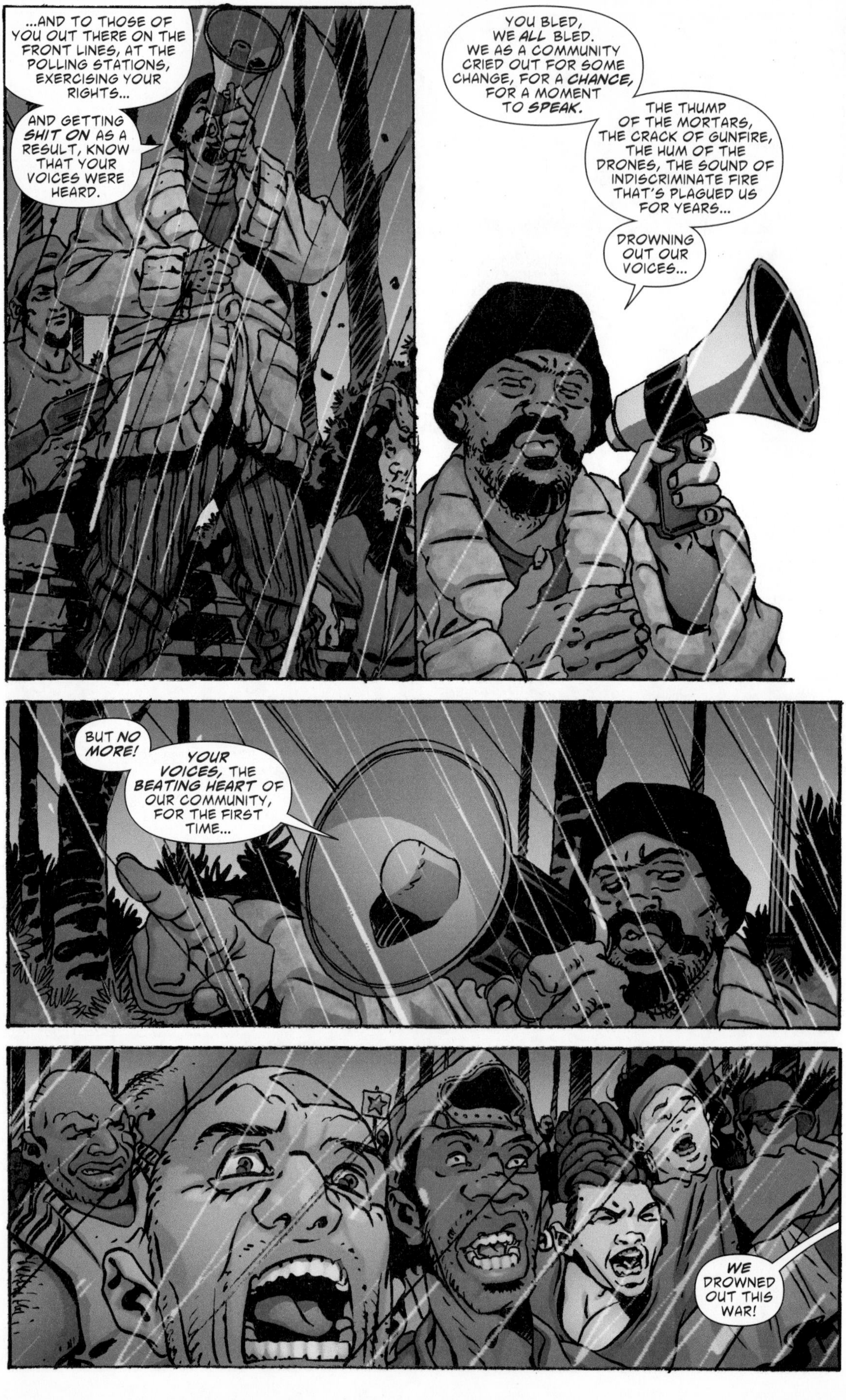
...AND TO THOSE OF YOU OUT THERE ON THE FRONT LINES, AT THE POLLING STATIONS, EXERCISING YOUR RIGHTS...
AND GETTING *SHIT ON* AS A RESULT, KNOW THAT YOUR VOICES WERE HEARD.
YOU BLED, WE *ALL* BLED. WE AS A COMMUNITY CRIED OUT FOR SOME CHANGE, FOR A *CHANCE,* FOR A MOMENT TO *SPEAK.*
THE THUMP OF THE MORTARS, THE CRACK OF GUNFIRE, THE HUM OF THE DRONES, THE SOUND OF INDISCRIMINATE FIRE THAT'S PLAGUED US FOR YEARS...
DROWNING OUT OUR VOICES...
BUT *NO MORE!*
YOUR VOICES, THE *BEATING HEART* OF OUR COMMUNITY, FOR THE FIRST TIME...
WE DROWNED OUT THIS WAR!

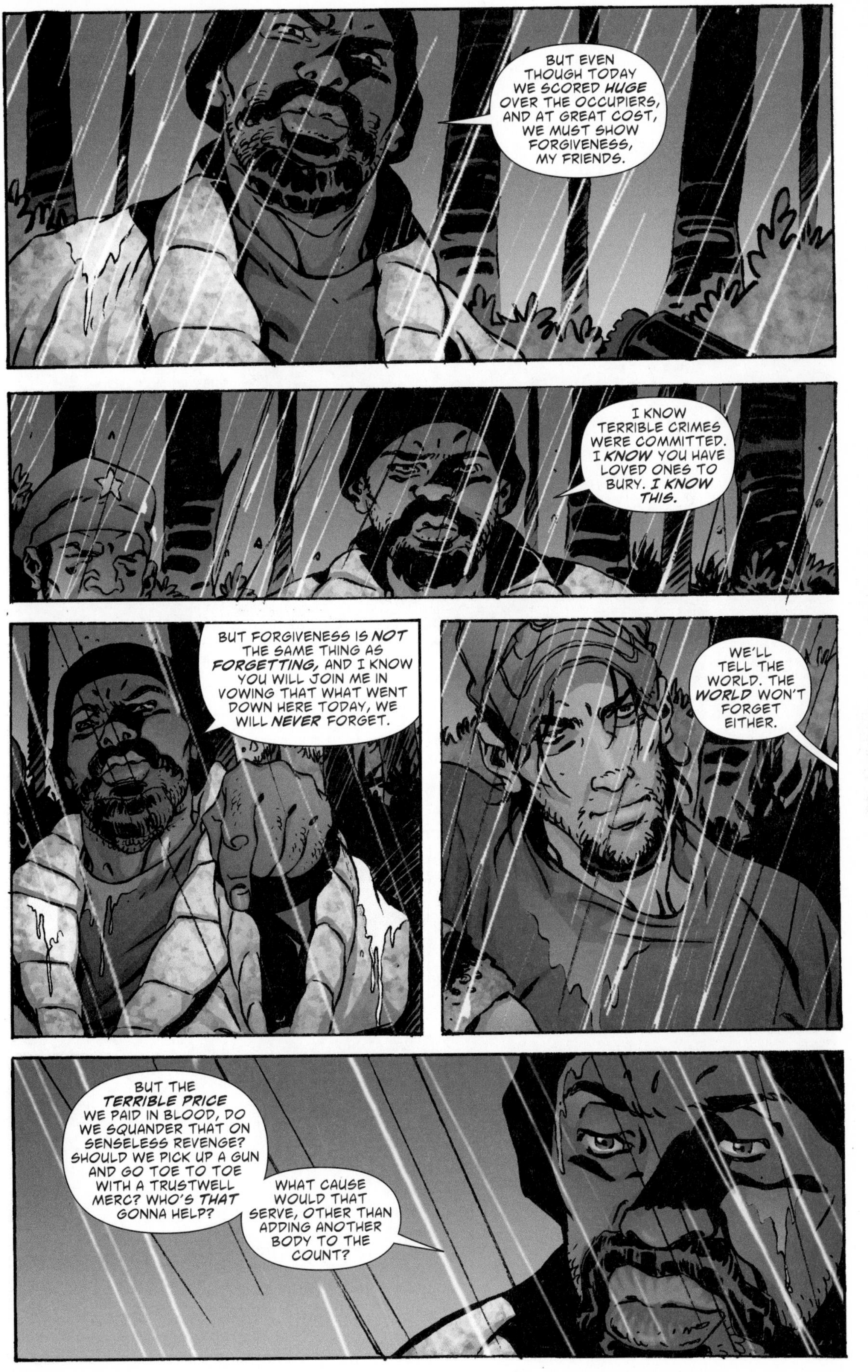
BUT EVEN THOUGH TODAY WE SCORED HUGE OVER THE OCCUPIERS, AND AT GREAT COST, WE MUST SHOW FORGIVENESS, MY FRIENDS.
I KNOW TERRIBLE CRIMES WERE COMMITTED. I KNOW YOU HAVE LOVED ONES TO BURY. I KNOW THIS.
BUT FORGIVENESS IS NOT THE SAME THING AS FORGETTING, AND I KNOW YOU WILL JOIN ME IN VOWING THAT WHAT WENT DOWN HERE TODAY, WE WILL NEVER FORGET.
WE'LL TELL THE WORLD. THE WORLD WON'T FORGET EITHER.
BUT THE TERRIBLE PRICE WE PAID IN BLOOD, DO WE SQUANDER THAT ON SENSELESS REVENGE? SHOULD WE PICK UP A GUN AND GO TOE TO TOE WITH A TRUSTWELL MERC? WHO'S THAT GONNA HELP?
WHAT CAUSE WOULD THAT SERVE, OTHER THAN ADDING ANOTHER BODY TO THE COUNT?

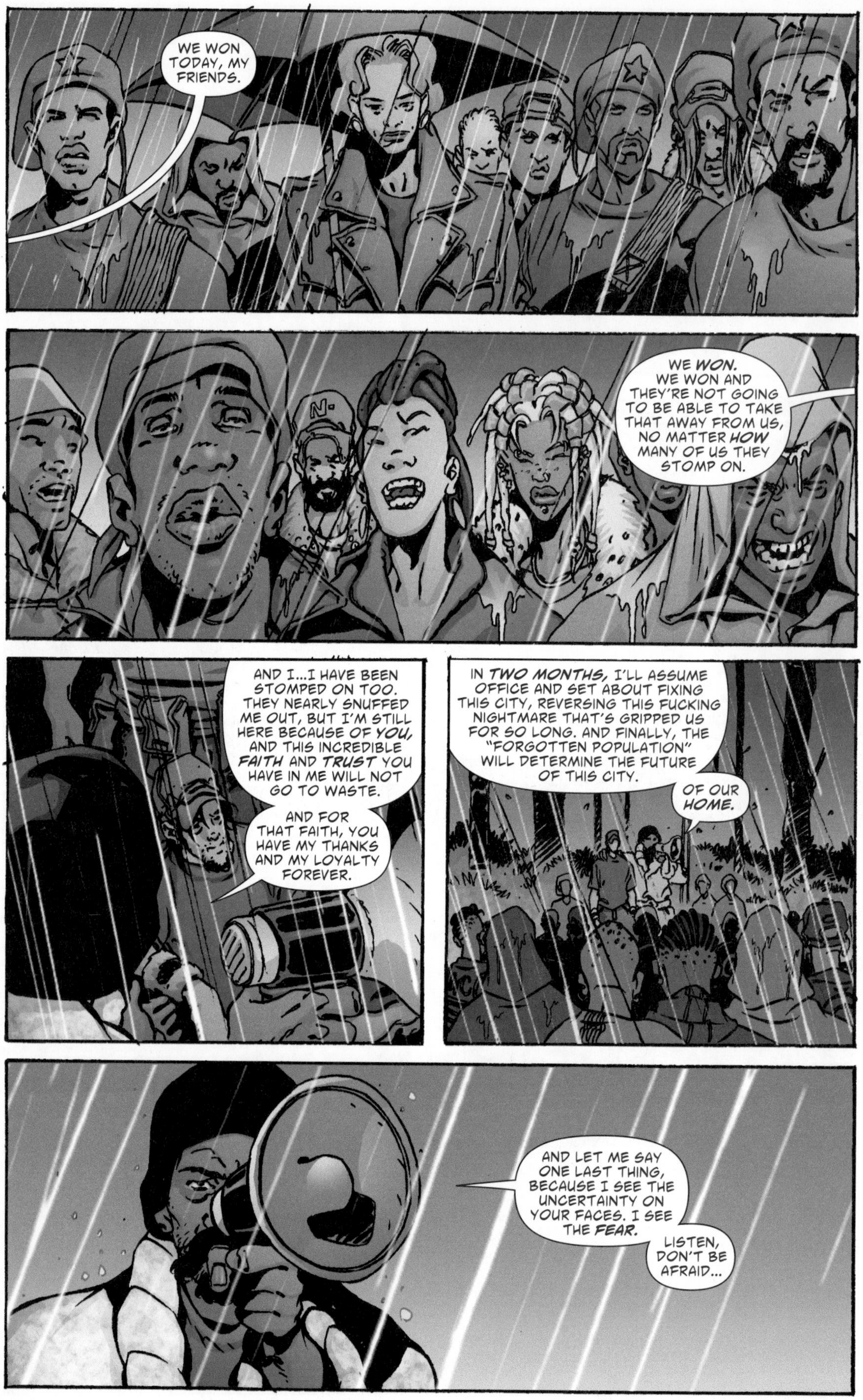
WE WON TODAY, MY FRIENDS.
WE *WON.* WE WON AND THEY'RE NOT GOING TO BE ABLE TO TAKE THAT AWAY FROM US, NO MATTER *HOW* MANY OF US THEY STOMP ON.
AND I...I HAVE BEEN STOMPED ON TOO. THEY NEARLY SNUFFED ME OUT, BUT I'M STILL HERE BECAUSE OF *YOU,* AND THIS INCREDIBLE *FAITH* AND *TRUST* YOU HAVE IN ME WILL NOT GO TO WASTE.
AND FOR THAT FAITH, YOU HAVE MY THANKS AND MY LOYALTY FOREVER.
IN *TWO MONTHS,* I'LL ASSUME OFFICE AND SET ABOUT FIXING THIS CITY, REVERSING THIS FUCKING NIGHTMARE THAT'S GRIPPED US FOR SO LONG. AND FINALLY, THE "FORGOTTEN POPULATION" WILL DETERMINE THE FUTURE OF THIS CITY.
OF OUR *HOME.*
AND LET ME SAY ONE LAST THING, BECAUSE I SEE THE UNCERTAINTY ON YOUR FACES. I SEE THE *FEAR.*
LISTEN, DON'T BE AFRAID...

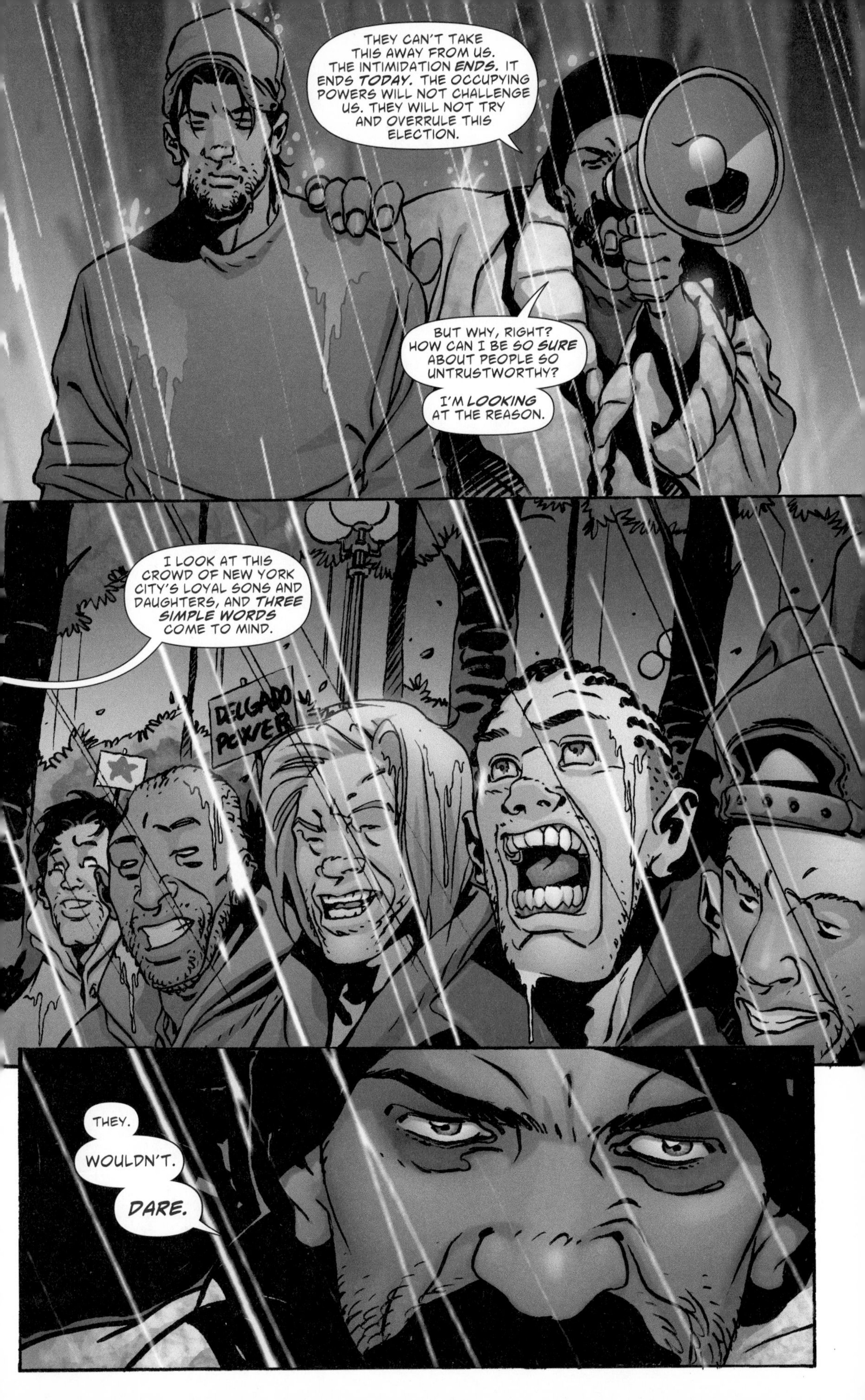
THEY CAN'T TAKE THIS AWAY FROM US. THE INTIMIDATION ENDS. IT ENDS TODAY. THE OCCUPYING POWERS WILL NOT CHALLENGE US. THEY WILL NOT TRY AND OVERRULE THIS ELECTION.
BUT WHY, RIGHT? HOW CAN I BE SO SURE ABOUT PEOPLE SO UNTRUSTWORTHY?
I'M LOOKING AT THE REASON.
I LOOK AT THIS CROWD OF NEW YORK CITY'S LOYAL SONS AND DAUGHTERS, AND THREE SIMPLE WORDS COME TO MIND.
DELGADO POWER
THEY.
WOULDN'T.
DARE.

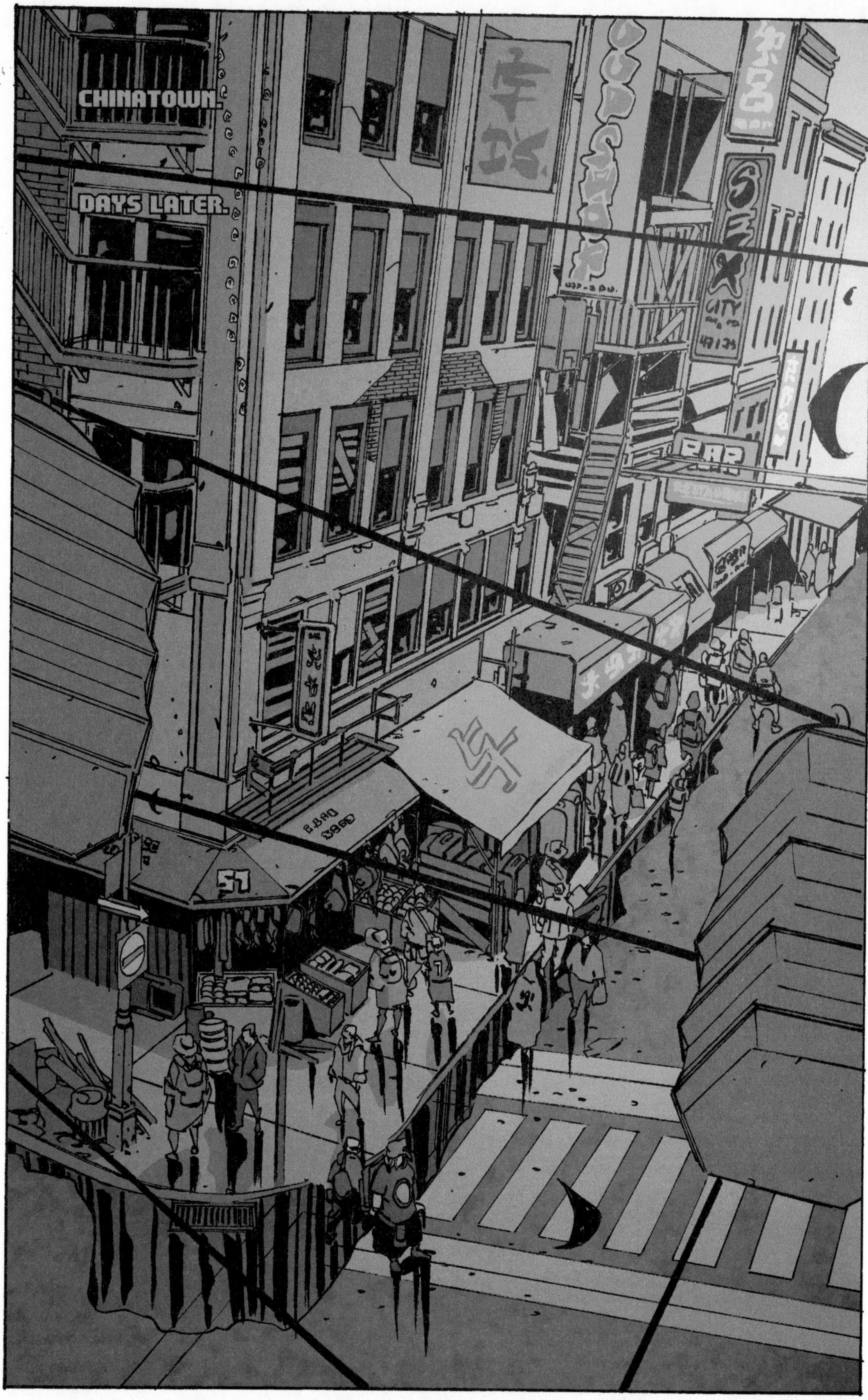
CHINATOWN.
DAYS LATER.

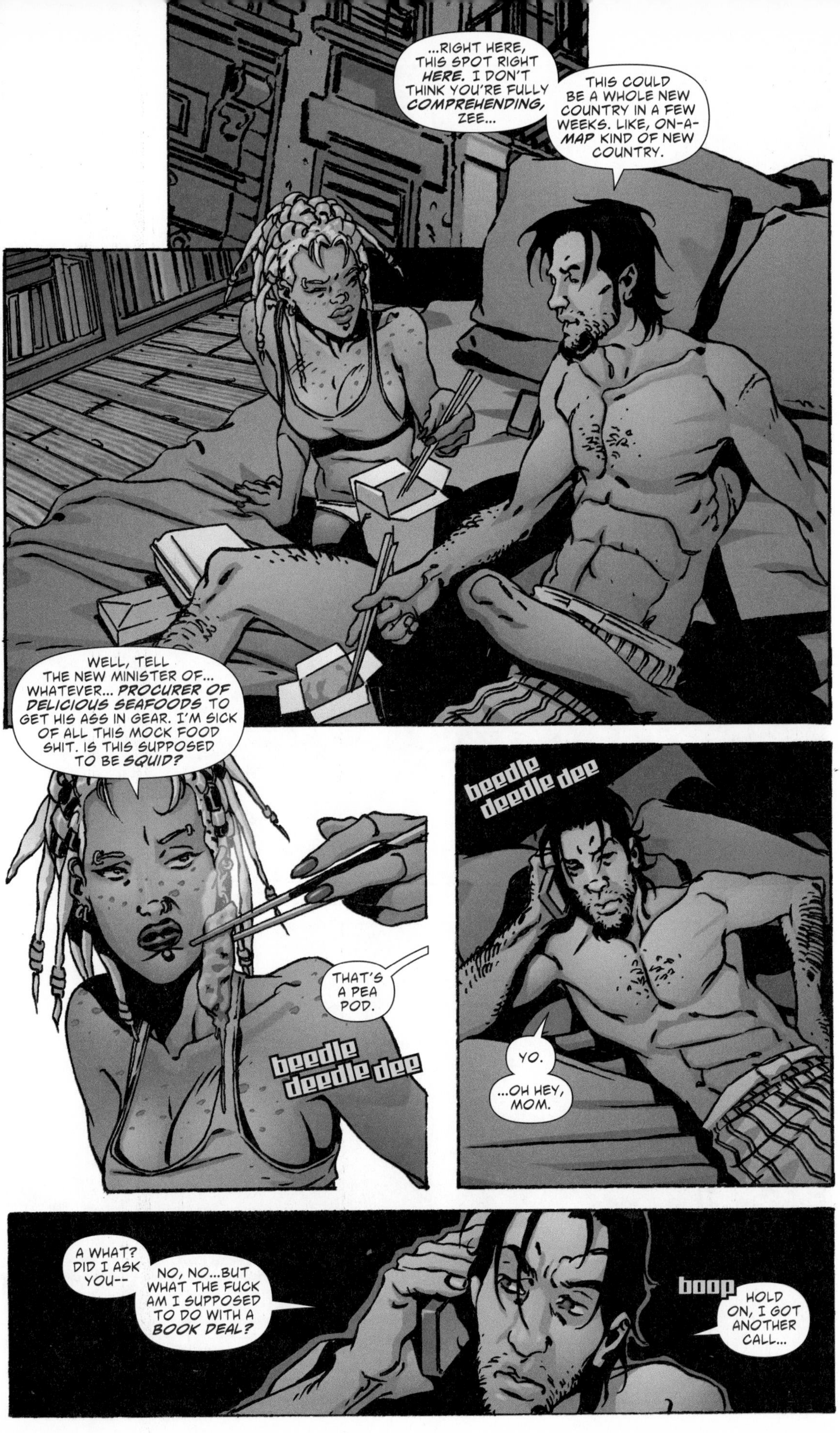
...RIGHT HERE, THIS SPOT RIGHT HERE. I DON'T THINK YOU'RE FULLY COMPREHENDING, ZEE...
THIS COULD BE A WHOLE NEW COUNTRY IN A FEW WEEKS. LIKE, ON-A-MAP KIND OF NEW COUNTRY.
WELL, TELL THE NEW MINISTER OF... WHATEVER... PROCURER OF DELICIOUS SEAFOODS TO GET HIS ASS IN GEAR. I'M SICK OF ALL THIS MOCK FOOD SHIT. IS THIS SUPPOSED TO BE SQUID?
THAT'S A PEA POD.
beedle deedle dee
beedle deedle dee
YO.
...OH HEY, MOM.
A WHAT? DID I ASK YOU--
NO, NO...BUT WHAT THE FUCK AM I SUPPOSED TO DO WITH A BOOK DEAL?
boop
HOLD ON, I GOT ANOTHER CALL...

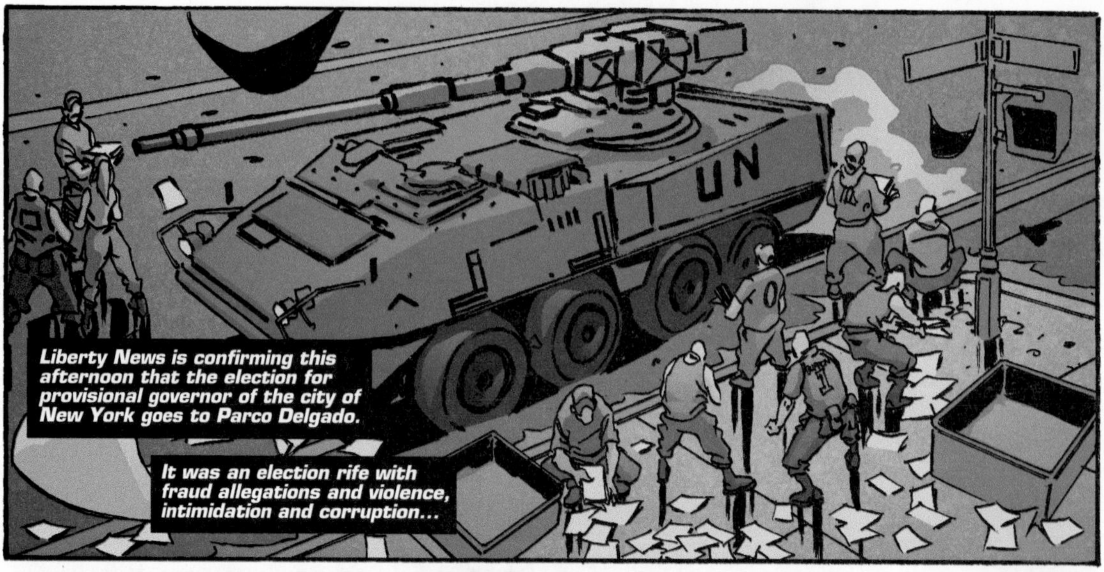
UN
Liberty News is confirming this afternoon that the election for provisional governor of the city of New York goes to Parco Delgado.
It was an election rife with fraud allegations and violence, intimidation and corruption...

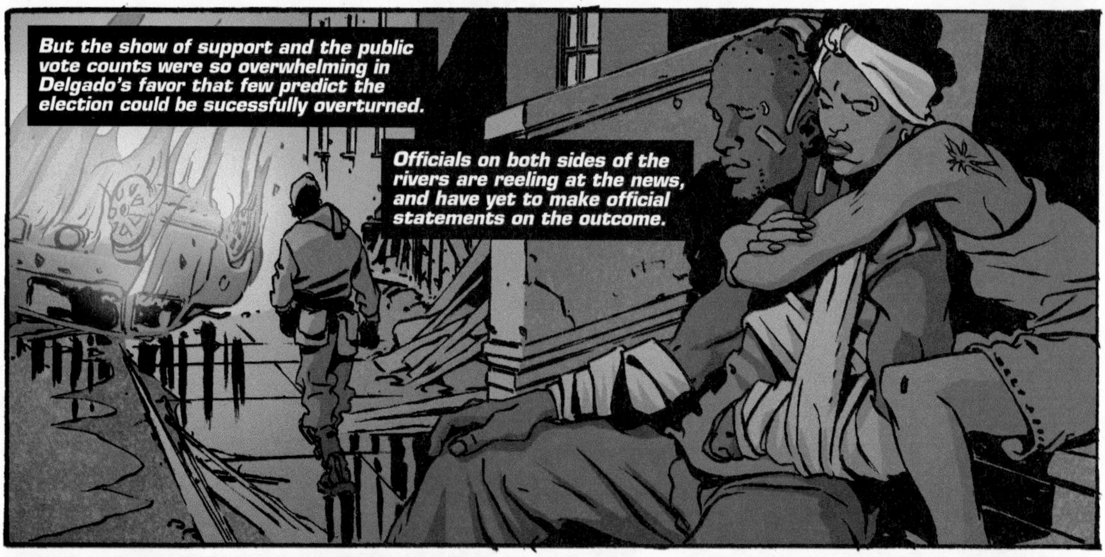
But the show of support and the public vote counts were so overwhelming in Delgado's favor that few predict the election could be sucessfully overturned.
Officials on both sides of the rivers are reeling at the news, and have yet to make official statements on the outcome.

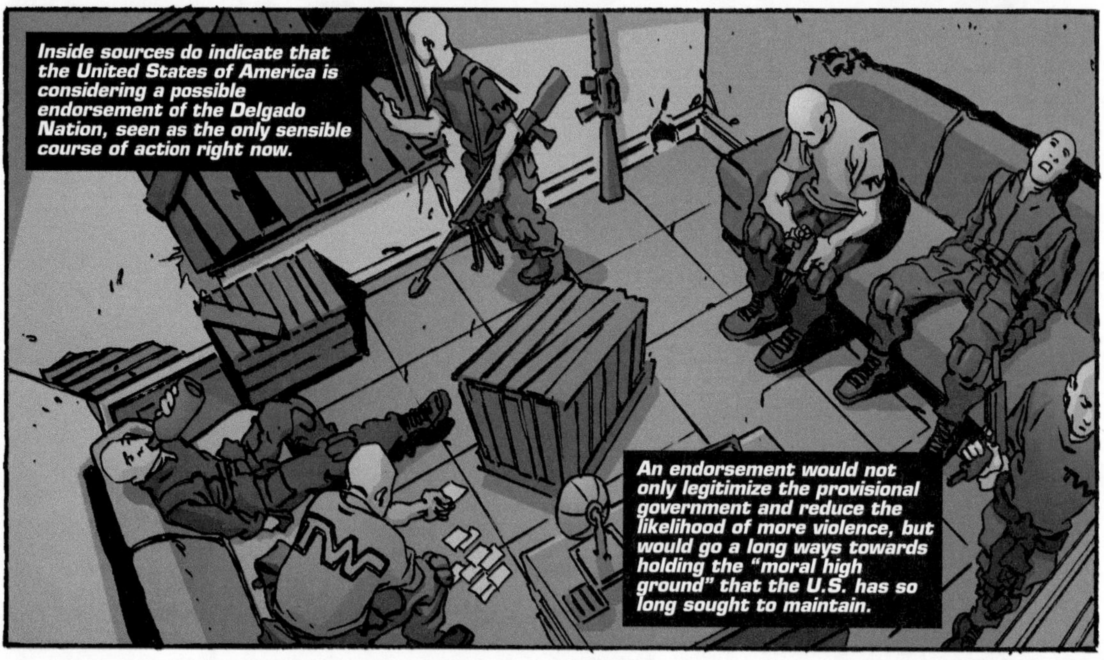
Inside sources do indicate that the United States of America is considering a possible endorsement of the Delgado Nation, seen as the only sensible course of action right now.
An endorsement would not only legitimize the provisional government and reduce the likelihood of more violence, but would go a long ways towards holding the "moral high ground" that the U.S. has so long sought to maintain.

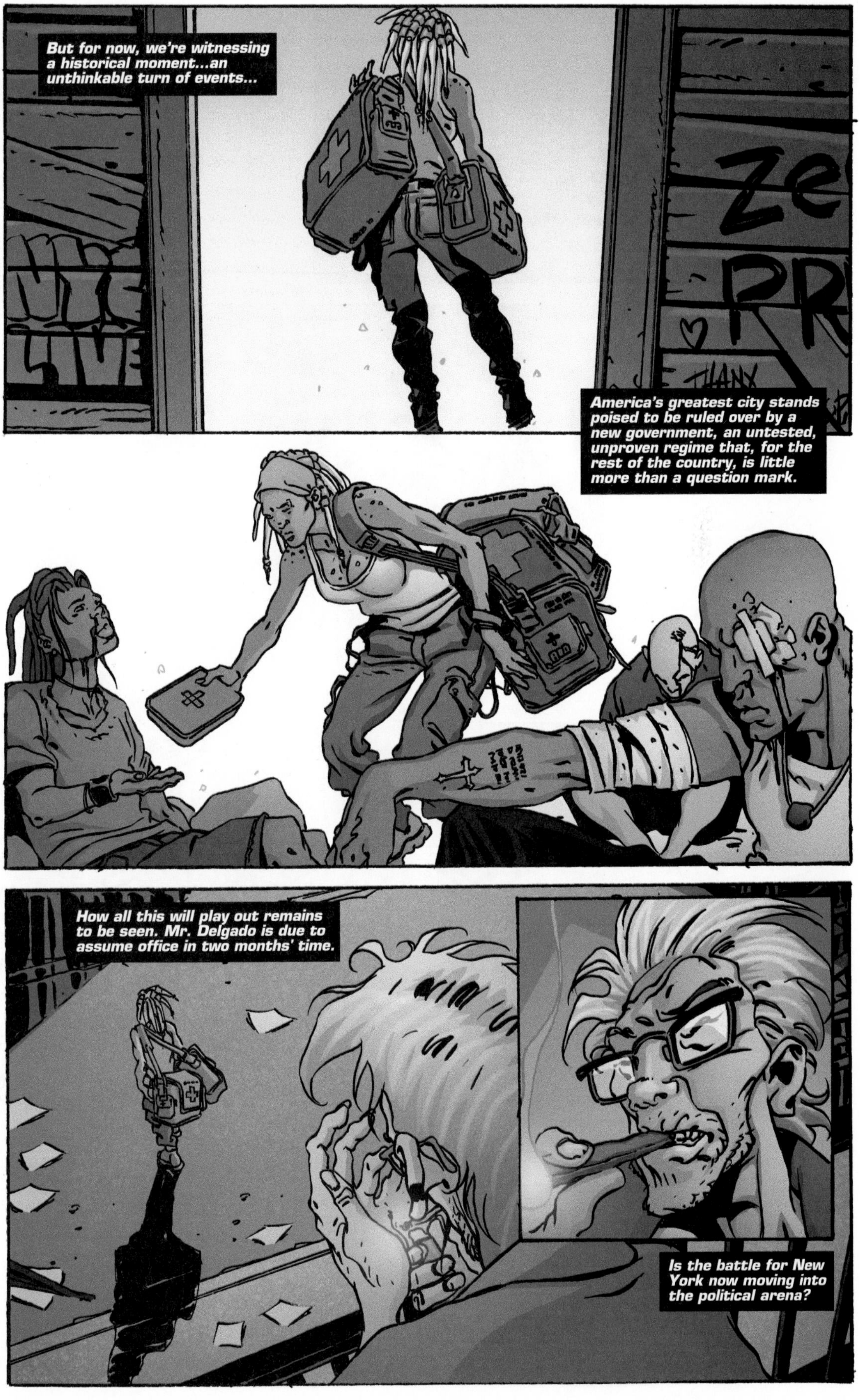

But for now, we're witnessing a historical moment...an unthinkable turn of events...
LIVE
ZE
PR
THANX
America's greatest city stands poised to be ruled over by a new government, an untested, unproven regime that, for the rest of the country, is little more than a question mark.
How all this will play out remains to be seen. Mr. Delgado is due to assume office in two months' time.
Is the battle for New York now moving into the political arena?

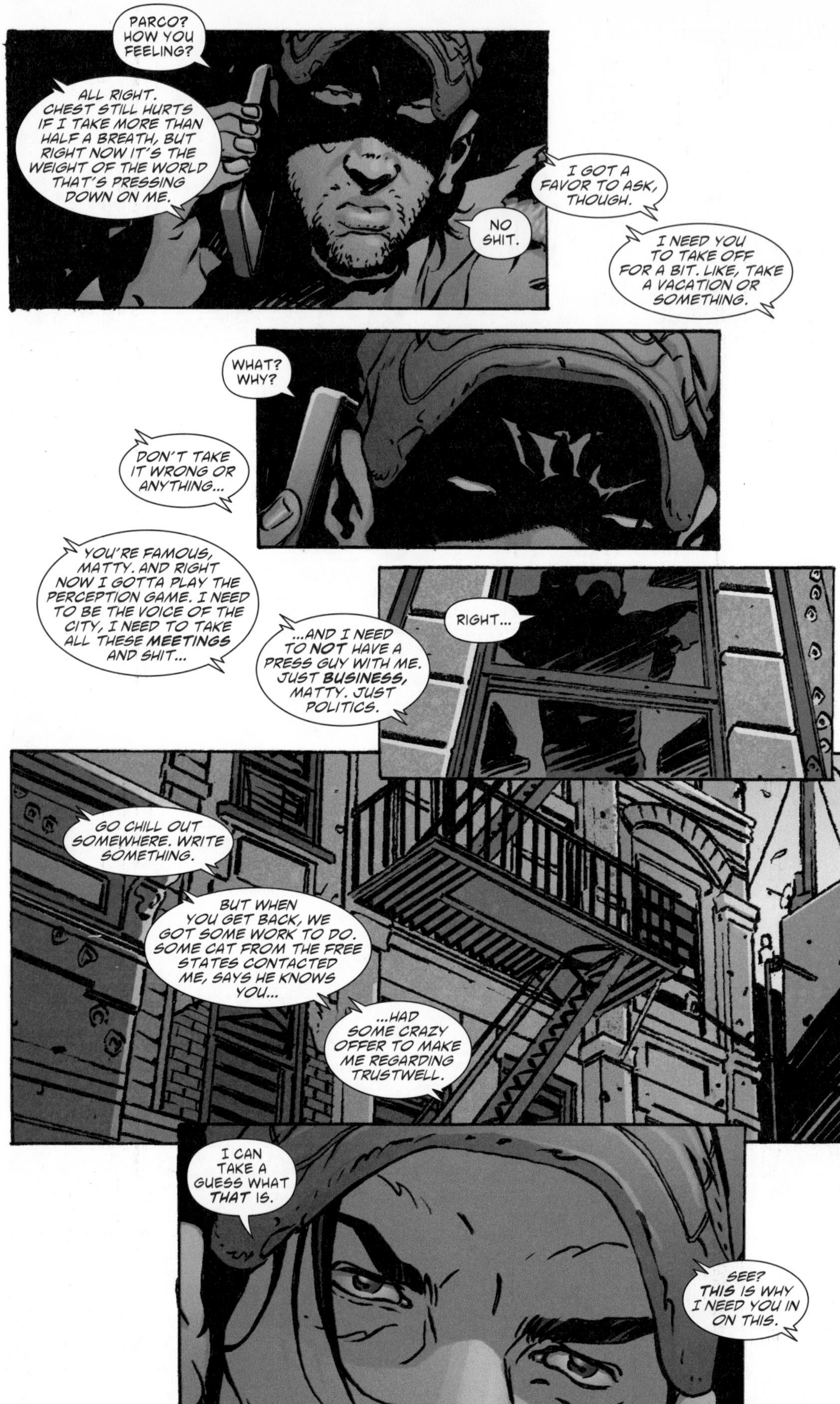
PARCO? HOW YOU FEELING?
ALL RIGHT. CHEST STILL HURTS IF I TAKE MORE THAN HALF A BREATH, BUT RIGHT NOW IT'S THE WEIGHT OF THE WORLD THAT'S PRESSING DOWN ON ME.
NO SHIT.
I GOT A FAVOR TO ASK, THOUGH.
I NEED YOU TO TAKE OFF FOR A BIT. LIKE, TAKE A VACATION OR SOMETHING.
WHAT? WHY?
DON'T TAKE IT WRONG OR ANYTHING...
YOU'RE FAMOUS, MATTY. AND RIGHT NOW I GOTTA PLAY THE PERCEPTION GAME. I NEED TO BE THE VOICE OF THE CITY, I NEED TO TAKE ALL THESE **MEETINGS** AND SHIT...
...AND I NEED TO **NOT** HAVE A PRESS GUY WITH ME. JUST **BUSINESS,** MATTY. JUST POLITICS.
RIGHT...
GO CHILL OUT SOMEWHERE. WRITE SOMETHING.
BUT WHEN YOU GET BACK, WE GOT SOME WORK TO DO. SOME CAT FROM THE FREE STATES CONTACTED ME, SAYS HE KNOWS YOU...
...HAD SOME CRAZY OFFER TO MAKE ME REGARDING TRUSTWELL.
I CAN TAKE A GUESS WHAT **THAT** IS.
SEE? **THIS** IS WHY I NEED YOU IN ON THIS.

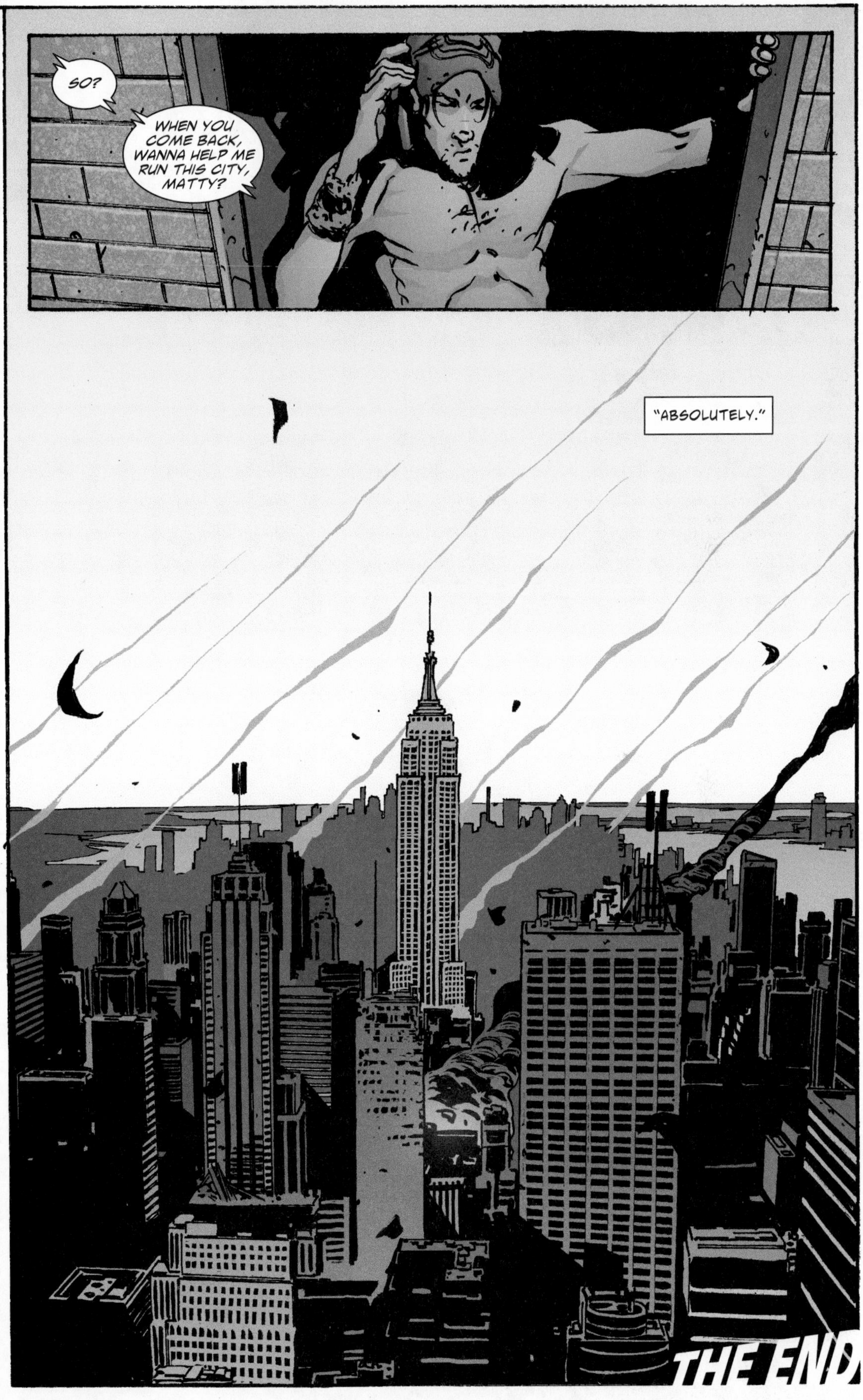
SO?
WHEN YOU COME BACK, WANNA HELP ME RUN THIS CITY, MATTY?
"ABSOLUTELY."
THE END

DMZ

THE ISLAND

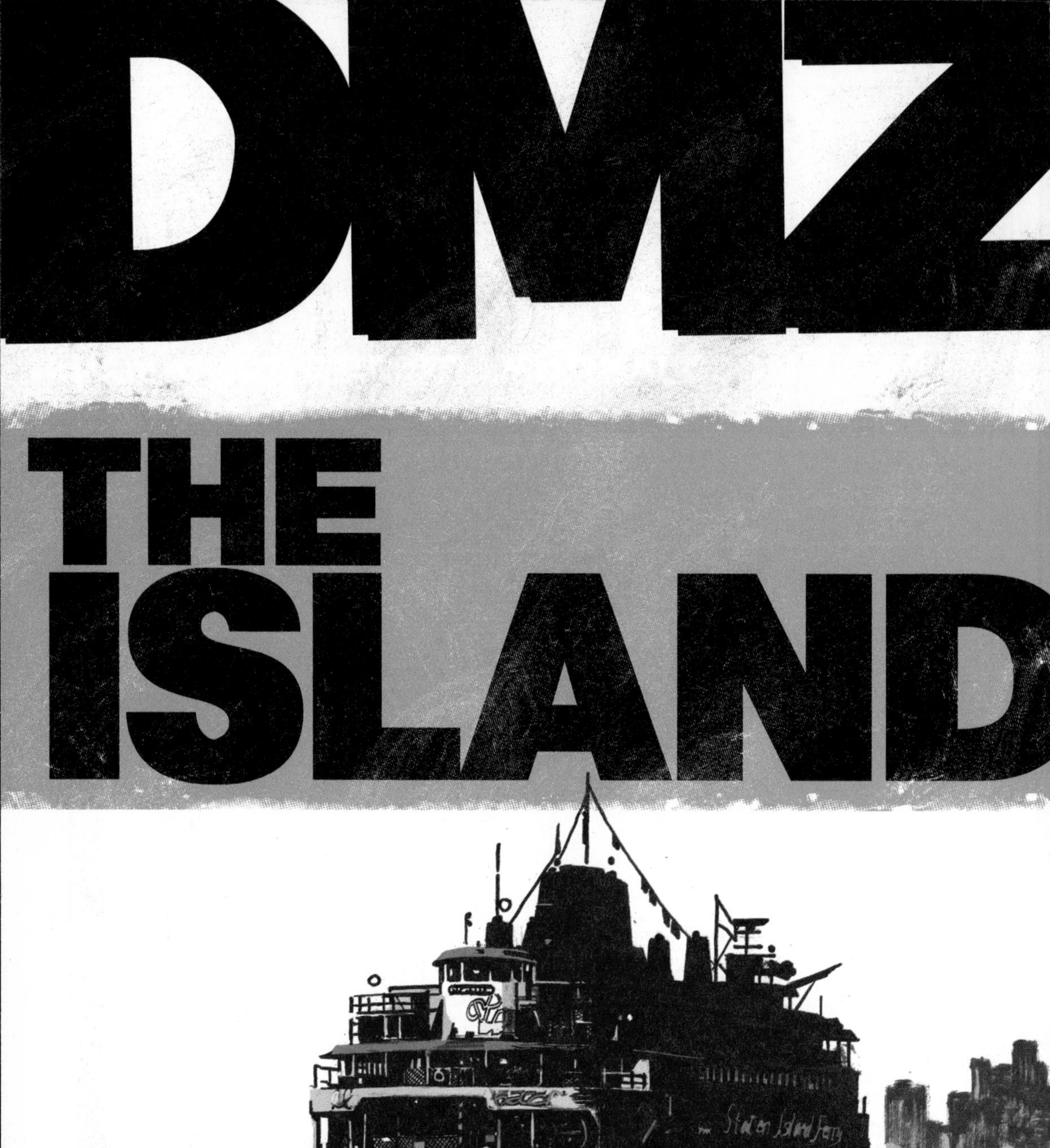
Staten Island Ferry

1 OF 2

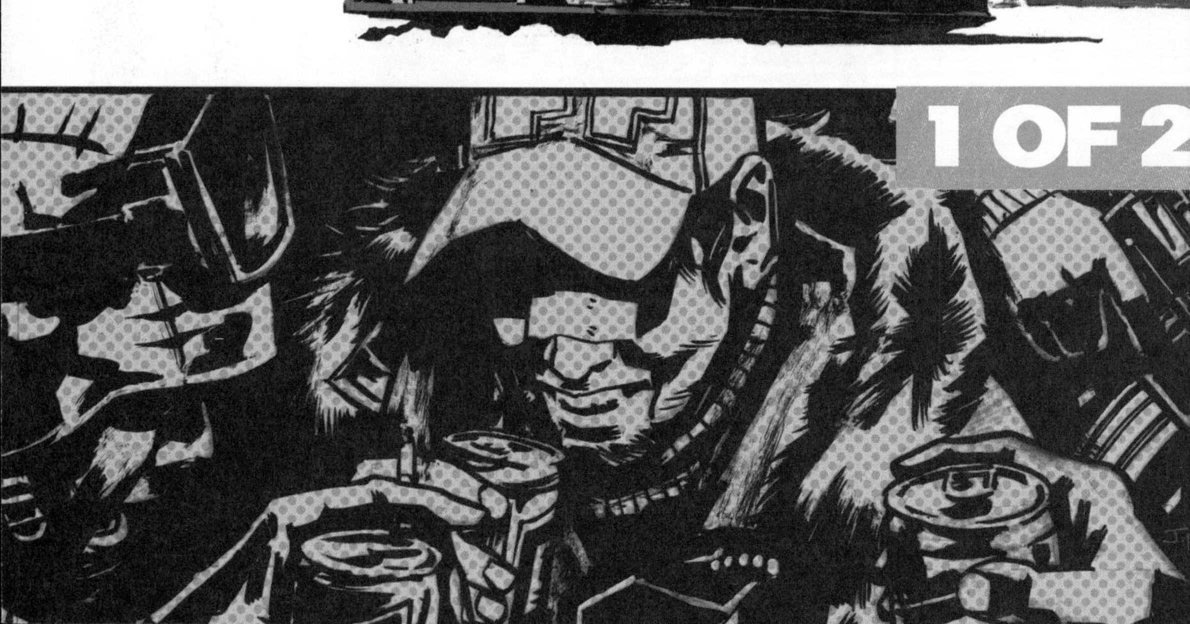

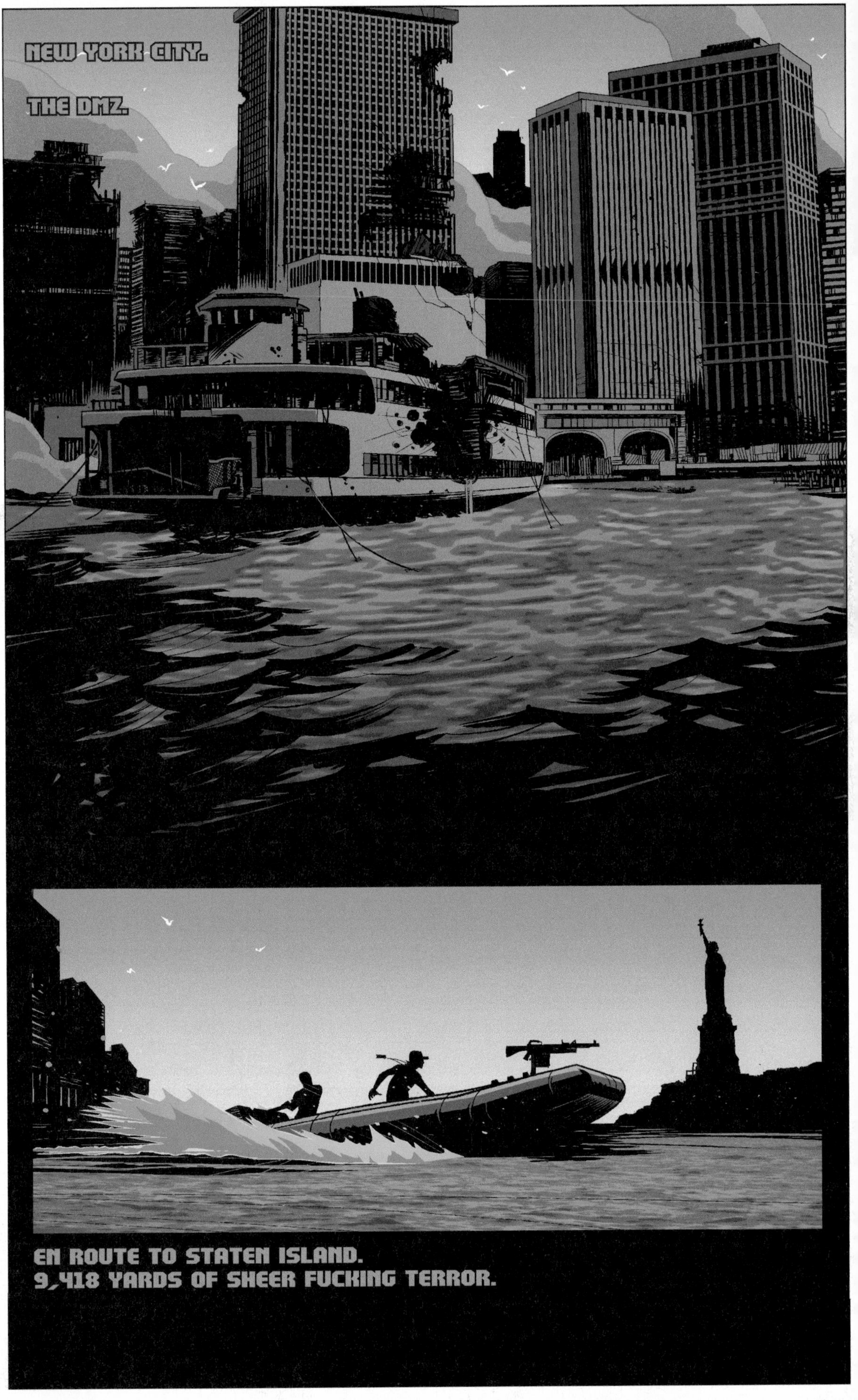
NEW YORK CITY.
THE DMZ.
EN ROUTE TO STATEN ISLAND.
9,418 YARDS OF SHEER FUCKING TERROR.

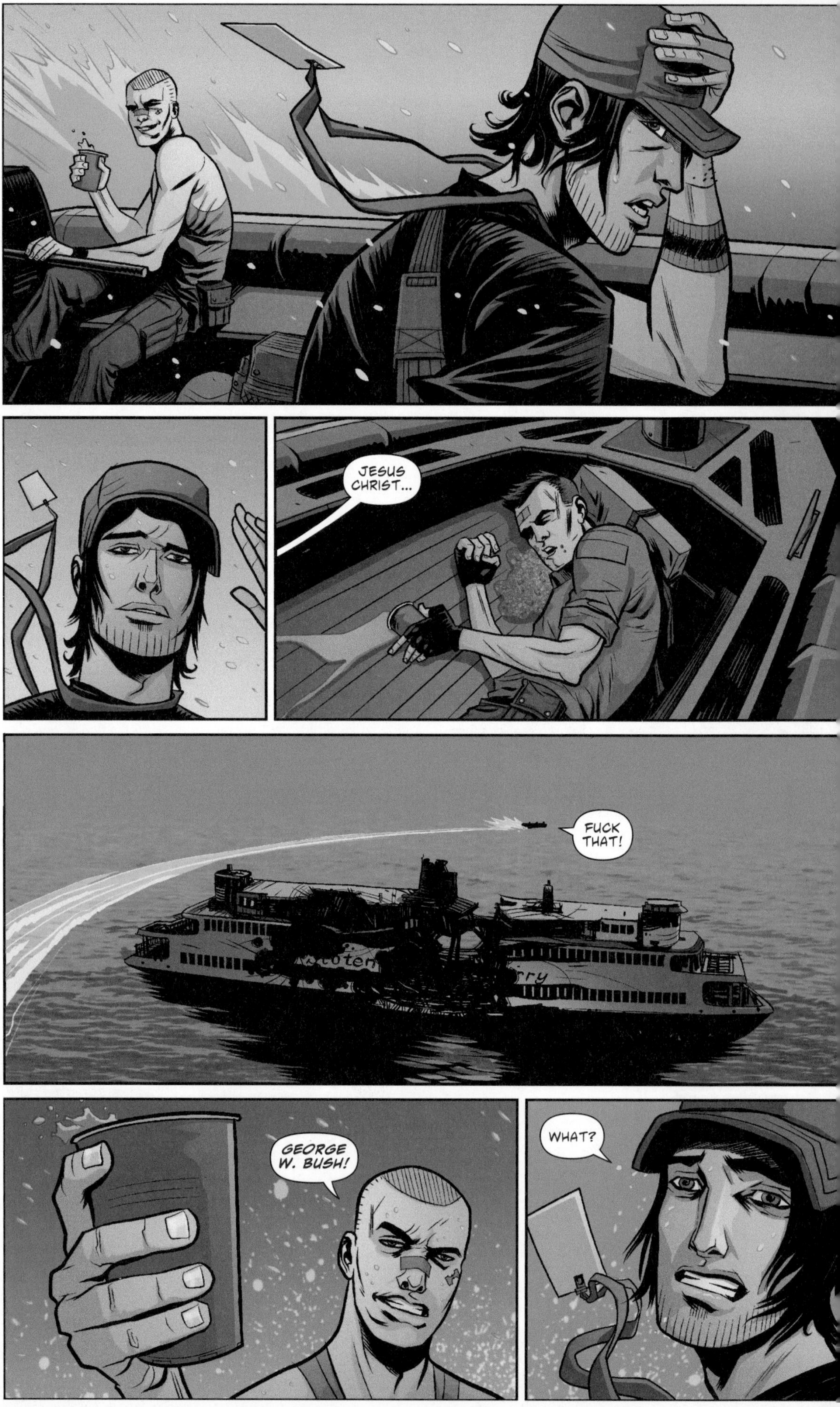
JESUS CHRIST...
FUCK THAT!
GEORGE W. BUSH!
WHAT?

THE ISLAND

PART 1 OF 2

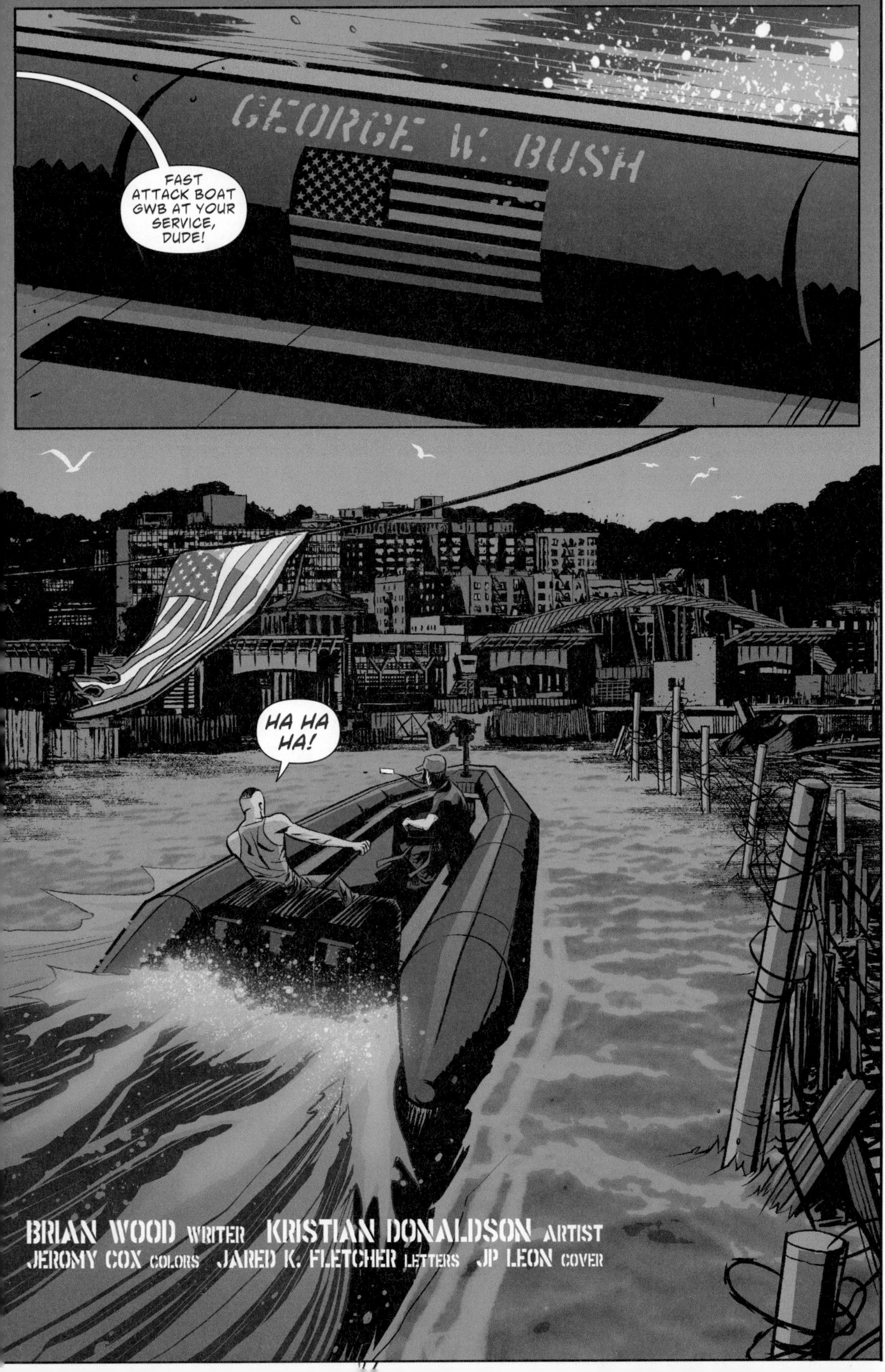
GEORGE W. BUSH
FAST ATTACK BOAT GWB AT YOUR SERVICE, DUDE!
HA HA HA!
BRIAN WOOD WRITER KRISTIAN DONALDSON ARTIST
JEROMY COX COLORS JARED K. FLETCHER LETTERS JP LEON COVER

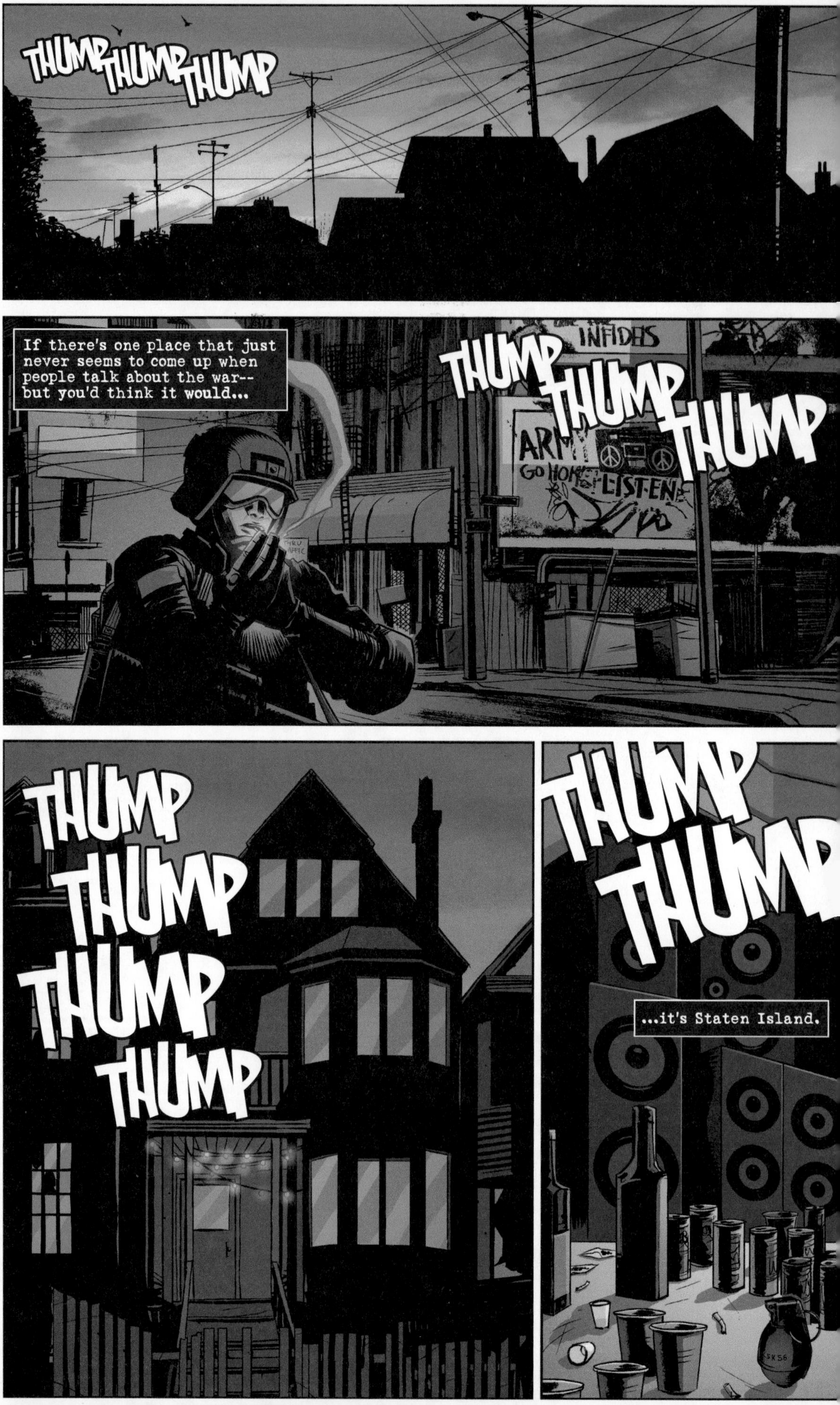
THUMP THUMP THUMP
If there's one place that just never seems to come up when people talk about the war--but you'd think it would...
INFIDELS
THUMP THUMP THUMP
THUMP THUMP THUMP THUMP
THUMP THUMP
...it's Staten Island.

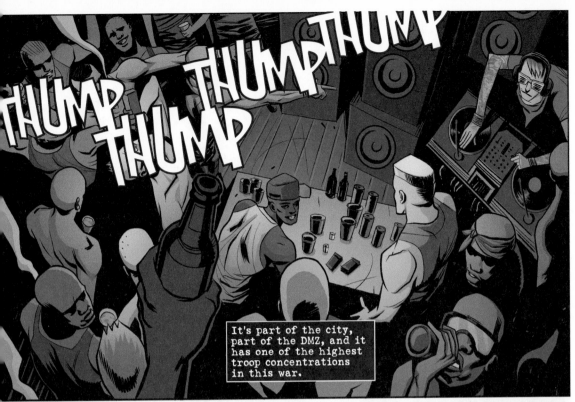

THUMP THUMP THUMP THUMP
It's part of the city, part of the DMZ, and it has one of the highest troop concentrations in this war.
All United States of America Army, straight grunts.
What happens here? Why so many guns, but so little noise?
What's the word on the ground?

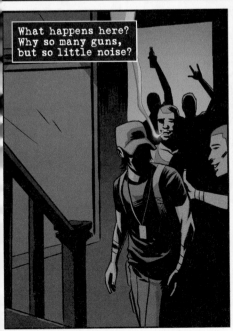

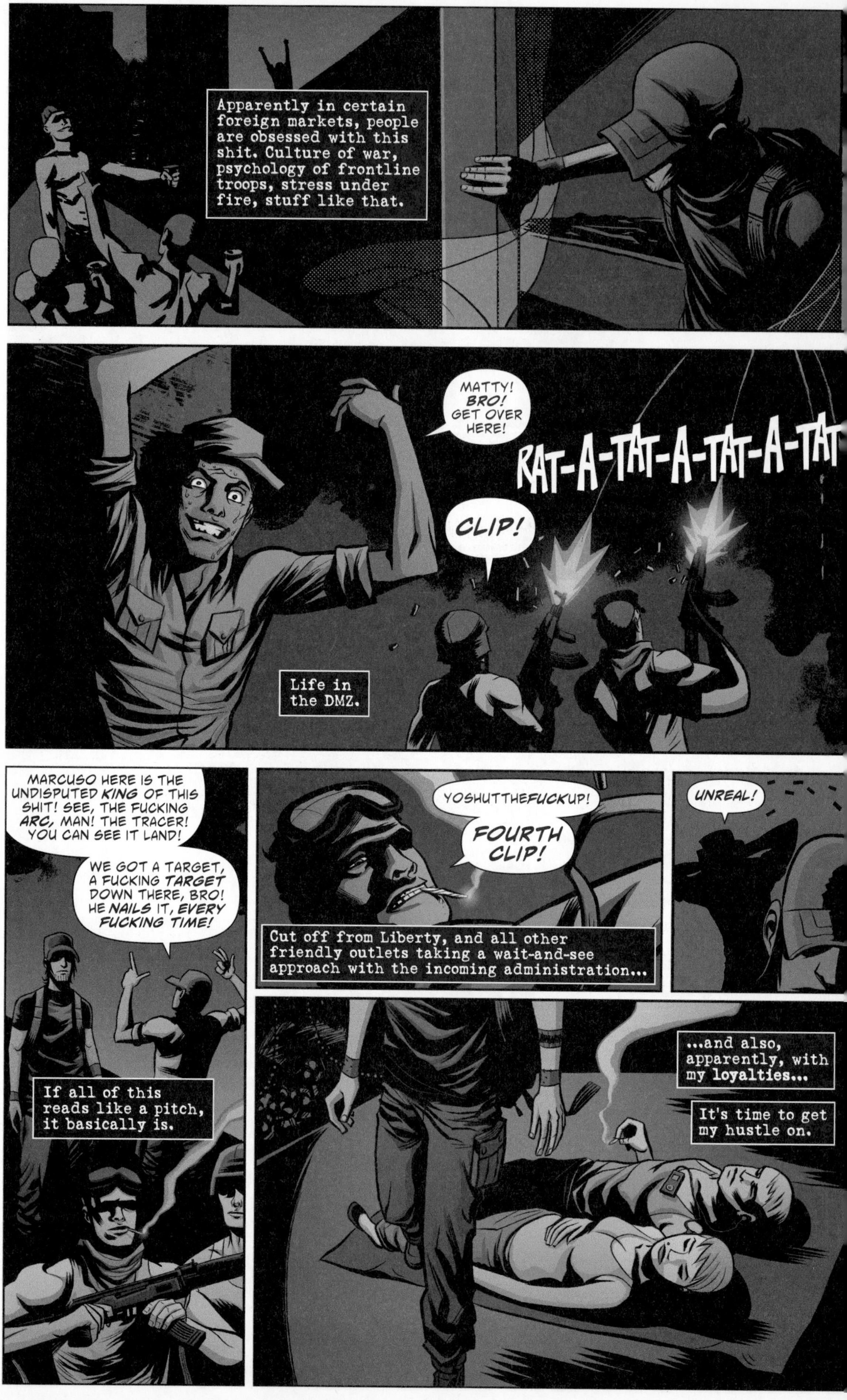

Apparently in certain foreign markets, people are obsessed with this shit. Culture of war, psychology of frontline troops, stress under fire, stuff like that.
MATTY! BRO! GET OVER HERE!
RAT-A-TAT-A-TAT-A-TAT
CLIP!
Life in the DMZ.
MARCUSO HERE IS THE UNDISPUTED KING OF THIS SHIT! SEE, THE FUCKING ARC, MAN! THE TRACER! YOU CAN SEE IT LAND!
WE GOT A TARGET, A FUCKING TARGET DOWN THERE, BRO! HE NAILS IT, EVERY FUCKING TIME!
If all of this reads like a pitch, it basically is.
YOSHUTTHEFUCKUP!
FOURTH CLIP!
Cut off from Liberty, and all other friendly outlets taking a wait-and-see approach with the incoming administration...
UNREAL!
...and also, apparently, with my loyalties...
It's time to get my hustle on.

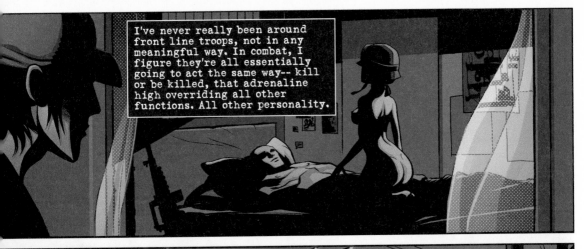

I've never really been around front line troops, not in any meaningful way. In combat, I figure they're all essentially going to act the same way-- kill or be killed, that adrenaline high overriding all other functions. All other personality.

But troops stationed somewhere, on base, standing by, keeping watch... what's that all about? What's their P.O.V.? What's it like to get this close to Manhattan and all you can do is stare at it from across the harbor?

Beyond the rah-rah shit, beyond the shit talk, beyond the sound bites...

These invisible troops in the forgotten borough.

What's their **deal**?

CLIP!

THERE'S GOTTA BE SOMETHING HERE...

ARE YOU MATTY ROTH?

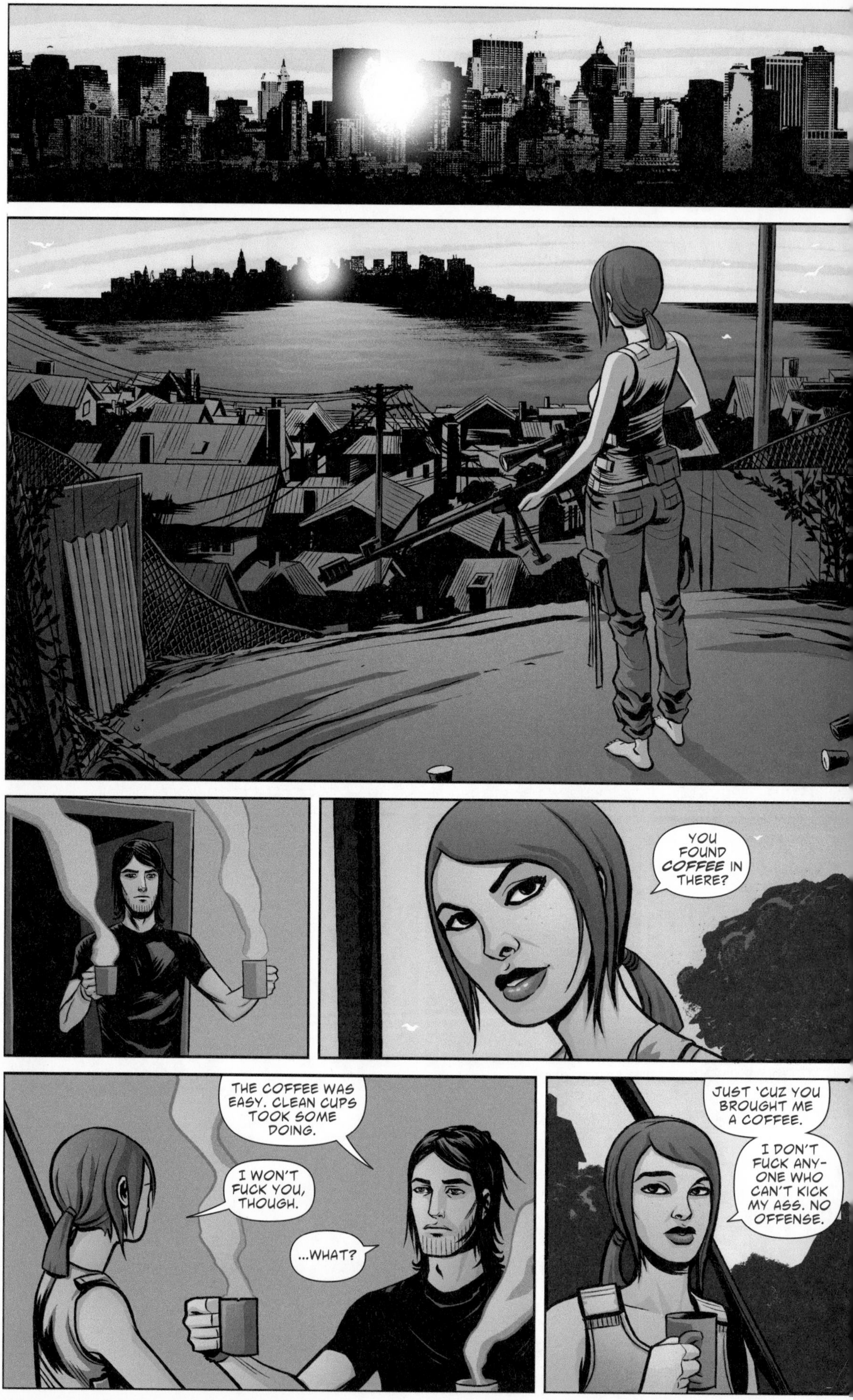
YOU FOUND COFFEE IN THERE?
THE COFFEE WAS EASY. CLEAN CUPS TOOK SOME DOING.
I WON'T FUCK YOU, THOUGH.
...WHAT?
JUST 'CUZ YOU BROUGHT ME A COFFEE.
I DON'T FUCK ANY-ONE WHO CAN'T KICK MY ASS. NO OFFENSE.

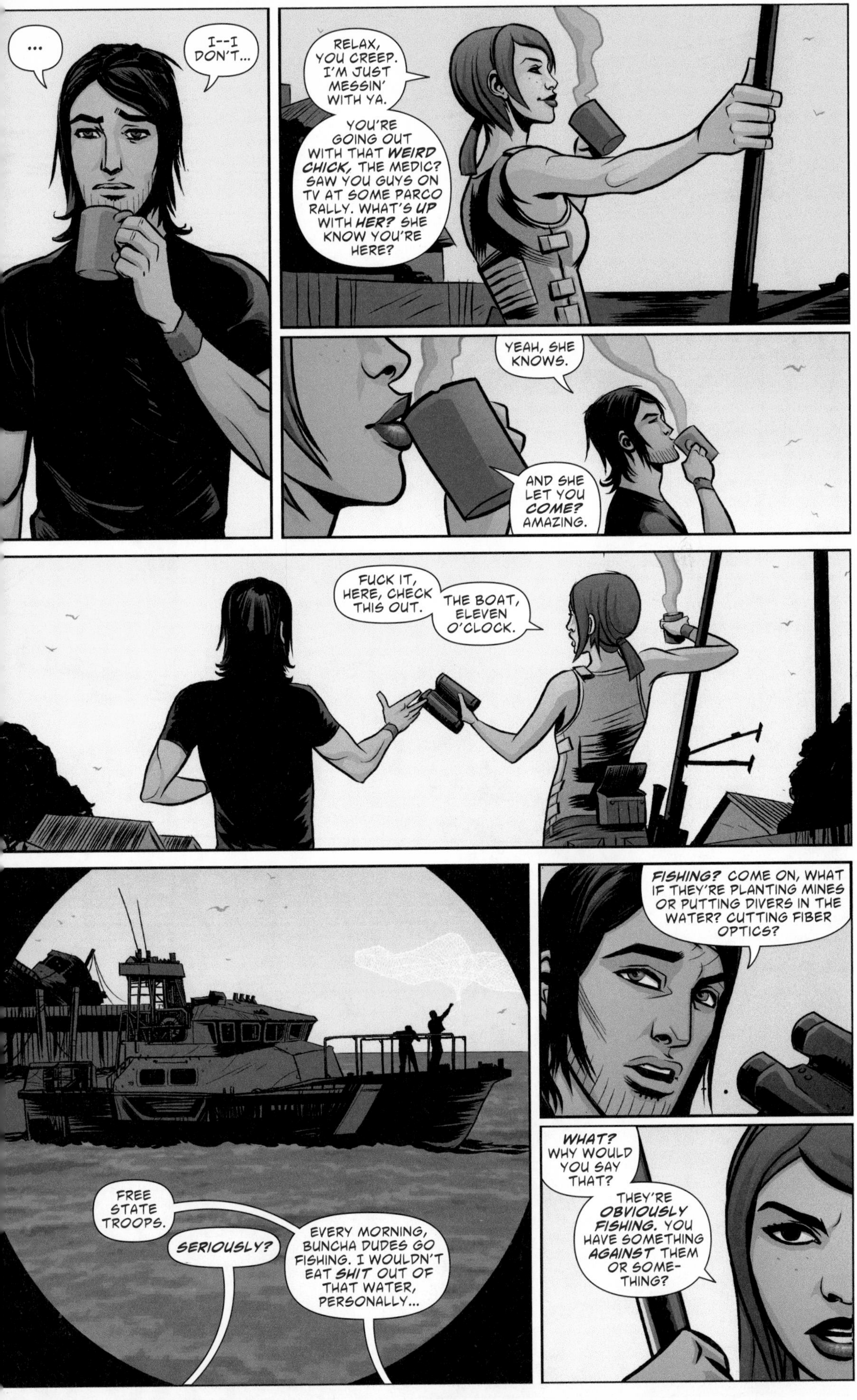
...
I--I DON'T...
RELAX, YOU CREEP. I'M JUST MESSIN' WITH YA.
YOU'RE GOING OUT WITH THAT WEIRD CHICK, THE MEDIC? SAW YOU GUYS ON TV AT SOME PARCO RALLY. WHAT'S UP WITH HER? SHE KNOW YOU'RE HERE?
YEAH, SHE KNOWS.
AND SHE LET YOU COME? AMAZING.
FUCK IT, HERE, CHECK THIS OUT.
THE BOAT, ELEVEN O'CLOCK.
FREE STATE TROOPS.
SERIOUSLY?
EVERY MORNING, BUNCHA DUDES GO FISHING. I WOULDN'T EAT SHIT OUT OF THAT WATER, PERSONALLY...
FISHING? COME ON, WHAT IF THEY'RE PLANTING MINES OR PUTTING DIVERS IN THE WATER? CUTTING FIBER OPTICS?
WHAT? WHY WOULD YOU SAY THAT?
THEY'RE OBVIOUSLY FISHING. YOU HAVE SOMETHING AGAINST THEM OR SOME-THING?

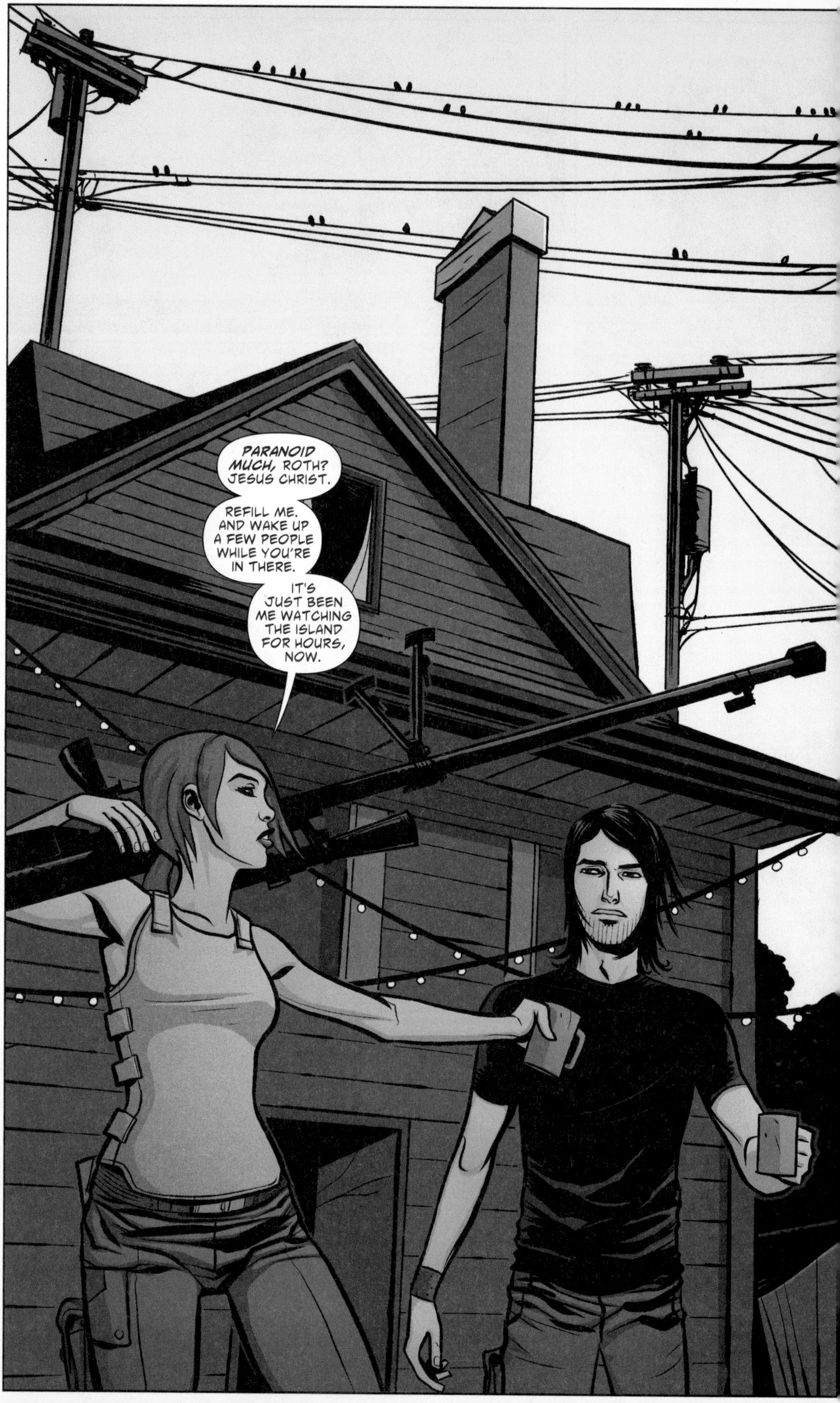
PARANOID MUCH, ROTH? JESUS CHRIST.
REFILL ME. AND WAKE UP A FEW PEOPLE WHILE YOU'RE IN THERE.
IT'S JUST BEEN ME WATCHING THE ISLAND FOR HOURS, NOW.

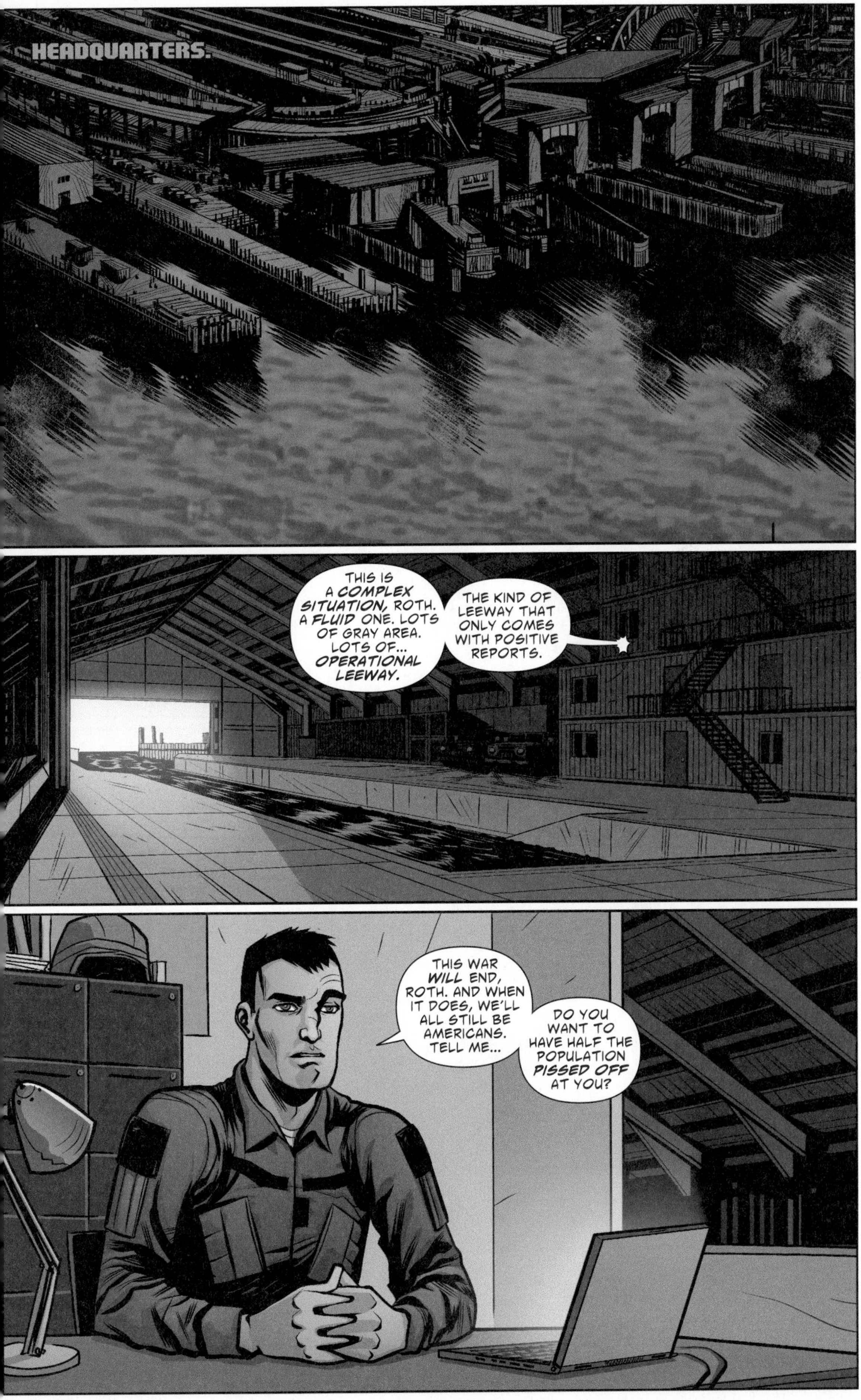
HEADQUARTERS.
THIS IS A COMPLEX SITUATION, ROTH. A FLUID ONE. LOTS OF GRAY AREA. LOTS OF... OPERATIONAL LEEWAY.
THE KIND OF LEEWAY THAT ONLY COMES WITH POSITIVE REPORTS.
THIS WAR WILL END, ROTH. AND WHEN IT DOES, WE'LL ALL STILL BE AMERICANS. TELL ME...
DO YOU WANT TO HAVE HALF THE POPULATION PISSED OFF AT YOU?

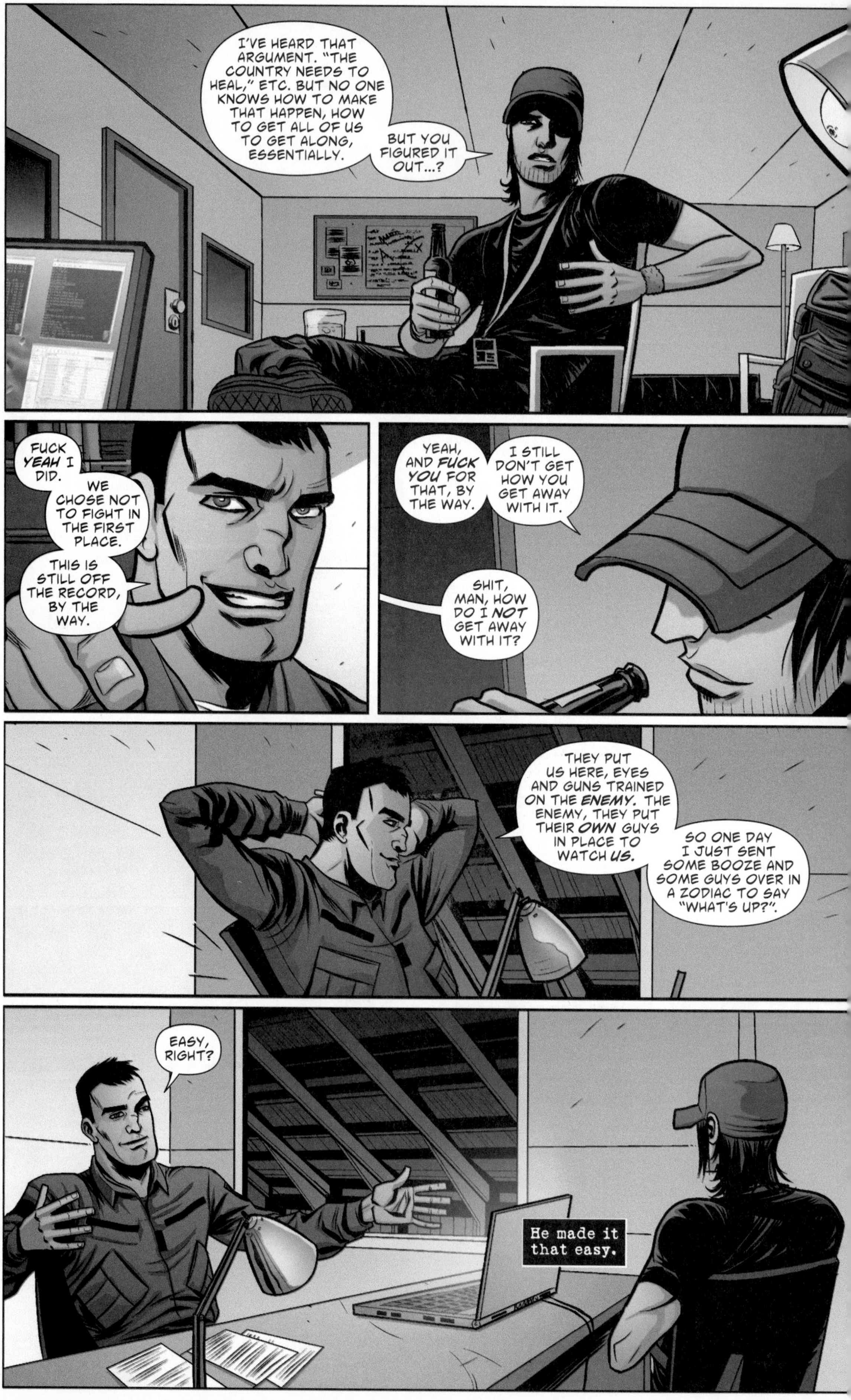
I'VE HEARD THAT ARGUMENT. "THE COUNTRY NEEDS TO HEAL," ETC. BUT NO ONE KNOWS HOW TO MAKE THAT HAPPEN, HOW TO GET ALL OF US TO GET ALONG, ESSENTIALLY.
BUT YOU FIGURED IT OUT...?
FUCK YEAH I DID.
WE CHOSE NOT TO FIGHT IN THE FIRST PLACE.
THIS IS STILL OFF THE RECORD, BY THE WAY.
YEAH, AND FUCK YOU FOR THAT, BY THE WAY.
I STILL DON'T GET HOW YOU GET AWAY WITH IT.
SHIT, MAN, HOW DO I NOT GET AWAY WITH IT?
THEY PUT US HERE, EYES AND GUNS TRAINED ON THE ENEMY. THE ENEMY, THEY PUT THEIR OWN GUYS IN PLACE TO WATCH US.
SO ONE DAY I JUST SENT SOME BOOZE AND SOME GUYS OVER IN A ZODIAC TO SAY "WHAT'S UP?".
EASY, RIGHT?
He made it that easy.

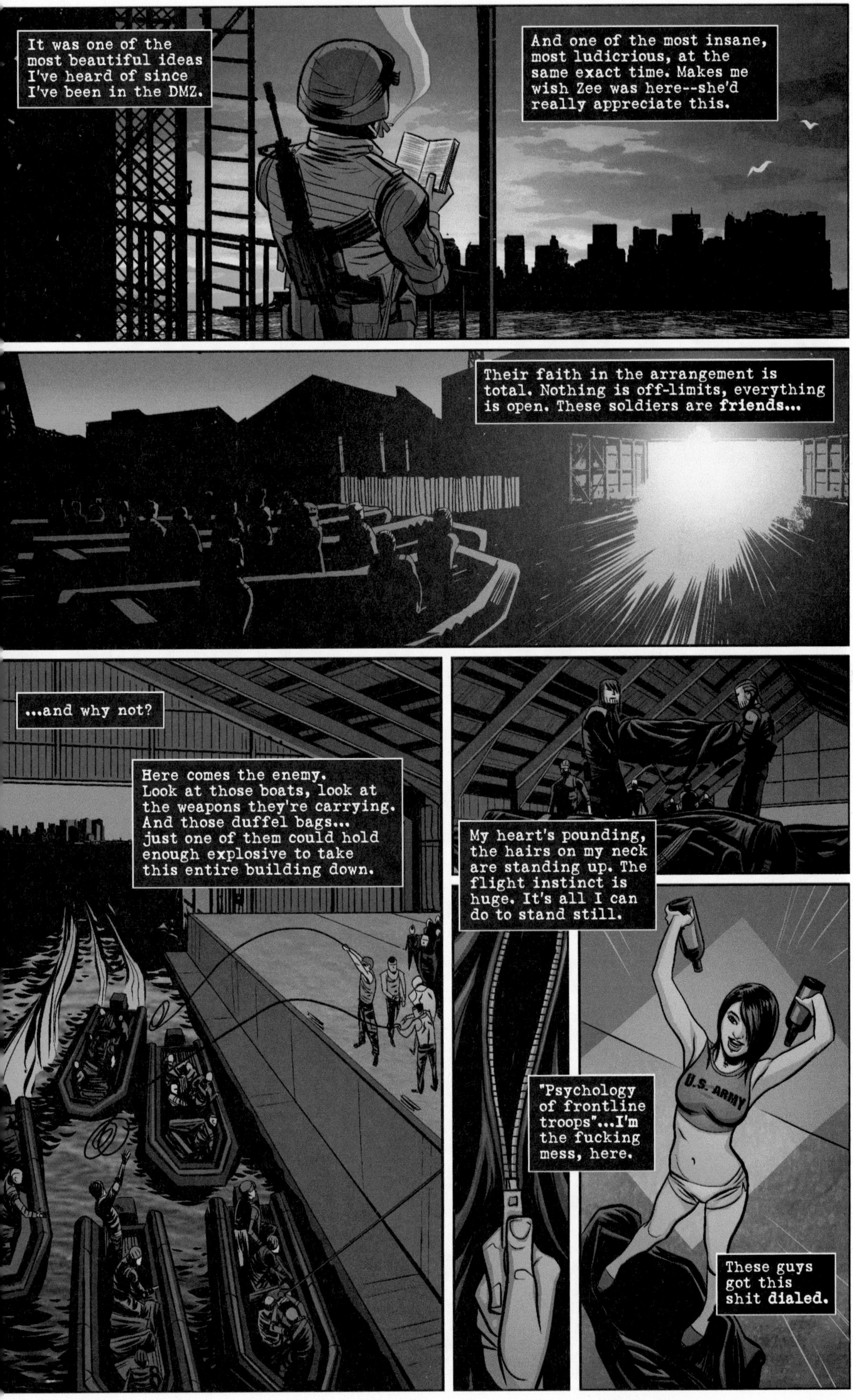
It was one of the most beautiful ideas I've heard of since I've been in the DMZ.
And one of the most insane, most ludicrious, at the same exact time. Makes me wish Zee was here--she'd really appreciate this.
Their faith in the arrangement is total. Nothing is off-limits, everything is open. These soldiers are **friends...**
...and why not?
Here comes the enemy. Look at those boats, look at the weapons they're carrying. And those duffel bags... just one of them could hold enough explosive to take this entire building down.
My heart's pounding, the hairs on my neck are standing up. The flight instinct is huge. It's all I can do to stand still.
"Psychology of frontline troops"...I'm the fucking mess, here.
U.S. ARMY
These guys got this shit **dialed.**

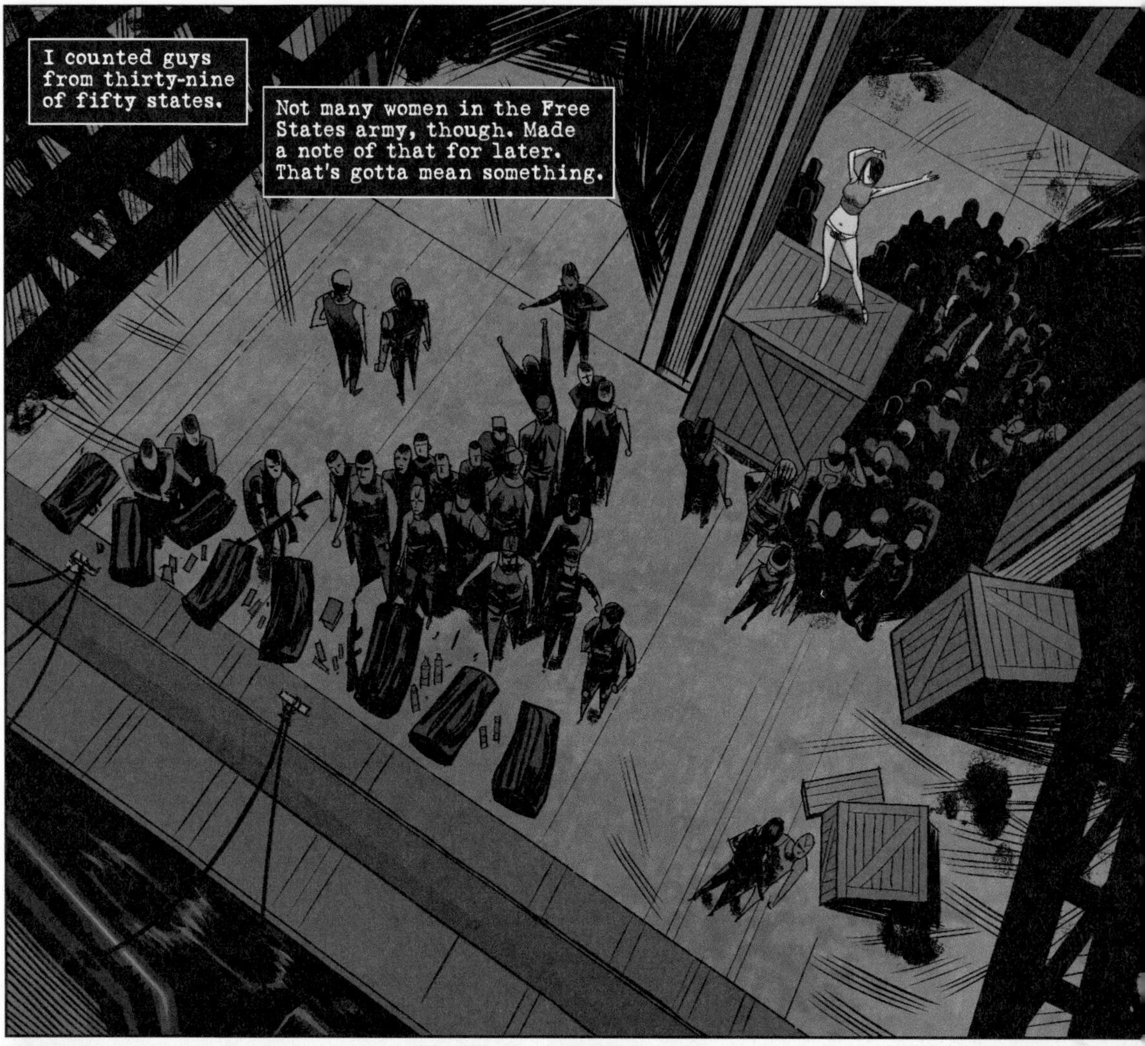
I counted guys from thirty-nine of fifty states.
Not many women in the Free States army, though. Made a note of that for later. That's gotta mean something.

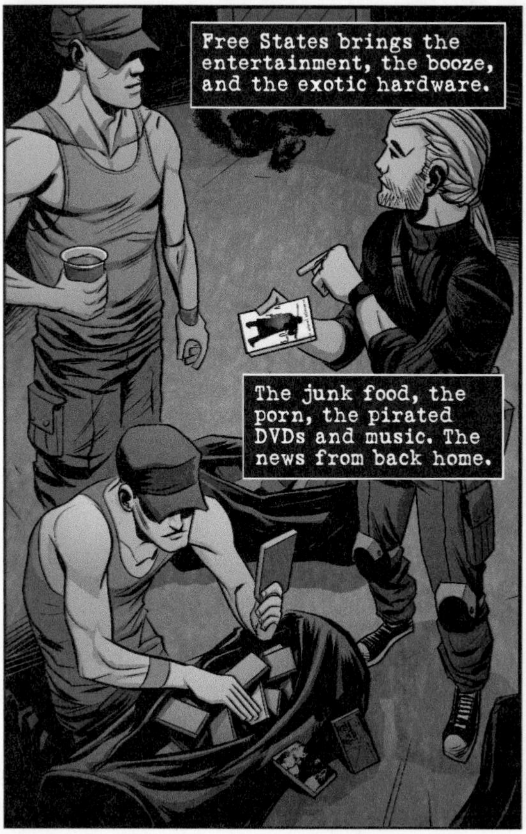
Free States brings the entertainment, the booze, and the exotic hardware.
The junk food, the porn, the pirated DVDs and music. The news from back home.

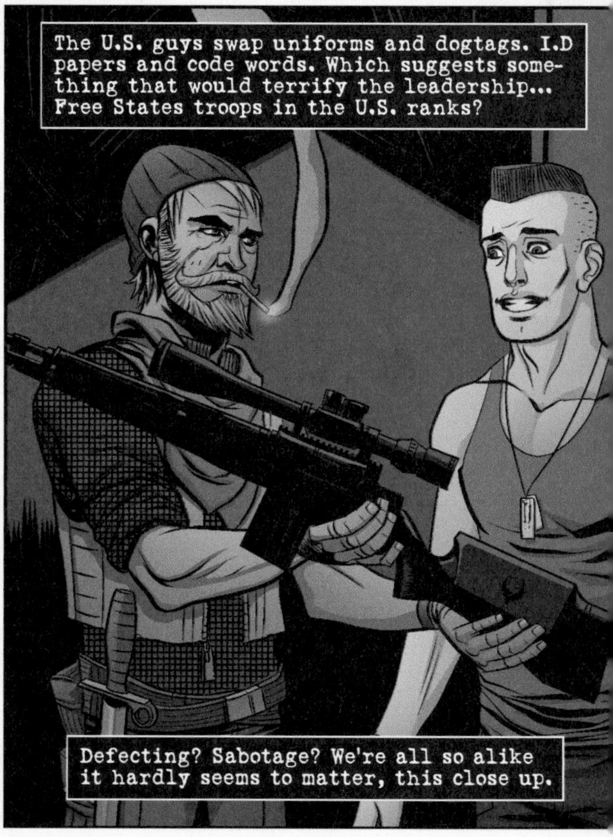
The U.S. guys swap uniforms and dogtags. I.D papers and code words. Which suggests something that would terrify the leadership... Free States troops in the U.S. ranks?
Defecting? Sabotage? We're all so alike it hardly seems to matter, this close up.

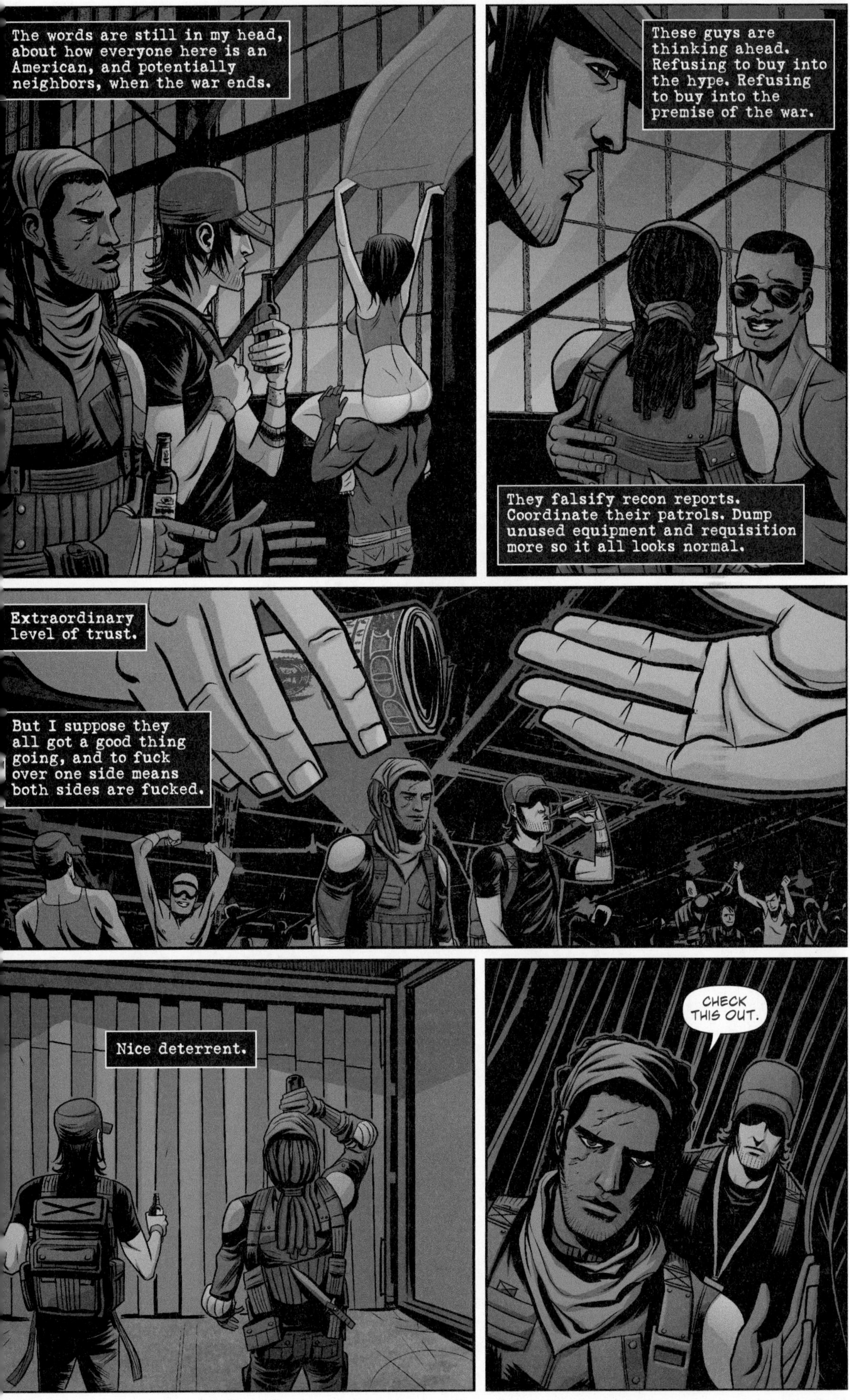

The words are still in my head, about how everyone here is an American, and potentially neighbors, when the war ends.
These guys are thinking ahead. Refusing to buy into the hype. Refusing to buy into the premise of the war.
They falsify recon reports. Coordinate their patrols. Dump unused equipment and requisition more so it all looks normal.
Extraordinary level of trust.
But I suppose they all got a good thing going, and to fuck over one side means both sides are fucked.
Nice deterrent.
CHECK THIS OUT.

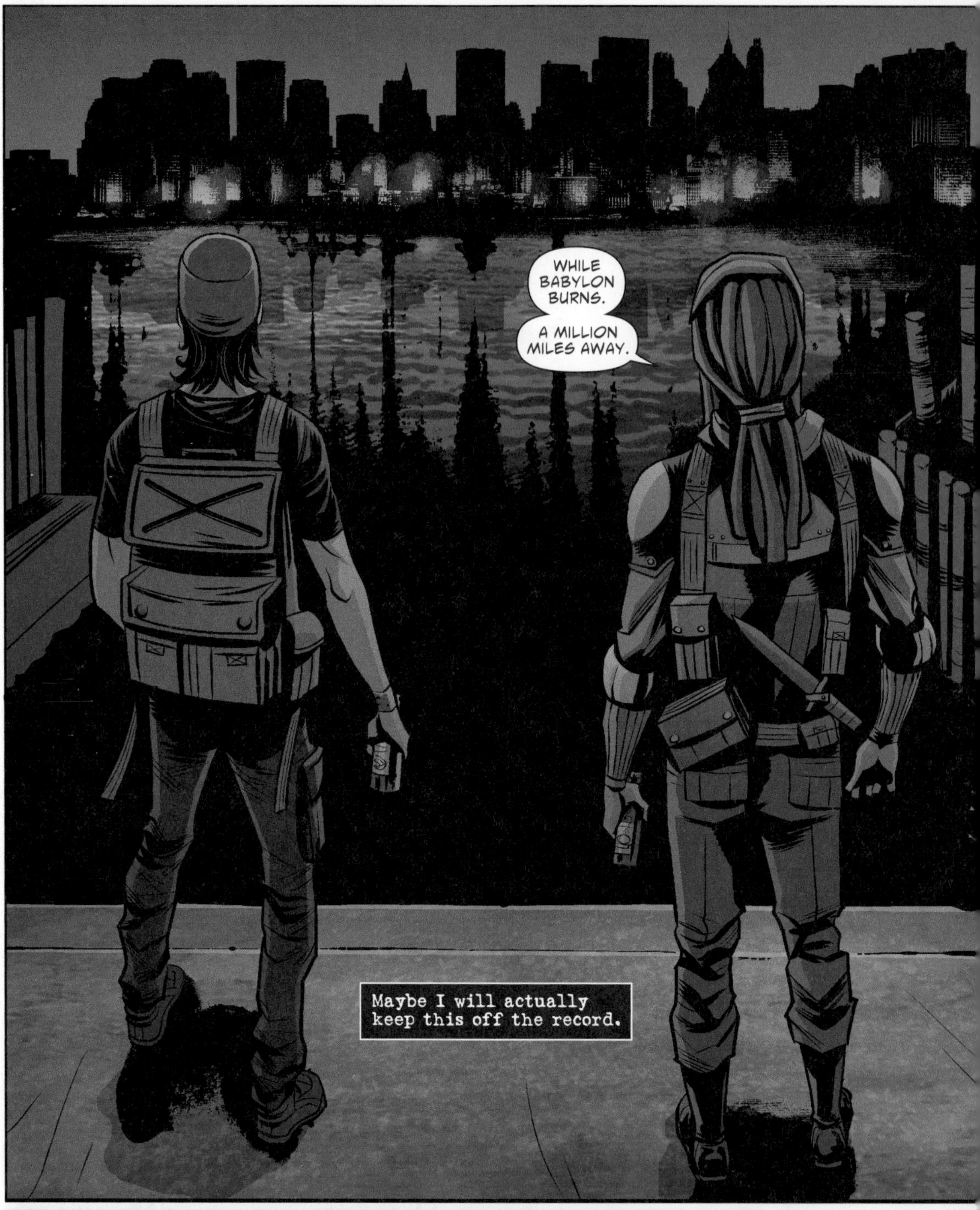
WHILE BABYLON BURNS.
A MILLION MILES AWAY.
Maybe I will actually keep this off the record.

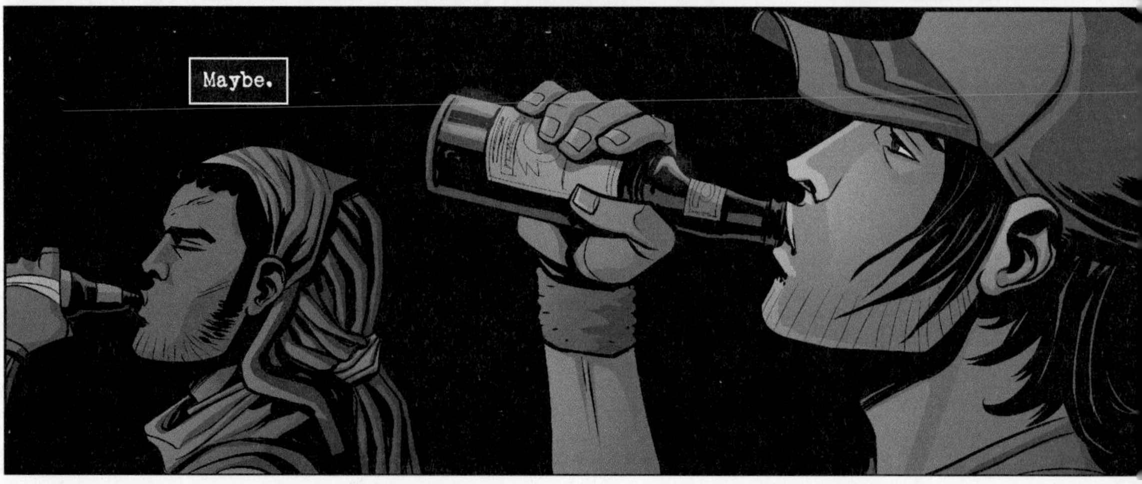
Maybe.

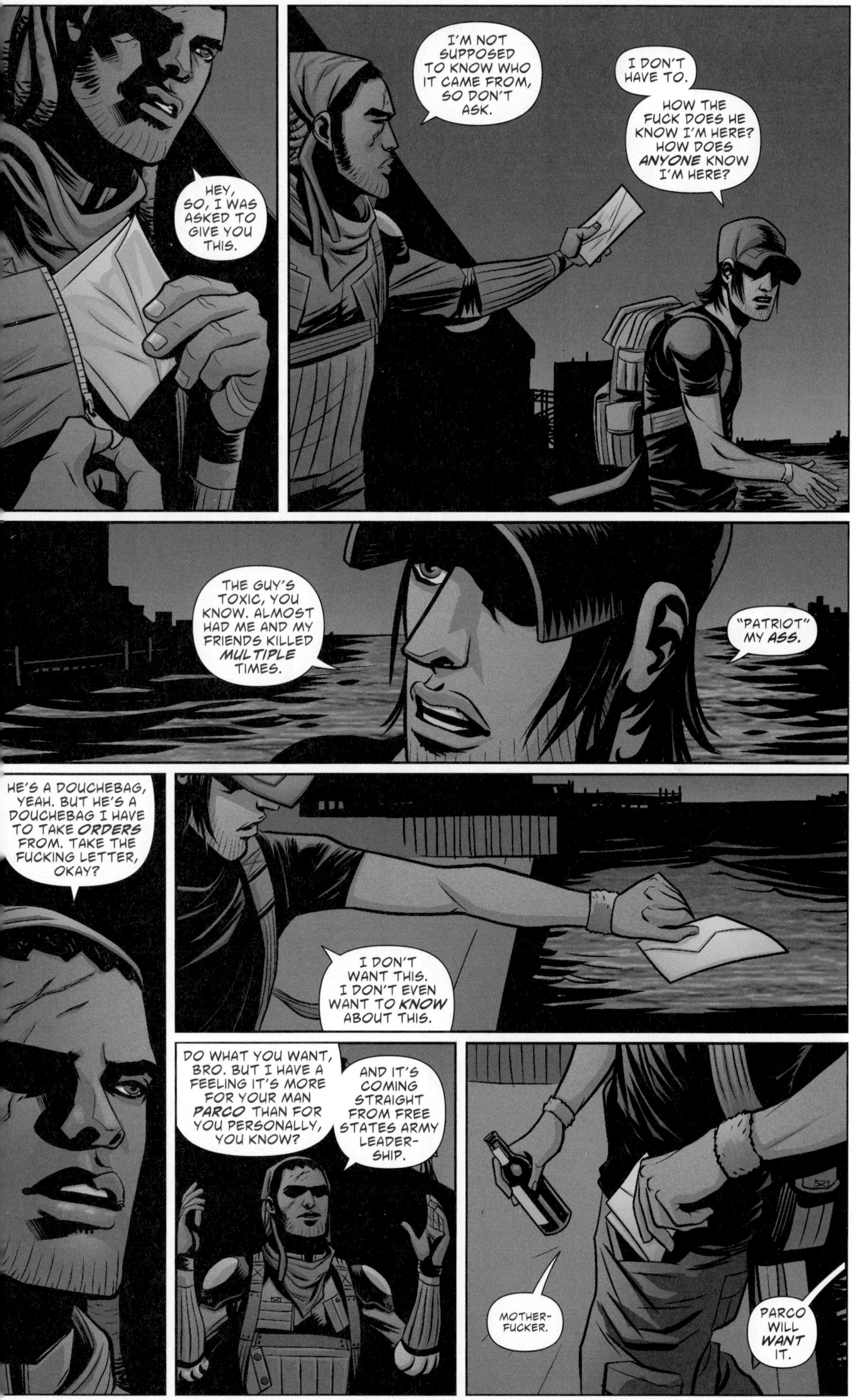
HEY, SO, I WAS ASKED TO GIVE YOU THIS.
I'M NOT SUPPOSED TO KNOW WHO IT CAME FROM, SO DON'T ASK.
I DON'T HAVE TO.
HOW THE FUCK DOES HE KNOW I'M HERE? HOW DOES ANYONE KNOW I'M HERE?
THE GUY'S TOXIC, YOU KNOW. ALMOST HAD ME AND MY FRIENDS KILLED MULTIPLE TIMES.
"PATRIOT" MY ASS.
HE'S A DOUCHEBAG, YEAH. BUT HE'S A DOUCHEBAG I HAVE TO TAKE ORDERS FROM. TAKE THE FUCKING LETTER, OKAY?
I DON'T WANT THIS. I DON'T EVEN WANT TO KNOW ABOUT THIS.
DO WHAT YOU WANT, BRO. BUT I HAVE A FEELING IT'S MORE FOR YOUR MAN PARCO THAN FOR YOU PERSONALLY, YOU KNOW?
AND IT'S COMING STRAIGHT FROM FREE STATES ARMY LEADER-SHIP.
MOTHER-FUCKER.
PARCO WILL WANT IT.

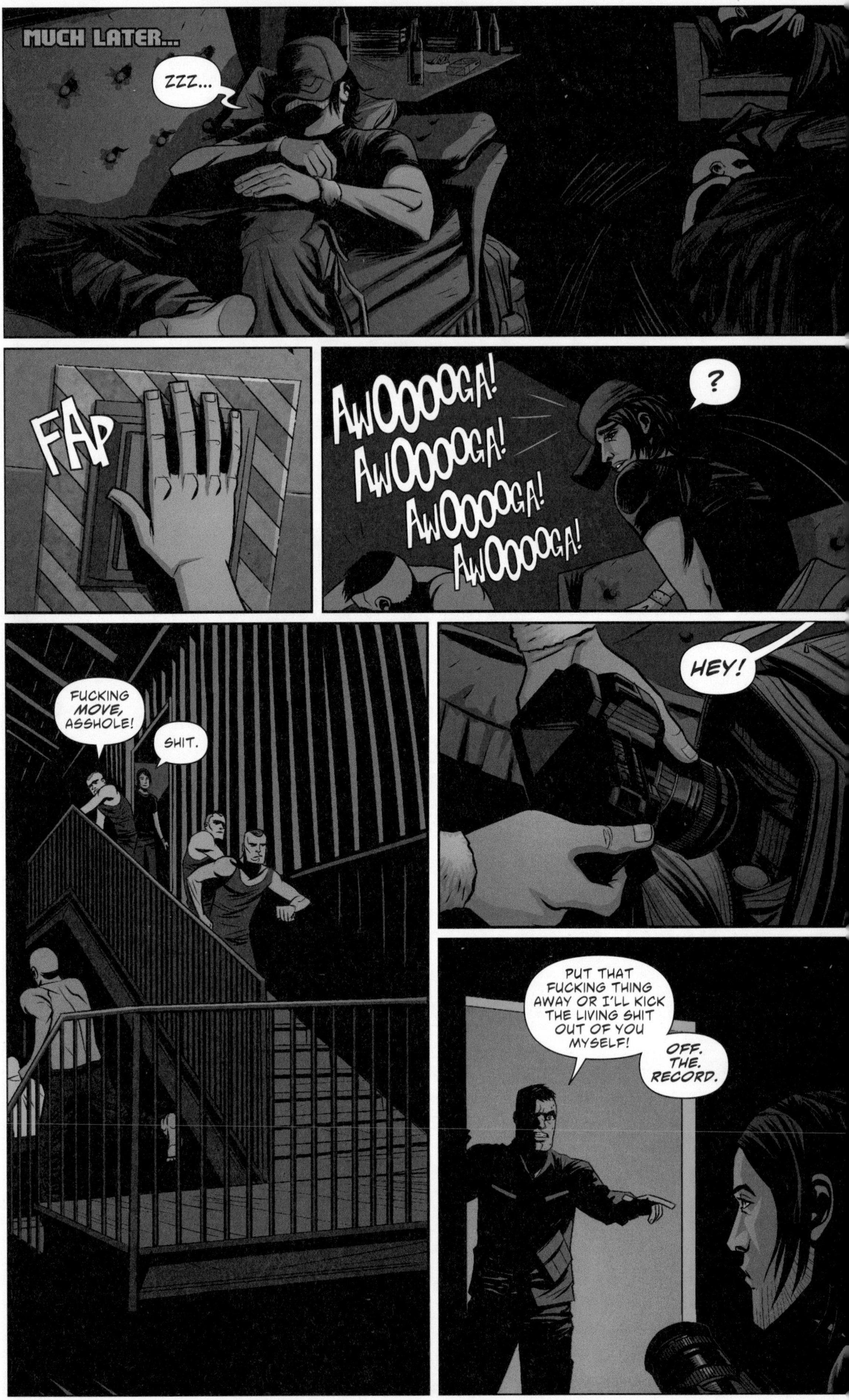
MUCH LATER...
ZZZ...
FAP
AWOOOOGA!
AWOOOOGA!
AWOOOOGA!
AWOOOOGA!
?
FUCKING MOVE, ASSHOLE!
SHIT.
HEY!
PUT THAT FUCKING THING AWAY OR I'LL KICK THE LIVING SHIT OUT OF YOU MYSELF!
OFF. THE. RECORD.

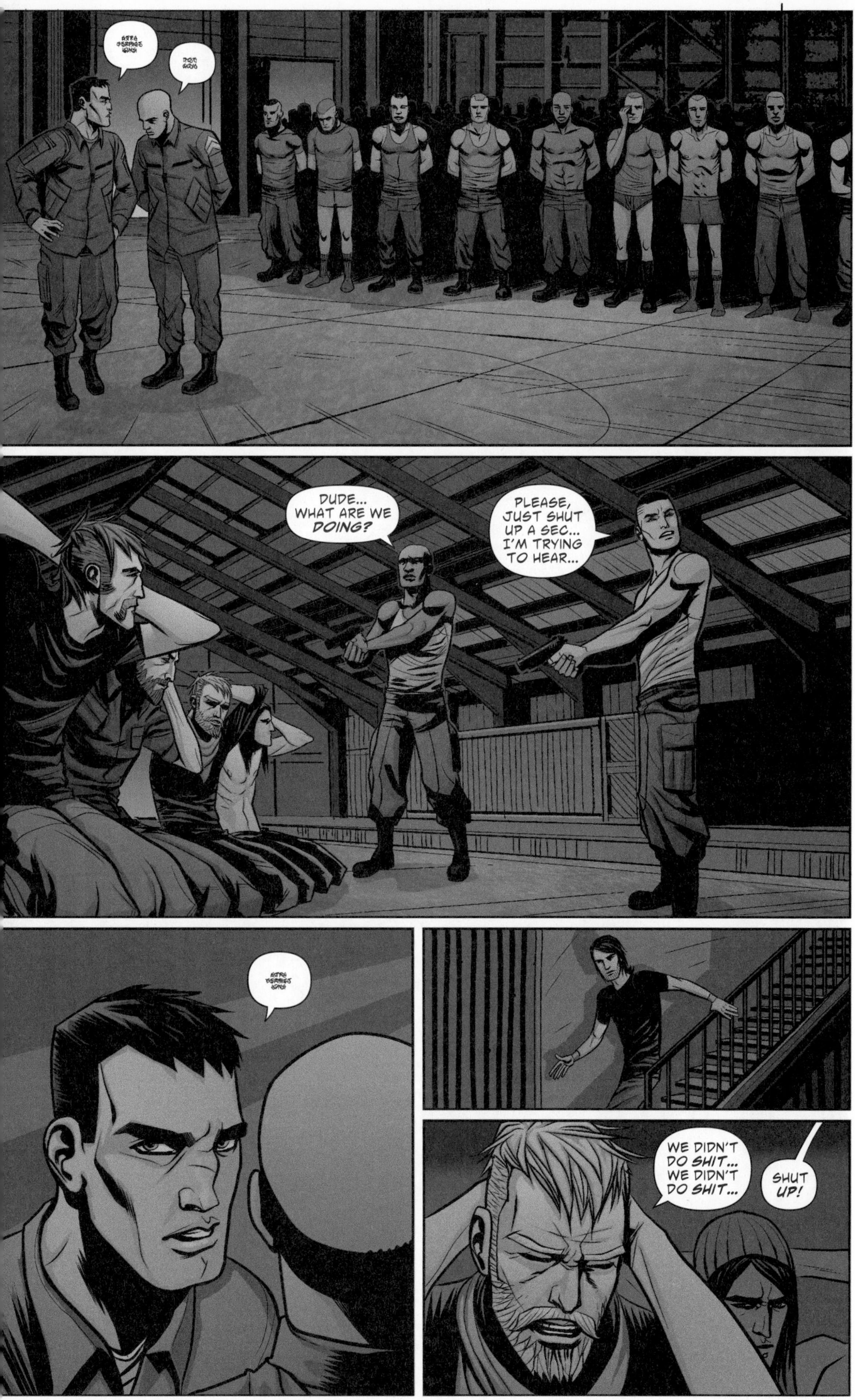
DUDE... WHAT ARE WE *DOING?*
PLEASE, JUST SHUT UP A SEC... I'M TRYING TO HEAR...
WE DIDN'T DO *SHIT*... WE DIDN'T DO *SHIT*...
SHUT *UP!*

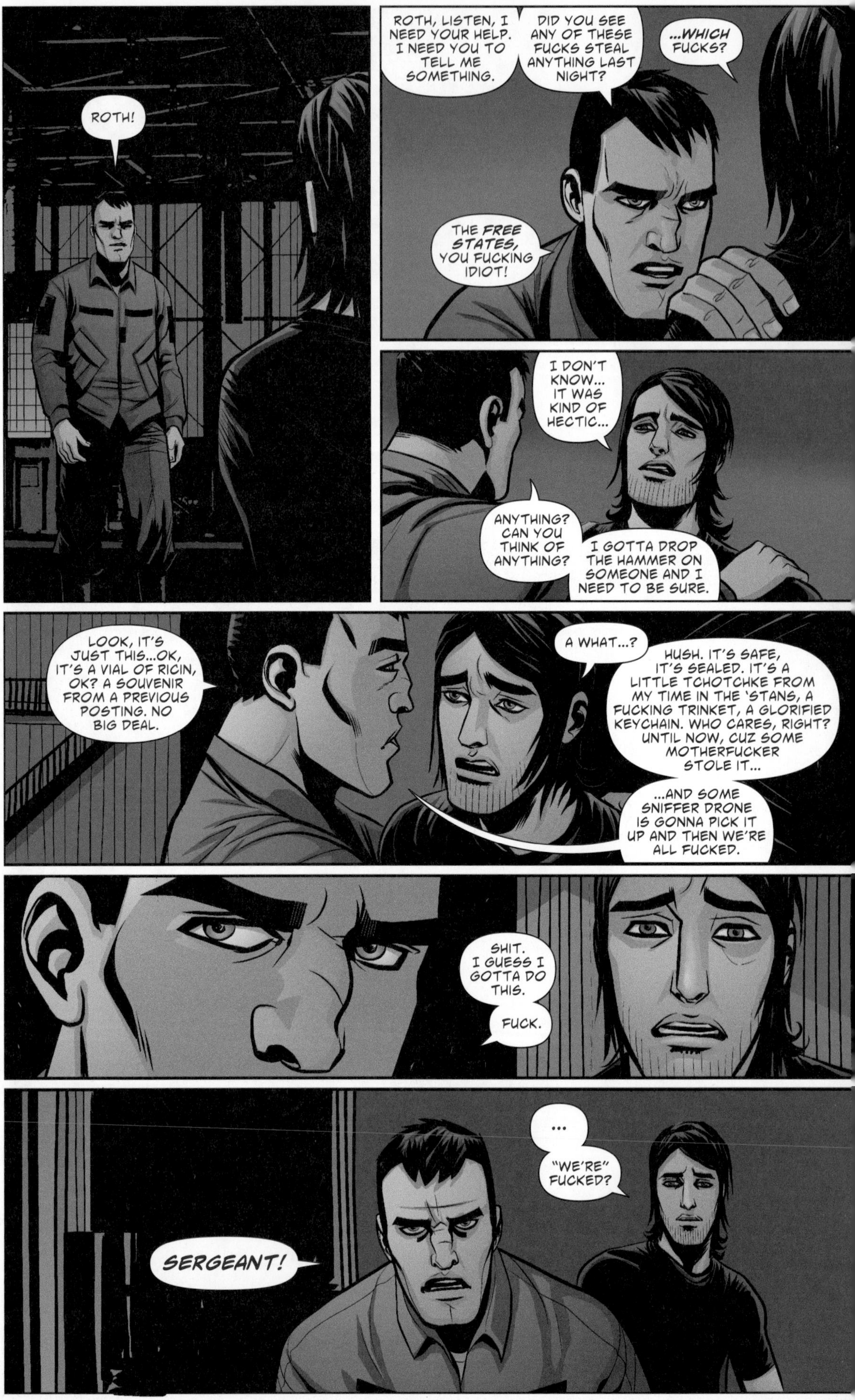
ROTH!
ROTH, LISTEN, I NEED YOUR HELP. I NEED YOU TO TELL ME SOMETHING.
DID YOU SEE ANY OF THESE FUCKS STEAL ANYTHING LAST NIGHT?
...WHICH FUCKS?
THE FREE STATES, YOU FUCKING IDIOT!
I DON'T KNOW... IT WAS KIND OF HECTIC...
ANYTHING? CAN YOU THINK OF ANYTHING?
I GOTTA DROP THE HAMMER ON SOMEONE AND I NEED TO BE SURE.
LOOK, IT'S JUST THIS...OK, IT'S A VIAL OF RICIN, OK? A SOUVENIR FROM A PREVIOUS POSTING. NO BIG DEAL.
A WHAT...?
HUSH. IT'S SAFE, IT'S SEALED. IT'S A LITTLE TCHOTCHKE FROM MY TIME IN THE 'STANS, A FUCKING TRINKET, A GLORIFIED KEYCHAIN. WHO CARES, RIGHT? UNTIL NOW, CUZ SOME MOTHERFUCKER STOLE IT...
...AND SOME SNIFFER DRONE IS GONNA PICK IT UP AND THEN WE'RE ALL FUCKED.
SHIT. I GUESS I GOTTA DO THIS.
FUCK.
...
"WE'RE" FUCKED?
SERGEANT!

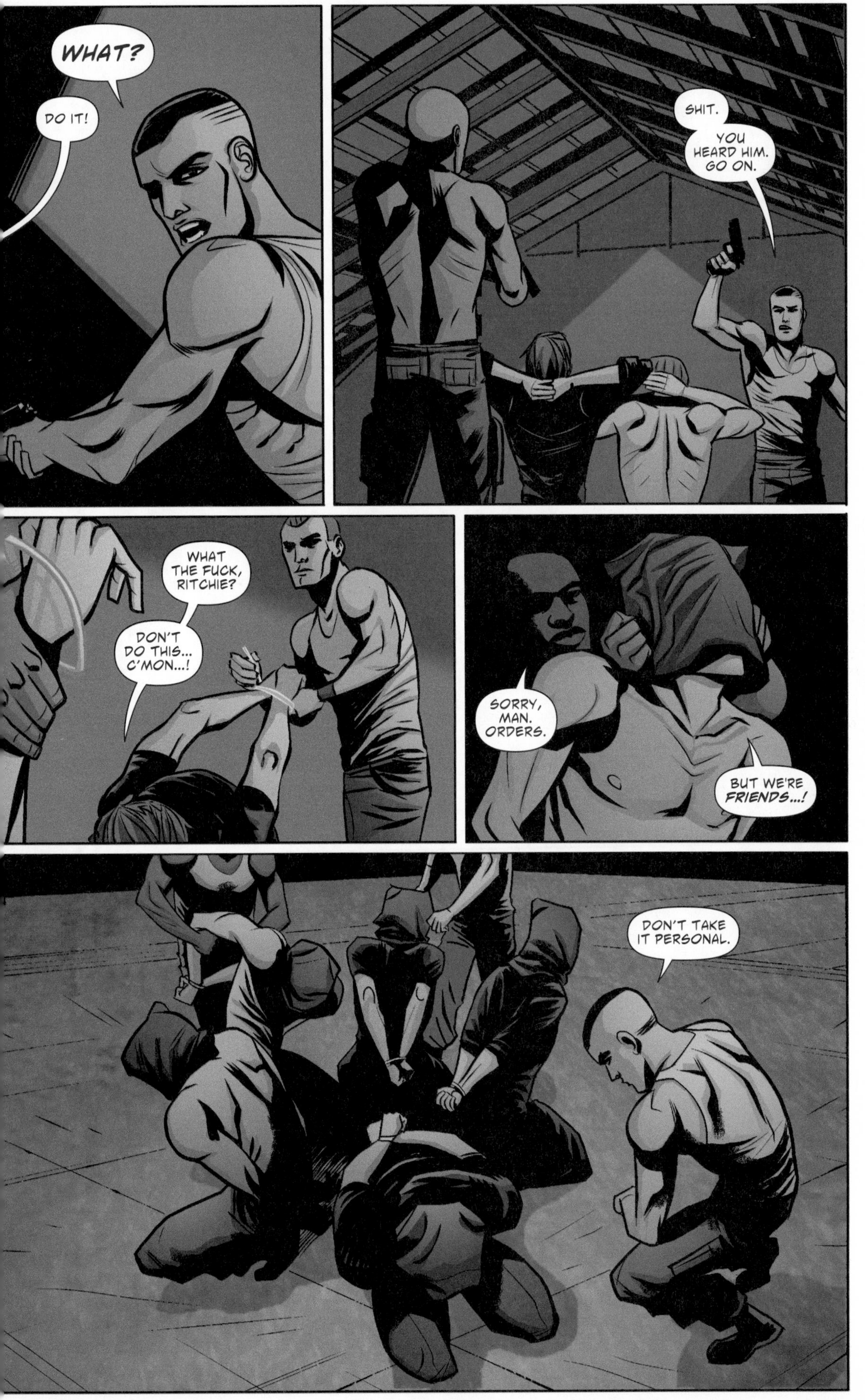
WHAT?
DO IT!
SHIT.
YOU HEARD HIM. GO ON.
WHAT THE FUCK, RITCHIE?
DON'T DO THIS... C'MON...!
SORRY, MAN. ORDERS.
BUT WE'RE FRIENDS...!
DON'T TAKE IT PERSONAL.

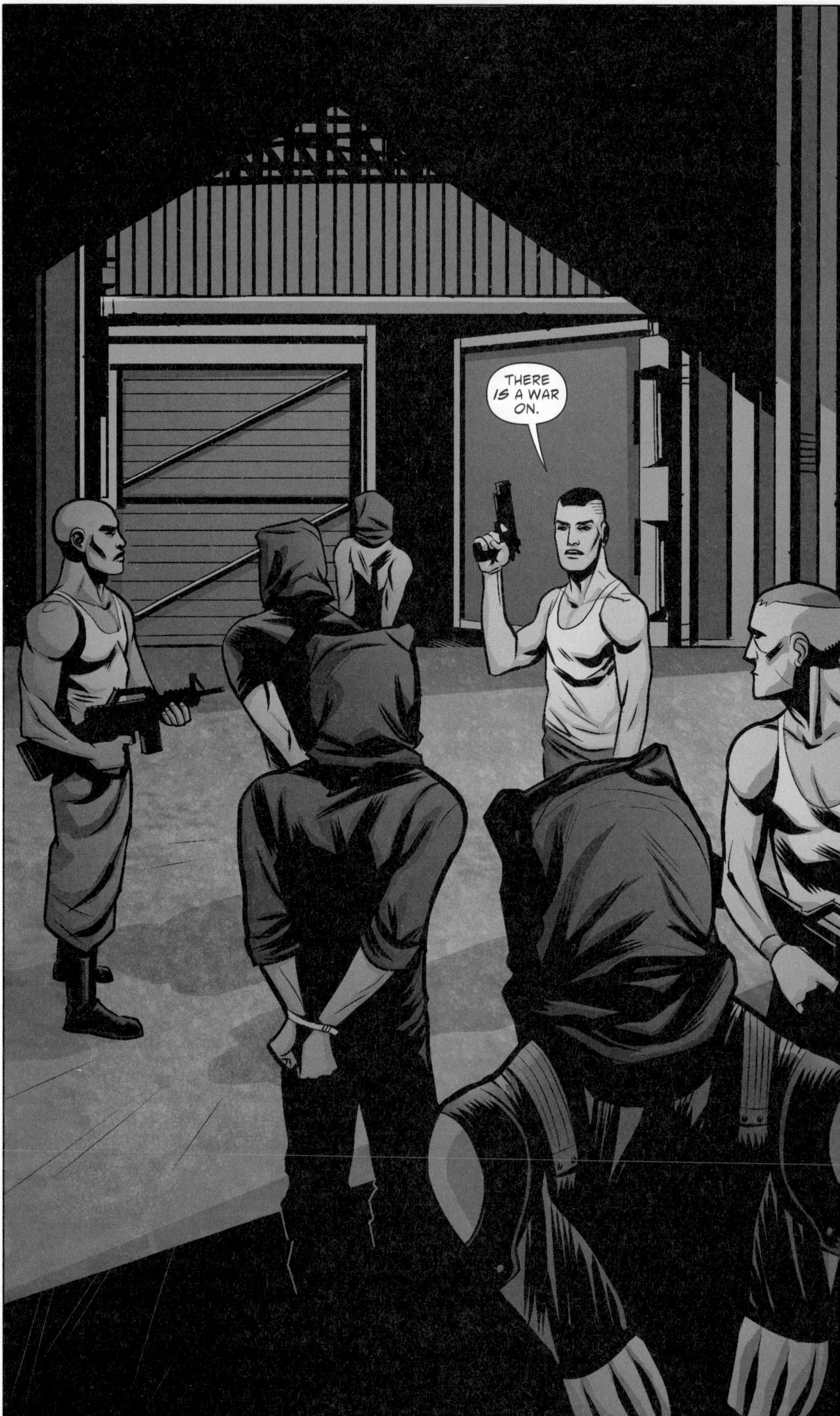
THERE IS A WAR ON.

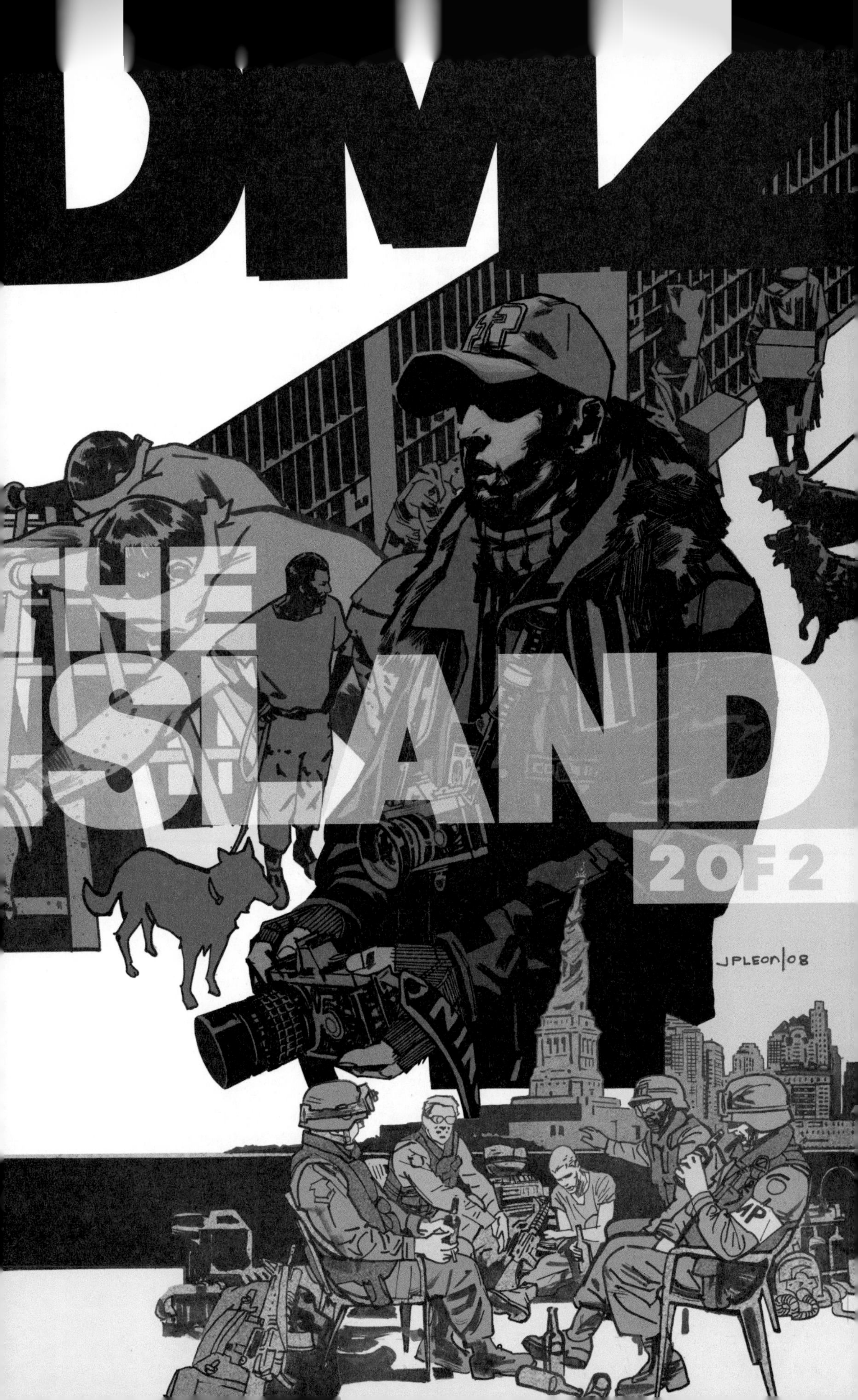
THE ISLAND
2 OF 2
JPLEON|08

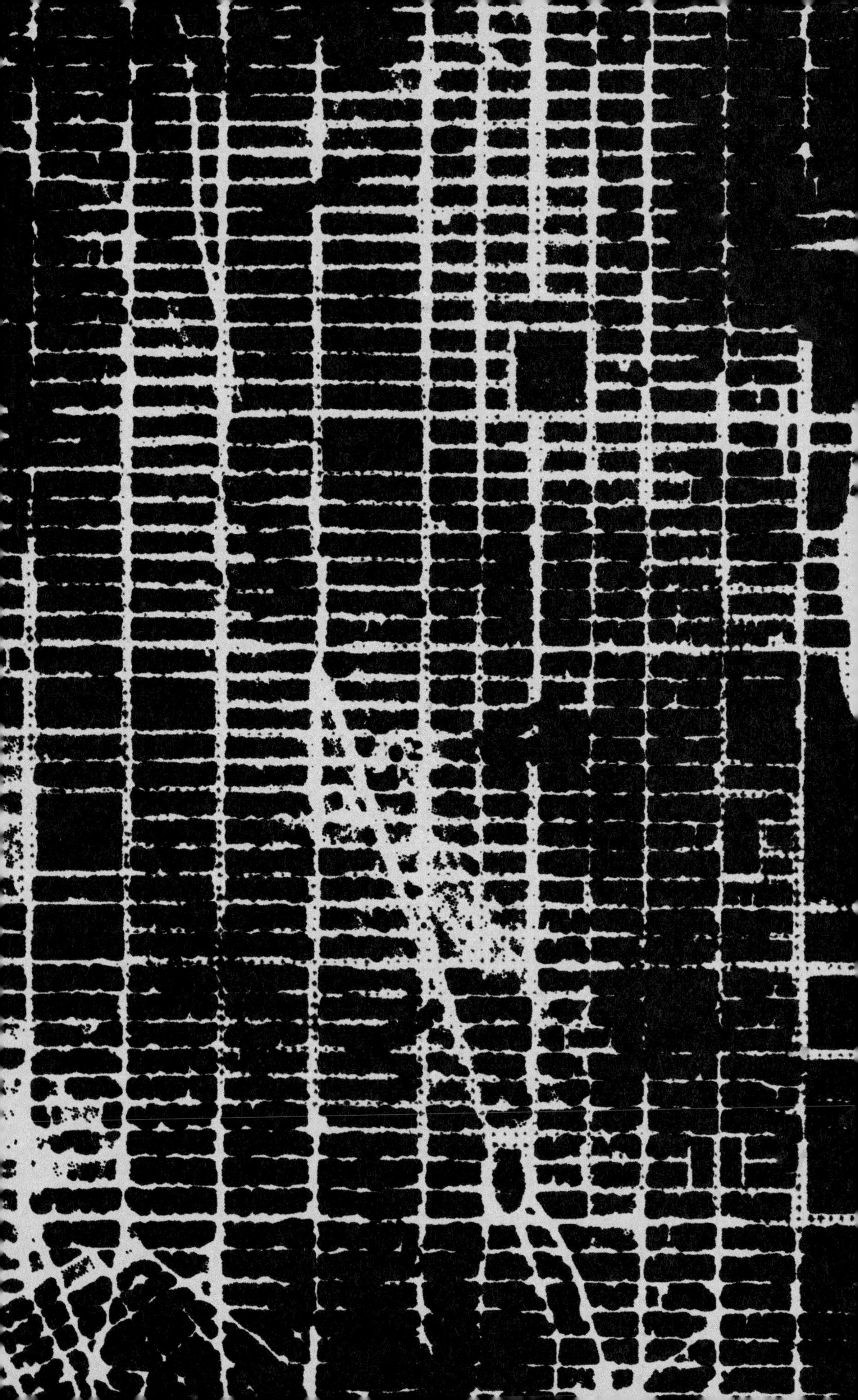

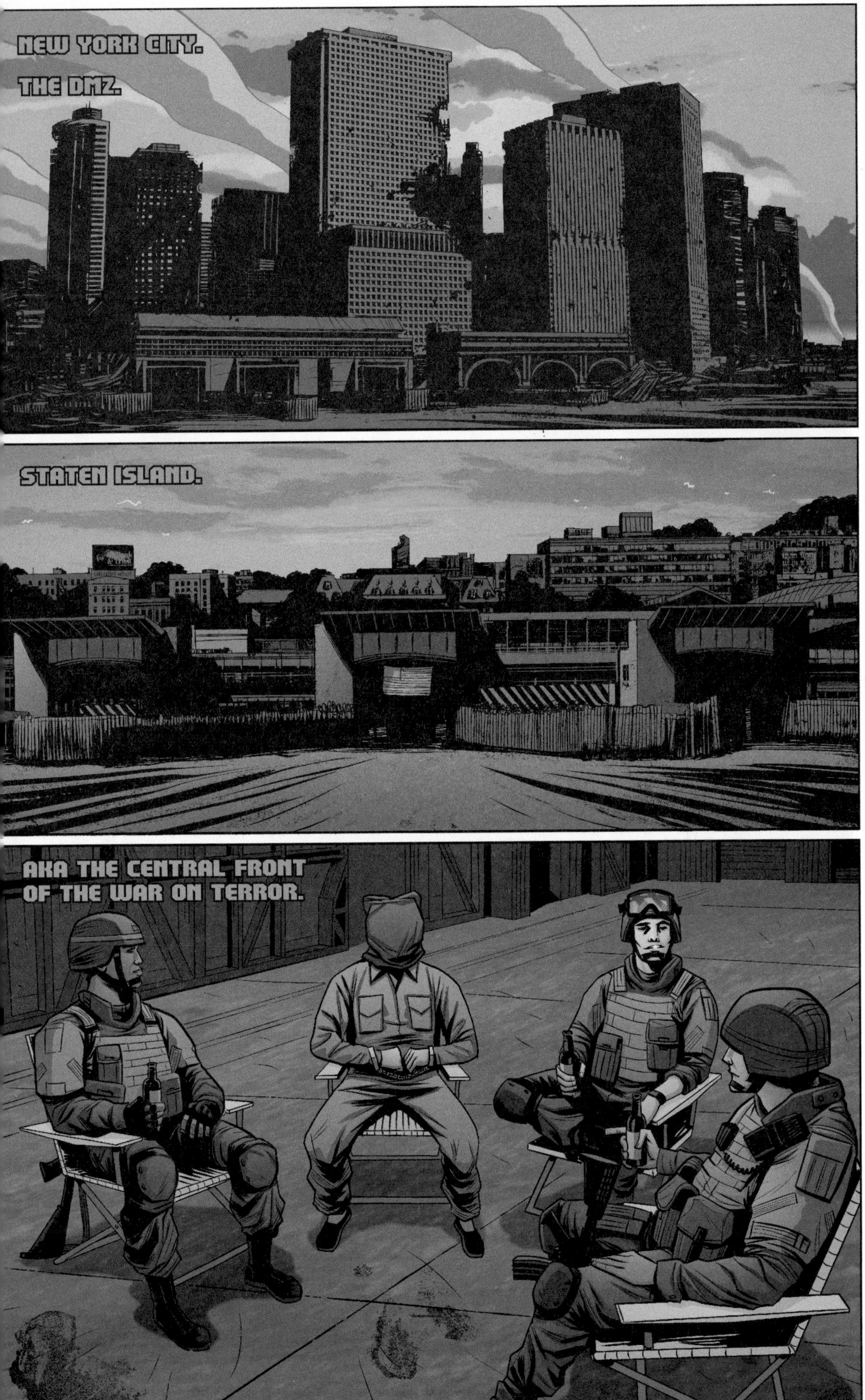
NEW YORK CITY.
THE DMZ.
STATEN ISLAND.
AKA THE CENTRAL FRONT OF THE WAR ON TERROR.

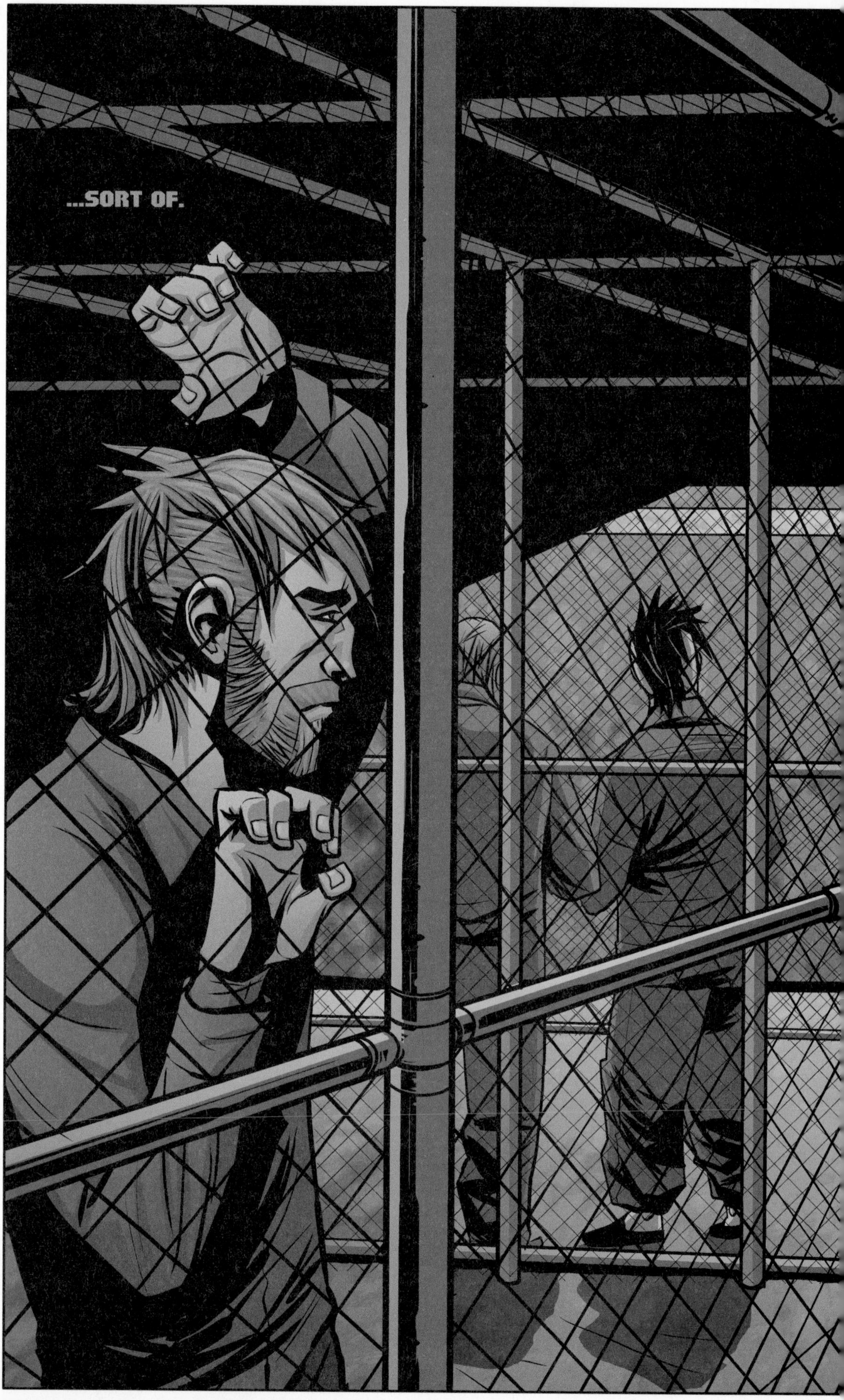
...SORT OF.

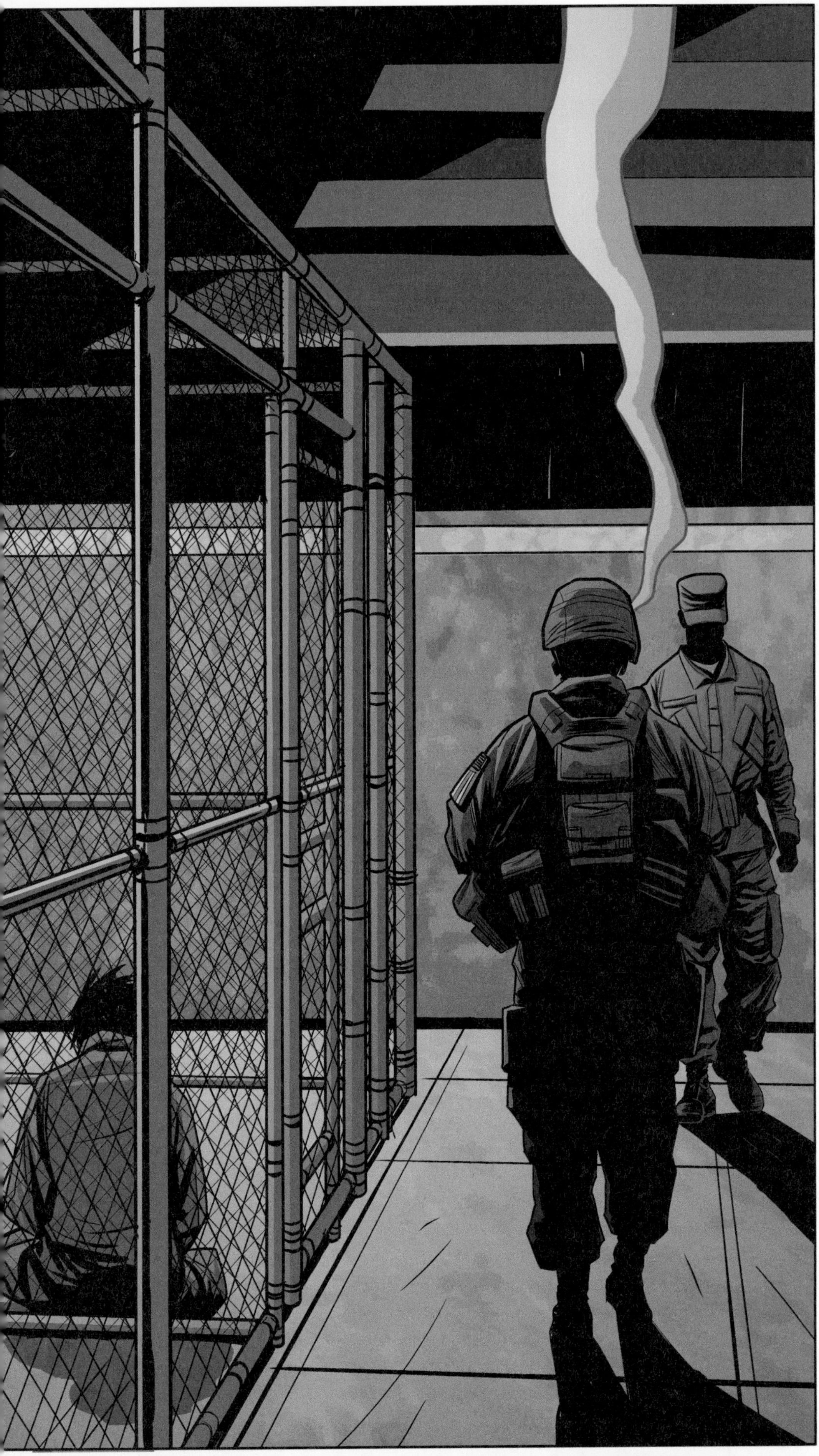

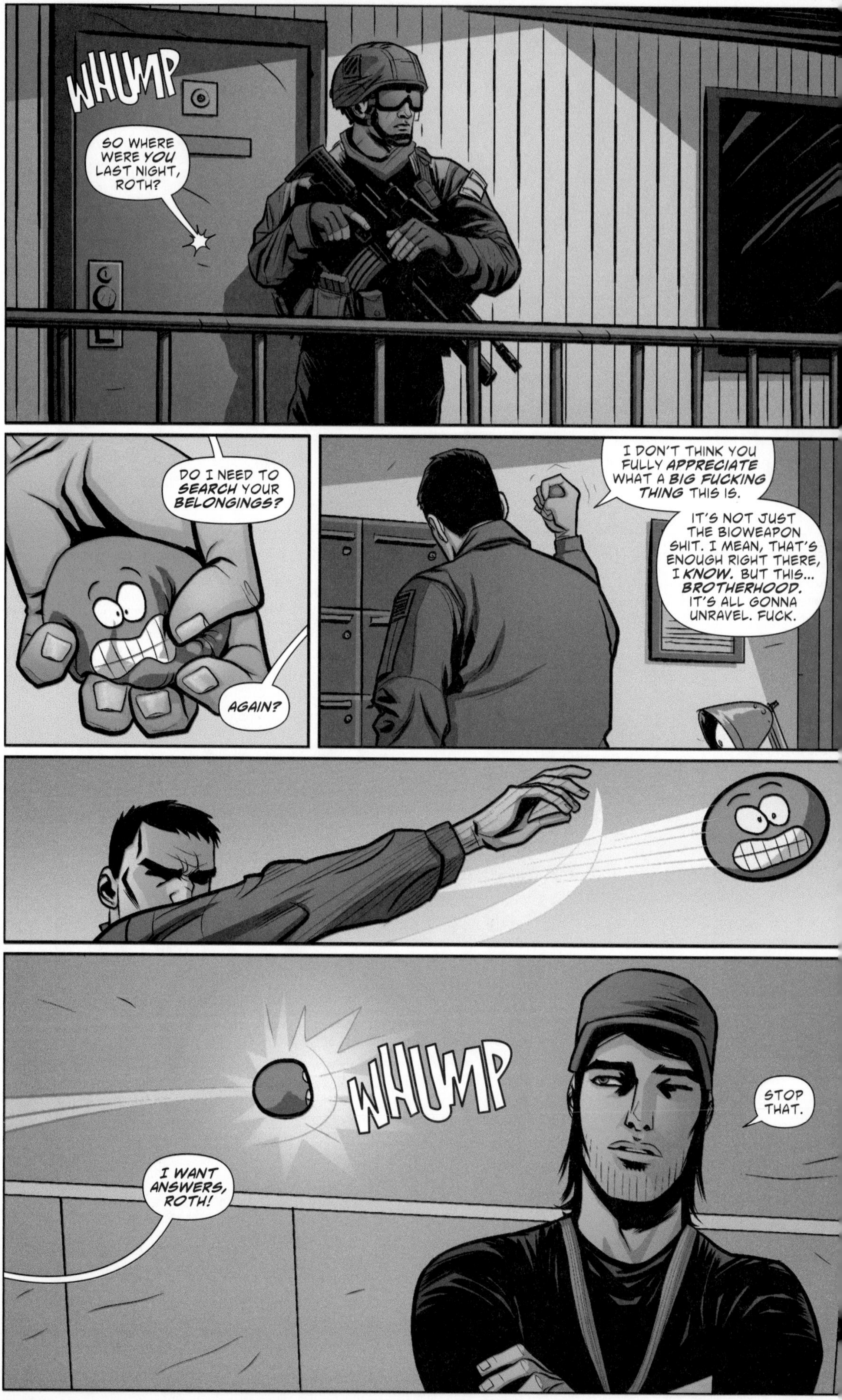
WHUMP
SO WHERE WERE YOU LAST NIGHT, ROTH?
DO I NEED TO SEARCH YOUR BELONGINGS?
AGAIN?
I DON'T THINK YOU FULLY APPRECIATE WHAT A BIG FUCKING THING THIS IS.
IT'S NOT JUST THE BIOWEAPON SHIT. I MEAN, THAT'S ENOUGH RIGHT THERE, I KNOW. BUT THIS... BROTHERHOOD. IT'S ALL GONNA UNRAVEL. FUCK.
WHUMP
STOP THAT.
I WANT ANSWERS, ROTH!

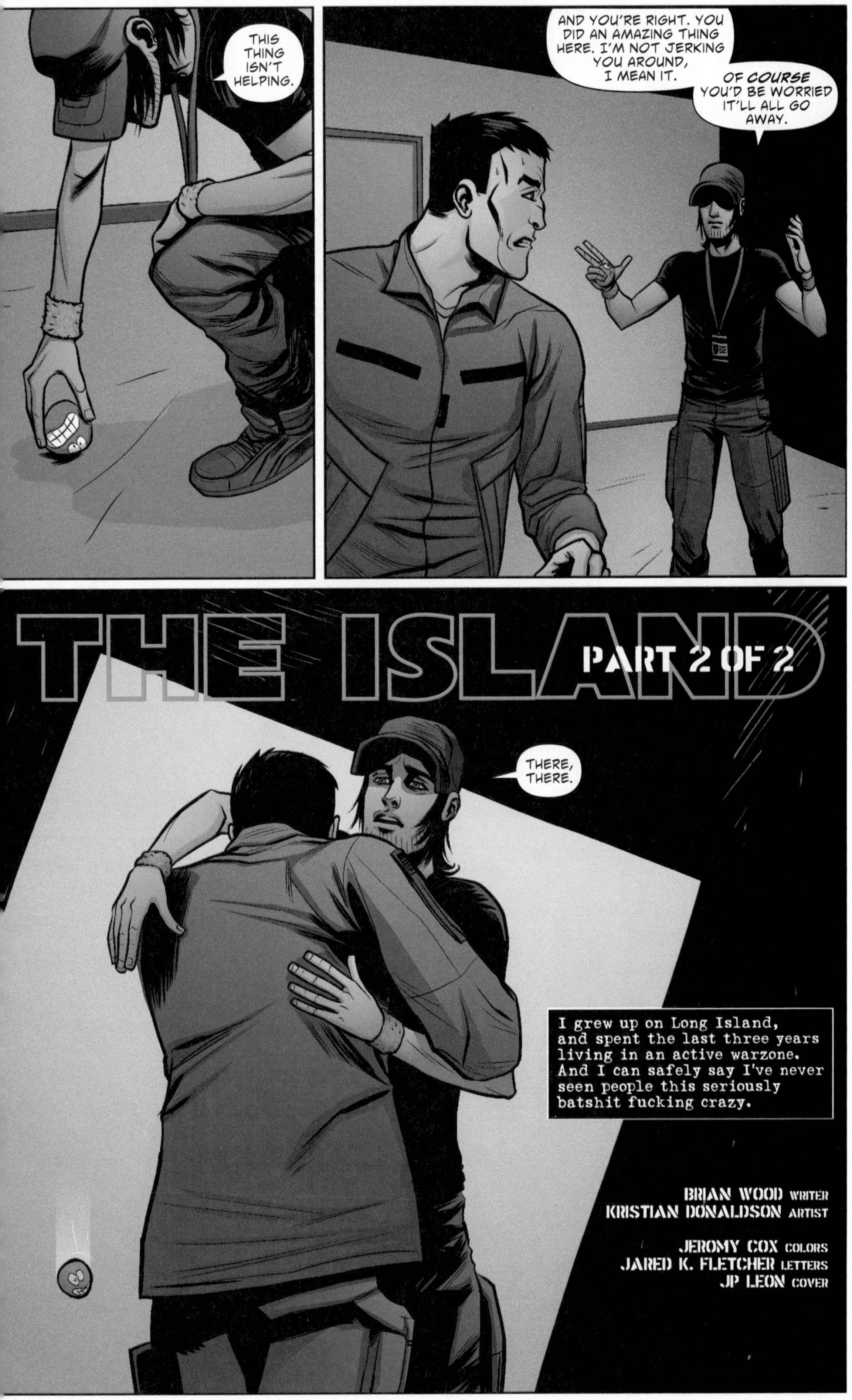
THIS THING ISN'T HELPING.
AND YOU'RE RIGHT. YOU DID AN AMAZING THING HERE. I'M NOT JERKING YOU AROUND, I MEAN IT.
OF COURSE YOU'D BE WORRIED IT'LL ALL GO AWAY.
THE ISLAND
PART 2 OF 2
THERE, THERE.
I grew up on Long Island, and spent the last three years living in an active warzone. And I can safely say I've never seen people this seriously batshit fucking crazy.
BRIAN WOOD WRITER
KRISTIAN DONALDSON ARTIST
JEROMY COX COLORS
JARED K. FLETCHER LETTERS
JP LEON COVER

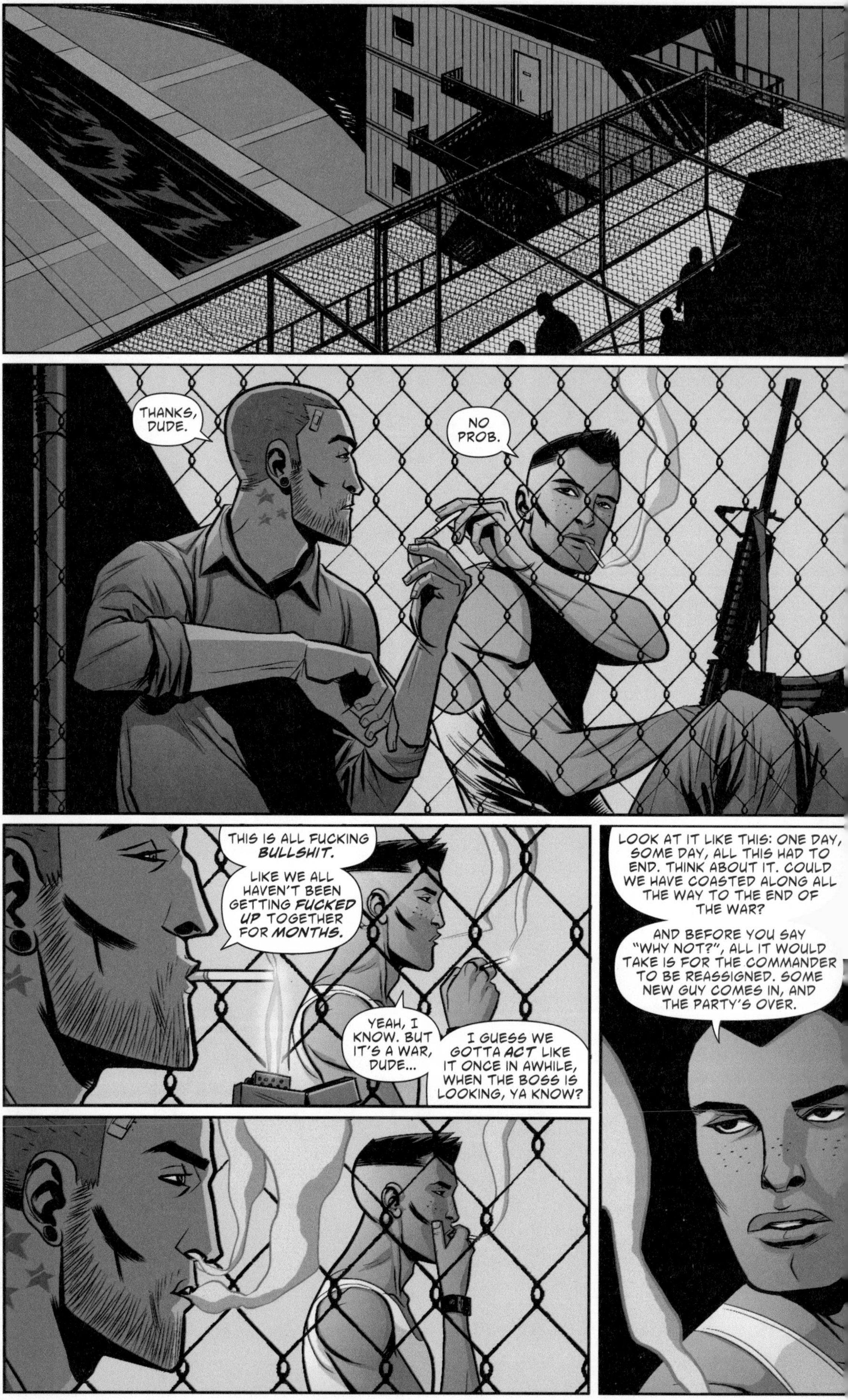
THANKS, DUDE.
NO PROB.
THIS IS ALL FUCKING BULLSHIT.
LIKE WE ALL HAVEN'T BEEN GETTING FUCKED UP TOGETHER FOR MONTHS.
YEAH, I KNOW. BUT IT'S A WAR, DUDE...
I GUESS WE GOTTA ACT LIKE IT ONCE IN AWHILE, WHEN THE BOSS IS LOOKING, YA KNOW?
LOOK AT IT LIKE THIS: ONE DAY, SOME DAY, ALL THIS HAD TO END. THINK ABOUT IT. COULD WE HAVE COASTED ALONG ALL THE WAY TO THE END OF THE WAR?
AND BEFORE YOU SAY "WHY NOT?", ALL IT WOULD TAKE IS FOR THE COMMANDER TO BE REASSIGNED. SOME NEW GUY COMES IN, AND THE PARTY'S OVER.

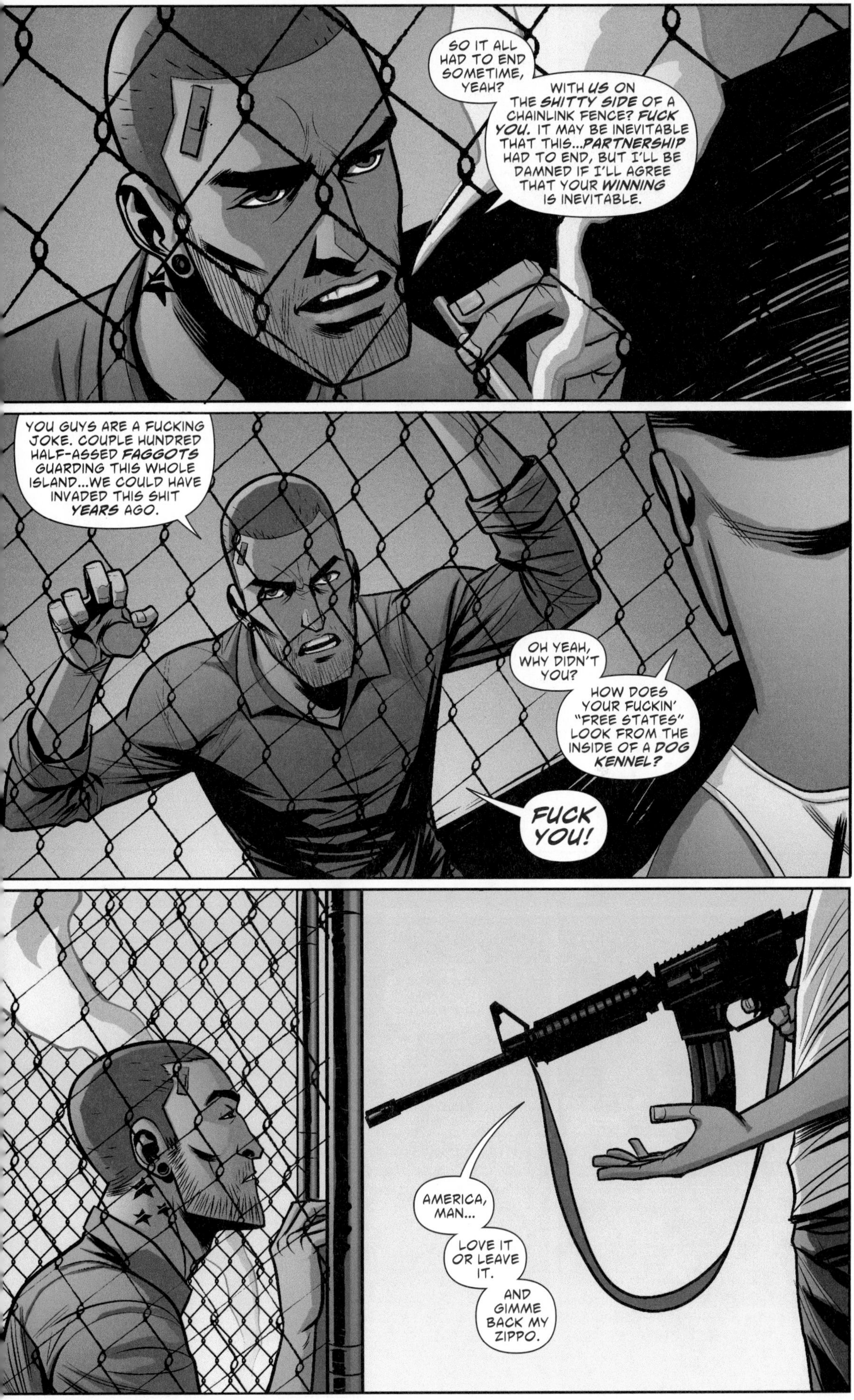

SO IT ALL HAD TO END SOMETIME, YEAH?
WITH *US* ON THE *SHITTY SIDE* OF A CHAINLINK FENCE? *FUCK YOU.* IT MAY BE INEVITABLE THAT THIS...*PARTNERSHIP* HAD TO END, BUT I'LL BE DAMNED IF I'LL AGREE THAT YOUR *WINNING* IS INEVITABLE.
YOU GUYS ARE A FUCKING JOKE. COUPLE HUNDRED HALF-ASSED *FAGGOTS* GUARDING THIS WHOLE ISLAND...WE COULD HAVE INVADED THIS SHIT *YEARS* AGO.
OH YEAH, WHY DIDN'T YOU?
HOW DOES YOUR FUCKIN' "FREE STATES" LOOK FROM THE INSIDE OF A *DOG KENNEL?*
FUCK YOU!
AMERICA, MAN...
LOVE IT OR LEAVE IT.
AND GIMME BACK MY ZIPPO.

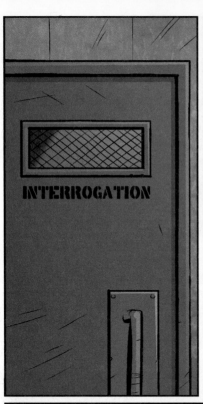

INTERROGATION

TELL ME WHERE IT IS.

...TELL YOU WHERE *WHAT* IS?

WHAP

GAHHHH!

Why am I here?

This is a **disaster**. These guys are panicking...they have no idea what they're doing.

WHAP

FUCK! THAT FUCKING *HURT*, MAN!

TELL ME WHERE THE VIAL IS, ASSHOLE!

And that makes this whole thing so dangerous.

WHERE IS IT?
A VIAL OF WHAT? OF WHAT? YOU FUCKING PSYCHO!
LOOK AT WHAT YOU'RE DOING!
Ricin is a toxin, one of nature's wonders that can be misused to kill people.
All it takes is a grain of it, inhaled. Massive organ failure, shock. I think you can literally end up shitting your insides out.
PULL HIS FINGERNAILS, MAN. PULL THOSE FUCKERS RIGHT THE FUCK OUT.
IT'LL WORK, I SWEAR.
...NO!
It dates back to World War One. All the major players in the last century used it, or at least considered it. A bona fide WMD.
AHHH!
TOO SHORT! THEY'RE ALL BITTEN DOWN, I CAN'T GET A GRIP!
JUST PULL ON THEM, DISLOCATE HIS FUCKING KNUCKLES INSTEAD!
FUCKING ASSHOLES!
And now there's a vial of it loose somewhere.
This feels like a bad movie.
...
HELLO?

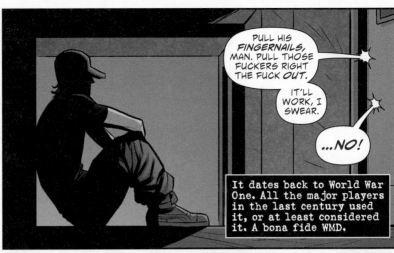

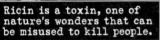

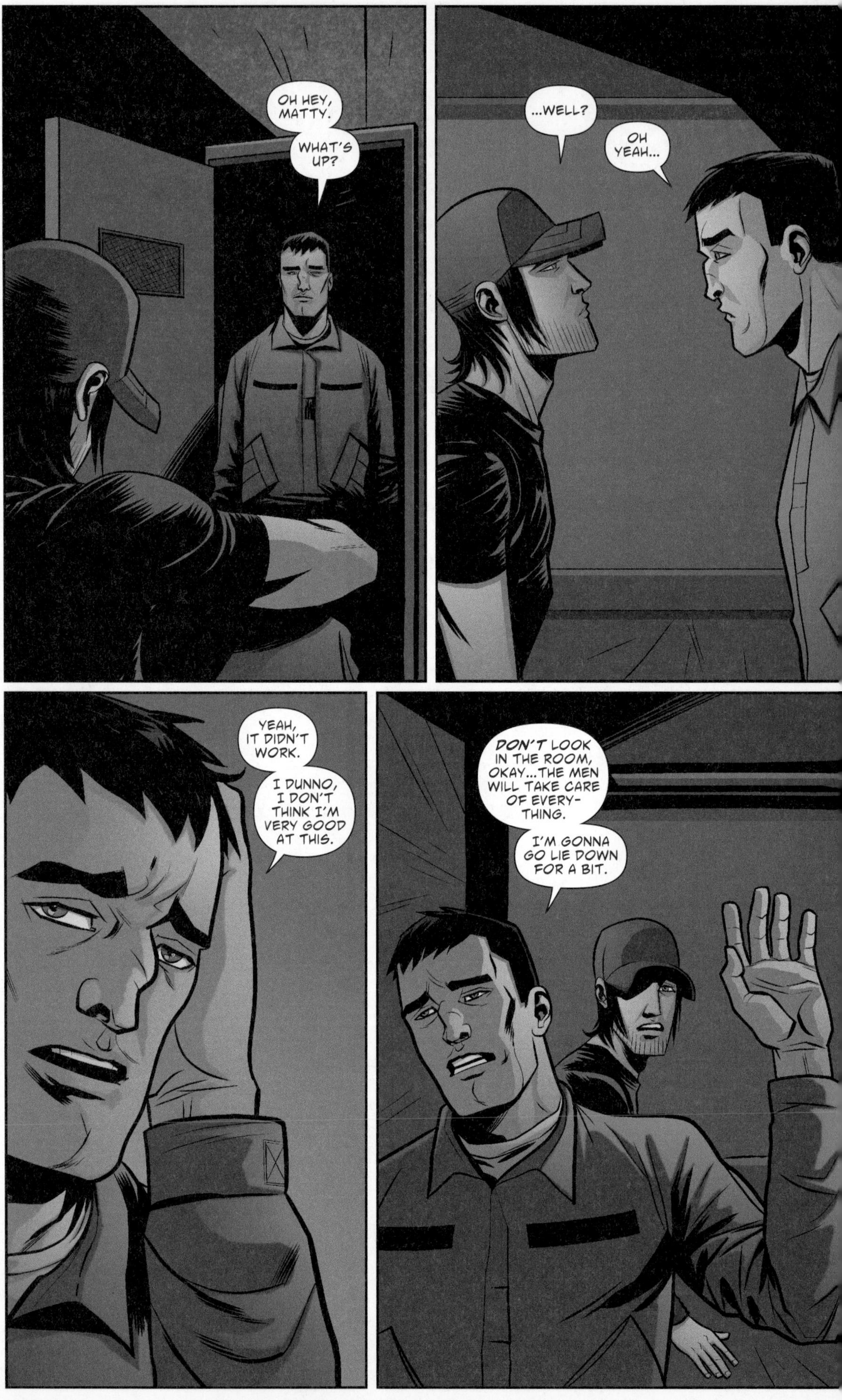
OH HEY, MATTY.
WHAT'S UP?
...WELL?
OH YEAH...
YEAH, IT DIDN'T WORK.
I DUNNO, I DON'T THINK I'M VERY GOOD AT THIS.
DON'T LOOK IN THE ROOM, OKAY...THE MEN WILL TAKE CARE OF EVERY-THING.
I'M GONNA GO LIE DOWN FOR A BIT.

U.S. MILITARY SURVEILLANCE STATION. GEOSTATIONARY ORBIT 35,000KM DIRECTLY ABOVE.

SIR? DO YOU HAVE A MINUTE?

STATEN ISLAND WATCH 1 HAS FAILED TO LOG STATUS, SIR.

HOW LONG?

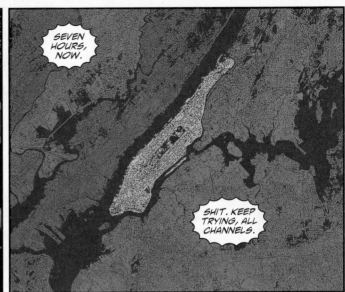

SEVEN HOURS, NOW.

SHIT. KEEP TRYING, ALL CHANNELS.

BIRDEYE 7, BIRDEYE 7, THIS IS CONTROL, COPY.

CONTROL, THIS IS BIRDEYE. GO AHEAD.

BIRDEYE, I NEED YOU TO BUZZ ISLAND WATCH 1, GIVE ME A VISUAL. GO IN LOW, THIS IS PROBABLY NOTHING. NO NEED TO RILE ANYONE UP.

COPY. STAND BY, CONTROL.

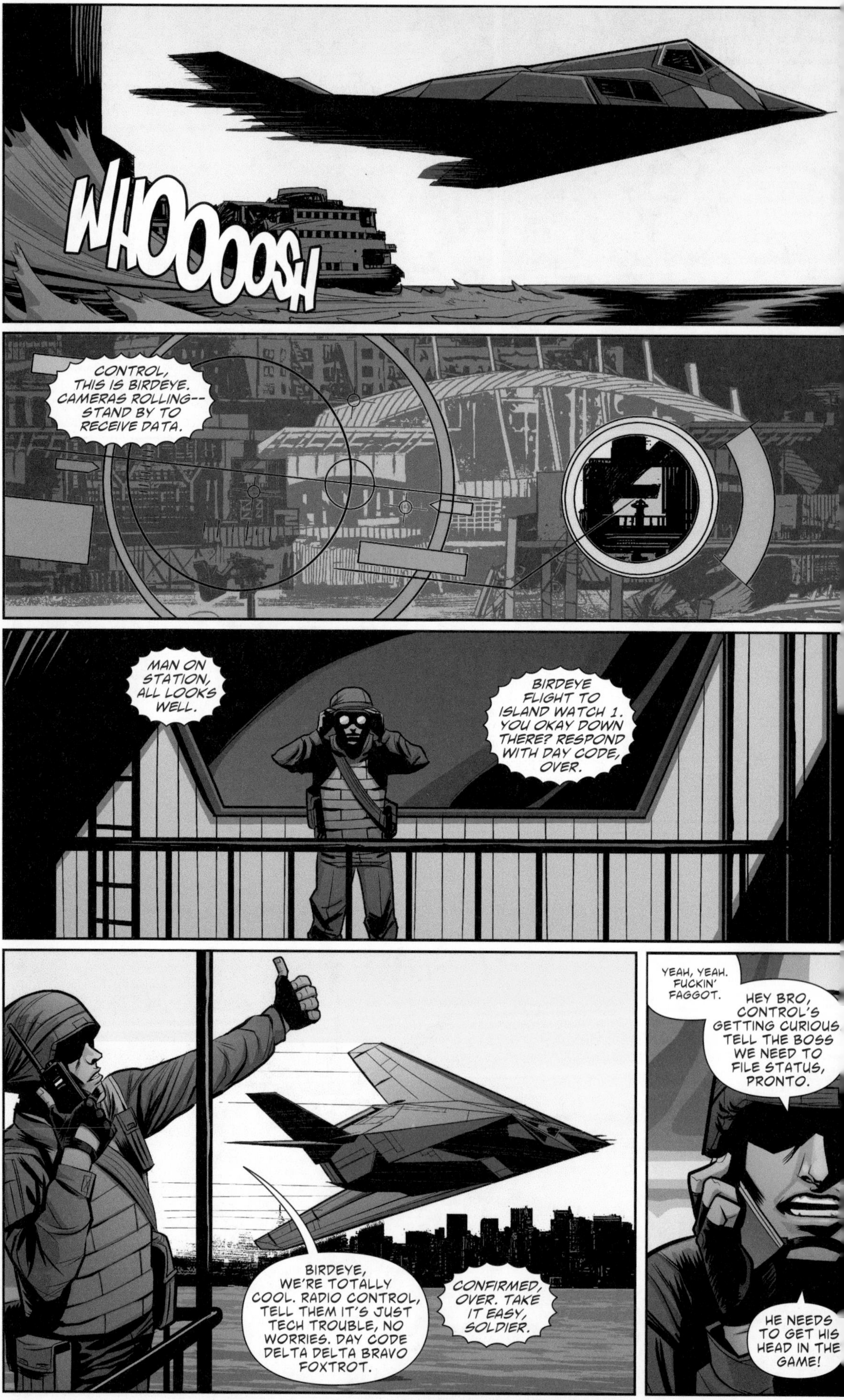
WHOOOOSH
CONTROL, THIS IS BIRDEYE. CAMERAS ROLLING-- STAND BY TO RECEIVE DATA.
MAN ON STATION, ALL LOOKS WELL.
BIRDEYE FLIGHT TO ISLAND WATCH 1. YOU OKAY DOWN THERE? RESPOND WITH DAY CODE, OVER.
BIRDEYE, WE'RE TOTALLY COOL. RADIO CONTROL, TELL THEM IT'S JUST TECH TROUBLE, NO WORRIES. DAY CODE DELTA DELTA BRAVO FOXTROT.
CONFIRMED, OVER. TAKE IT EASY, SOLDIER.
YEAH, YEAH. FUCKIN' FAGGOT.
HEY BRO, CONTROL'S GETTING CURIOUS. TELL THE BOSS WE NEED TO FILE STATUS, PRONTO.
HE NEEDS TO GET HIS HEAD IN THE GAME!

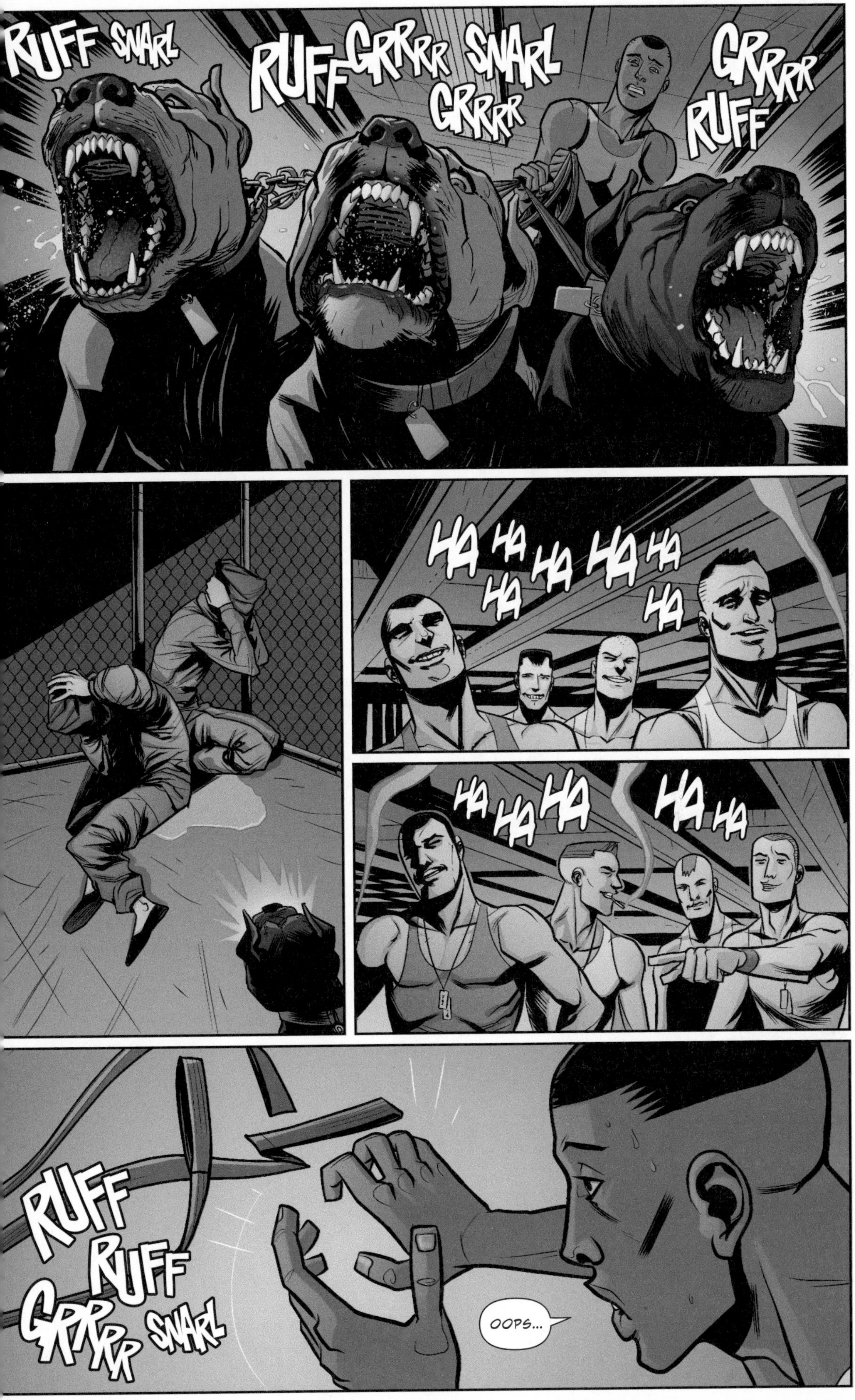
RUFF SNARL
RUFF GRRRRR SNARL GRRRRR
GRRRRR RUFF
HA HA HA HA HA HA HA HA
HA HA HA HA HA HA HA
RUFF RUFF GRRRR SNARL
OOPS...

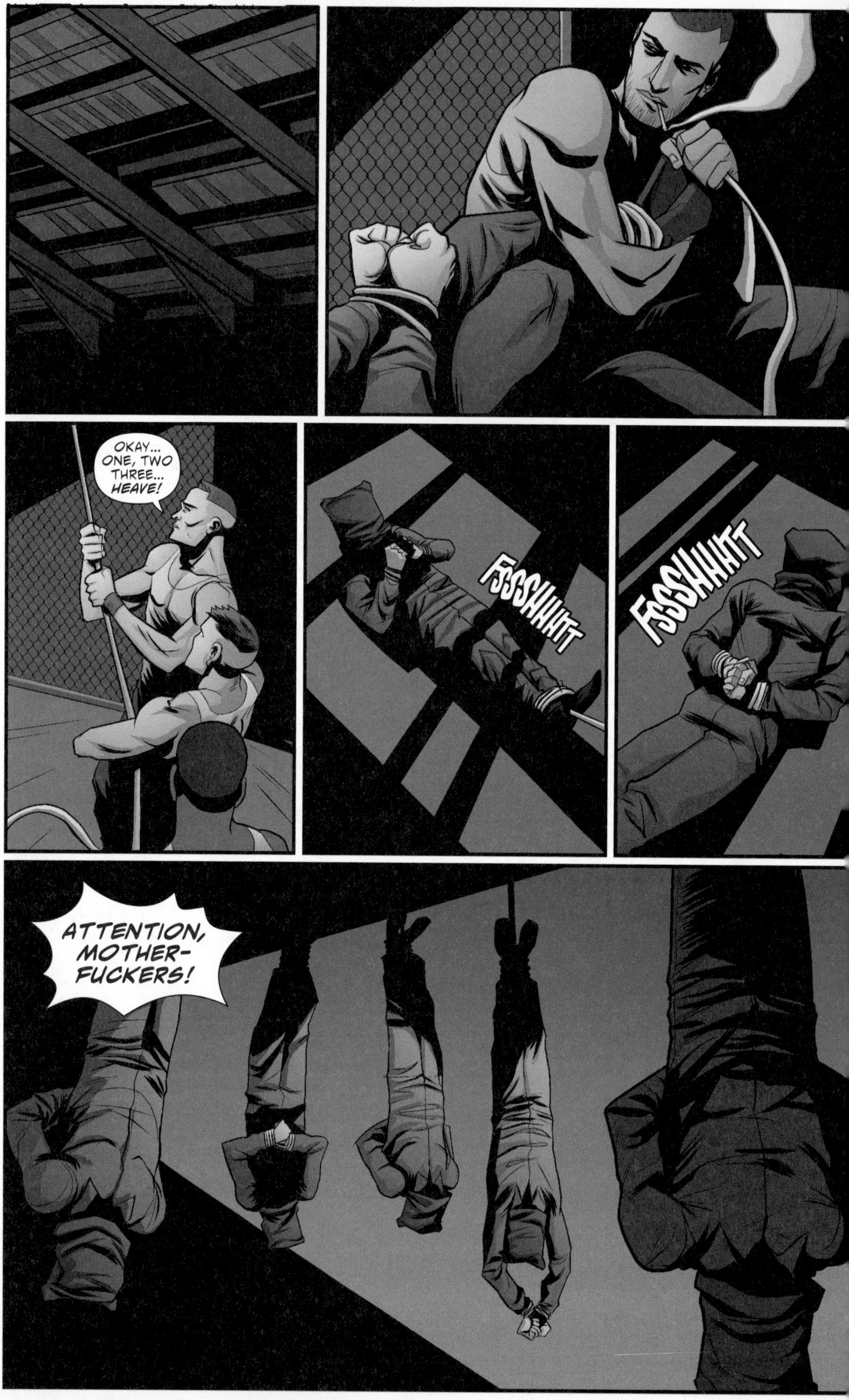
OKAY... ONE, TWO THREE... HEAVE!
FSSSHHHTT
FSSSHHHTT
ATTENTION, MOTHER-FUCKERS!

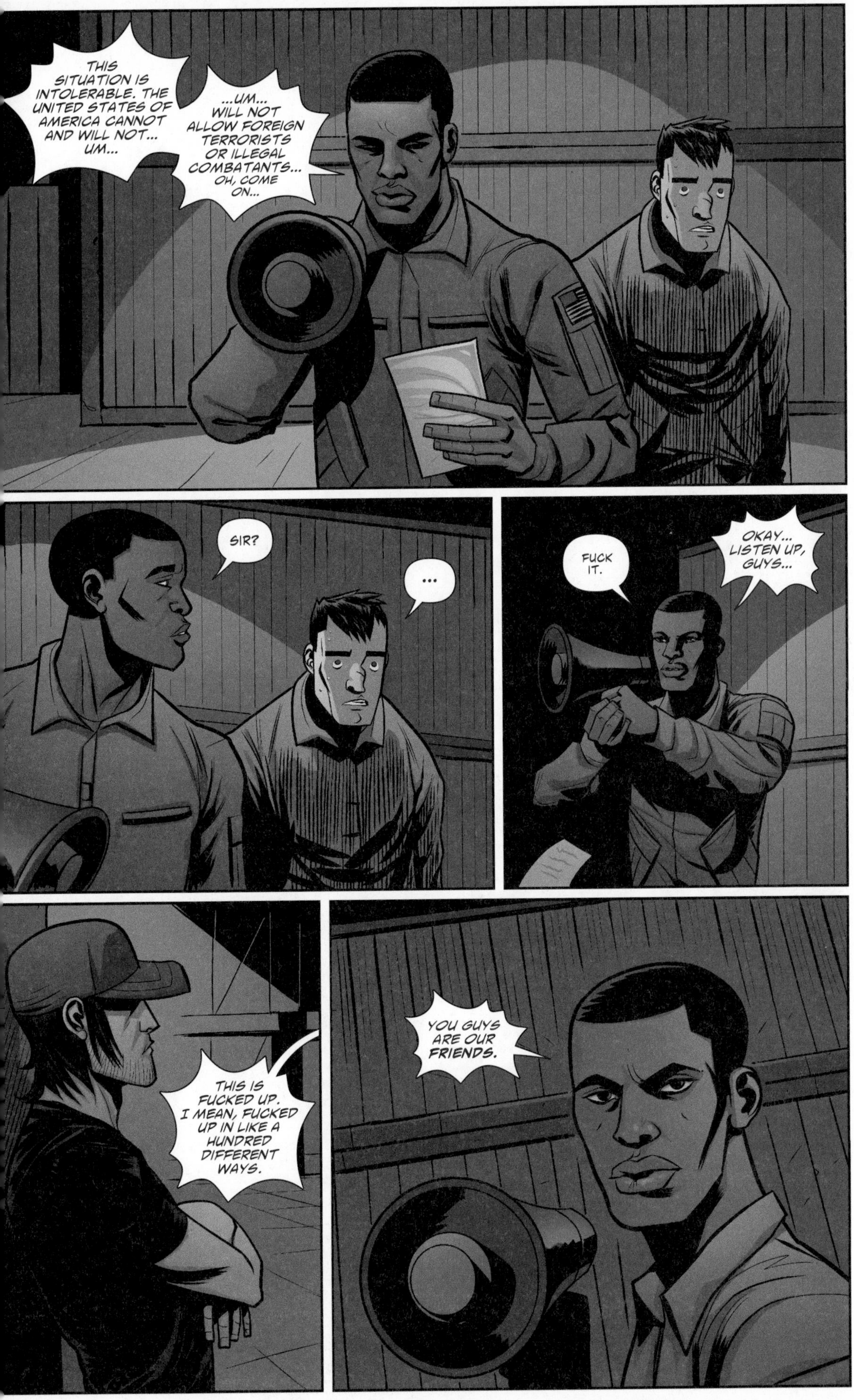
THIS SITUATION IS INTOLERABLE. THE UNITED STATES OF AMERICA CANNOT AND WILL NOT... UM...
...UM... WILL NOT ALLOW FOREIGN TERRORISTS OR ILLEGAL COMBATANTS... OH, COME ON...
SIR?
...
FUCK IT.
OKAY... LISTEN UP, GUYS...
THIS IS FUCKED UP. I MEAN, FUCKED UP IN LIKE A HUNDRED DIFFERENT WAYS.
YOU GUYS ARE OUR FRIENDS.

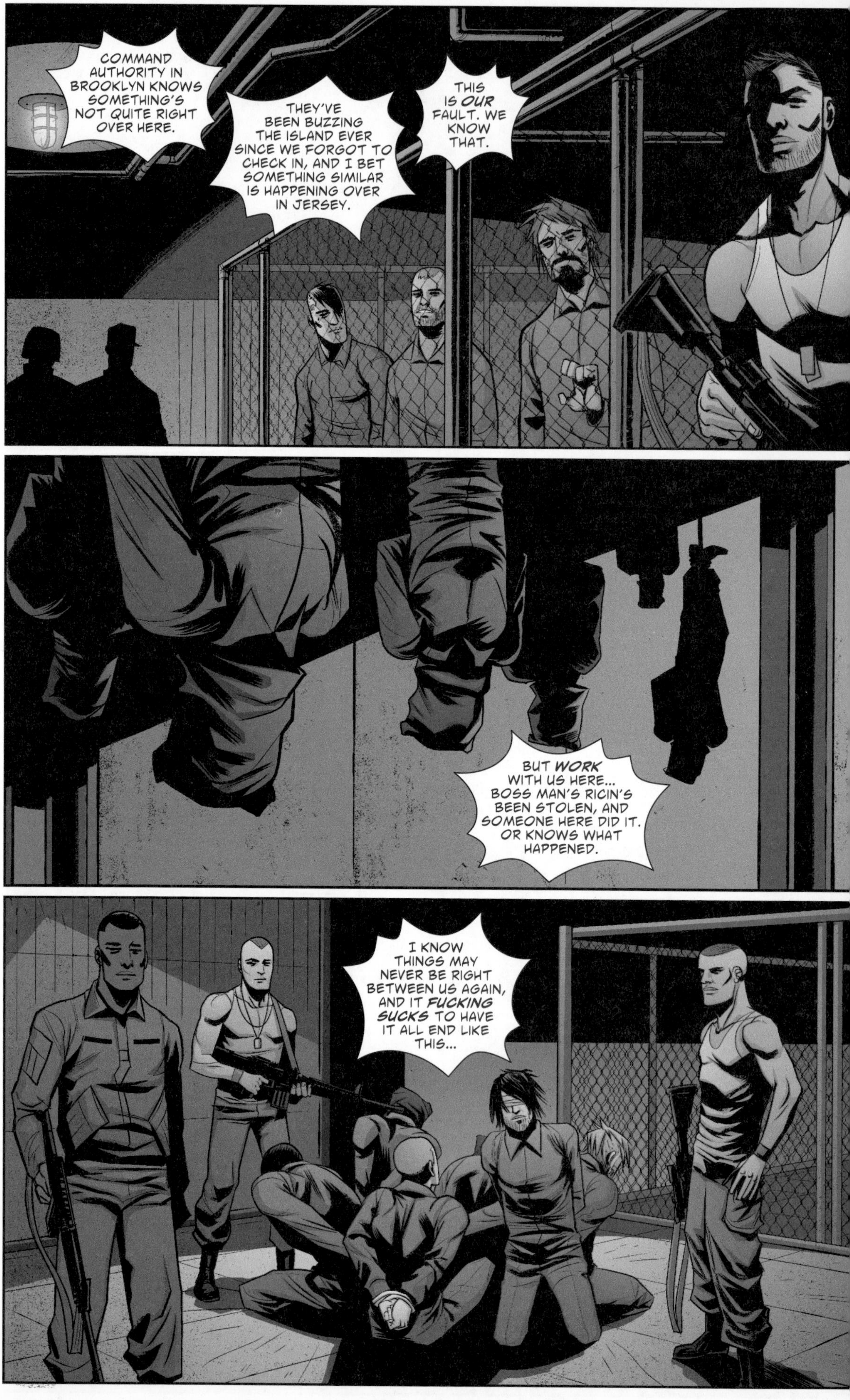
COMMAND AUTHORITY IN BROOKLYN KNOWS SOMETHING'S NOT QUITE RIGHT OVER HERE.
THEY'VE BEEN BUZZING THE ISLAND EVER SINCE WE FORGOT TO CHECK IN, AND I BET SOMETHING SIMILAR IS HAPPENING OVER IN JERSEY.
THIS IS *OUR* FAULT. WE KNOW THAT.
BUT *WORK* WITH US HERE... BOSS MAN'S RICIN'S BEEN STOLEN, AND SOMEONE HERE DID IT. OR KNOWS WHAT HAPPENED.
I KNOW THINGS MAY NEVER BE RIGHT BETWEEN US AGAIN, AND IT *FUCKING SUCKS* TO HAVE IT ALL END LIKE THIS...

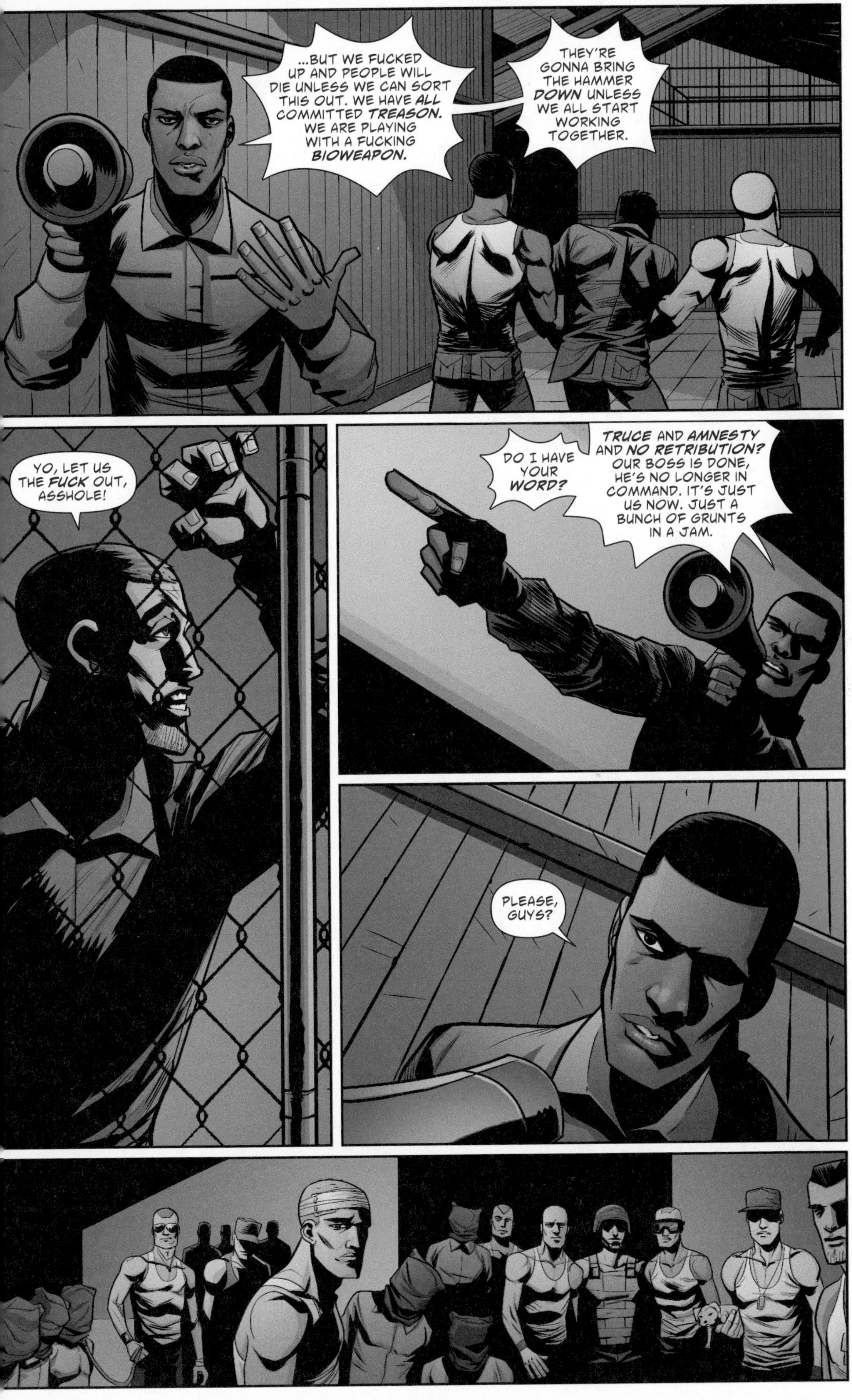
...BUT WE FUCKED UP AND PEOPLE WILL DIE UNLESS WE CAN SORT THIS OUT. WE HAVE ALL COMMITTED TREASON. WE ARE PLAYING WITH A FUCKING BIOWEAPON.
THEY'RE GONNA BRING THE HAMMER DOWN UNLESS WE ALL START WORKING TOGETHER.
YO, LET US THE FUCK OUT, ASSHOLE!
DO I HAVE YOUR WORD?
TRUCE AND AMNESTY AND NO RETRIBUTION? OUR BOSS IS DONE, HE'S NO LONGER IN COMMAND. IT'S JUST US NOW. JUST A BUNCH OF GRUNTS IN A JAM.
PLEASE, GUYS?

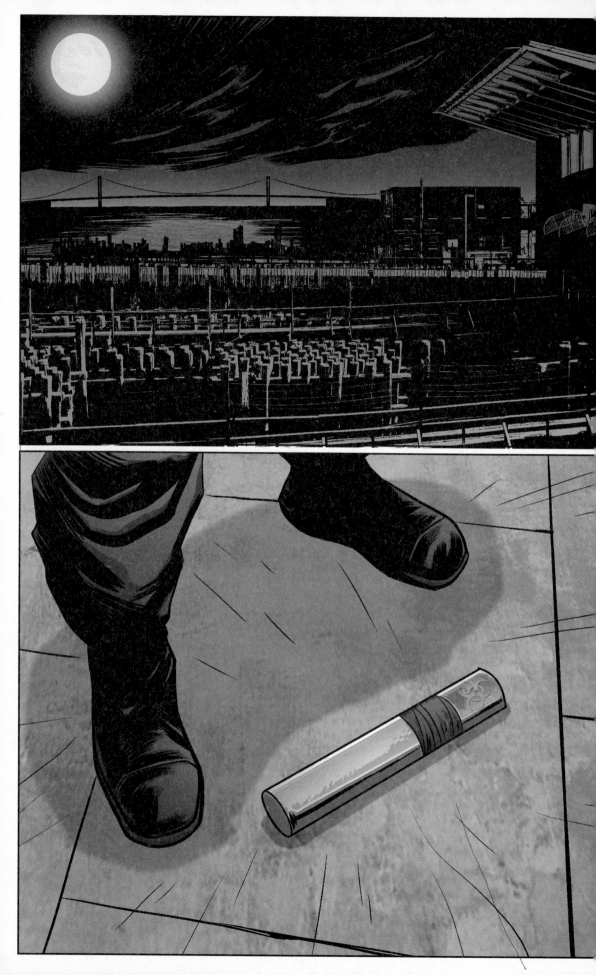

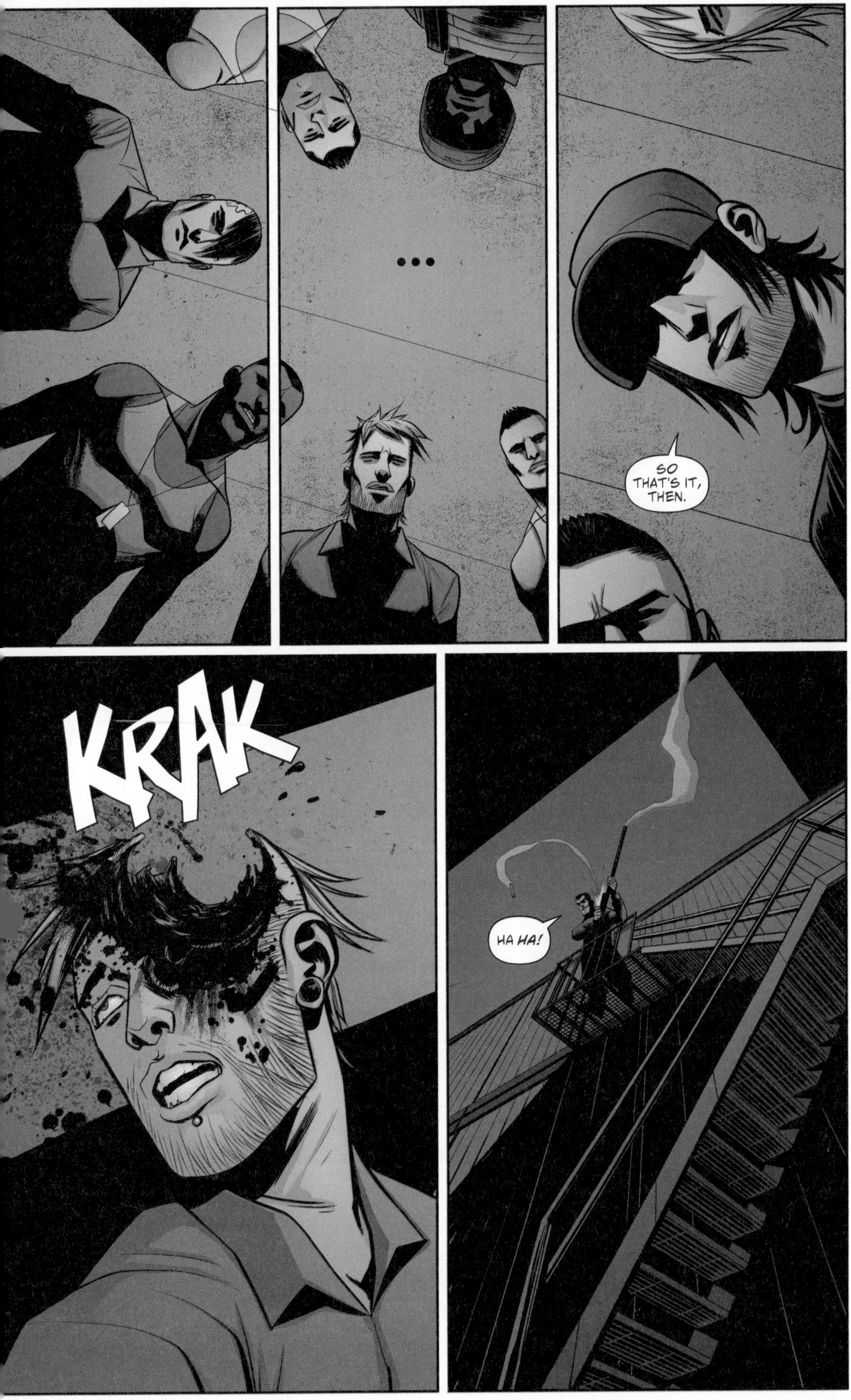
...
SO THAT'S IT, THEN.
KRAK
HA HA!

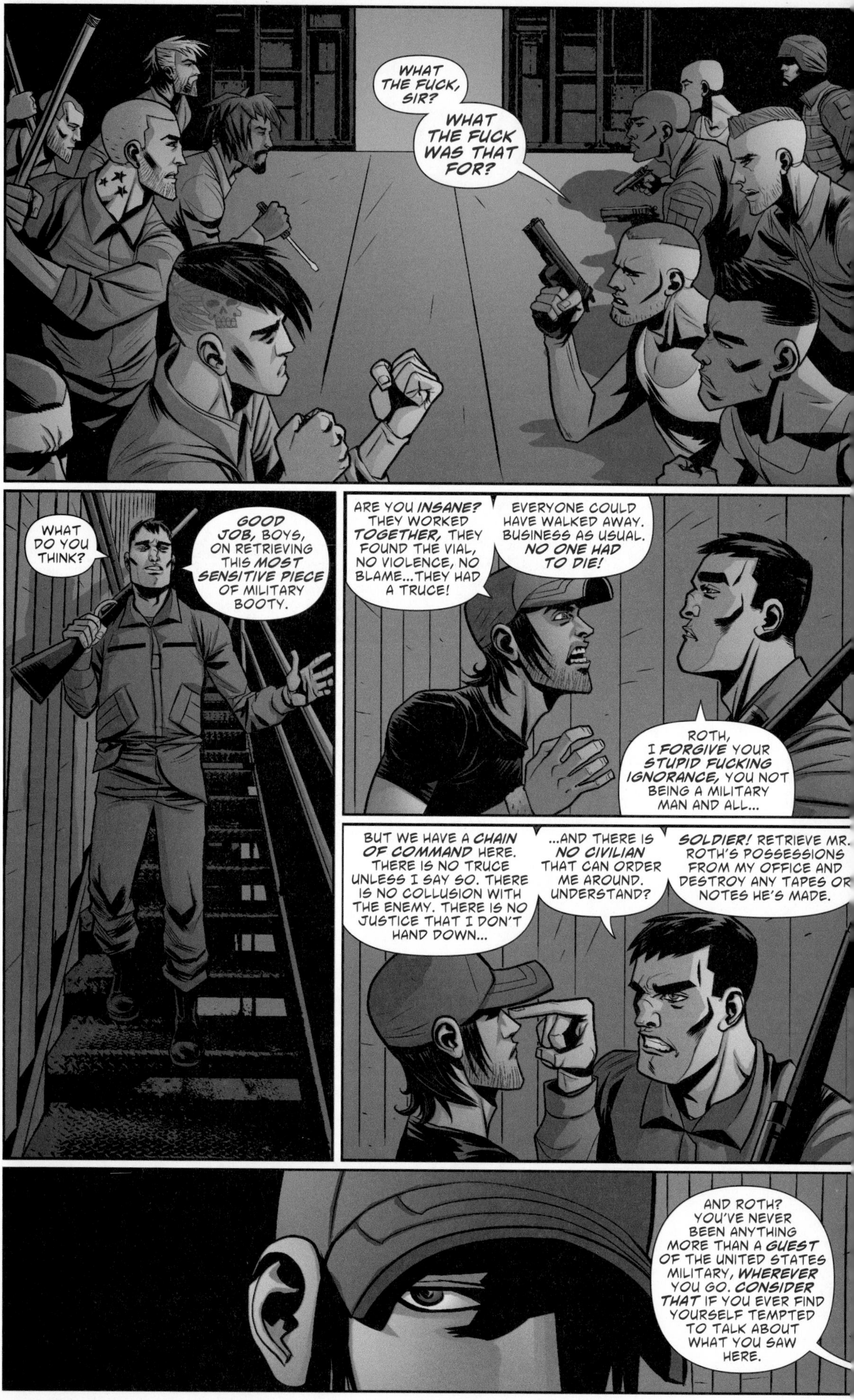
WHAT THE FUCK, SIR?
WHAT THE FUCK WAS THAT FOR?
WHAT DO YOU THINK?
GOOD JOB, BOYS, ON RETRIEVING THIS MOST SENSITIVE PIECE OF MILITARY BOOTY.
ARE YOU INSANE? THEY WORKED TOGETHER, THEY FOUND THE VIAL, NO VIOLENCE, NO BLAME...THEY HAD A TRUCE!
EVERYONE COULD HAVE WALKED AWAY. BUSINESS AS USUAL. NO ONE HAD TO DIE!
ROTH, I FORGIVE YOUR STUPID FUCKING IGNORANCE, YOU NOT BEING A MILITARY MAN AND ALL...
BUT WE HAVE A CHAIN OF COMMAND HERE. THERE IS NO TRUCE UNLESS I SAY SO. THERE IS NO COLLUSION WITH THE ENEMY. THERE IS NO JUSTICE THAT I DON'T HAND DOWN...
...AND THERE IS NO CIVILIAN THAT CAN ORDER ME AROUND. UNDERSTAND?
SOLDIER! RETRIEVE MR. ROTH'S POSSESSIONS FROM MY OFFICE AND DESTROY ANY TAPES OR NOTES HE'S MADE.
AND ROTH? YOU'VE NEVER BEEN ANYTHING MORE THAN A GUEST OF THE UNITED STATES MILITARY, WHEREVER YOU GO. CONSIDER THAT IF YOU EVER FIND YOURSELF TEMPTED TO TALK ABOUT WHAT YOU SAW HERE.

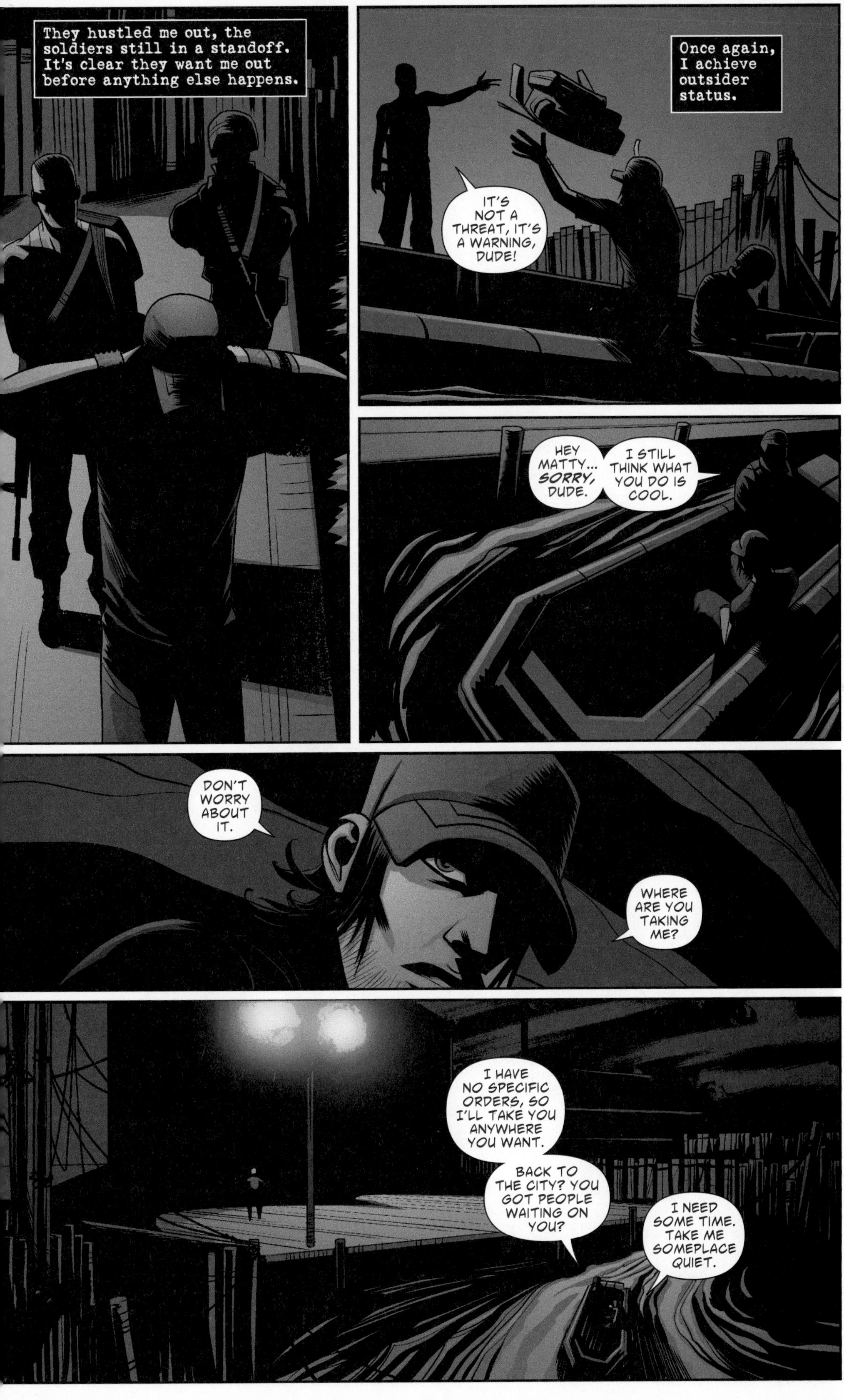
They hustled me out, the soldiers still in a standoff. It's clear they want me out before anything else happens.
Once again, I achieve outsider status.
IT'S NOT A THREAT, IT'S A WARNING, DUDE!
HEY MATTY... SORRY, DUDE.
I STILL THINK WHAT YOU DO IS COOL.
DON'T WORRY ABOUT IT.
WHERE ARE YOU TAKING ME?
I HAVE NO SPECIFIC ORDERS, SO I'LL TAKE YOU ANYWHERE YOU WANT.
BACK TO THE CITY? YOU GOT PEOPLE WAITING ON YOU?
I NEED SOME TIME. TAKE ME SOMEPLACE QUIET.

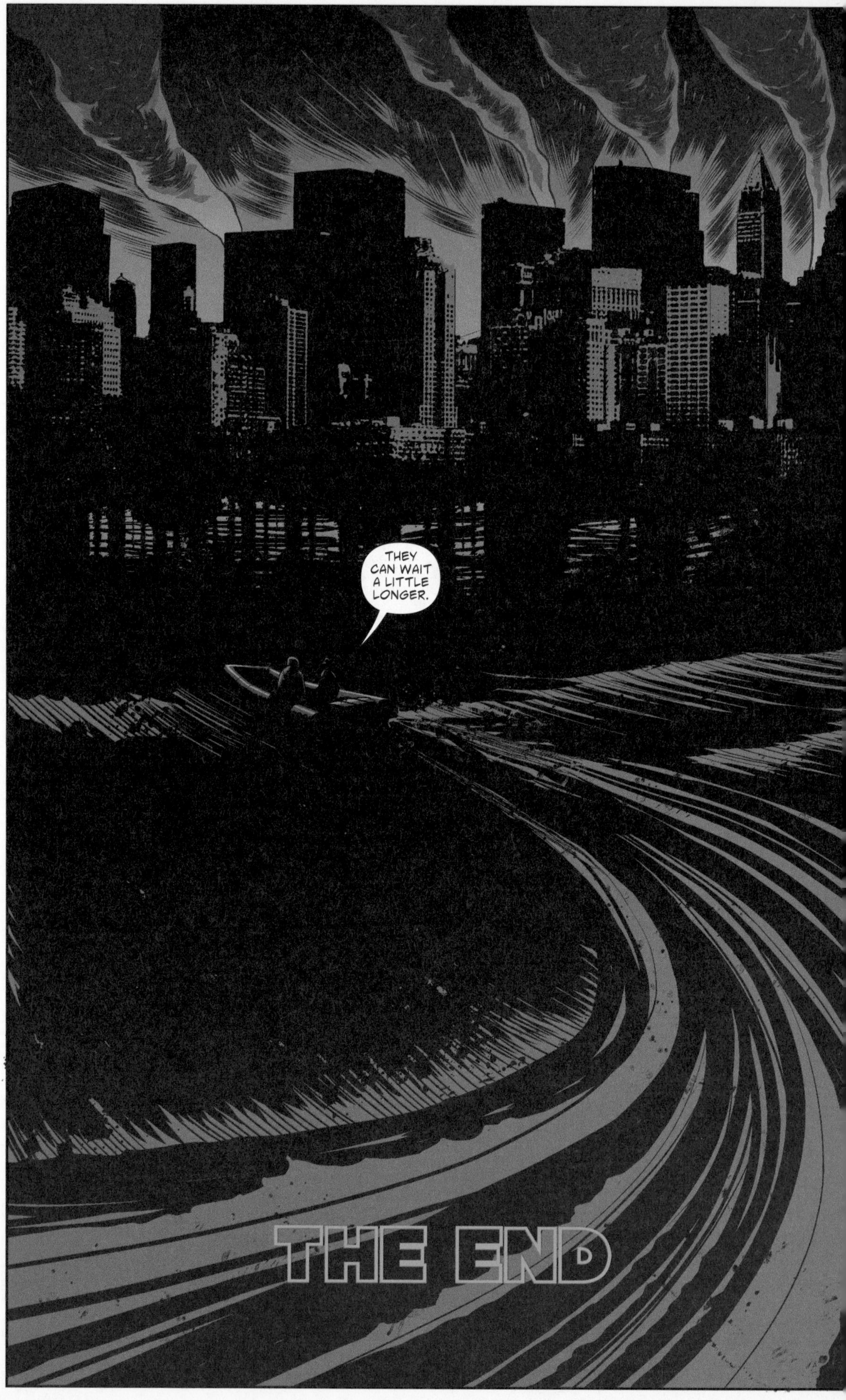
THEY CAN WAIT A LITTLE LONGER.
THE END

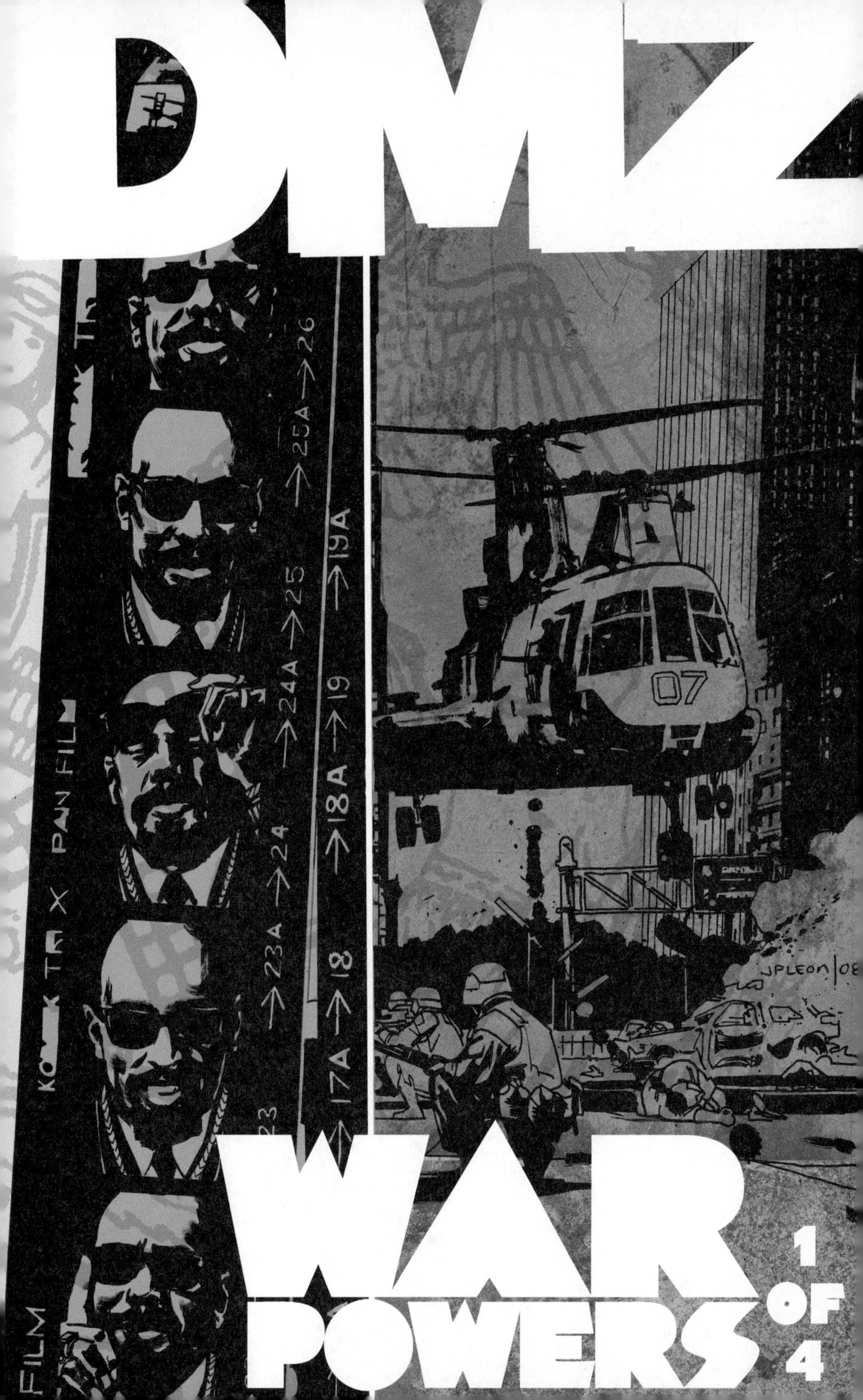
DMZ
07
JPLEON/08
WAR POWERS
1 OF 4

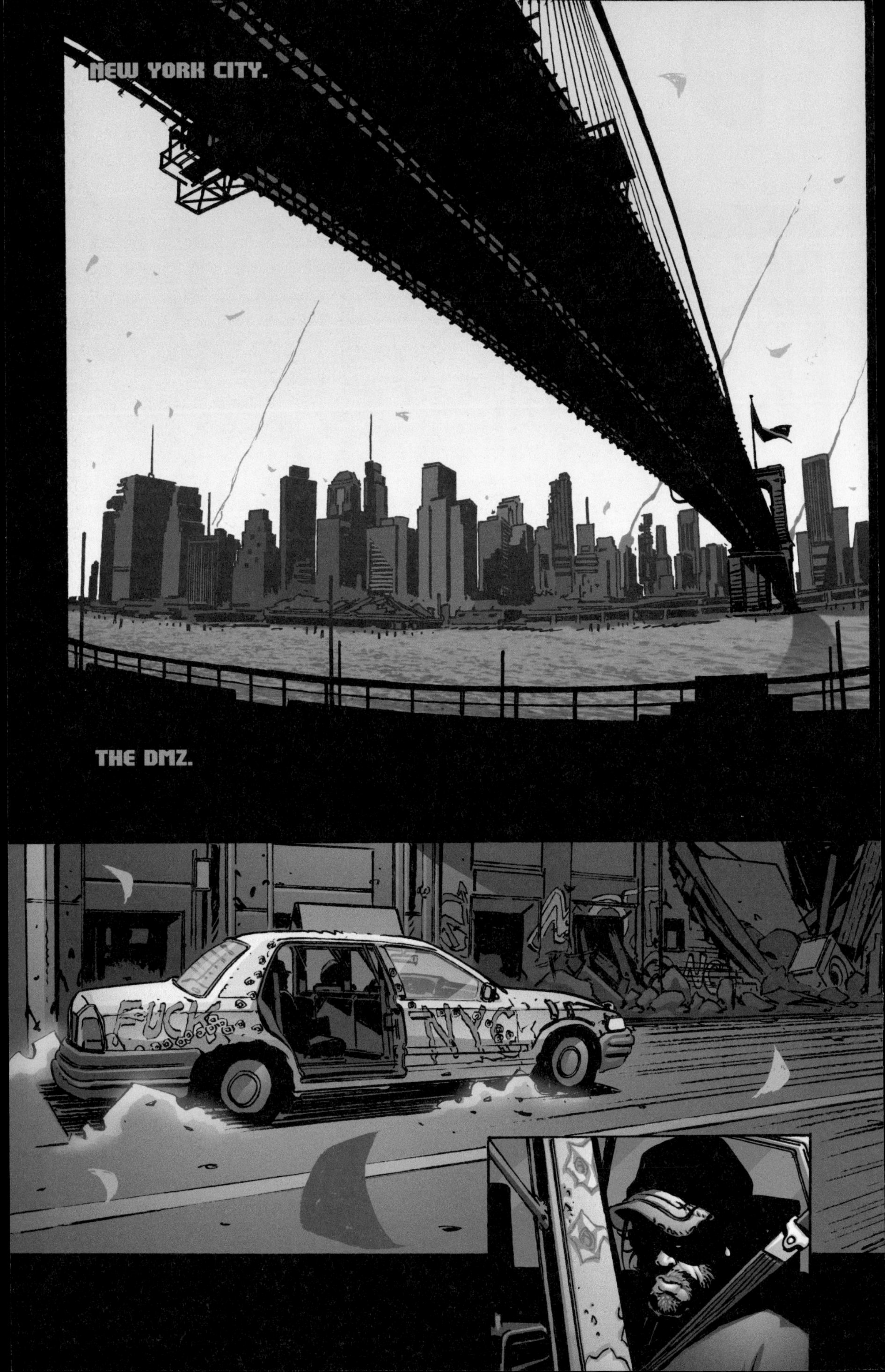
NEW YORK CITY.
THE DMZ.
FUCK NYC

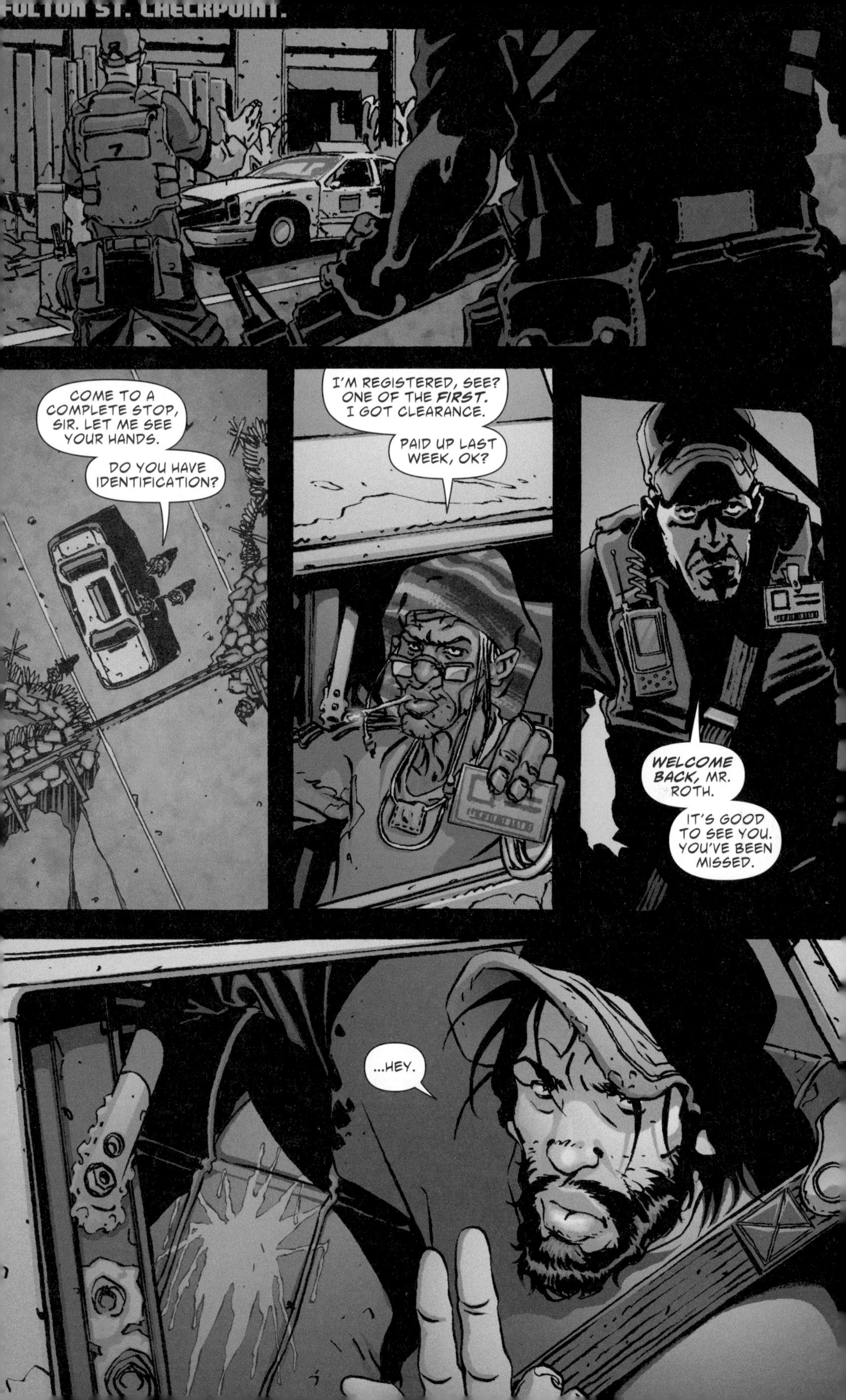
FULTON ST. CHECKPOINT.
COME TO A COMPLETE STOP, SIR. LET ME SEE YOUR HANDS.
DO YOU HAVE IDENTIFICATION?
I'M REGISTERED, SEE? ONE OF THE FIRST. I GOT CLEARANCE.
PAID UP LAST WEEK, OK?
WELCOME BACK, MR. ROTH.
IT'S GOOD TO SEE YOU. YOU'VE BEEN MISSED.
...HEY.

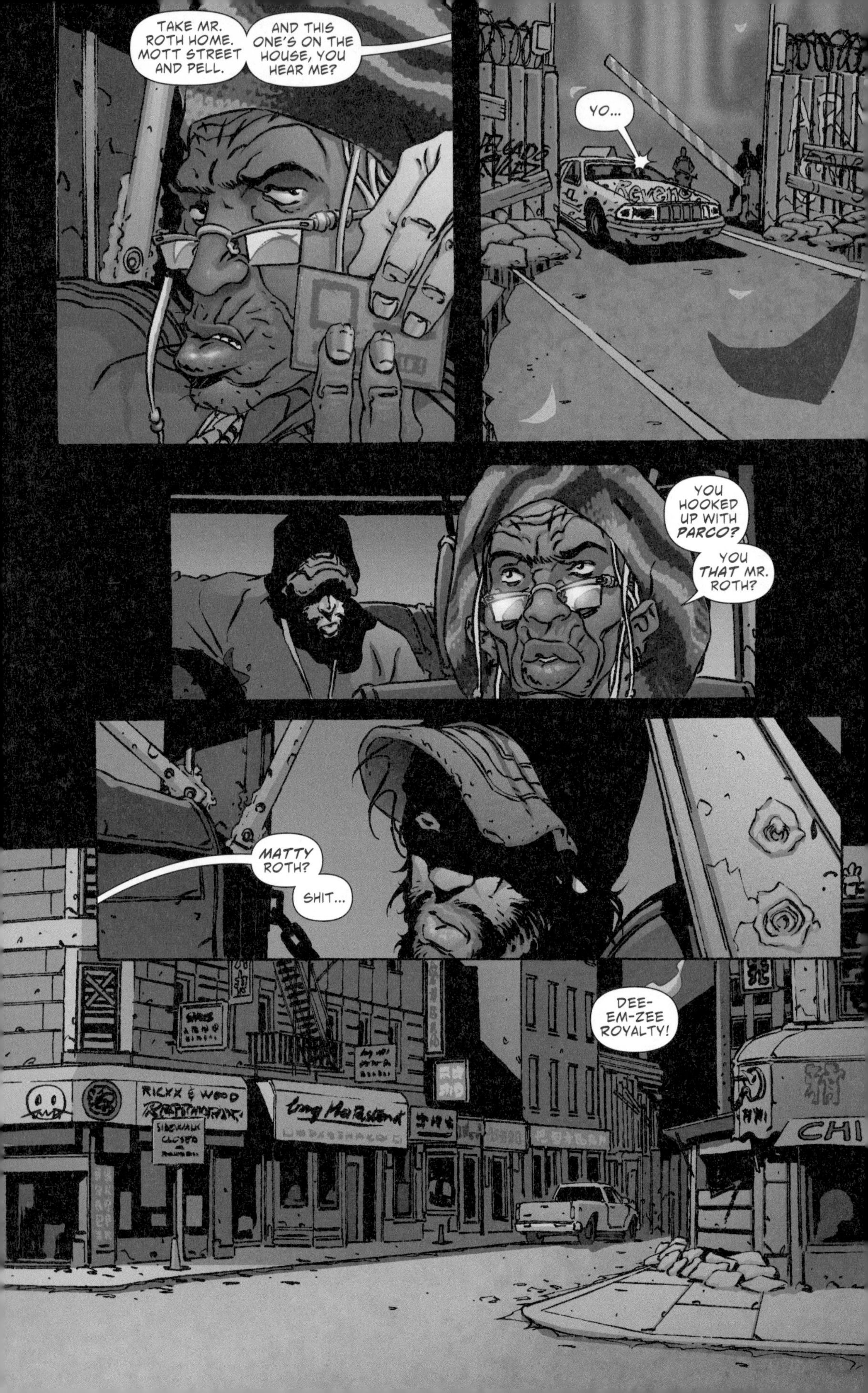
TAKE MR. ROTH HOME. MOTT STREET AND PELL.
AND THIS ONE'S ON THE HOUSE, YOU HEAR ME?
YO...
YOU HOOKED UP WITH PARCO?
YOU THAT MR. ROTH?
MATTY ROTH?
SHIT...
DEE-EM-ZEE ROYALTY!
CHI

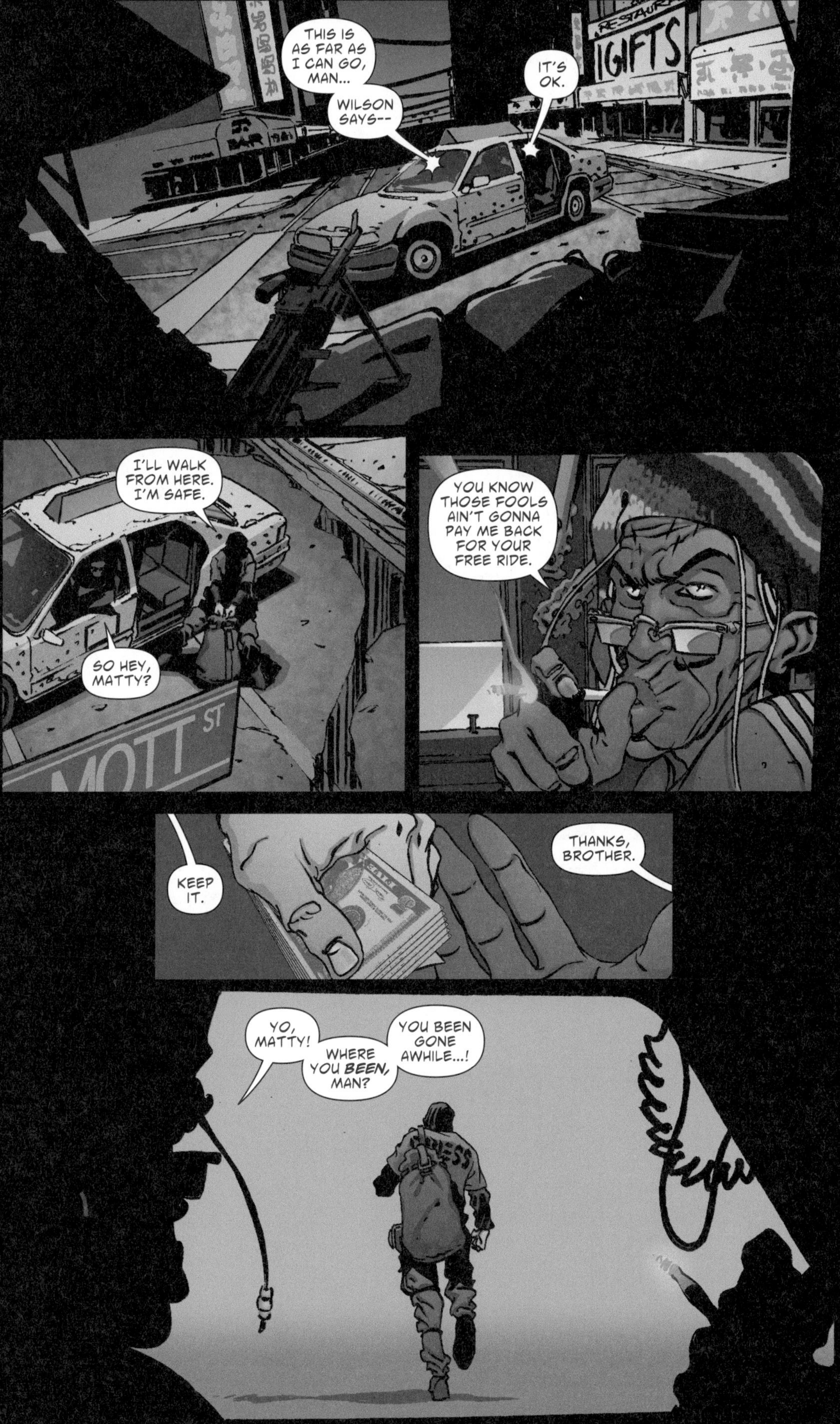
THIS IS AS FAR AS I CAN GO, MAN...
WILSON SAYS--
IT'S OK.
RESTAURANT
GIFTS
I'LL WALK FROM HERE. I'M SAFE.
SO HEY, MATTY?
MOTT ST
YOU KNOW THOSE FOOLS AIN'T GONNA PAY ME BACK FOR YOUR FREE RIDE.
KEEP IT.
THANKS, BROTHER.
YO, MATTY!
WHERE YOU *BEEN,* MAN?
YOU BEEN GONE AWHILE...!

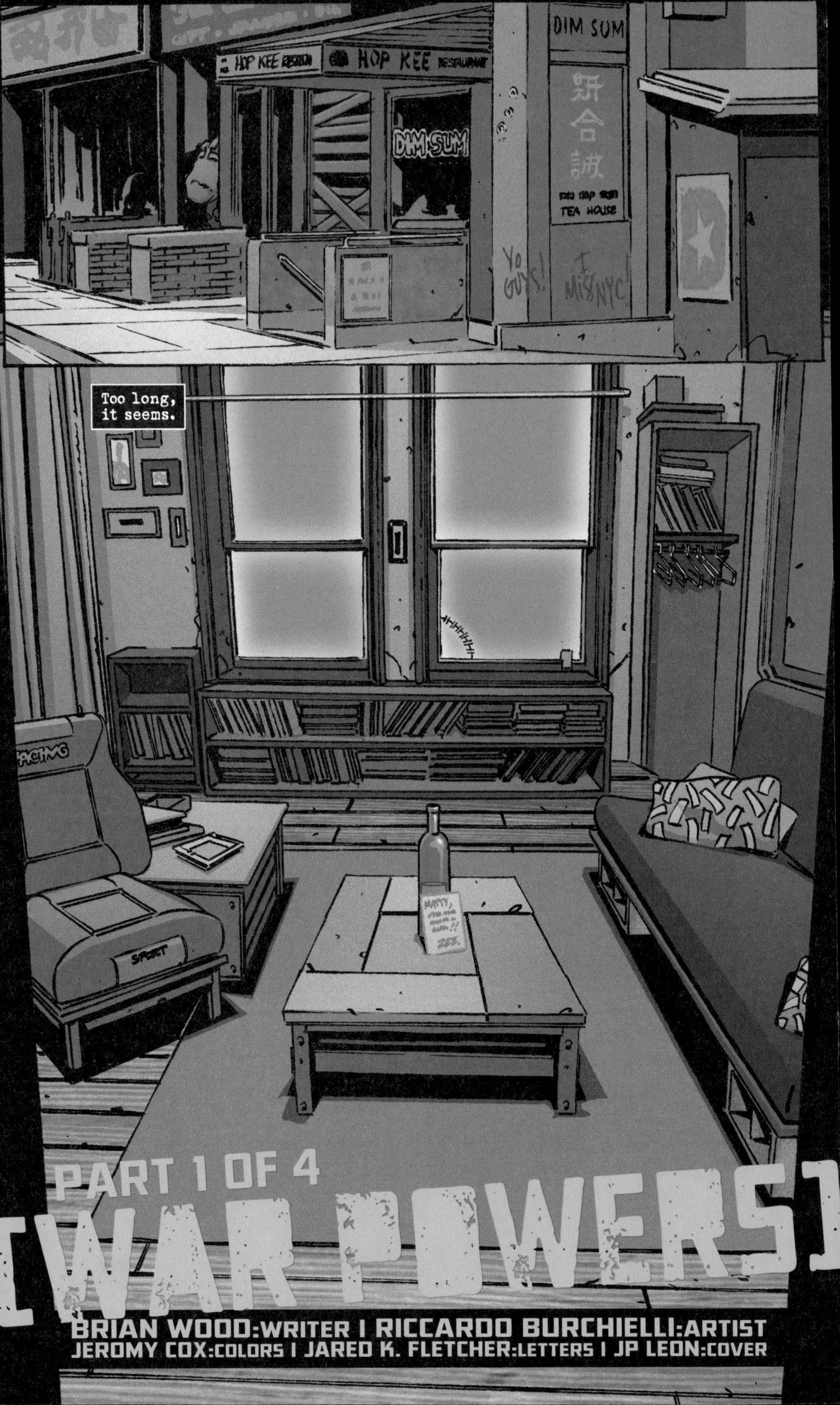
DIM SUM
HOP KEE RESTAURANT
HOP KEE
DIM SUM
TEA HOUSE
Yo GUYS!
I MISS NYC!
Too long, it seems.
PART 1 OF 4
[WAR POWERS]
BRIAN WOOD:WRITER I RICCARDO BURCHIELLI:ARTIST
JEROMY COX:COLORS I JARED K. FLETCHER:LETTERS I JP LEON:COVER

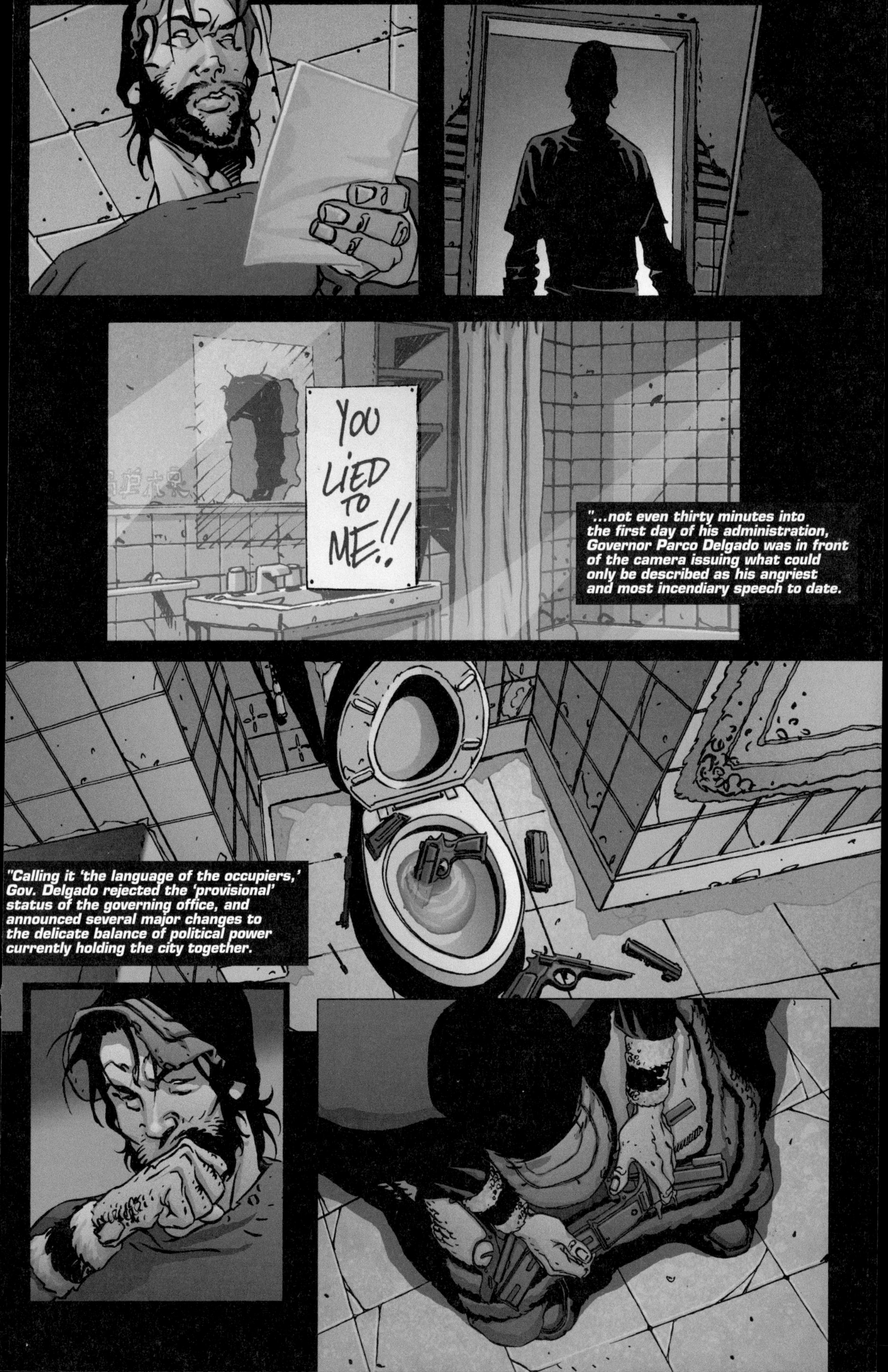
YOU LIED TO ME!!
"...not even thirty minutes into the first day of his administration, Governor Parco Delgado was in front of the camera issuing what could only be described as his angriest and most incendiary speech to date.
"Calling it 'the language of the occupiers,' Gov. Delgado rejected the 'provisional' status of the governing office, and announced several major changes to the delicate balance of political power currently holding the city together.

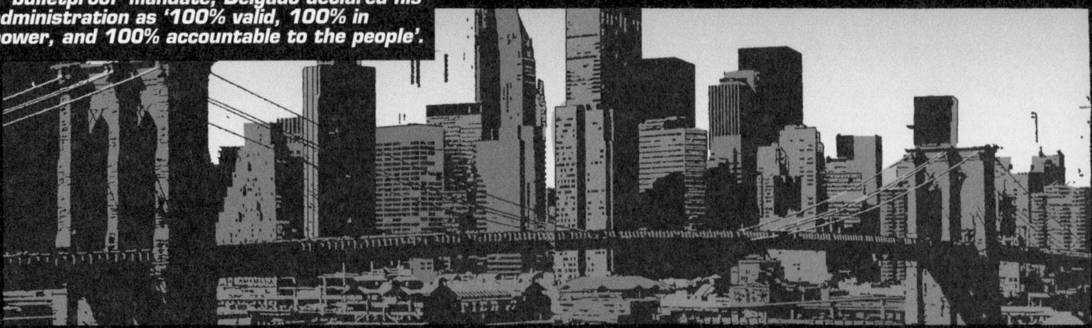
"Claiming a landslide victory in the polls and a 'bulletproof' mandate, Delgado declared his administration as '100% valid, 100% in power, and 100% accountable to the people'.

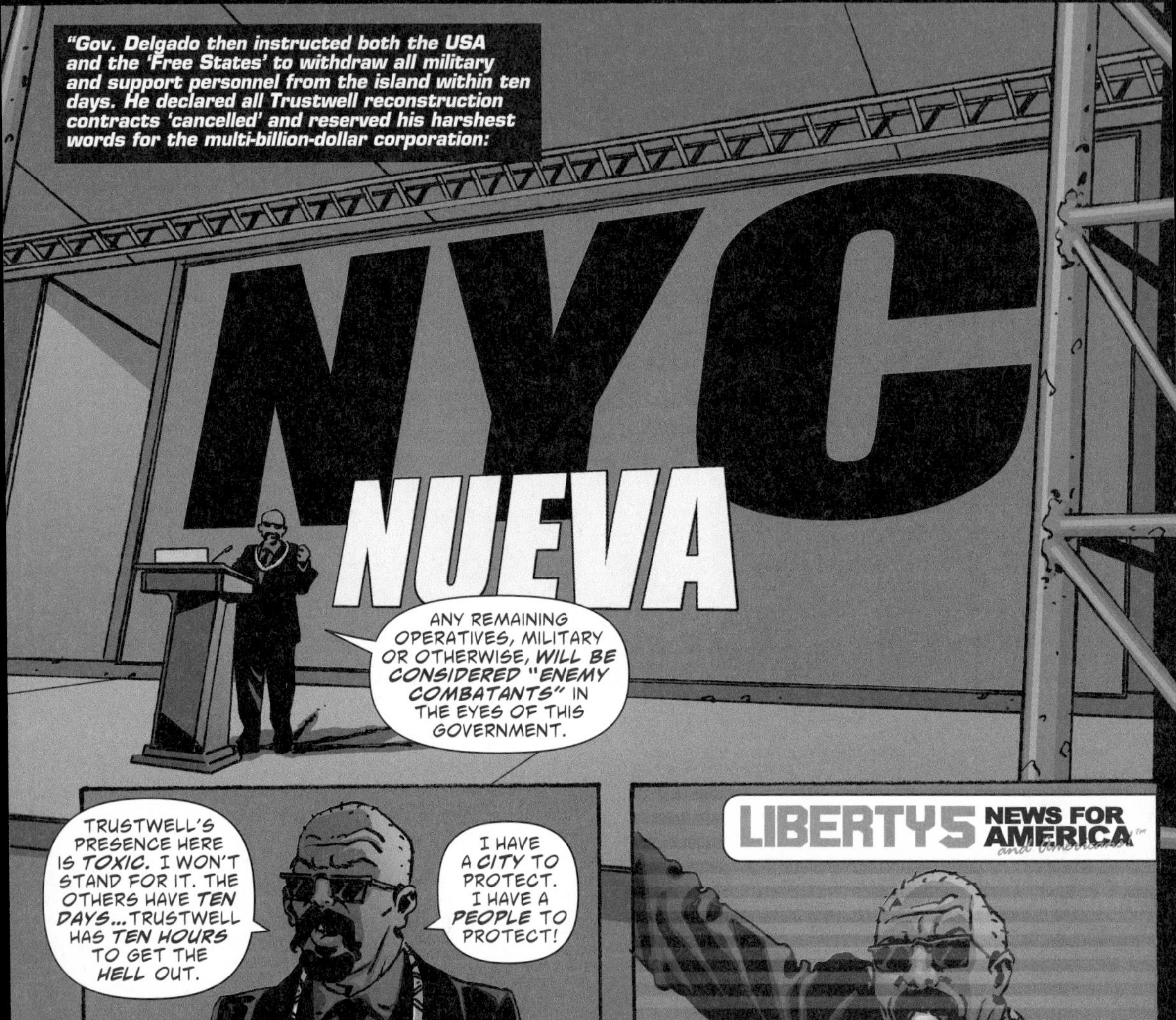
"Gov. Delgado then instructed both the USA and the 'Free States' to withdraw all military and support personnel from the island within ten days. He declared all Trustwell reconstruction contracts 'cancelled' and reserved his harshest words for the multi-billion-dollar corporation:
NYC
NUEVA
ANY REMAINING OPERATIVES, MILITARY OR OTHERWISE, *WILL BE CONSIDERED "ENEMY COMBATANTS"* IN THE EYES OF THIS GOVERNMENT.

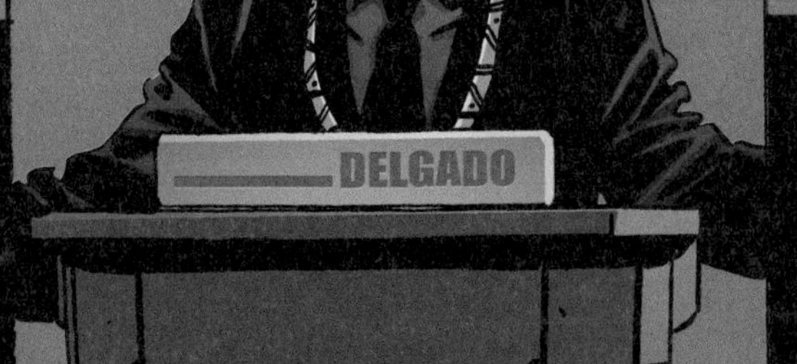
TRUSTWELL'S PRESENCE HERE IS *TOXIC*. I WON'T STAND FOR IT. THE OTHERS HAVE *TEN DAYS*... TRUSTWELL HAS *TEN HOURS* TO GET THE *HELL* OUT.
I HAVE A *CITY* TO PROTECT. I HAVE A *PEOPLE* TO PROTECT!
DELGADO

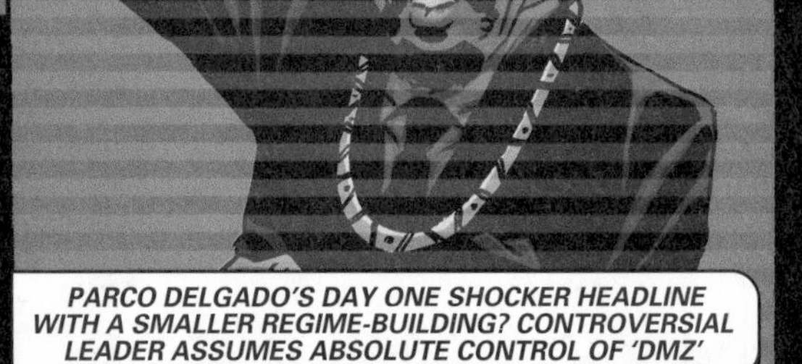
LIBERTY5 NEWS FOR AMERICA
PARCO DELGADO'S DAY ONE SHOCKER HEADLINE WITH A SMALLER REGIME-BUILDING? CONTROVERSIAL LEADER ASSUMES ABSOLUTE CONTROL OF 'DMZ'

"In the past, Trustwell has always used its contracts, issued by legal authority by the United States of America, to defend its actions as lawful and constitutional. It's unclear at this time if that defense will hold up.

"They have yet to comment."

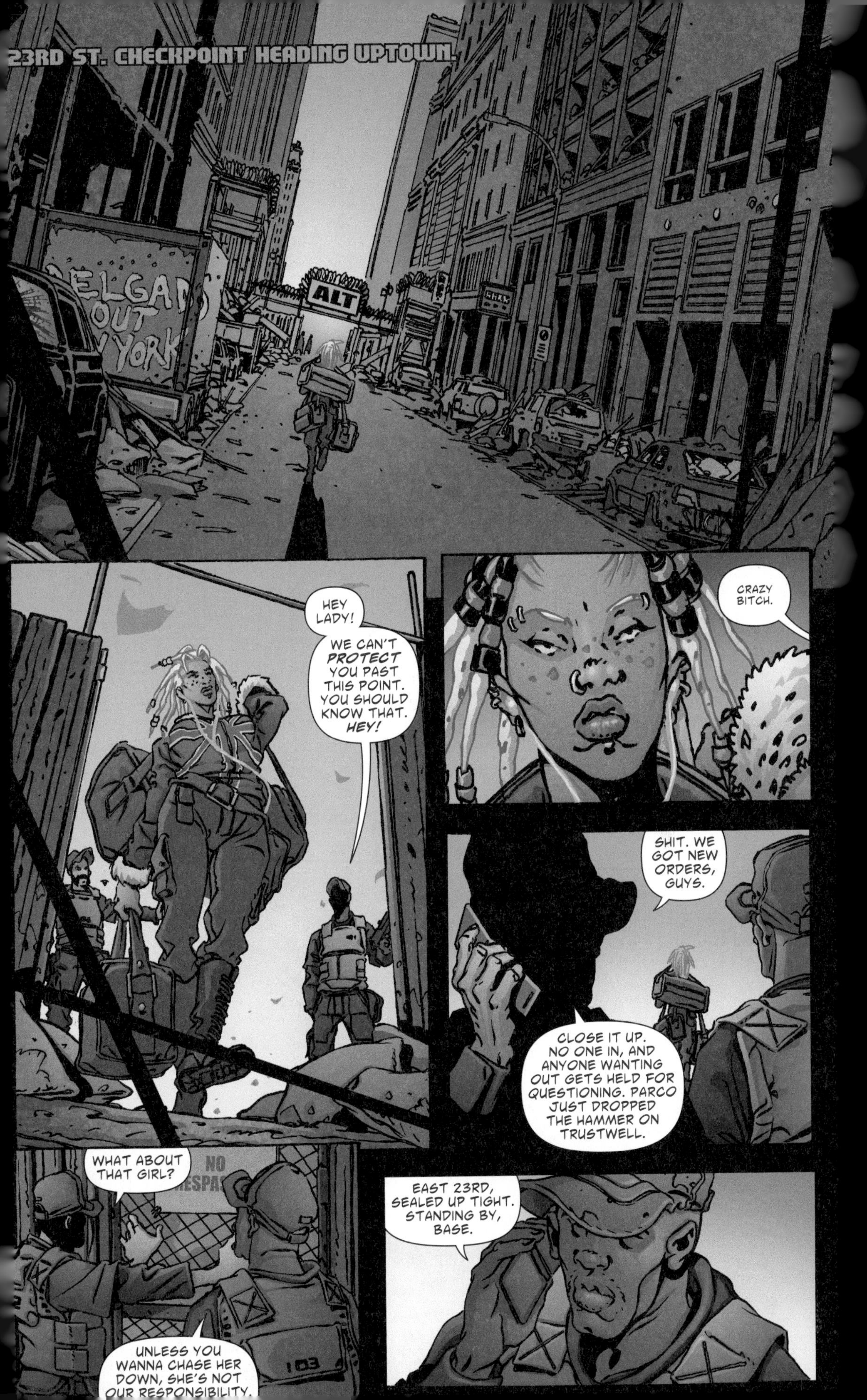
23RD ST. CHECKPOINT HEADING UPTOWN.
DELGADO OUT NEW YORK
ALT
HEY LADY!
WE CAN'T *PROTECT* YOU PAST THIS POINT. YOU SHOULD KNOW THAT. *HEY!*
CRAZY BITCH.
SHIT. WE GOT NEW ORDERS, GUYS.
CLOSE IT UP. NO ONE IN, AND ANYONE WANTING OUT GETS HELD FOR QUESTIONING. PARCO JUST DROPPED THE HAMMER ON TRUSTWELL.
WHAT ABOUT THAT GIRL?
UNLESS YOU WANNA CHASE HER DOWN, SHE'S NOT OUR RESPONSIBILITY.
EAST 23RD, SEALED UP TIGHT. STANDING BY, BASE.

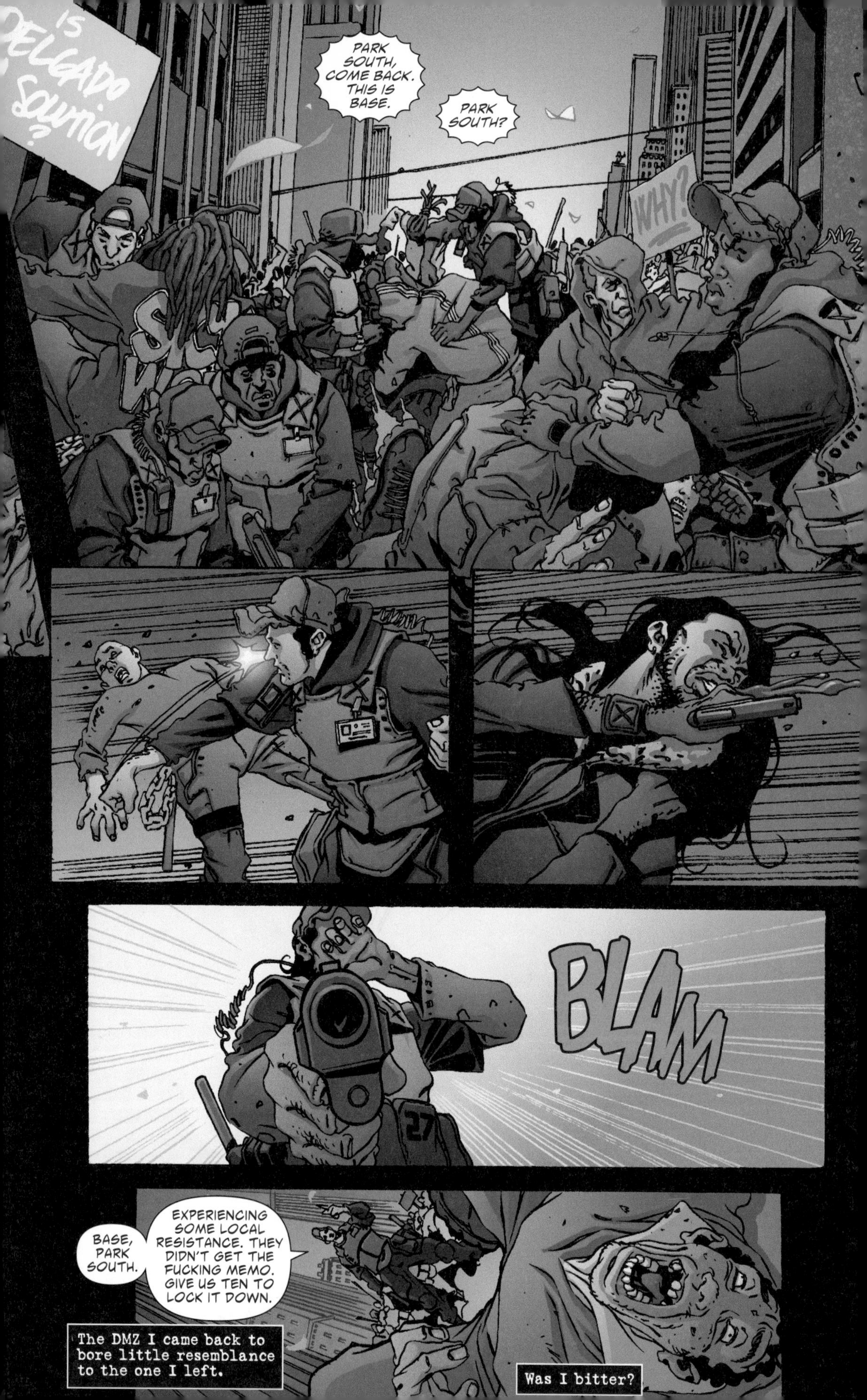
IS DELGADO A SOLUTION?
PARK SOUTH, COME BACK. THIS IS BASE.
PARK SOUTH?
WHY?
BLAM
BASE, PARK SOUTH.
EXPERIENCING SOME LOCAL RESISTANCE. THEY DIDN'T GET THE FUCKING MEMO. GIVE US TEN TO LOCK IT DOWN.
The DMZ I came back to bore little resemblance to the one I left.
Was I bitter?

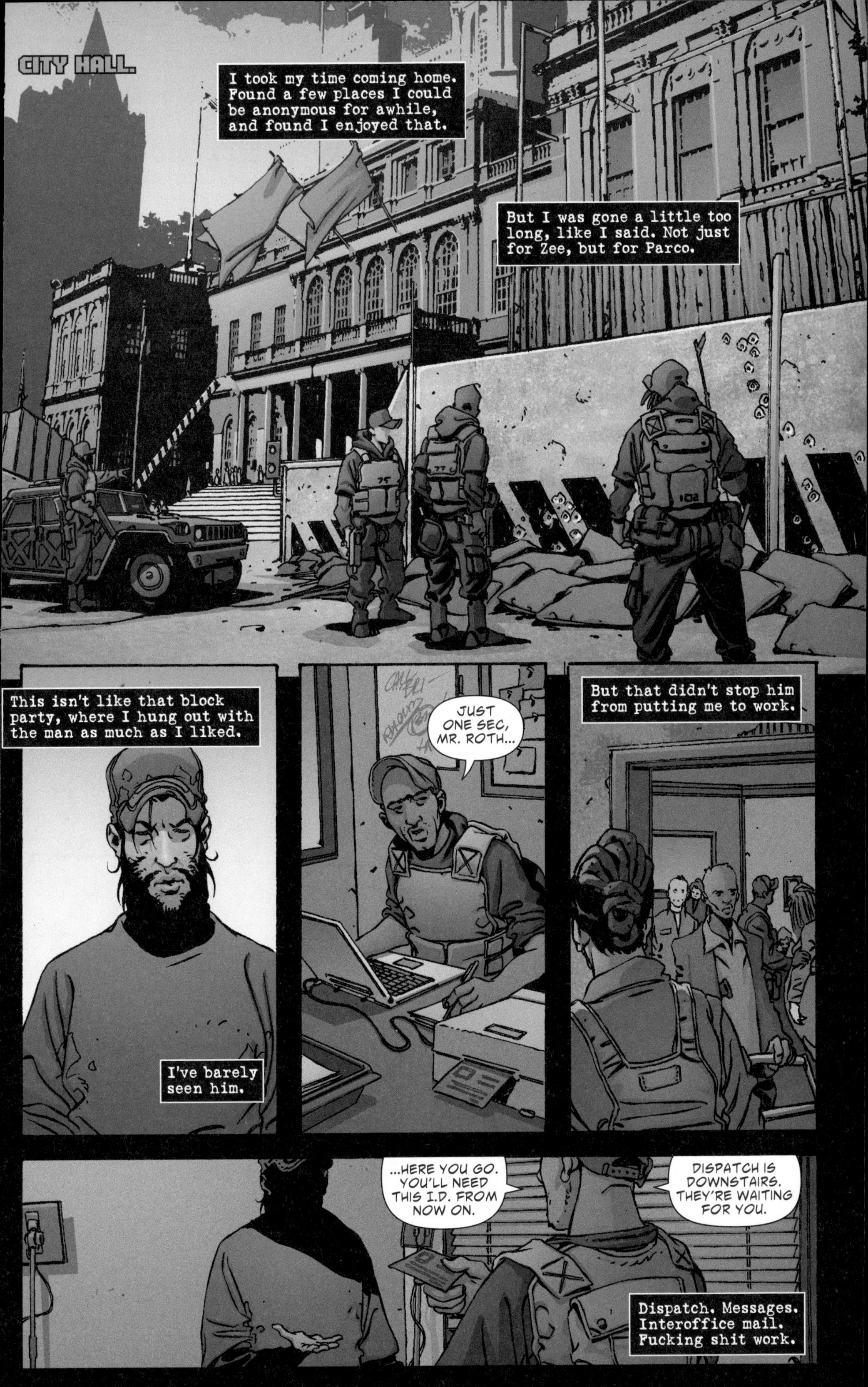
CITY HALL.
I took my time coming home. Found a few places I could be anonymous for awhile, and found I enjoyed that.
But I was gone a little too long, like I said. Not just for Zee, but for Parco.
This isn't like that block party, where I hung out with the man as much as I liked.
I've barely seen him.
JUST ONE SEC, MR. ROTH...
But that didn't stop him from putting me to work.
...HERE YOU GO. YOU'LL NEED THIS I.D. FROM NOW ON.
DISPATCH IS DOWNSTAIRS. THEY'RE WAITING FOR YOU.
Dispatch. Messages. Interoffice mail. Fucking shit work.

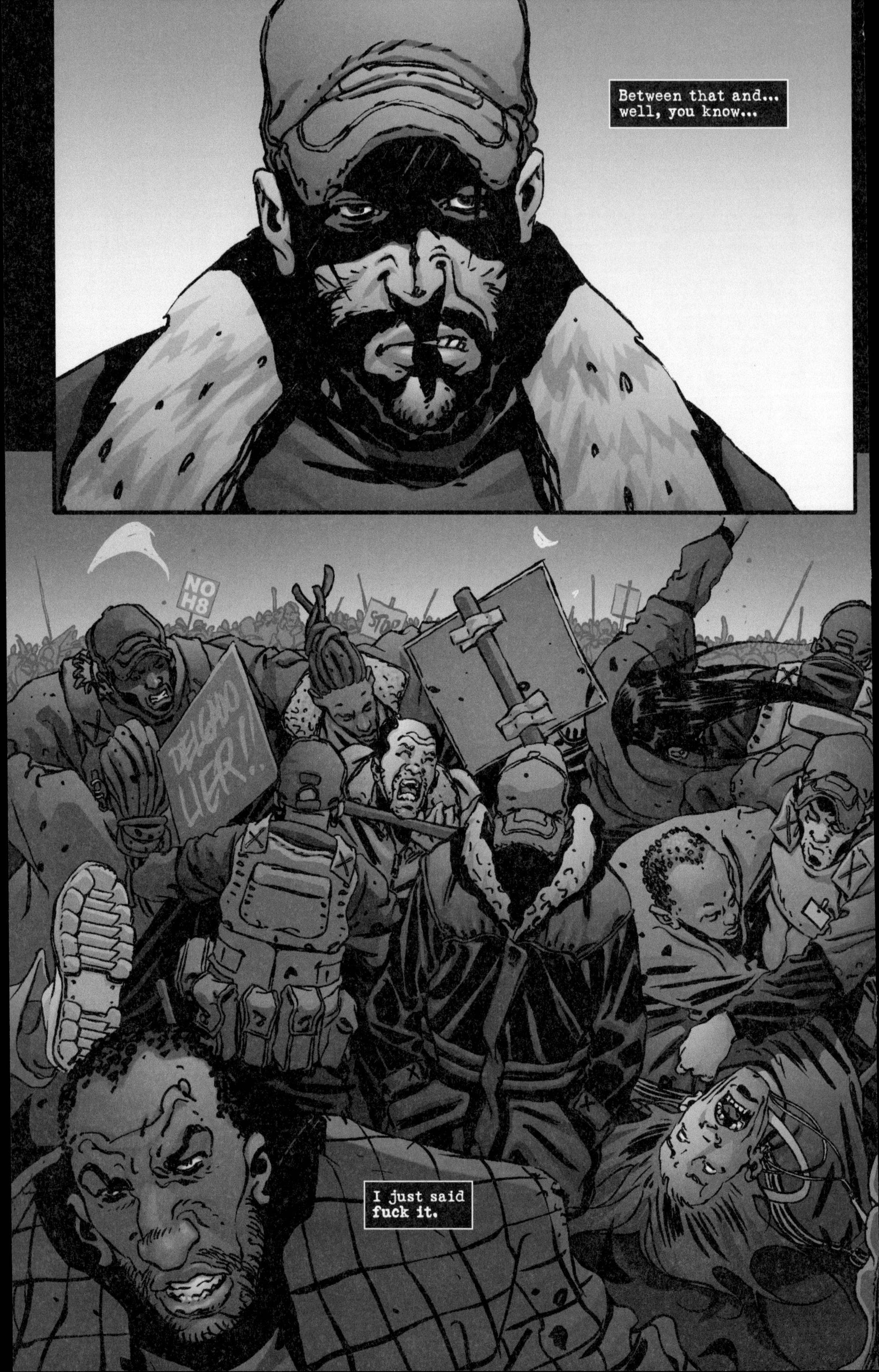
Between that and...
well, you know...
NO H8
STOP
DELGADO LIER!!
I just said
fuck it.

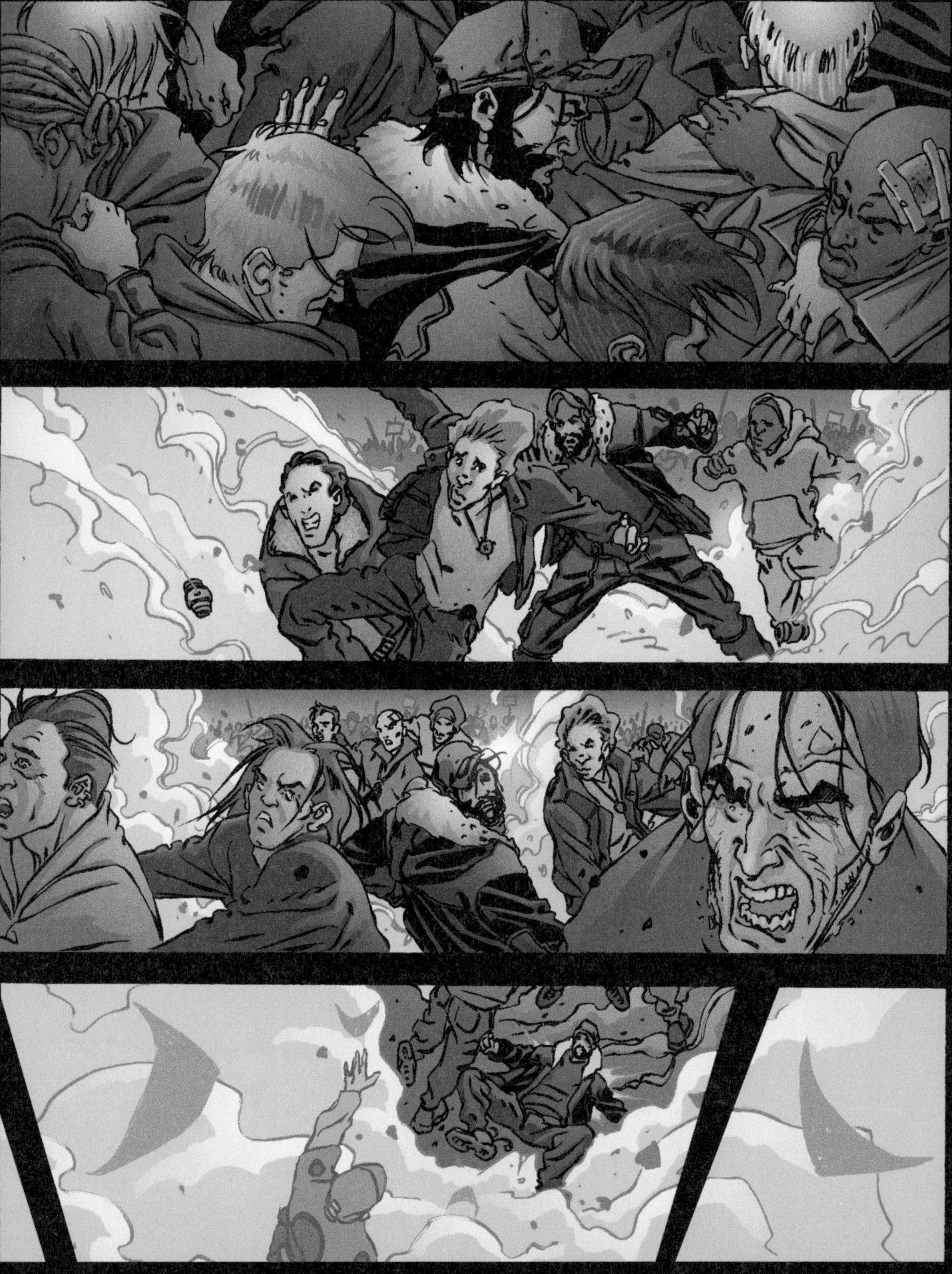

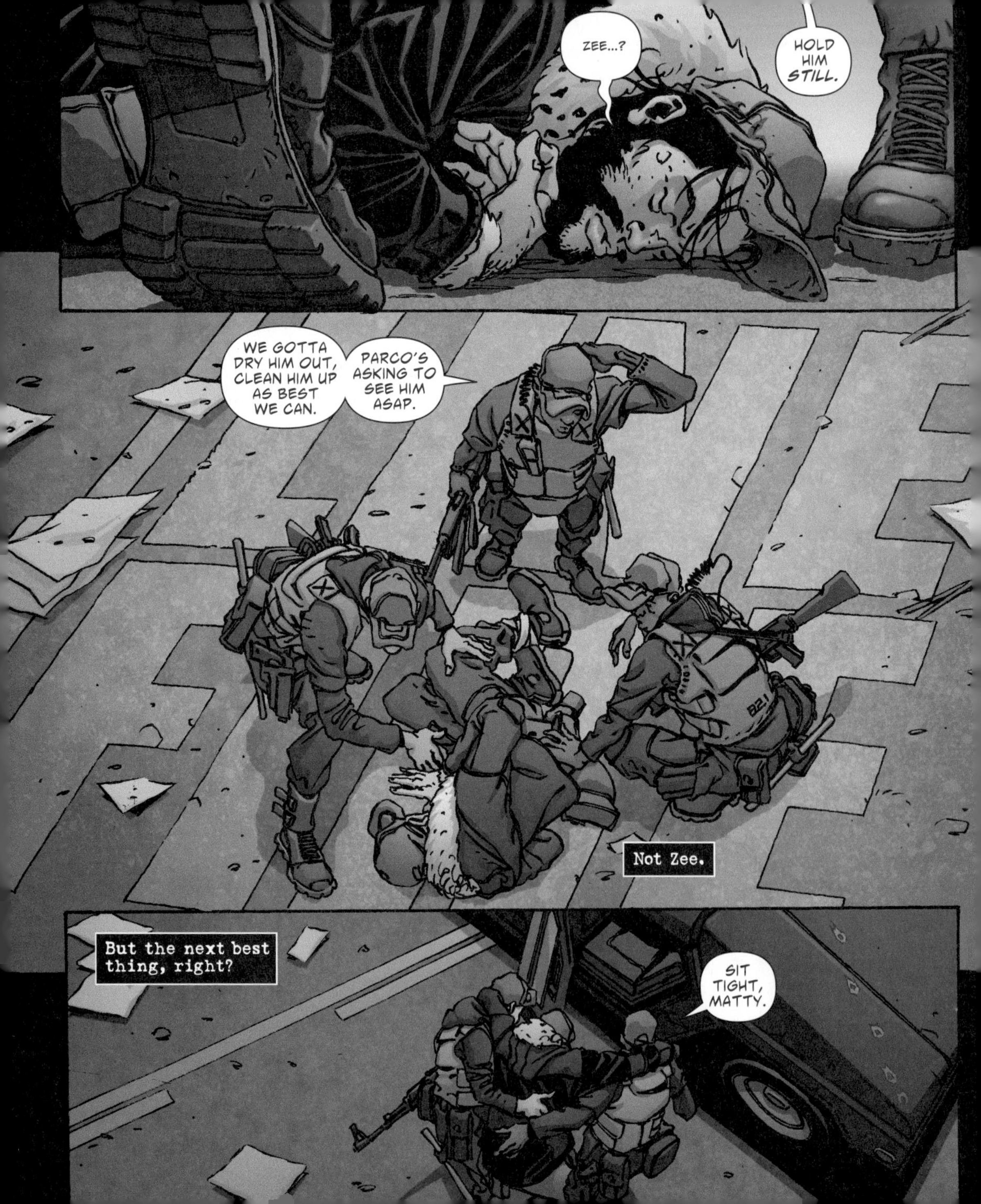
ZEE...?
HOLD HIM STILL.
WE GOTTA DRY HIM OUT, CLEAN HIM UP AS BEST WE CAN.
PARCO'S ASKING TO SEE HIM ASAP.
Not Zee.
But the next best thing, right?
SIT TIGHT, MATTY.

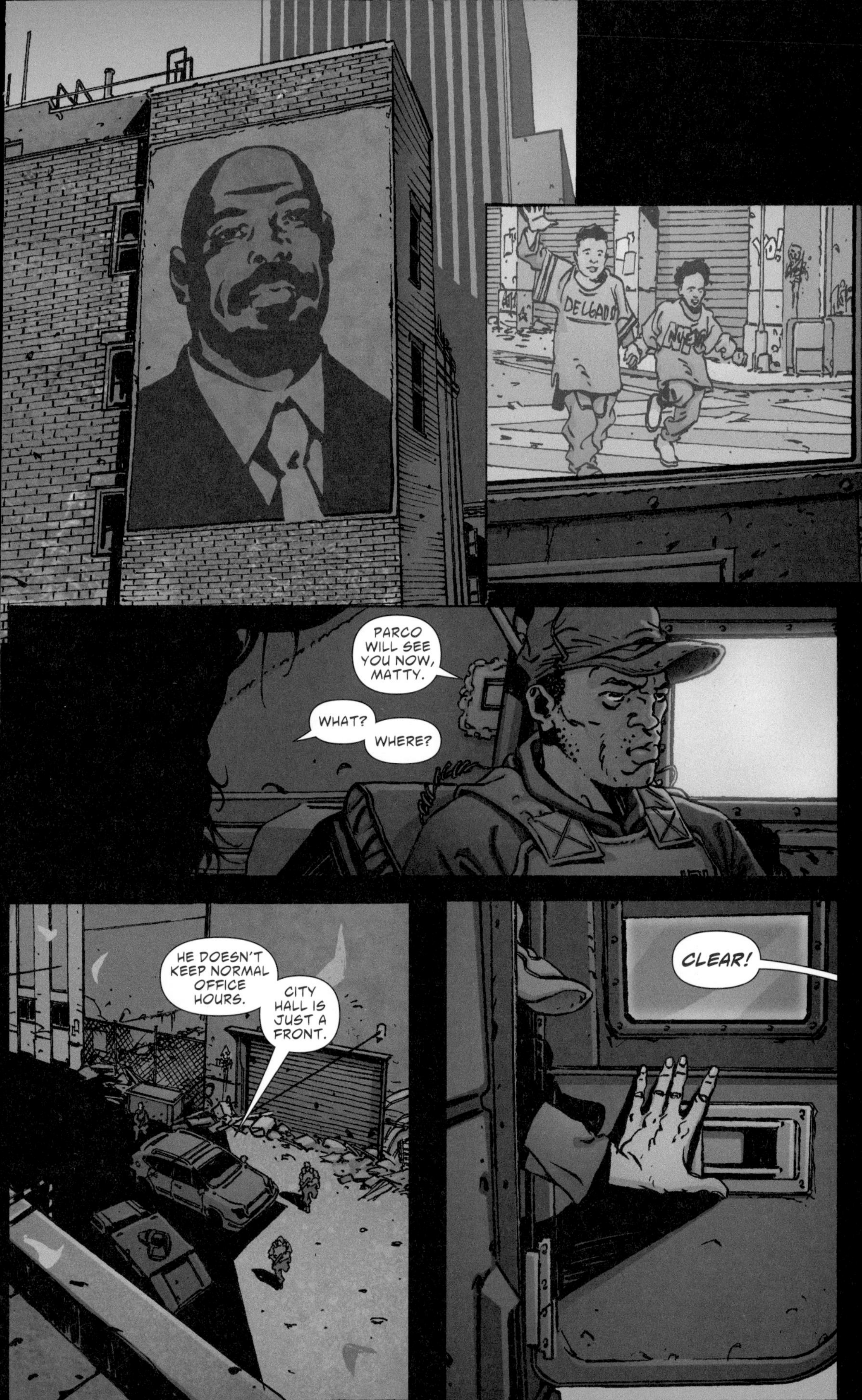

DELGADO
NYC
YO!
PARCO WILL SEE YOU NOW, MATTY.
WHAT?
WHERE?
HE DOESN'T KEEP NORMAL OFFICE HOURS.
CITY HALL IS JUST A FRONT.
CLEAR!

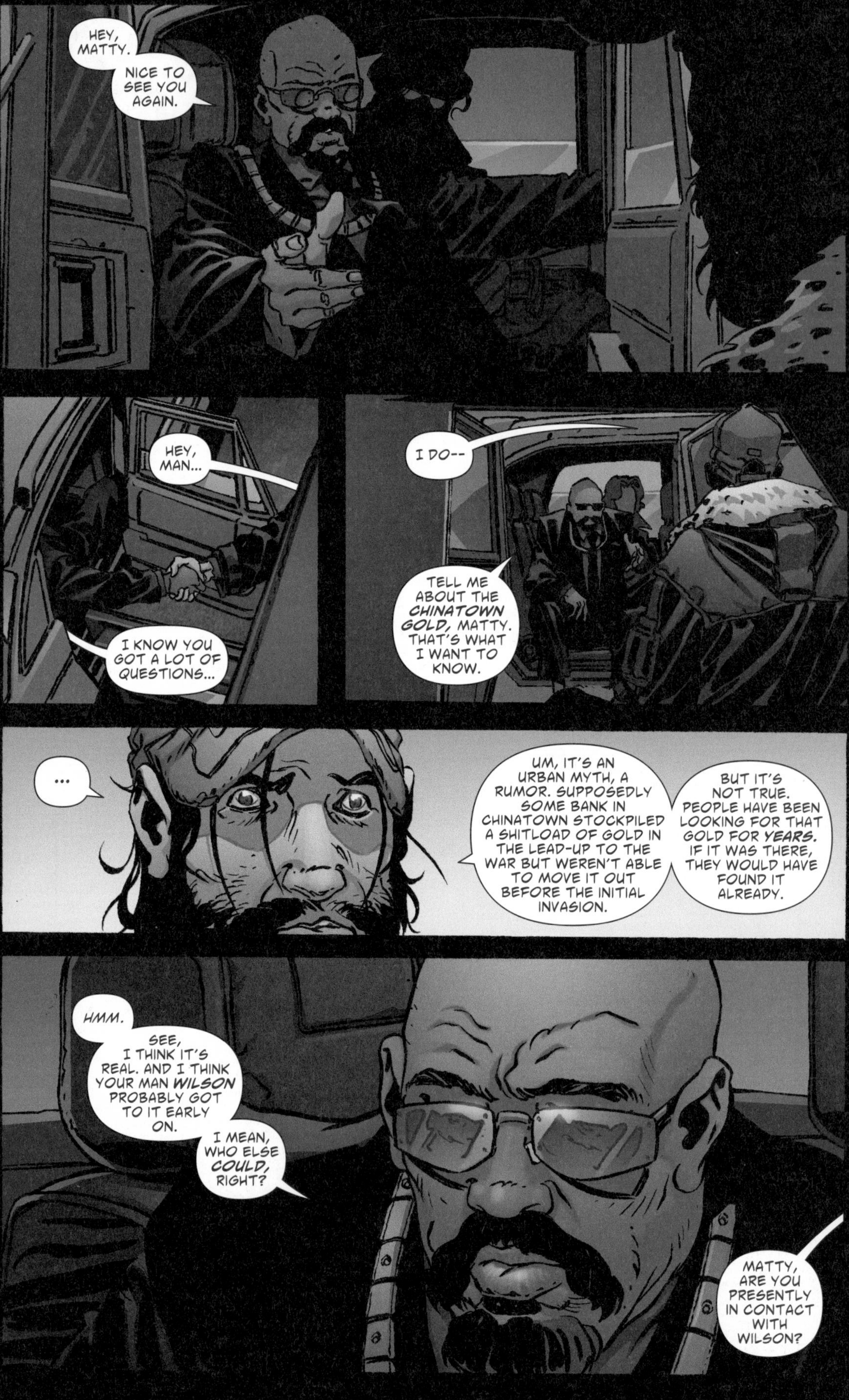
HEY, MATTY.
NICE TO SEE YOU AGAIN.
HEY, MAN...
I KNOW YOU GOT A LOT OF QUESTIONS...
I DO--
TELL ME ABOUT THE CHINATOWN GOLD, MATTY. THAT'S WHAT I WANT TO KNOW.
...
UM, IT'S AN URBAN MYTH, A RUMOR. SUPPOSEDLY SOME BANK IN CHINATOWN STOCKPILED A SHITLOAD OF GOLD IN THE LEAD-UP TO THE WAR BUT WEREN'T ABLE TO MOVE IT OUT BEFORE THE INITIAL INVASION.
BUT IT'S NOT TRUE. PEOPLE HAVE BEEN LOOKING FOR THAT GOLD FOR YEARS. IF IT WAS THERE, THEY WOULD HAVE FOUND IT ALREADY.
HMM.
SEE, I THINK IT'S REAL. AND I THINK YOUR MAN WILSON PROBABLY GOT TO IT EARLY ON.
I MEAN, WHO ELSE COULD, RIGHT?
MATTY, ARE YOU PRESENTLY IN CONTACT WITH WILSON?

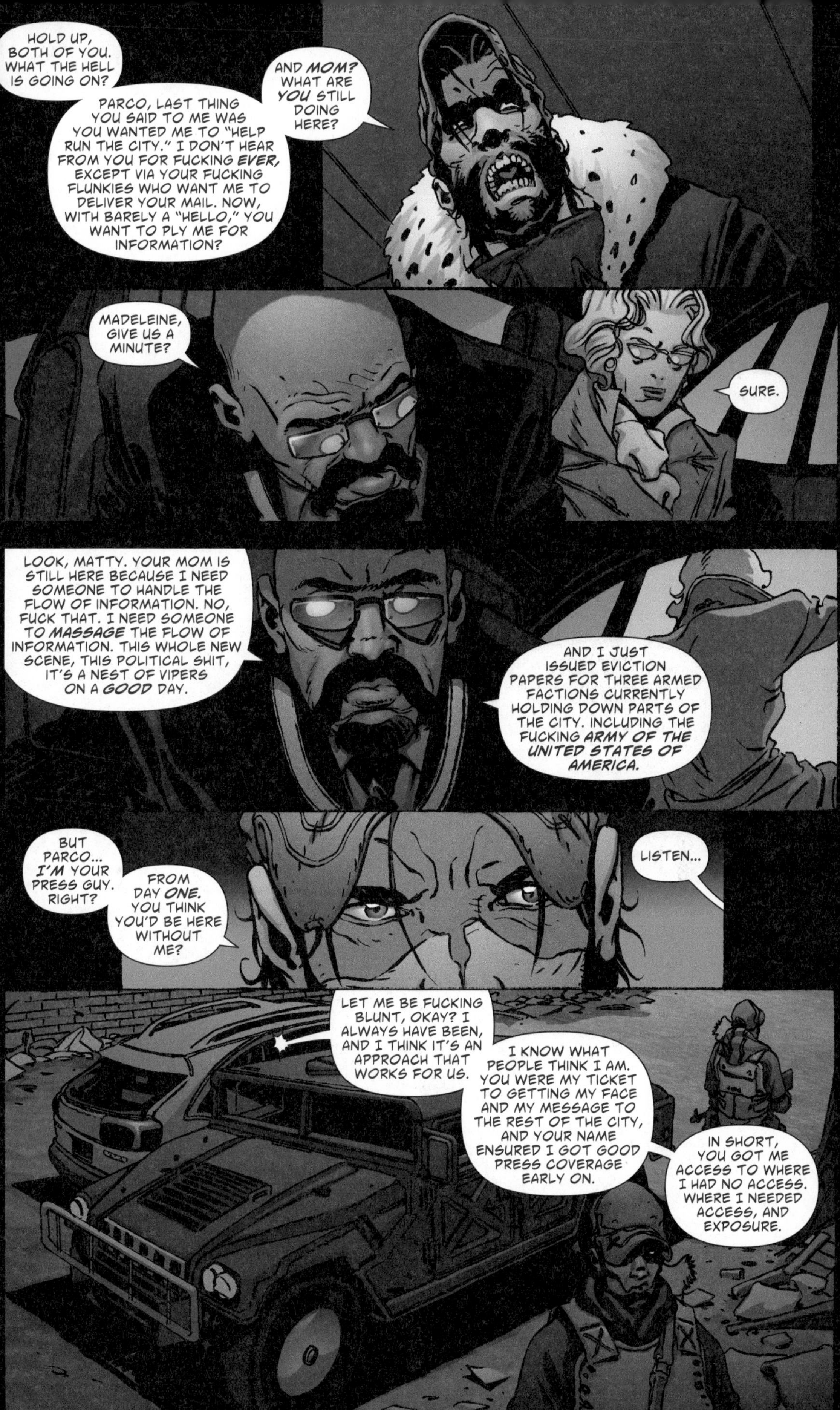
HOLD UP, BOTH OF YOU. WHAT THE HELL IS GOING ON?
PARCO, LAST THING YOU SAID TO ME WAS YOU WANTED ME TO "HELP RUN THE CITY." I DON'T HEAR FROM YOU FOR FUCKING *EVER,* EXCEPT VIA YOUR FUCKING FLUNKIES WHO WANT ME TO DELIVER YOUR MAIL. NOW, WITH BARELY A "HELLO," YOU WANT TO PLY ME FOR INFORMATION?
AND *MOM?* WHAT ARE *YOU* STILL DOING HERE?
MADELEINE, GIVE US A MINUTE?
SURE.
LOOK, MATTY. YOUR MOM IS STILL HERE BECAUSE I NEED SOMEONE TO HANDLE THE FLOW OF INFORMATION. NO, FUCK THAT. I NEED SOMEONE TO *MASSAGE* THE FLOW OF INFORMATION. THIS WHOLE NEW SCENE, THIS POLITICAL SHIT, IT'S A NEST OF VIPERS ON A *GOOD* DAY.
AND I JUST ISSUED EVICTION PAPERS FOR THREE ARMED FACTIONS CURRENTLY HOLDING DOWN PARTS OF THE CITY. INCLUDING THE FUCKING *ARMY OF THE UNITED STATES OF AMERICA.*
BUT PARCO... *I'M* YOUR PRESS GUY. RIGHT?
FROM DAY *ONE.* YOU THINK YOU'D BE HERE WITHOUT ME?
LISTEN...
LET ME BE FUCKING BLUNT, OKAY? I ALWAYS HAVE BEEN, AND I THINK IT'S AN APPROACH THAT WORKS FOR US.
I KNOW WHAT PEOPLE THINK I AM. YOU WERE MY TICKET TO GETTING MY FACE AND MY MESSAGE TO THE REST OF THE CITY, AND YOUR NAME ENSURED I GOT GOOD PRESS COVERAGE EARLY ON.
IN SHORT, YOU GOT ME ACCESS TO WHERE I HAD NO ACCESS. WHERE I NEEDED ACCESS, AND EXPOSURE.

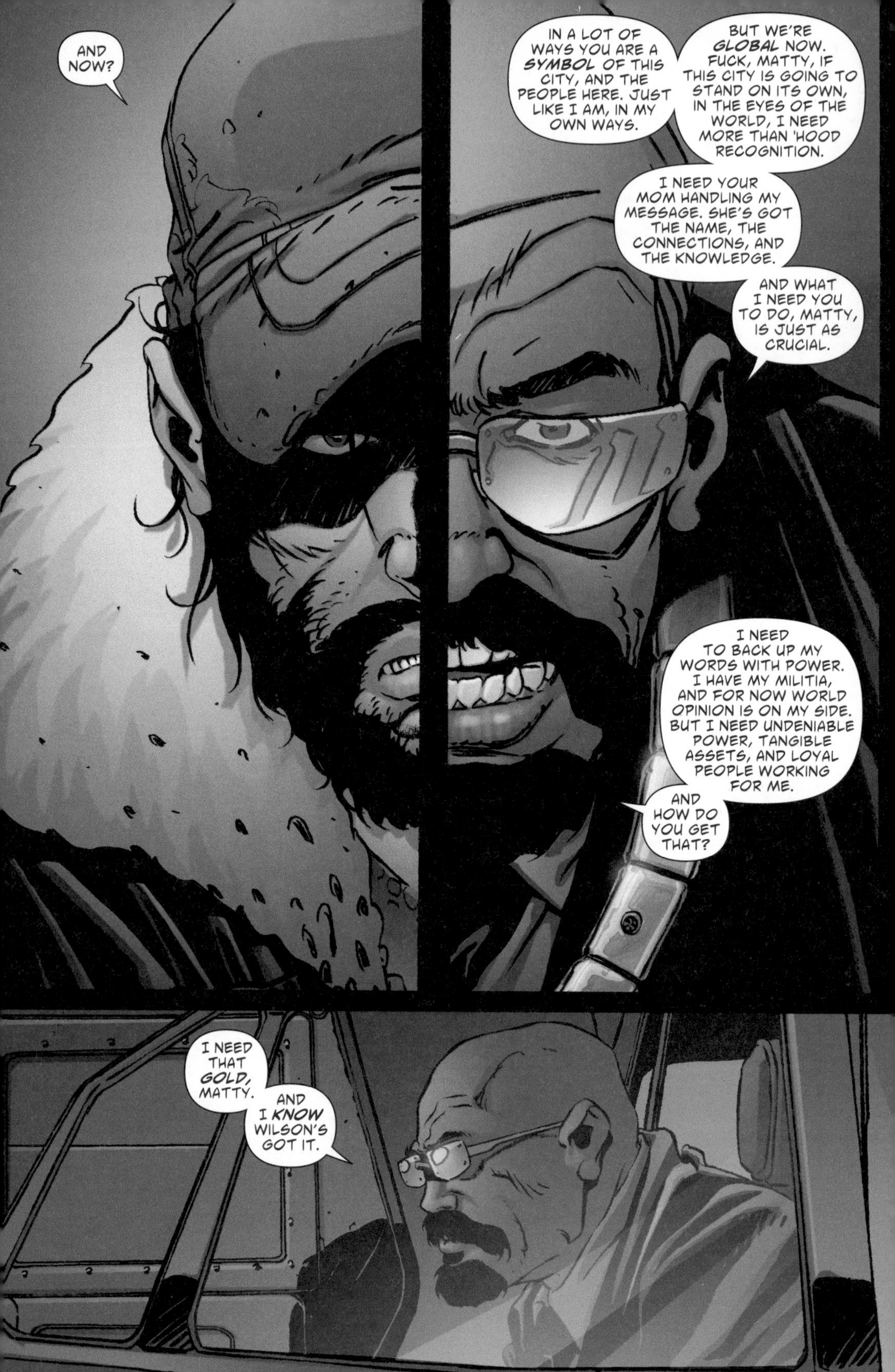
AND NOW?
IN A LOT OF WAYS YOU ARE A SYMBOL OF THIS CITY, AND THE PEOPLE HERE. JUST LIKE I AM, IN MY OWN WAYS.
BUT WE'RE GLOBAL NOW. FUCK, MATTY, IF THIS CITY IS GOING TO STAND ON ITS OWN, IN THE EYES OF THE WORLD, I NEED MORE THAN 'HOOD RECOGNITION.
I NEED YOUR MOM HANDLING MY MESSAGE. SHE'S GOT THE NAME, THE CONNECTIONS, AND THE KNOWLEDGE.
AND WHAT I NEED YOU TO DO, MATTY, IS JUST AS CRUCIAL.
I NEED TO BACK UP MY WORDS WITH POWER. I HAVE MY MILITIA, AND FOR NOW WORLD OPINION IS ON MY SIDE. BUT I NEED UNDENIABLE POWER, TANGIBLE ASSETS, AND LOYAL PEOPLE WORKING FOR ME.
AND HOW DO YOU GET THAT?
I NEED THAT GOLD, MATTY.
AND I KNOW WILSON'S GOT IT.

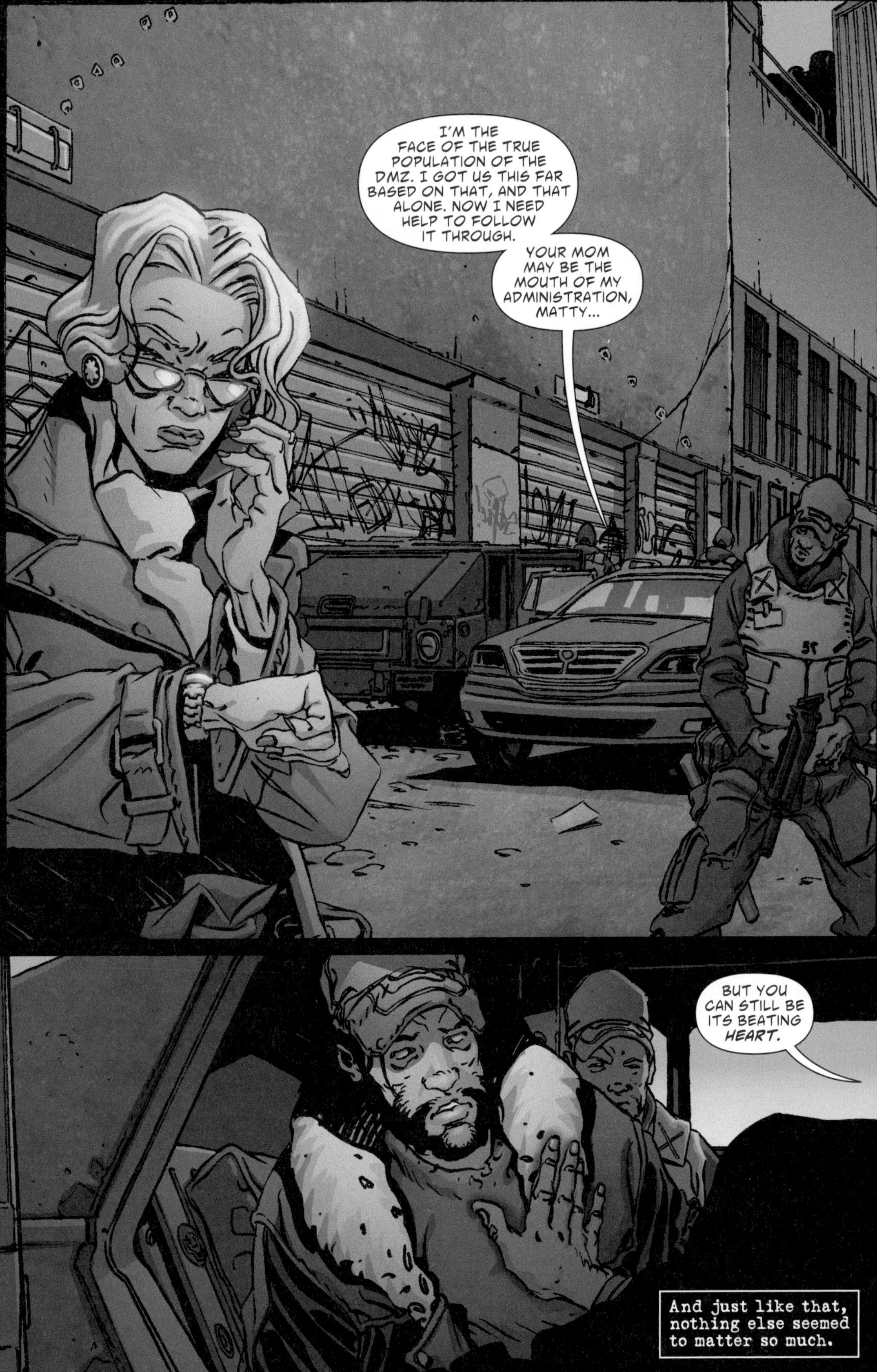
I'M THE FACE OF THE TRUE POPULATION OF THE DMZ. I GOT US THIS FAR BASED ON THAT, AND THAT ALONE. NOW I NEED HELP TO FOLLOW IT THROUGH.
YOUR MOM MAY BE THE MOUTH OF MY ADMINISTRATION, MATTY...
BUT YOU CAN STILL BE ITS BEATING *HEART.*
And just like that, nothing else seemed to matter so much.

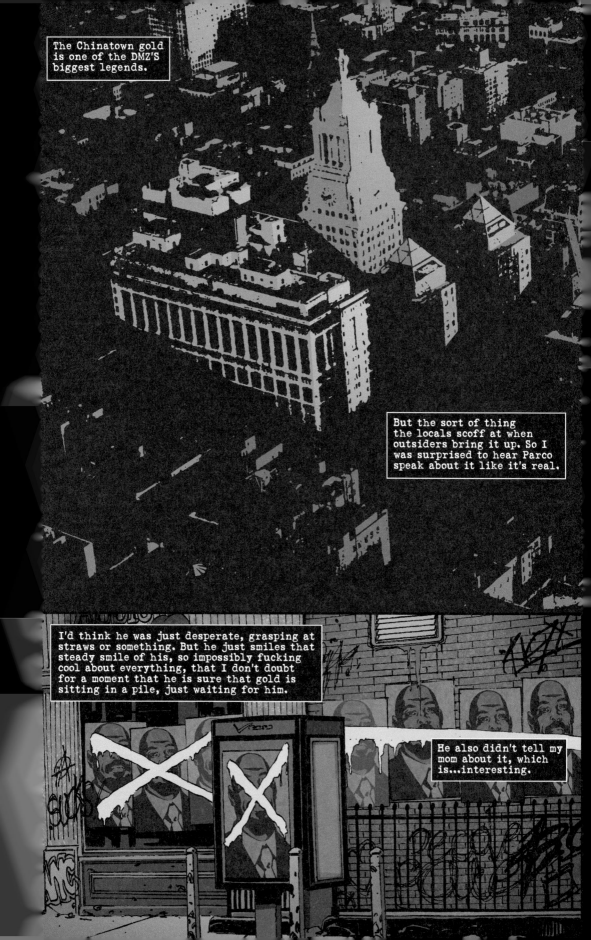

The Chinatown gold is one of the DMZ'S biggest legends.

But the sort of thing the locals scoff at when outsiders bring it up. So I was surprised to hear Parco speak about it like it's real.

I'd think he was just desperate, grasping at straws or something. But he just smiles that steady smile of his, so impossibly fucking cool about everything, that I don't doubt for a moment that he is sure that gold is sitting in a pile, just waiting for him.

He also didn't tell my mom about it, which is...interesting.

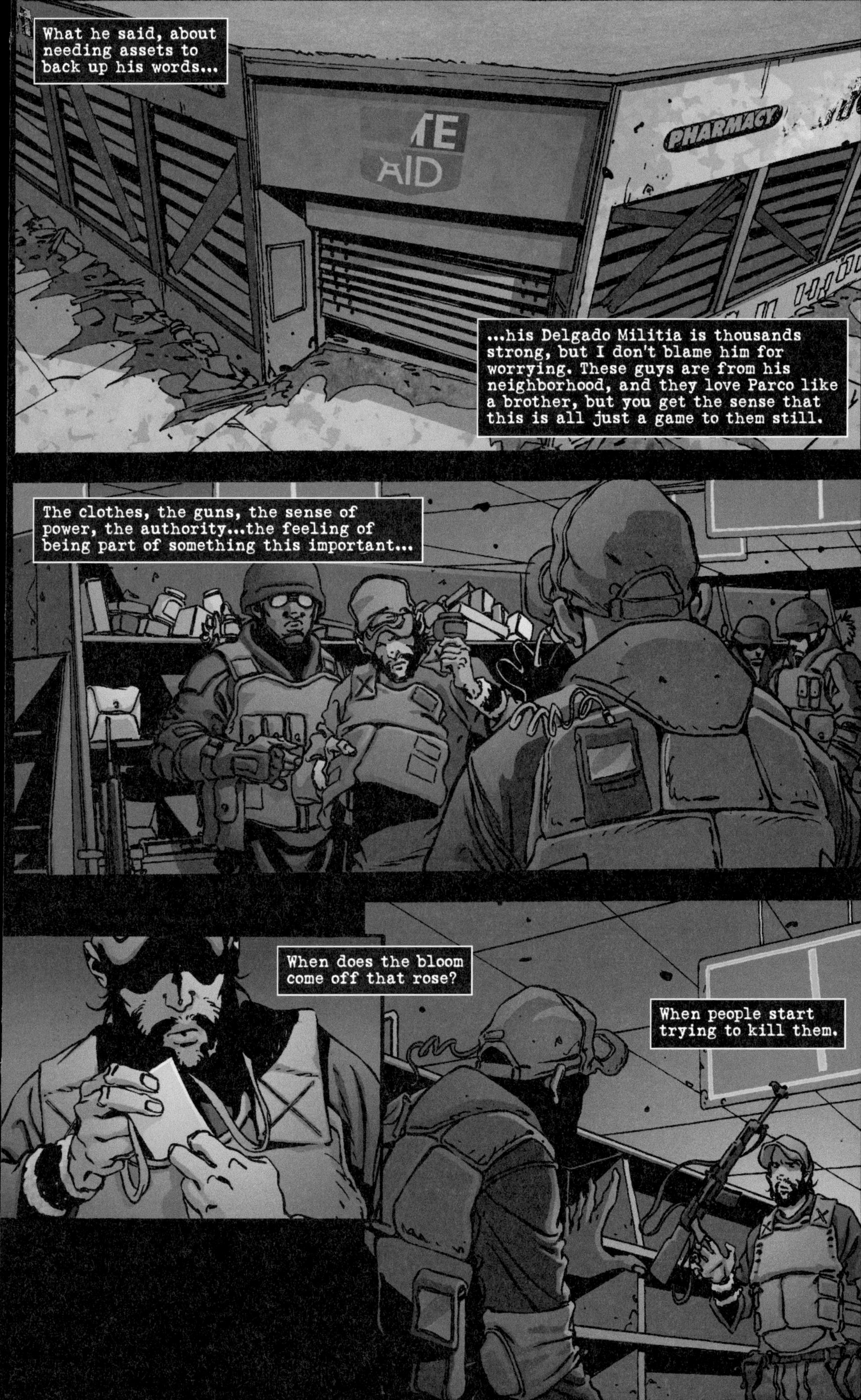
What he said, about needing assets to back up his words...
TE AID
PHARMACY
...his Delgado Militia is thousands strong, but I don't blame him for worrying. These guys are from his neighborhood, and they love Parco like a brother, but you get the sense that this is all just a game to them still.
The clothes, the guns, the sense of power, the authority...the feeling of being part of something this important...
When does the bloom come off that rose?
When people start trying to kill them.

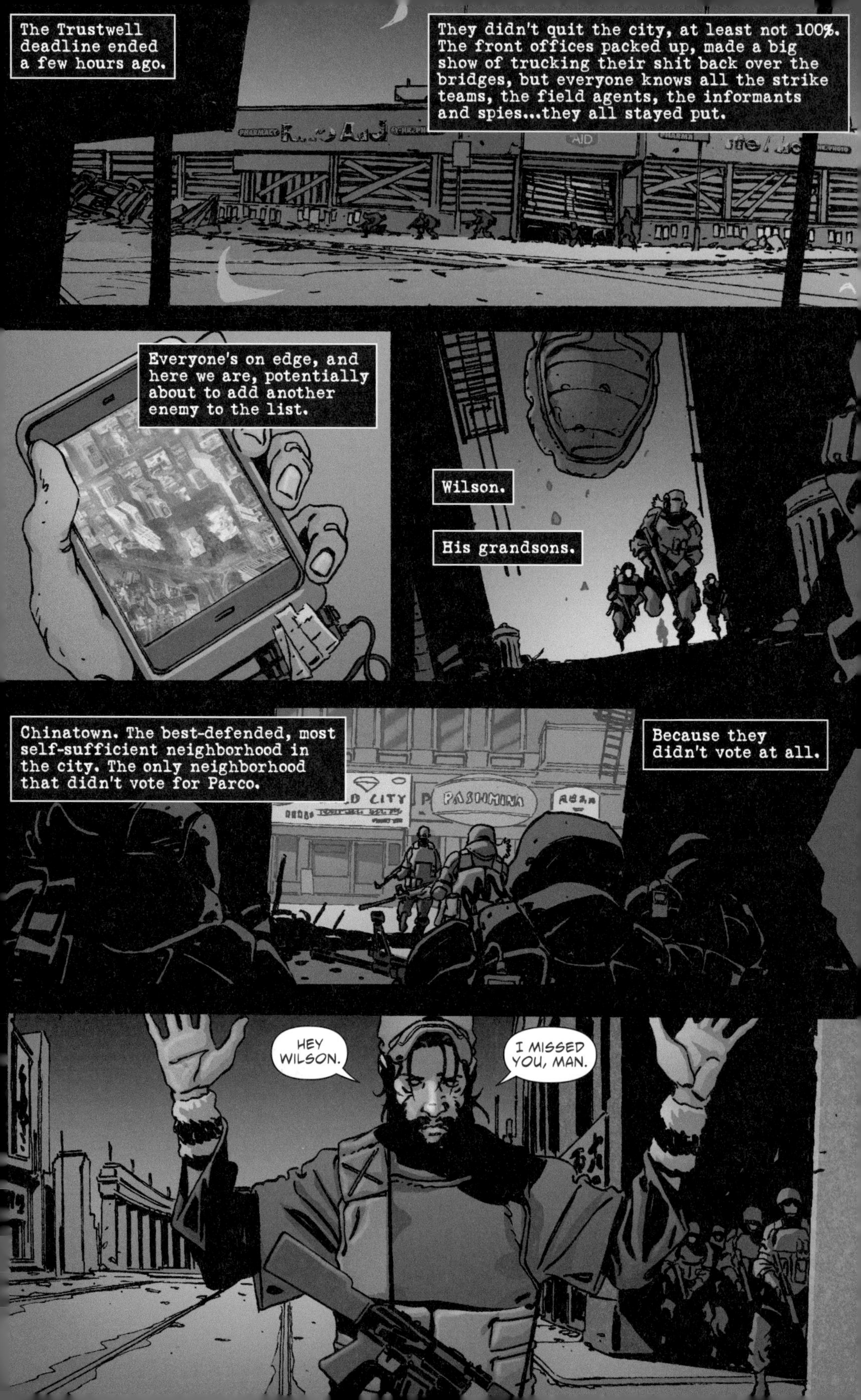
The Trustwell deadline ended a few hours ago.
They didn't quit the city, at least not 100%. The front offices packed up, made a big show of trucking their shit back over the bridges, but everyone knows all the strike teams, the field agents, the informants and spies...they all stayed put.
Everyone's on edge, and here we are, potentially about to add another enemy to the list.
Wilson.
His grandsons.
Chinatown. The best-defended, most self-sufficient neighborhood in the city. The only neighborhood that didn't vote for Parco.
Because they didn't vote at all.
HEY WILSON.
I MISSED YOU, MAN.

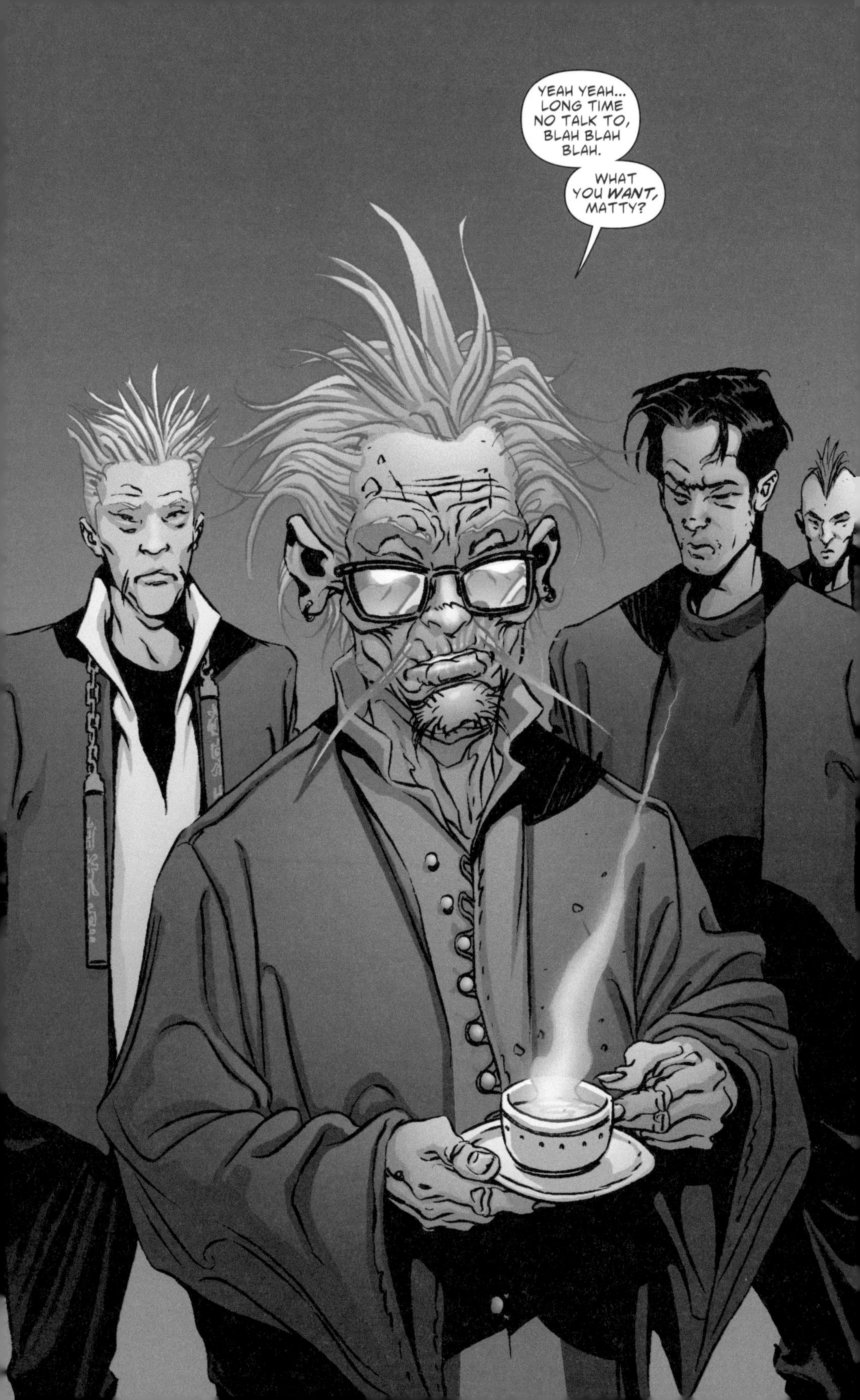
YEAH YEAH... LONG TIME NO TALK TO, BLAH BLAH BLAH.
WHAT YOU *WANT,* MATTY?

DMZ

WAR POWERS

2 OF 4

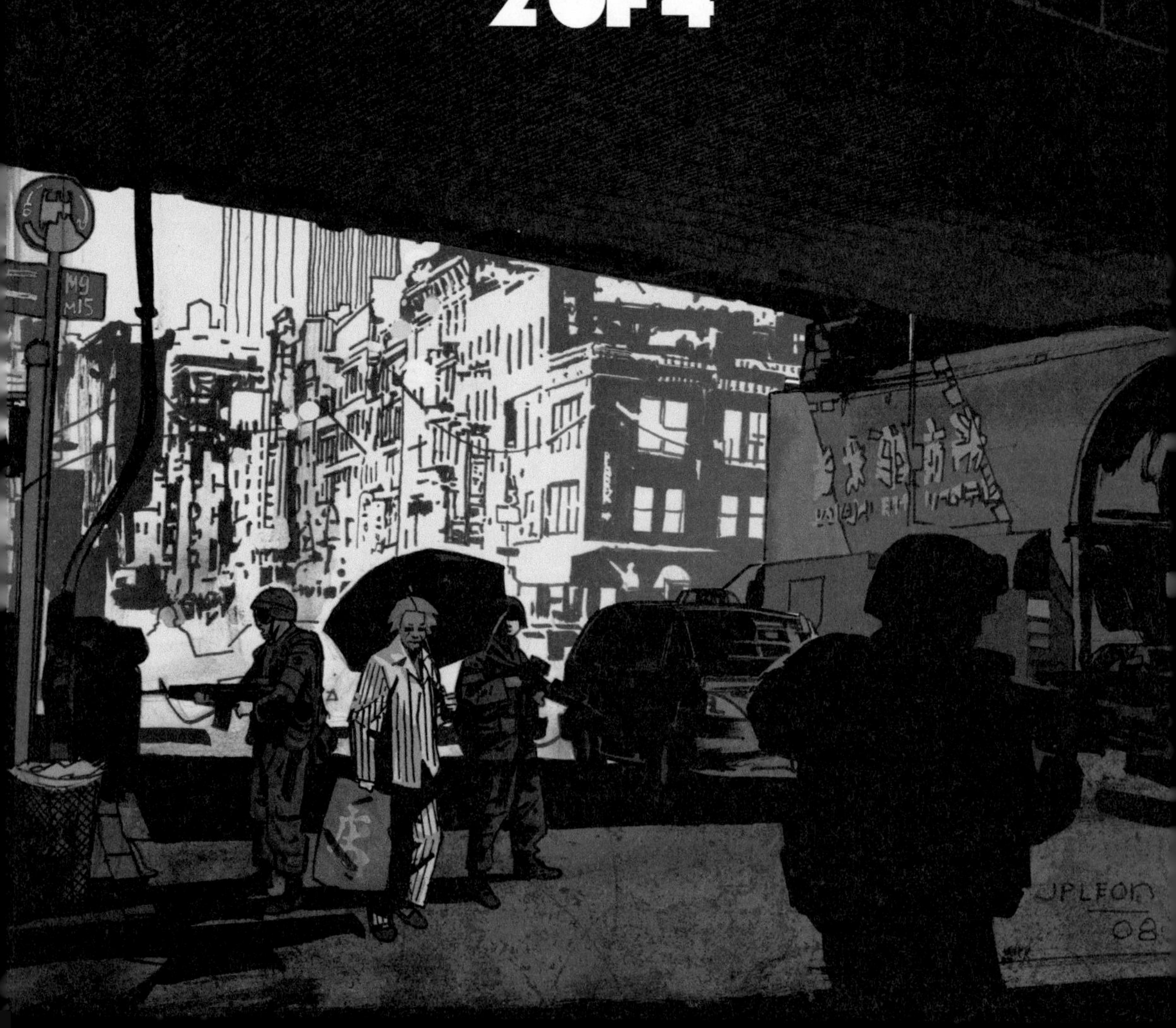
M9
M15
JPLEON
08

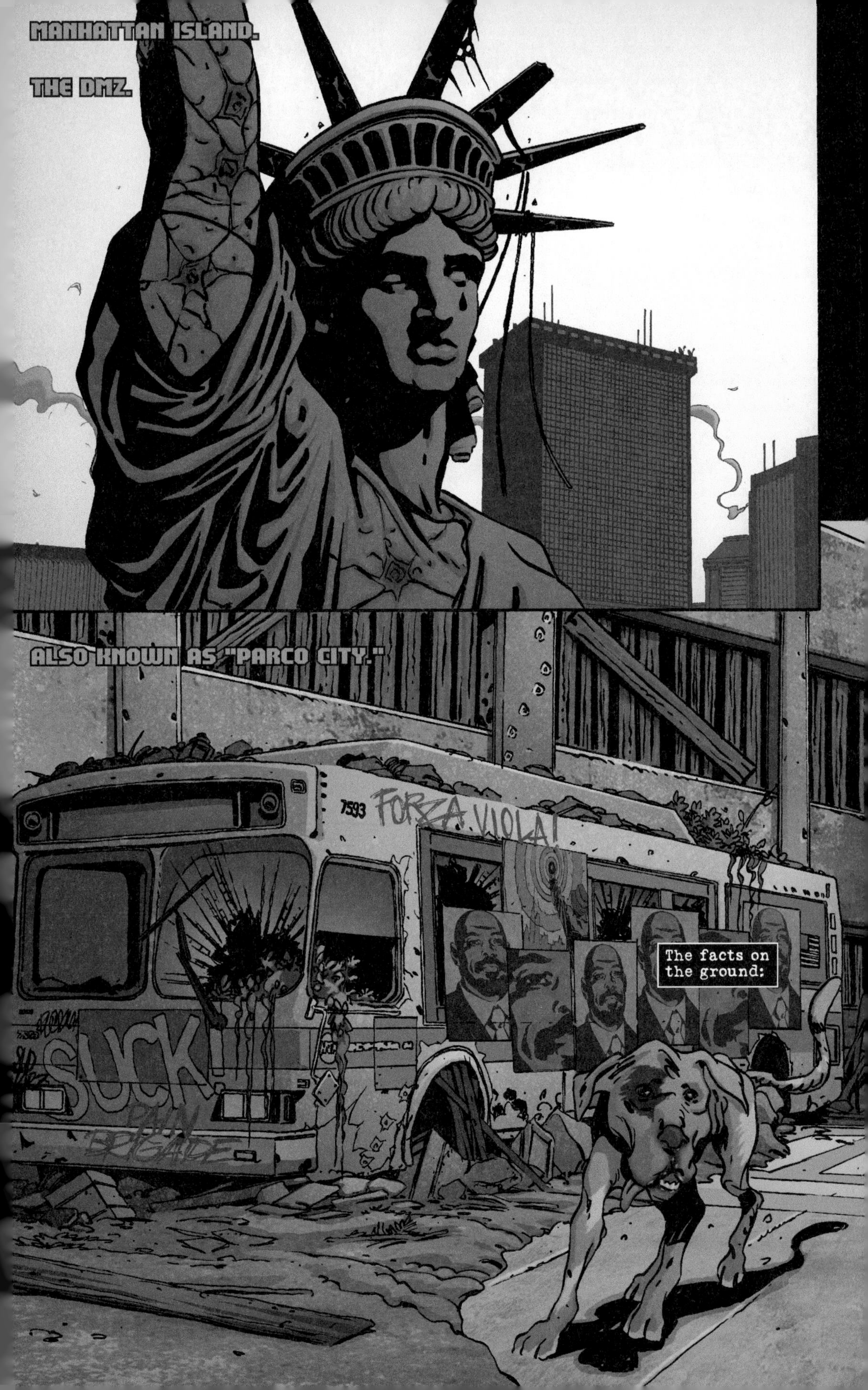
MANHATTAN ISLAND.
THE DMZ.
ALSO KNOWN AS "PARCO CITY."
7593
FORZA VIOLA!
SUCK!
The facts on the ground:

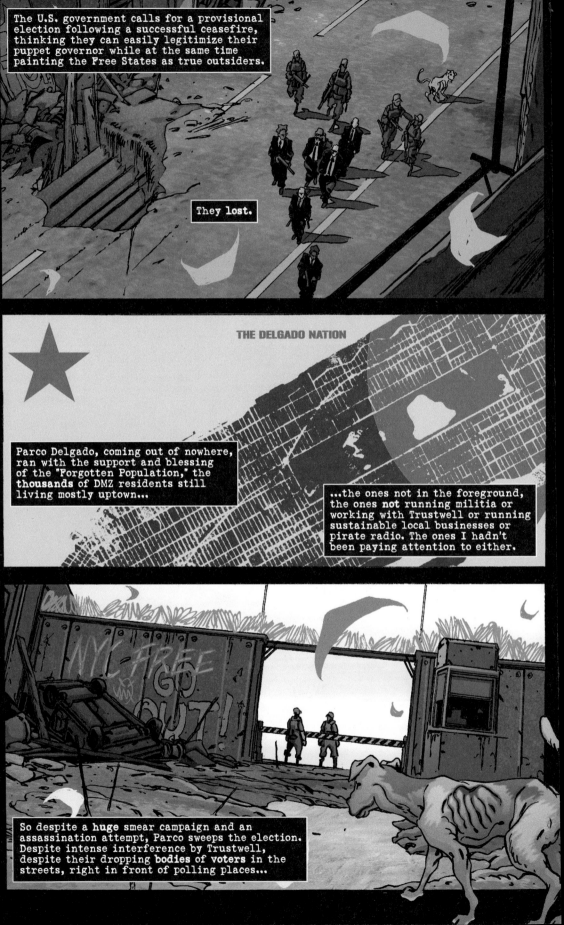

The U.S. government calls for a provisional election following a successful ceasefire, thinking they can easily legitimize their puppet governor while at the same time painting the Free States as true outsiders.

They **lost**.

THE DELGADO NATION

Parco Delgado, coming out of nowhere, ran with the support and blessing of the "Forgotten Population," the **thousands** of DMZ residents still living mostly uptown...

...the ones not in the foreground, the ones **not** running militia or working with Trustwell or running sustainable local businesses or pirate radio. The ones I hadn't been paying attention to either.

So despite a **huge** smear campaign and an assassination attempt, Parco sweeps the election. Despite intense interference by Trustwell, despite their dropping **bodies** of **voters** in the streets, right in front of polling places...

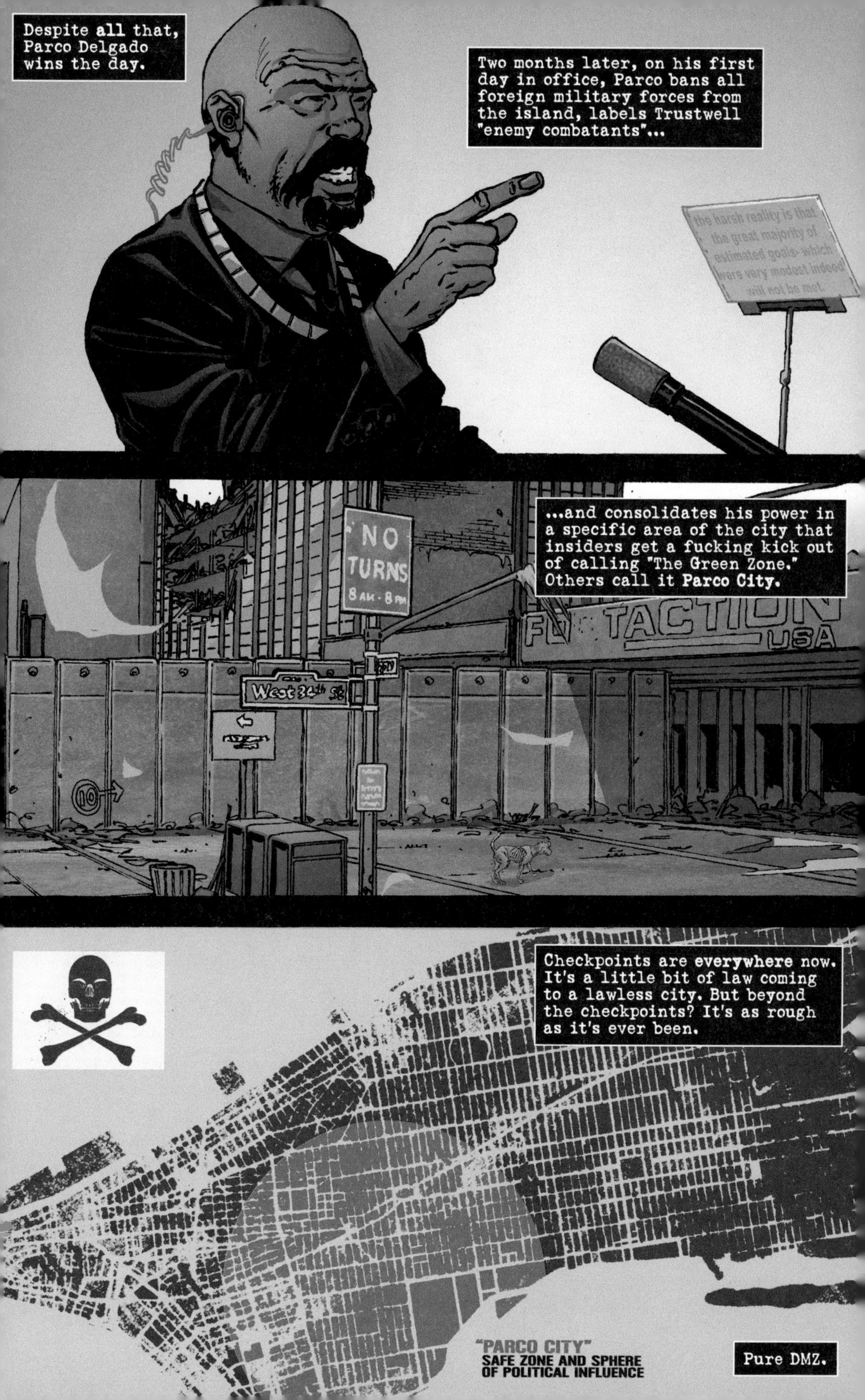

Despite **all** that, Parco Delgado wins the day.
Two months later, on his first day in office, Parco bans all foreign military forces from the island, labels Trustwell "enemy combatants"...
the harsh reality is that the great majority of estimated goals- which were very modest indeed- will not be met.
...and consolidates his power in a specific area of the city that insiders get a fucking kick out of calling "The Green Zone." Others call it **Parco City.**
NO TURNS 8 AM - 8 PM
West 34th St
TACTION
USA
Checkpoints are **everywhere** now. It's a little bit of law coming to a lawless city. But beyond the checkpoints? It's as rough as it's ever been.
"PARCO CITY"
SAFE ZONE AND SPHERE OF POLITICAL INFLUENCE
Pure DMZ.

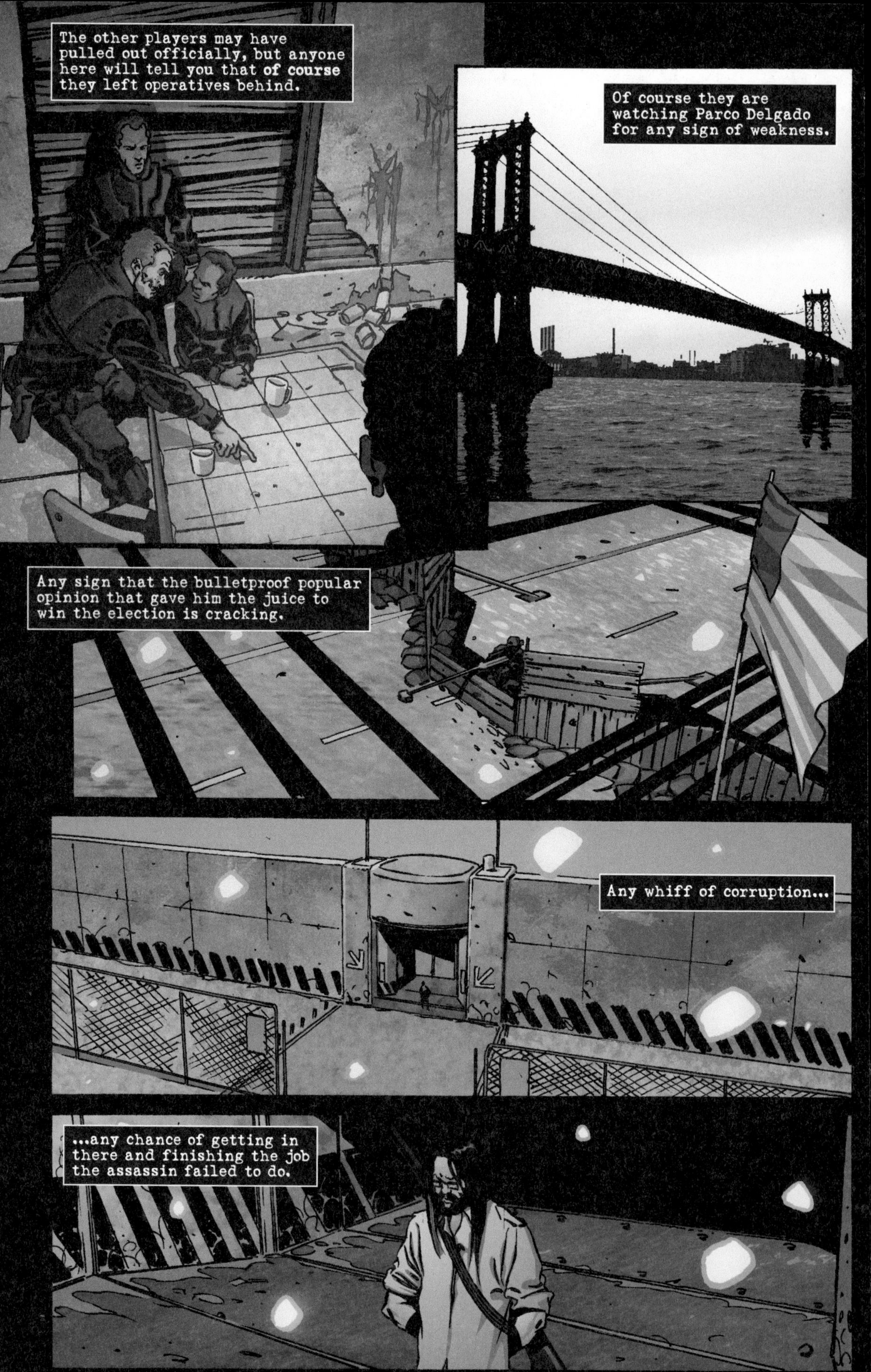
The other players may have pulled out officially, but anyone here will tell you that **of course** they left operatives behind.
Of course they are watching Parco Delgado for any sign of weakness.
Any sign that the bulletproof popular opinion that gave him the juice to win the election is cracking.
Any whiff of corruption...
...any chance of getting in there and finishing the job the assassin failed to do.

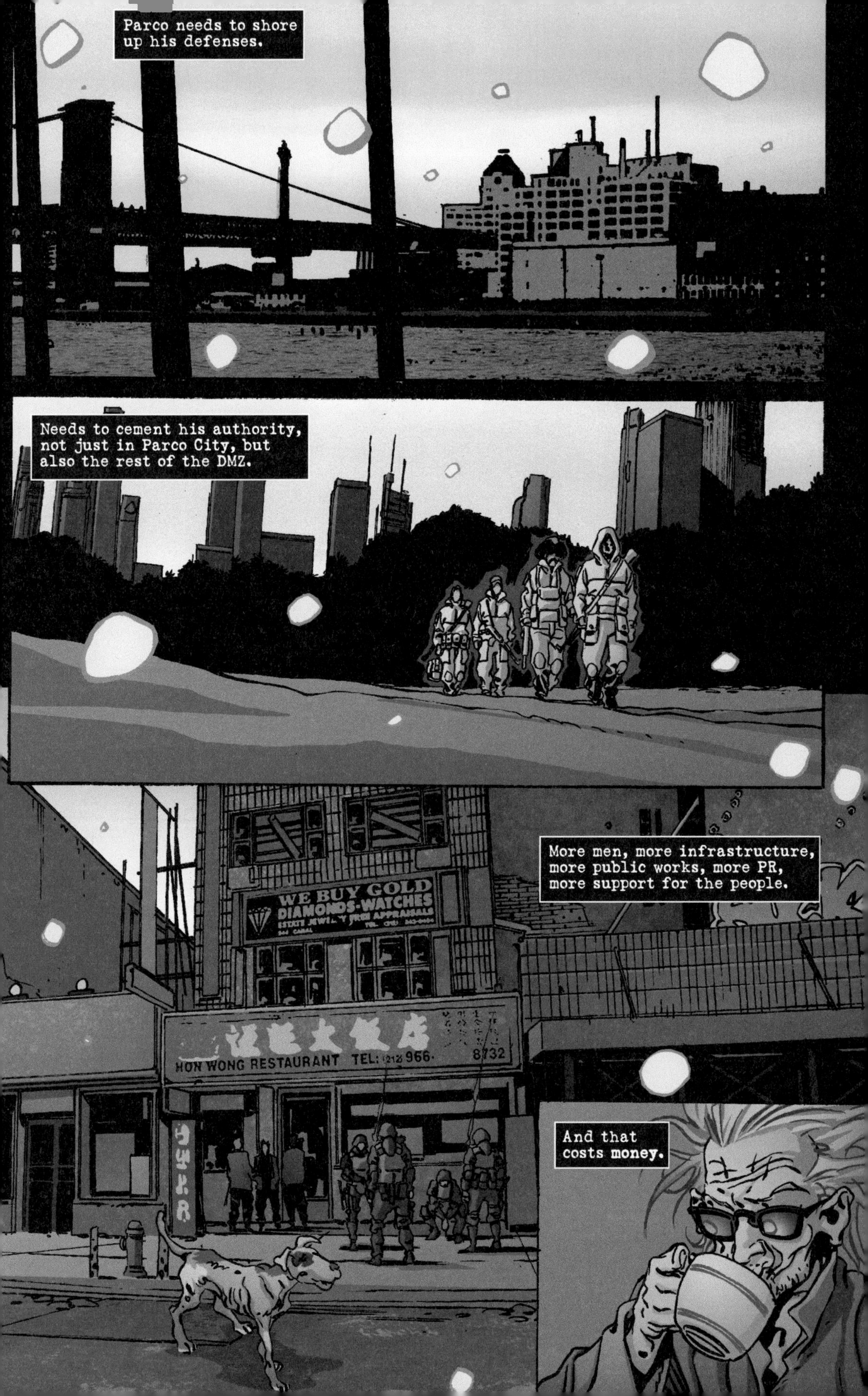
Parco needs to shore up his defenses.
Needs to cement his authority, not just in Parco City, but also the rest of the DMZ.
WE BUY GOLD
DIAMONDS-WATCHES
HON WONG RESTAURANT
More men, more infrastructure, more public works, more PR, more support for the people.
And that costs money.

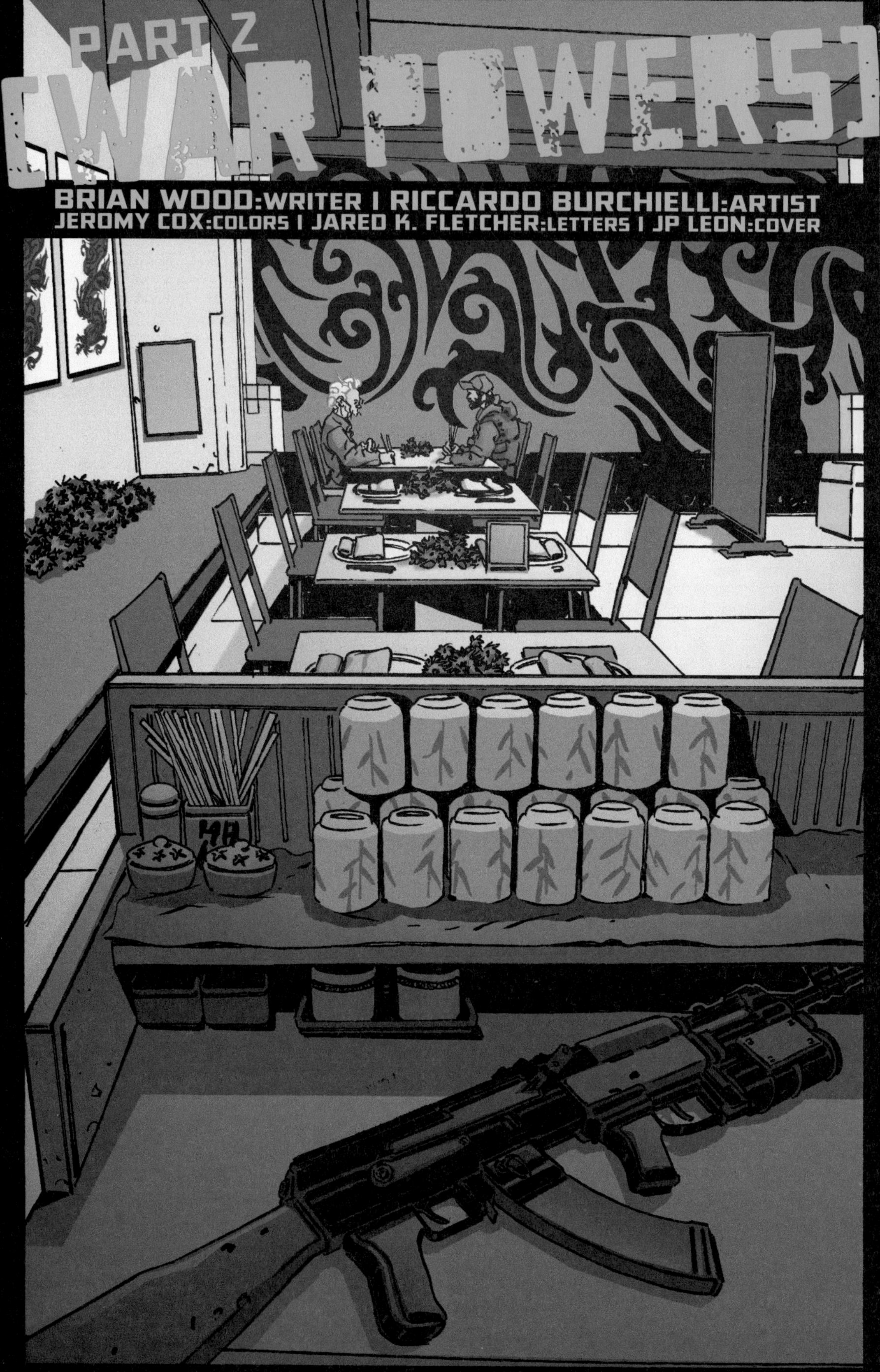
PART 2
[WAR POWERS]
BRIAN WOOD:WRITER I RICCARDO BURCHIELLI:ARTIST
JEROMY COX:COLORS I JARED K. FLETCHER:LETTERS I JP LEON:COVER

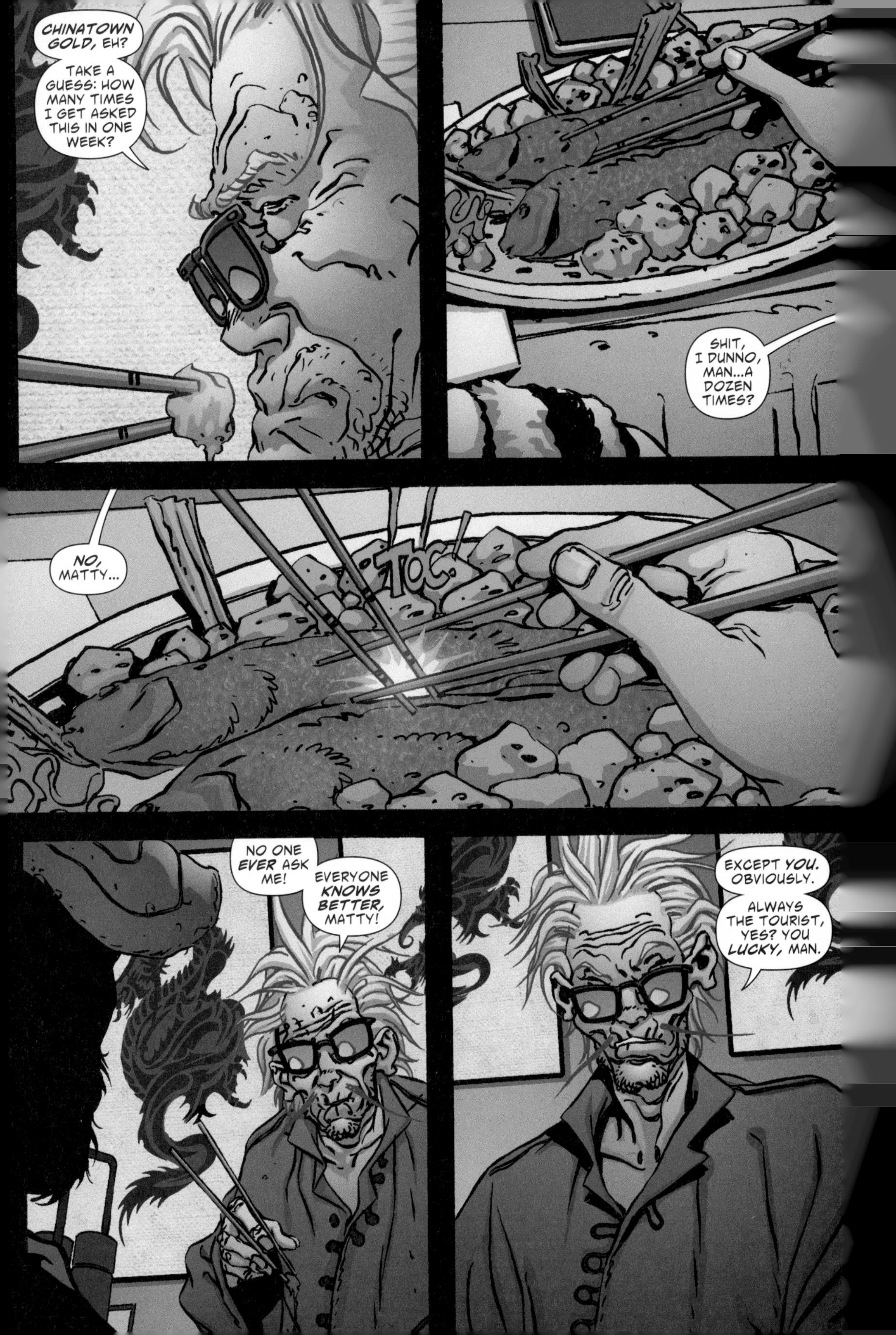
CHINATOWN GOLD, EH?
TAKE A GUESS: HOW MANY TIMES I GET ASKED THIS IN ONE WEEK?
SHIT, I DUNNO, MAN...A DOZEN TIMES?
NO, MATTY...
TOC!
NO ONE EVER ASK ME!
EVERYONE KNOWS BETTER, MATTY!
EXCEPT YOU. OBVIOUSLY.
ALWAYS THE TOURIST, YES? YOU LUCKY, MAN.

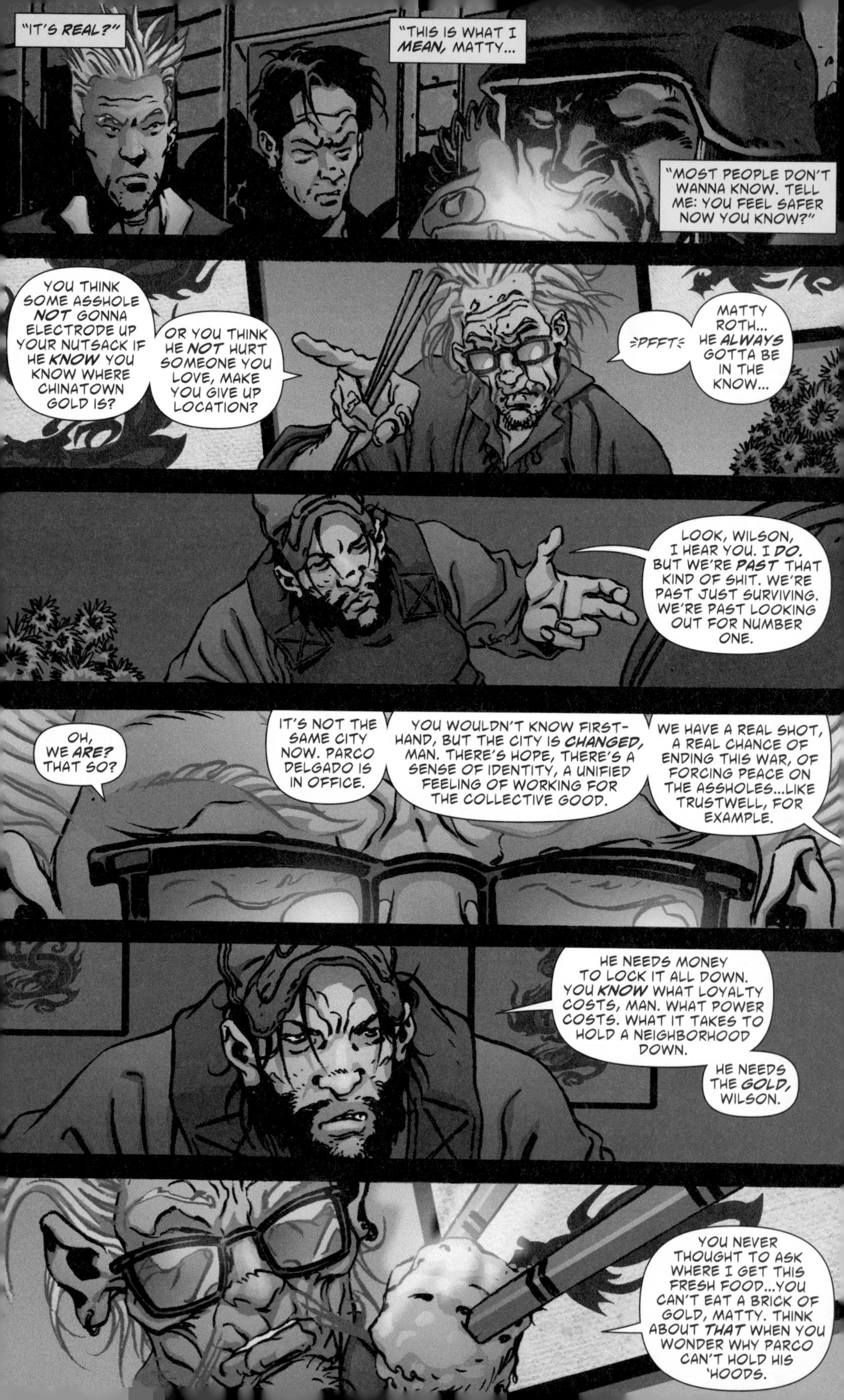
"IT'S REAL?"
"THIS IS WHAT I MEAN, MATTY...
"MOST PEOPLE DON'T WANNA KNOW. TELL ME: YOU FEEL SAFER NOW YOU KNOW?"
YOU THINK SOME ASSHOLE NOT GONNA ELECTRODE UP YOUR NUTSACK IF HE KNOW YOU KNOW WHERE CHINATOWN GOLD IS?
OR YOU THINK HE NOT HURT SOMEONE YOU LOVE, MAKE YOU GIVE UP LOCATION?
≈PFFT≈
MATTY ROTH... HE ALWAYS GOTTA BE IN THE KNOW...
LOOK, WILSON, I HEAR YOU. I DO. BUT WE'RE PAST THAT KIND OF SHIT. WE'RE PAST JUST SURVIVING. WE'RE PAST LOOKING OUT FOR NUMBER ONE.
OH, WE ARE? THAT SO?
IT'S NOT THE SAME CITY NOW. PARCO DELGADO IS IN OFFICE.
YOU WOULDN'T KNOW FIRST-HAND, BUT THE CITY IS CHANGED, MAN. THERE'S HOPE, THERE'S A SENSE OF IDENTITY, A UNIFIED FEELING OF WORKING FOR THE COLLECTIVE GOOD.
WE HAVE A REAL SHOT, A REAL CHANCE OF ENDING THIS WAR, OF FORCING PEACE ON THE ASSHOLES...LIKE TRUSTWELL, FOR EXAMPLE.
HE NEEDS MONEY TO LOCK IT ALL DOWN. YOU KNOW WHAT LOYALTY COSTS, MAN. WHAT POWER COSTS. WHAT IT TAKES TO HOLD A NEIGHBORHOOD DOWN.
HE NEEDS THE GOLD, WILSON.
YOU NEVER THOUGHT TO ASK WHERE I GET THIS FRESH FOOD...YOU CAN'T EAT A BRICK OF GOLD, MATTY. THINK ABOUT THAT WHEN YOU WONDER WHY PARCO CAN'T HOLD HIS 'HOODS.

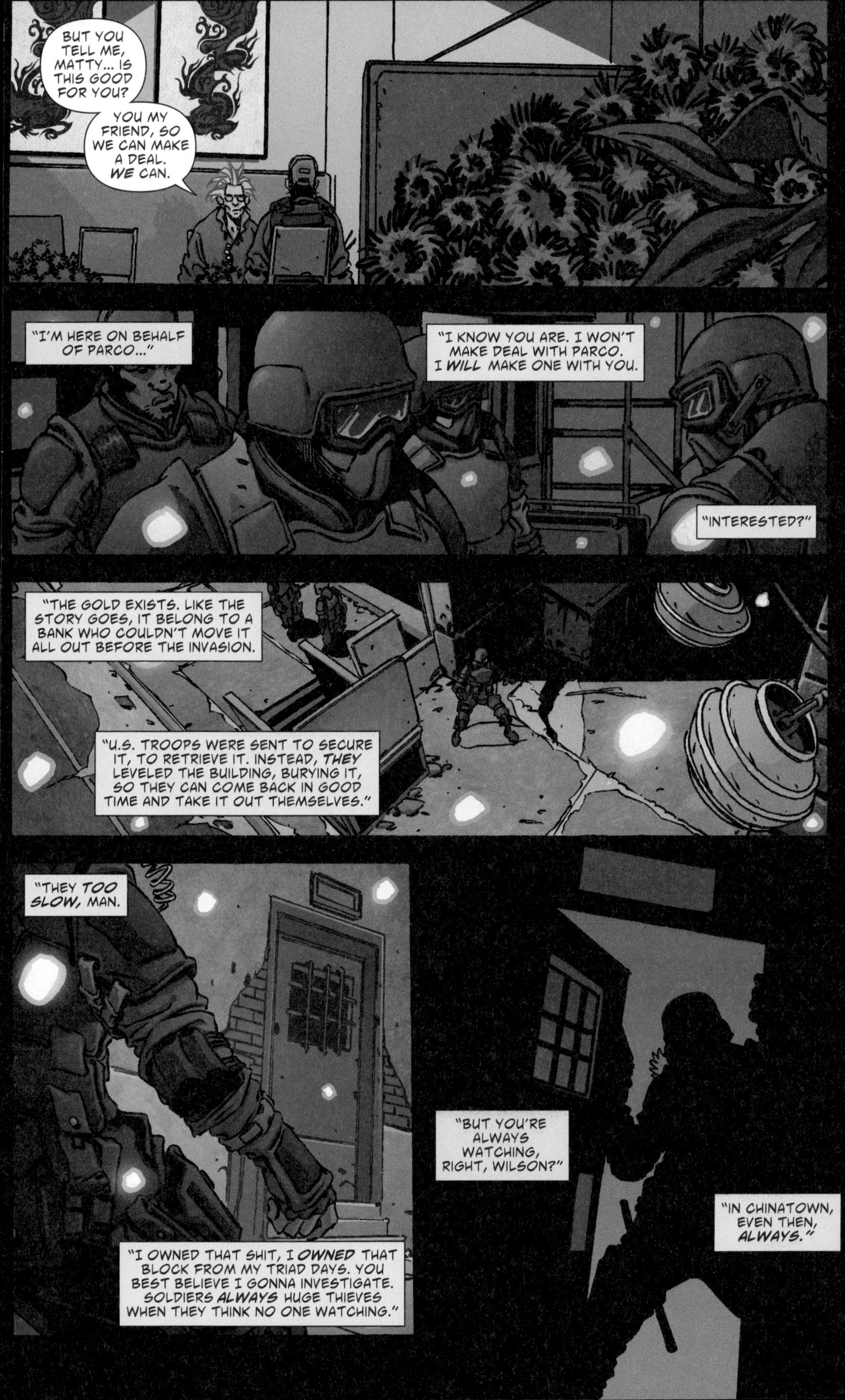
BUT YOU TELL ME, MATTY... IS THIS GOOD FOR YOU?
YOU MY FRIEND, SO WE CAN MAKE A DEAL. WE CAN.
"I'M HERE ON BEHALF OF PARCO..."
"I KNOW YOU ARE. I WON'T MAKE DEAL WITH PARCO. I WILL MAKE ONE WITH YOU.
"INTERESTED?"
"THE GOLD EXISTS. LIKE THE STORY GOES, IT BELONG TO A BANK WHO COULDN'T MOVE IT ALL OUT BEFORE THE INVASION.
"U.S. TROOPS WERE SENT TO SECURE IT, TO RETRIEVE IT. INSTEAD, THEY LEVELED THE BUILDING, BURYING IT, SO THEY CAN COME BACK IN GOOD TIME AND TAKE IT OUT THEMSELVES."
"THEY TOO SLOW, MAN.
"I OWNED THAT SHIT, I OWNED THAT BLOCK FROM MY TRIAD DAYS. YOU BEST BELIEVE I GONNA INVESTIGATE. SOLDIERS ALWAYS HUGE THIEVES WHEN THEY THINK NO ONE WATCHING."
"BUT YOU'RE ALWAYS WATCHING, RIGHT, WILSON?"
"IN CHINATOWN, EVEN THEN, ALWAYS."

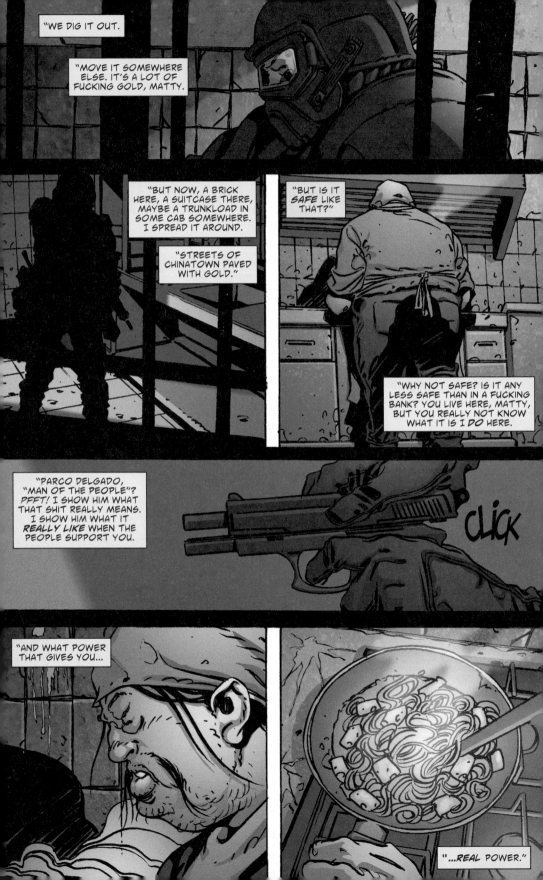

"WE DIG IT OUT.

"MOVE IT SOMEWHERE ELSE. IT'S A LOT OF FUCKING GOLD, MATTY.

"BUT NOW, A BRICK HERE, A SUITCASE THERE, MAYBE A TRUNKLOAD IN SOME CAB SOMEWHERE. I SPREAD IT AROUND.

"STREETS OF CHINATOWN PAVED WITH GOLD."

"BUT IS IT SAFE LIKE THAT?"

"WHY NOT SAFE? IS IT ANY LESS SAFE THAN IN A FUCKING BANK? YOU LIVE HERE, MATTY, BUT YOU REALLY NOT KNOW WHAT IT IS I DO HERE.

"PARCO DELGADO, "MAN OF THE PEOPLE"? PFFT! I SHOW HIM WHAT THAT SHIT REALLY MEANS. I SHOW HIM WHAT IT REALLY LIKE WHEN THE PEOPLE SUPPORT YOU.

CLICK

"AND WHAT POWER THAT GIVES YOU...

"...REAL POWER."

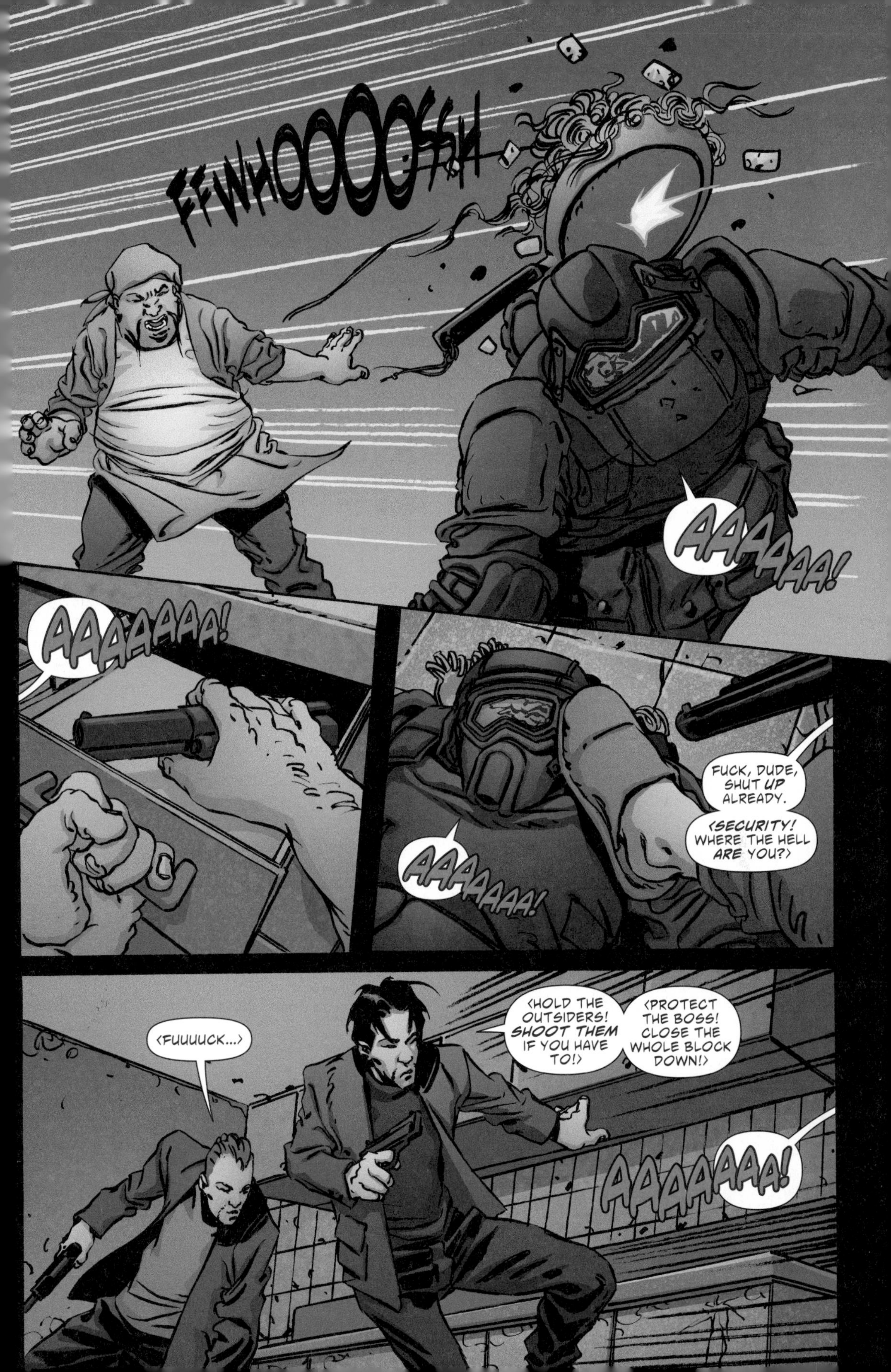
FFWHOOOOOSSH
AAAAAAA!
AAAAAAA!
AAAAAAA!
FUCK, DUDE, SHUT UP ALREADY.
<SECURITY! WHERE THE HELL ARE YOU?>
<FUUUUCK...>
<HOLD THE OUTSIDERS! SHOOT THEM IF YOU HAVE TO!>
<PROTECT THE BOSS! CLOSE THE WHOLE BLOCK DOWN!>
AAAAAAA!

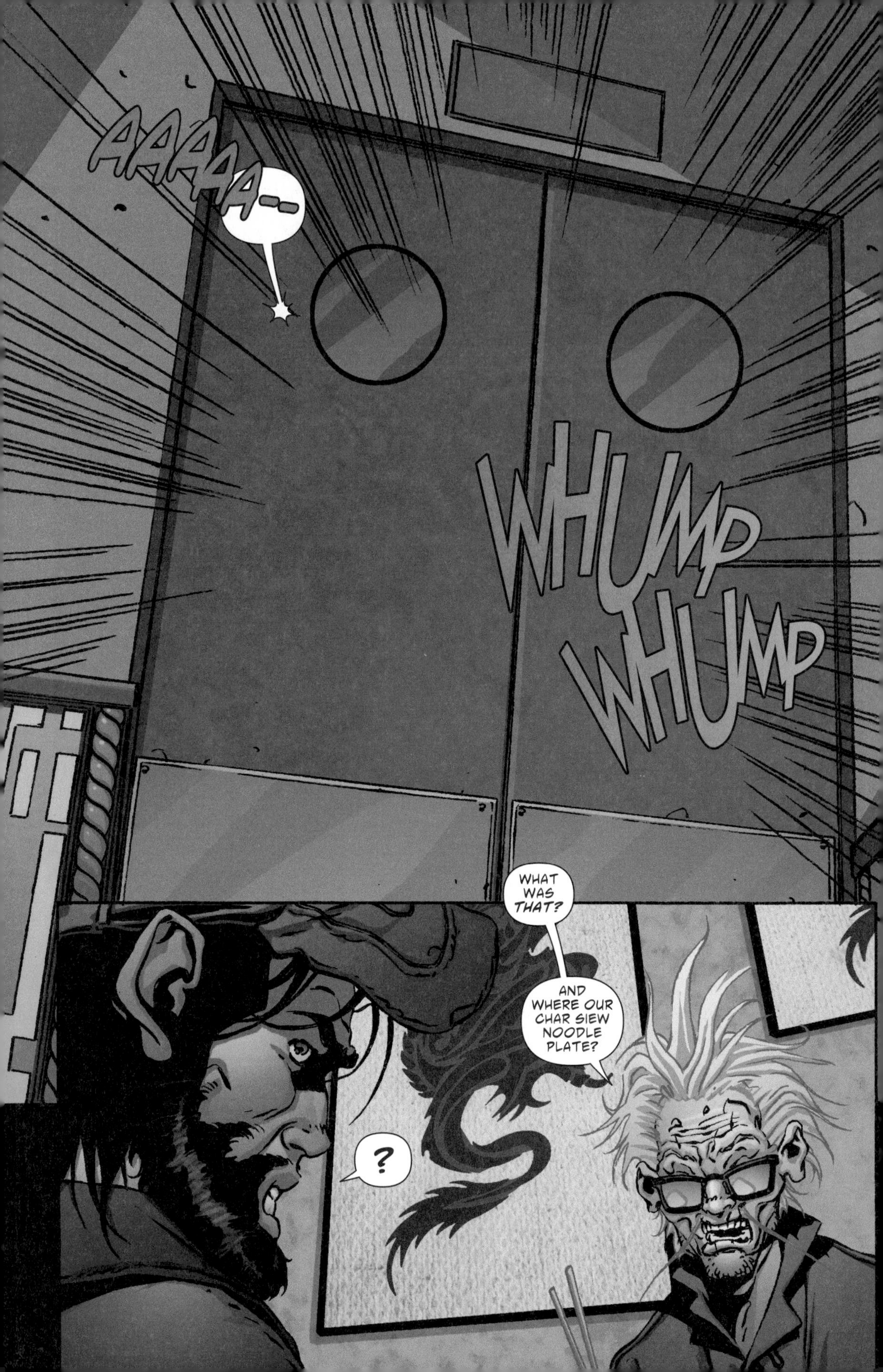
AAAAA--
WHUMP
WHUMP
WHAT WAS THAT?
AND WHERE OUR CHAR SIEW NOODLE PLATE?
?

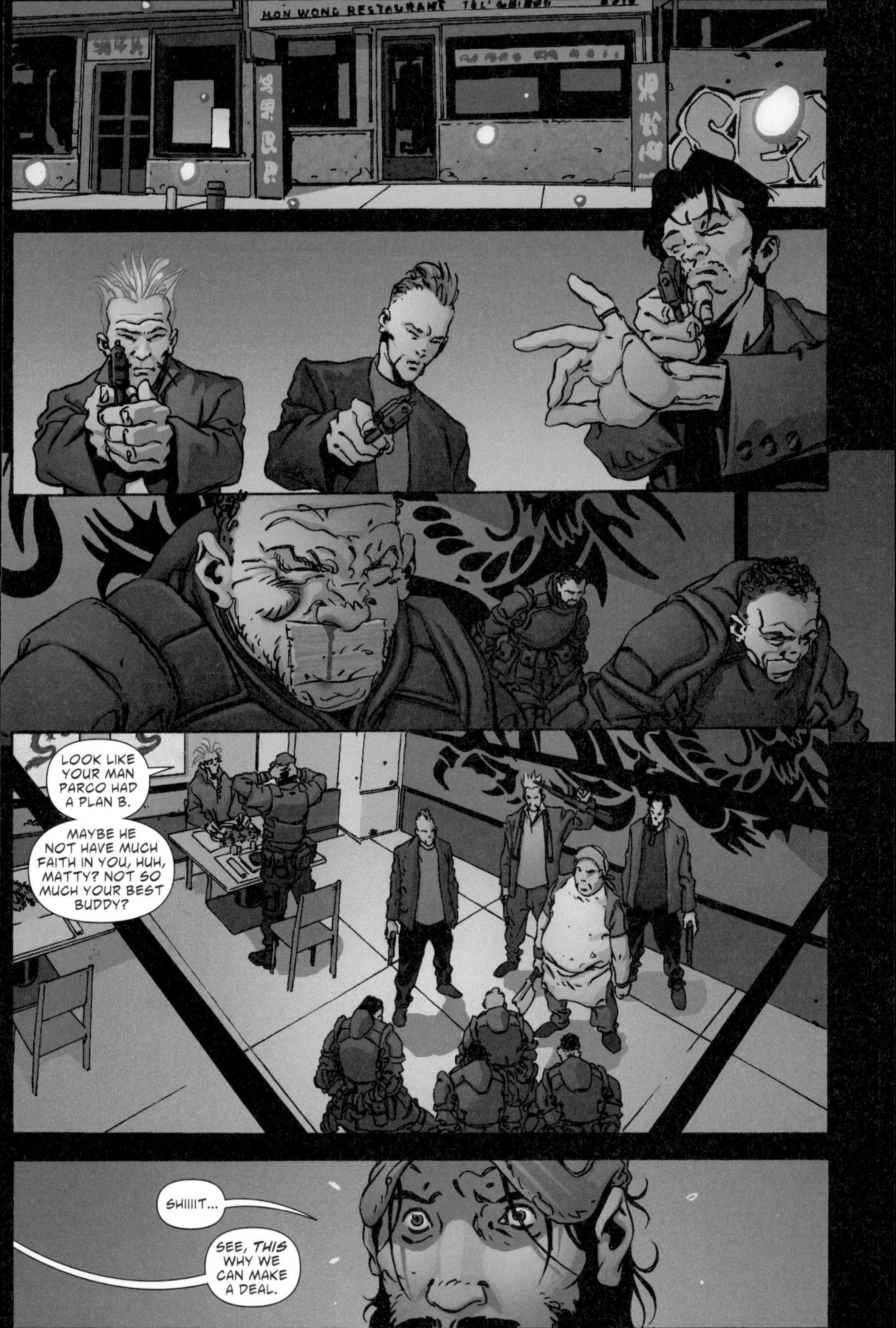
MON WONG RESTAURANT
LOOK LIKE YOUR MAN PARCO HAD A PLAN B.
MAYBE HE NOT HAVE MUCH FAITH IN YOU, HUH, MATTY? NOT SO MUCH YOUR BEST BUDDY?
SHIIIIT...
SEE, *THIS* WHY WE CAN MAKE A DEAL.

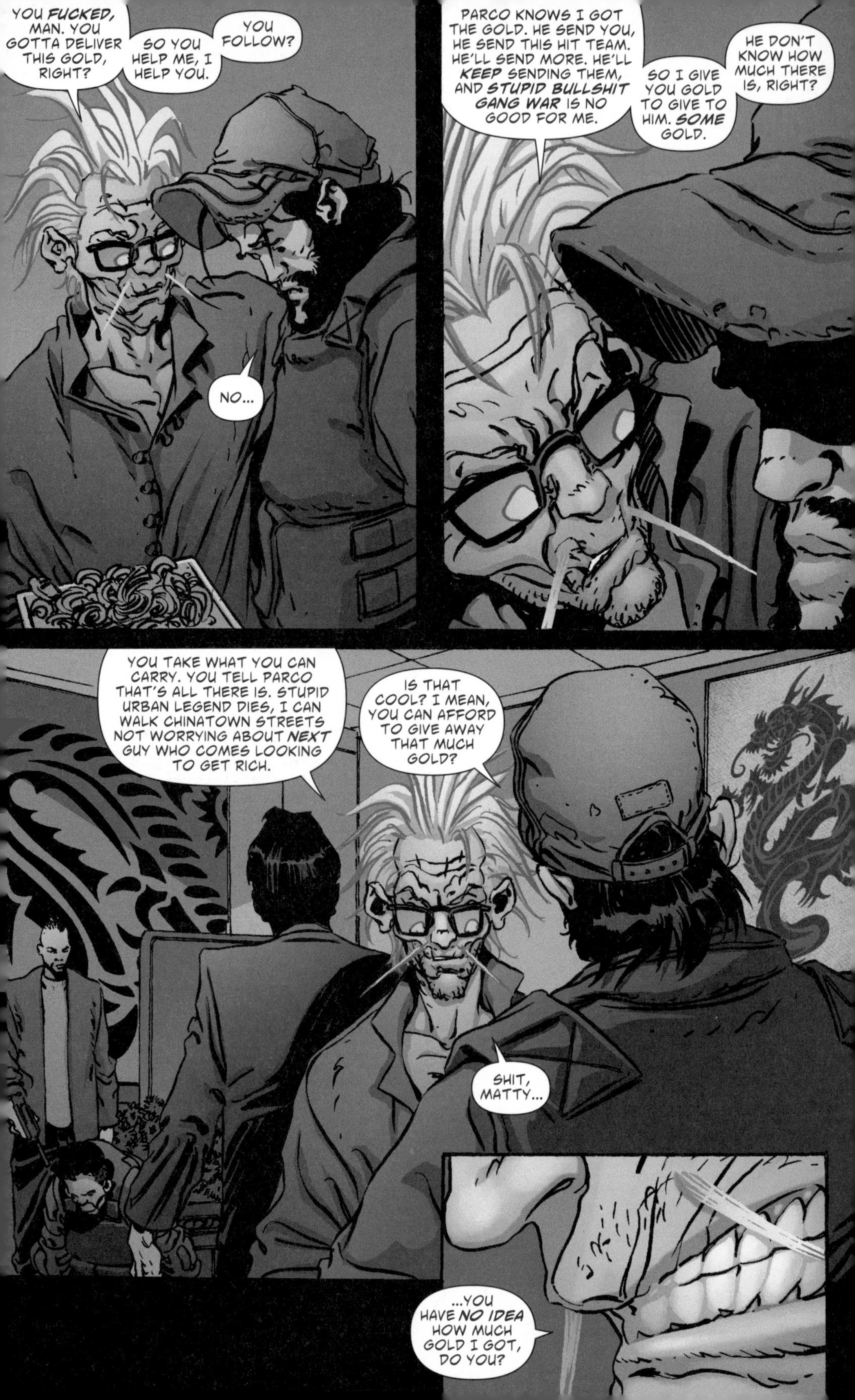
YOU *FUCKED*, MAN. YOU GOTTA DELIVER THIS GOLD, RIGHT?
SO YOU HELP ME, I HELP YOU.
YOU FOLLOW?
NO...
PARCO KNOWS I GOT THE GOLD. HE SEND YOU, HE SEND THIS HIT TEAM. HE'LL SEND MORE. HE'LL *KEEP* SENDING THEM, AND *STUPID BULLSHIT GANG WAR* IS NO GOOD FOR ME.
SO I GIVE YOU GOLD TO GIVE TO HIM. *SOME* GOLD.
HE DON'T KNOW HOW MUCH THERE IS, RIGHT?
YOU TAKE WHAT YOU CAN CARRY. YOU TELL PARCO THAT'S ALL THERE IS. STUPID URBAN LEGEND DIES, I CAN WALK CHINATOWN STREETS NOT WORRYING ABOUT *NEXT* GUY WHO COMES LOOKING TO GET RICH.
IS THAT COOL? I MEAN, YOU CAN AFFORD TO GIVE AWAY THAT MUCH GOLD?
SHIT, MATTY...
...YOU HAVE *NO IDEA* HOW MUCH GOLD I GOT, DO YOU?

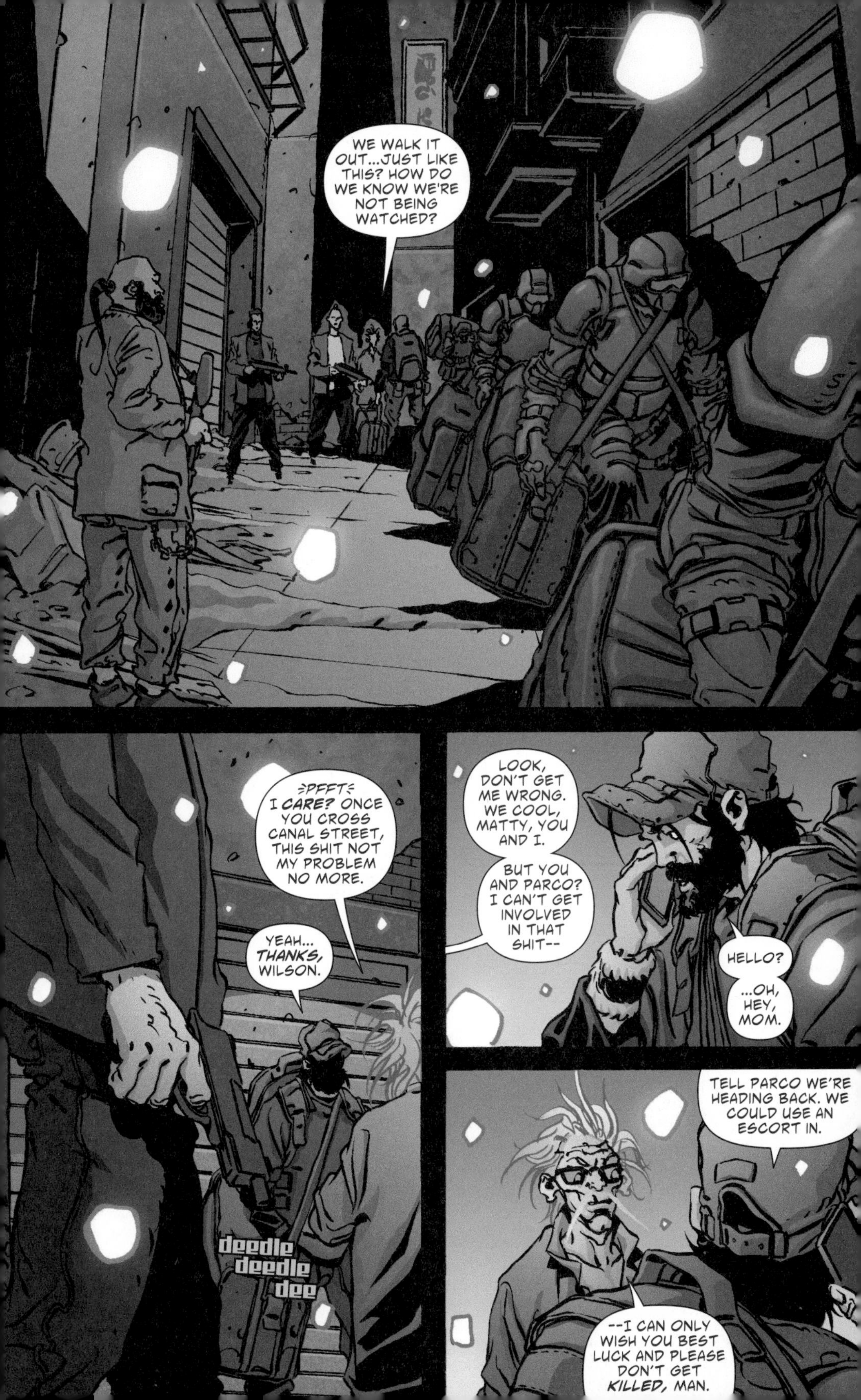
WE WALK IT OUT...JUST LIKE THIS? HOW DO WE KNOW WE'RE NOT BEING WATCHED?
=PFFT= I CARE? ONCE YOU CROSS CANAL STREET, THIS SHIT NOT MY PROBLEM NO MORE.
YEAH... THANKS, WILSON.
deedle deedle dee
LOOK, DON'T GET ME WRONG. WE COOL, MATTY, YOU AND I.
BUT YOU AND PARCO? I CAN'T GET INVOLVED IN THAT SHIT--
HELLO?
...OH, HEY, MOM.
TELL PARCO WE'RE HEADING BACK. WE COULD USE AN ESCORT IN.
--I CAN ONLY WISH YOU BEST LUCK AND PLEASE DON'T GET KILLED, MAN.

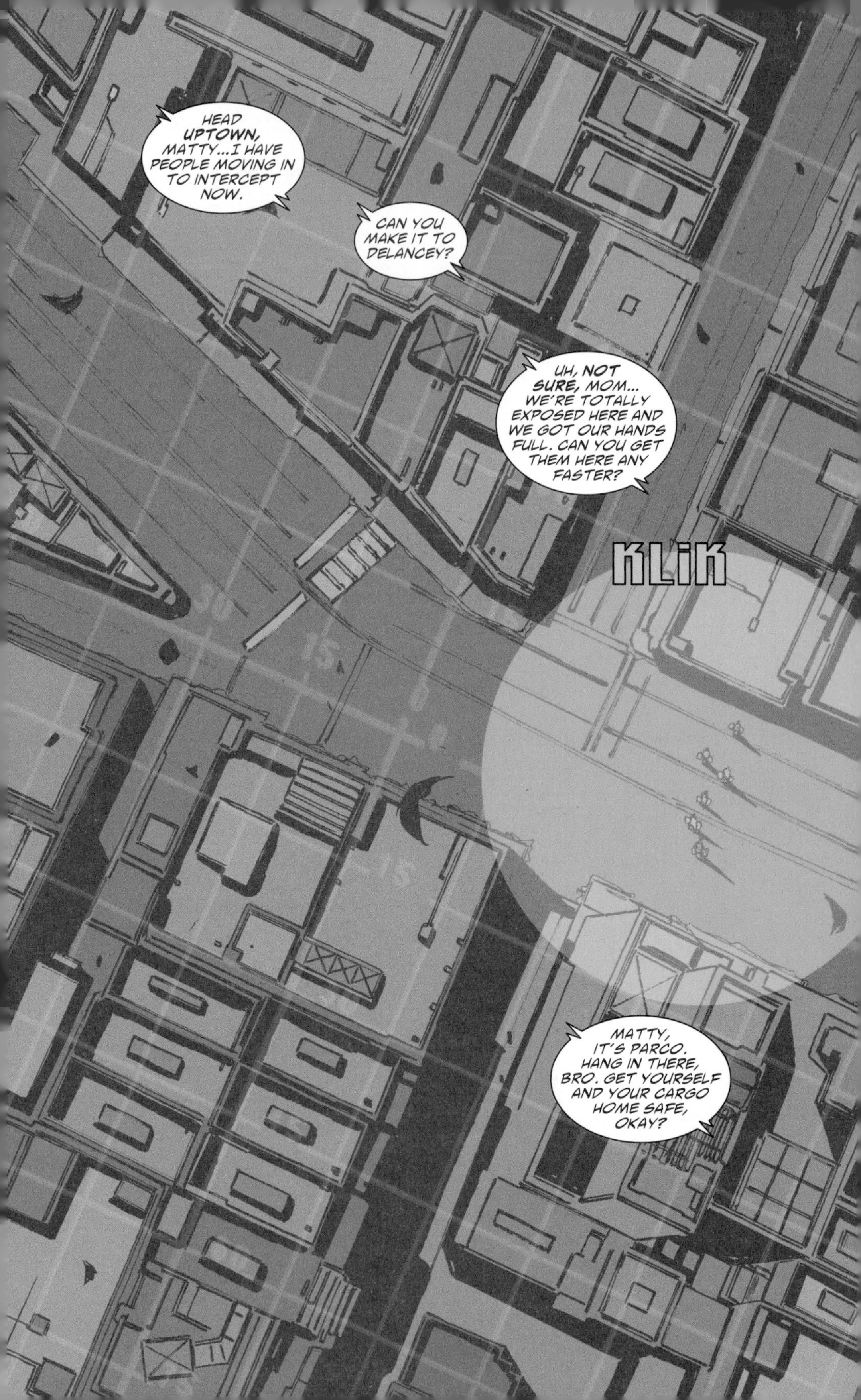
HEAD **UPTOWN,** MATTY...I HAVE PEOPLE MOVING IN TO INTERCEPT NOW.
CAN YOU MAKE IT TO DELANCEY?
UH, **NOT SURE,** MOM... WE'RE TOTALLY EXPOSED HERE AND WE GOT OUR HANDS FULL. CAN YOU GET THEM HERE ANY FASTER?
KLIK
MATTY, IT'S PARCO. HANG IN THERE, BRO. GET YOURSELF AND YOUR CARGO HOME SAFE, OKAY?

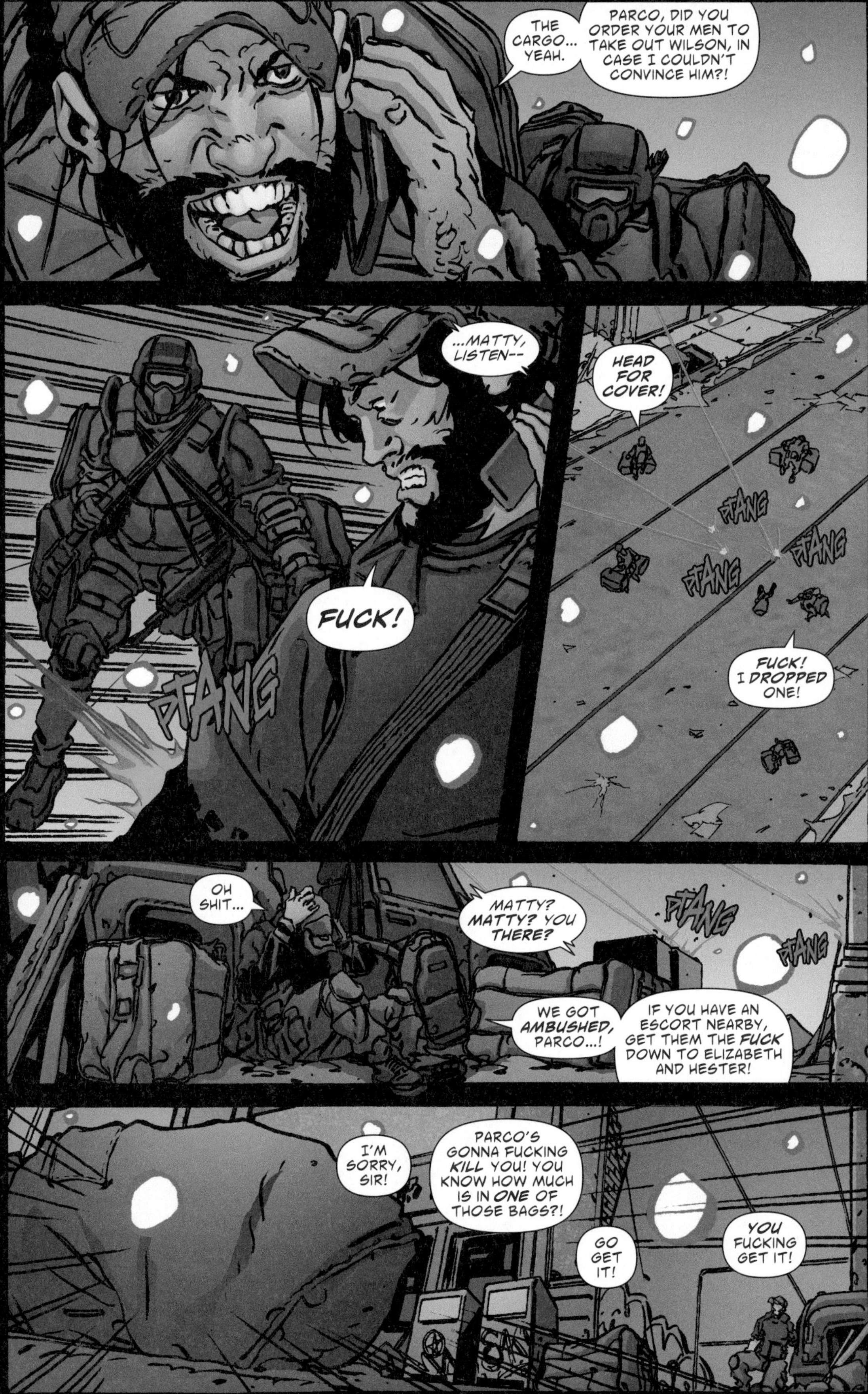
THE CARGO... YEAH.
PARCO, DID YOU ORDER YOUR MEN TO TAKE OUT WILSON, IN CASE I COULDN'T CONVINCE HIM?!
...MATTY, LISTEN--
FUCK!
PTANG
HEAD FOR COVER!
PTANG
PTANG
PTANG
FUCK! I DROPPED ONE!
OH SHIT...
MATTY? MATTY? YOU THERE?
PTANG
PTANG
WE GOT AMBUSHED, PARCO...!
IF YOU HAVE AN ESCORT NEARBY, GET THEM THE FUCK DOWN TO ELIZABETH AND HESTER!
I'M SORRY, SIR!
PARCO'S GONNA FUCKING KILL YOU! YOU KNOW HOW MUCH IS IN ONE OF THOSE BAGS?!
GO GET IT!
YOU FUCKING GET IT!

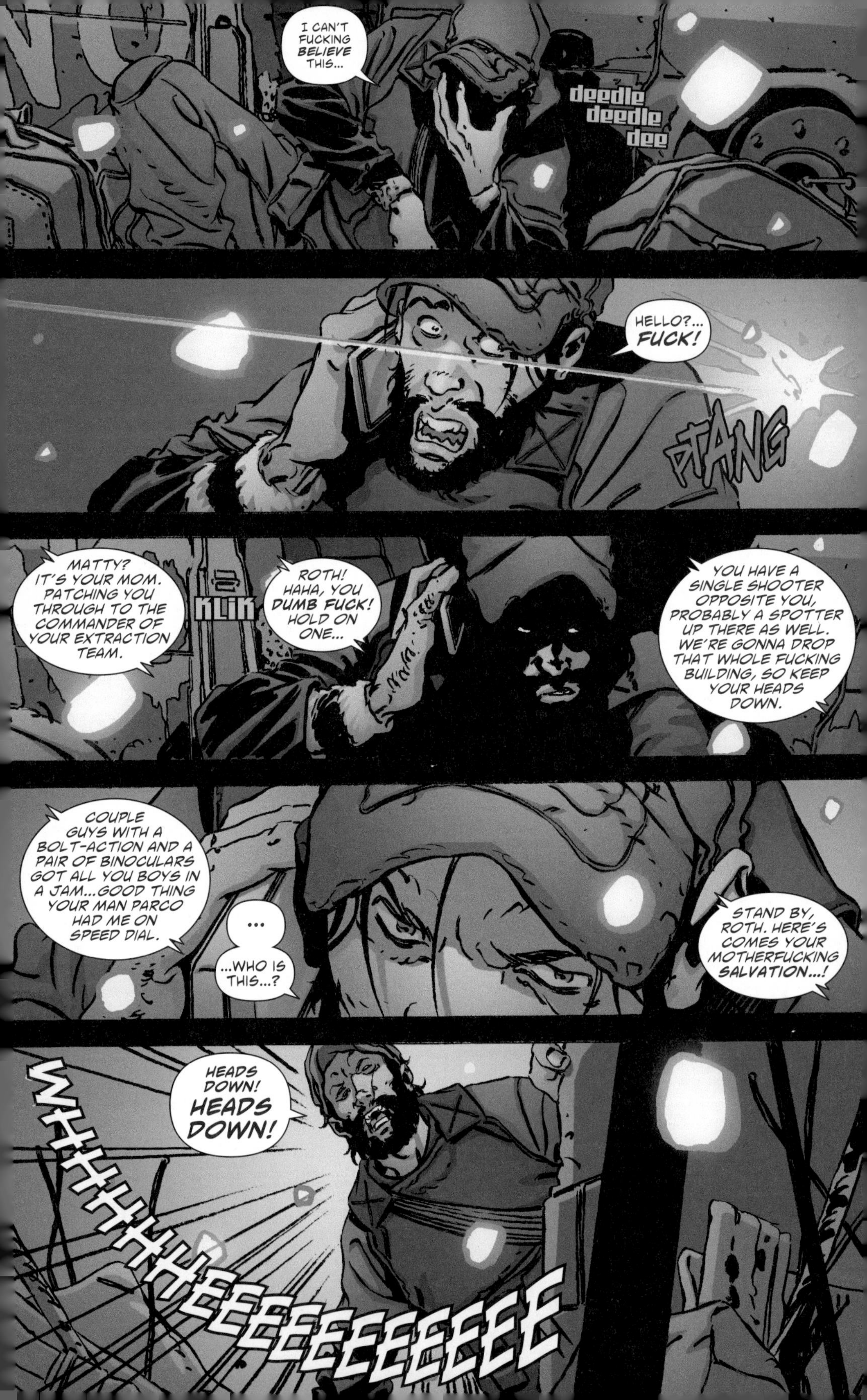
I CAN'T FUCKING BELIEVE THIS...
deedle deedle dee
HELLO?... FUCK!
PTANG
MATTY? IT'S YOUR MOM. PATCHING YOU THROUGH TO THE COMMANDER OF YOUR EXTRACTION TEAM.
KLIK
ROTH! HAHA, YOU DUMB FUCK! HOLD ON ONE...
YOU HAVE A SINGLE SHOOTER OPPOSITE YOU, PROBABLY A SPOTTER UP THERE AS WELL. WE'RE GONNA DROP THAT WHOLE FUCKING BUILDING, SO KEEP YOUR HEADS DOWN.
COUPLE GUYS WITH A BOLT-ACTION AND A PAIR OF BINOCULARS GOT ALL YOU BOYS IN A JAM...GOOD THING YOUR MAN PARCO HAD ME ON SPEED DIAL.
...
...WHO IS THIS...?
STAND BY, ROTH. HERE'S COMES YOUR MOTHERFUCKING SALVATION...!
HEADS DOWN! HEADS DOWN!
WHHHHHHEEEEEEEEEEEEE

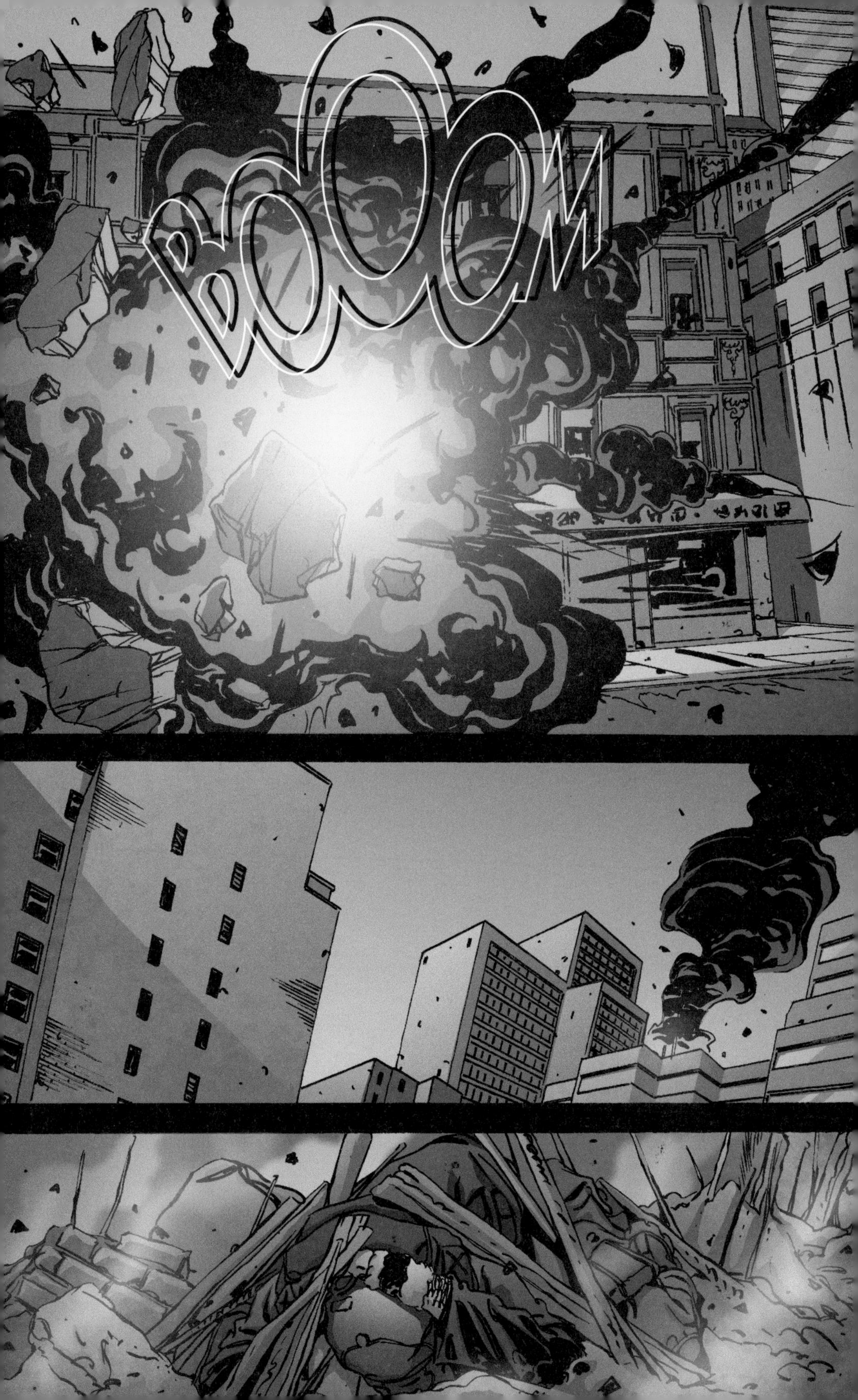
BOOOM

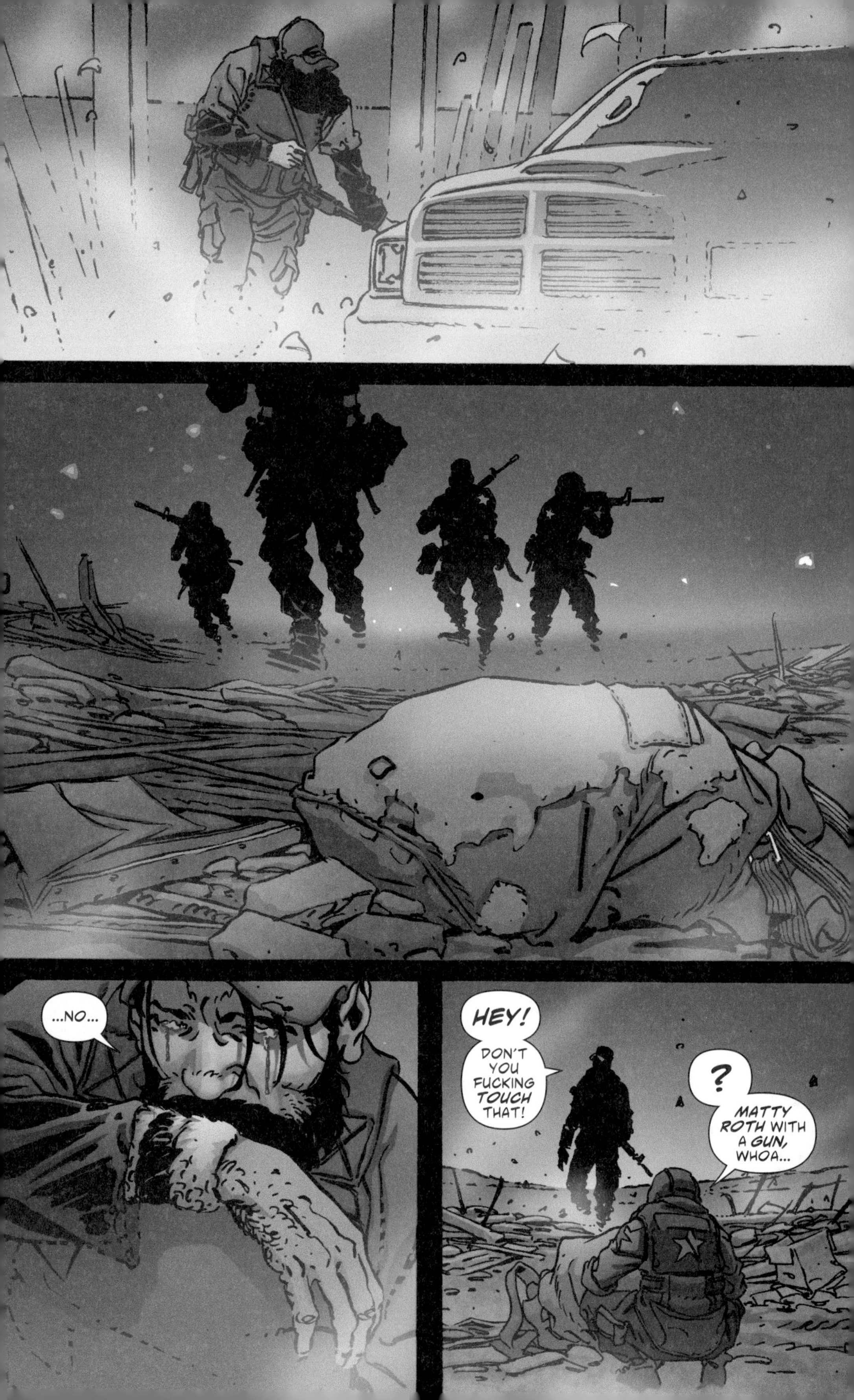
...NO...
HEY!
DON'T YOU FUCKING TOUCH THAT!
?
MATTY ROTH WITH A GUN, WHOA...

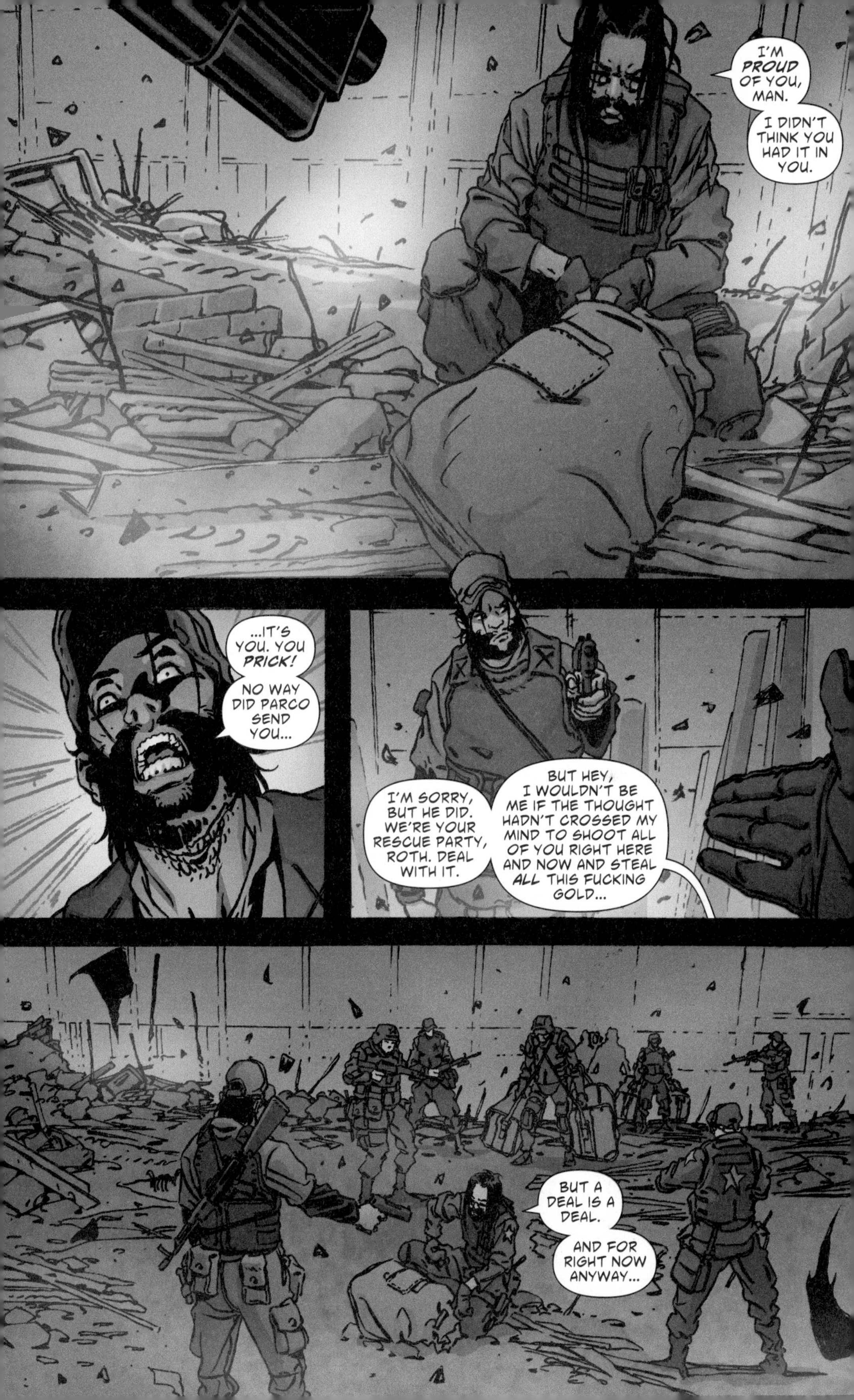
I'M PROUD OF YOU, MAN.
I DIDN'T THINK YOU HAD IT IN YOU.
...IT'S YOU. YOU PRICK!
NO WAY DID PARCO SEND YOU...
I'M SORRY, BUT HE DID. WE'RE YOUR RESCUE PARTY, ROTH. DEAL WITH IT.
BUT HEY, I WOULDN'T BE ME IF THE THOUGHT HADN'T CROSSED MY MIND TO SHOOT ALL OF YOU RIGHT HERE AND NOW AND STEAL ALL THIS FUCKING GOLD...
BUT A DEAL IS A DEAL.
AND FOR RIGHT NOW ANYWAY...

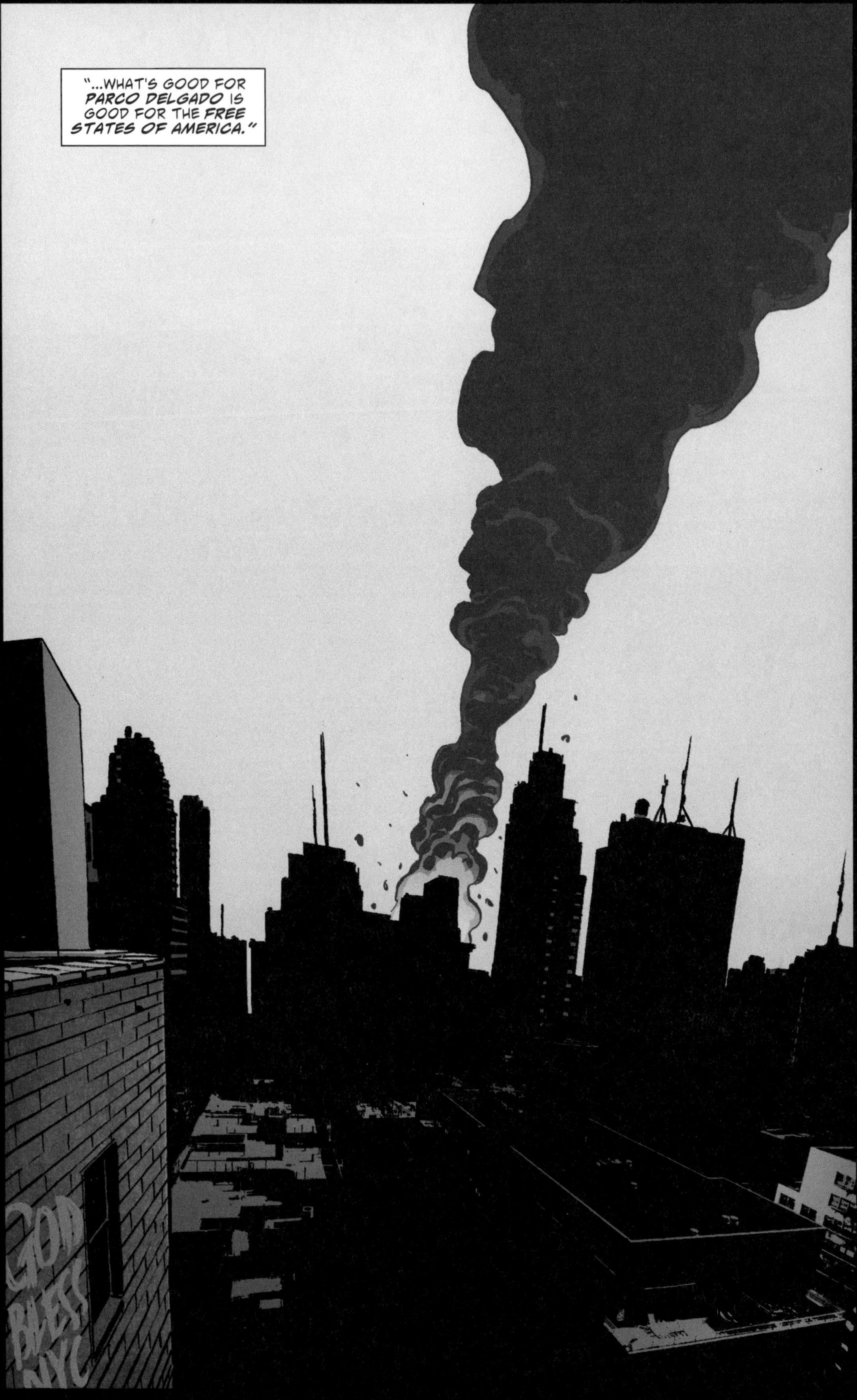
"...WHAT'S GOOD FOR *PARCO DELGADO* IS GOOD FOR THE *FREE STATES OF AMERICA.*"
GOD BLESS NYC

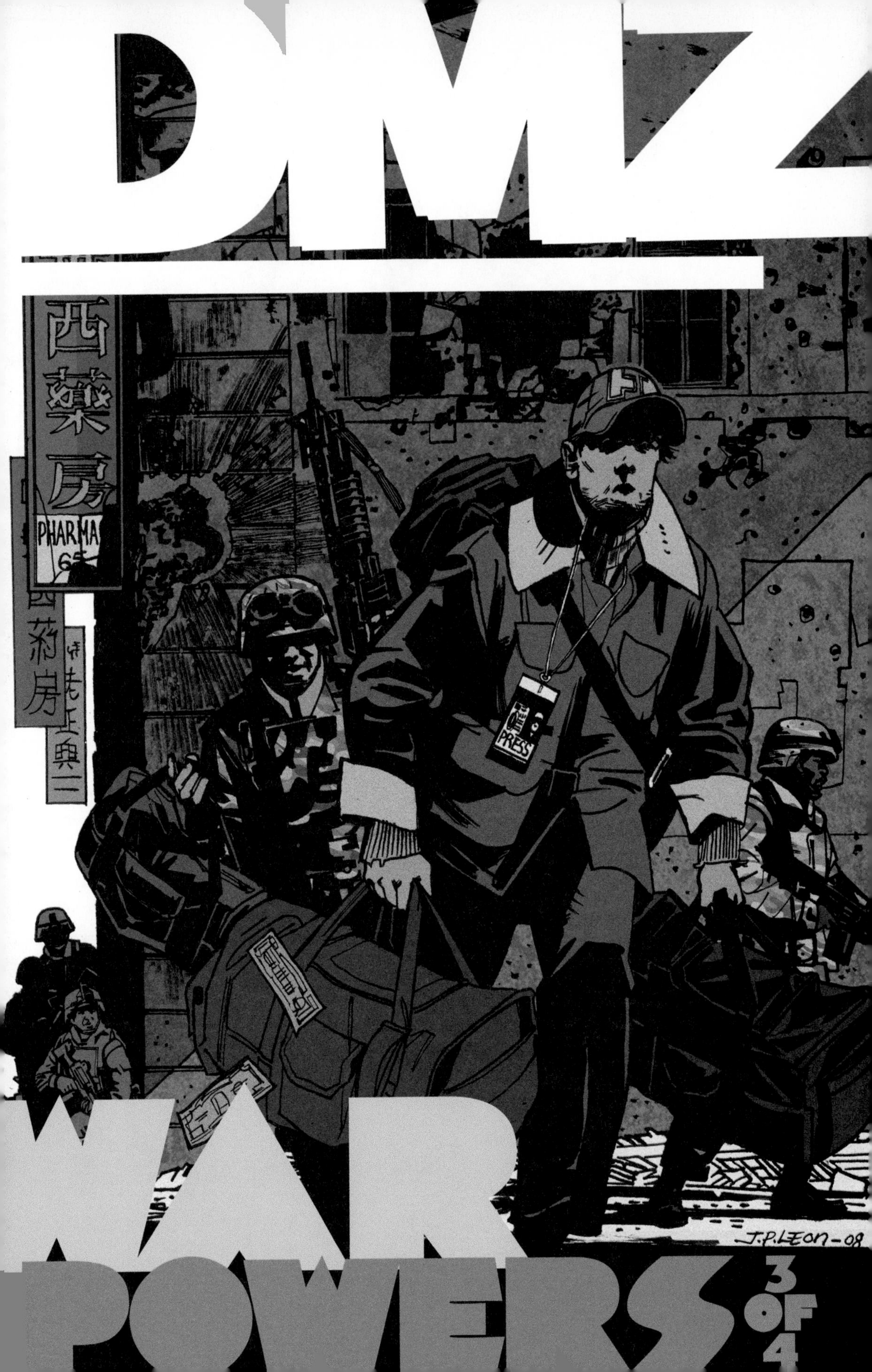
DMZ
西藥房
PHARMA
65
PRESS
J.P.LEON-08
WAR POWERS
3 OF 4

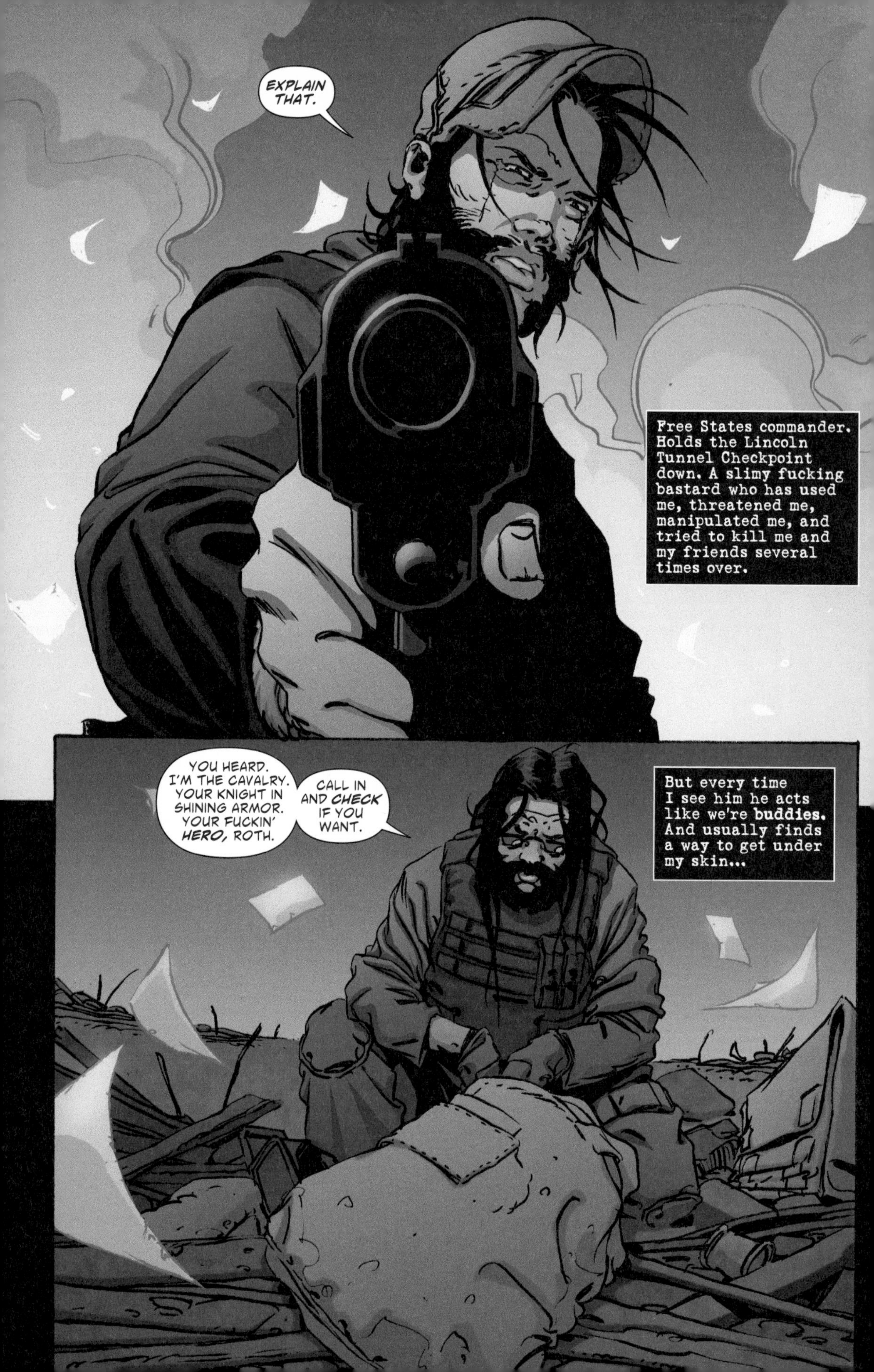
EXPLAIN THAT.
Free States commander. Holds the Lincoln Tunnel Checkpoint down. A slimy fucking bastard who has used me, threatened me, manipulated me, and tried to kill me and my friends several times over.
YOU HEARD. I'M THE CAVALRY. YOUR KNIGHT IN SHINING ARMOR. YOUR FUCKIN' HERO, ROTH.
CALL IN AND CHECK IF YOU WANT.
But every time I see him he acts like we're buddies. And usually finds a way to get under my skin...

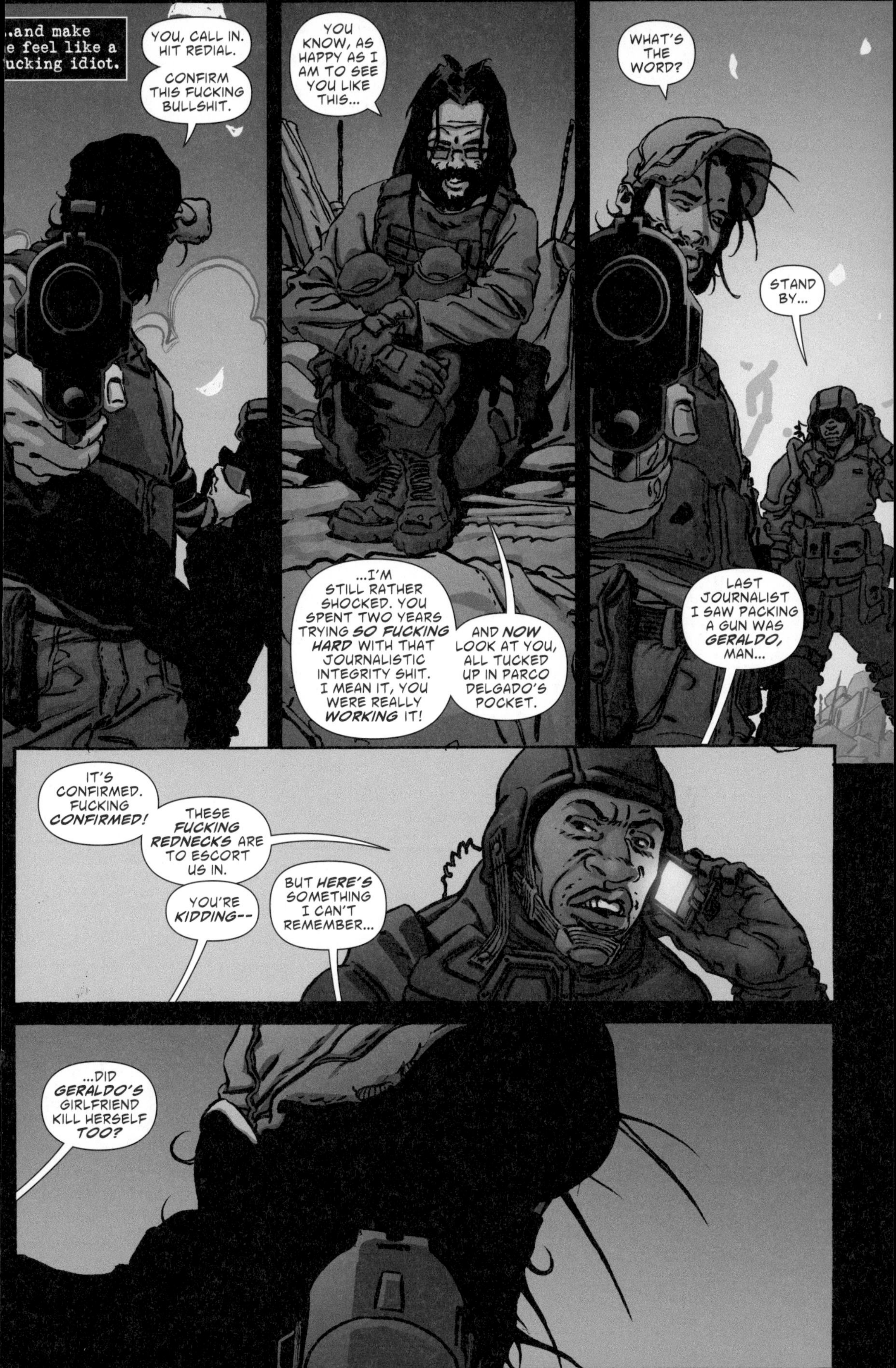
..and make
e feel like a
ucking idiot.
YOU, CALL IN. HIT REDIAL.
CONFIRM THIS FUCKING BULLSHIT.
YOU KNOW, AS HAPPY AS I AM TO SEE YOU LIKE THIS...
...I'M STILL RATHER SHOCKED. YOU SPENT TWO YEARS TRYING SO FUCKING HARD WITH THAT JOURNALISTIC INTEGRITY SHIT. I MEAN IT, YOU WERE REALLY WORKING IT!
AND NOW LOOK AT YOU, ALL TUCKED UP IN PARCO DELGADO'S POCKET.
WHAT'S THE WORD?
STAND BY...
LAST JOURNALIST I SAW PACKING A GUN WAS GERALDO, MAN...
IT'S CONFIRMED. FUCKING CONFIRMED!
THESE FUCKING REDNECKS ARE TO ESCORT US IN.
YOU'RE KIDDING--
BUT HERE'S SOMETHING I CAN'T REMEMBER...
...DID GERALDO'S GIRLFRIEND KILL HERSELF TOO?

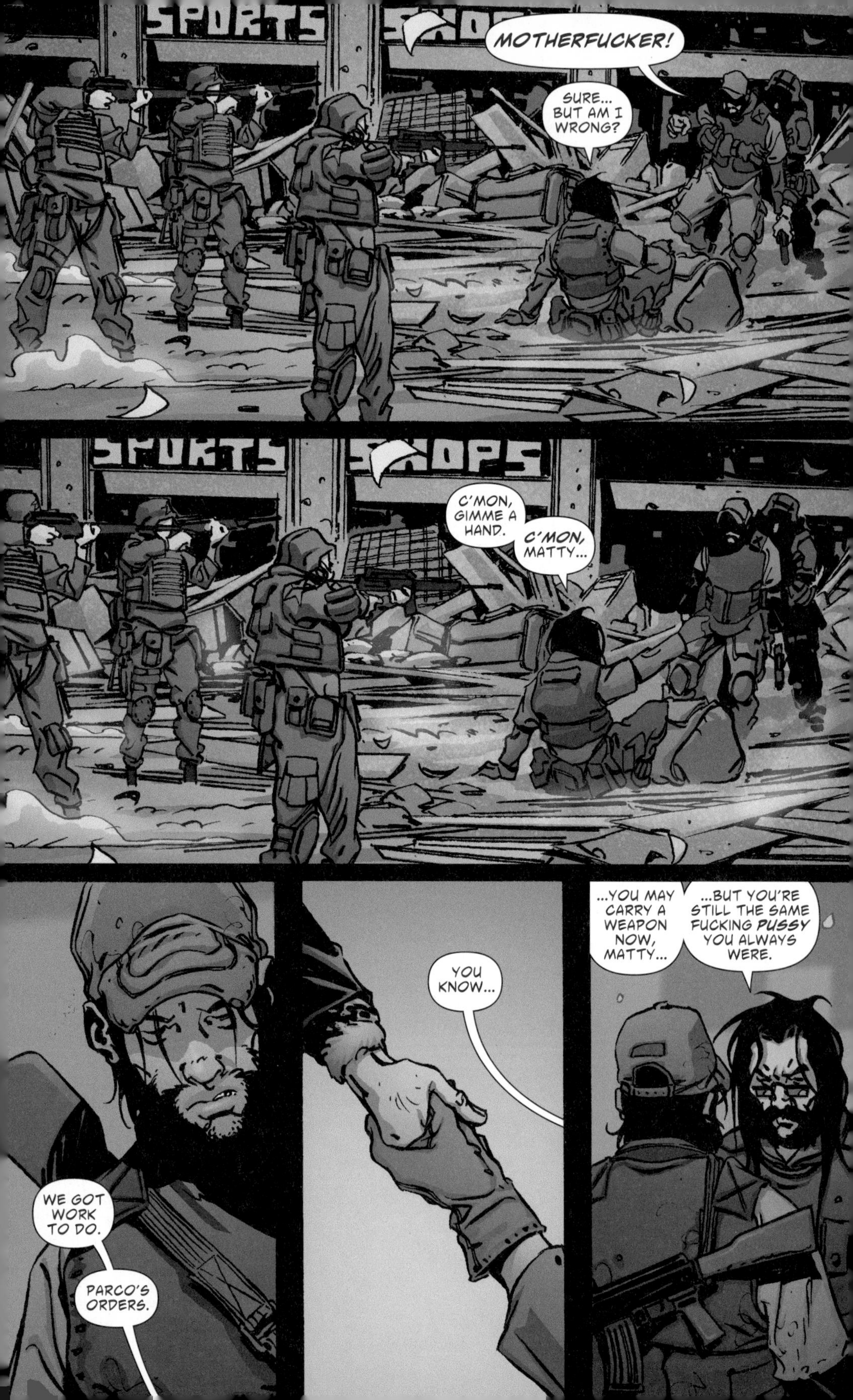
SPORTS SHOPS
MOTHERFUCKER!
SURE... BUT AM I WRONG?
SPORTS SHOPS
C'MON, GIMME A HAND.
C'MON, MATTY...
WE GOT WORK TO DO.
PARCO'S ORDERS.
YOU KNOW...
...YOU MAY CARRY A WEAPON NOW, MATTY...
...BUT YOU'RE STILL THE SAME FUCKING *PUSSY* YOU ALWAYS WERE.

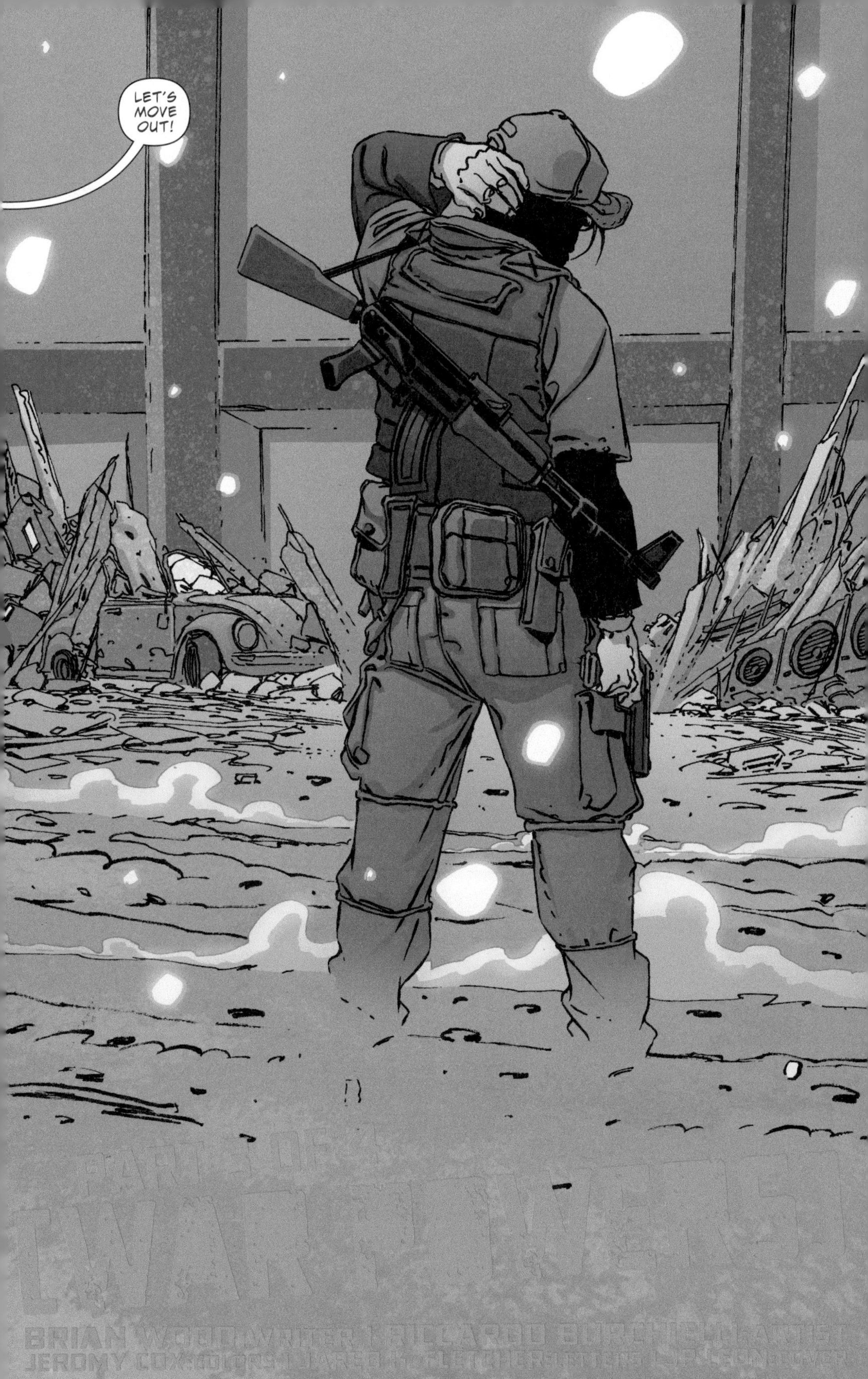
LET'S MOVE OUT!
PART 1 OF 4
BRIAN WOOD WRITER
RICCARDO BURCHIELLI ARTIST
JEROMY COX COLORS

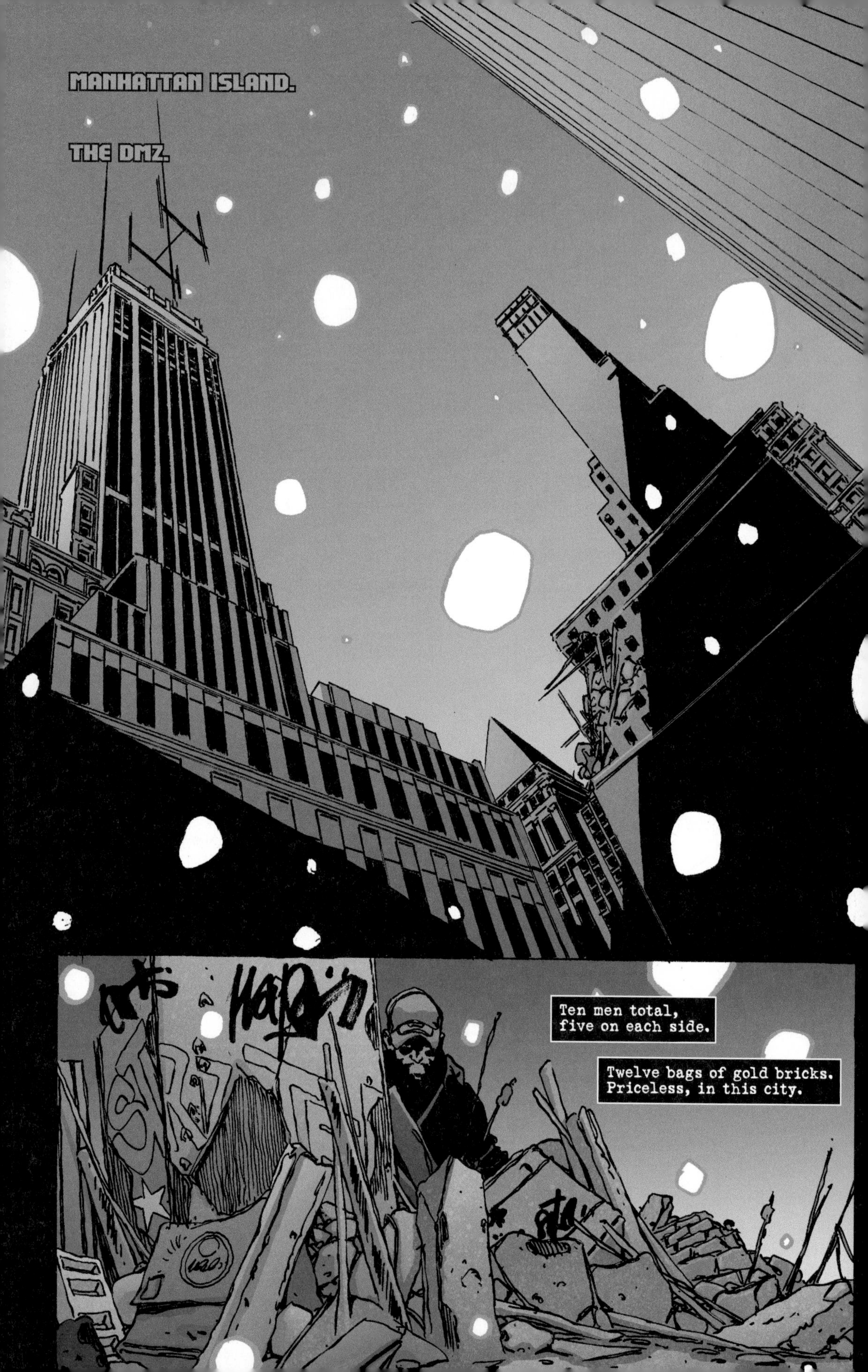
MANHATTAN ISLAND.
THE DMZ.
Ten men total, five on each side.
Twelve bags of gold bricks. Priceless, in this city.

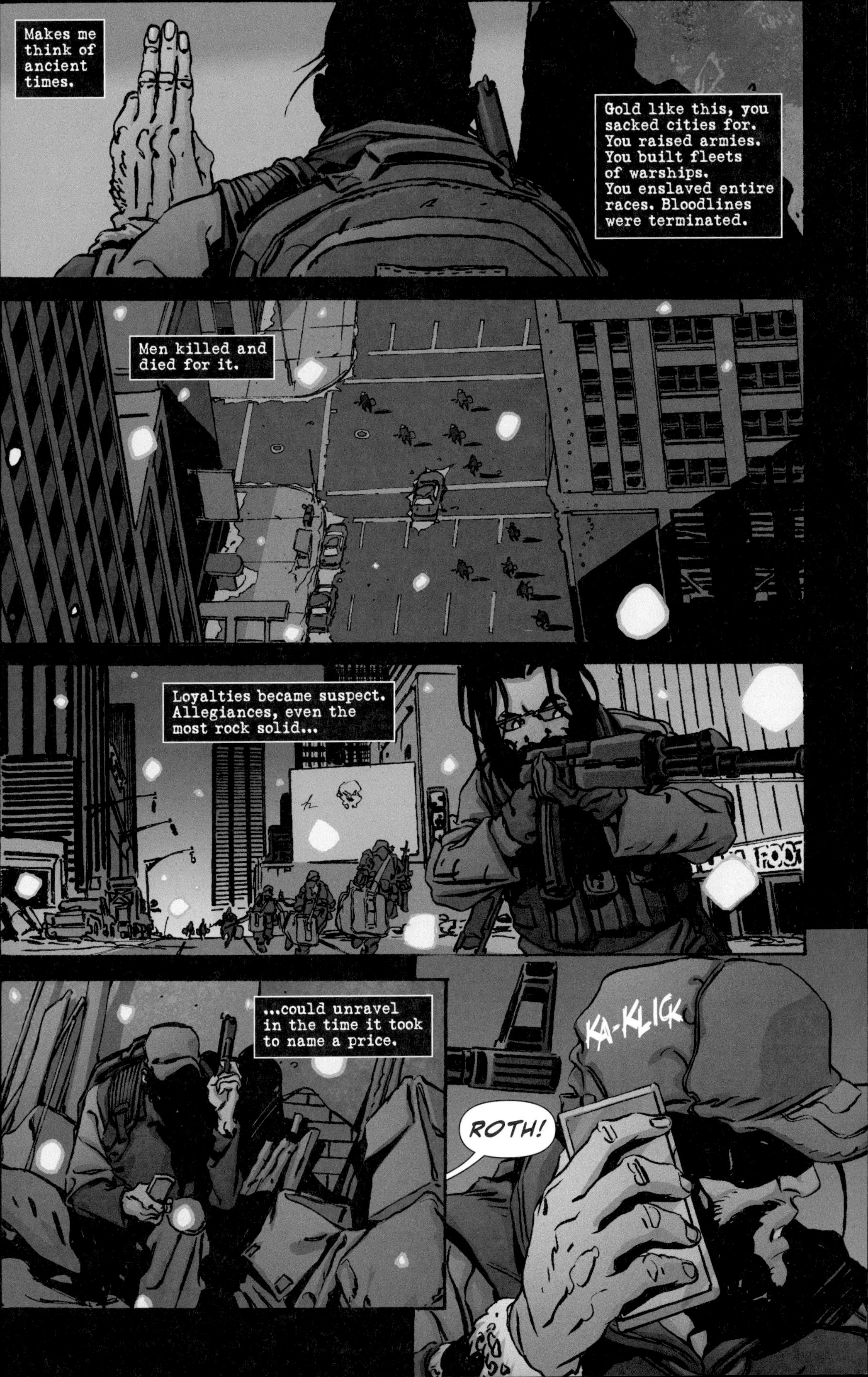
Makes me think of ancient times.
Gold like this, you sacked cities for. You raised armies. You built fleets of warships. You enslaved entire races. Bloodlines were terminated.
Men killed and died for it.
Loyalties became suspect. Allegiances, even the most rock solid...
...could unravel in the time it took to name a price.
KA-KLICK
ROTH!

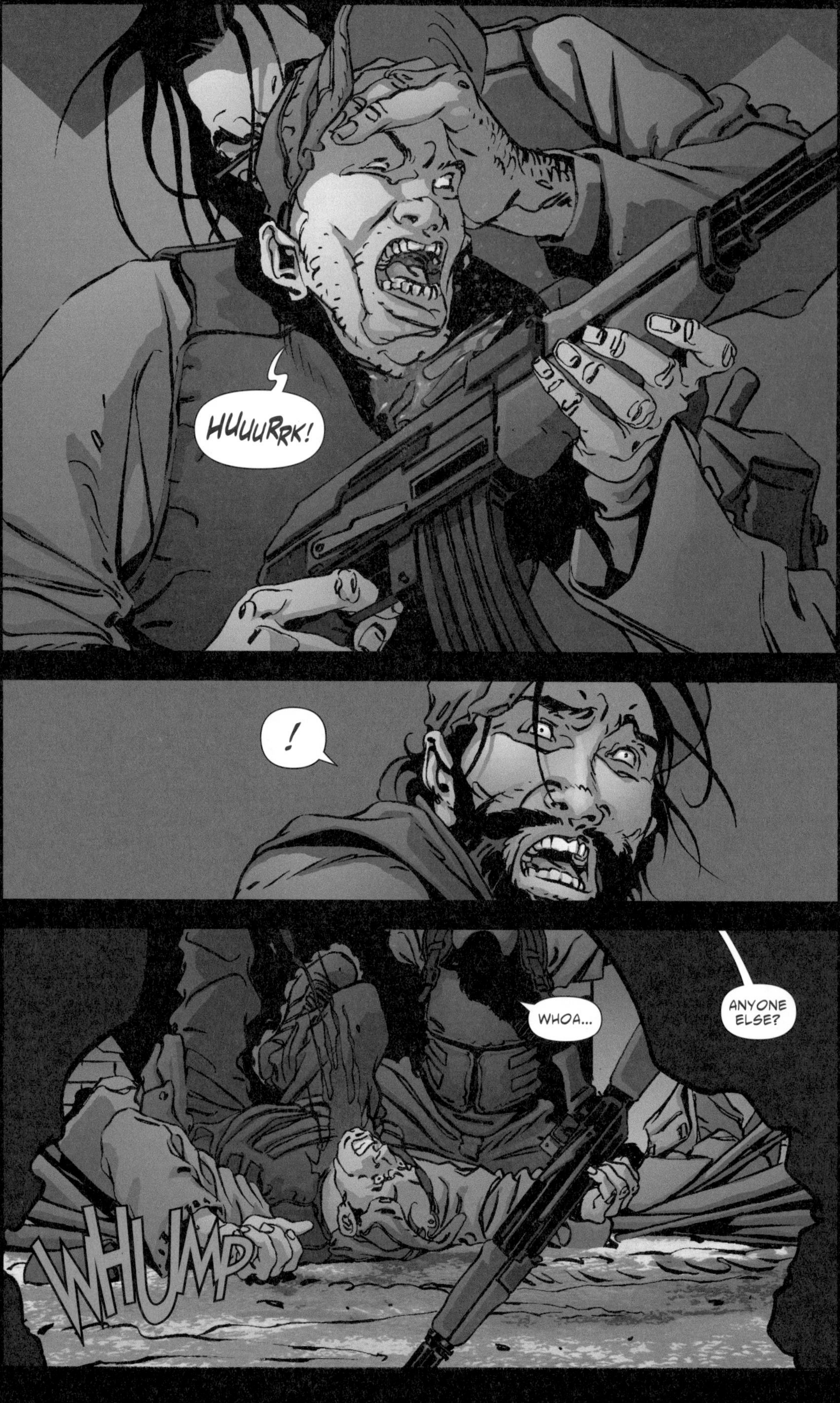
HUUURRK!
!
WHOA...
ANYONE ELSE?
WHUMP

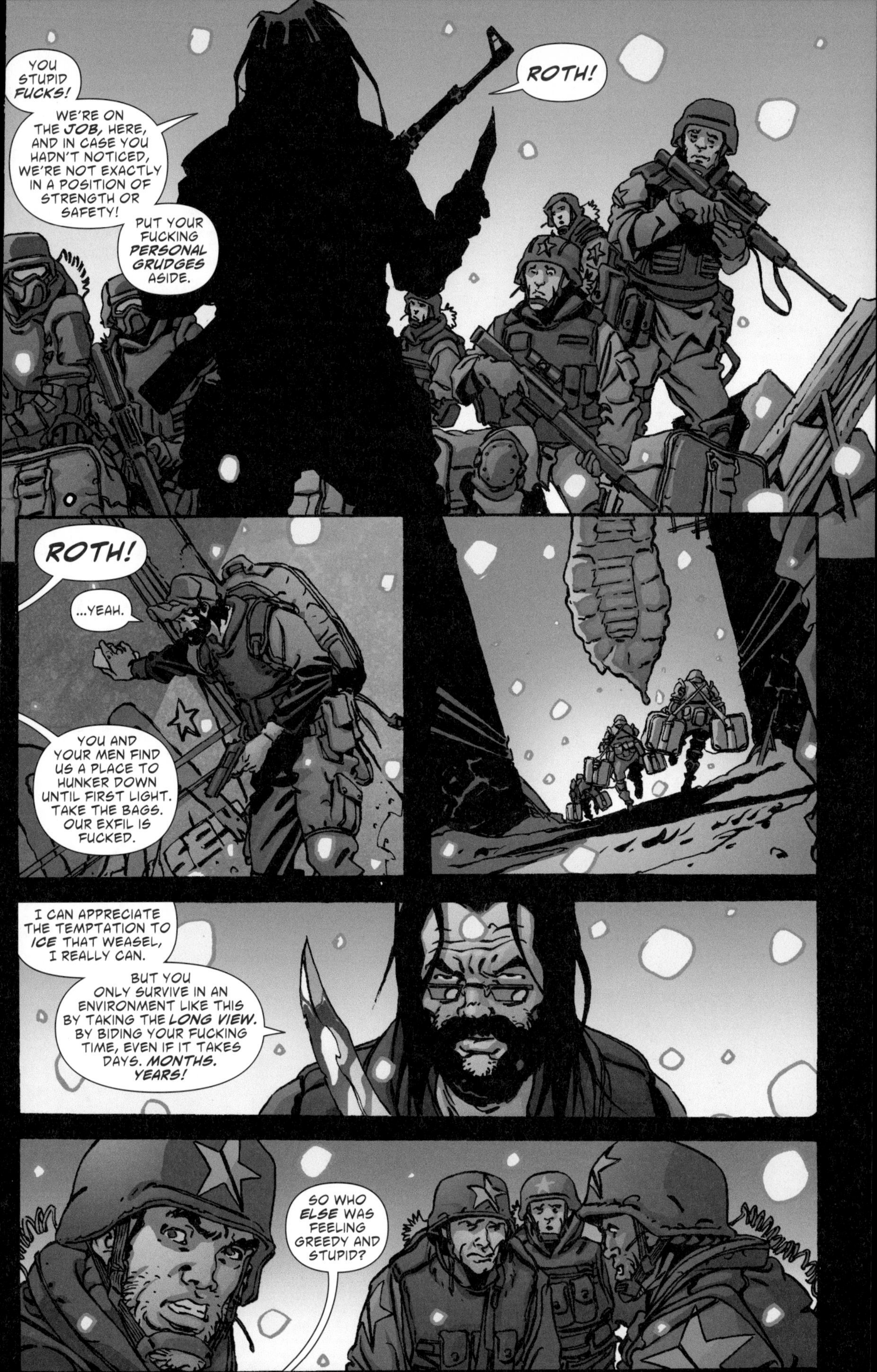

YOU STUPID FUCKS!
WE'RE ON THE JOB, HERE, AND IN CASE YOU HADN'T NOTICED, WE'RE NOT EXACTLY IN A POSITION OF STRENGTH OR SAFETY!
PUT YOUR FUCKING PERSONAL GRUDGES ASIDE.
ROTH!
ROTH!
...YEAH.
YOU AND YOUR MEN FIND US A PLACE TO HUNKER DOWN UNTIL FIRST LIGHT. TAKE THE BAGS. OUR EXFIL IS FUCKED.
I CAN APPRECIATE THE TEMPTATION TO ICE THAT WEASEL, I REALLY CAN.
BUT YOU ONLY SURVIVE IN AN ENVIRONMENT LIKE THIS BY TAKING THE LONG VIEW. BY BIDING YOUR FUCKING TIME, EVEN IF IT TAKES DAYS. MONTHS. YEARS!
SO WHO ELSE WAS FEELING GREEDY AND STUPID?

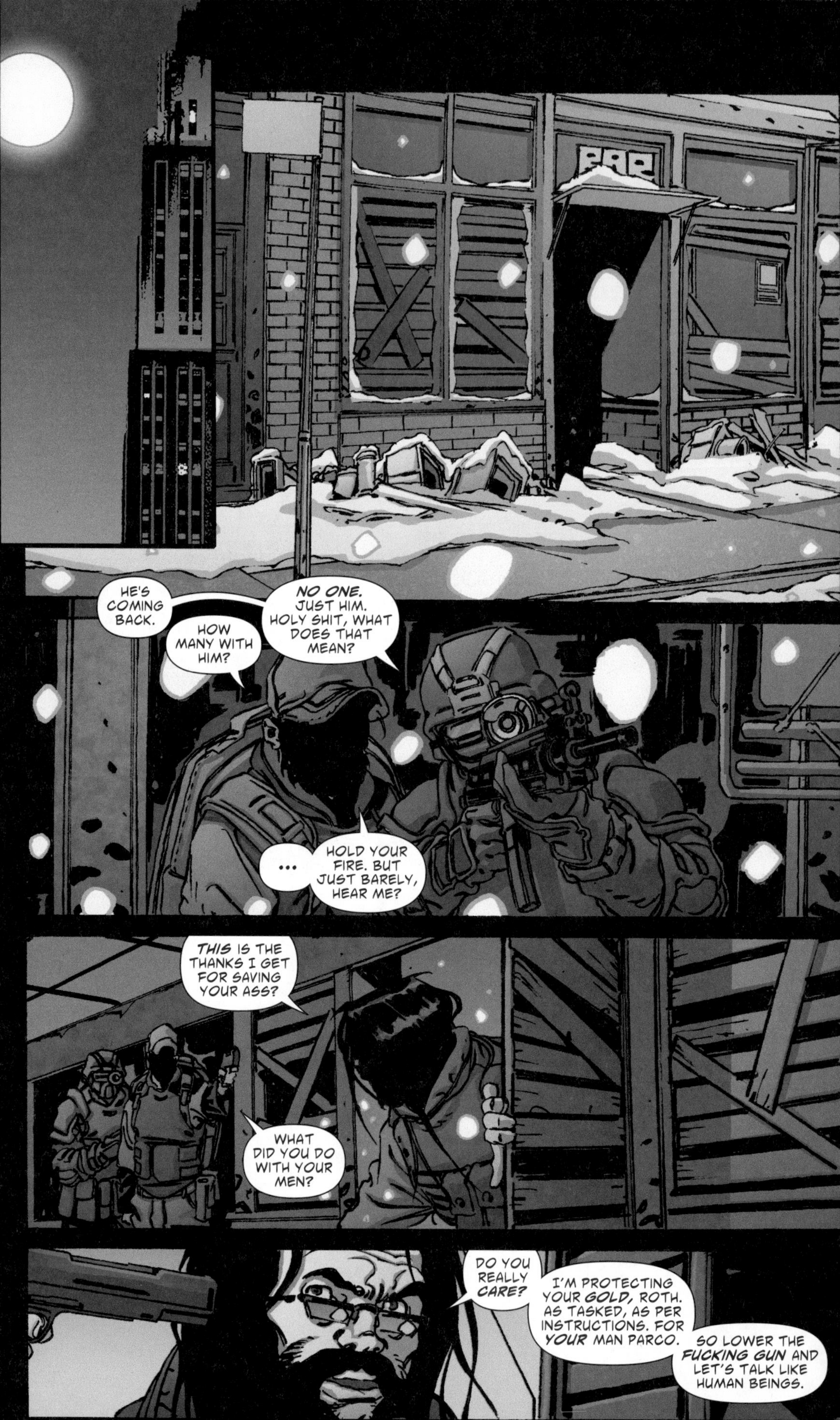
HE'S COMING BACK.
HOW MANY WITH HIM?
NO ONE. JUST HIM. HOLY SHIT, WHAT DOES THAT MEAN?
...
HOLD YOUR FIRE. BUT JUST BARELY, HEAR ME?
THIS IS THE THANKS I GET FOR SAVING YOUR ASS?
WHAT DID YOU DO WITH YOUR MEN?
DO YOU REALLY CARE?
I'M PROTECTING YOUR GOLD, ROTH. AS TASKED, AS PER INSTRUCTIONS. FOR YOUR MAN PARCO.
SO LOWER THE FUCKING GUN AND LET'S TALK LIKE HUMAN BEINGS.

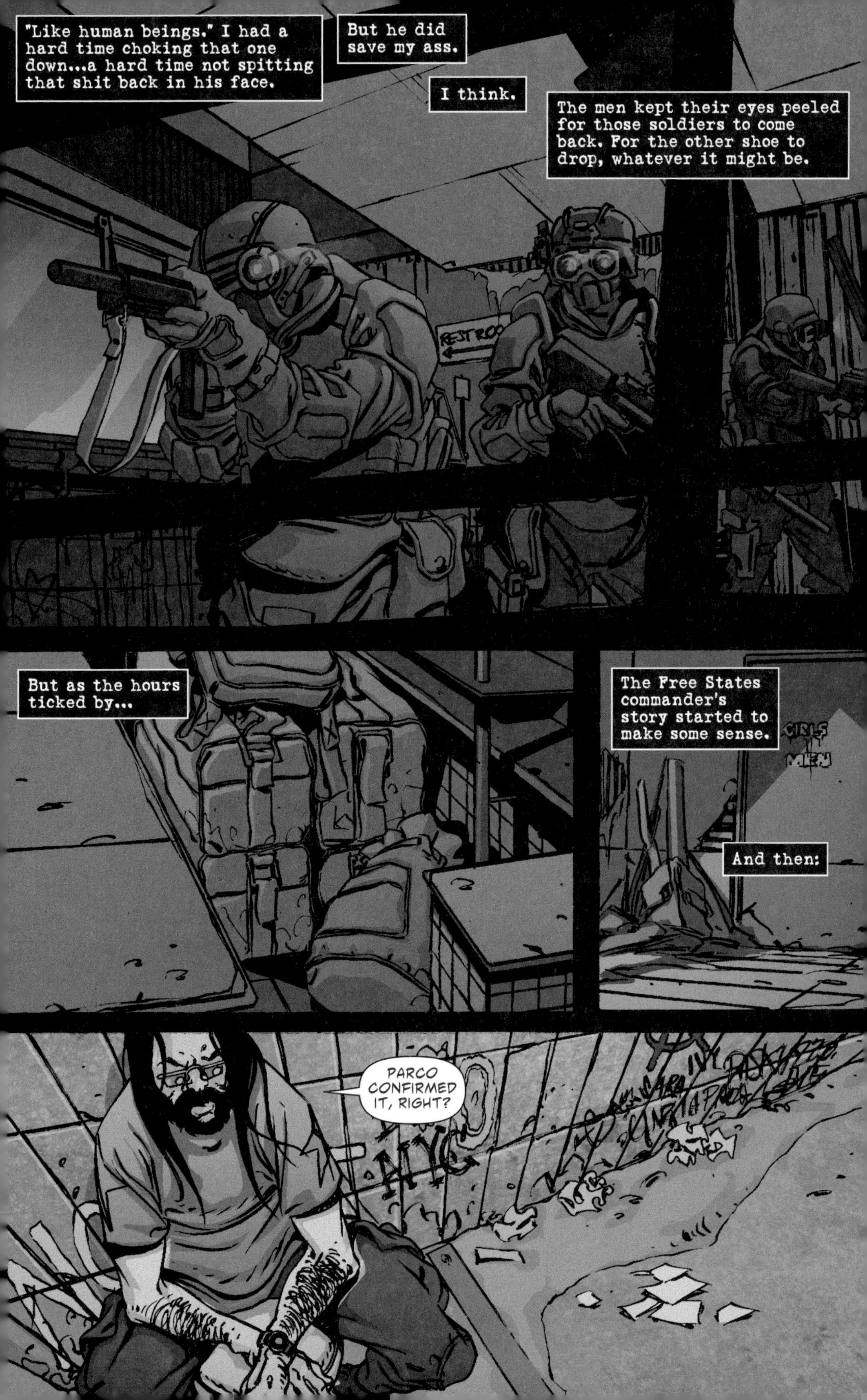
"Like human beings." I had a hard time choking that one down...a hard time not spitting that shit back in his face.
But he did save my ass.
I think.
The men kept their eyes peeled for those soldiers to come back. For the other shoe to drop, whatever it might be.
But as the hours ticked by...
The Free States commander's story started to make some sense.
And then:
PARCO CONFIRMED IT, RIGHT?

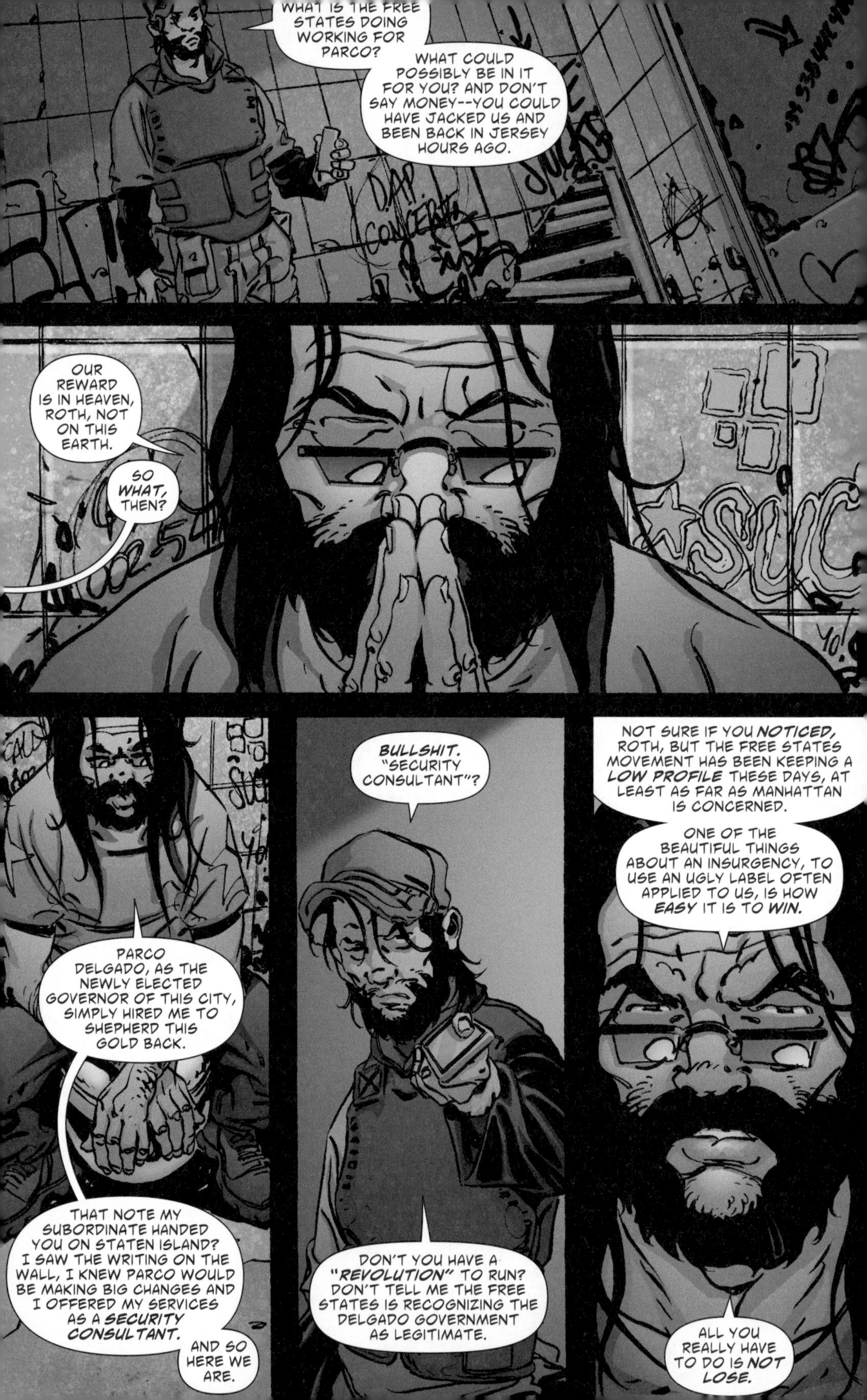
WHAT IS THE FREE STATES DOING WORKING FOR PARCO?
WHAT COULD POSSIBLY BE IN IT FOR YOU? AND DON'T SAY MONEY--YOU COULD HAVE JACKED US AND BEEN BACK IN JERSEY HOURS AGO.
OUR REWARD IS IN HEAVEN, ROTH, NOT ON THIS EARTH.
SO *WHAT*, THEN?
PARCO DELGADO, AS THE NEWLY ELECTED GOVERNOR OF THIS CITY, SIMPLY HIRED ME TO SHEPHERD THIS GOLD BACK.
THAT NOTE MY SUBORDINATE HANDED YOU ON STATEN ISLAND? I SAW THE WRITING ON THE WALL, I KNEW PARCO WOULD BE MAKING BIG CHANGES AND I OFFERED MY SERVICES AS A *SECURITY CONSULTANT.*
AND SO HERE WE ARE.
BULLSHIT. "SECURITY CONSULTANT"?
DON'T YOU HAVE A *"REVOLUTION"* TO RUN? DON'T TELL ME THE FREE STATES IS RECOGNIZING THE DELGADO GOVERNMENT AS LEGITIMATE.
NOT SURE IF YOU *NOTICED,* ROTH, BUT THE FREE STATES MOVEMENT HAS BEEN KEEPING A *LOW PROFILE* THESE DAYS, AT LEAST AS FAR AS MANHATTAN IS CONCERNED.
ONE OF THE BEAUTIFUL THINGS ABOUT AN INSURGENCY, TO USE AN UGLY LABEL OFTEN APPLIED TO US, IS HOW *EASY* IT IS TO *WIN.*
ALL YOU REALLY HAVE TO DO IS *NOT LOSE.*

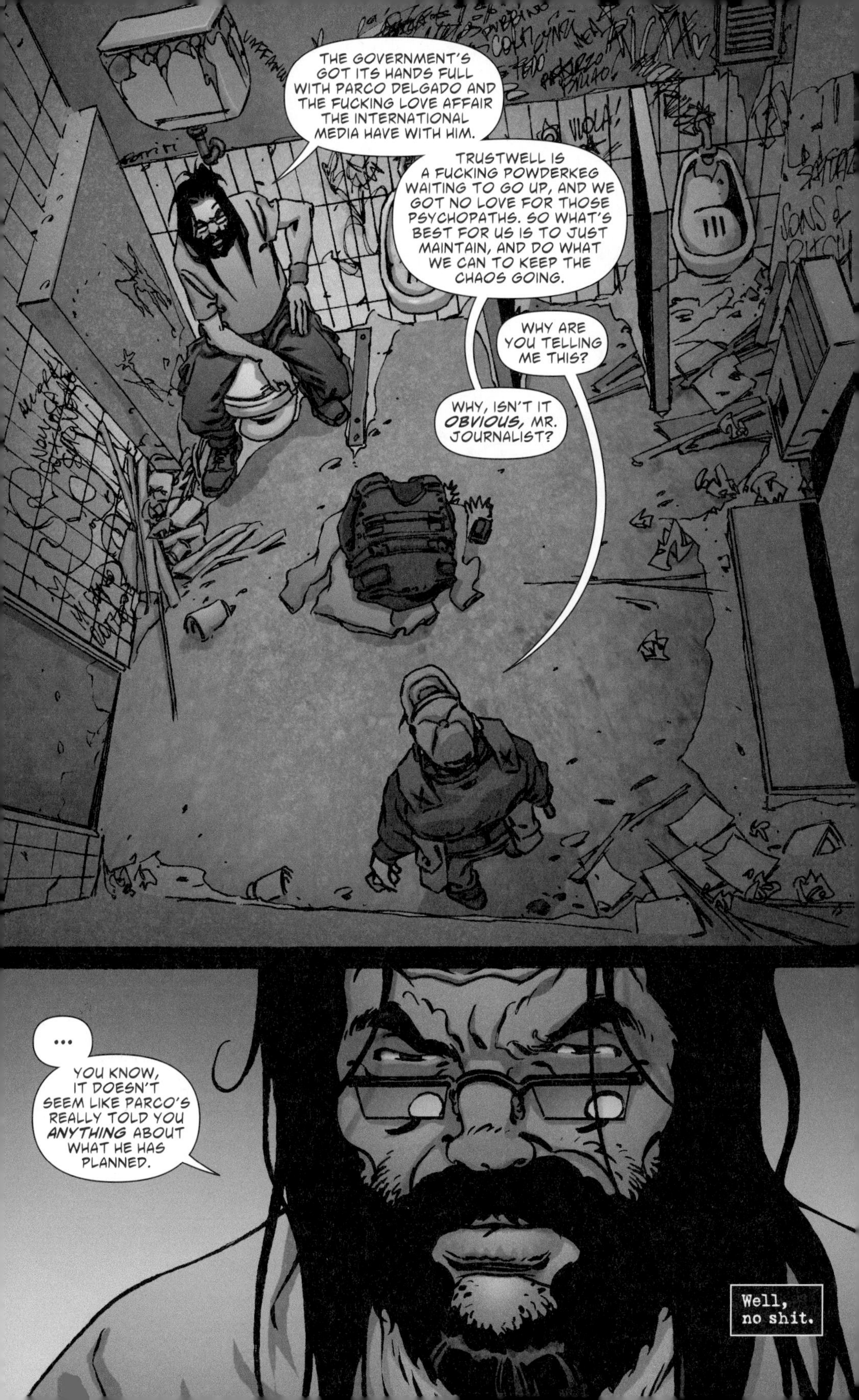
THE GOVERNMENT'S GOT ITS HANDS FULL WITH PARCO DELGADO AND THE FUCKING LOVE AFFAIR THE INTERNATIONAL MEDIA HAVE WITH HIM.
TRUSTWELL IS A FUCKING POWDERKEG WAITING TO GO UP, AND WE GOT NO LOVE FOR THOSE PSYCHOPATHS. SO WHAT'S BEST FOR US IS TO JUST MAINTAIN, AND DO WHAT WE CAN TO KEEP THE CHAOS GOING.
WHY ARE YOU TELLING ME THIS?
WHY, ISN'T IT *OBVIOUS,* MR. JOURNALIST?
...
YOU KNOW, IT DOESN'T SEEM LIKE PARCO'S REALLY TOLD YOU *ANYTHING* ABOUT WHAT HE HAS PLANNED.
Well, no shit.

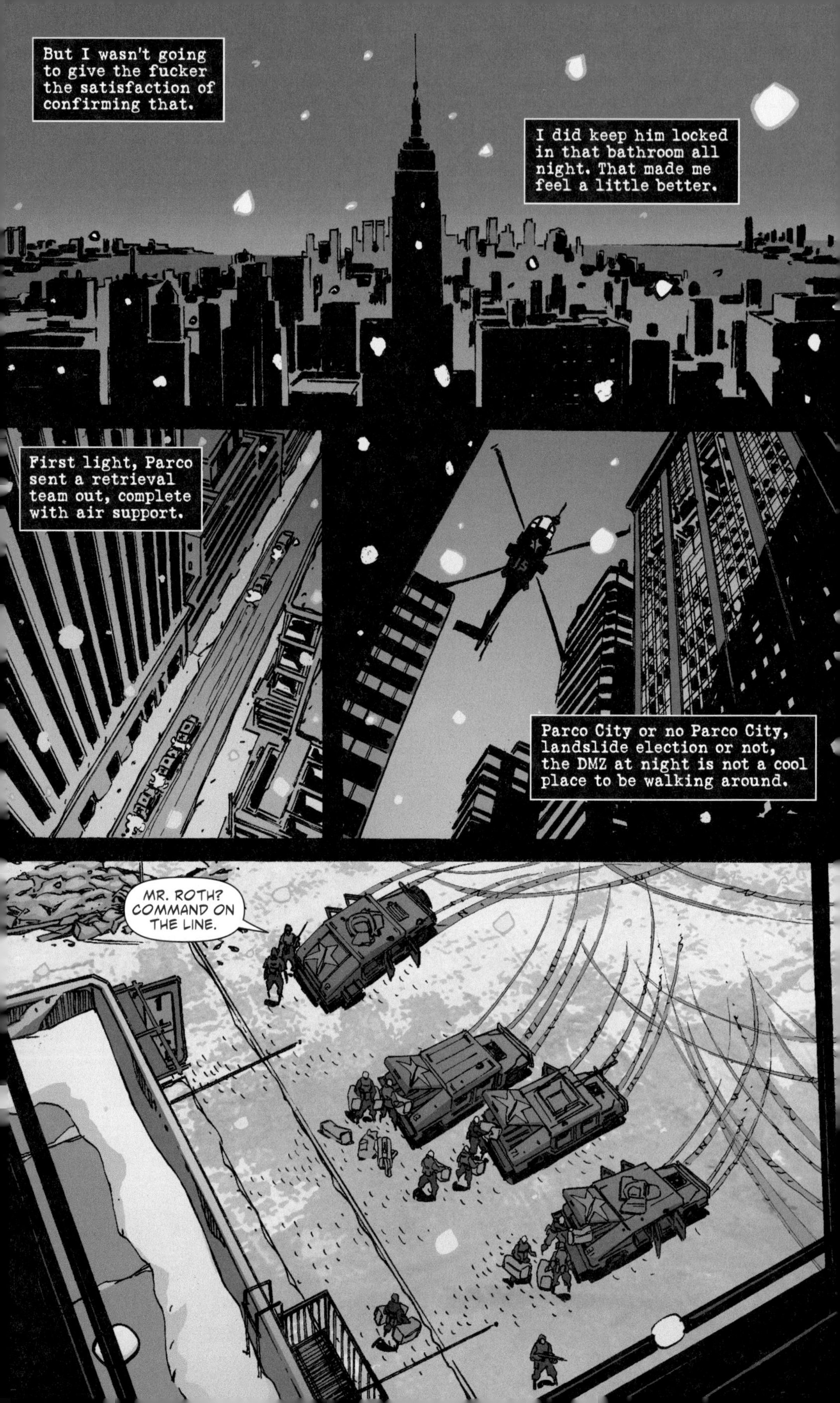
But I wasn't going to give the fucker the satisfaction of confirming that.
I did keep him locked in that bathroom all night. That made me feel a little better.
First light, Parco sent a retrieval team out, complete with air support.
Parco City or no Parco City, landslide election or not, the DMZ at night is not a cool place to be walking around.
MR. ROTH? COMMAND ON THE LINE.

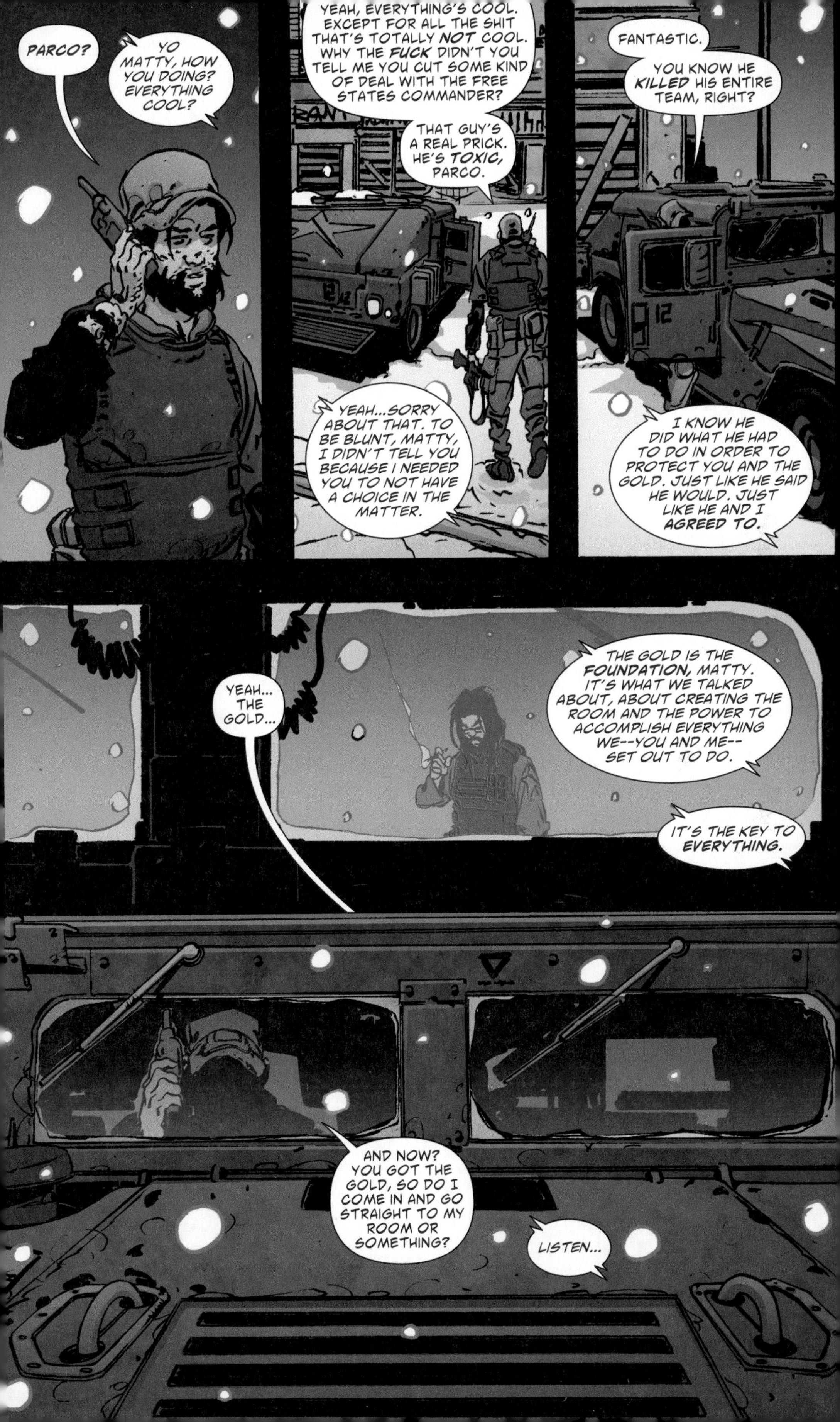
PARCO?
YO MATTY, HOW YOU DOING? EVERYTHING COOL?
YEAH, EVERYTHING'S COOL. EXCEPT FOR ALL THE SHIT THAT'S TOTALLY NOT COOL. WHY THE FUCK DIDN'T YOU TELL ME YOU CUT SOME KIND OF DEAL WITH THE FREE STATES COMMANDER?
THAT GUY'S A REAL PRICK. HE'S TOXIC, PARCO.
YEAH...SORRY ABOUT THAT. TO BE BLUNT, MATTY, I DIDN'T TELL YOU BECAUSE I NEEDED YOU TO NOT HAVE A CHOICE IN THE MATTER.
FANTASTIC.
YOU KNOW HE KILLED HIS ENTIRE TEAM, RIGHT?
I KNOW HE DID WHAT HE HAD TO DO IN ORDER TO PROTECT YOU AND THE GOLD. JUST LIKE HE SAID HE WOULD. JUST LIKE HE AND I AGREED TO.
YEAH... THE GOLD...
THE GOLD IS THE FOUNDATION, MATTY. IT'S WHAT WE TALKED ABOUT, ABOUT CREATING THE ROOM AND THE POWER TO ACCOMPLISH EVERYTHING WE--YOU AND ME--SET OUT TO DO.
IT'S THE KEY TO EVERYTHING.
AND NOW? YOU GOT THE GOLD, SO DO I COME IN AND GO STRAIGHT TO MY ROOM OR SOMETHING?
LISTEN...

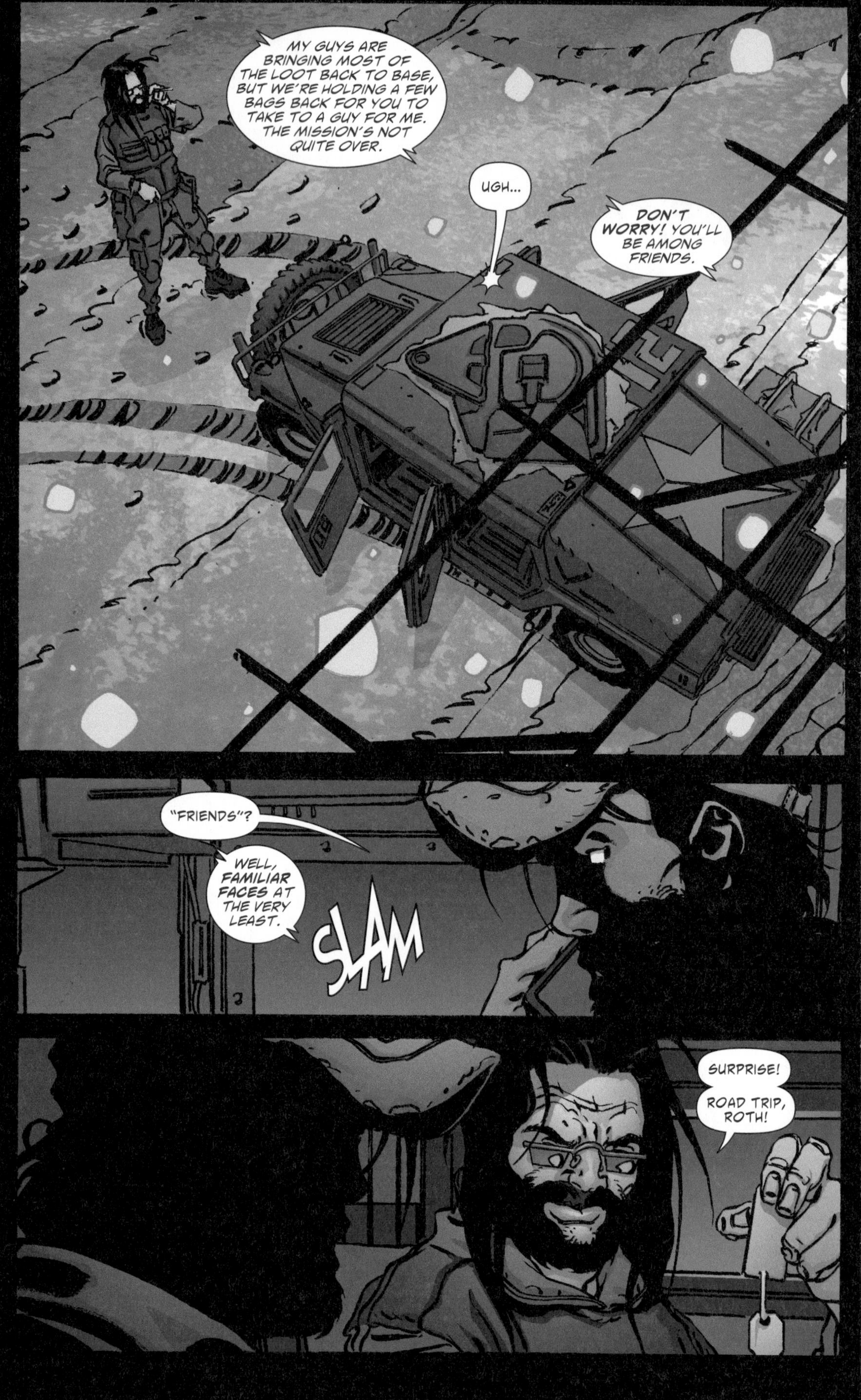
MY GUYS ARE BRINGING MOST OF THE LOOT BACK TO BASE, BUT WE'RE HOLDING A FEW BAGS BACK FOR YOU TO TAKE TO A GUY FOR ME. THE MISSION'S NOT QUITE OVER.
UGH...
DON'T WORRY! YOU'LL BE AMONG FRIENDS.
"FRIENDS"?
WELL, FAMILIAR FACES AT THE VERY LEAST.
SLAM
SURPRISE!
ROAD TRIP, ROTH!

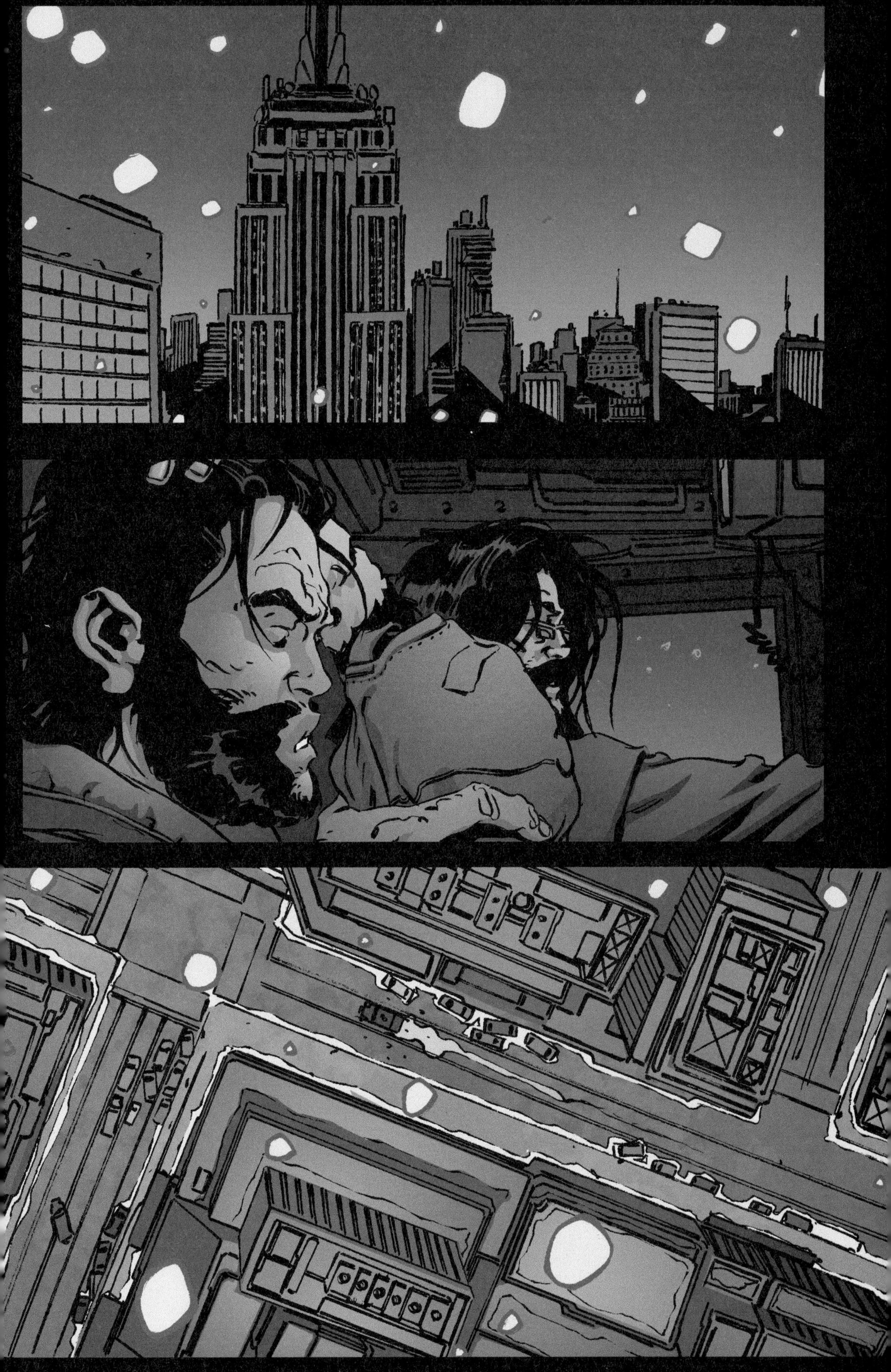

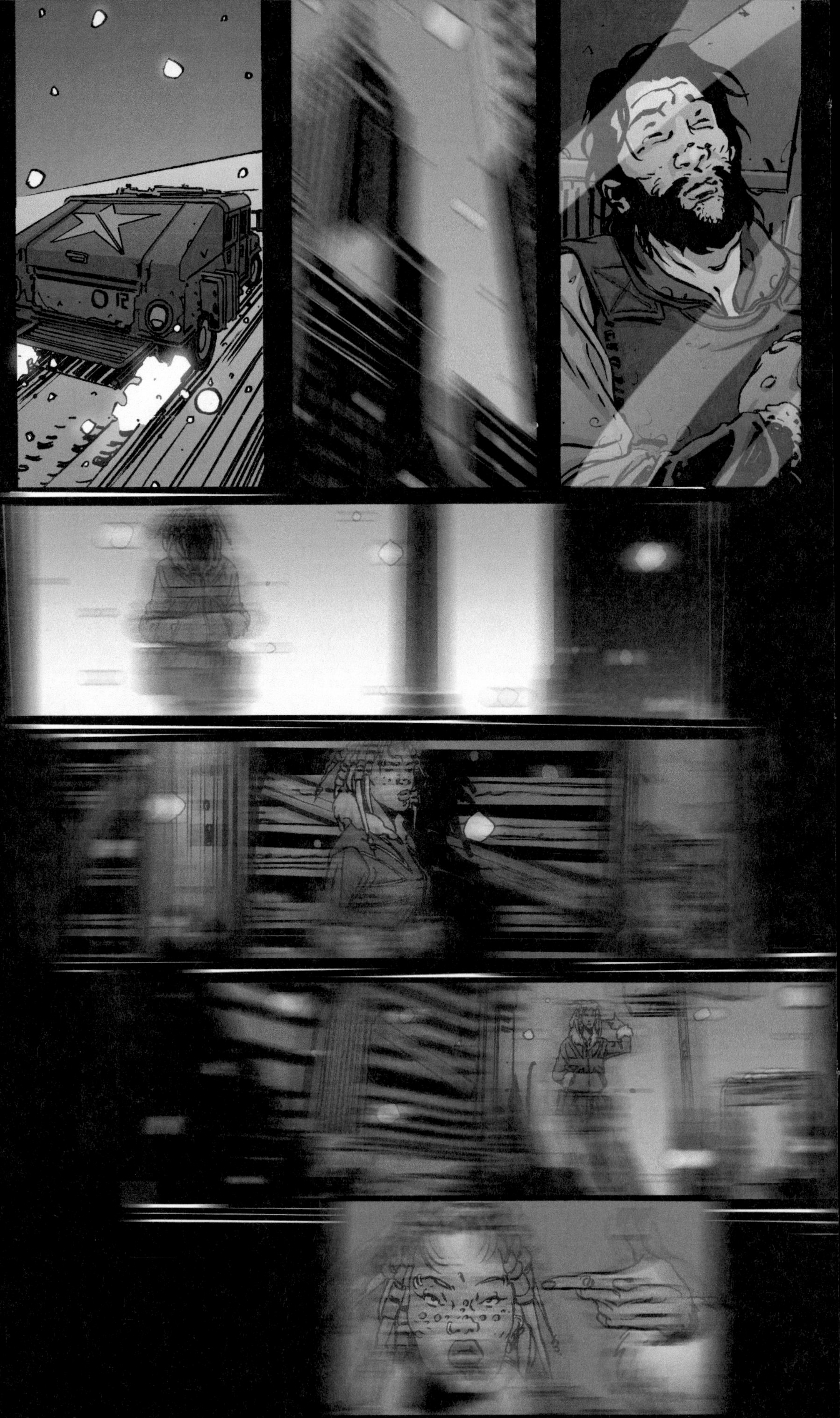

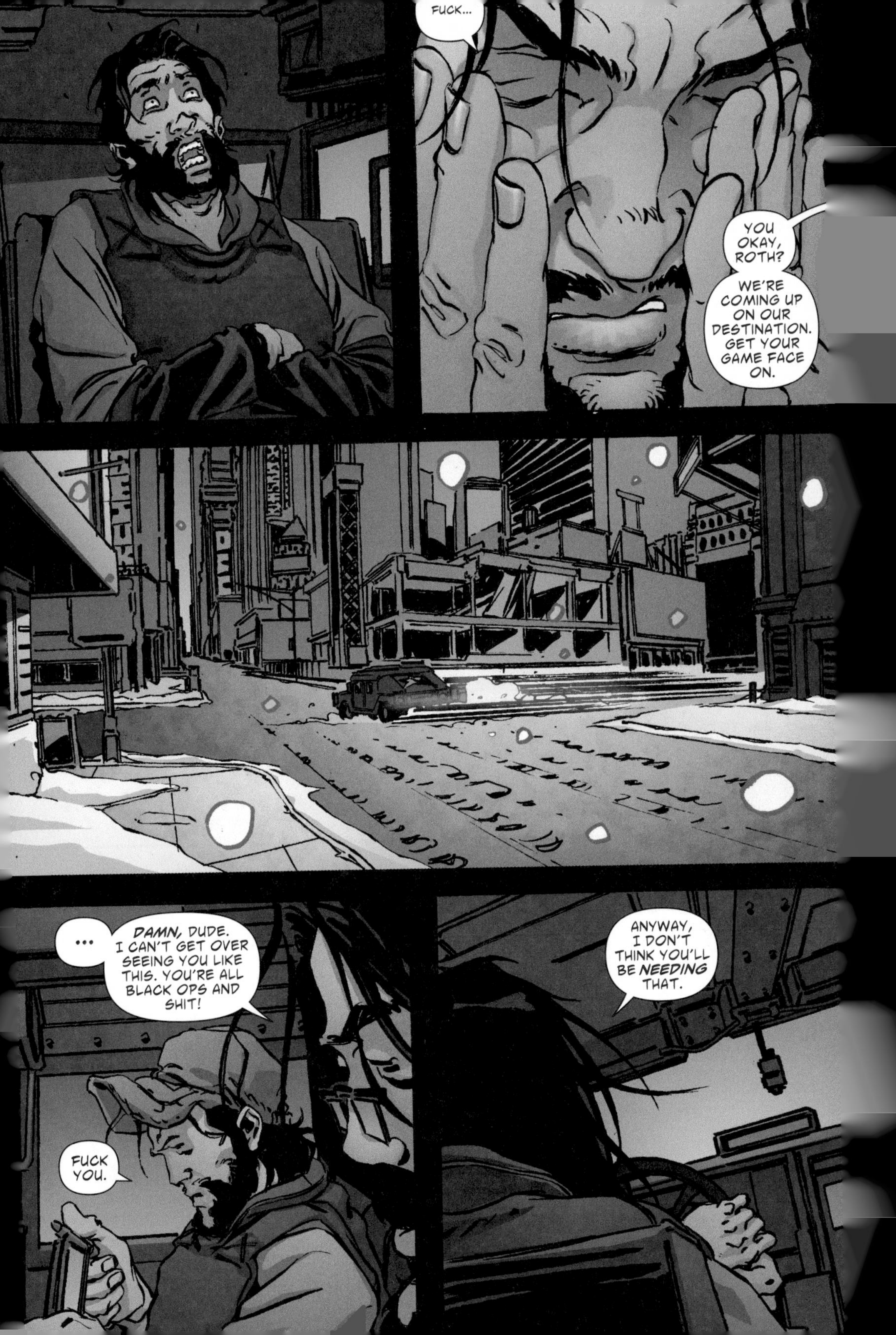
FUCK...
YOU OKAY, ROTH?
WE'RE COMING UP ON OUR DESTINATION. GET YOUR GAME FACE ON.
...
DAMN, DUDE. I CAN'T GET OVER SEEING YOU LIKE THIS. YOU'RE ALL BLACK OPS AND SHIT!
FUCK YOU.
ANYWAY, I DON'T THINK YOU'LL BE NEEDING THAT.

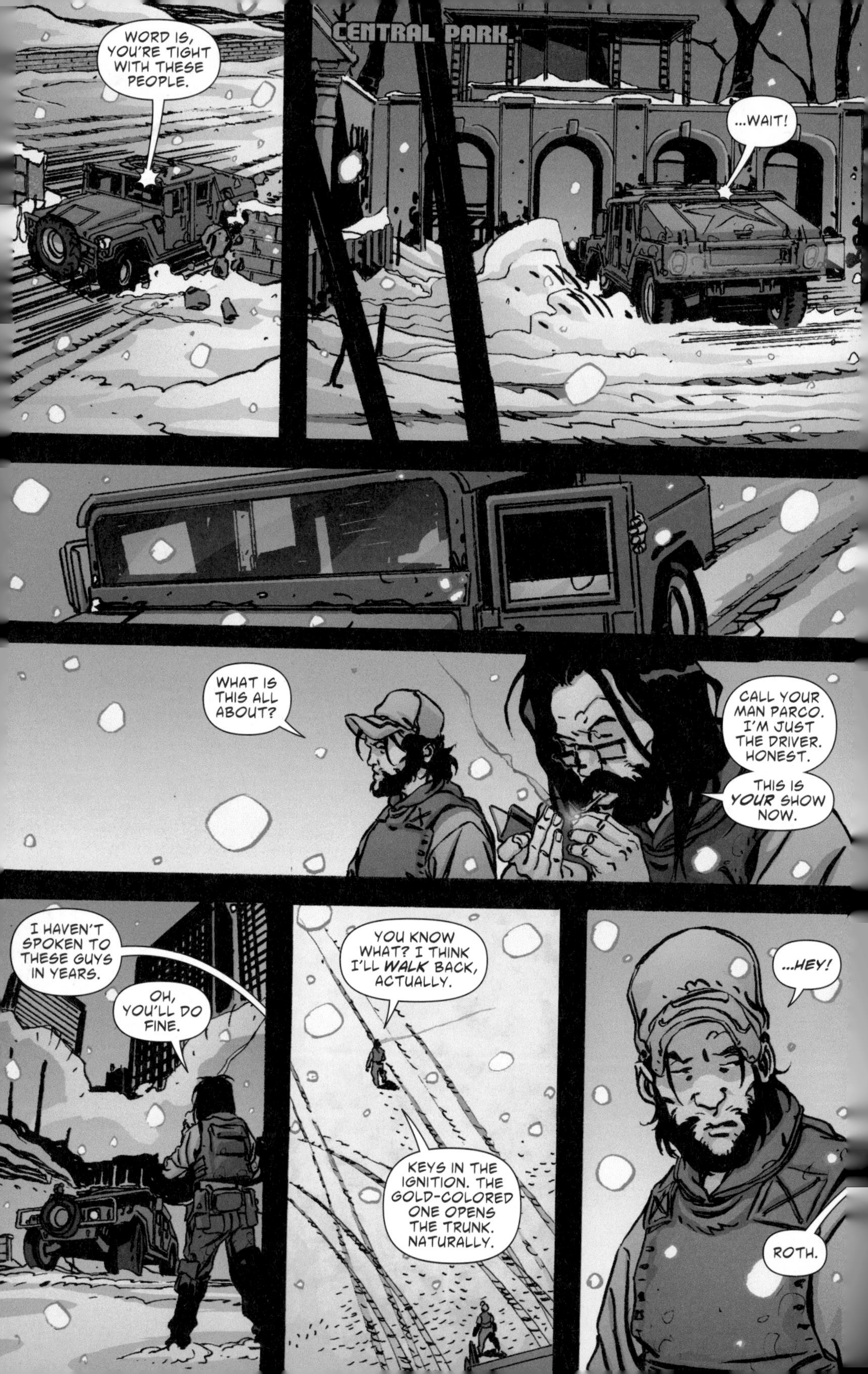
CENTRAL PARK
WORD IS, YOU'RE TIGHT WITH THESE PEOPLE.
...WAIT!
WHAT IS THIS ALL ABOUT?
CALL YOUR MAN PARCO. I'M JUST THE DRIVER. HONEST.
THIS IS YOUR SHOW NOW.
I HAVEN'T SPOKEN TO THESE GUYS IN YEARS.
OH, YOU'LL DO FINE.
YOU KNOW WHAT? I THINK I'LL WALK BACK, ACTUALLY.
KEYS IN THE IGNITION. THE GOLD-COLORED ONE OPENS THE TRUNK. NATURALLY.
...HEY!
ROTH.

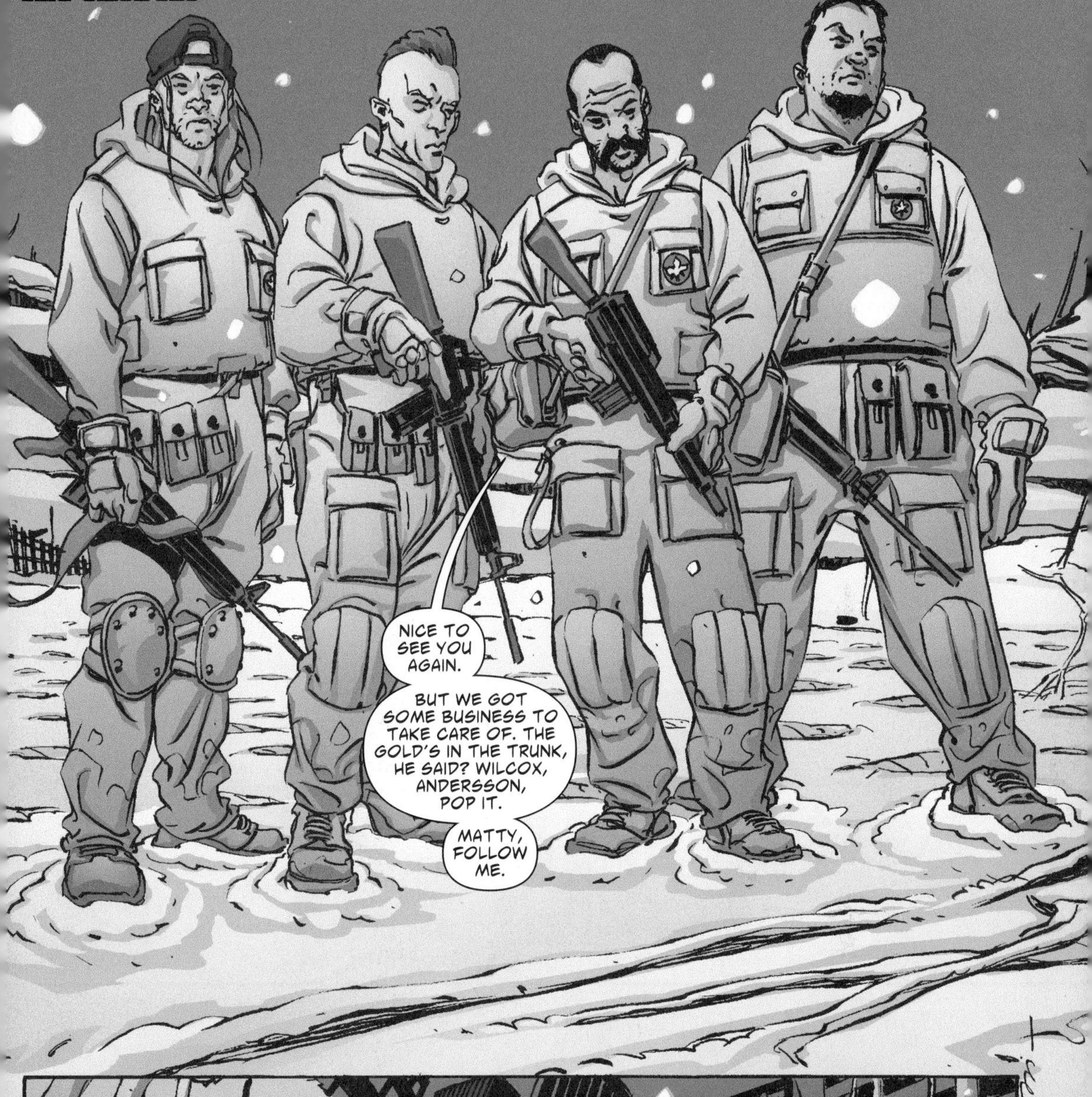
NICE TO SEE YOU AGAIN.
BUT WE GOT SOME BUSINESS TO TAKE CARE OF. THE GOLD'S IN THE TRUNK, HE SAID? WILCOX, ANDERSSON, POP IT.
MATTY, FOLLOW ME.

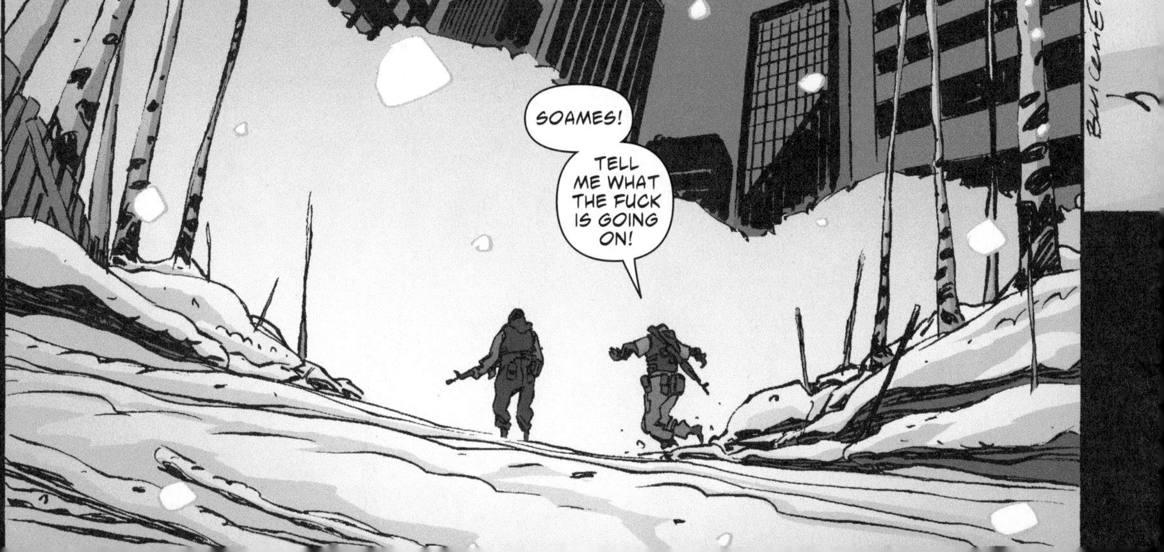
SOAMES!
TELL ME WHAT THE FUCK IS GOING ON!

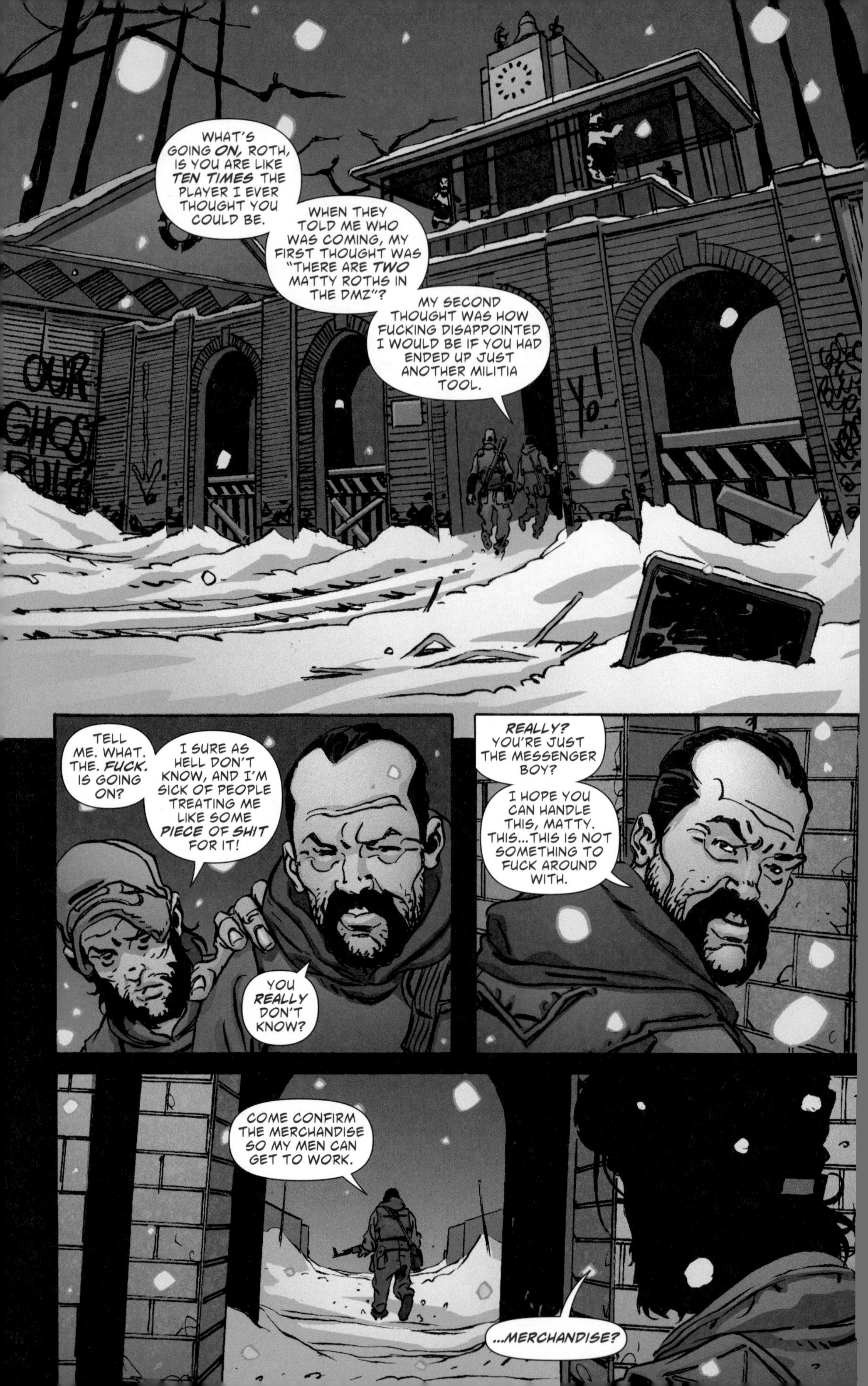

WHAT'S GOING ON, ROTH, IS YOU ARE LIKE TEN TIMES THE PLAYER I EVER THOUGHT YOU COULD BE.
WHEN THEY TOLD ME WHO WAS COMING, MY FIRST THOUGHT WAS "THERE ARE TWO MATTY ROTHS IN THE DMZ"?
MY SECOND THOUGHT WAS HOW FUCKING DISAPPOINTED I WOULD BE IF YOU HAD ENDED UP JUST ANOTHER MILITIA TOOL.
OUR GHOST RULES
YO!
TELL ME. WHAT. THE. FUCK. IS GOING ON?
I SURE AS HELL DON'T KNOW, AND I'M SICK OF PEOPLE TREATING ME LIKE SOME PIECE OF SHIT FOR IT!
YOU REALLY DON'T KNOW?
REALLY? YOU'RE JUST THE MESSENGER BOY?
I HOPE YOU CAN HANDLE THIS, MATTY. THIS...THIS IS NOT SOMETHING TO FUCK AROUND WITH.
COME CONFIRM THE MERCHANDISE SO MY MEN CAN GET TO WORK.
...MERCHANDISE?

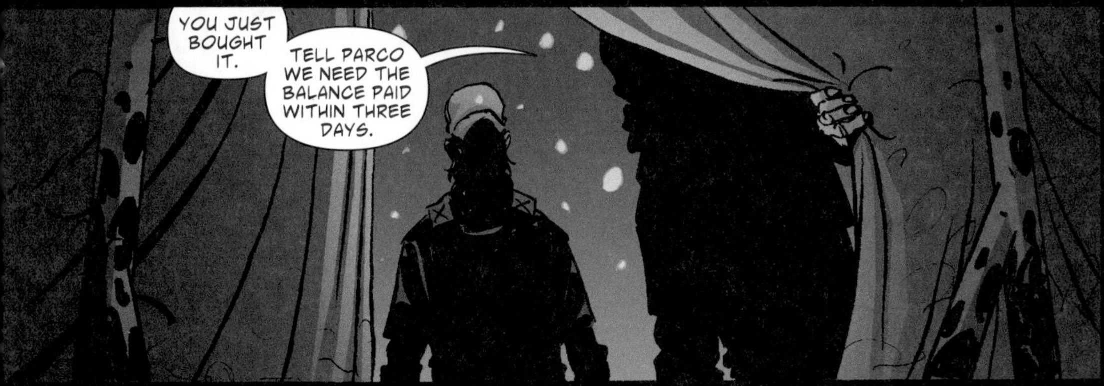
YOU JUST BOUGHT IT.
TELL PARCO WE NEED THE BALANCE PAID WITHIN THREE DAYS.

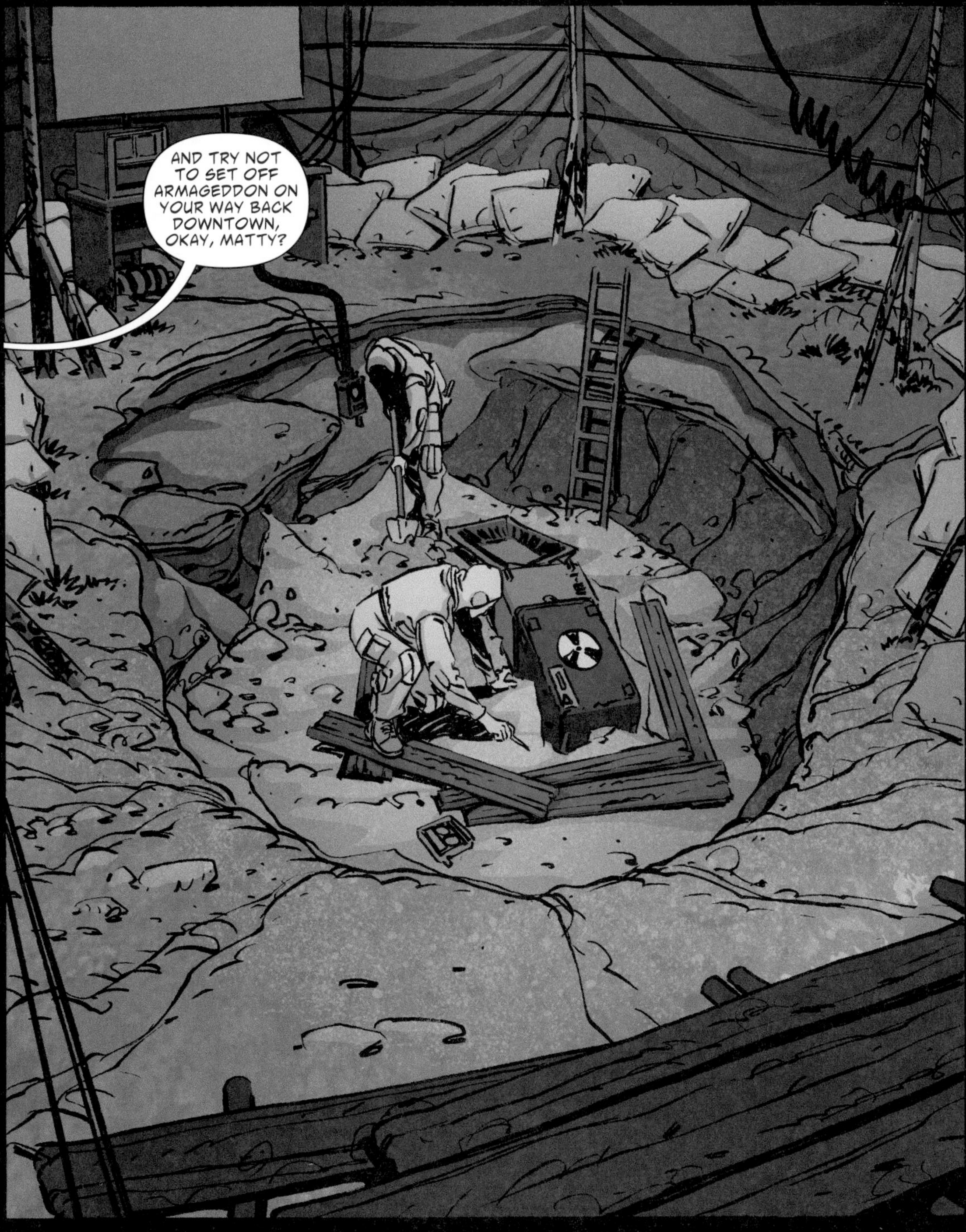
AND TRY NOT TO SET OFF ARMAGEDDON ON YOUR WAY BACK DOWNTOWN, OKAY, MATTY?

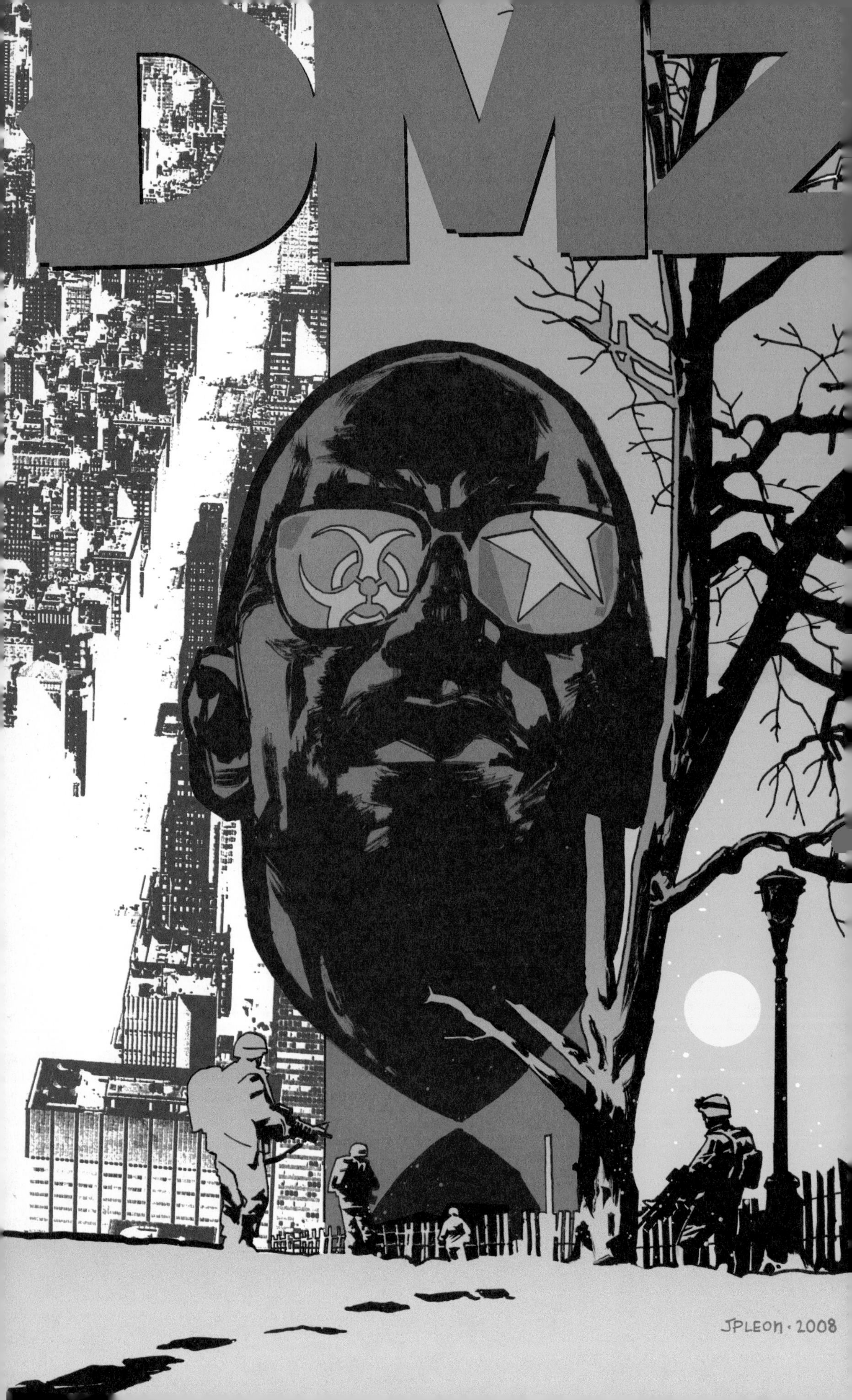
DMZ
JPLEON · 2008

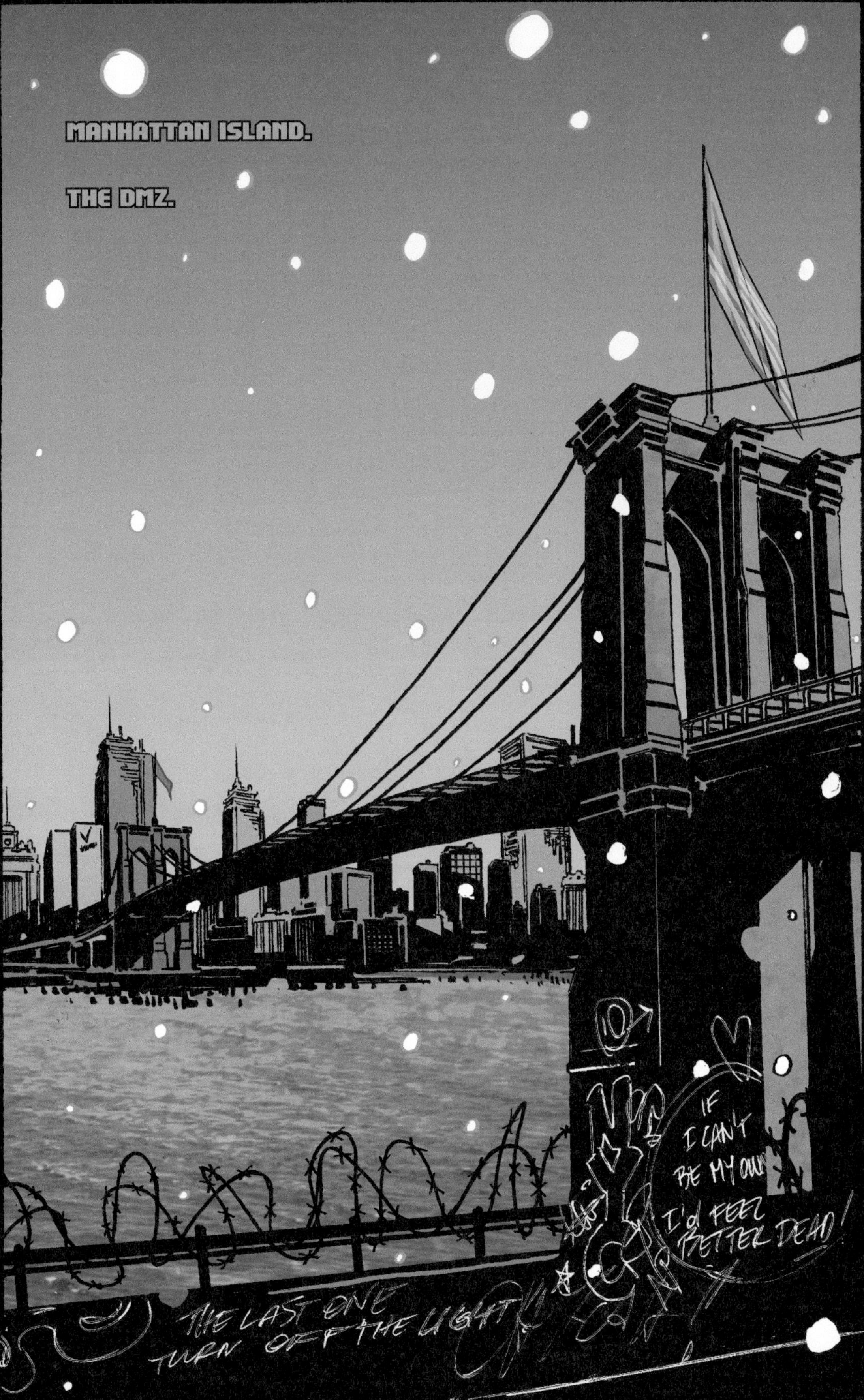
MANHATTAN ISLAND.
THE DMZ.
IF I CAN'T BE MY OWN I'd FEEL BETTER DEAD!
THE LAST ONE TURN OFF THE LIGHT!!

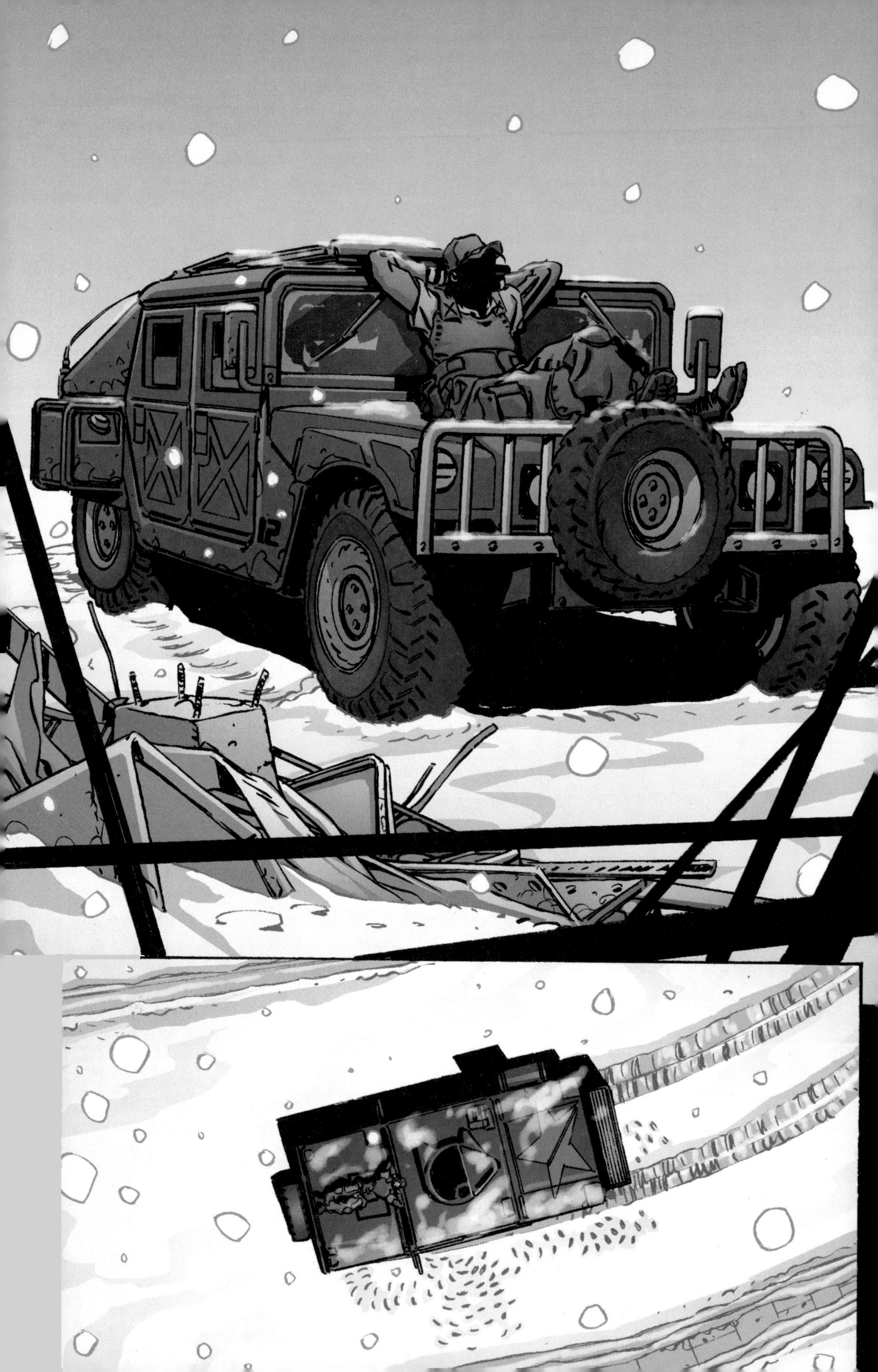

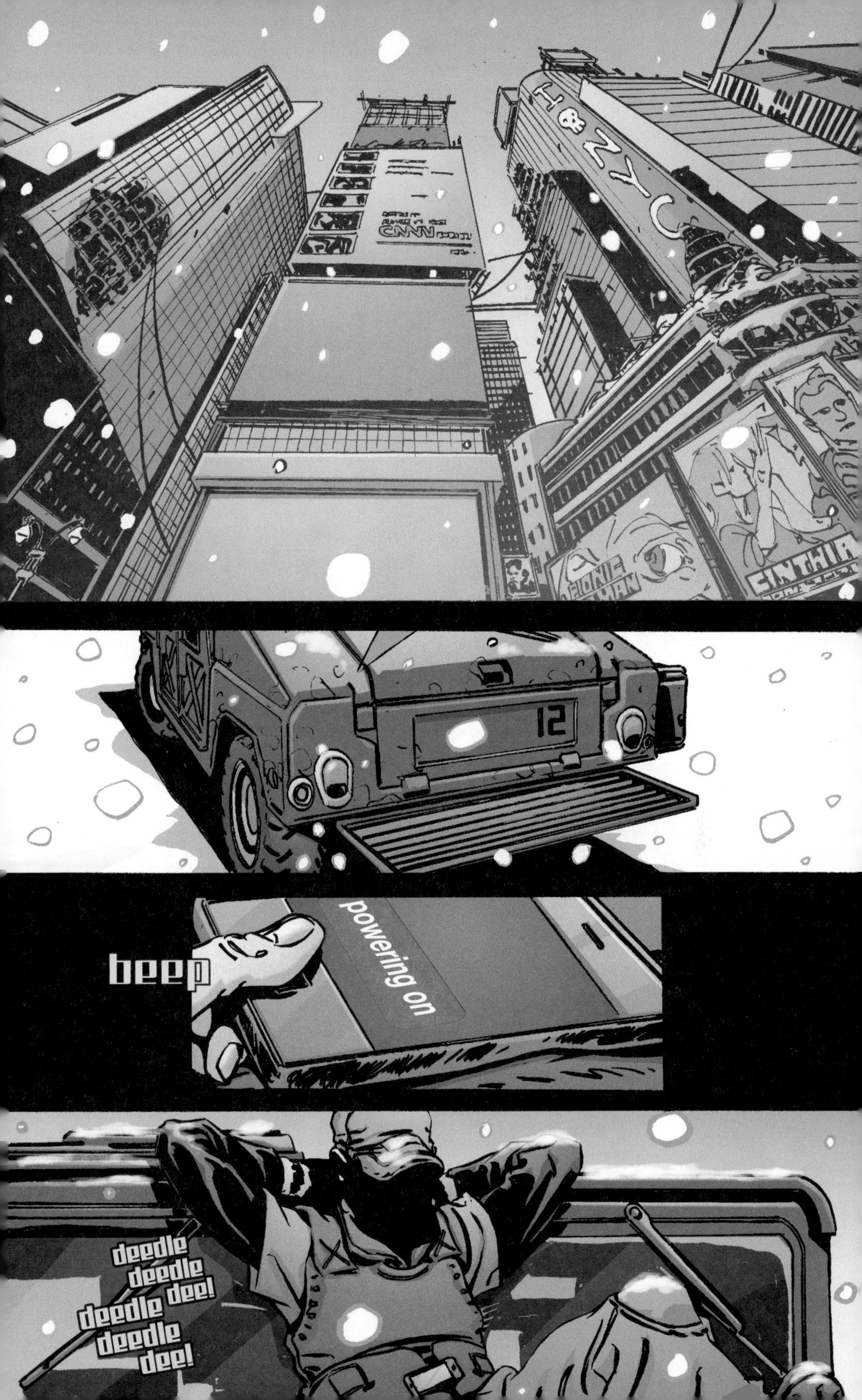
CNN
NYC
12
beep
powering on
deedle
deedle
dee!
deedle
deedle
dee!

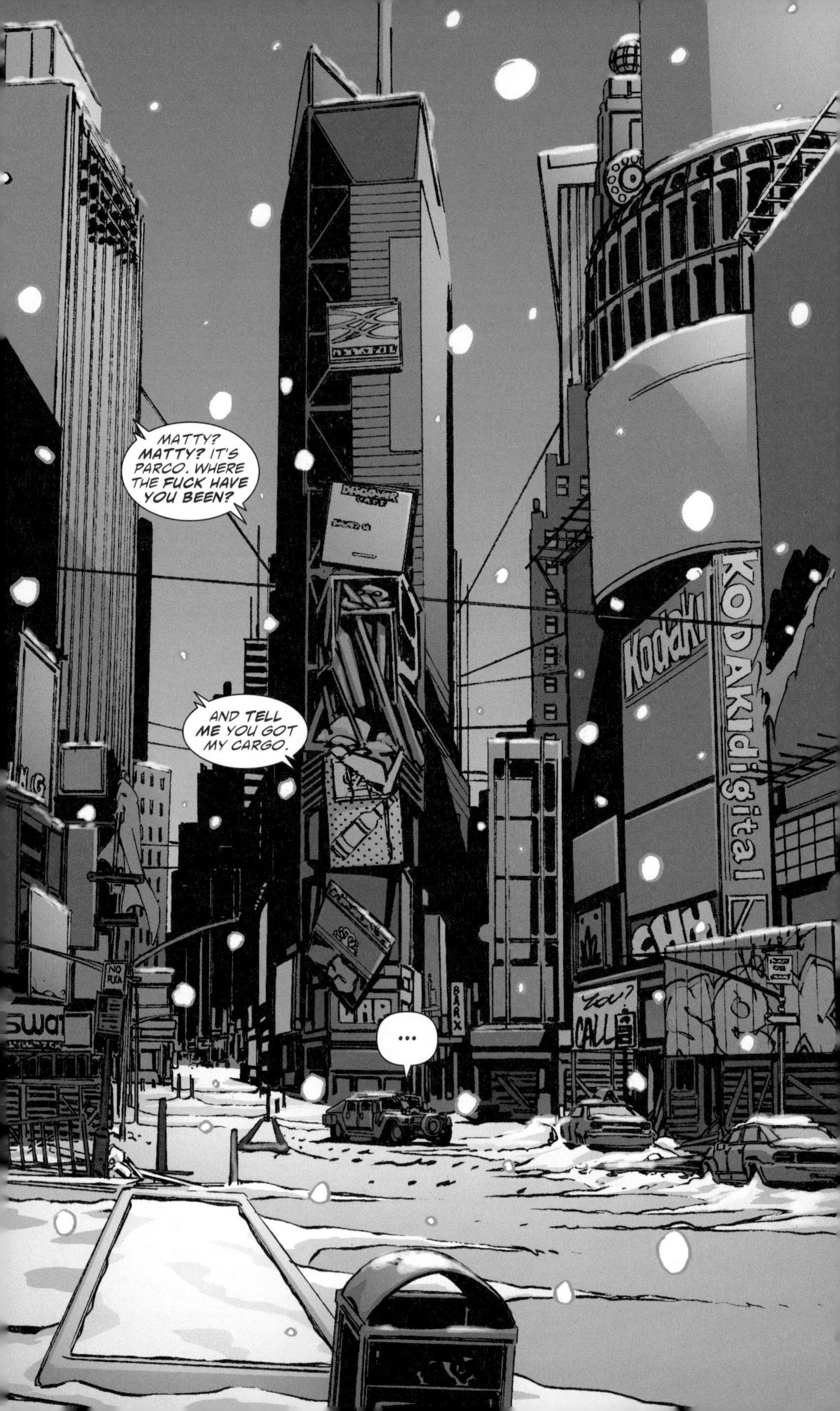
MATTY? MATTY? IT'S PARCO. WHERE THE FUCK HAVE YOU BEEN?
AND TELL ME YOU GOT MY CARGO.
...

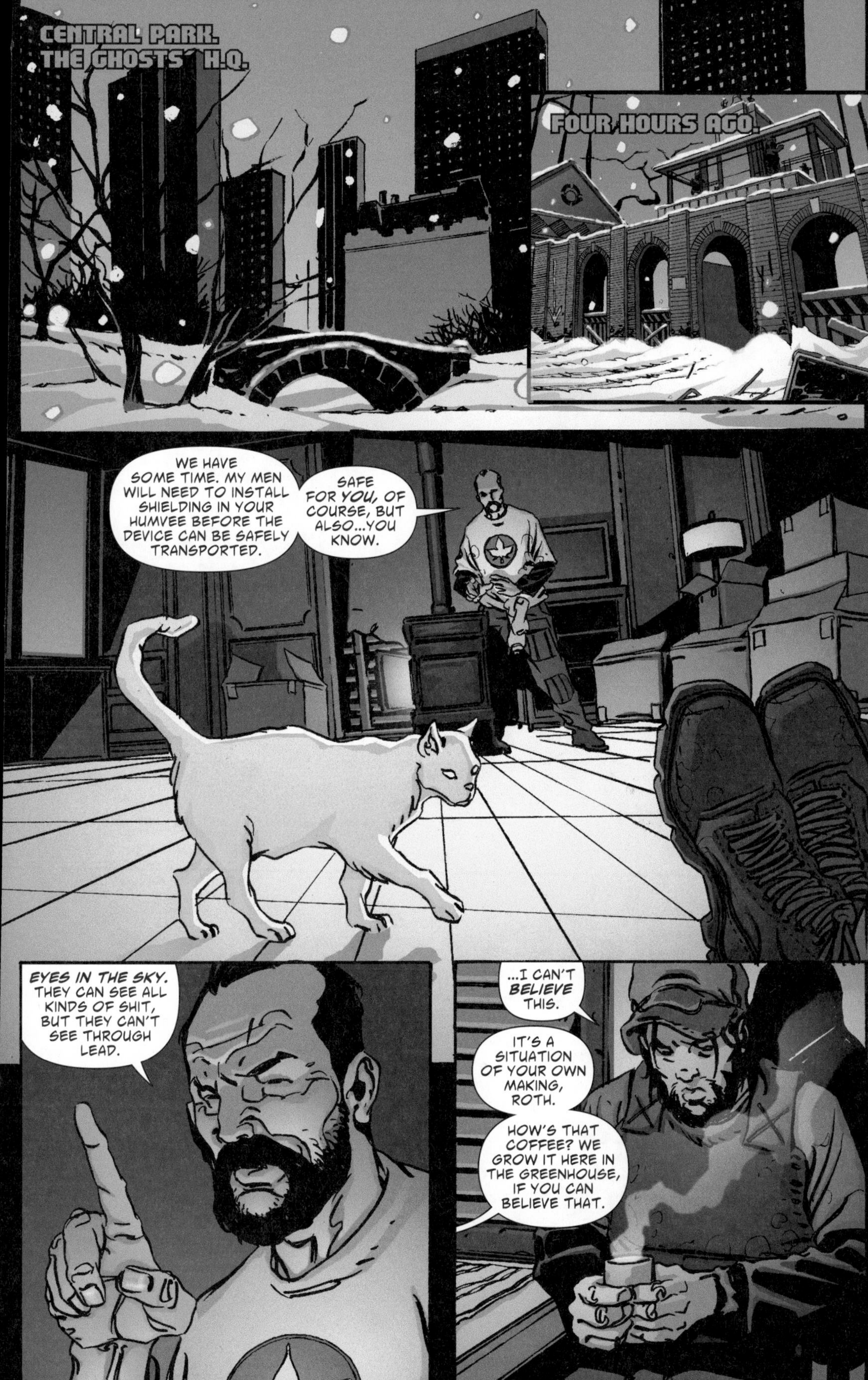
CENTRAL PARK. THE GHOSTS' H.Q.
FOUR HOURS AGO.
WE HAVE SOME TIME. MY MEN WILL NEED TO INSTALL SHIELDING IN YOUR HUMVEE BEFORE THE DEVICE CAN BE SAFELY TRANSPORTED.
SAFE FOR *YOU,* OF COURSE, BUT ALSO...YOU KNOW.
EYES IN THE SKY. THEY CAN SEE ALL KINDS OF SHIT, BUT THEY CAN'T SEE THROUGH LEAD.
...I CAN'T *BELIEVE* THIS.
IT'S A SITUATION OF YOUR OWN MAKING, ROTH.
HOW'S THAT COFFEE? WE GROW IT HERE IN THE GREENHOUSE, IF YOU CAN BELIEVE THAT.

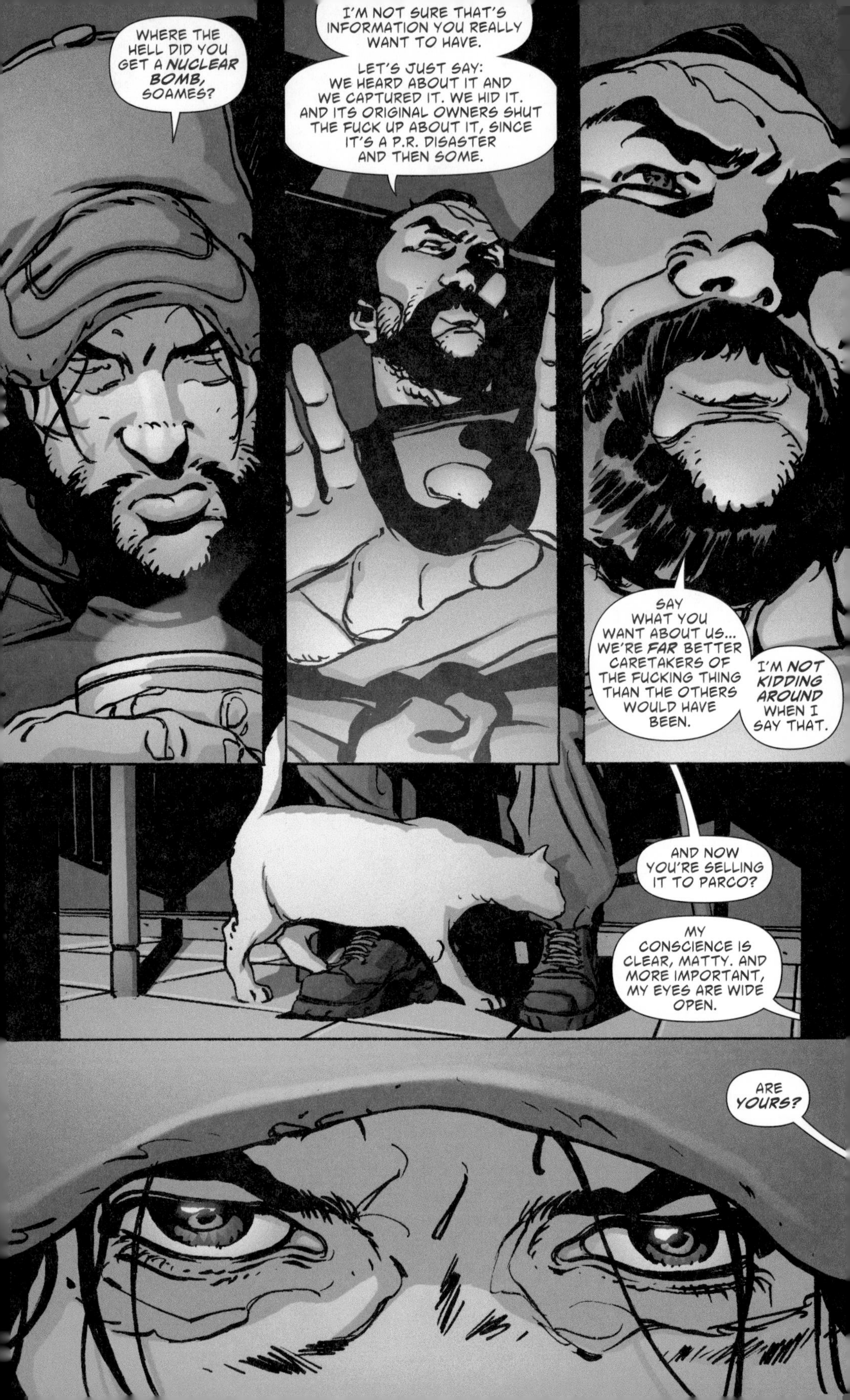
WHERE THE HELL DID YOU GET A NUCLEAR BOMB, SOAMES?
I'M NOT SURE THAT'S INFORMATION YOU REALLY WANT TO HAVE.
LET'S JUST SAY: WE HEARD ABOUT IT AND WE CAPTURED IT. WE HID IT. AND ITS ORIGINAL OWNERS SHUT THE FUCK UP ABOUT IT, SINCE IT'S A P.R. DISASTER AND THEN SOME.
SAY WHAT YOU WANT ABOUT US... WE'RE FAR BETTER CARETAKERS OF THE FUCKING THING THAN THE OTHERS WOULD HAVE BEEN.
I'M NOT KIDDING AROUND WHEN I SAY THAT.
AND NOW YOU'RE SELLING IT TO PARCO?
MY CONSCIENCE IS CLEAR, MATTY. AND MORE IMPORTANT, MY EYES ARE WIDE OPEN.
ARE YOURS?

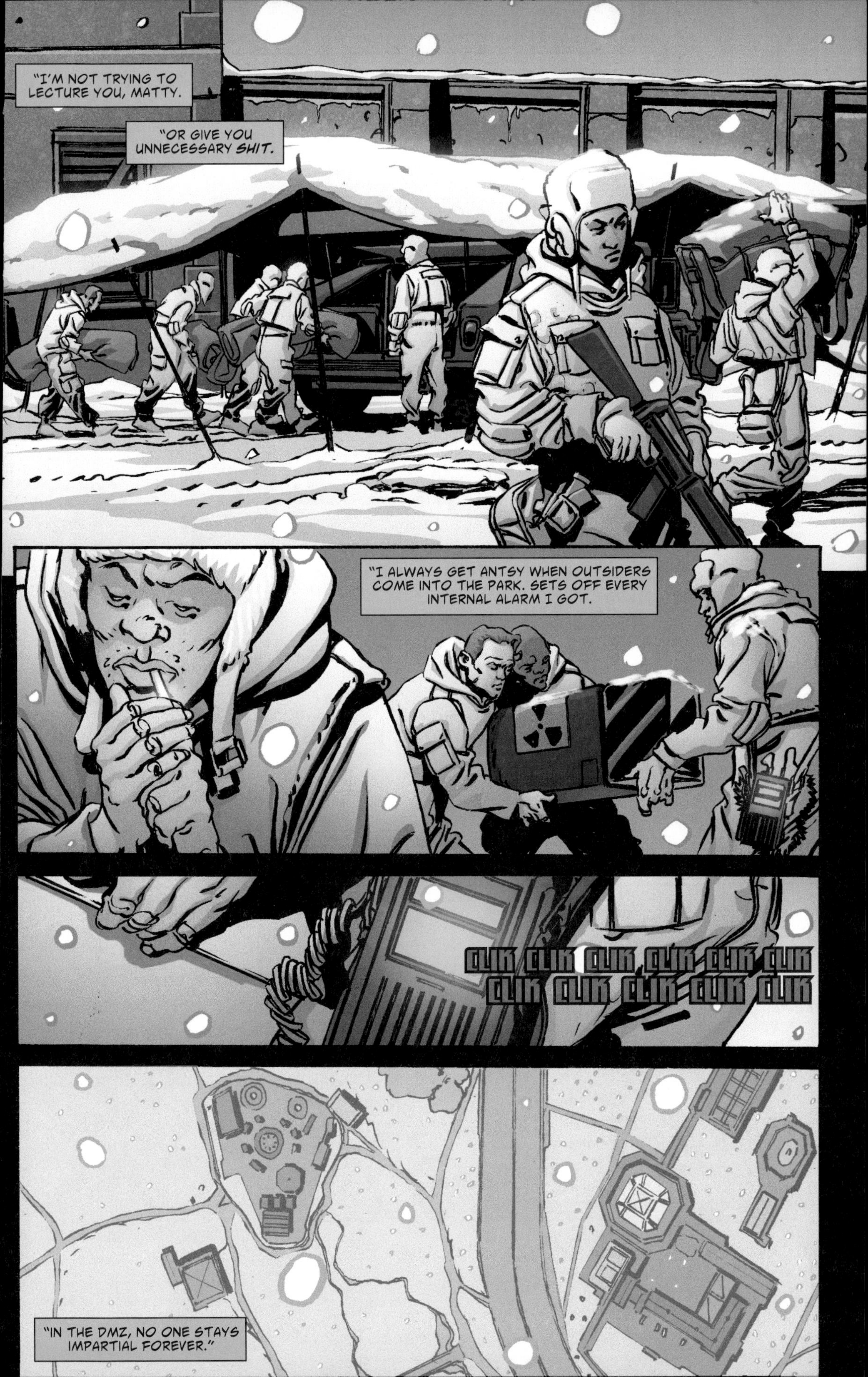
"I'M NOT TRYING TO LECTURE YOU, MATTY.
"OR GIVE YOU UNNECESSARY SHIT.
"I ALWAYS GET ANTSY WHEN OUTSIDERS COME INTO THE PARK. SETS OFF EVERY INTERNAL ALARM I GOT.
CLIK CLIK CLIK CLIK CLIK CLIK CLIK CLIK CLIK CLIK CLIK
"IN THE DMZ, NO ONE STAYS IMPARTIAL FOREVER."

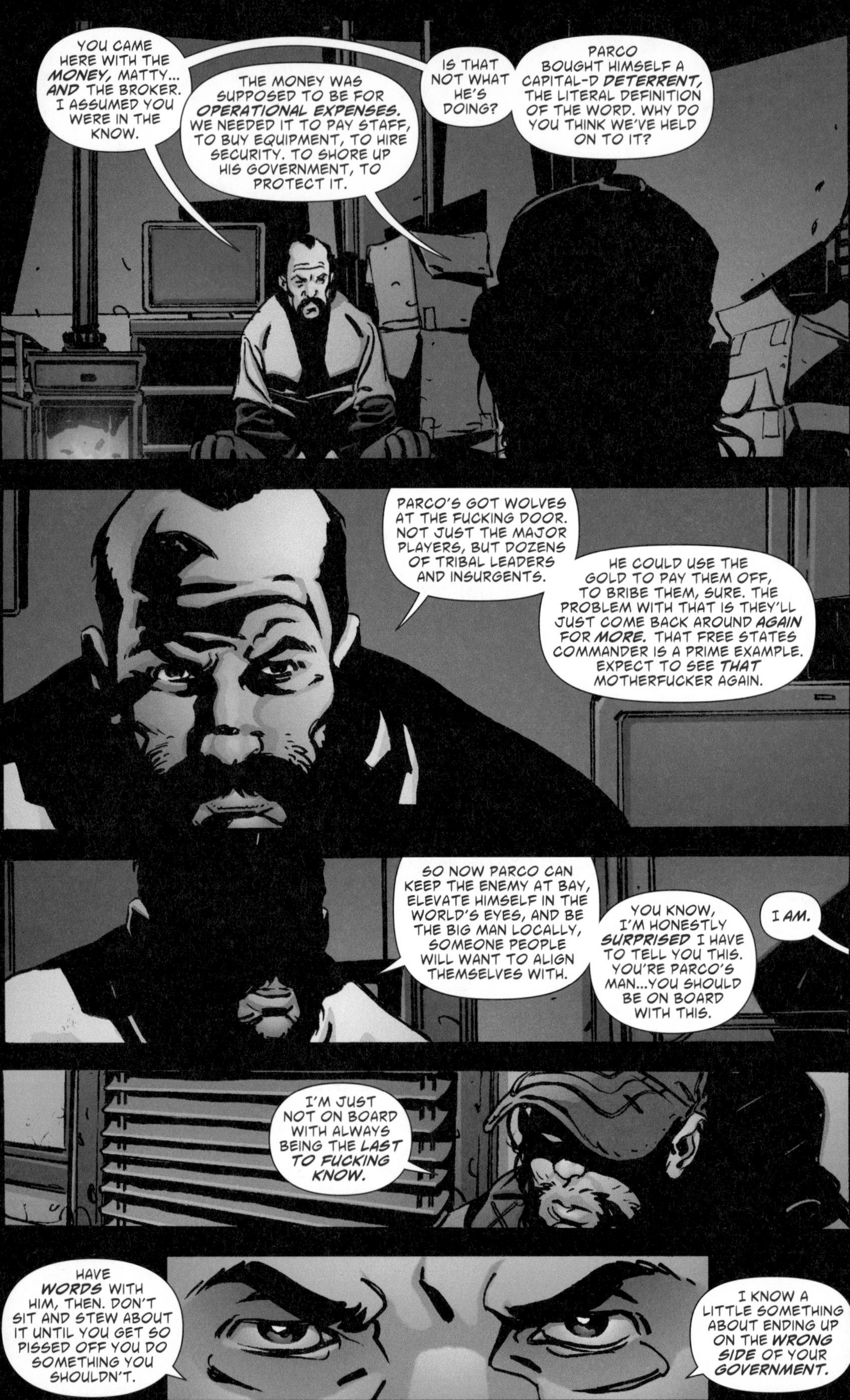

YOU CAME HERE WITH THE MONEY, MATTY... AND THE BROKER. I ASSUMED YOU WERE IN THE KNOW.
THE MONEY WAS SUPPOSED TO BE FOR OPERATIONAL EXPENSES. WE NEEDED IT TO PAY STAFF, TO BUY EQUIPMENT, TO HIRE SECURITY. TO SHORE UP HIS GOVERNMENT, TO PROTECT IT.
IS THAT NOT WHAT HE'S DOING?
PARCO BOUGHT HIMSELF A CAPITAL-D DETERRENT, THE LITERAL DEFINITION OF THE WORD. WHY DO YOU THINK WE'VE HELD ON TO IT?
PARCO'S GOT WOLVES AT THE FUCKING DOOR. NOT JUST THE MAJOR PLAYERS, BUT DOZENS OF TRIBAL LEADERS AND INSURGENTS.
HE COULD USE THE GOLD TO PAY THEM OFF, TO BRIBE THEM, SURE. THE PROBLEM WITH THAT IS THEY'LL JUST COME BACK AROUND AGAIN FOR MORE. THAT FREE STATES COMMANDER IS A PRIME EXAMPLE. EXPECT TO SEE THAT MOTHERFUCKER AGAIN.
SO NOW PARCO CAN KEEP THE ENEMY AT BAY, ELEVATE HIMSELF IN THE WORLD'S EYES, AND BE THE BIG MAN LOCALLY, SOMEONE PEOPLE WILL WANT TO ALIGN THEMSELVES WITH.
YOU KNOW, I'M HONESTLY SURPRISED I HAVE TO TELL YOU THIS. YOU'RE PARCO'S MAN...YOU SHOULD BE ON BOARD WITH THIS.
I AM.
I'M JUST NOT ON BOARD WITH ALWAYS BEING THE LAST TO FUCKING KNOW.
HAVE WORDS WITH HIM, THEN. DON'T SIT AND STEW ABOUT IT UNTIL YOU GET SO PISSED OFF YOU DO SOMETHING YOU SHOULDN'T.
I KNOW A LITTLE SOMETHING ABOUT ENDING UP ON THE WRONG SIDE OF YOUR GOVERNMENT.

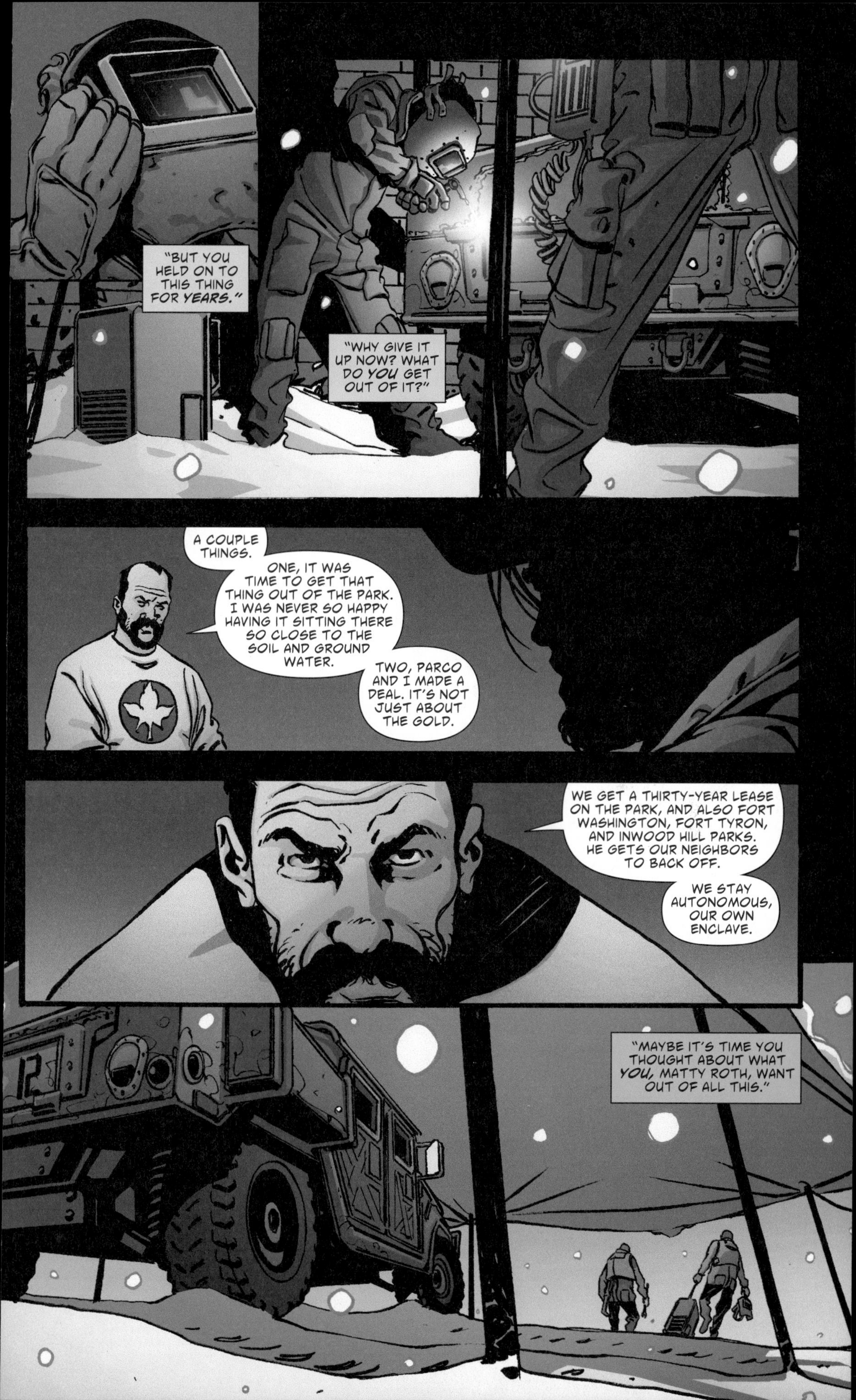
"BUT YOU HELD ON TO THIS THING FOR YEARS."
"WHY GIVE IT UP NOW? WHAT DO YOU GET OUT OF IT?"
A COUPLE THINGS.
ONE, IT WAS TIME TO GET THAT THING OUT OF THE PARK. I WAS NEVER SO HAPPY HAVING IT SITTING THERE SO CLOSE TO THE SOIL AND GROUND WATER.
TWO, PARCO AND I MADE A DEAL. IT'S NOT JUST ABOUT THE GOLD.
WE GET A THIRTY-YEAR LEASE ON THE PARK, AND ALSO FORT WASHINGTON, FORT TYRON, AND INWOOD HILL PARKS. HE GETS OUR NEIGHBORS TO BACK OFF.
WE STAY AUTONOMOUS, OUR OWN ENCLAVE.
"MAYBE IT'S TIME YOU THOUGHT ABOUT WHAT YOU, MATTY ROTH, WANT OUT OF ALL THIS."
12

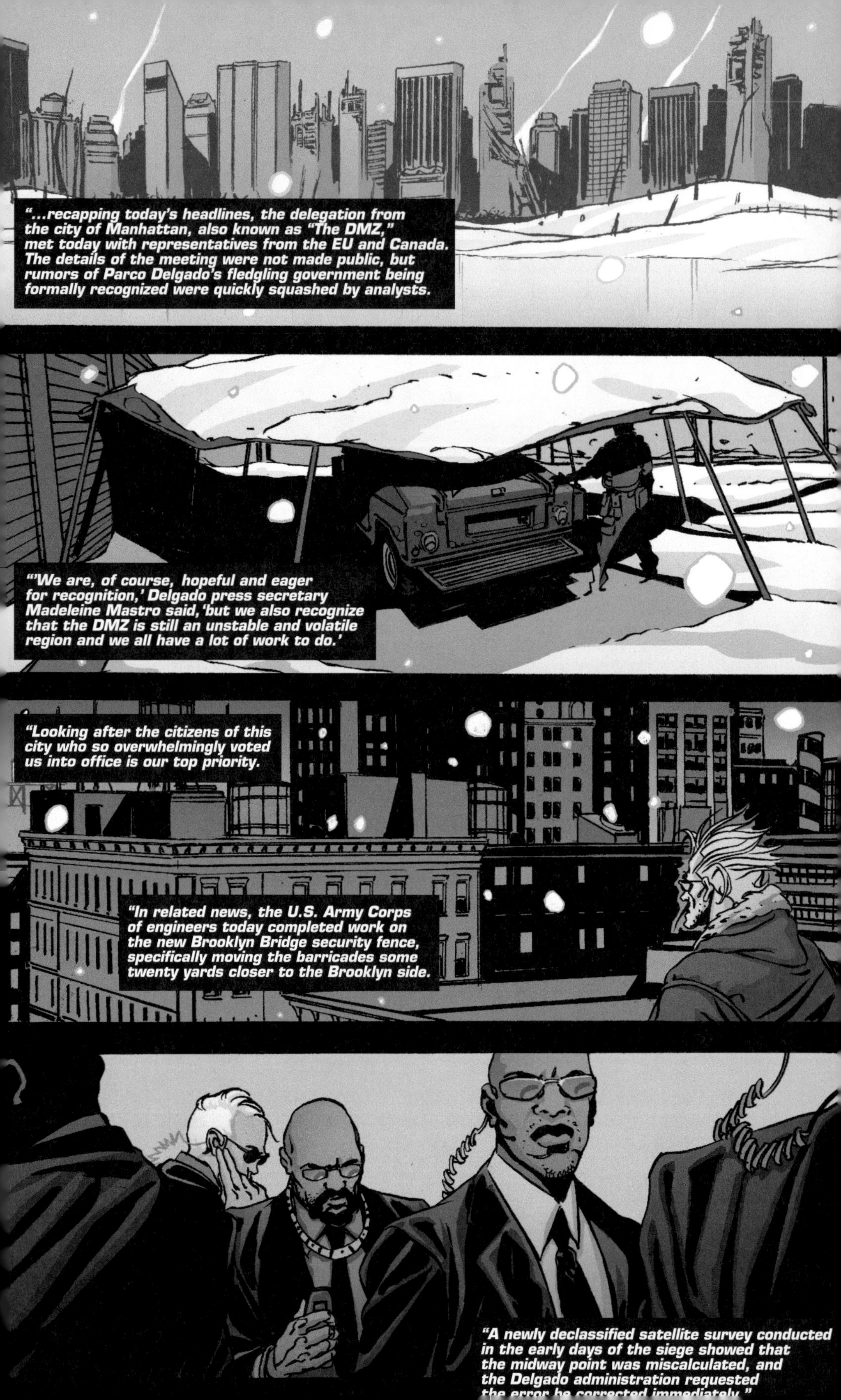
"...recapping today's headlines, the delegation from the city of Manhattan, also known as "The DMZ," met today with representatives from the EU and Canada. The details of the meeting were not made public, but rumors of Parco Delgado's fledgling government being formally recognized were quickly squashed by analysts.
"'We are, of course, hopeful and eager for recognition,' Delgado press secretary Madeleine Mastro said, 'but we also recognize that the DMZ is still an unstable and volatile region and we all have a lot of work to do.'
"Looking after the citizens of this city who so overwhelmingly voted us into office is our top priority.
"In related news, the U.S. Army Corps of engineers today completed work on the new Brooklyn Bridge security fence, specifically moving the barricades some twenty yards closer to the Brooklyn side.
"A newly declassified satellite survey conducted in the early days of the siege showed that the midway point was miscalculated, and the Delgado administration requested the error be corrected immediately."

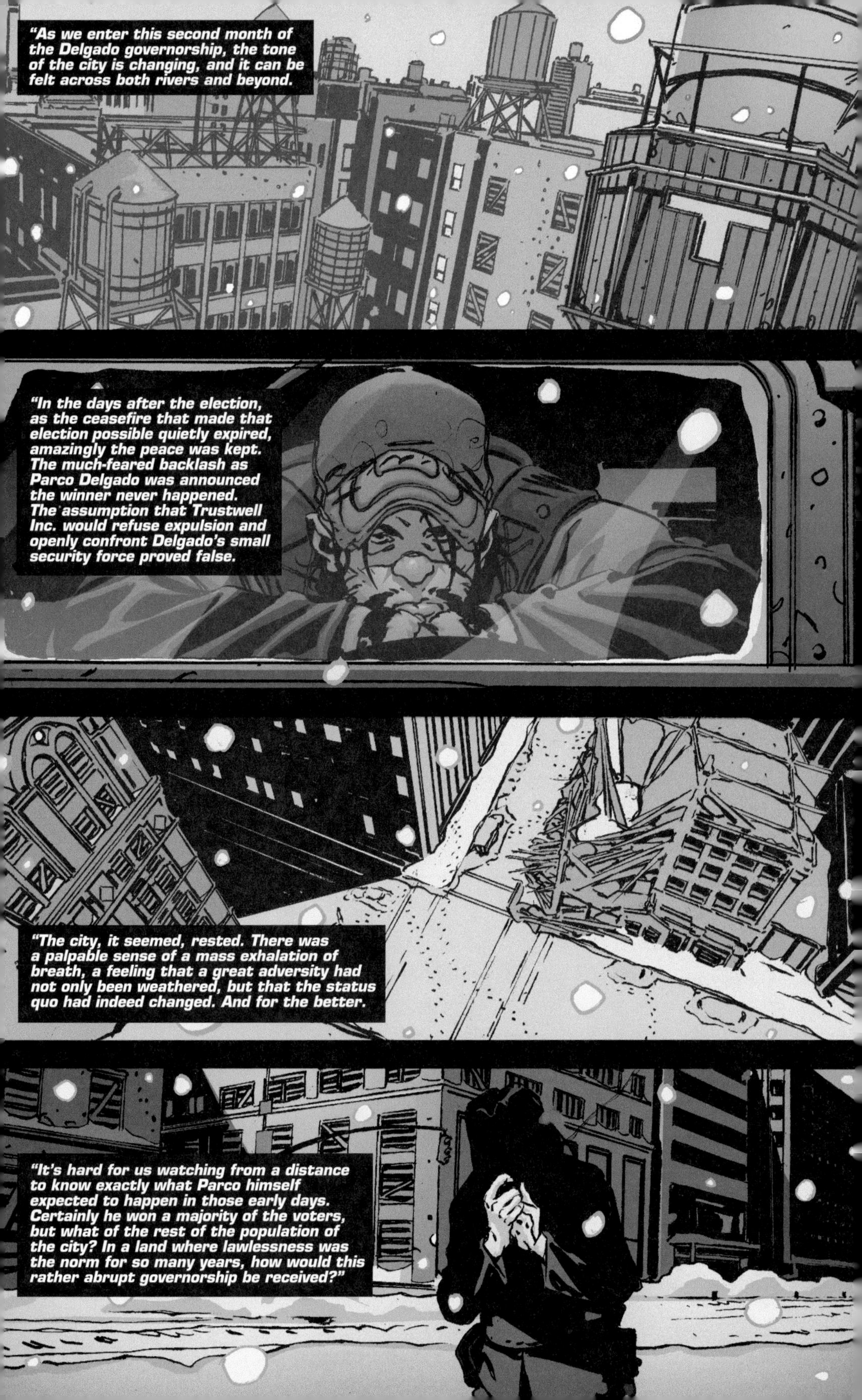
"As we enter this second month of the Delgado governorship, the tone of the city is changing, and it can be felt across both rivers and beyond.
"In the days after the election, as the ceasefire that made that election possible quietly expired, amazingly the peace was kept. The much-feared backlash as Parco Delgado was announced the winner never happened. The assumption that Trustwell Inc. would refuse expulsion and openly confront Delgado's small security force proved false.
"The city, it seemed, rested. There was a palpable sense of a mass exhalation of breath, a feeling that a great adversity had not only been weathered, but that the status quo had indeed changed. And for the better.
"It's hard for us watching from a distance to know exactly what Parco himself expected to happen in those early days. Certainly he won a majority of the voters, but what of the rest of the population of the city? In a land where lawlessness was the norm for so many years, how would this rather abrupt governorship be received?"

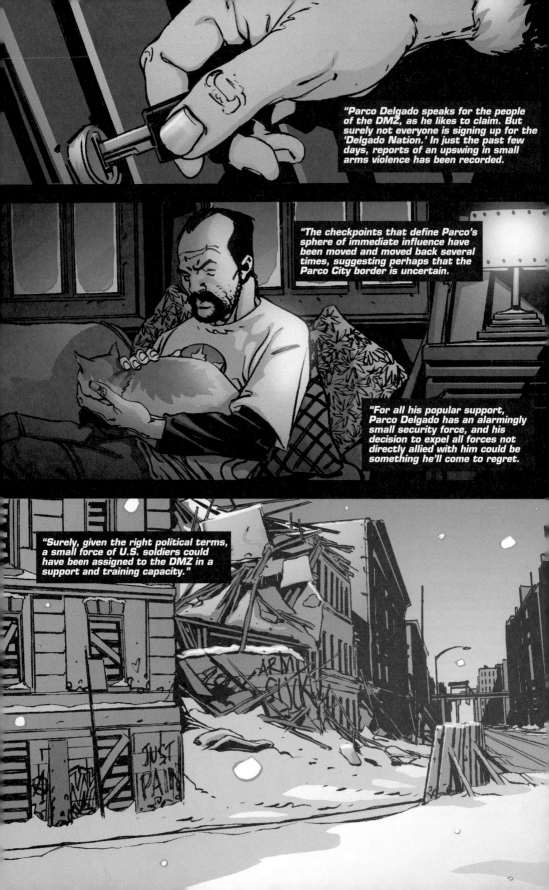

"Parco Delgado speaks for the people of the DMZ, as he likes to claim. But surely not everyone is signing up for the 'Delgado Nation.' In just the past few days, reports of an upswing in small arms violence has been recorded.

"The checkpoints that define Parco's sphere of immediate influence have been moved and moved back several times, suggesting perhaps that the Parco City border is uncertain.

"For all his popular support, Parco Delgado has an alarmingly small security force, and his decision to expel all forces not directly allied with him could be something he'll come to regret.

"Surely, given the right political terms, a small force of U.S. soldiers could have been assigned to the DMZ in a support and training capacity."

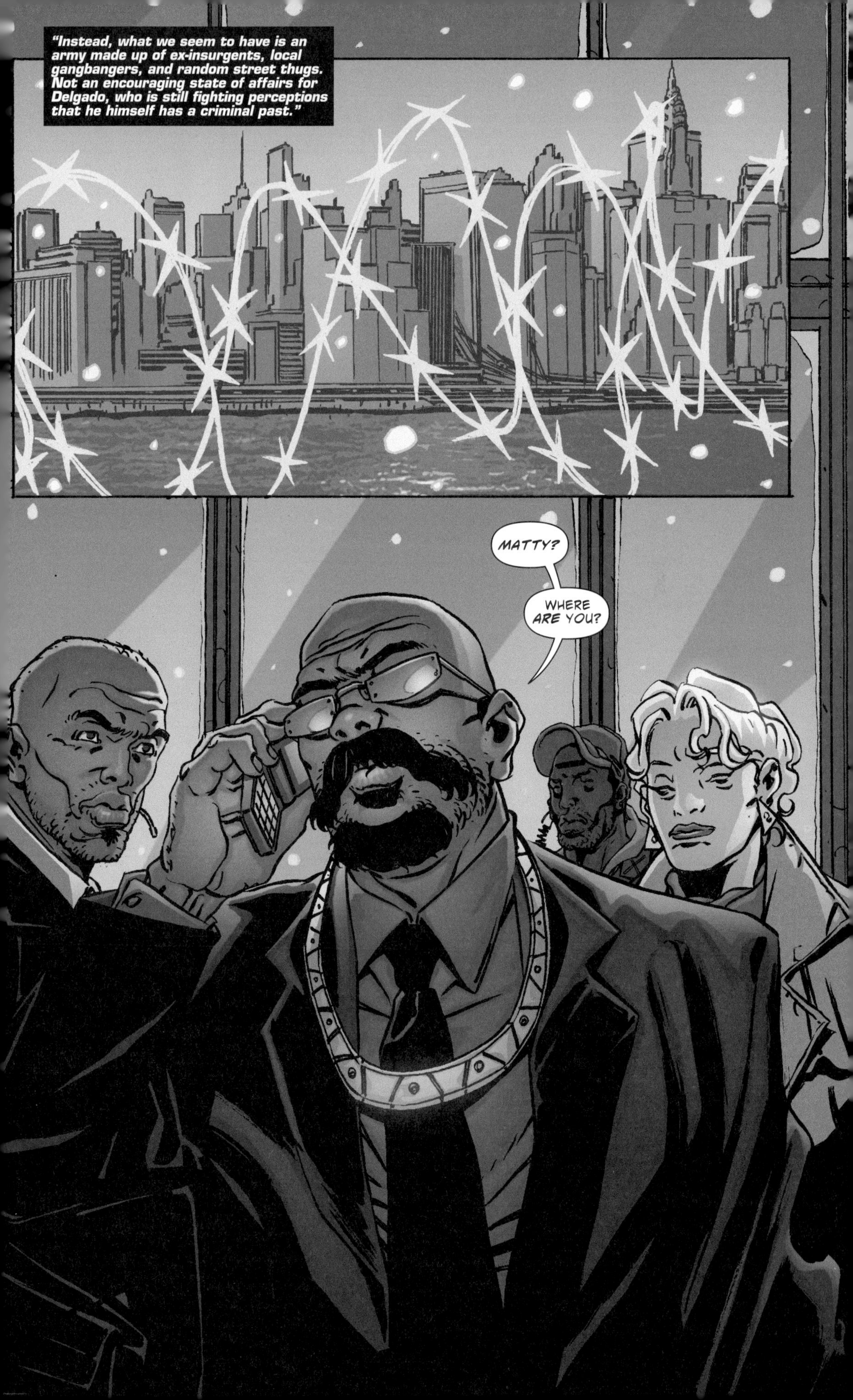
"Instead, what we seem to have is an army made up of ex-insurgents, local gangbangers, and random street thugs. Not an encouraging state of affairs for Delgado, who is still fighting perceptions that he himself has a criminal past."
MATTY?
WHERE ARE YOU?

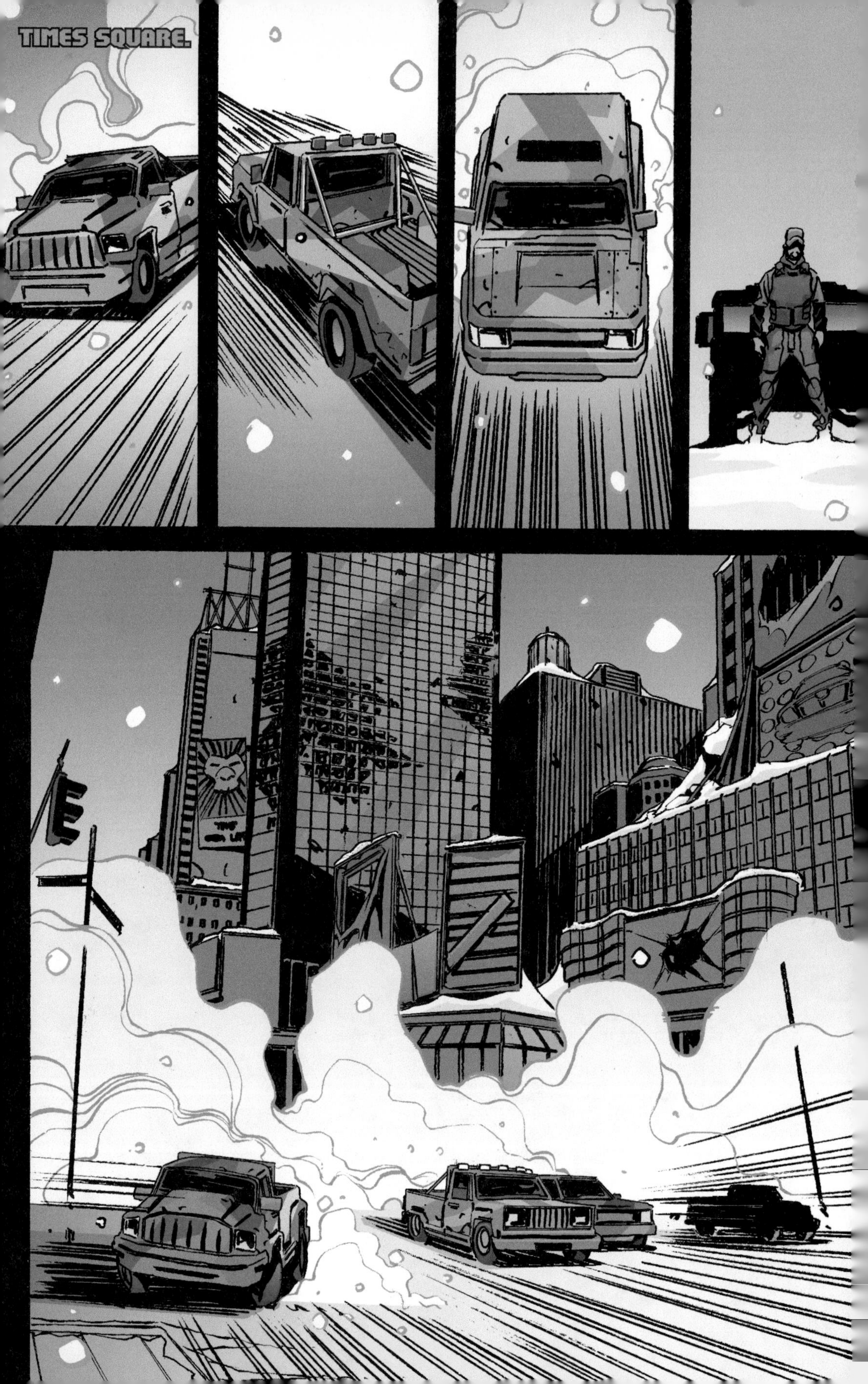
TIMES SQUARE.

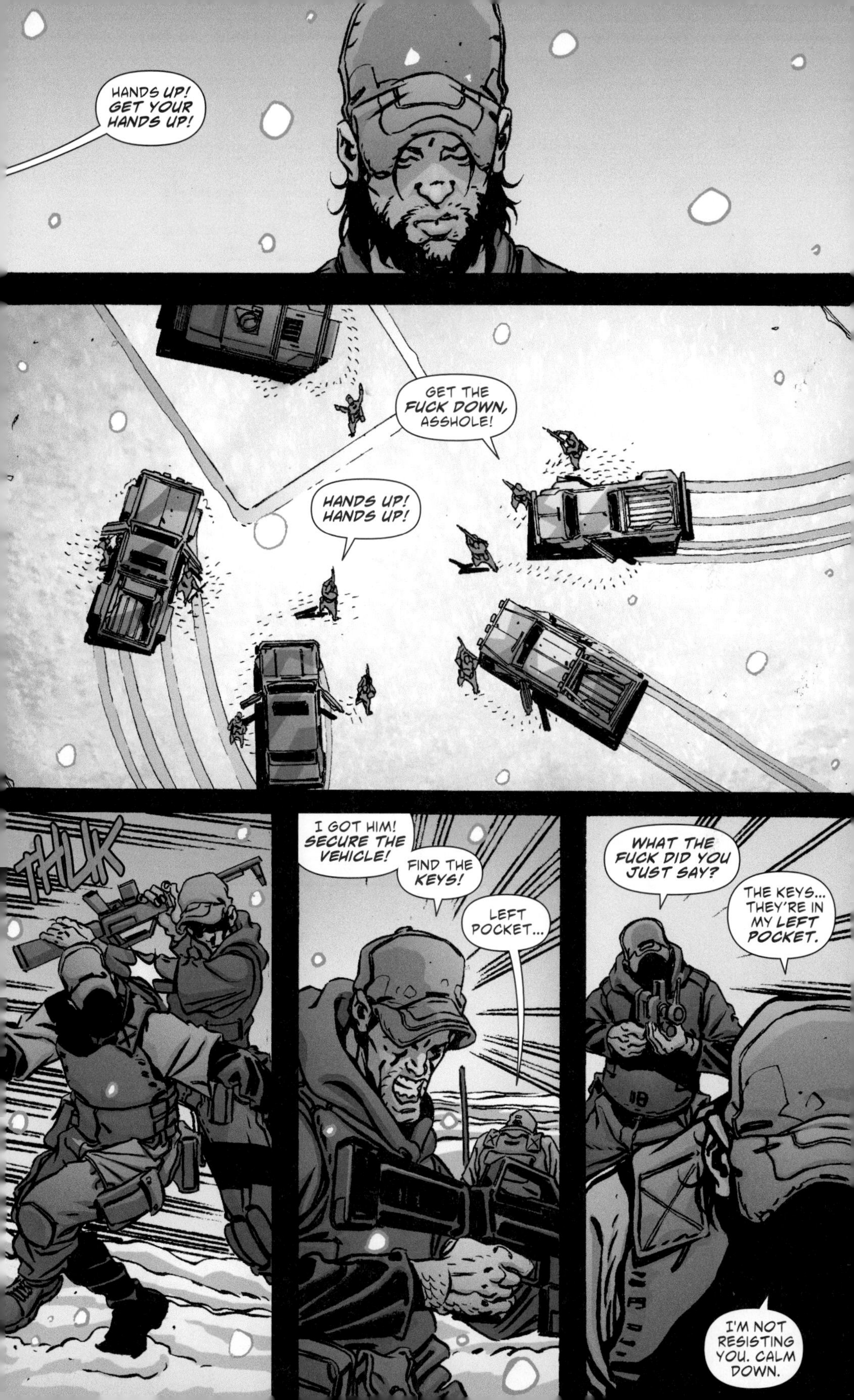
HANDS UP! GET YOUR HANDS UP!
GET THE FUCK DOWN, ASSHOLE!
HANDS UP! HANDS UP!
THUK
I GOT HIM! SECURE THE VEHICLE!
FIND THE KEYS!
LEFT POCKET...
WHAT THE FUCK DID YOU JUST SAY?
THE KEYS... THEY'RE IN MY LEFT POCKET.
I'M NOT RESISTING YOU. CALM DOWN.

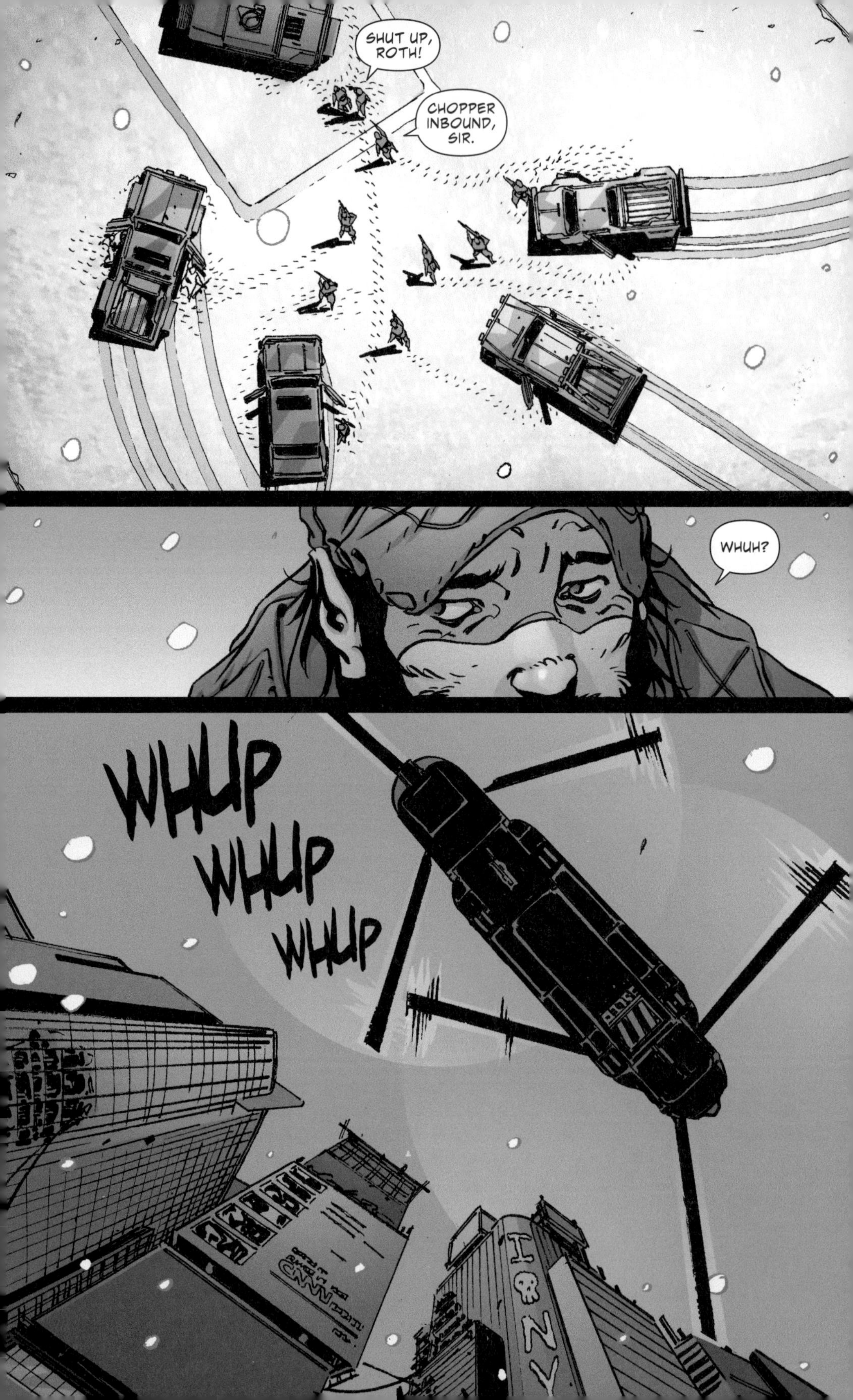
SHUT UP, ROTH!
CHOPPER INBOUND, SIR.
WHUH?
WHUP
WHUP
WHUP

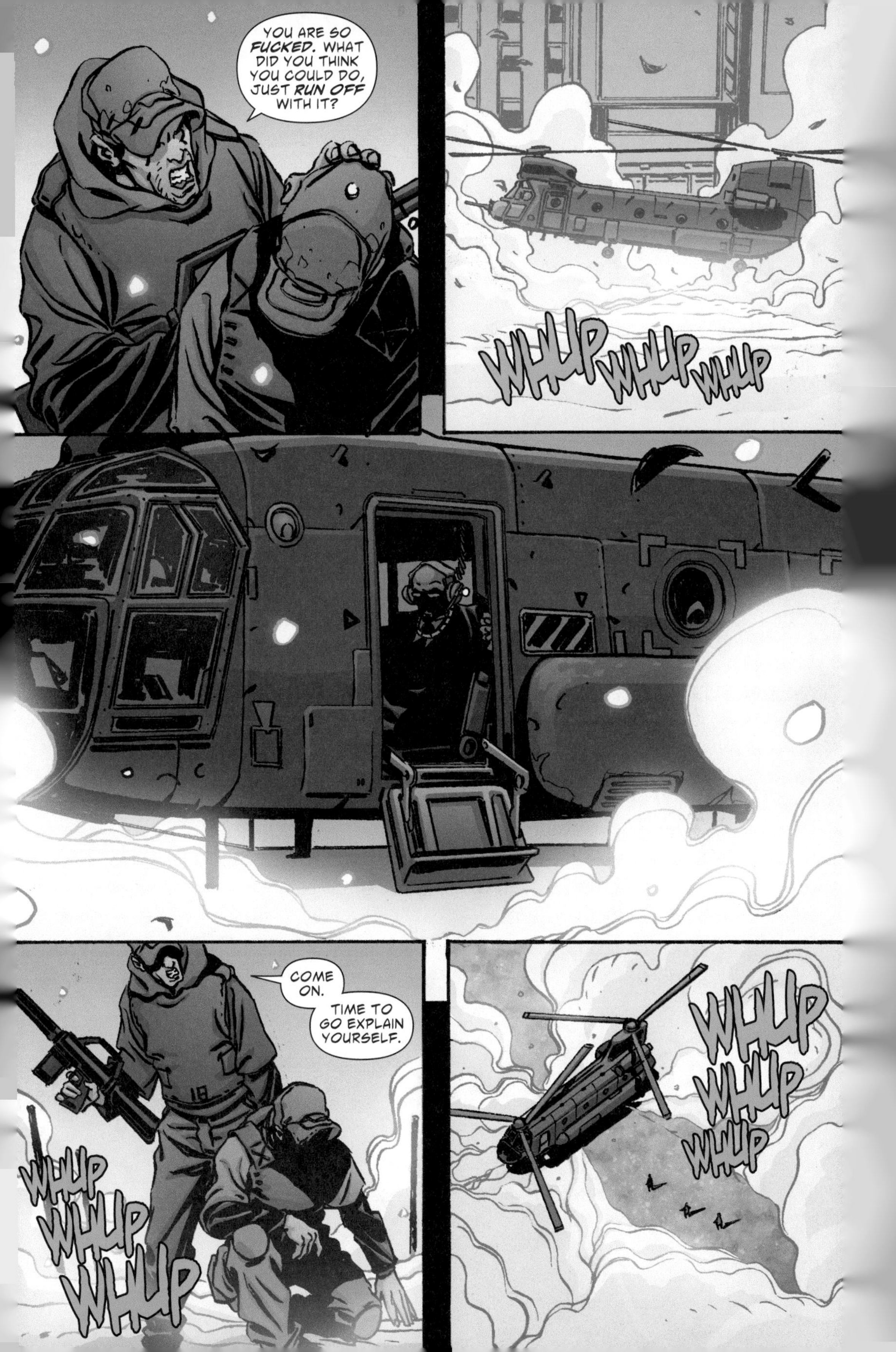
YOU ARE SO FUCKED. WHAT DID YOU THINK YOU COULD DO, JUST RUN OFF WITH IT?
WHUP WHUP WHUP
COME ON.
TIME TO GO EXPLAIN YOURSELF.
WHUP WHUP WHUP
WHUP WHUP WHUP

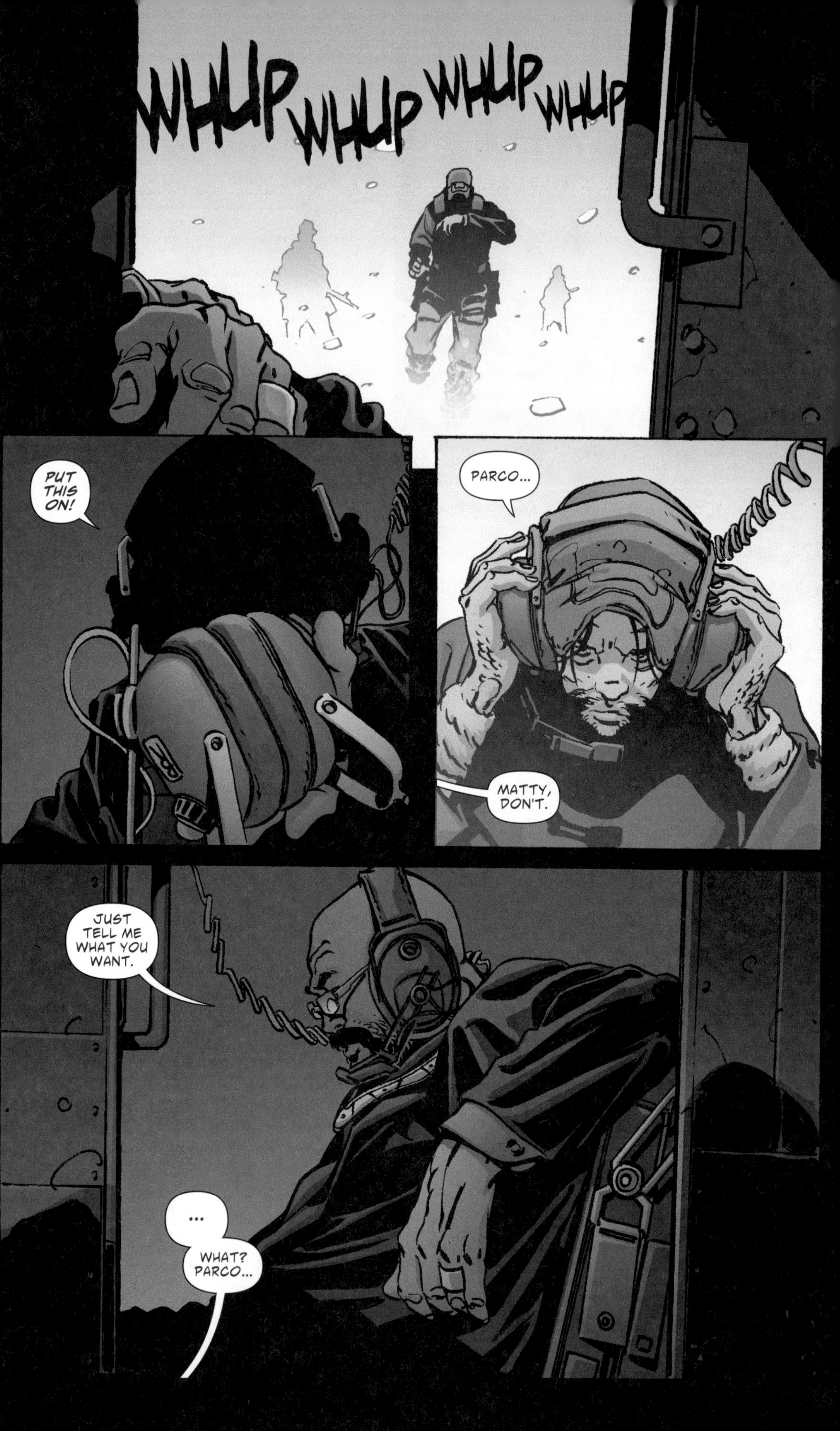
WHUP WHUP WHUP WHUP
PUT THIS ON!
PARCO...
MATTY, DON'T.
JUST TELL ME WHAT YOU WANT.
...
WHAT? PARCO...

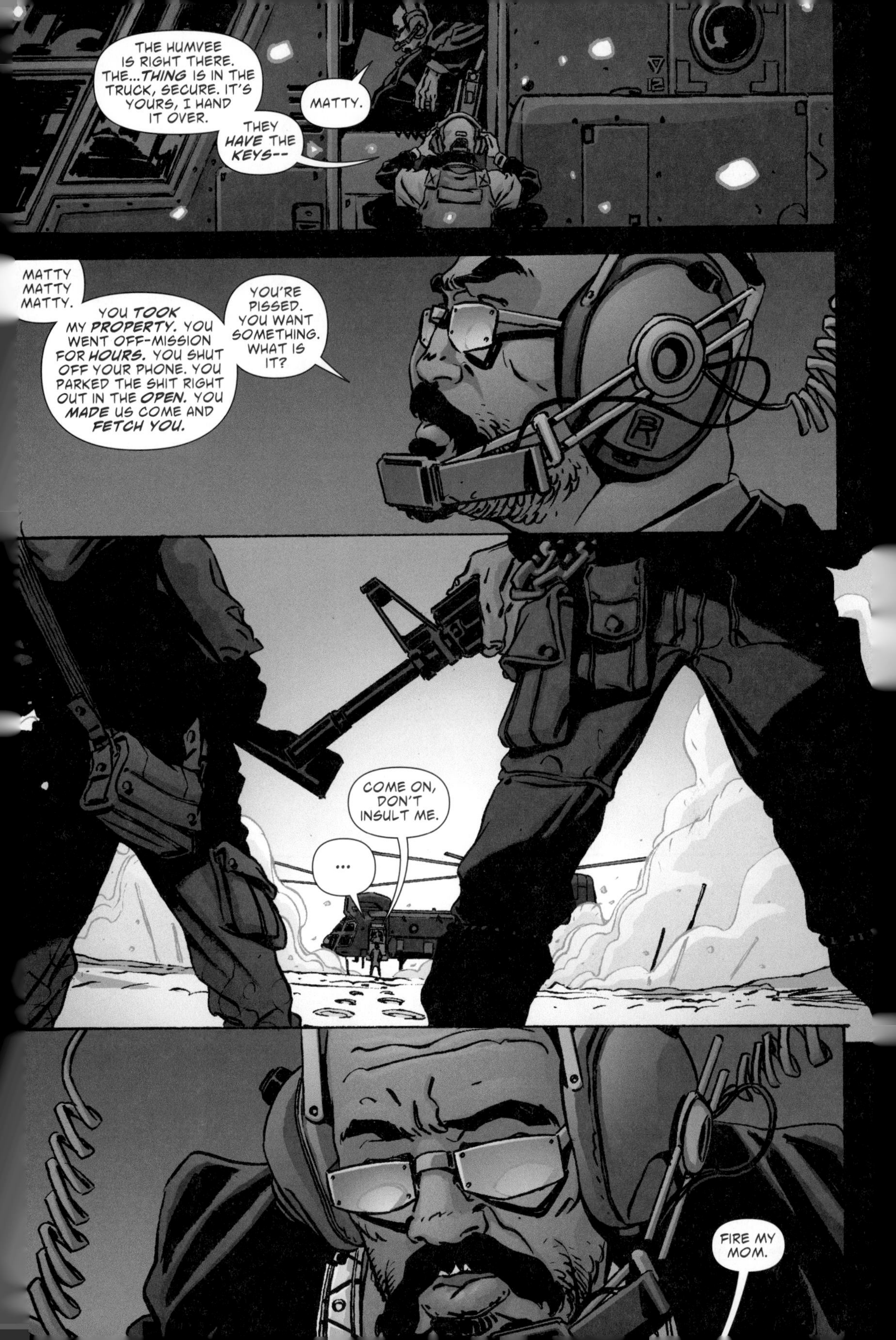
THE HUMVEE IS RIGHT THERE. THE...THING IS IN THE TRUCK, SECURE. IT'S YOURS, I HAND IT OVER.
THEY HAVE THE KEYS--
MATTY.
MATTY MATTY MATTY.
YOU TOOK MY PROPERTY. YOU WENT OFF-MISSION FOR HOURS. YOU SHUT OFF YOUR PHONE. YOU PARKED THE SHIT RIGHT OUT IN THE OPEN. YOU MADE US COME AND FETCH YOU.
YOU'RE PISSED. YOU WANT SOMETHING. WHAT IS IT?
COME ON, DON'T INSULT ME.
...
FIRE MY MOM.

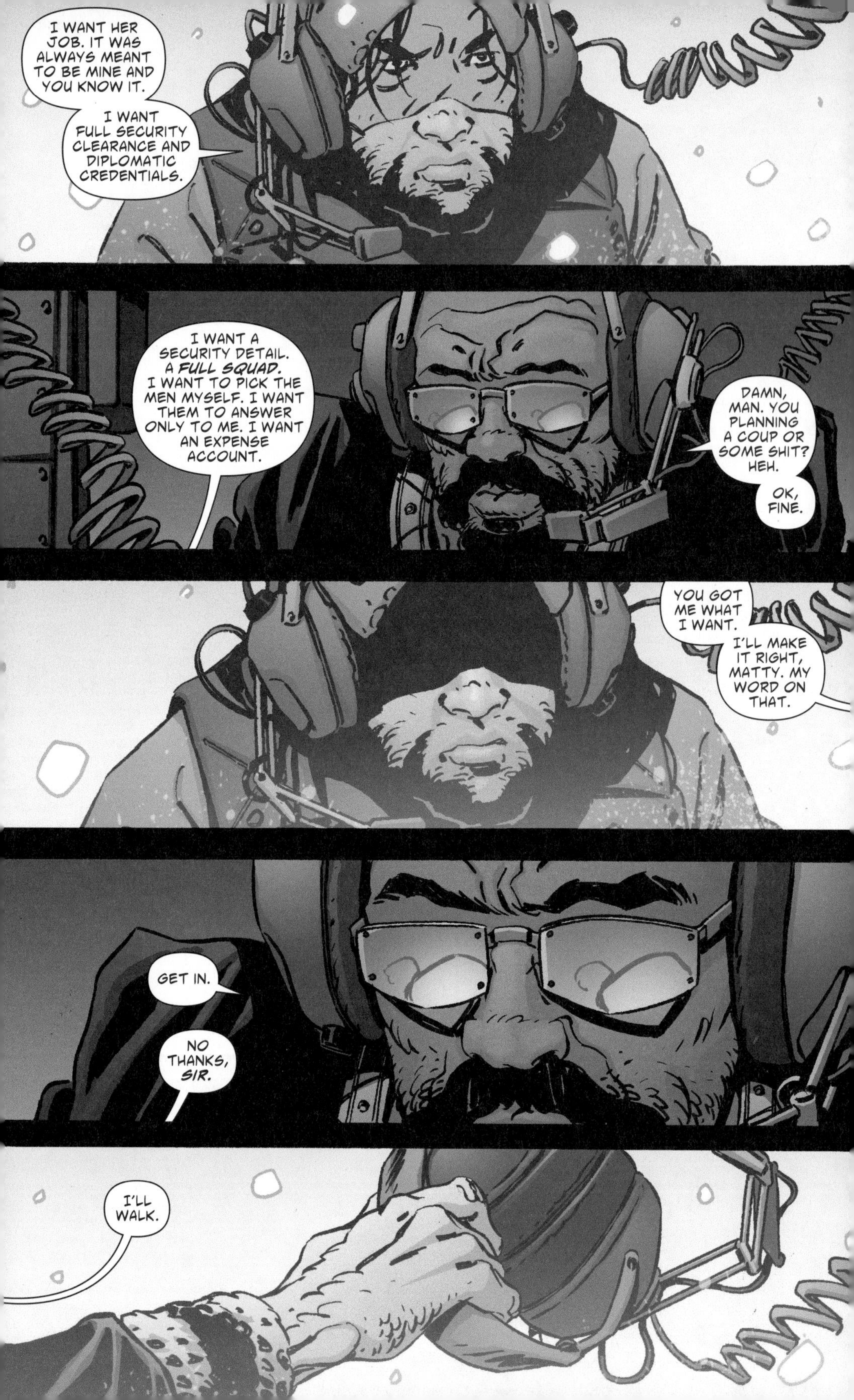
I WANT HER JOB. IT WAS ALWAYS MEANT TO BE MINE AND YOU KNOW IT.
I WANT FULL SECURITY CLEARANCE AND DIPLOMATIC CREDENTIALS.
I WANT A SECURITY DETAIL. A FULL SQUAD. I WANT TO PICK THE MEN MYSELF. I WANT THEM TO ANSWER ONLY TO ME. I WANT AN EXPENSE ACCOUNT.
DAMN, MAN. YOU PLANNING A COUP OR SOME SHIT? HEH.
OK, FINE.
YOU GOT ME WHAT I WANT.
I'LL MAKE IT RIGHT, MATTY. MY WORD ON THAT.
GET IN.
NO THANKS, SIR.
I'LL WALK.

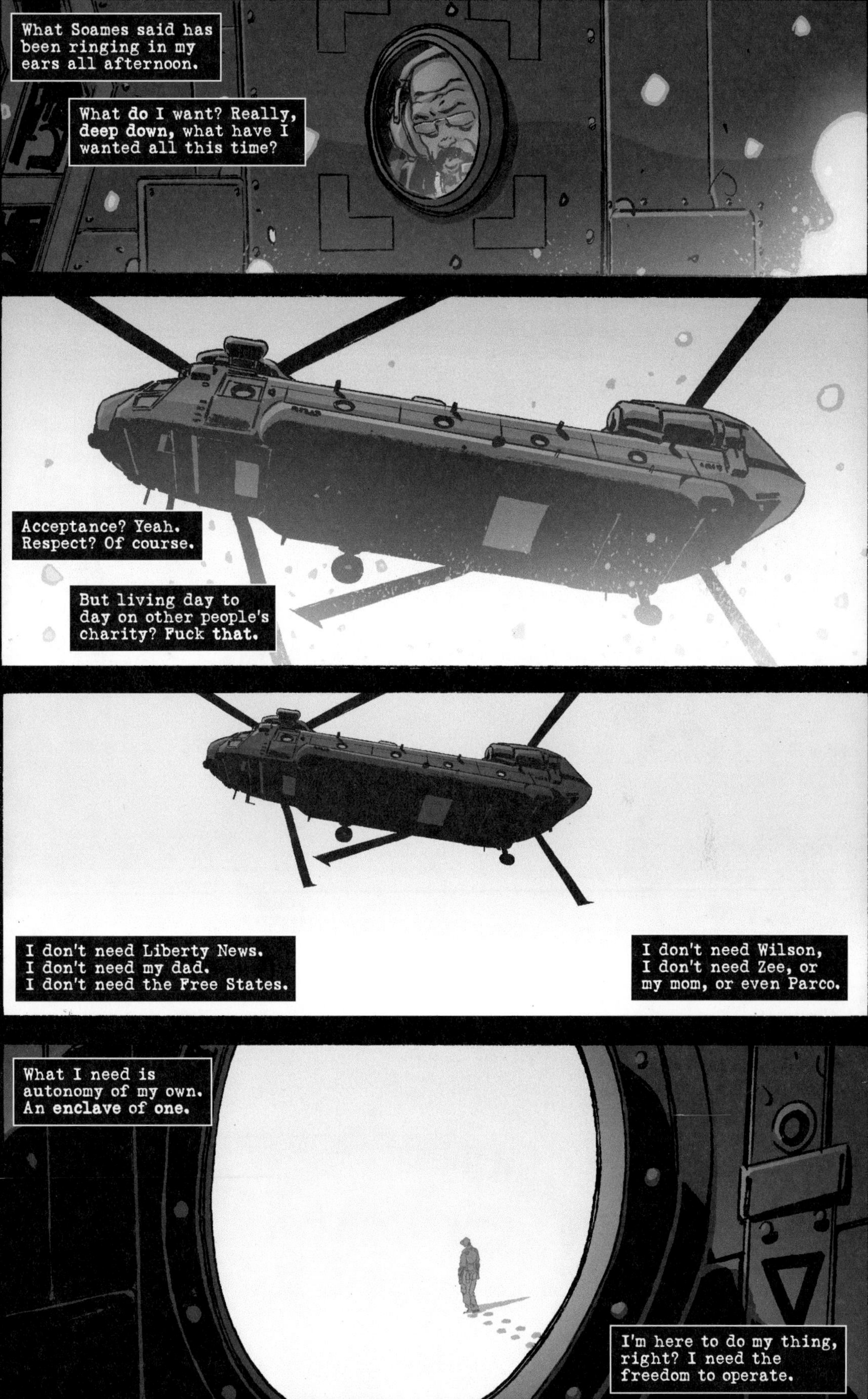
What Soames said has been ringing in my ears all afternoon.
What do I want? Really, deep down, what have I wanted all this time?
Acceptance? Yeah. Respect? Of course.
But living day to day on other people's charity? Fuck that.
I don't need Liberty News. I don't need my dad. I don't need the Free States.
I don't need Wilson, I don't need Zee, or my mom, or even Parco.
What I need is autonomy of my own. An enclave of one.
I'm here to do my thing, right? I need the freedom to operate.

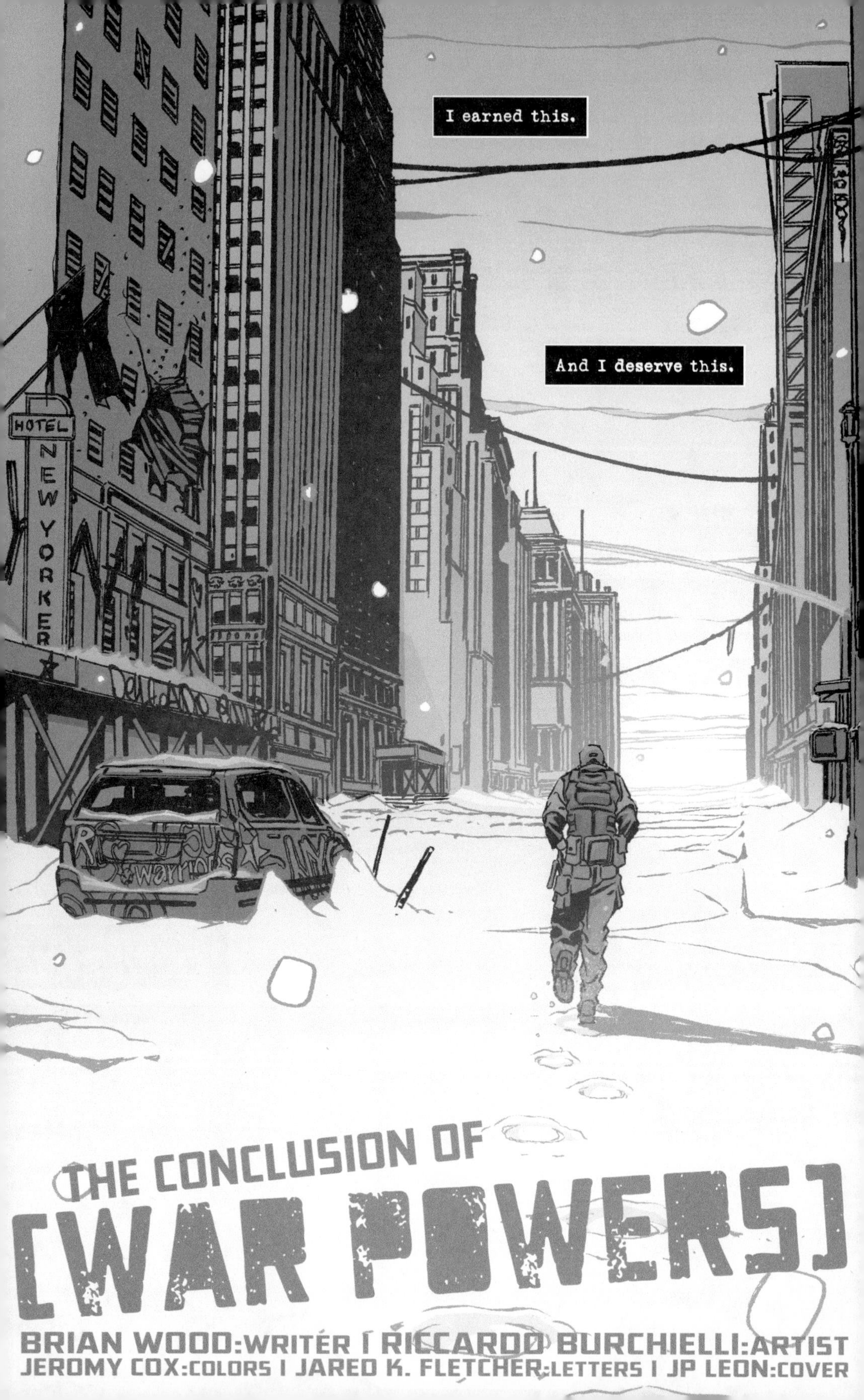
I earned this.
And I deserve this.
HOTEL NEW YORKER
THE CONCLUSION OF
[WAR POWERS]
BRIAN WOOD:WRITER | RICCARDO BURCHIELLI:ARTIST
JEROMY COX:COLORS | JARED K. FLETCHER:LETTERS | JP LEON:COVER

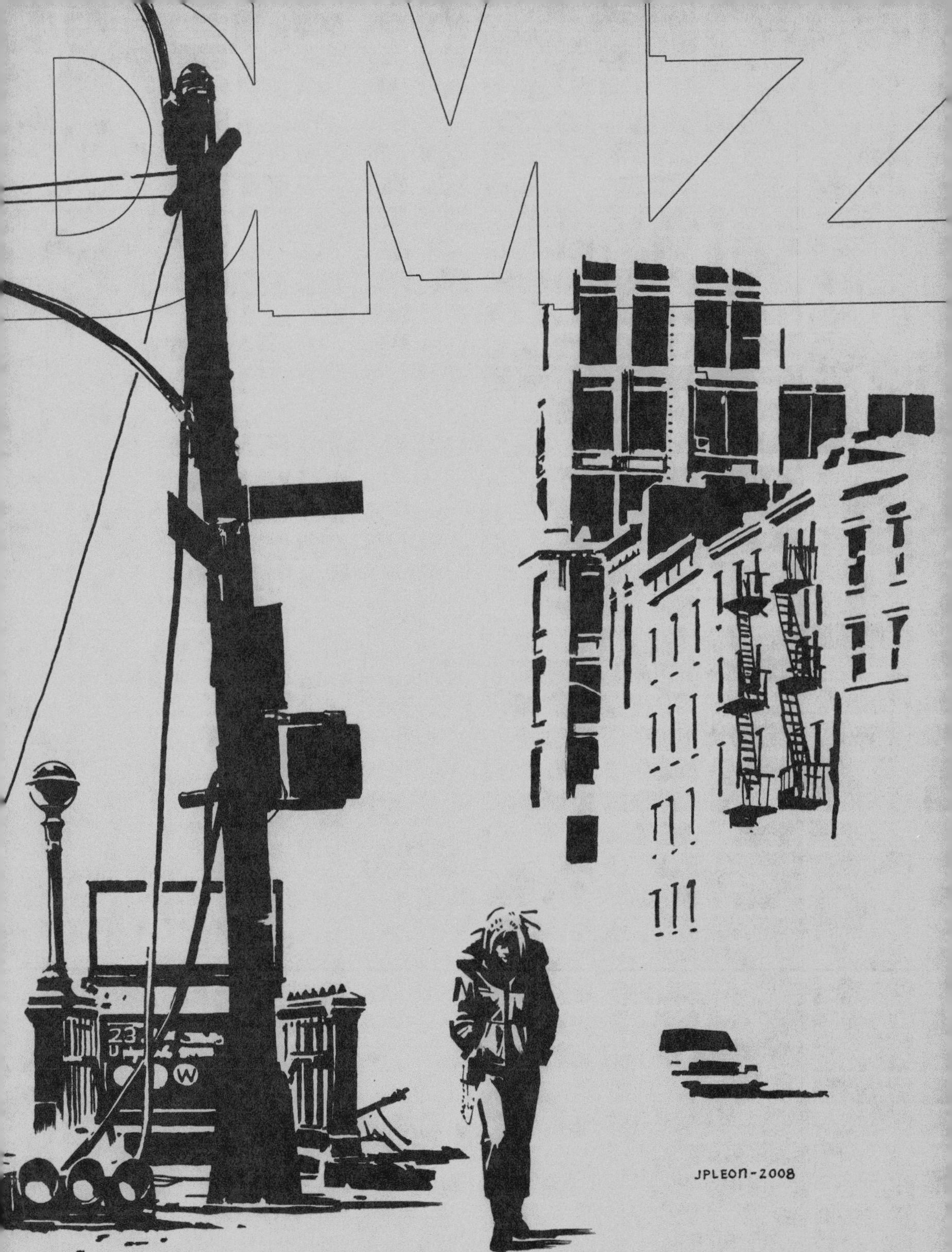
DMZ
23
W
JPLEON-2008

ZEE, DMZ

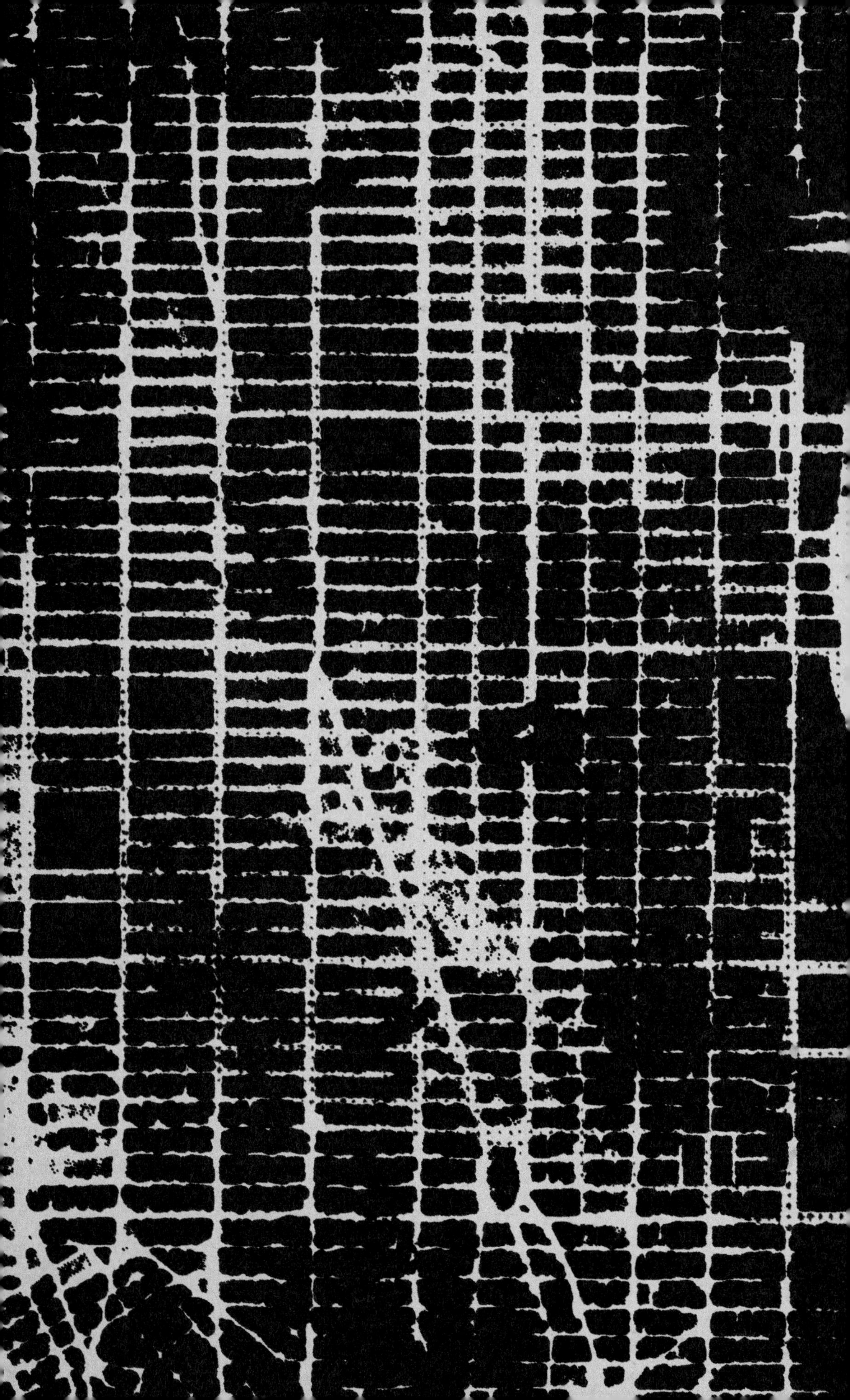

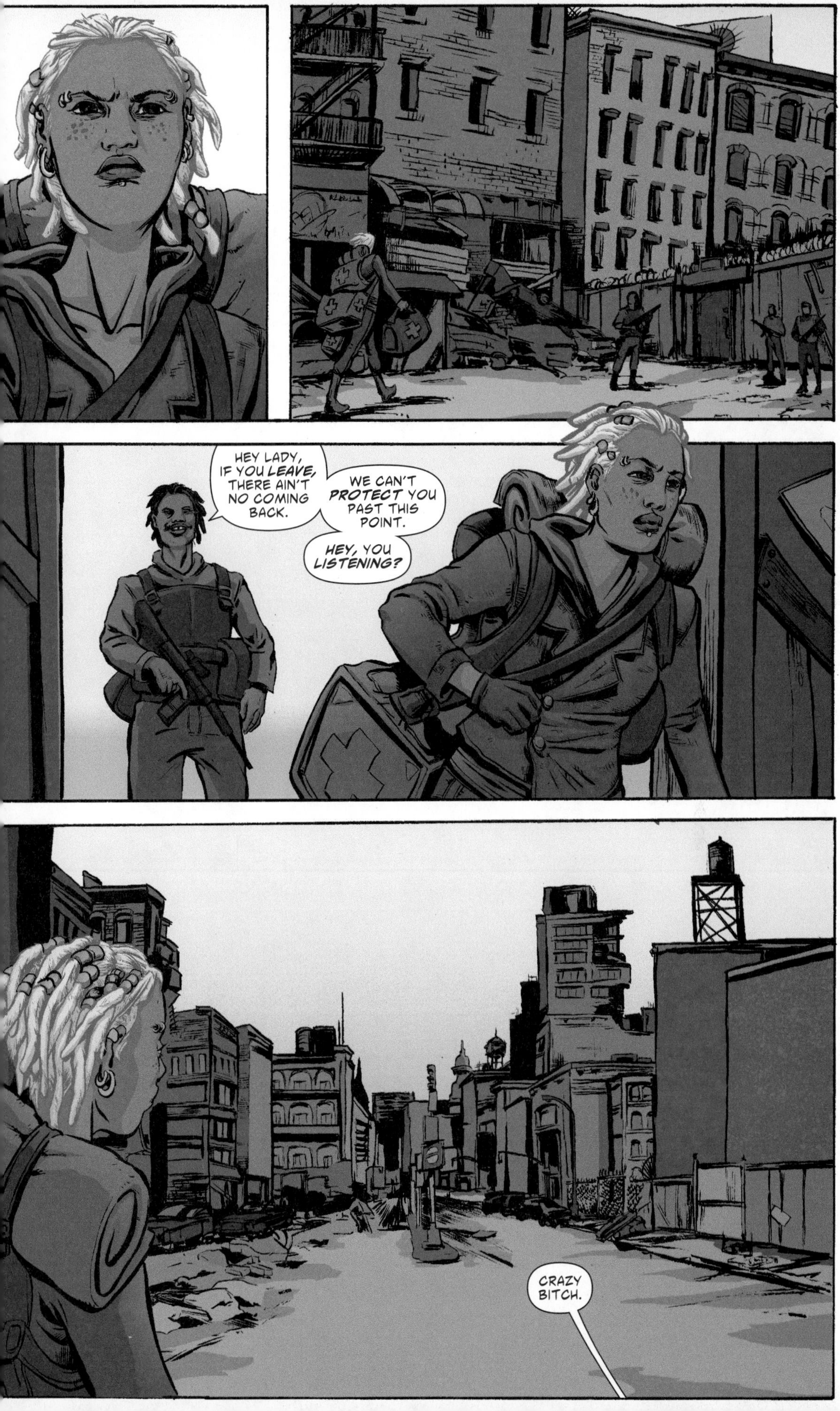
HEY LADY, IF YOU LEAVE, THERE AIN'T NO COMING BACK.
WE CAN'T PROTECT YOU PAST THIS POINT.
HEY, YOU LISTENING?
CRAZY BITCH.

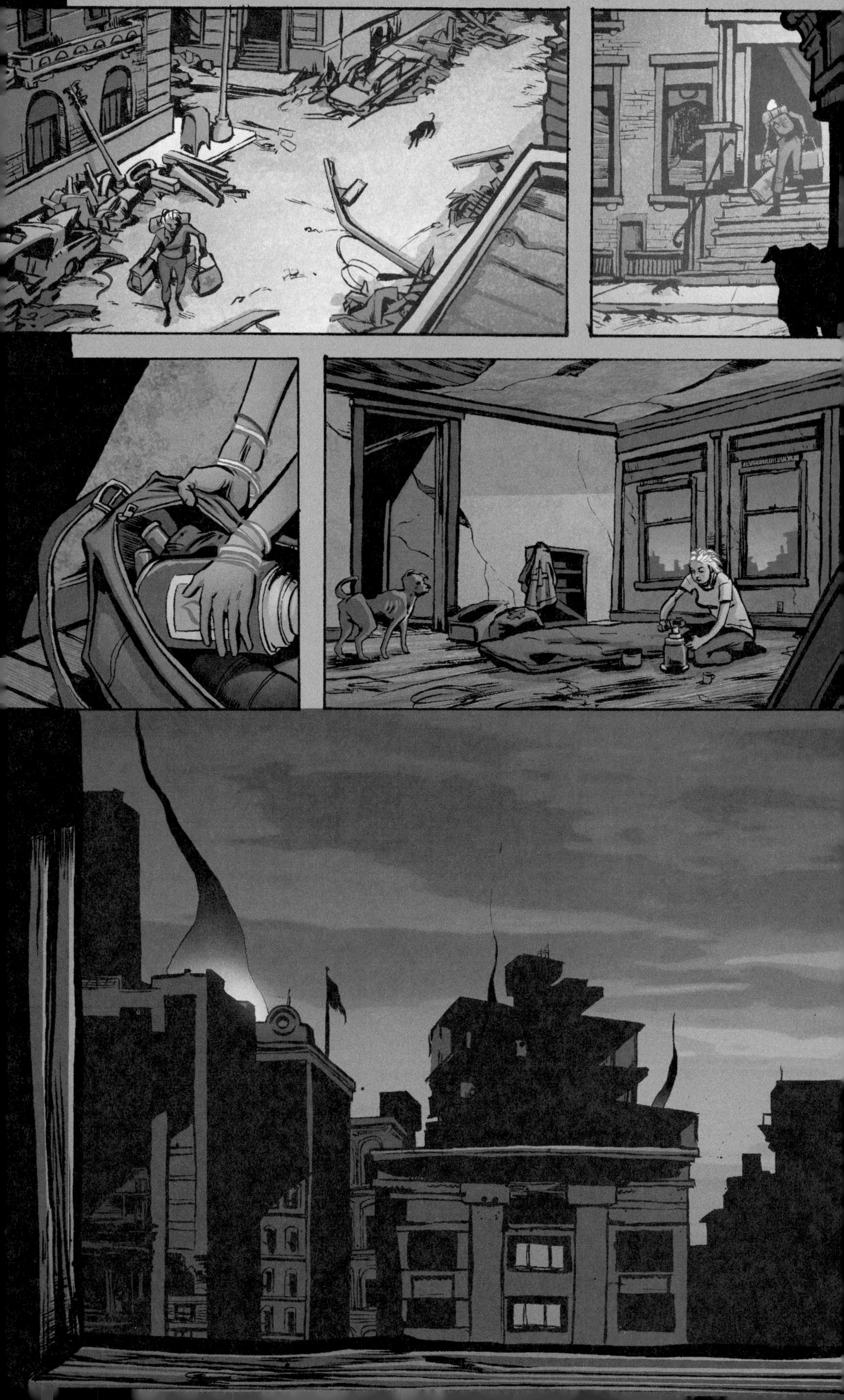

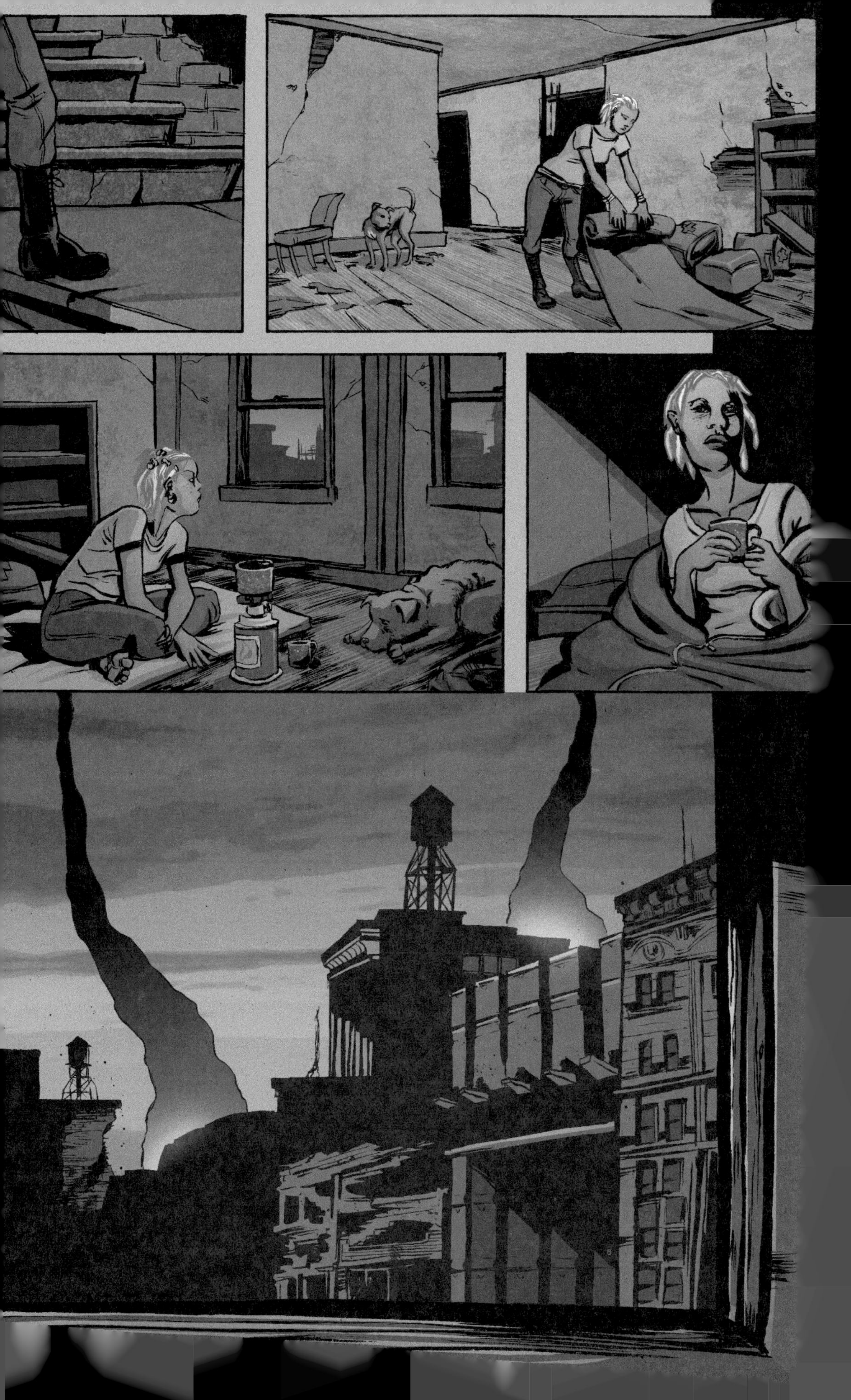

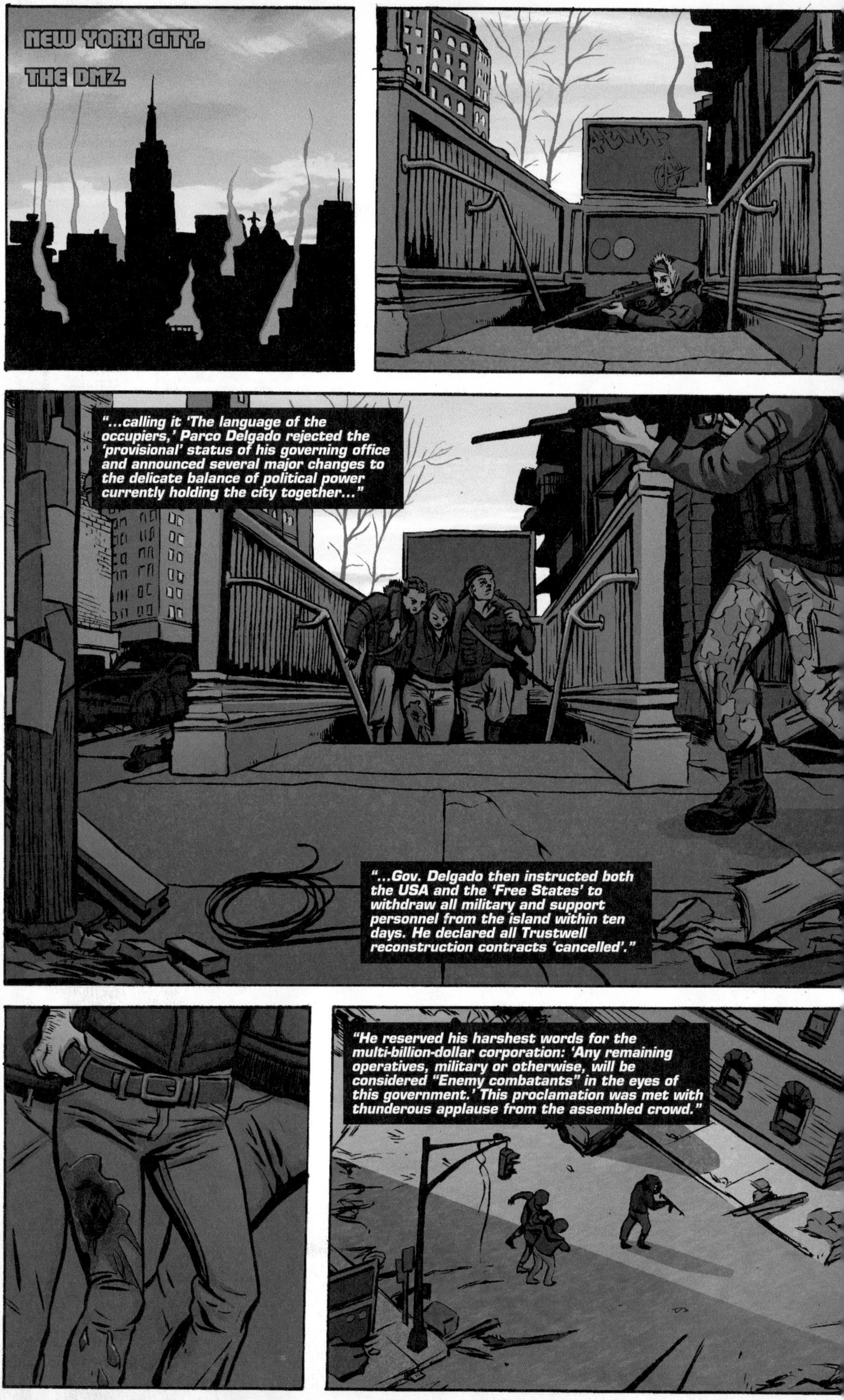
NEW YORK CITY.
THE DMZ.
"...calling it 'The language of the occupiers,' Parco Delgado rejected the 'provisional' status of his governing office and announced several major changes to the delicate balance of political power currently holding the city together..."
"...Gov. Delgado then instructed both the USA and the 'Free States' to withdraw all military and support personnel from the island within ten days. He declared all Trustwell reconstruction contracts 'cancelled'."
"He reserved his harshest words for the multi-billion-dollar corporation: 'Any remaining operatives, military or otherwise, will be considered "Enemy combatants" in the eyes of this government.' This proclamation was met with thunderous applause from the assembled crowd."

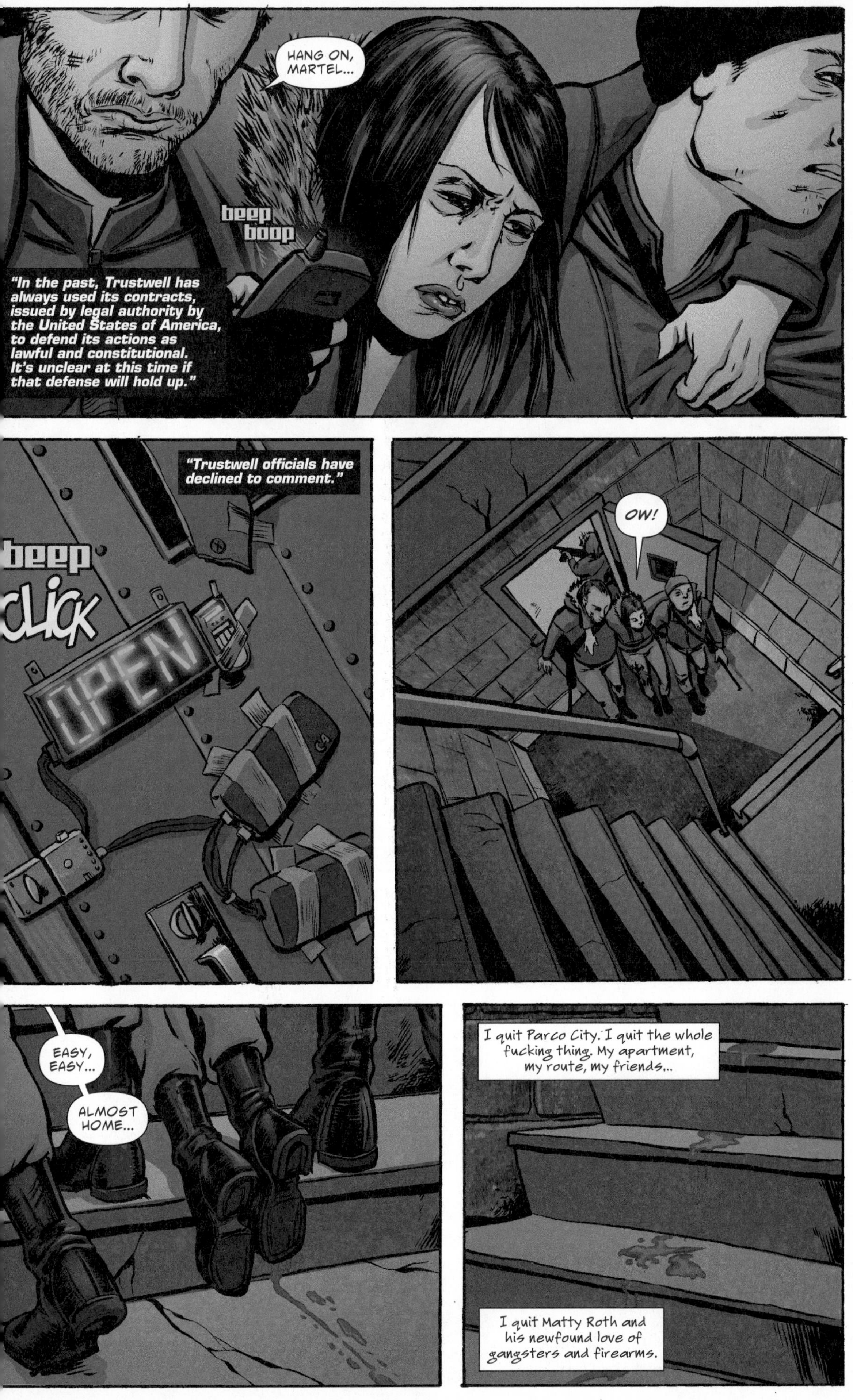
HANG ON, MARTEL...
beep
boop
"In the past, Trustwell has always used its contracts, issued by legal authority by the United States of America, to defend its actions as lawful and constitutional. It's unclear at this time if that defense will hold up."
"Trustwell officials have declined to comment."
beep
CLICK
OPEN
OW!
EASY, EASY...
ALMOST HOME...
I quit Parco City. I quit the whole fucking thing. My apartment, my route, my friends...
I quit Matty Roth and his newfound love of gangsters and firearms.

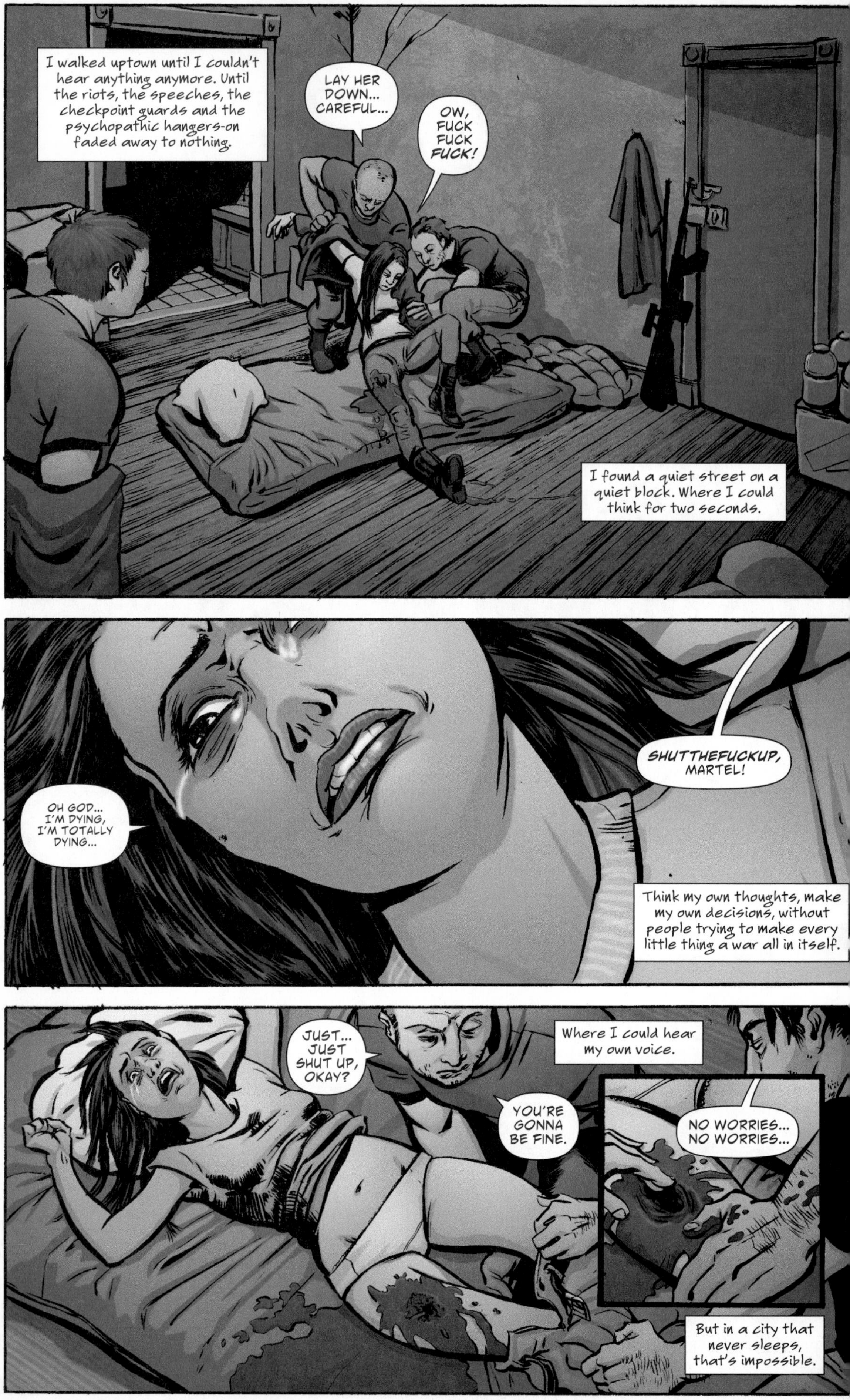
I walked uptown until I couldn't hear anything anymore. Until the riots, the speeches, the checkpoint guards and the psychopathic hangers-on faded away to nothing.
LAY HER DOWN... CAREFUL...
OW, FUCK FUCK FUCK!
I found a quiet street on a quiet block. Where I could think for two seconds.
SHUTTHEFUCKUP, MARTEL!
OH GOD... I'M DYING, I'M TOTALLY DYING...
Think my own thoughts, make my own decisions, without people trying to make every little thing a war all in itself.
JUST... JUST SHUT UP, OKAY?
Where I could hear my own voice.
YOU'RE GONNA BE FINE.
NO WORRIES... NO WORRIES...
But in a city that never sleeps, that's impossible.

OWWW! OH GOD...!

I could hear her screaming two blocks away.

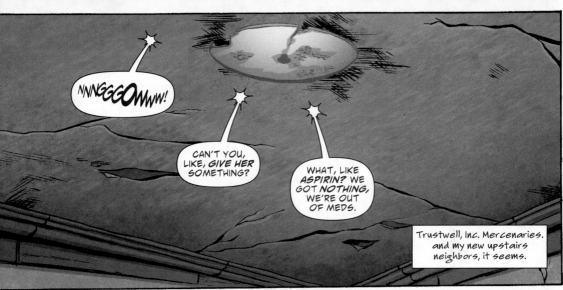

NNNGGOWWW!

CAN'T YOU, LIKE, *GIVE HER* SOMETHING?

WHAT, LIKE *ASPIRIN?* WE GOT *NOTHING,* WE'RE OUT OF MEDS.

Trustwell, Inc. Mercenaries. and my new upstairs neighbors, it seems.

FUCK! SHE'S BLEEDING TO DEATH!

OWWWW...

DUDE, SHUT UP! HANG ON, MARTEL, OKAY? LISTEN TO ME, LISTEN TO MY VOICE...

No one has hurt this city more than Trustwell. Mutilated it, raped it, robbed it. There's hundreds of these little cells scattered all over the island.

They are the worst of the worst, and it sounds like one of them is about to check out for good. Right above my head. ANd all I have to do is just sit here and do nothing.

MARTEL? *MARTEL?*

...

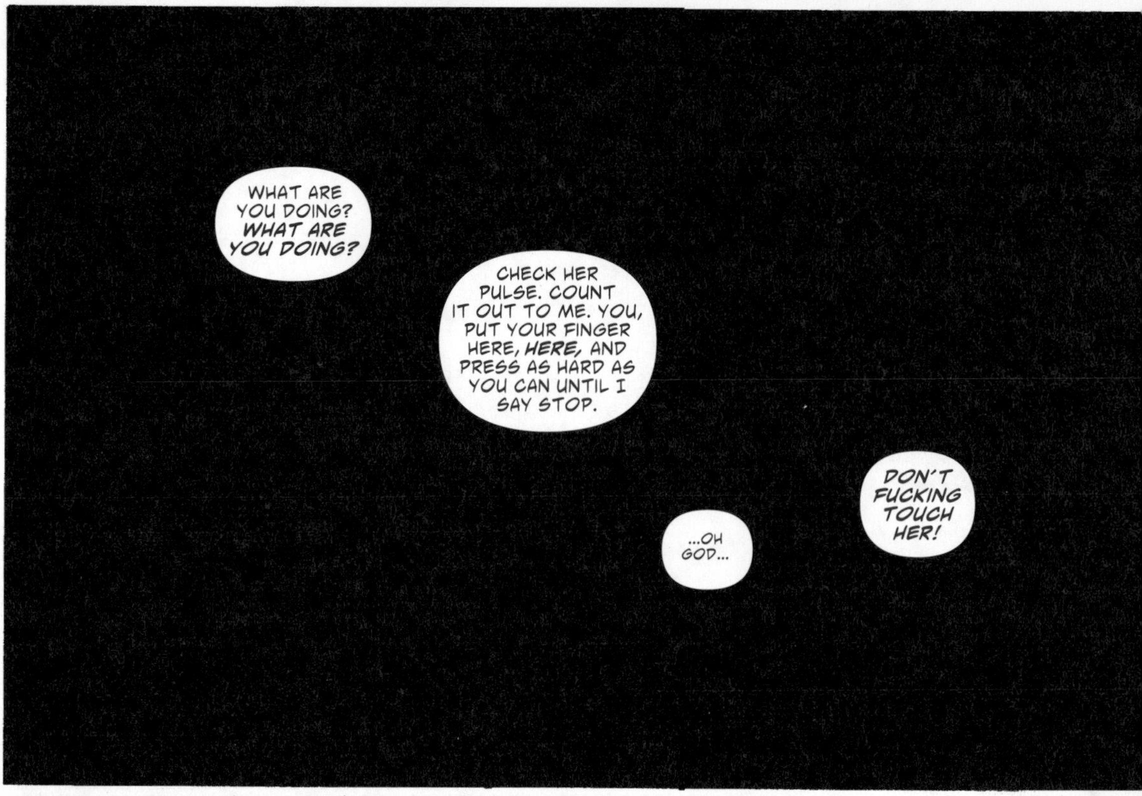
WHAT ARE YOU DOING? WHAT ARE YOU DOING?
CHECK HER PULSE. COUNT IT OUT TO ME. YOU, PUT YOUR FINGER HERE, HERE, AND PRESS AS HARD AS YOU CAN UNTIL I SAY STOP.
...OH GOD...
DON'T FUCKING TOUCH HER!

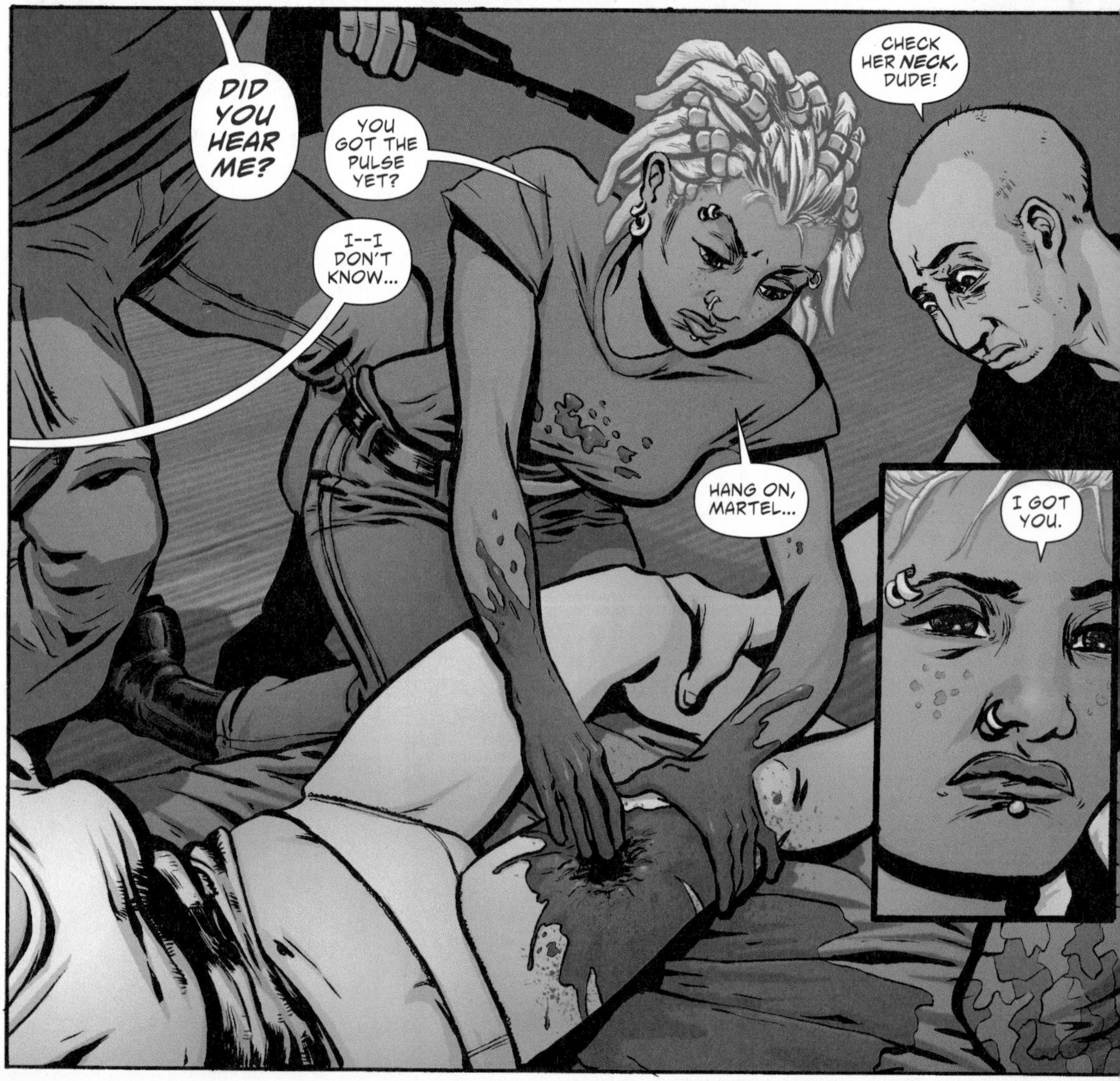
DID YOU HEAR ME?
YOU GOT THE PULSE YET?
I--I DON'T KNOW...
CHECK HER NECK, DUDE!
HANG ON, MARTEL...
I GOT YOU.

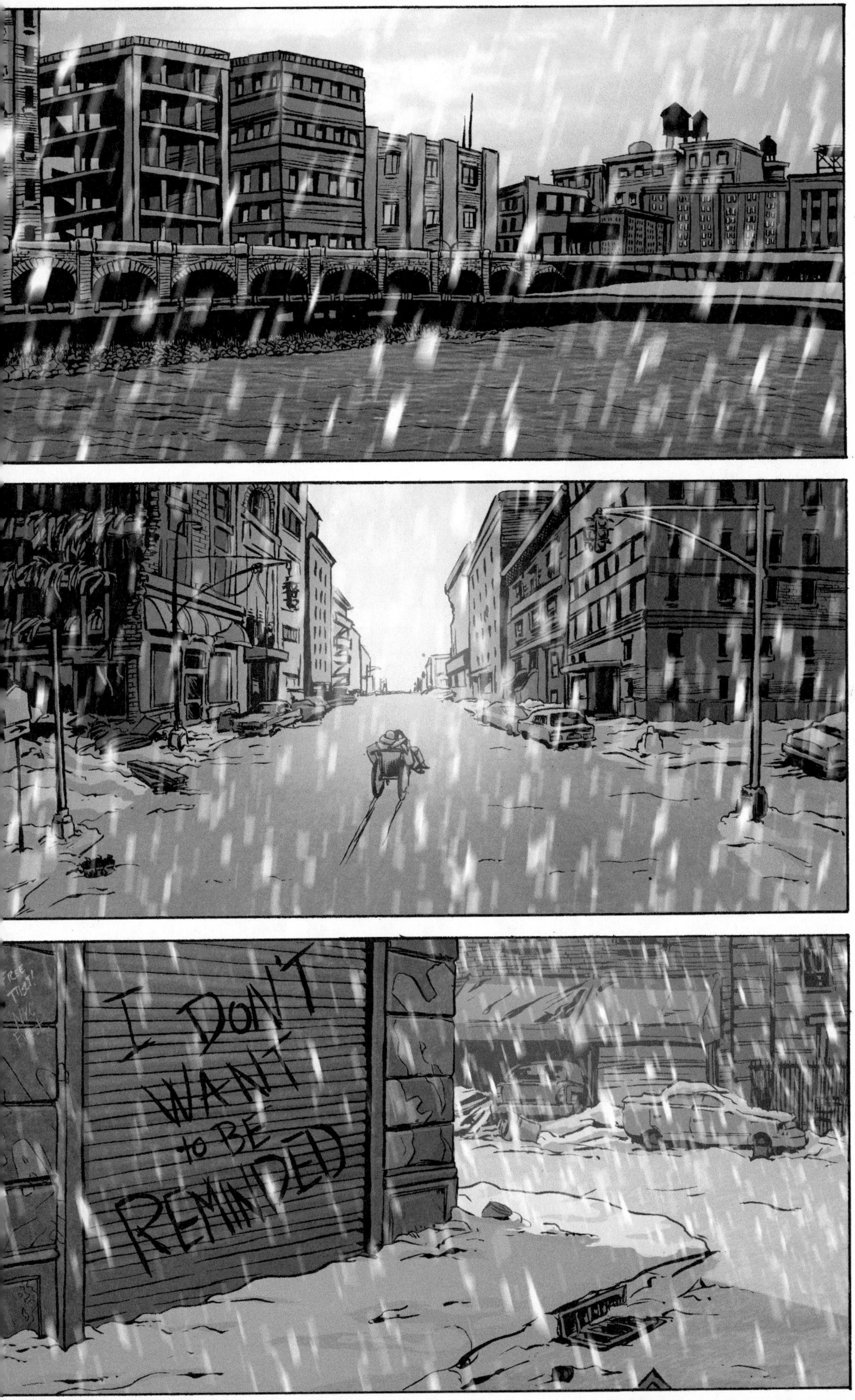

I DON'T WANT to BE REMINDED

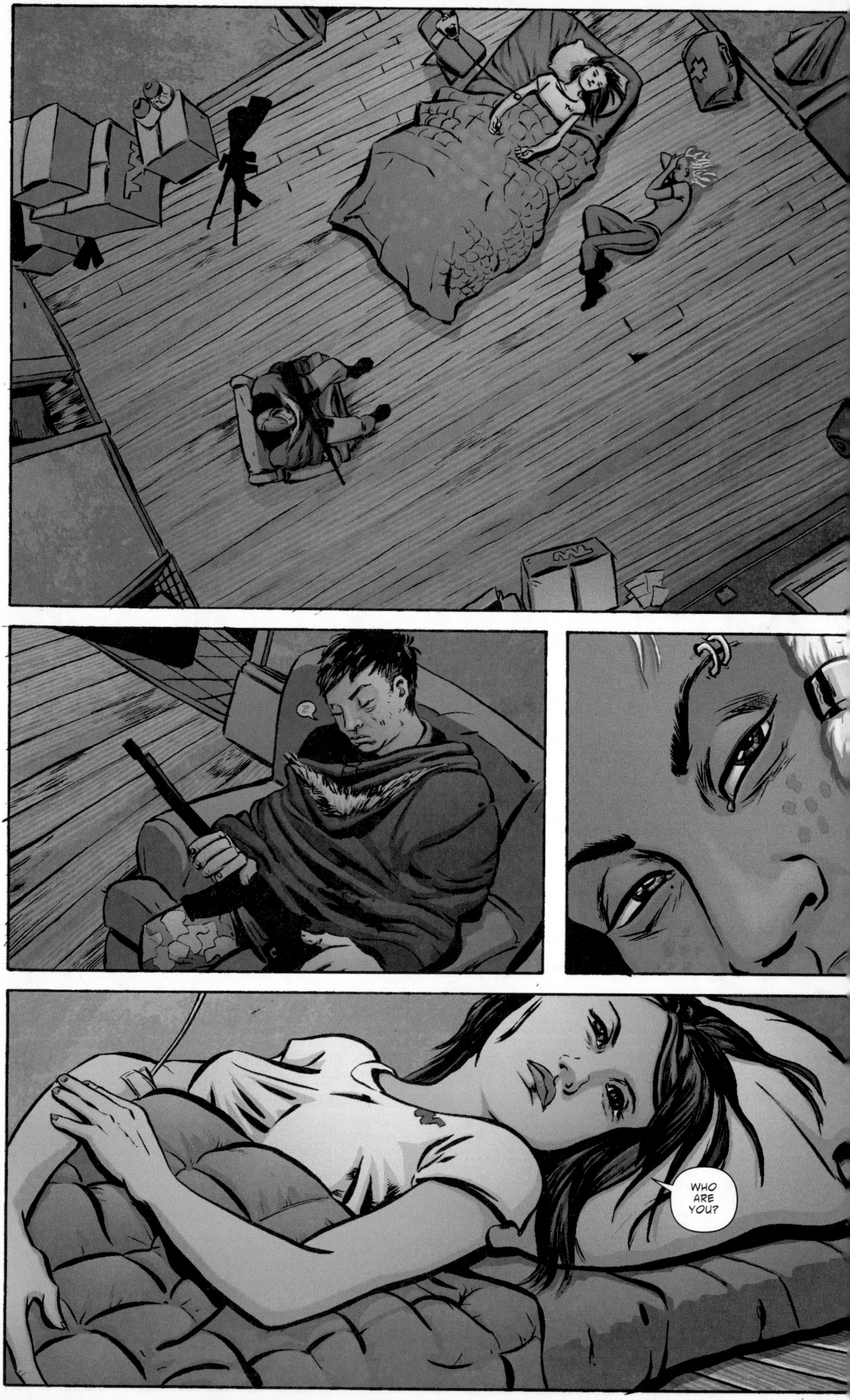

WHO ARE YOU?

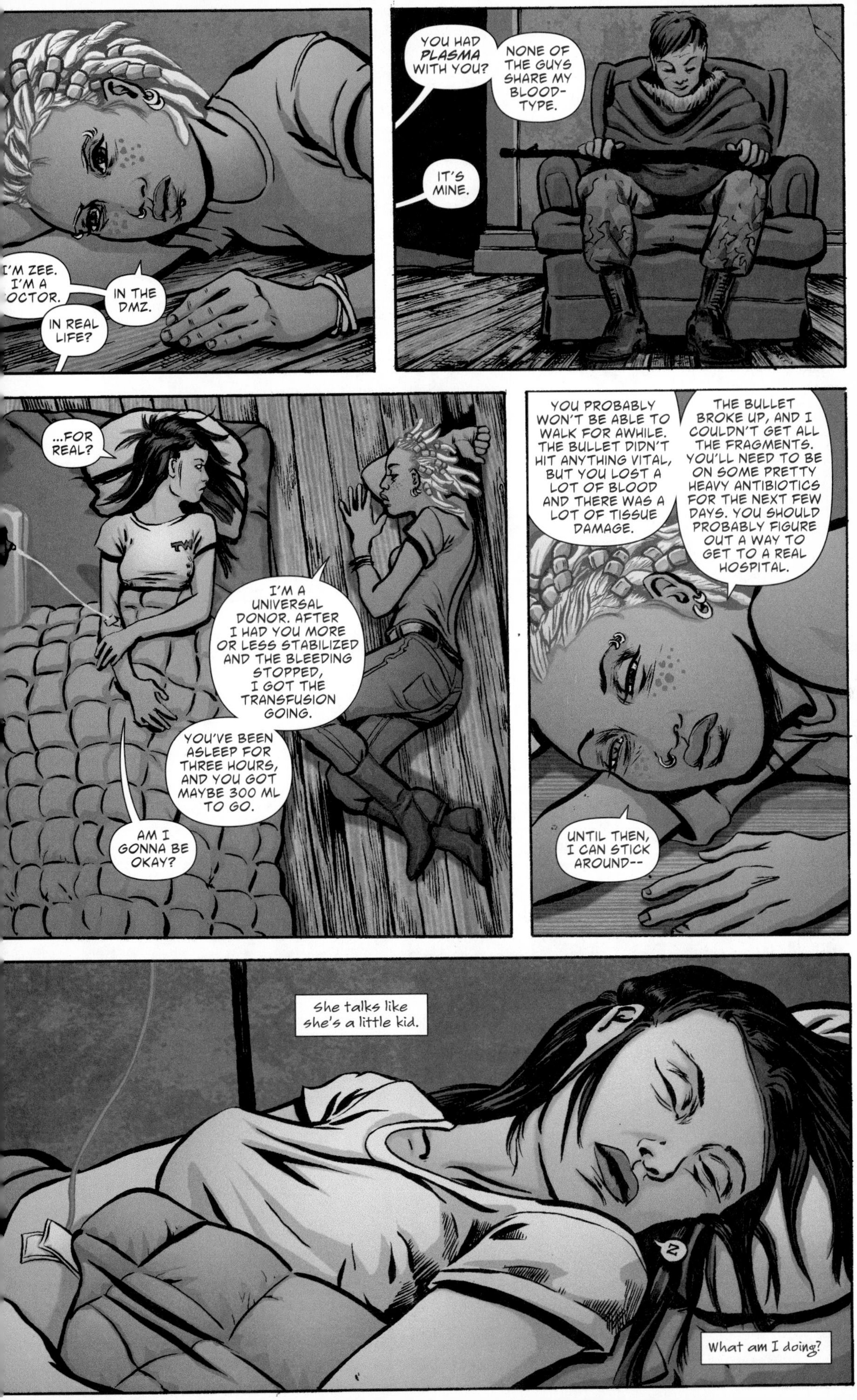
I'M ZEE. I'M A DOCTOR.
IN REAL LIFE?
IN THE DMZ.
YOU HAD PLASMA WITH YOU?
NONE OF THE GUYS SHARE MY BLOOD-TYPE.
IT'S MINE.
...FOR REAL?
I'M A UNIVERSAL DONOR. AFTER I HAD YOU MORE OR LESS STABILIZED AND THE BLEEDING STOPPED, I GOT THE TRANSFUSION GOING.
YOU'VE BEEN ASLEEP FOR THREE HOURS, AND YOU GOT MAYBE 300 ML TO GO.
AM I GONNA BE OKAY?
YOU PROBABLY WON'T BE ABLE TO WALK FOR AWHILE. THE BULLET DIDN'T HIT ANYTHING VITAL, BUT YOU LOST A LOT OF BLOOD AND THERE WAS A LOT OF TISSUE DAMAGE.
THE BULLET BROKE UP, AND I COULDN'T GET ALL THE FRAGMENTS. YOU'LL NEED TO BE ON SOME PRETTY HEAVY ANTIBIOTICS FOR THE NEXT FEW DAYS. YOU SHOULD PROBABLY FIGURE OUT A WAY TO GET TO A REAL HOSPITAL.
UNTIL THEN, I CAN STICK AROUND--
She talks like she's a little kid.
What am I doing?

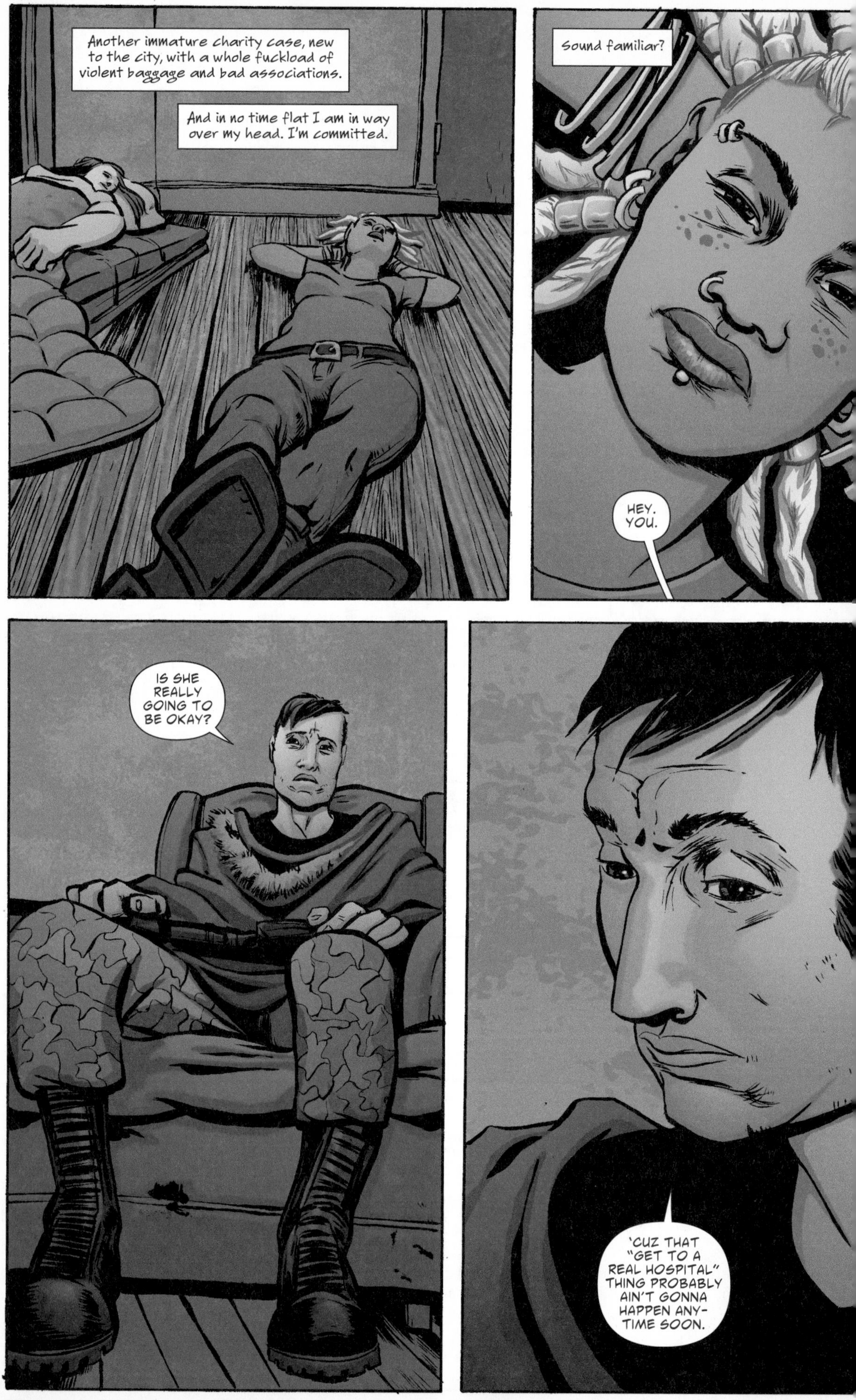
Another immature charity case, new to the city, with a whole fuckload of violent baggage and bad associations.
And in no time flat I am in way over my head. I'm committed.
Sound familiar?
HEY. YOU.
IS SHE REALLY GOING TO BE OKAY?
'CUZ THAT "GET TO A REAL HOSPITAL" THING PROBABLY AIN'T GONNA HAPPEN ANY-TIME SOON.

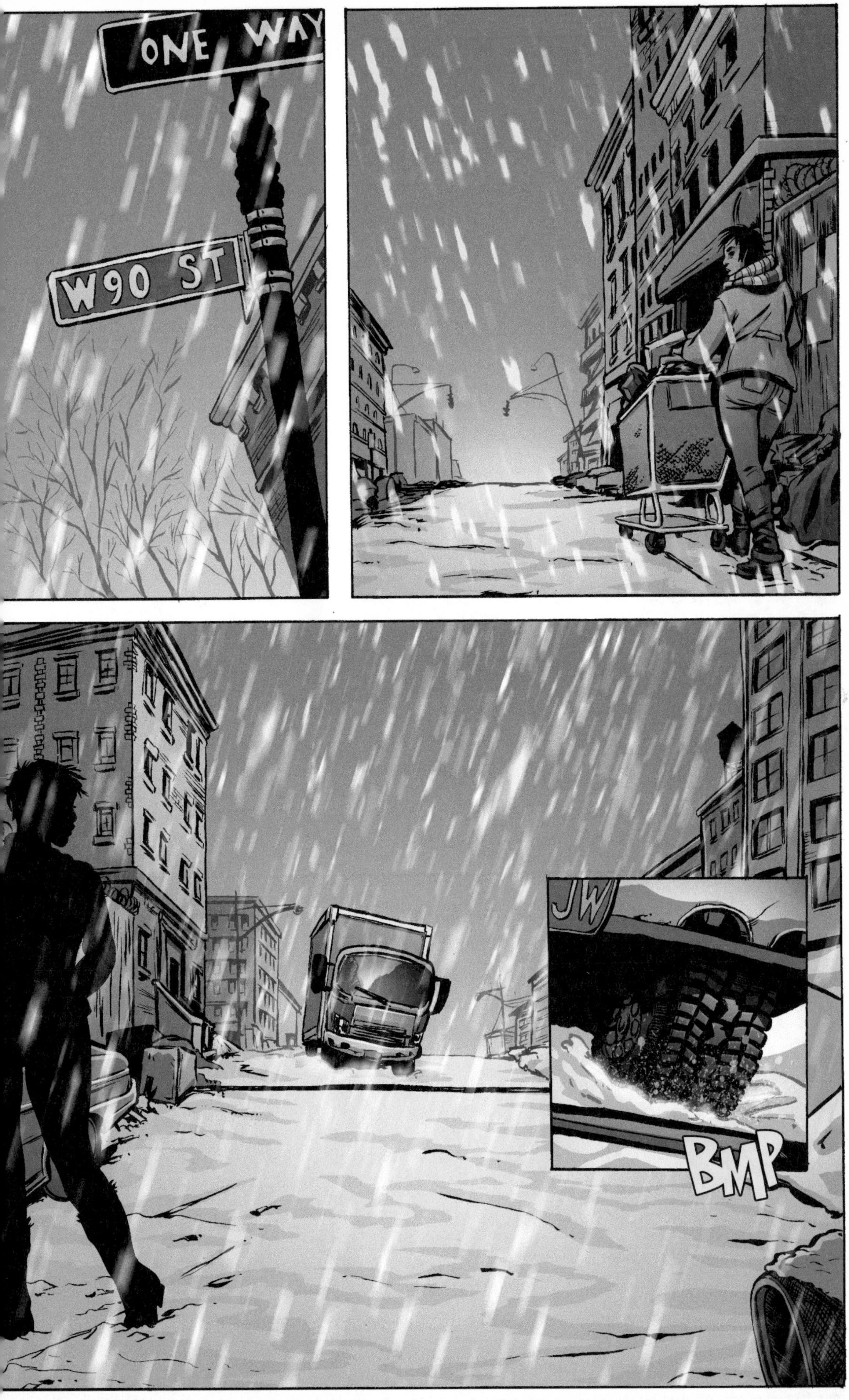
ONE WAY
W90 ST
JW
BMP

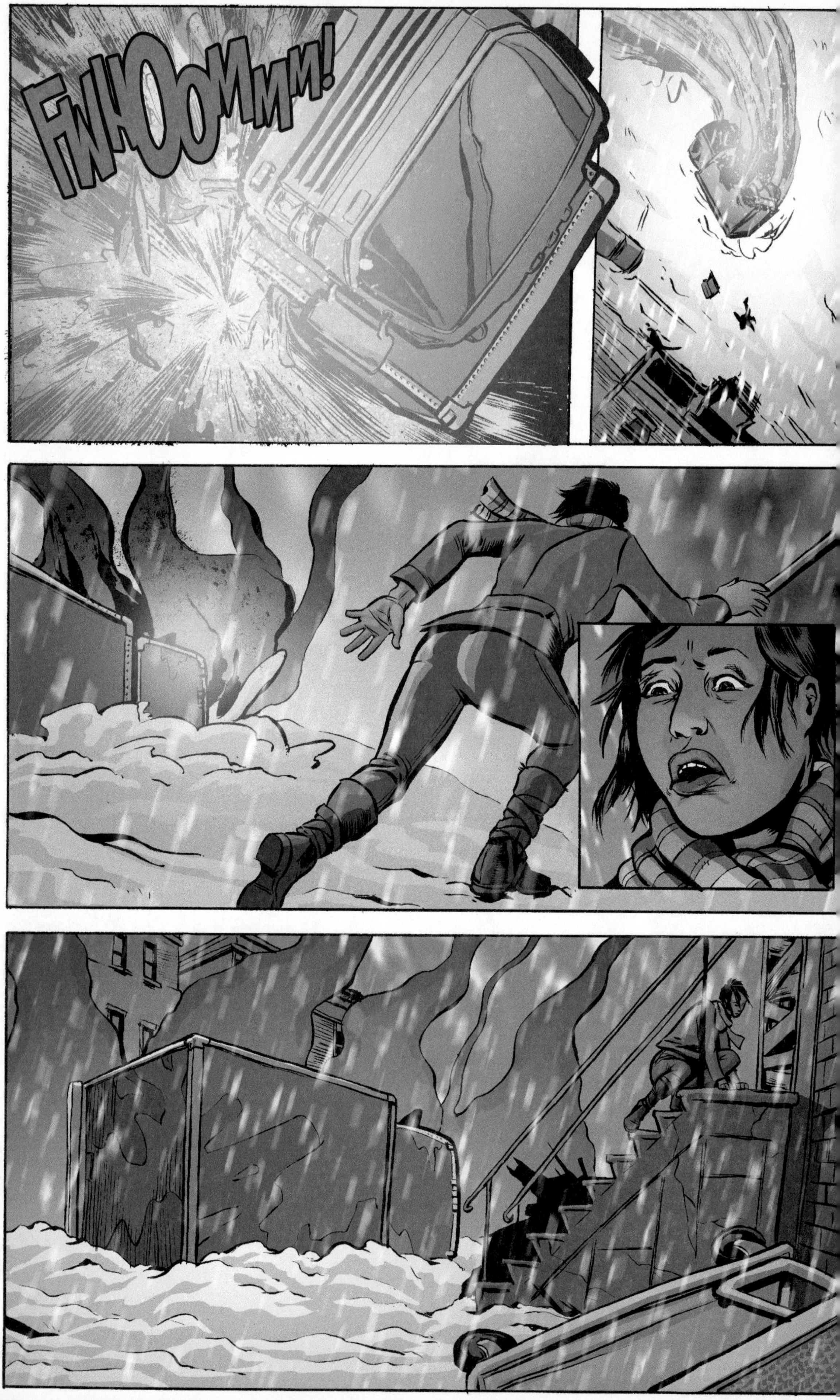
FWHOOMMM!

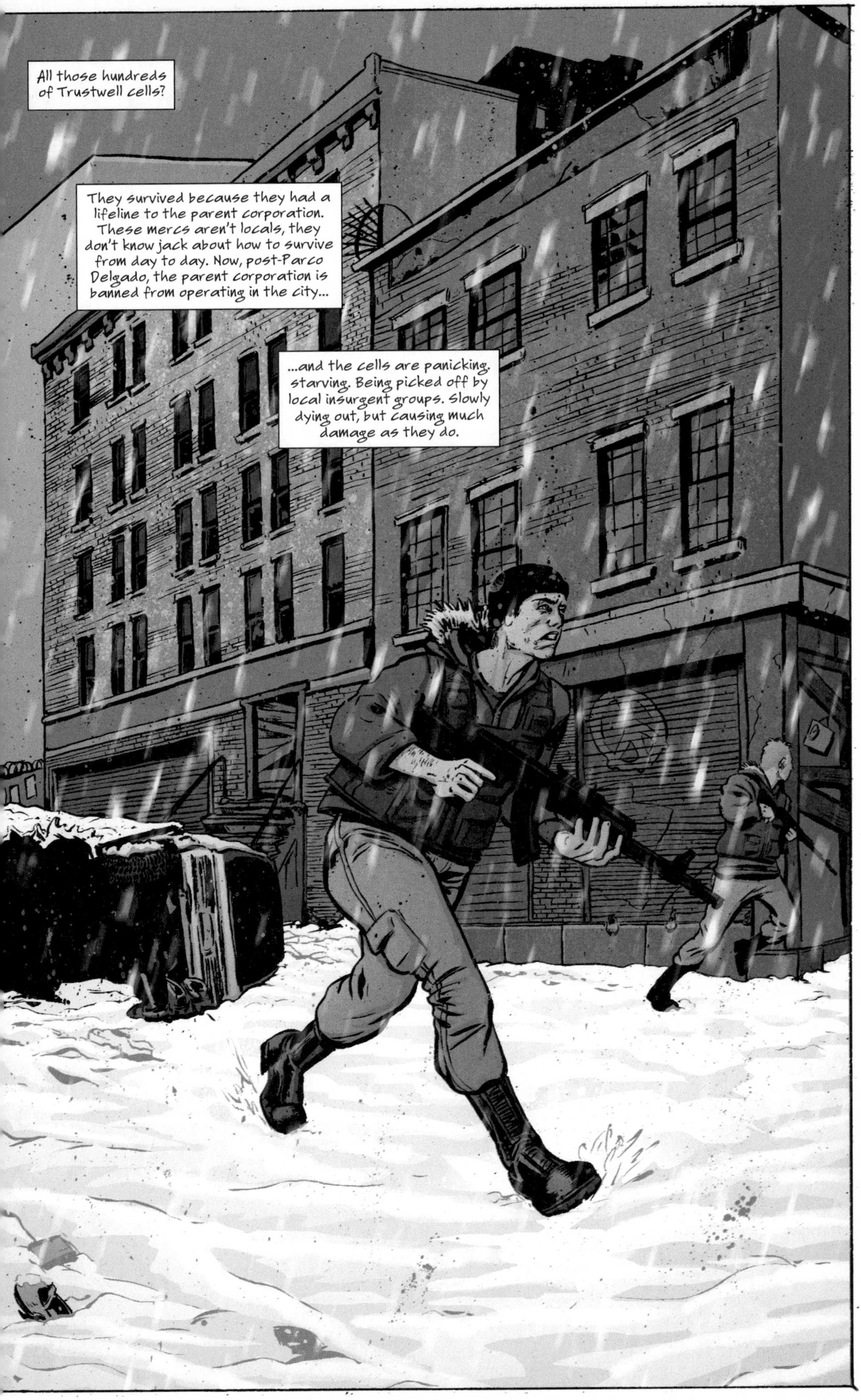
All those hundreds of Trustwell cells?
They survived because they had a lifeline to the parent corporation. These mercs aren't locals, they don't know jack about how to survive from day to day. Now, post-Parco Delgado, the parent corporation is banned from operating in the city...
...and the cells are panicking. starving. Being picked off by local insurgent groups. Slowly dying out, but causing much damage as they do.

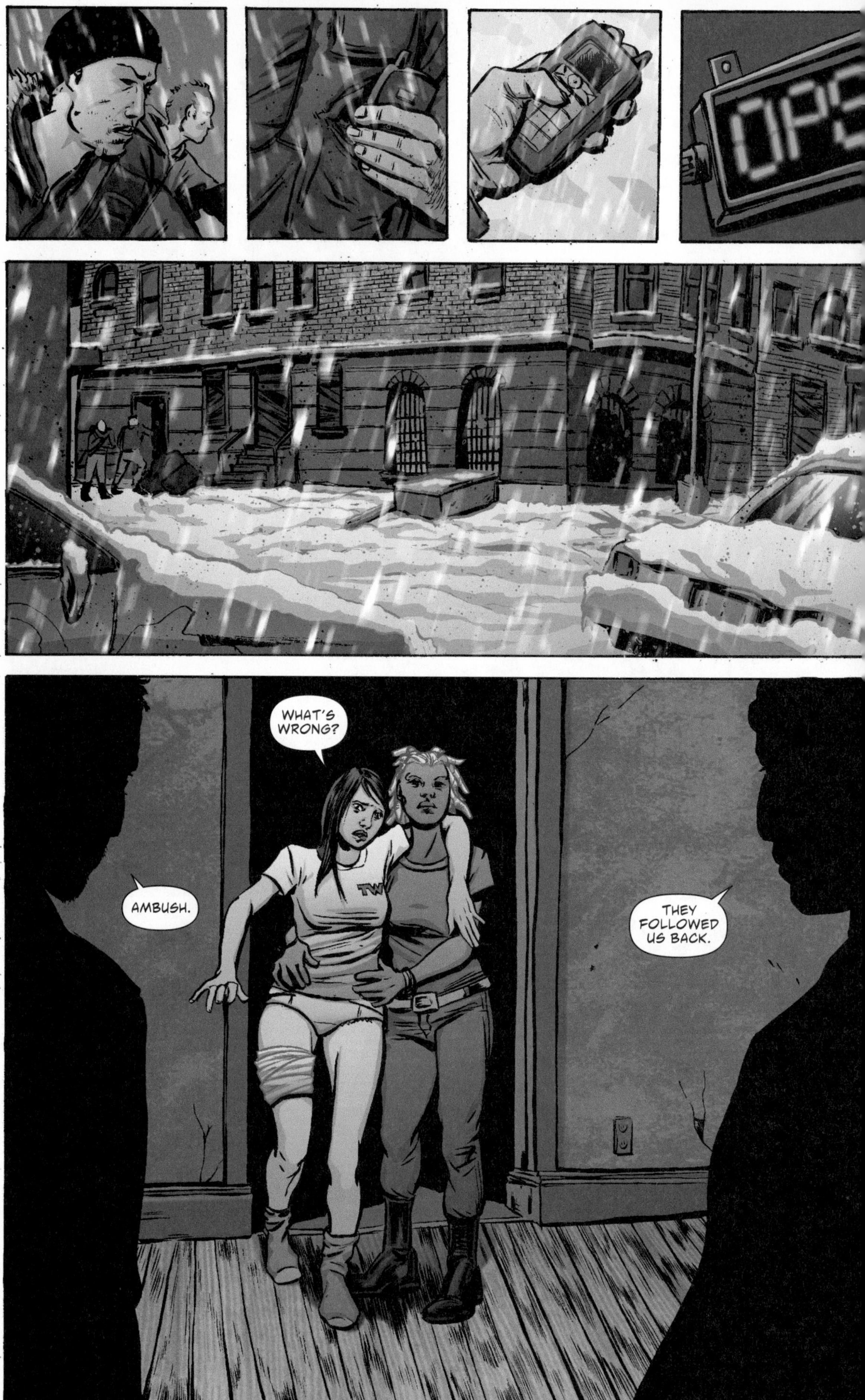
OPS
WHAT'S WRONG?
AMBUSH.
THEY FOLLOWED US BACK.

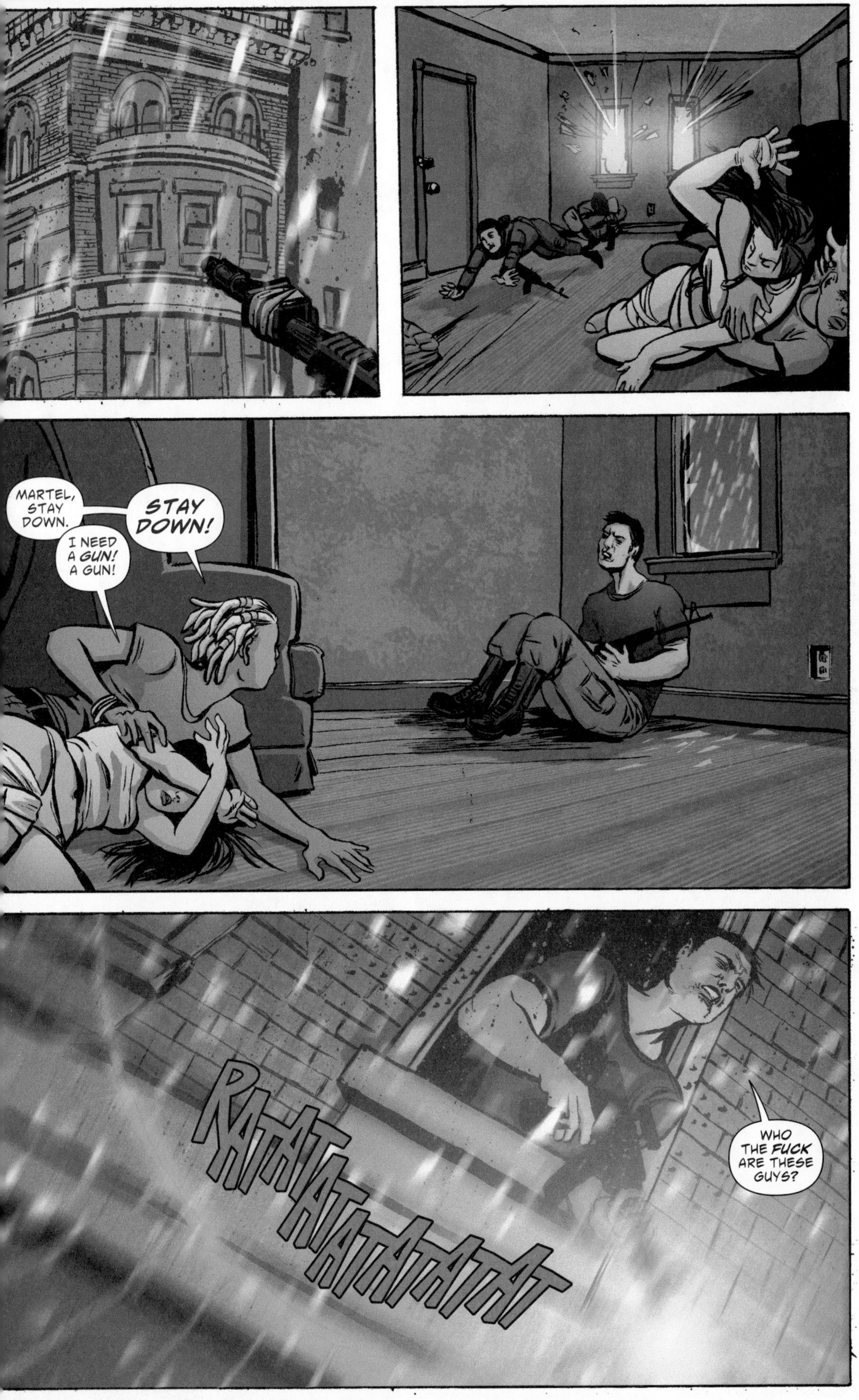
MARTEL, STAY DOWN.
STAY DOWN!
I NEED A GUN! A GUN!
RATATATATATATATAT
WHO THE FUCK ARE THESE GUYS?

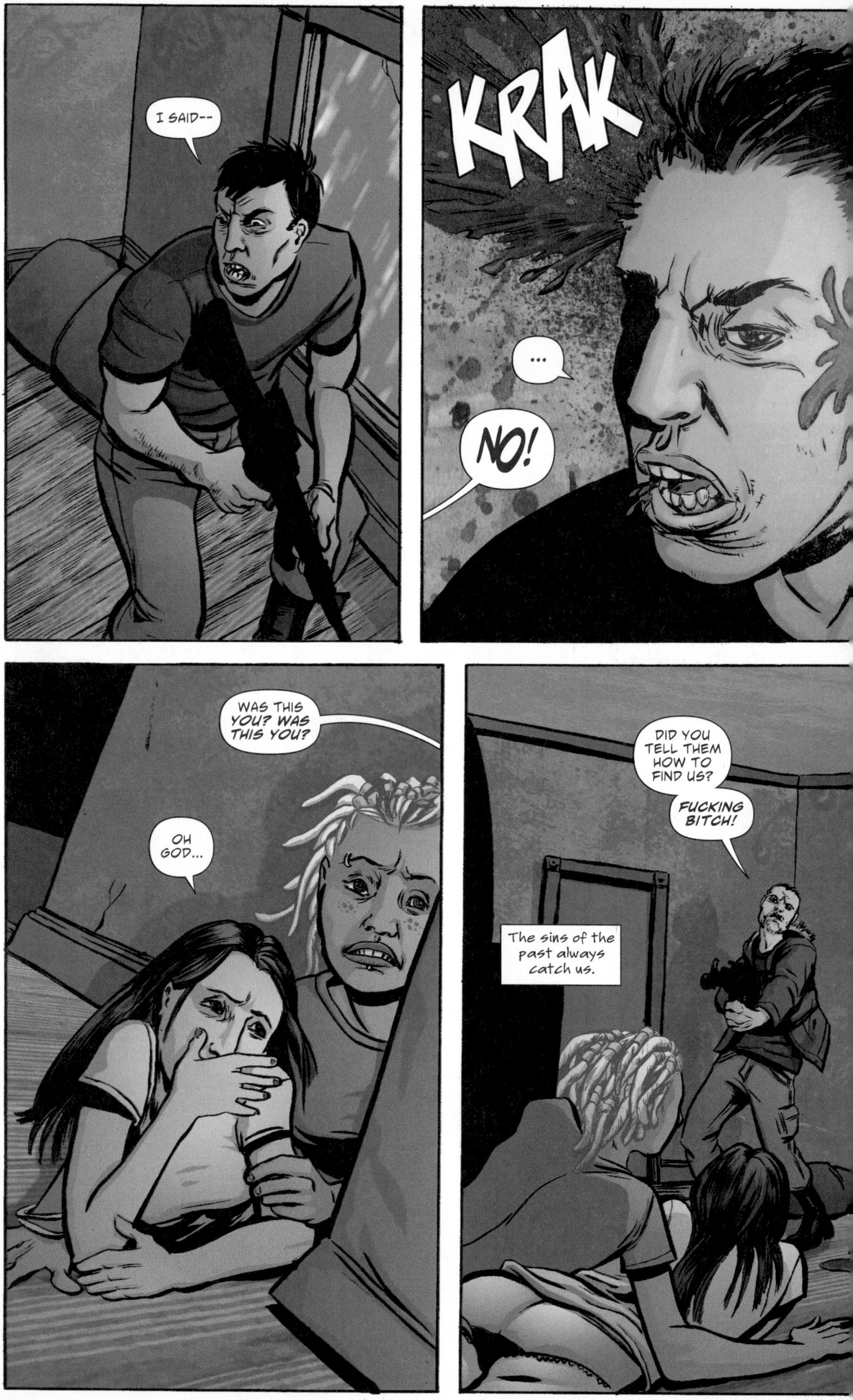
I SAID--
KRAK
...
NO!
WAS THIS YOU? WAS THIS YOU?
OH GOD...
DID YOU TELL THEM HOW TO FIND US?
FUCKING BITCH!
The sins of the past always catch us.

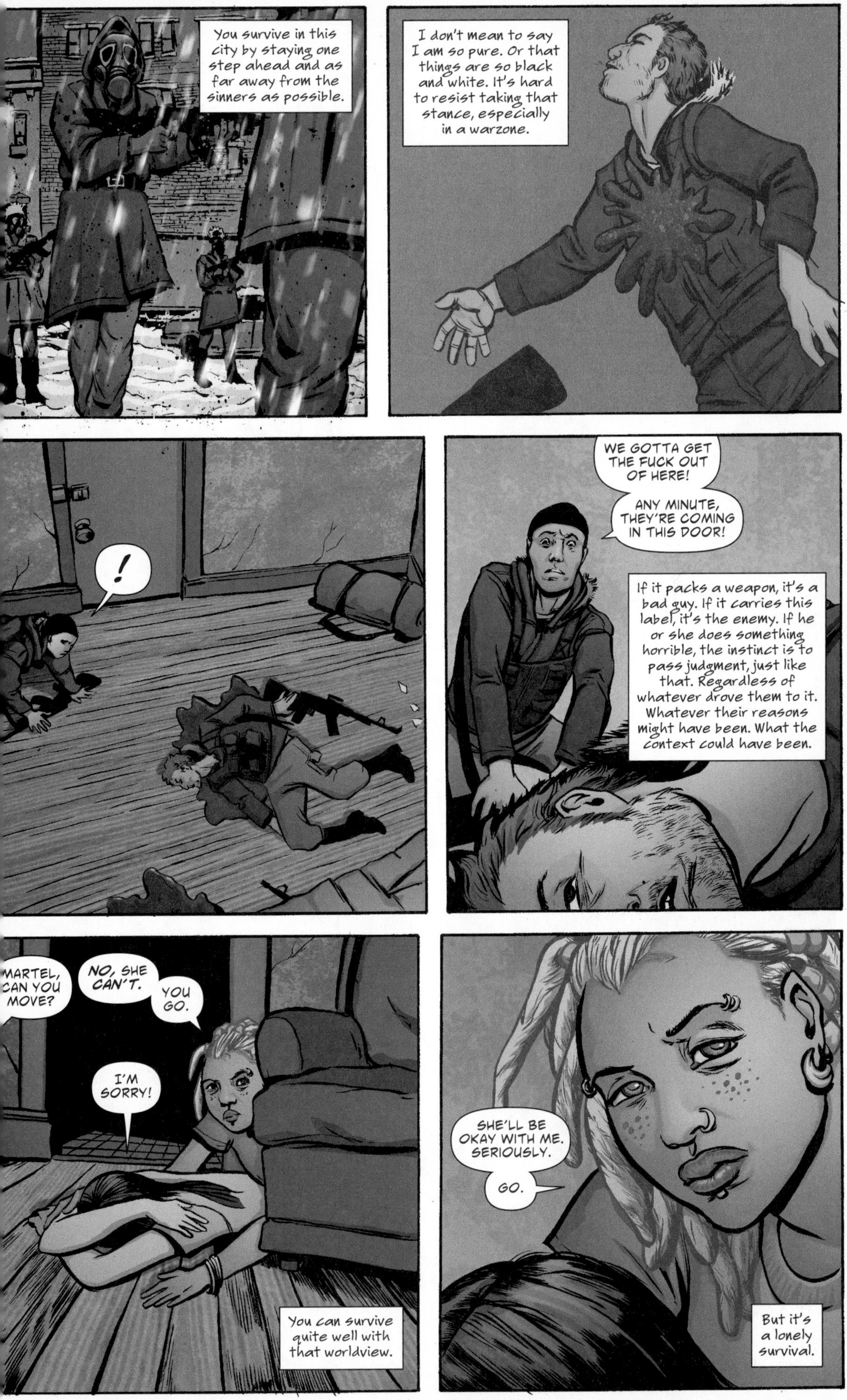
You survive in this city by staying one step ahead and as far away from the sinners as possible.
I don't mean to say I am so pure. Or that things are so black and white. It's hard to resist taking that stance, especially in a warzone.
!
WE GOTTA GET THE FUCK OUT OF HERE!
ANY MINUTE, THEY'RE COMING IN THIS DOOR!
If it packs a weapon, it's a bad guy. If it carries this label, it's the enemy. If he or she does something horrible, the instinct is to pass judgment, just like that. Regardless of whatever drove them to it. Whatever their reasons might have been. What the context could have been.
MARTEL, CAN YOU MOVE?
NO, SHE CAN'T.
YOU GO.
I'M SORRY!
You can survive quite well with that worldview.
SHE'LL BE OKAY WITH ME. SERIOUSLY.
GO.
But it's a lonely survival.

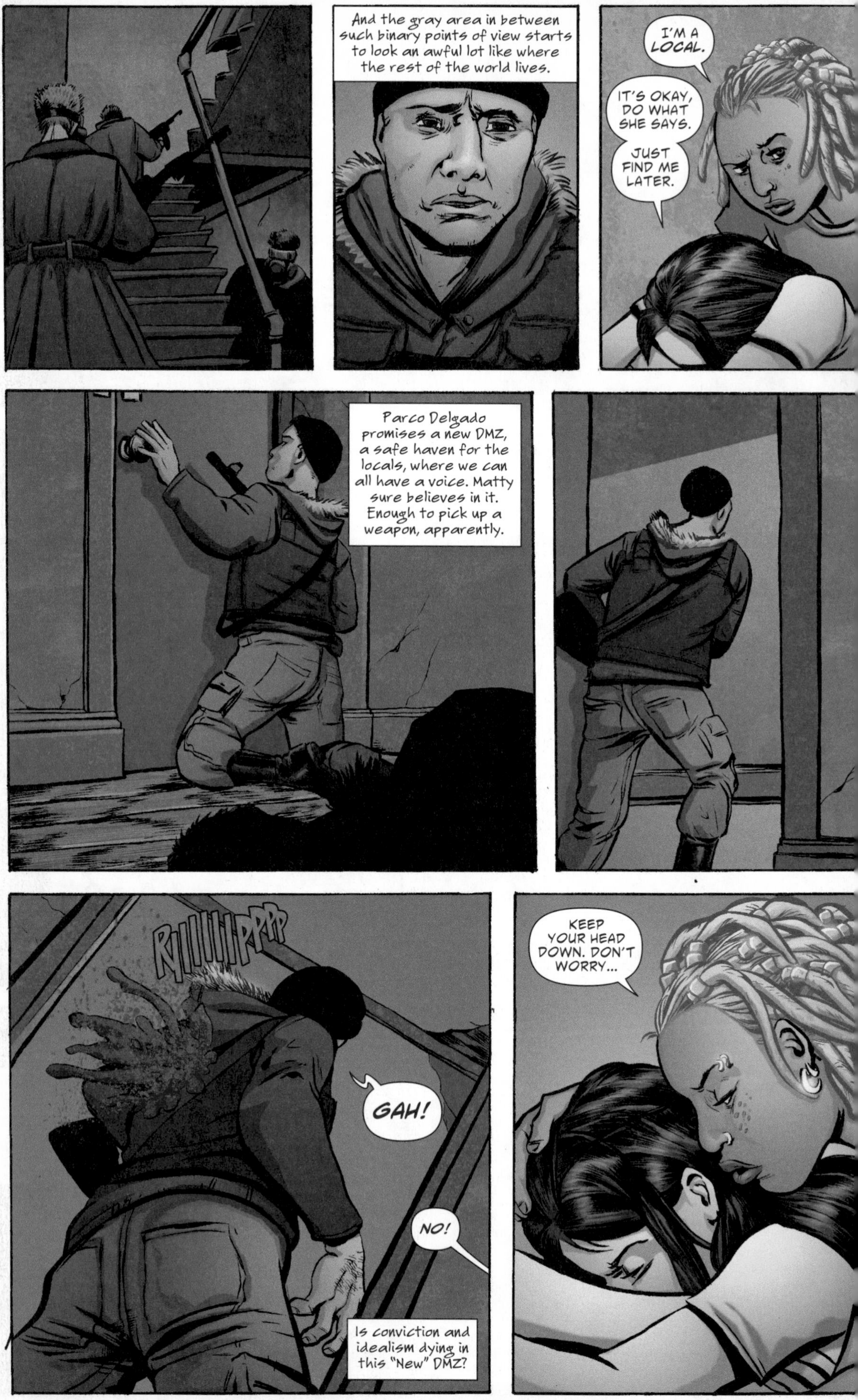

And the gray area in between such binary points of view starts to look an awful lot like where the rest of the world lives.
I'M A LOCAL.
IT'S OKAY, DO WHAT SHE SAYS.
JUST FIND ME LATER.
Parco Delgado promises a new DMZ, a safe haven for the locals, where we can all have a voice. Matty sure believes in it. Enough to pick up a weapon, apparently.
RIIIIIPPPP
GAH!
NO!
Is conviction and idealism dying in this "New" DMZ?
KEEP YOUR HEAD DOWN. DON'T WORRY...

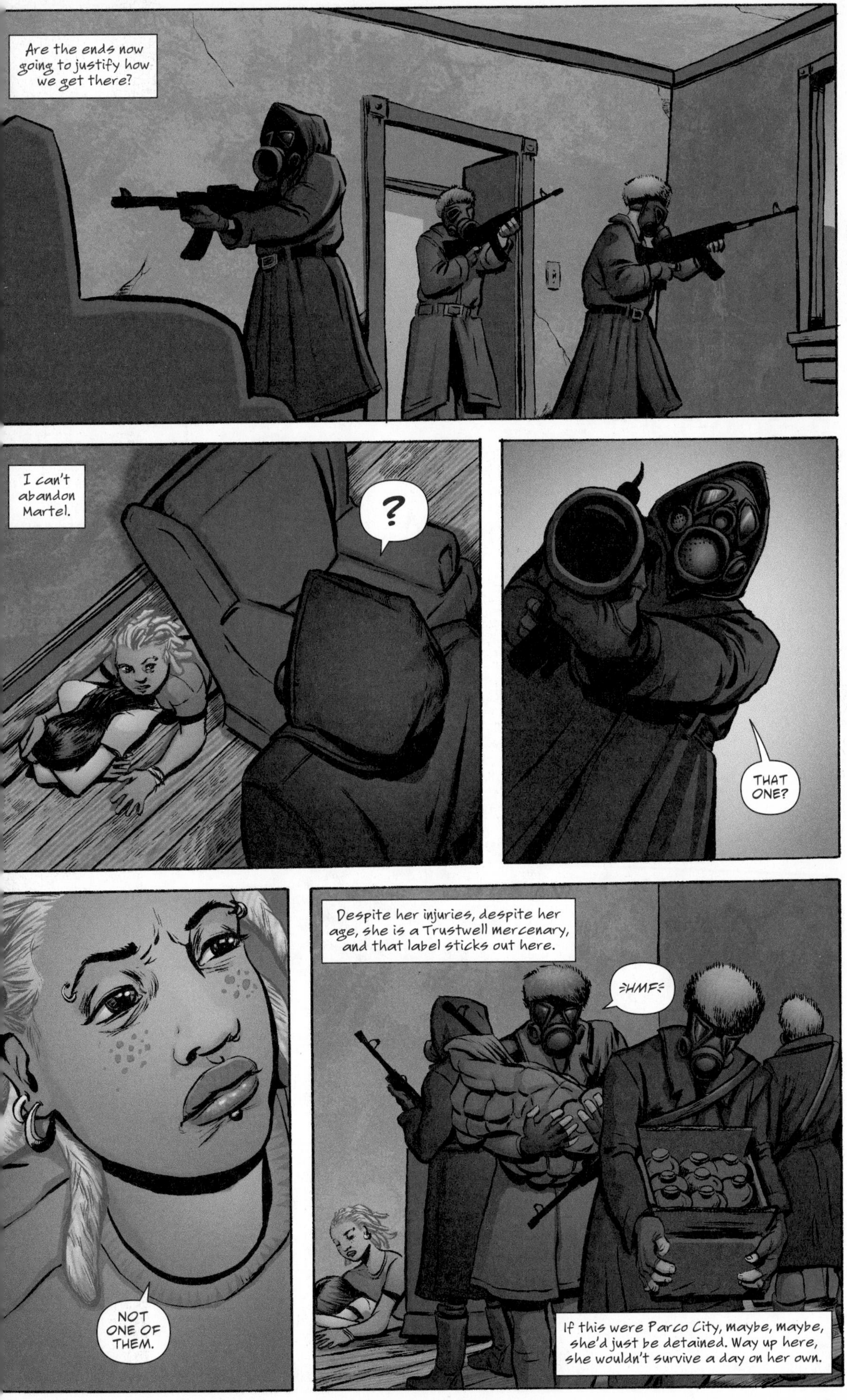
Are the ends now going to justify how we get there?
I can't abandon Martel.
?
THAT ONE?
NOT ONE OF THEM.
Despite her injuries, despite her age, she is a Trustwell mercenary, and that label sticks out here.
HMF
If this were Parco City, maybe, maybe, she'd just be detained. Way up here, she wouldn't survive a day on her own.

Unless she's with me.
Call it some kind of new conviction.
ZEE+DMZ
BRIAN WOOD writer
NIKKI COOK artist
JEROMY COX colors
JARED K. FLETCHER letters
JP LEON cover

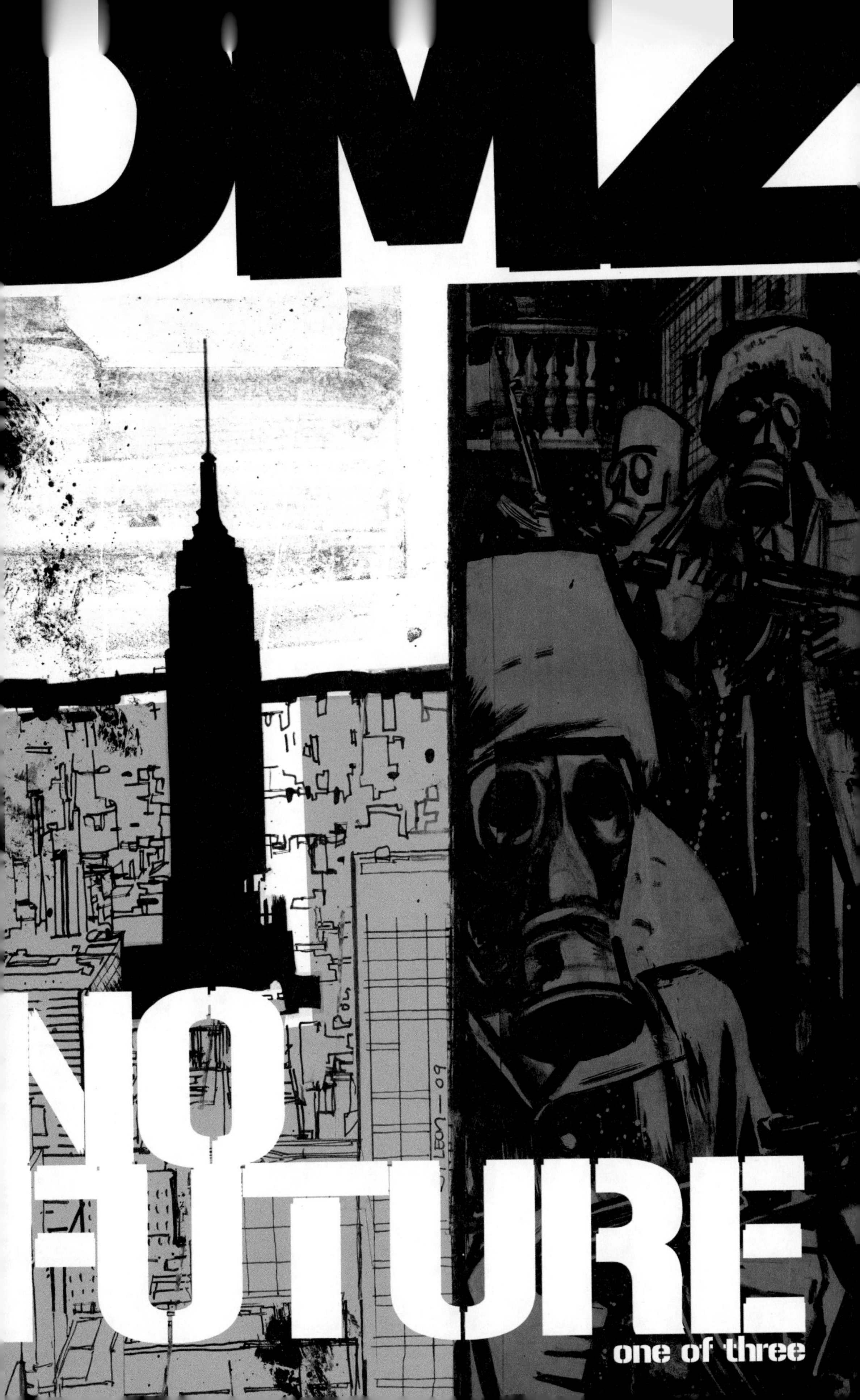
DMZ
NO FUTURE
one of three
LEON-09

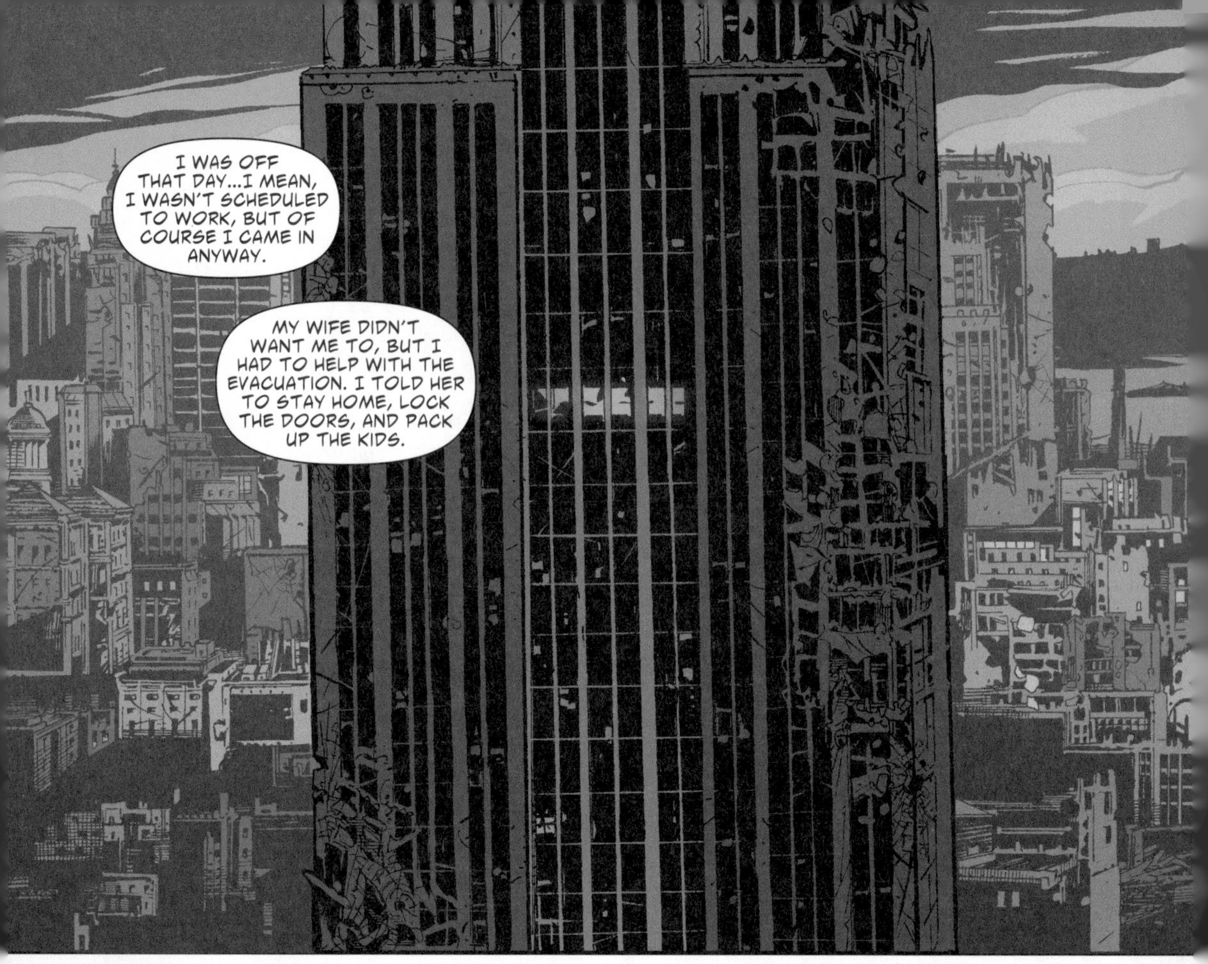
I WAS OFF THAT DAY...I MEAN, I WASN'T SCHEDULED TO WORK, BUT OF COURSE I CAME IN ANYWAY.
MY WIFE DIDN'T WANT ME TO, BUT I HAD TO HELP WITH THE EVACUATION. I TOLD HER TO STAY HOME, LOCK THE DOORS, AND PACK UP THE KIDS.

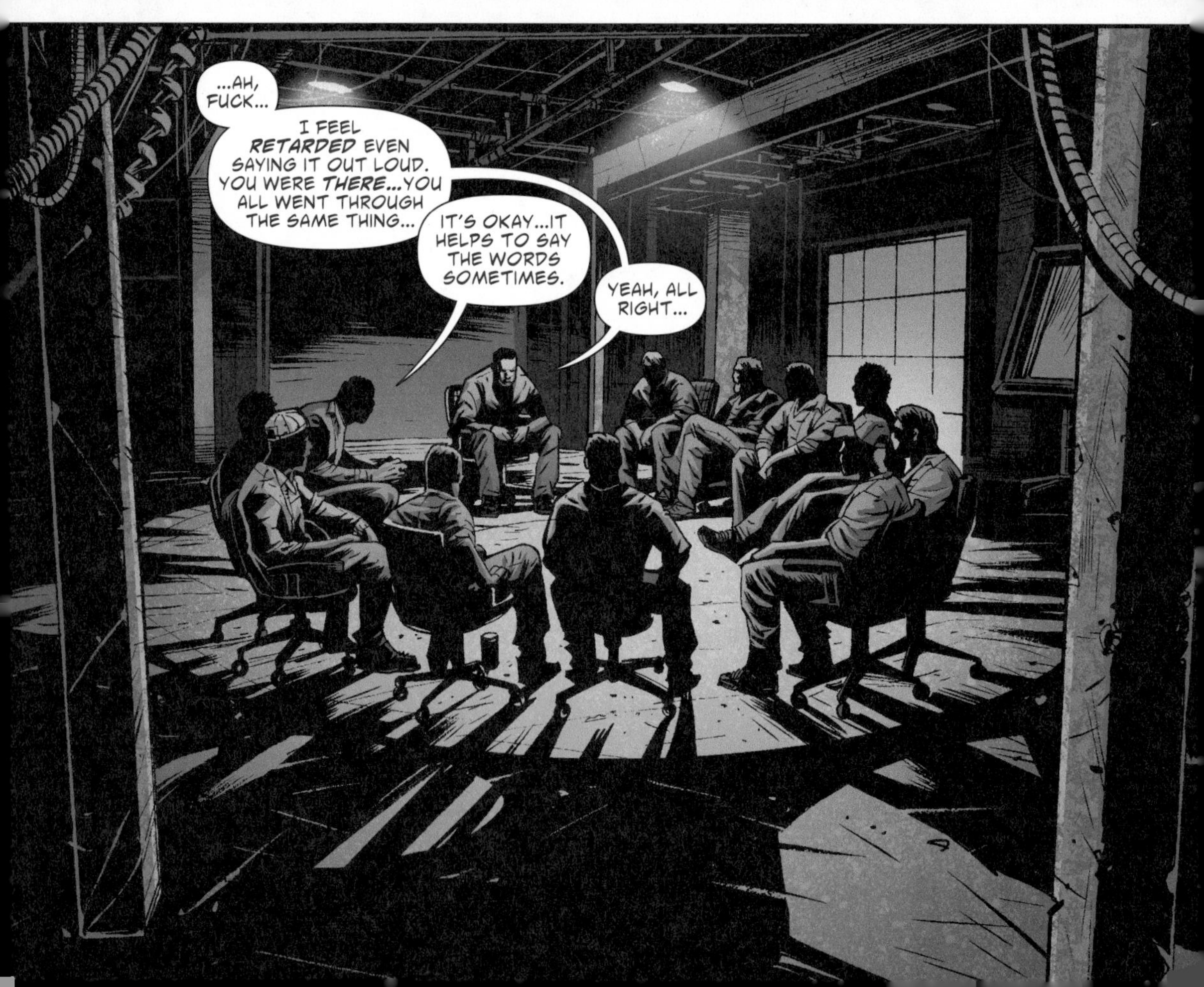
...AH, FUCK...
I FEEL *RETARDED* EVEN SAYING IT OUT LOUD. YOU WERE *THERE*...YOU ALL WENT THROUGH THE SAME THING...
IT'S OKAY...IT HELPS TO SAY THE WORDS SOMETIMES.
YEAH, ALL RIGHT...

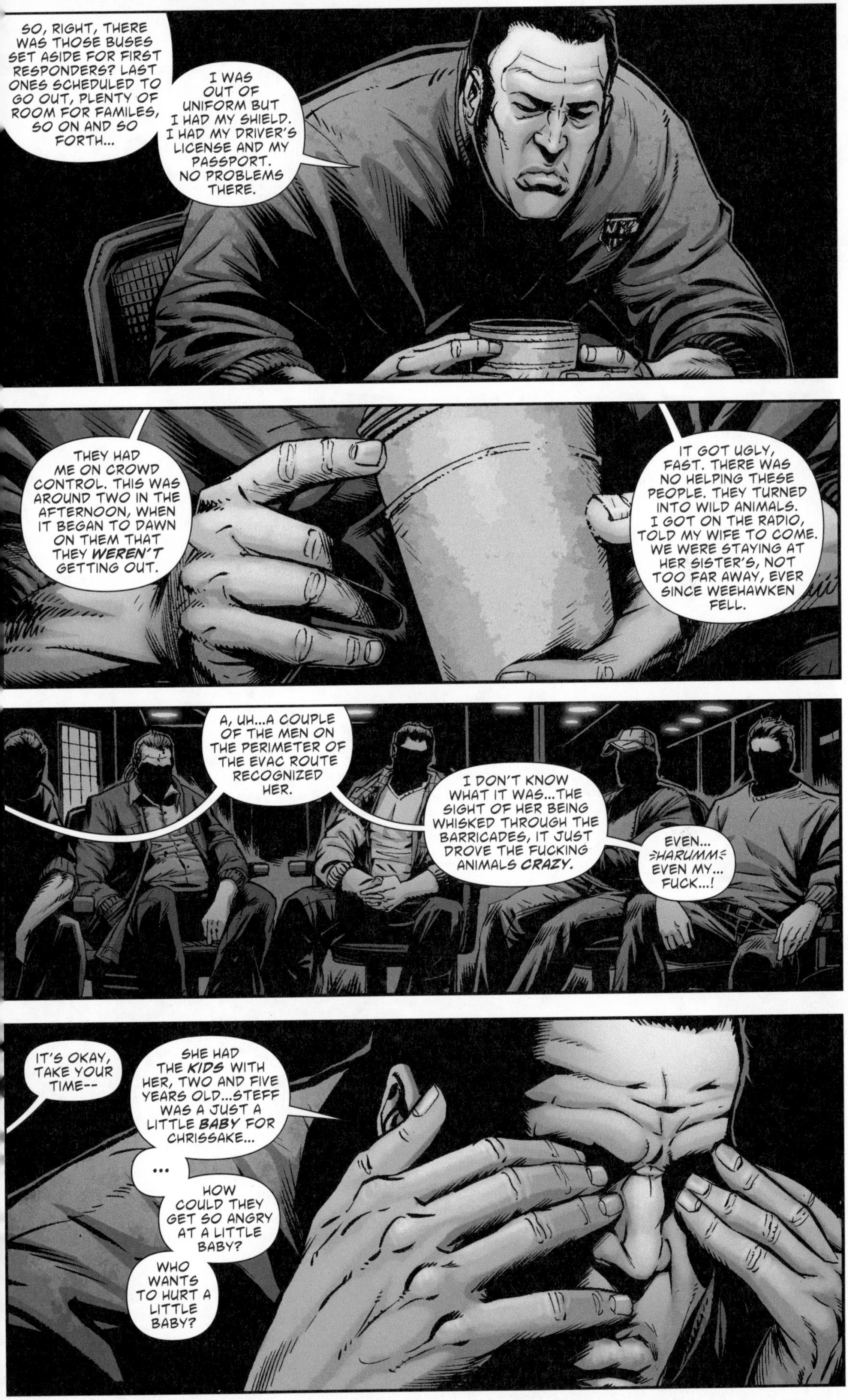
SO, RIGHT, THERE WAS THOSE BUSES SET ASIDE FOR FIRST RESPONDERS? LAST ONES SCHEDULED TO GO OUT, PLENTY OF ROOM FOR FAMILES, SO ON AND SO FORTH...
I WAS OUT OF UNIFORM BUT I HAD MY SHIELD. I HAD MY DRIVER'S LICENSE AND MY PASSPORT. NO PROBLEMS THERE.
THEY HAD ME ON CROWD CONTROL. THIS WAS AROUND TWO IN THE AFTERNOON, WHEN IT BEGAN TO DAWN ON THEM THAT THEY WEREN'T GETTING OUT.
IT GOT UGLY, FAST. THERE WAS NO HELPING THESE PEOPLE. THEY TURNED INTO WILD ANIMALS. I GOT ON THE RADIO, TOLD MY WIFE TO COME. WE WERE STAYING AT HER SISTER'S, NOT TOO FAR AWAY, EVER SINCE WEEHAWKEN FELL.
A, UH...A COUPLE OF THE MEN ON THE PERIMETER OF THE EVAC ROUTE RECOGNIZED HER.
I DON'T KNOW WHAT IT WAS...THE SIGHT OF HER BEING WHISKED THROUGH THE BARRICADES, IT JUST DROVE THE FUCKING ANIMALS CRAZY.
EVEN... HARUMM EVEN MY... FUCK...!
IT'S OKAY, TAKE YOUR TIME--
SHE HAD THE KIDS WITH HER, TWO AND FIVE YEARS OLD...STEFF WAS A JUST A LITTLE BABY FOR CHRISSAKE...
...
HOW COULD THEY GET SO ANGRY AT A LITTLE BABY?
WHO WANTS TO HURT A LITTLE BABY?

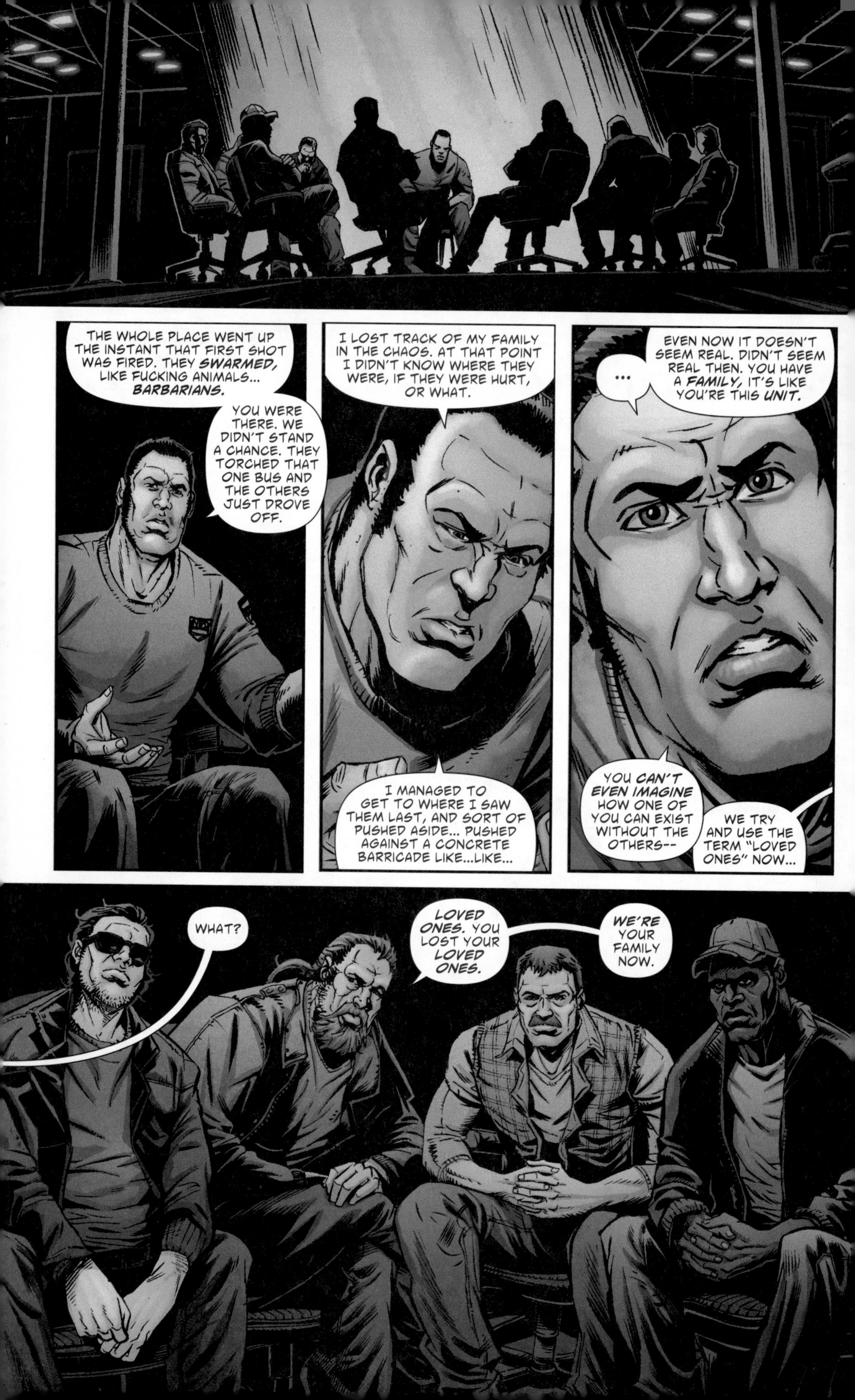
THE WHOLE PLACE WENT UP THE INSTANT THAT FIRST SHOT WAS FIRED. THEY SWARMED, LIKE FUCKING ANIMALS... BARBARIANS.
YOU WERE THERE. WE DIDN'T STAND A CHANCE. THEY TORCHED THAT ONE BUS AND THE OTHERS JUST DROVE OFF.
I LOST TRACK OF MY FAMILY IN THE CHAOS. AT THAT POINT I DIDN'T KNOW WHERE THEY WERE, IF THEY WERE HURT, OR WHAT.
I MANAGED TO GET TO WHERE I SAW THEM LAST, AND SORT OF PUSHED ASIDE... PUSHED AGAINST A CONCRETE BARRICADE LIKE...LIKE...
...
EVEN NOW IT DOESN'T SEEM REAL. DIDN'T SEEM REAL THEN. YOU HAVE A FAMILY, IT'S LIKE YOU'RE THIS UNIT.
YOU CAN'T EVEN IMAGINE HOW ONE OF YOU CAN EXIST WITHOUT THE OTHERS--
WE TRY AND USE THE TERM "LOVED ONES" NOW...
WHAT?
LOVED ONES. YOU LOST YOUR LOVED ONES.
WE'RE YOUR FAMILY NOW.

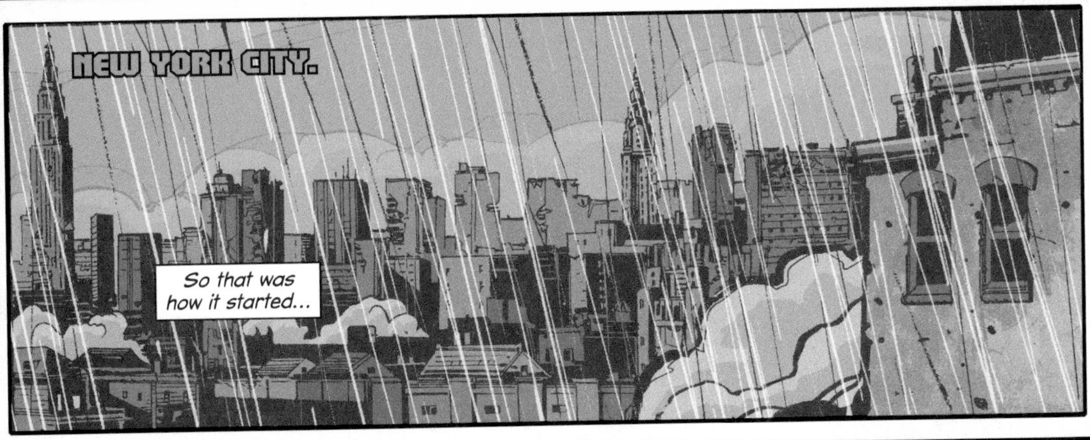
NEW YORK CITY.
So that was how it started...

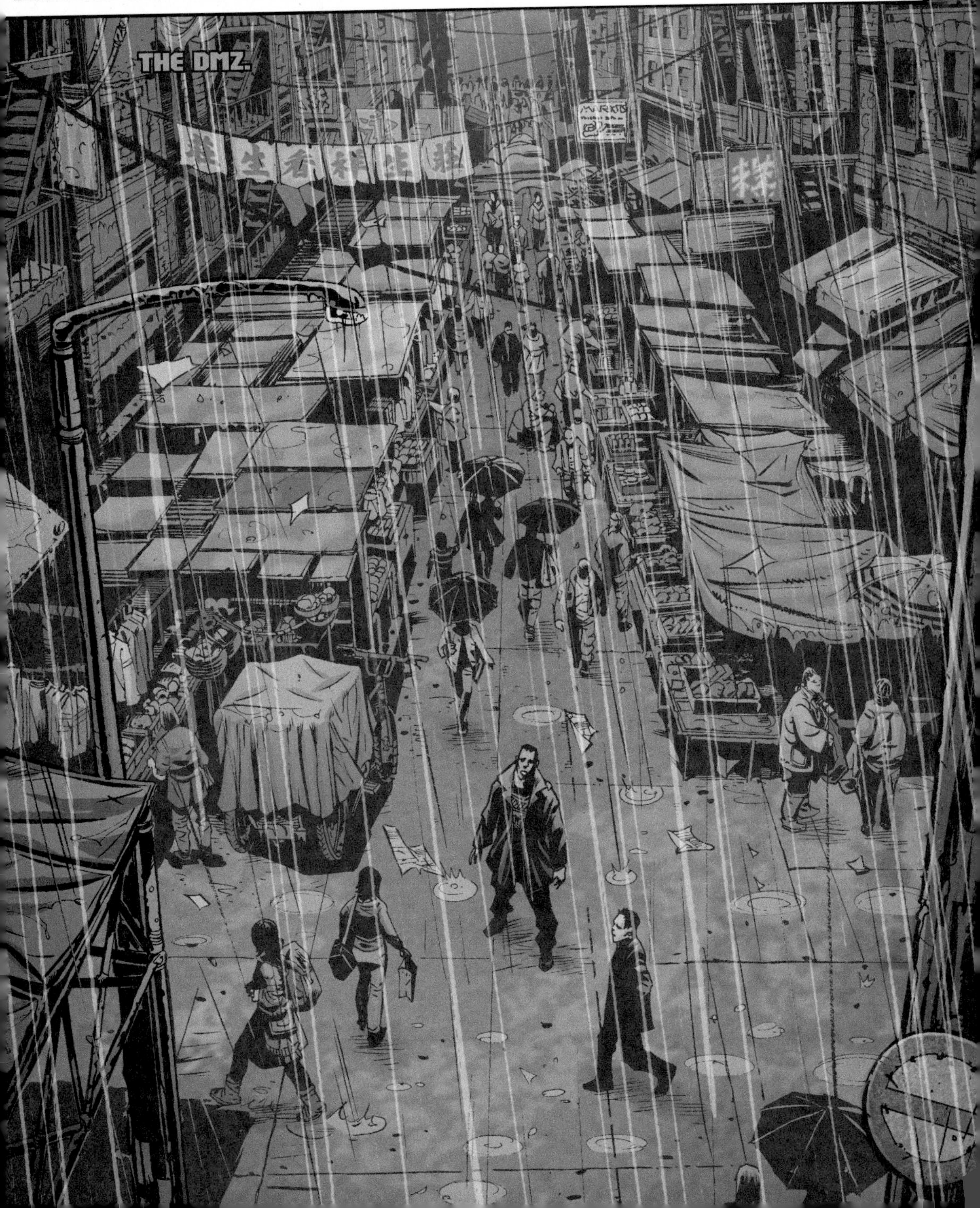
THE DMZ.

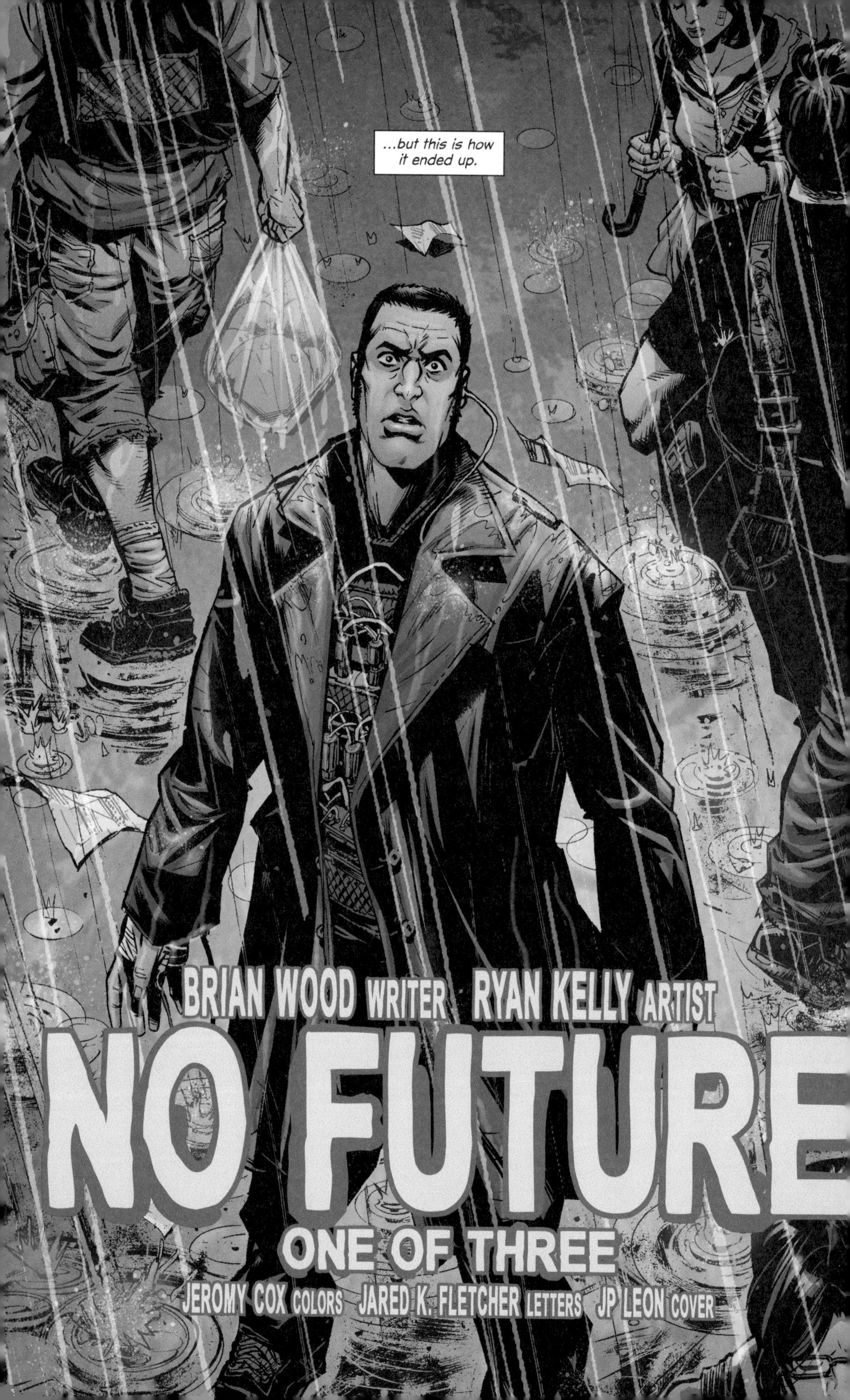
...but this is how it ended up.
BRIAN WOOD WRITER RYAN KELLY ARTIST
NO FUTURE
ONE OF THREE
JEROMY COX COLORS JARED K. FLETCHER LETTERS JP LEON COVER

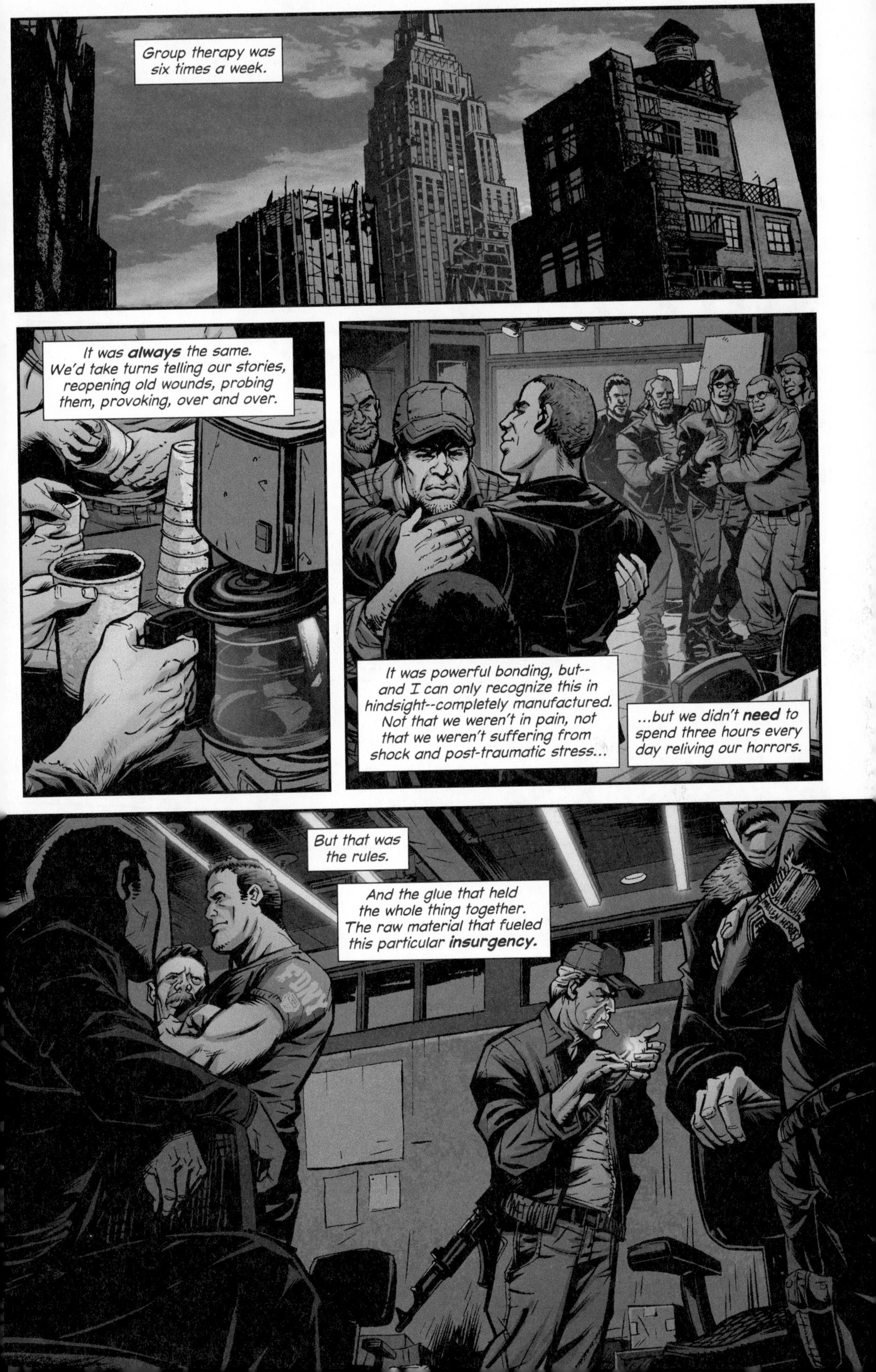
Group therapy was six times a week.
It was **always** the same. We'd take turns telling our stories, reopening old wounds, probing them, provoking, over and over.
It was powerful bonding, but--and I can only recognize this in hindsight--completely manufactured. Not that we weren't in pain, not that we weren't suffering from shock and post-traumatic stress...
...but we didn't **need** to spend three hours every day reliving our horrors.
But that was the rules.
And the glue that held the whole thing together. The raw material that fueled this particular **insurgency.**
FDNY

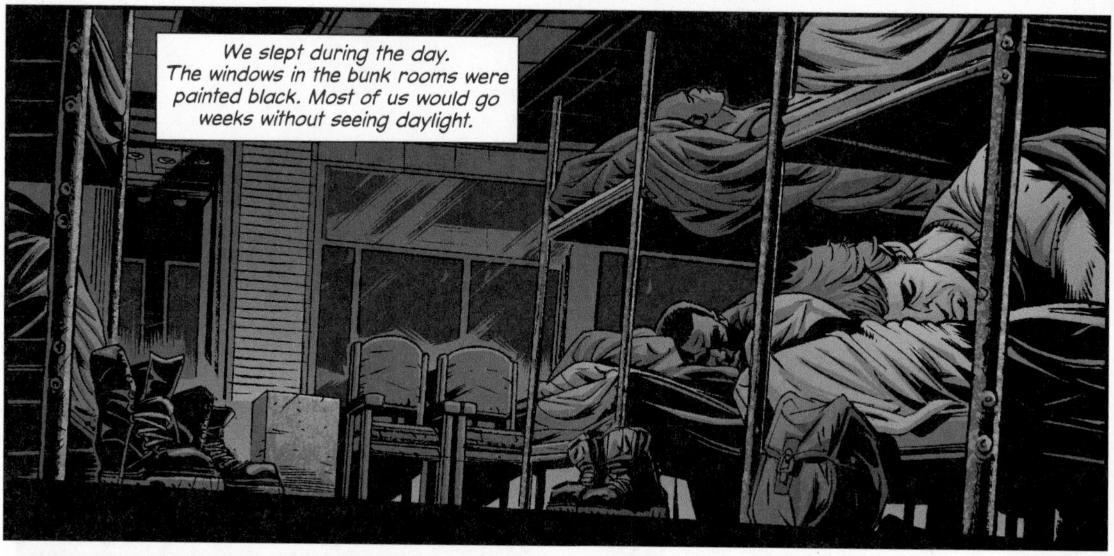
We slept during the day. The windows in the bunk rooms were painted black. Most of us would go weeks without seeing daylight.

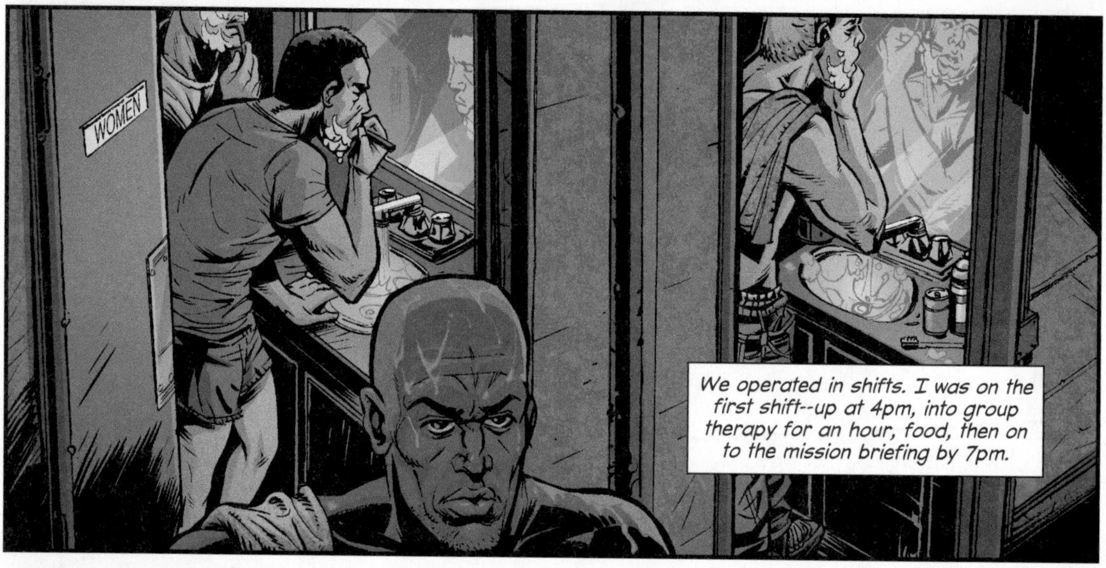
WOMEN
We operated in shifts. I was on the first shift--up at 4pm, into group therapy for an hour, food, then on to the mission briefing by 7pm.

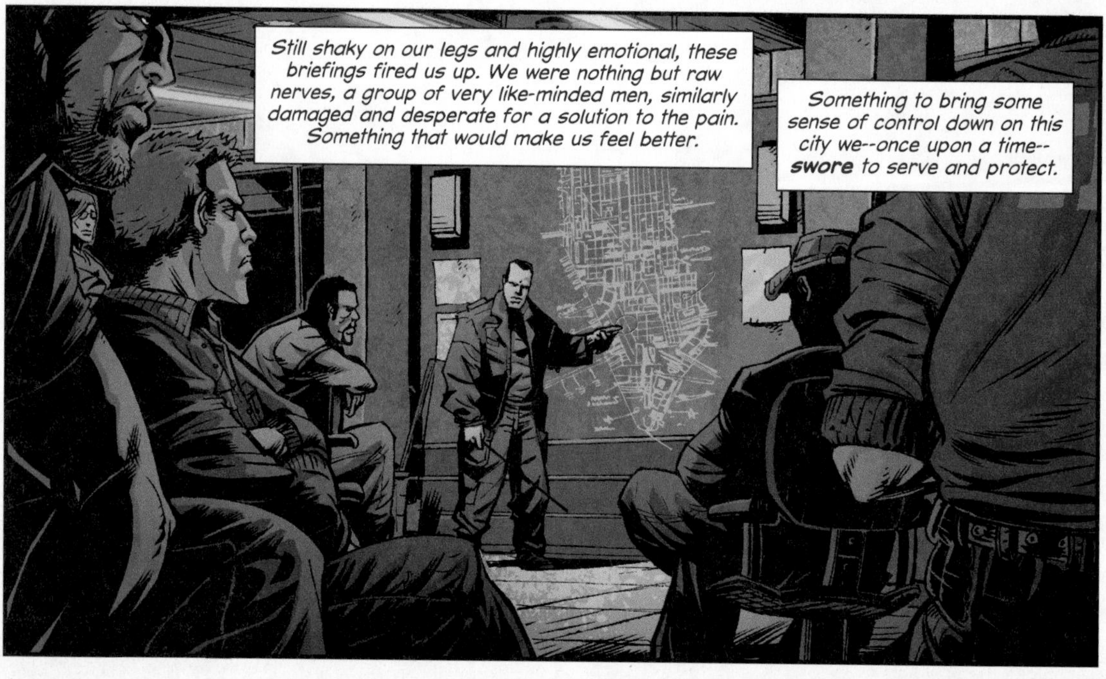
Still shaky on our legs and highly emotional, these briefings fired us up. We were nothing but raw nerves, a group of very like-minded men, similarly damaged and desperate for a solution to the pain. Something that would make us feel better.
Something to bring some sense of control down on this city we--once upon a time--**swore** to serve and protect.

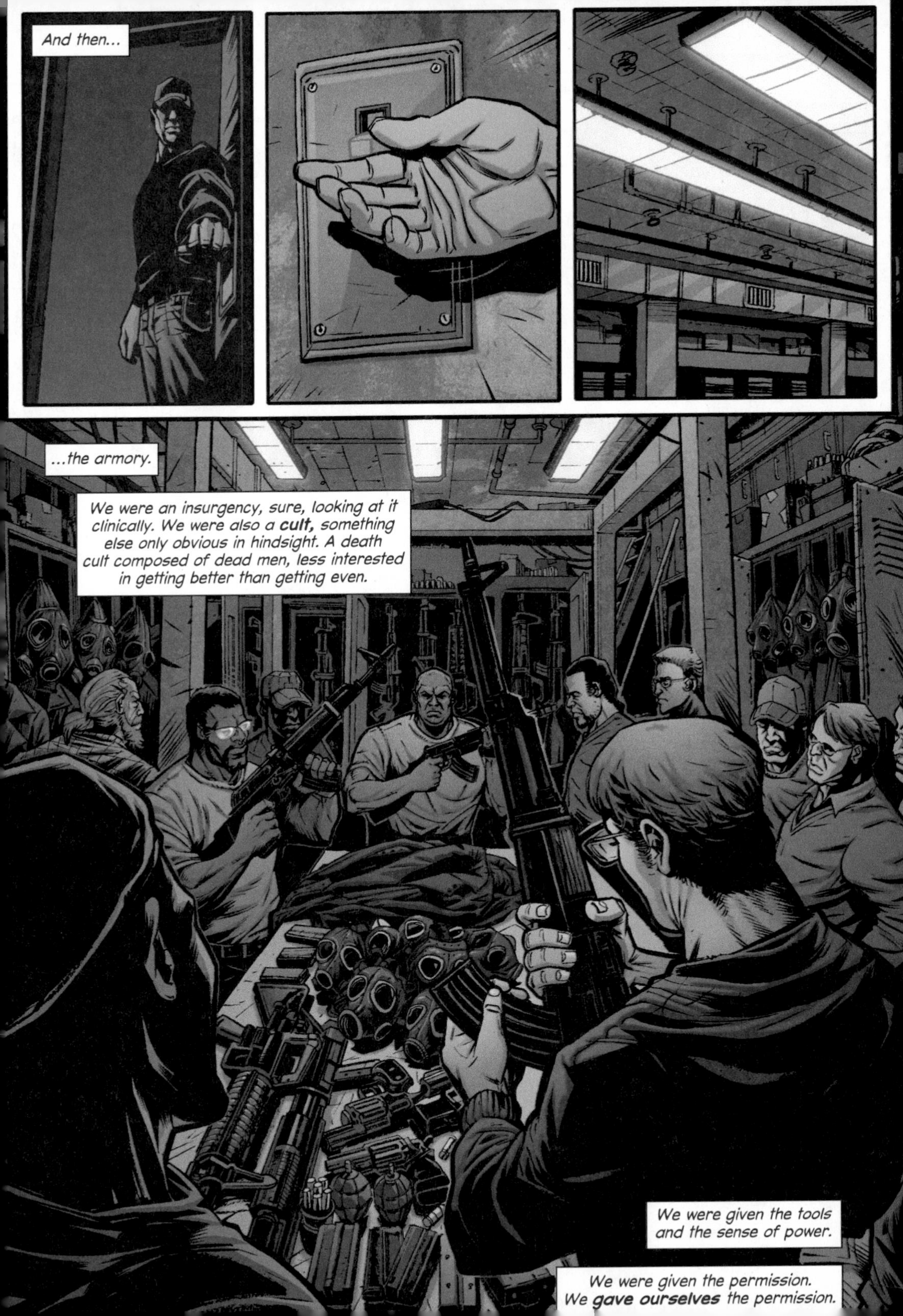
And then...
...the armory.
We were an insurgency, sure, looking at it clinically. We were also a **cult,** something else only obvious in hindsight. A death cult composed of dead men, less interested in getting better than getting even.
We were given the tools and the sense of power.
We were given the permission. We **gave ourselves** the permission.

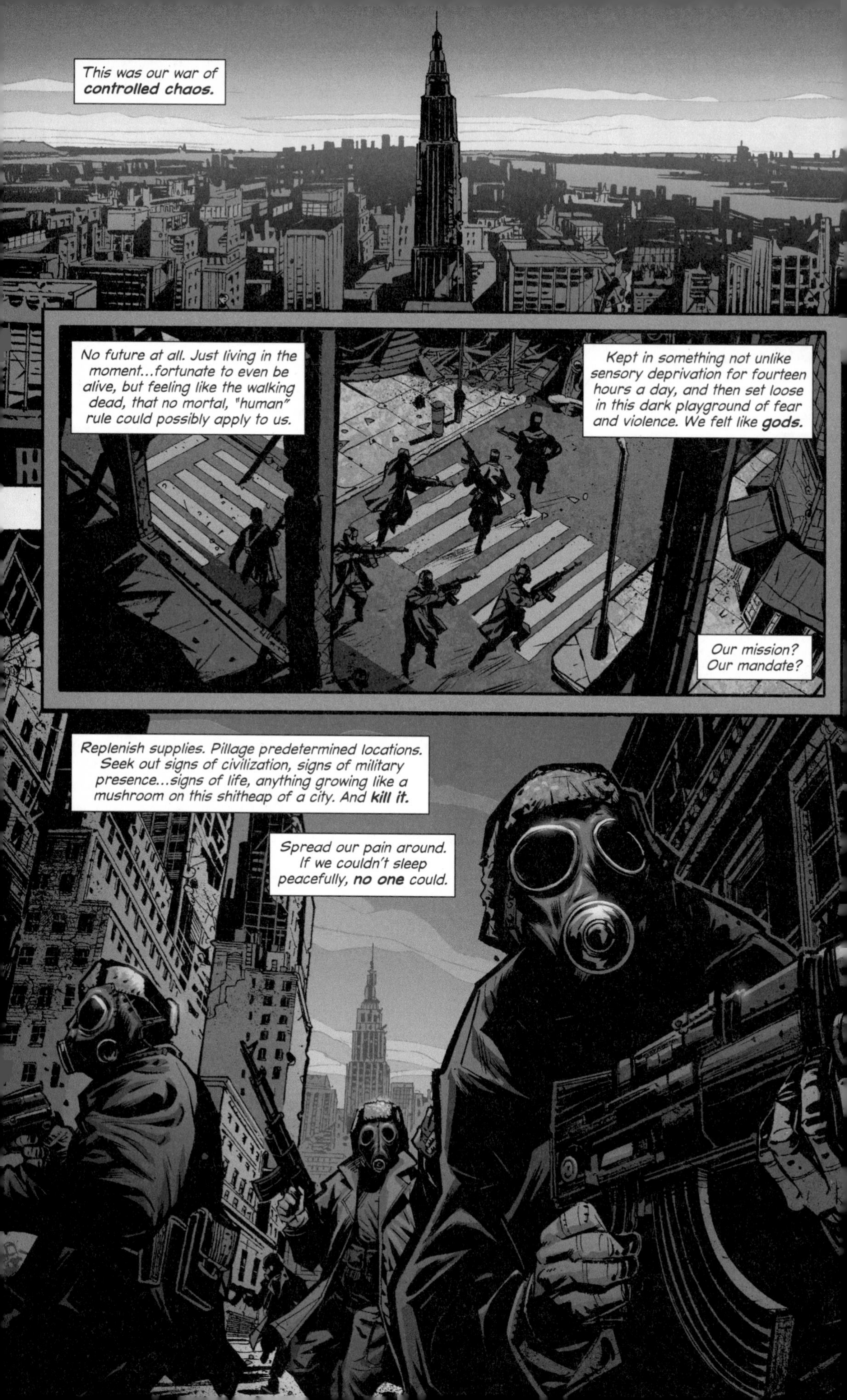
This was our war of **controlled chaos.**
No future at all. Just living in the moment...fortunate to even be alive, but feeling like the walking dead, that no mortal, "human" rule could possibly apply to us.
Kept in something not unlike sensory deprivation for fourteen hours a day, and then set loose in this dark playground of fear and violence. We felt like **gods.**
Our mission? Our mandate?
Replenish supplies. Pillage predetermined locations. Seek out signs of civilization, signs of military presence...signs of life, anything growing like a mushroom on this shitheap of a city. And **kill it.**
Spread our pain around. If we couldn't sleep peacefully, **no one** could.

HOLD UP.

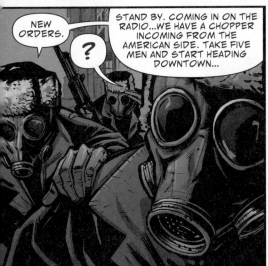

NEW ORDERS.

?

STAND BY. COMING IN ON THE RADIO...WE HAVE A CHOPPER INCOMING FROM THE AMERICAN SIDE. TAKE FIVE MEN AND START HEADING DOWNTOWN...

On specific missions, communication with home base was limited to one individual. The flow of information was cleverly managed...so we were only told what we needed to know in that moment.

ORDERS?

WILL ADVISE ON ROUTE. WE HAVE SPOTTERS TRACKING THE CHOPPER.

DON'T ENGAGE UNTIL YOU HEAR FROM ME. THIS COULD BE MORE THAN A TYPICAL HIT-AND-RUN...

No time to make a judgment call... no time to weigh consequences.

YOU GOT IT.

B SQUAD, ON ME! FIND ME SOMETHING WITH GAS, PRONTO!

Only time to twitch and react.

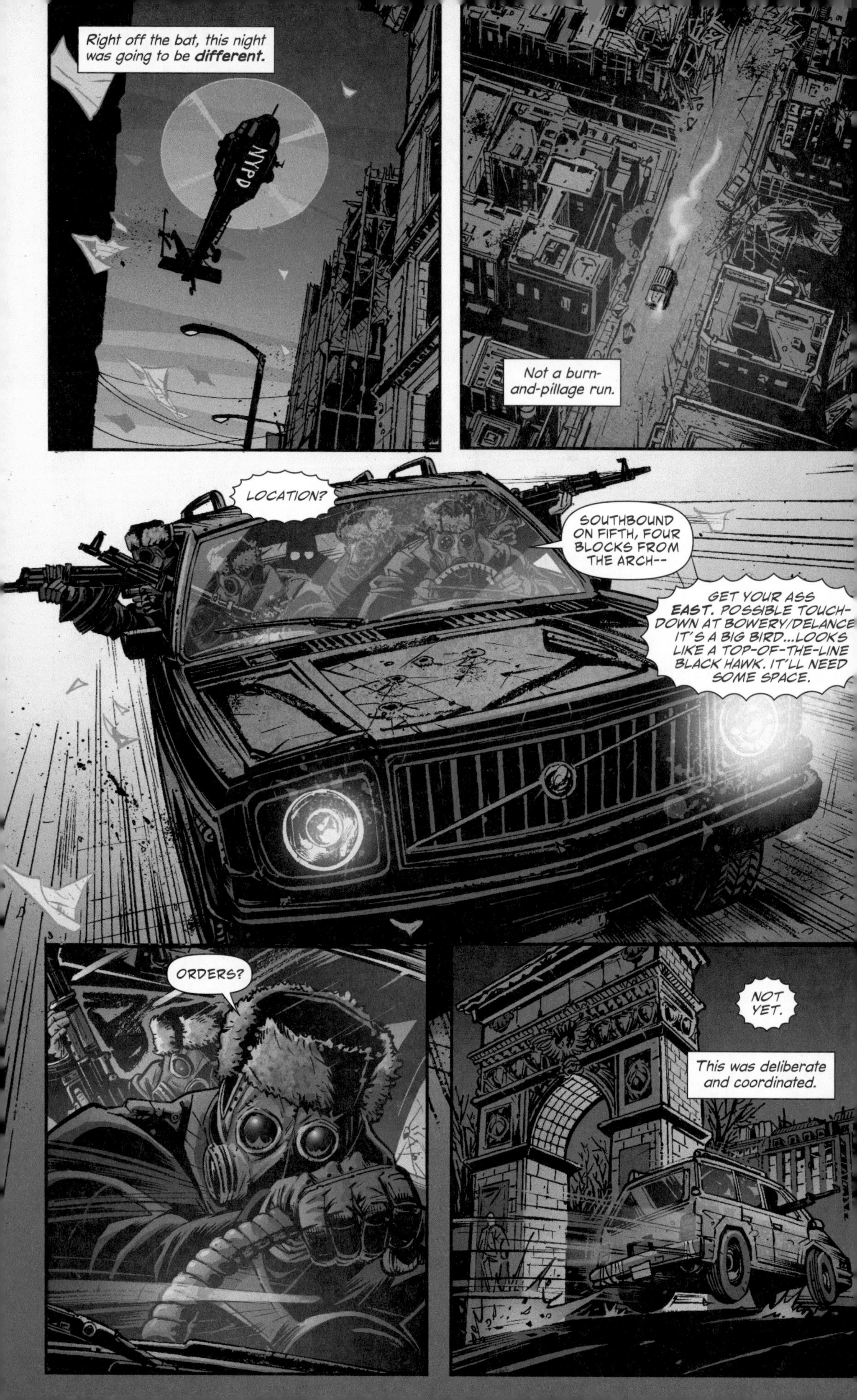
Right off the bat, this night was going to be **different.**
NYPD
Not a burn-and-pillage run.
LOCATION?
SOUTHBOUND ON FIFTH, FOUR BLOCKS FROM THE ARCH--
GET YOUR ASS **EAST.** POSSIBLE TOUCH-DOWN AT BOWERY/DELANCEY. IT'S A BIG BIRD...LOOKS LIKE A TOP-OF-THE-LINE BLACK HAWK. IT'LL NEED SOME SPACE.
ORDERS?
NOT YET.
This was deliberate and coordinated.

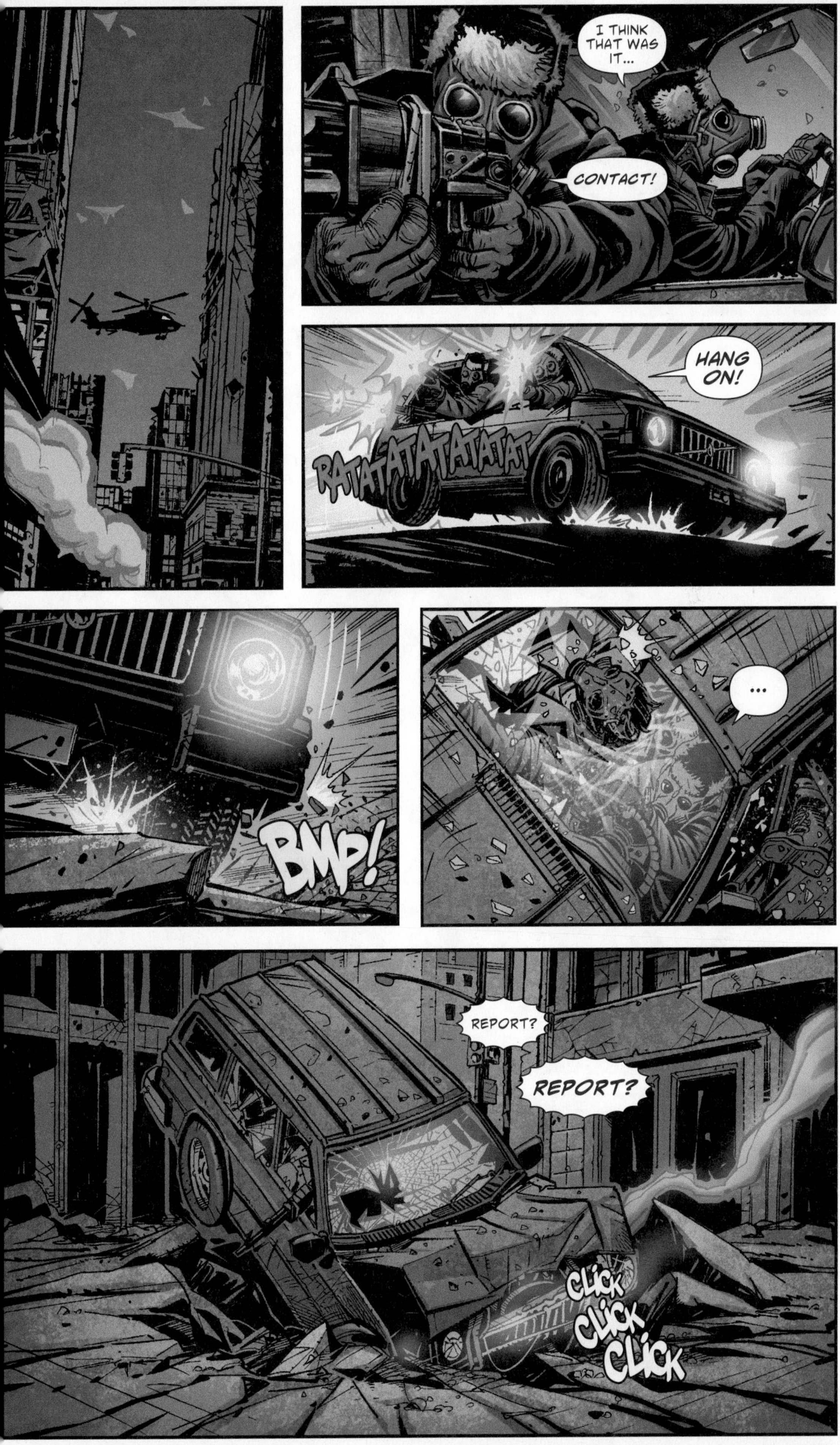
I THINK THAT WAS IT...
CONTACT!
HANG ON!
RATATATATATATAT
BMP!
...
REPORT?
REPORT?
CLICK
CLICK
CLICK

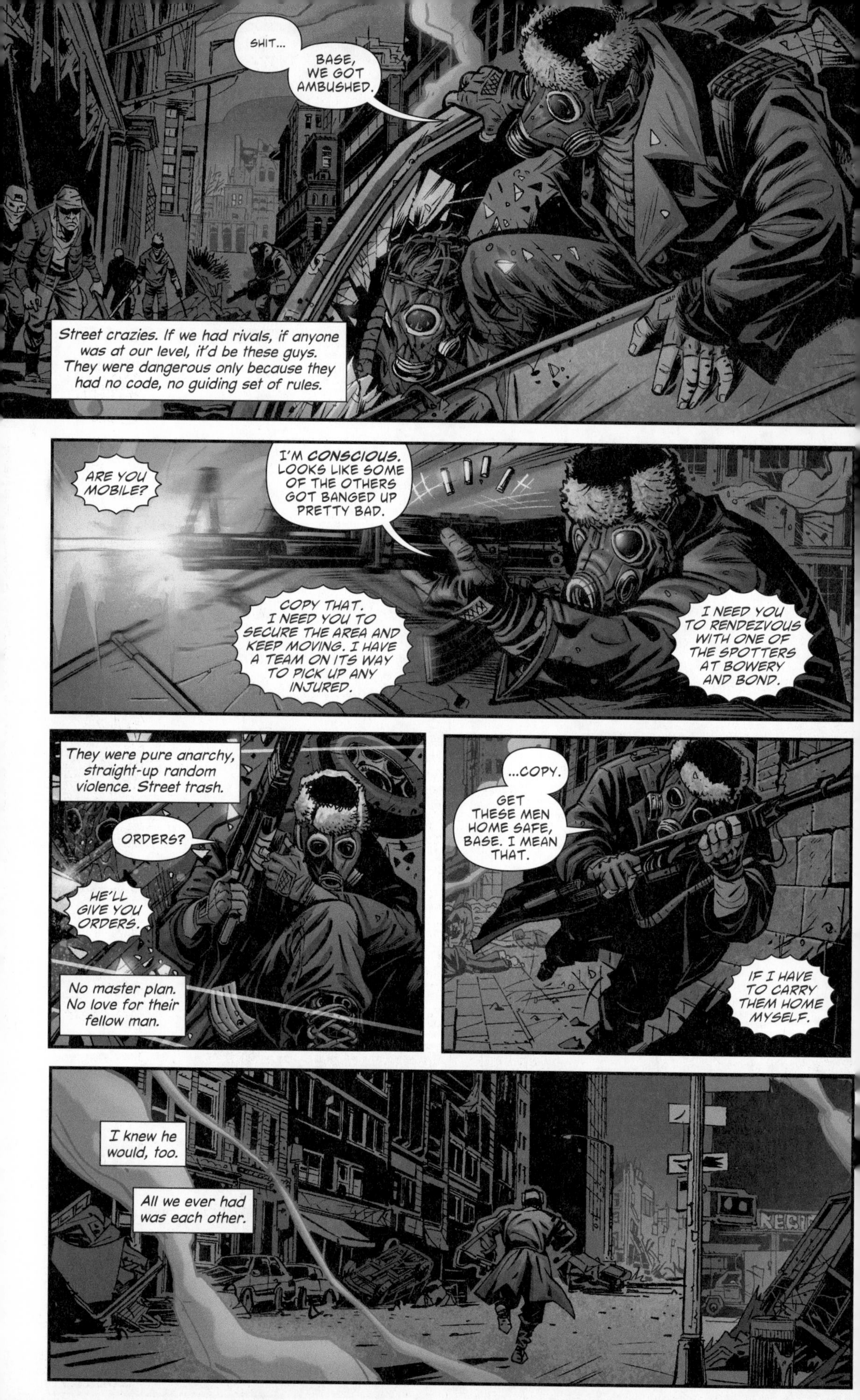
SHIT...
BASE, WE GOT AMBUSHED.
Street crazies. If we had rivals, if anyone was at our level, it'd be these guys. They were dangerous only because they had no code, no guiding set of rules.
ARE YOU MOBILE?
I'M CONSCIOUS. LOOKS LIKE SOME OF THE OTHERS GOT BANGED UP PRETTY BAD.
COPY THAT. I NEED YOU TO SECURE THE AREA AND KEEP MOVING. I HAVE A TEAM ON ITS WAY TO PICK UP ANY INJURED.
I NEED YOU TO RENDEZVOUS WITH ONE OF THE SPOTTERS AT BOWERY AND BOND.
They were pure anarchy, straight-up random violence. Street trash.
ORDERS?
HE'LL GIVE YOU ORDERS.
No master plan. No love for their fellow man.
...COPY.
GET THESE MEN HOME SAFE, BASE. I MEAN THAT.
IF I HAVE TO CARRY THEM HOME MYSELF.
I knew he would, too.
All we ever had was each other.

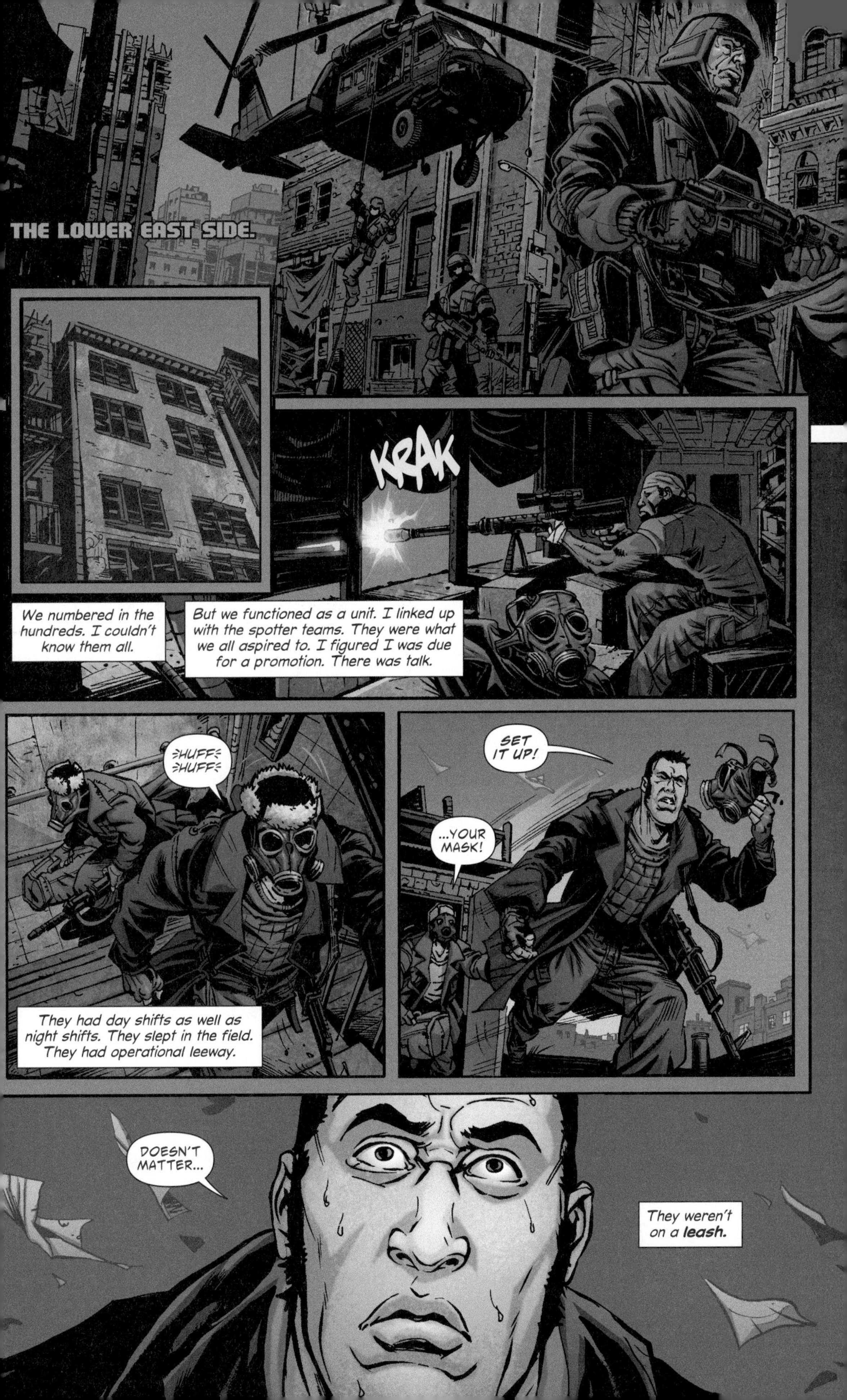
THE LOWER EAST SIDE.
KRAK
We numbered in the hundreds. I couldn't know them all.
But we functioned as a unit. I linked up with the spotter teams. They were what we all aspired to. I figured I was due for a promotion. There was talk.
HUFF HUFF
They had day shifts as well as night shifts. They slept in the field. They had operational leeway.
SET IT UP!
...YOUR MASK!
DOESN'T MATTER...
They weren't on a leash.

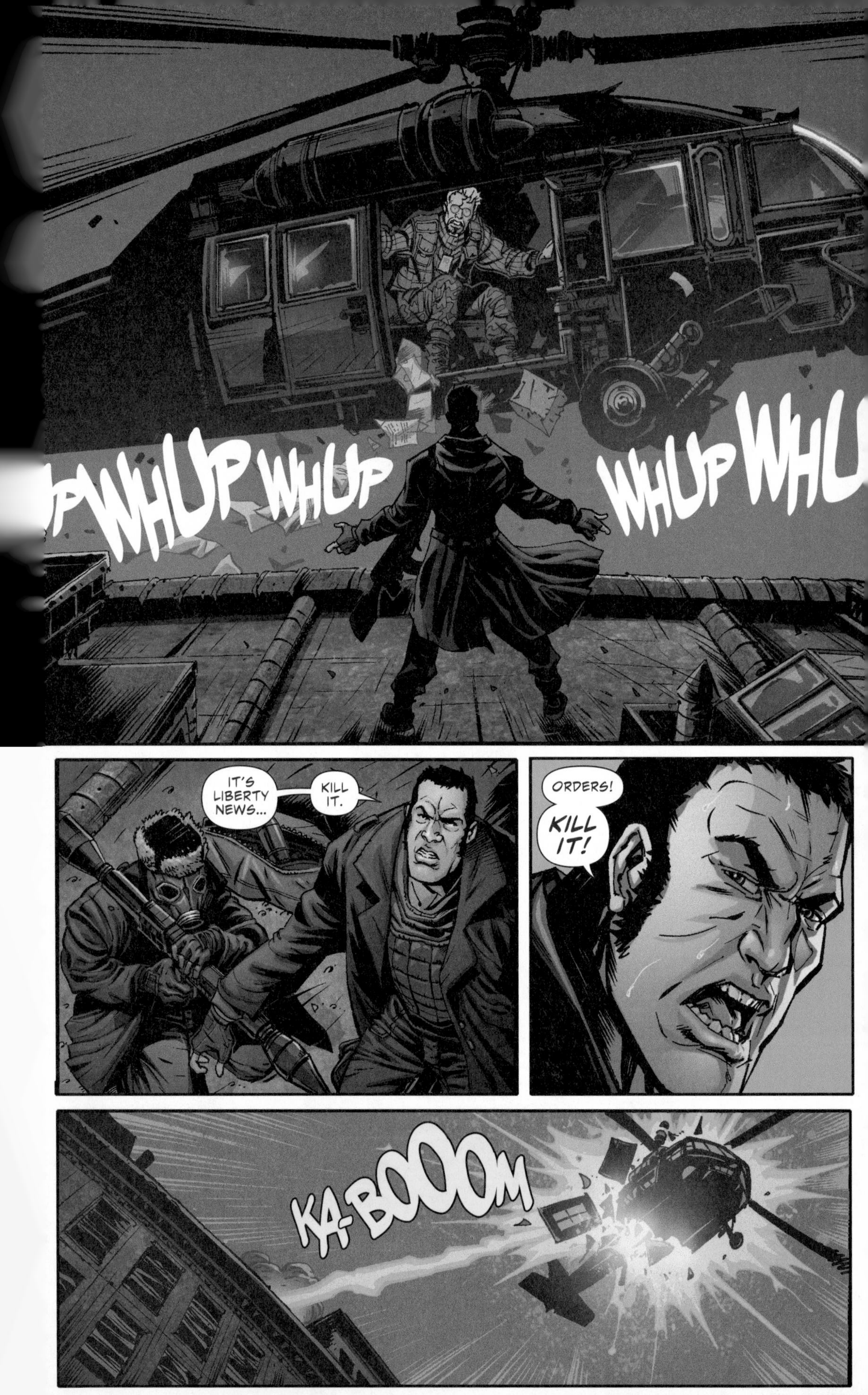
WHUP WHUP
WHUP WHU
IT'S LIBERTY NEWS...
KILL IT.
ORDERS!
KILL IT!
KA-BOOOM

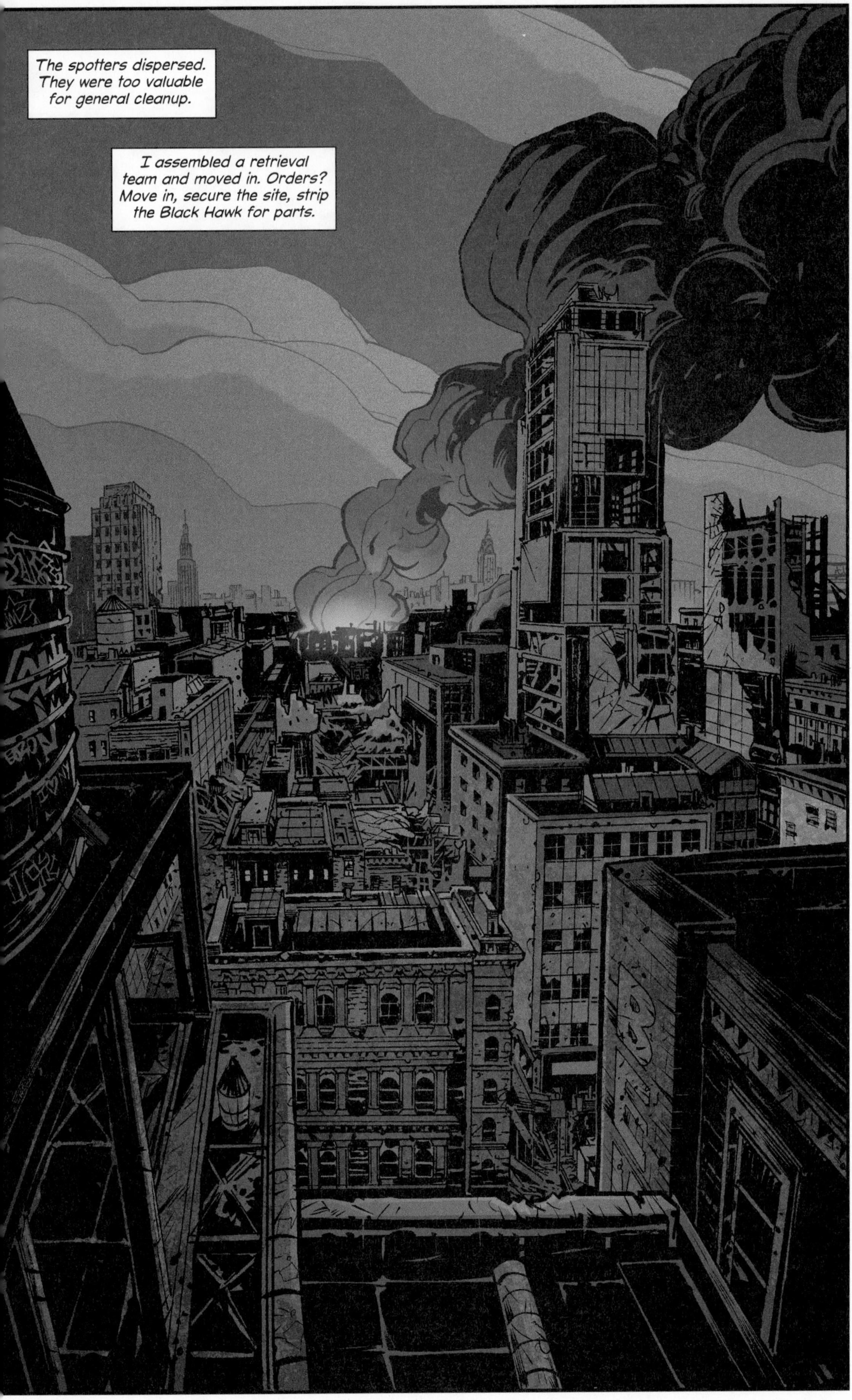
The spotters dispersed. They were too valuable for general cleanup.
I assembled a retrieval team and moved in. Orders? Move in, secure the site, strip the Black Hawk for parts.

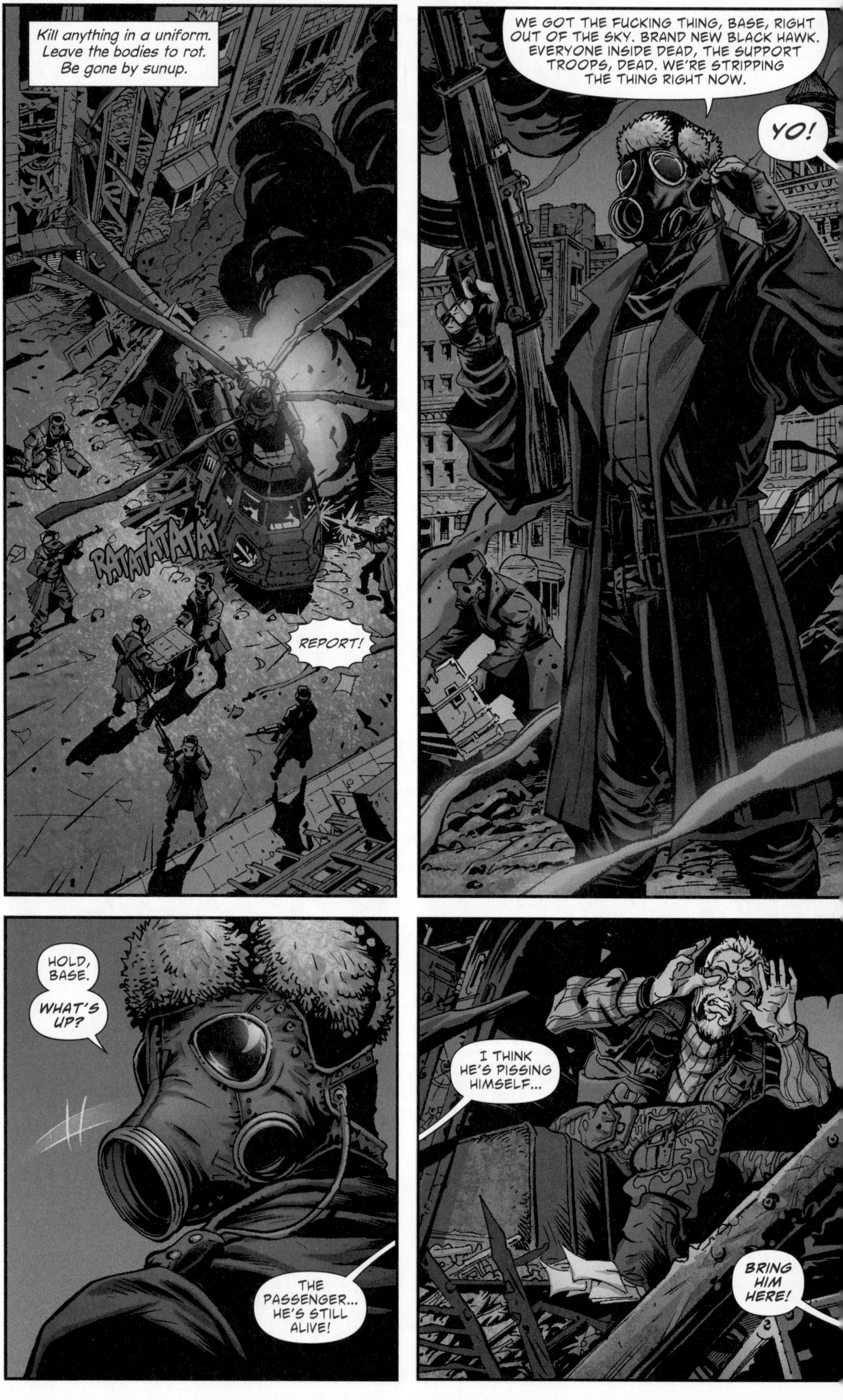
Kill anything in a uniform. Leave the bodies to rot. Be gone by sunup.
RATATATATAT
REPORT!
WE GOT THE FUCKING THING, BASE, RIGHT OUT OF THE SKY. BRAND NEW BLACK HAWK. EVERYONE INSIDE DEAD, THE SUPPORT TROOPS, DEAD. WE'RE STRIPPING THE THING RIGHT NOW.
YO!
HOLD, BASE.
WHAT'S UP?
THE PASSENGER... HE'S STILL ALIVE!
I THINK HE'S PISSING HIMSELF...
BRING HIM HERE!

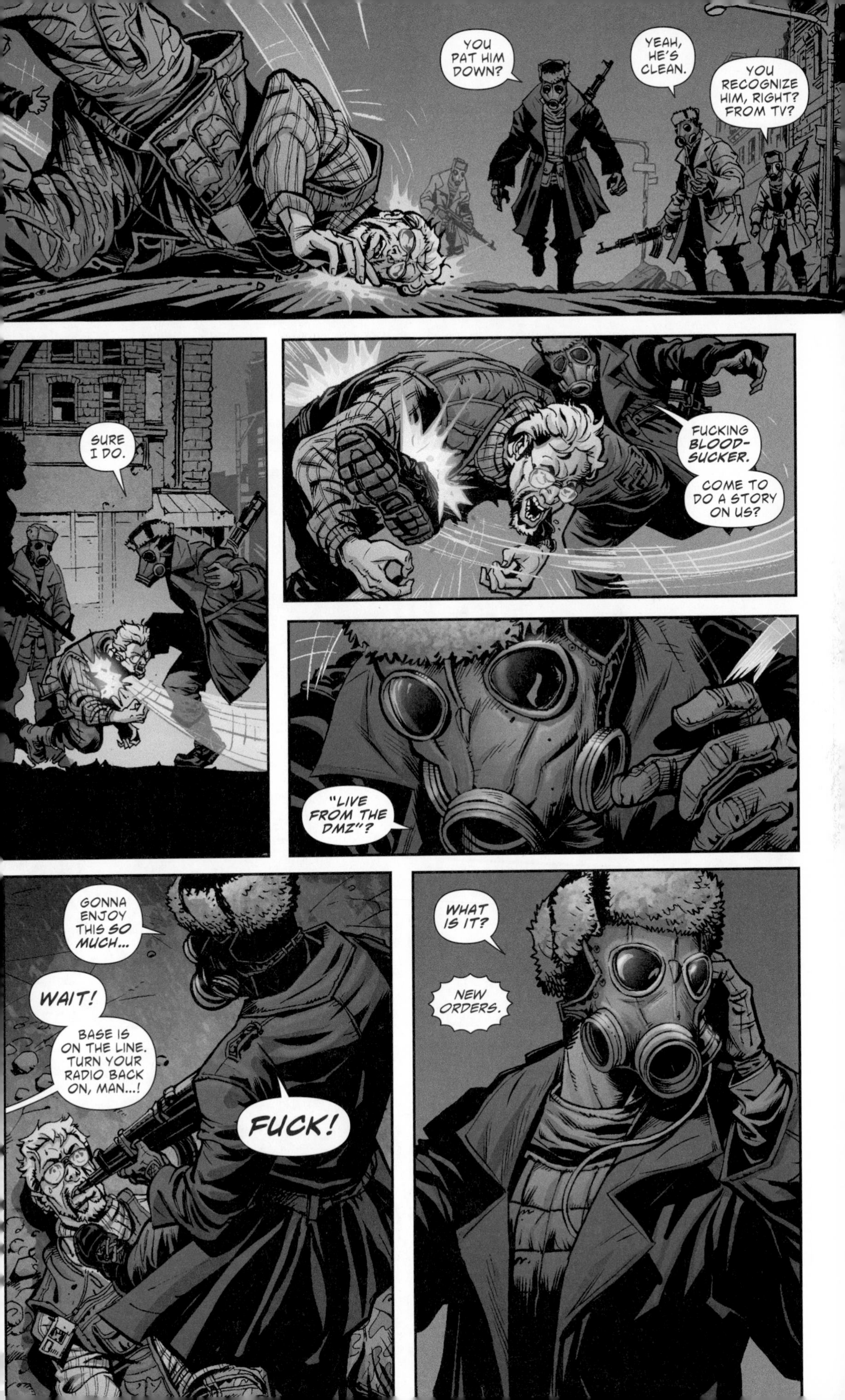
YOU PAT HIM DOWN?
YEAH, HE'S CLEAN.
YOU RECOGNIZE HIM, RIGHT? FROM TV?
SURE I DO.
FUCKING BLOOD-SUCKER.
COME TO DO A STORY ON US?
"LIVE FROM THE DMZ"?
GONNA ENJOY THIS SO MUCH...
WAIT!
BASE IS ON THE LINE. TURN YOUR RADIO BACK ON, MAN...!
FUCK!
WHAT IS IT?
NEW ORDERS.

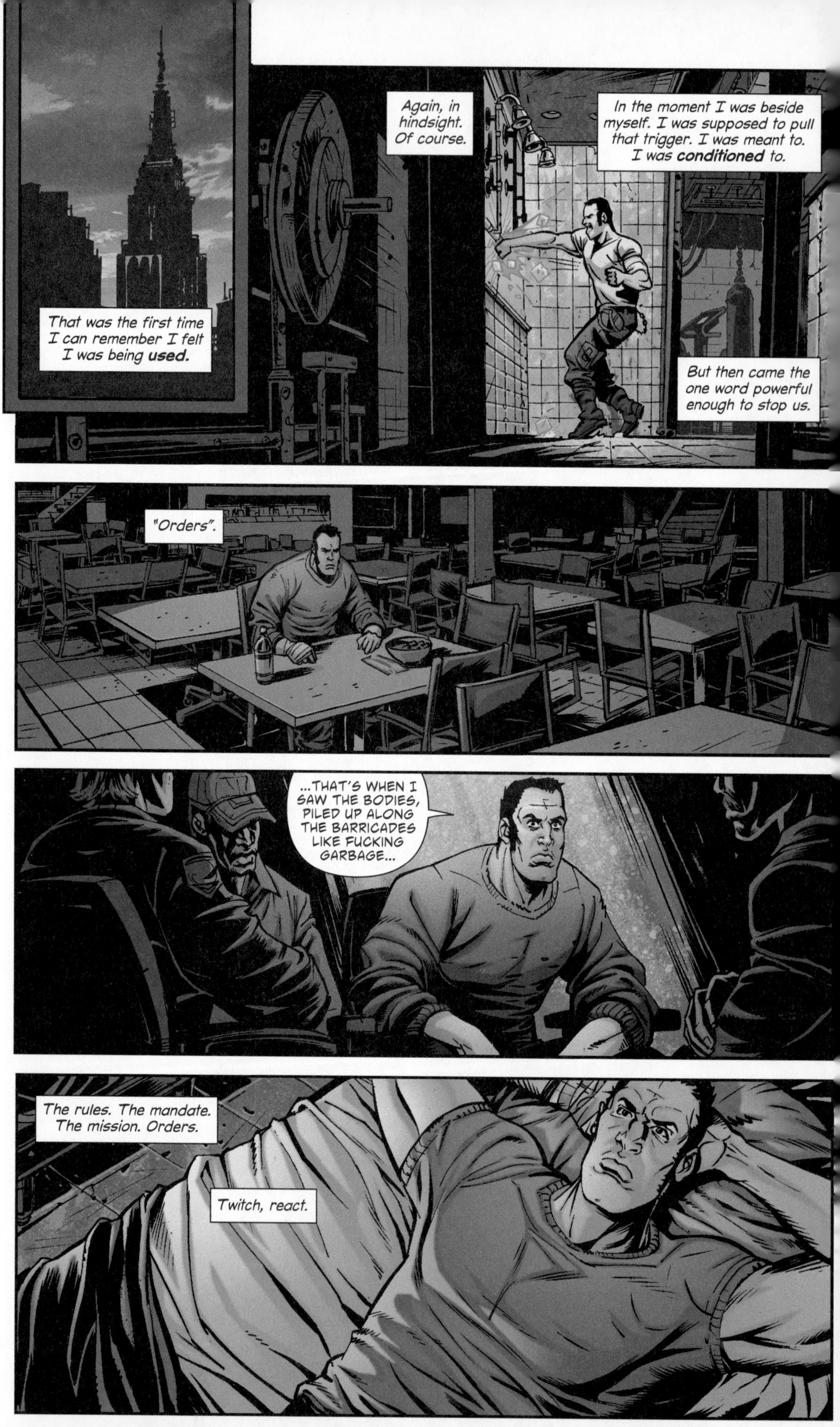
That was the first time I can remember I felt I was being **used.**
Again, in hindsight. Of course.
In the moment I was beside myself. I was supposed to pull that trigger. I was meant to. I was **conditioned** to.
But then came the one word powerful enough to stop us.
"Orders".
...THAT'S WHEN I SAW THE BODIES, PILED UP ALONG THE BARRICADES LIKE FUCKING GARBAGE...
The rules. The mandate. The mission. Orders.
Twitch, react.

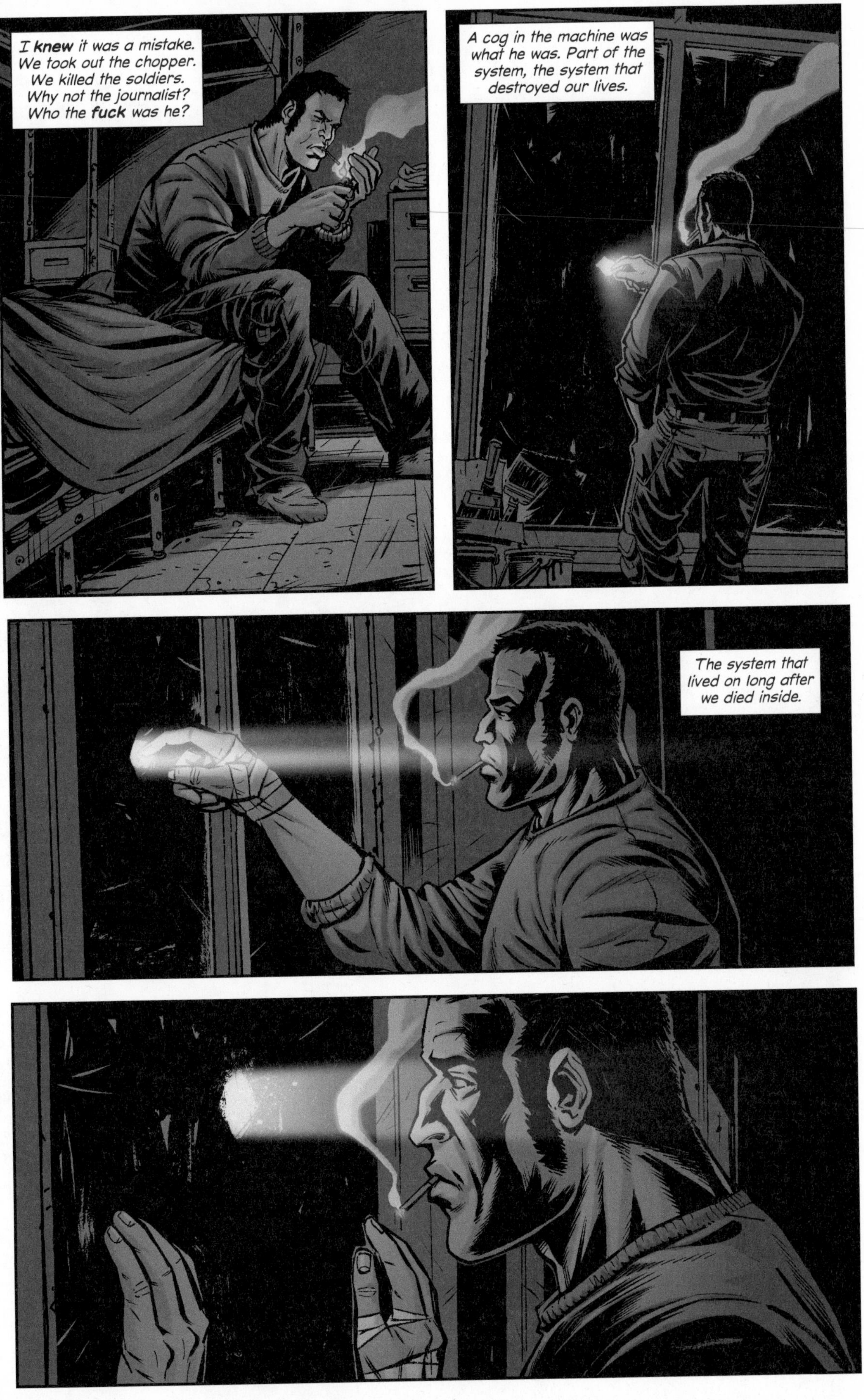
I knew it was a mistake. We took out the chopper. We killed the soldiers. Why not the journalist? Who the fuck was he?
A cog in the machine was what he was. Part of the system, the system that destroyed our lives.
The system that lived on long after we died inside.

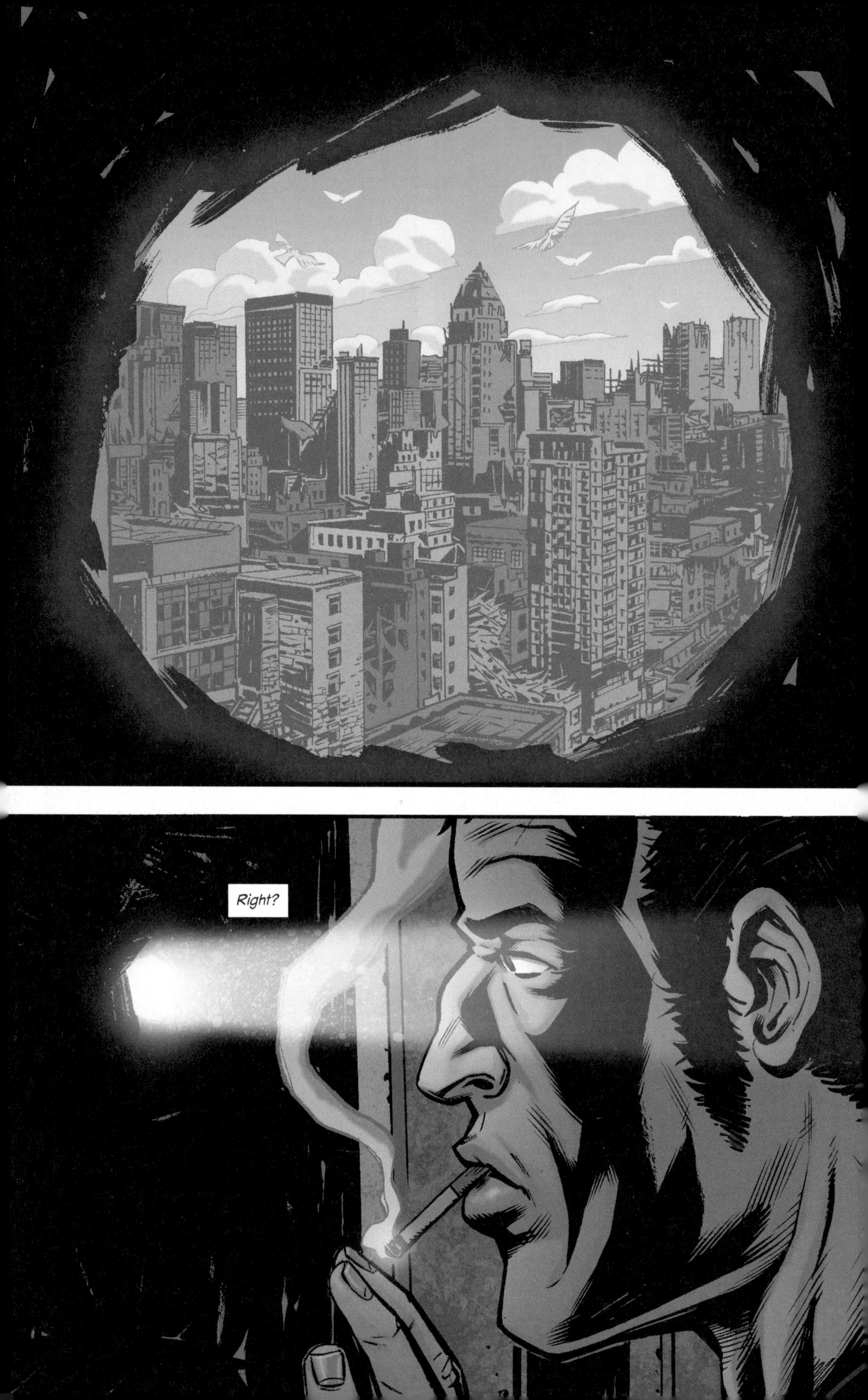
Right?

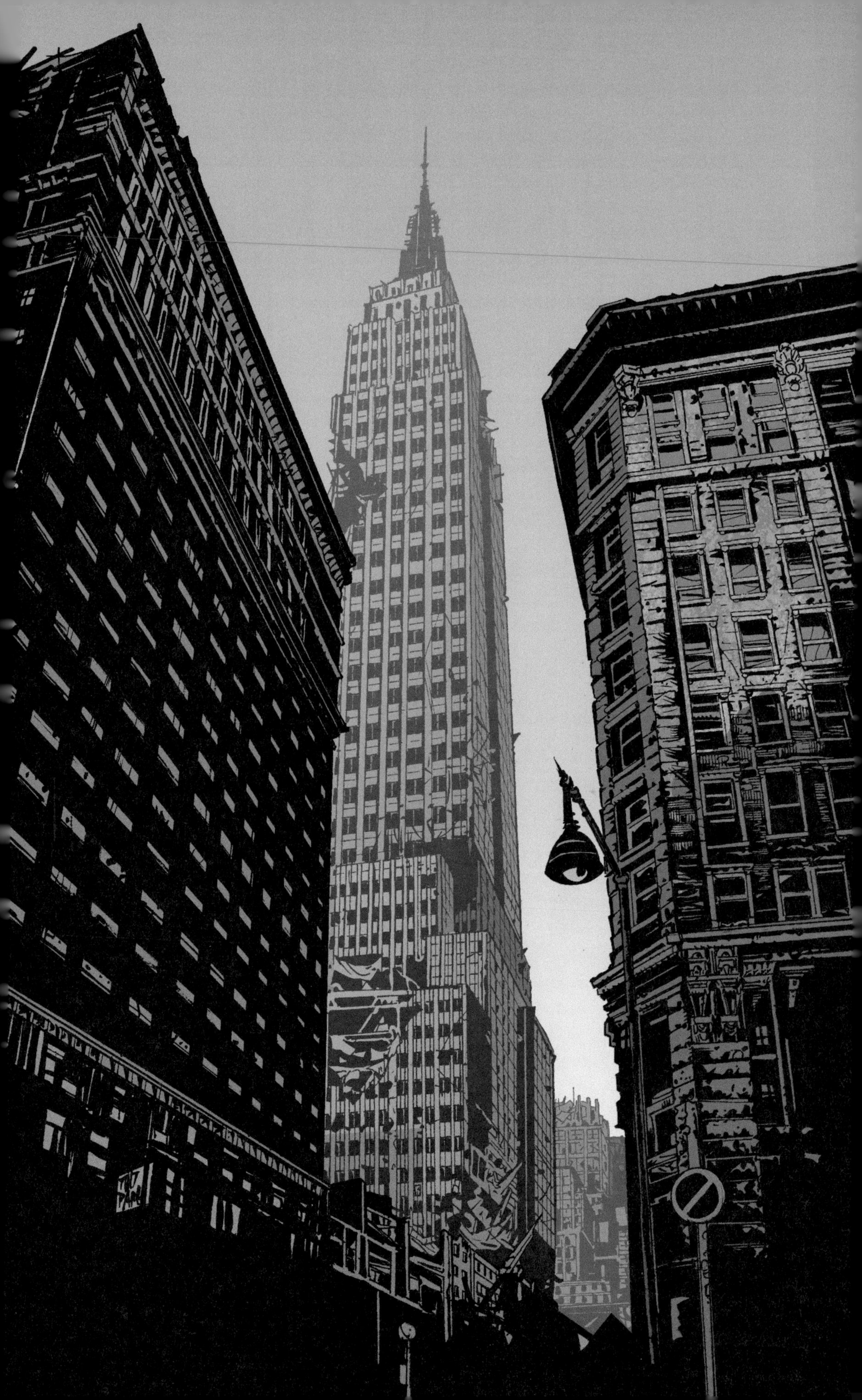

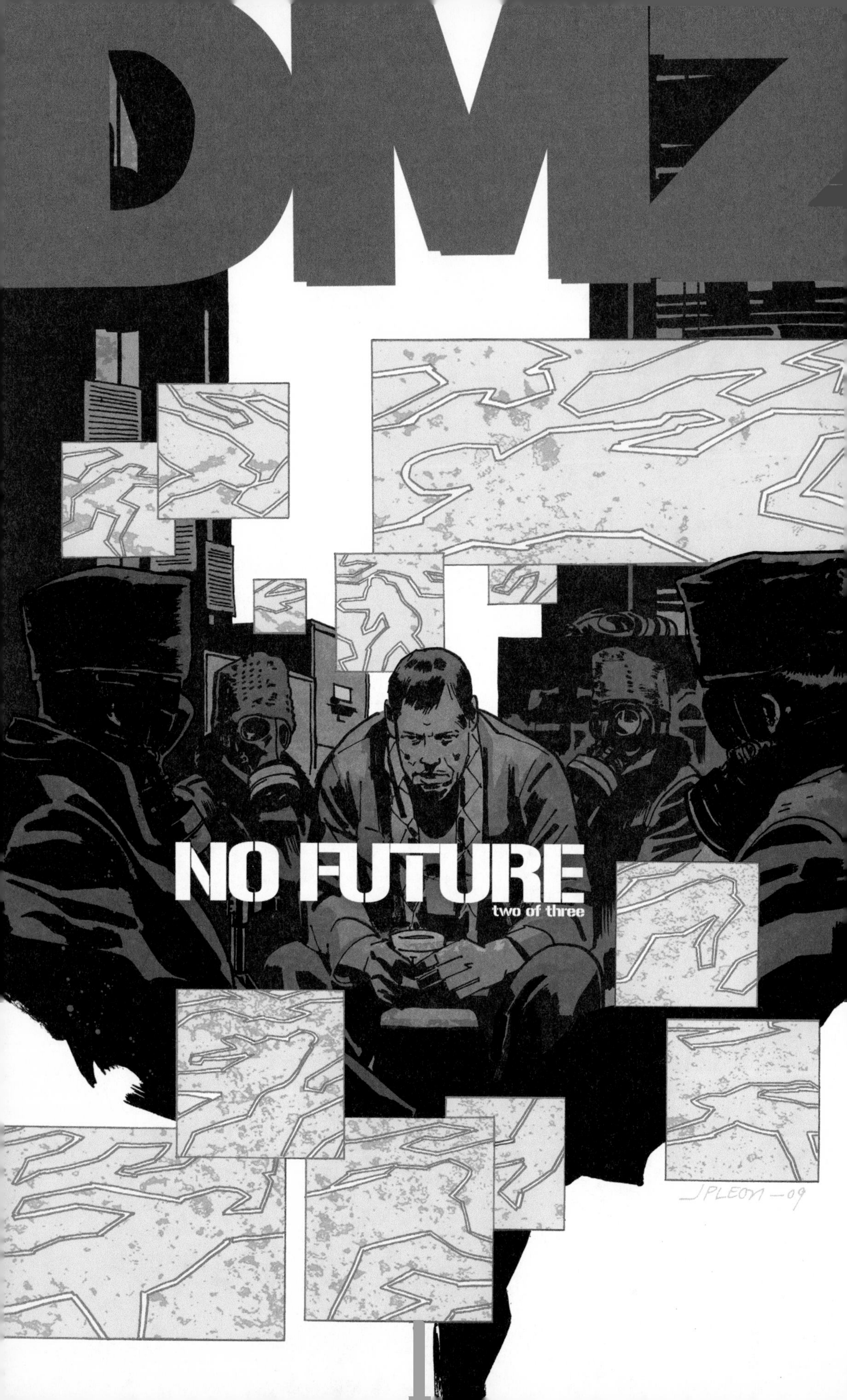
DMZ
NO FUTURE
two of three
JPLEON -09

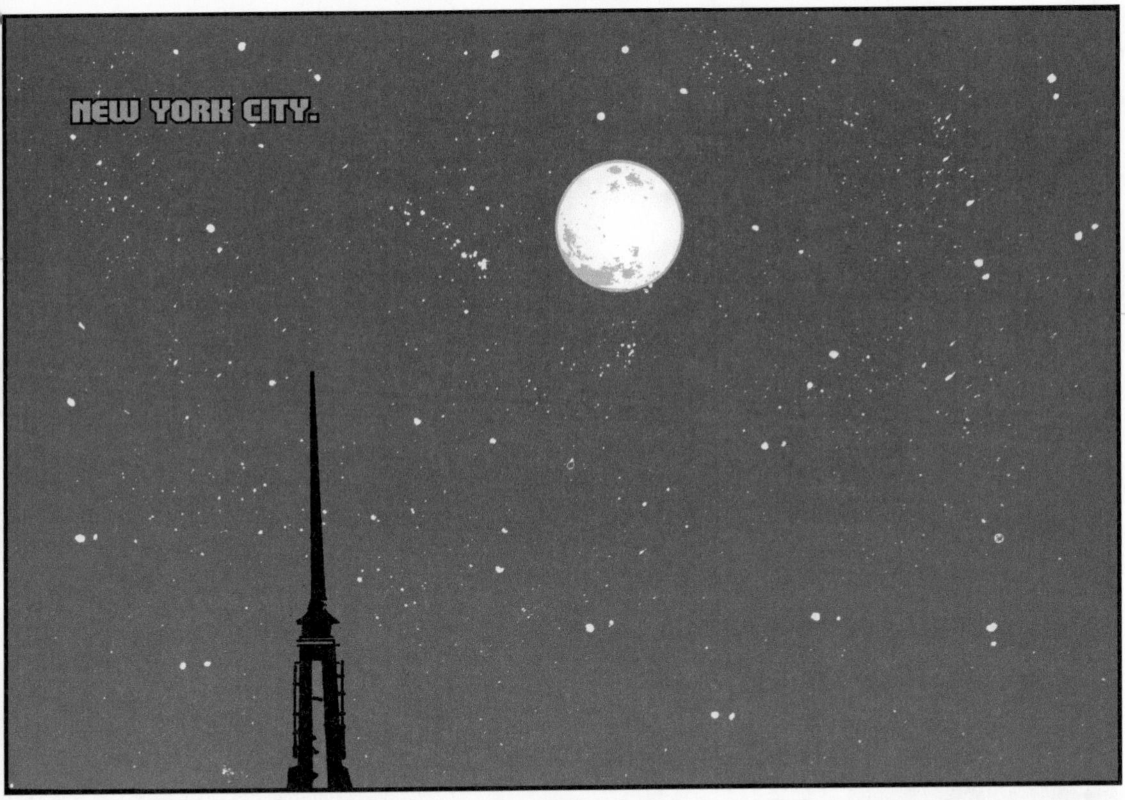
NEW YORK CITY.

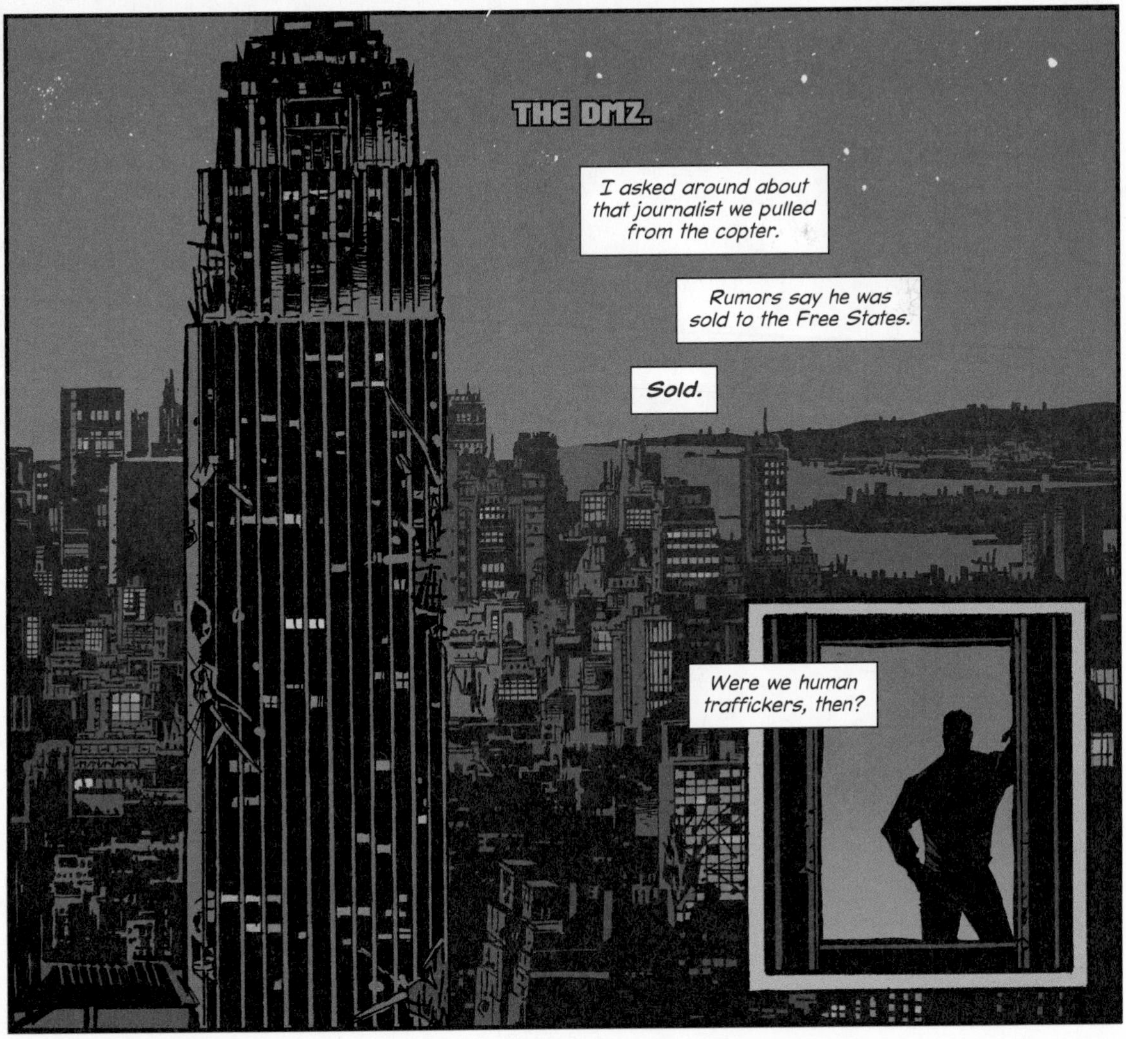
THE DMZ.
I asked around about that journalist we pulled from the copter.
Rumors say he was sold to the Free States.
Sold.
Were we human traffickers, then?

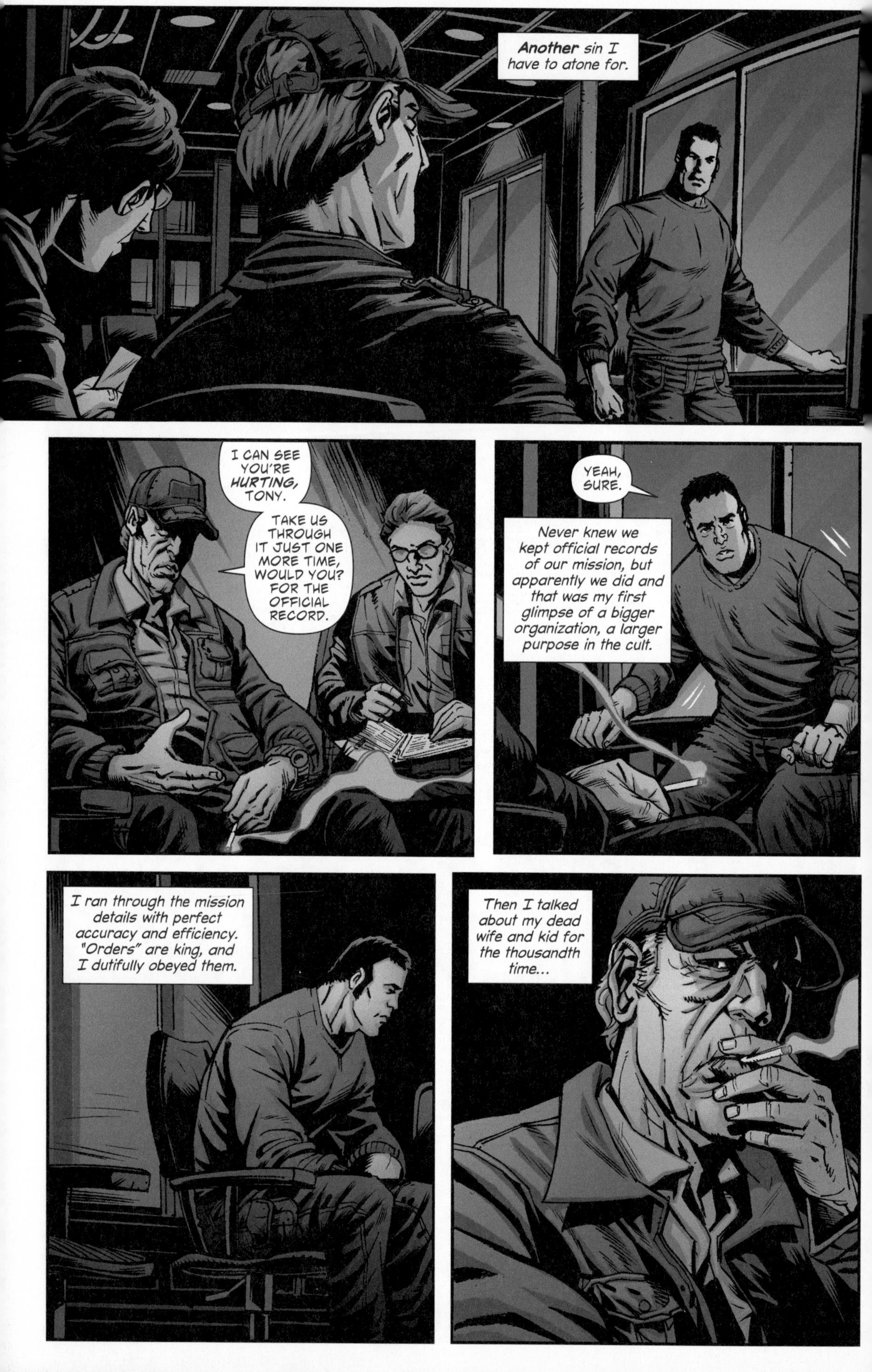
Another sin I have to atone for.
I CAN SEE YOU'RE ***HURTING,*** TONY.
TAKE US THROUGH IT JUST ONE MORE TIME, WOULD YOU? FOR THE OFFICIAL RECORD.
YEAH, SURE.
Never knew we kept official records of our mission, but apparently we did and that was my first glimpse of a bigger organization, a larger purpose in the cult.
I ran through the mission details with perfect accuracy and efficiency. "Orders" are king, and I dutifully obeyed them.
Then I talked about my dead wife and kid for the thousandth time...

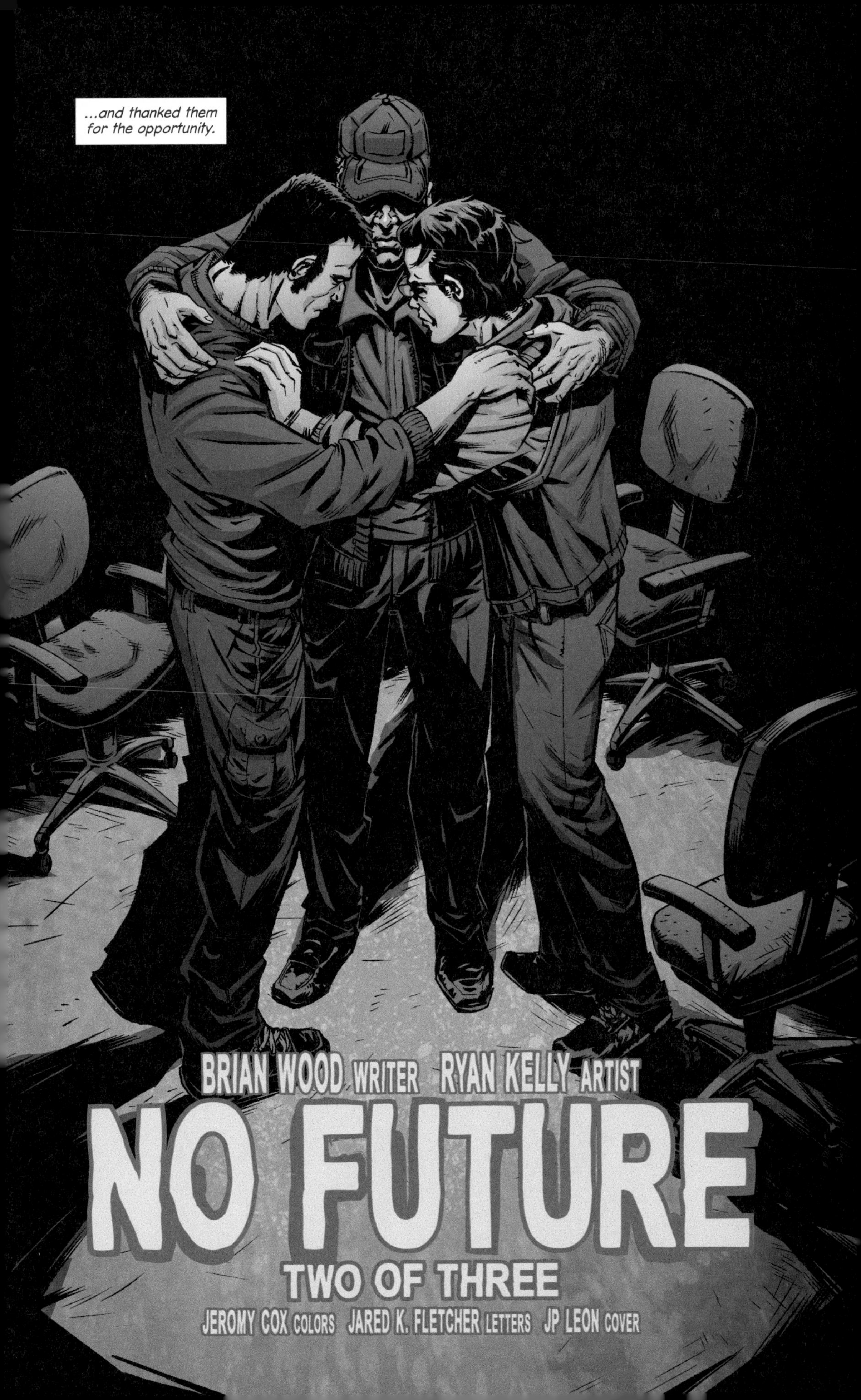
...and thanked them for the opportunity.
BRIAN WOOD WRITER RYAN KELLY ARTIST
NO FUTURE
TWO OF THREE
JEROMY COX COLORS JARED K. FLETCHER LETTERS JP LEON COVER

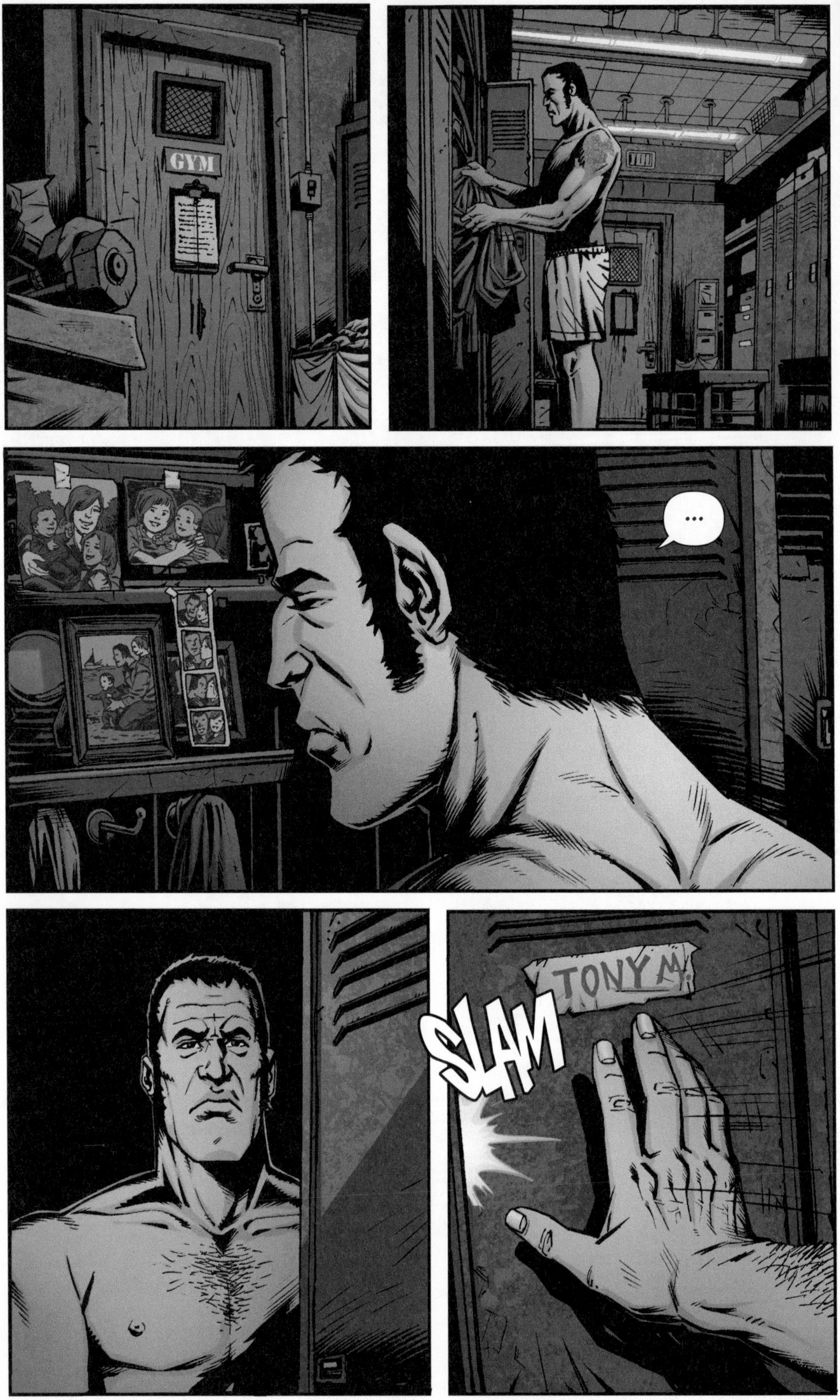
GYM
...
TONY M.
SLAM

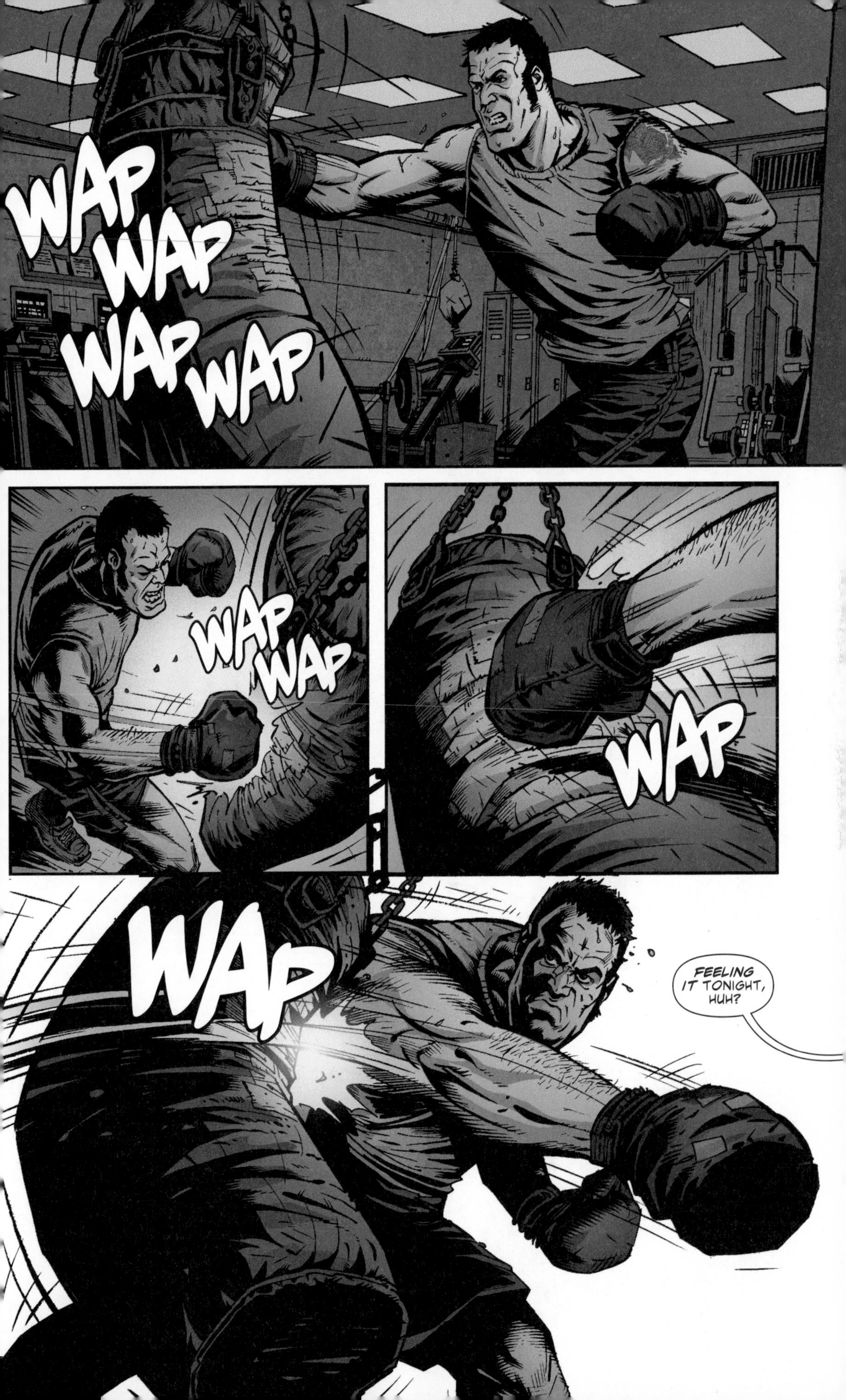
WAP
WAP
WAP
WAP
WAP
WAP
WAP
WAP
FEELING IT TONIGHT, HUH?

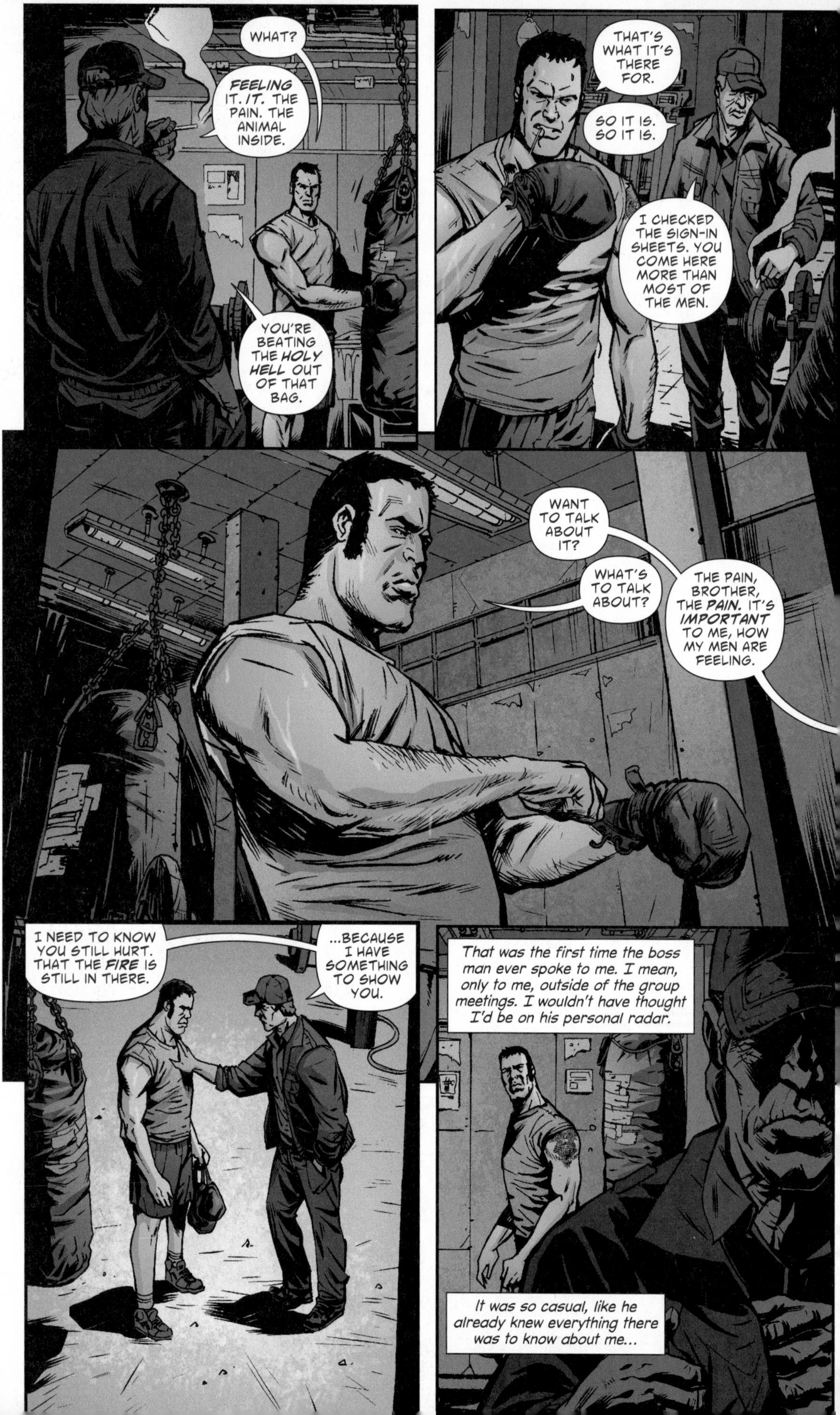
WHAT?
FEELING IT. IT. THE PAIN. THE ANIMAL INSIDE.
YOU'RE BEATING THE HOLY HELL OUT OF THAT BAG.
THAT'S WHAT IT'S THERE FOR.
SO IT IS. SO IT IS.
I CHECKED THE SIGN-IN SHEETS. YOU COME HERE MORE THAN MOST OF THE MEN.
WANT TO TALK ABOUT IT?
WHAT'S TO TALK ABOUT?
THE PAIN, BROTHER, THE PAIN. IT'S IMPORTANT TO ME, HOW MY MEN ARE FEELING.
I NEED TO KNOW YOU STILL HURT. THAT THE FIRE IS STILL IN THERE.
...BECAUSE I HAVE SOMETHING TO SHOW YOU.
That was the first time the boss man ever spoke to me. I mean, only to me, outside of the group meetings. I wouldn't have thought I'd be on his personal radar.
It was so casual, like he already knew everything there was to know about me...

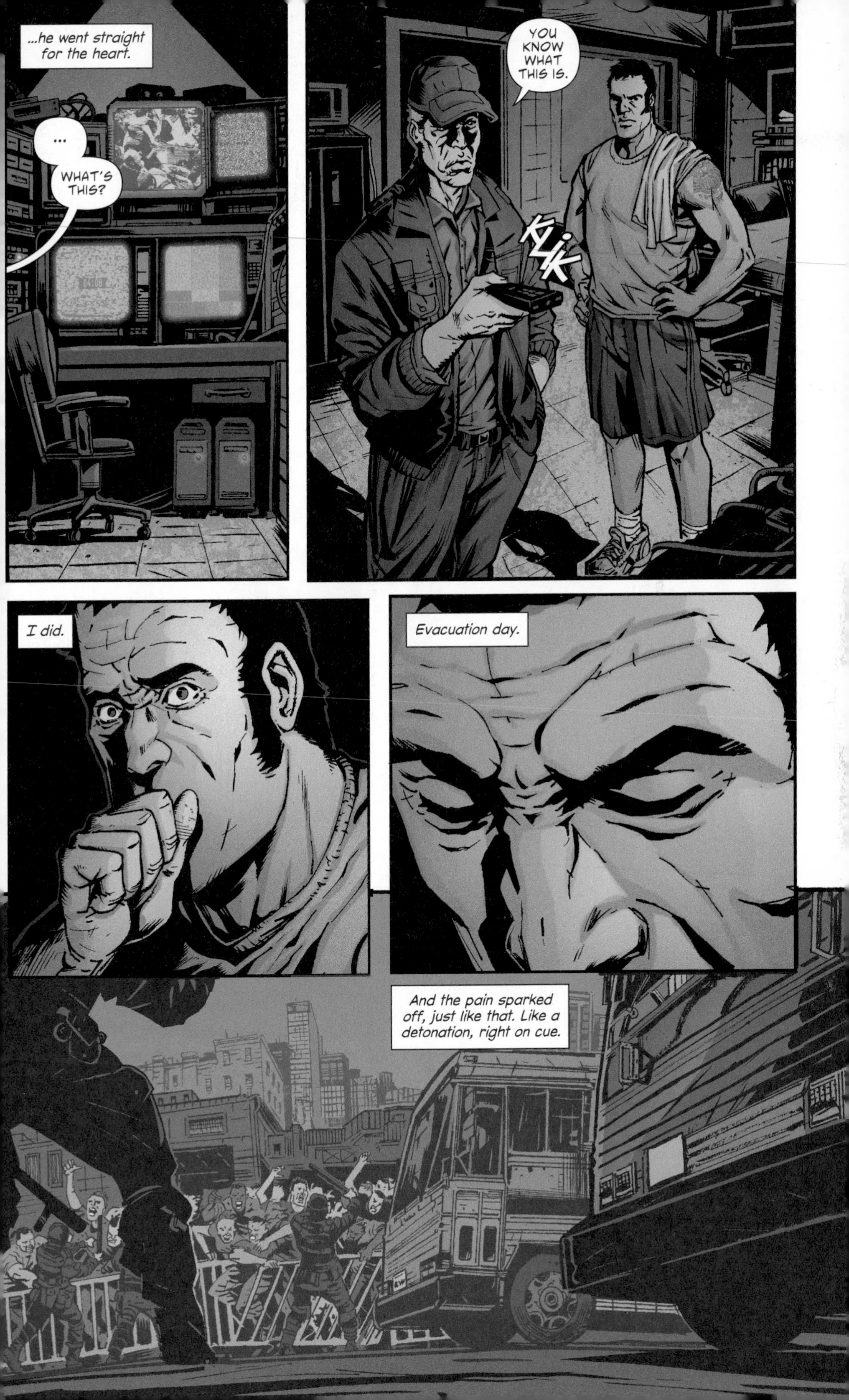
...he went straight for the heart.
...
WHAT'S THIS?
YOU KNOW WHAT THIS IS.
KLIK
I did.
Evacuation day.
And the pain sparked off, just like that. Like a detonation, right on cue.

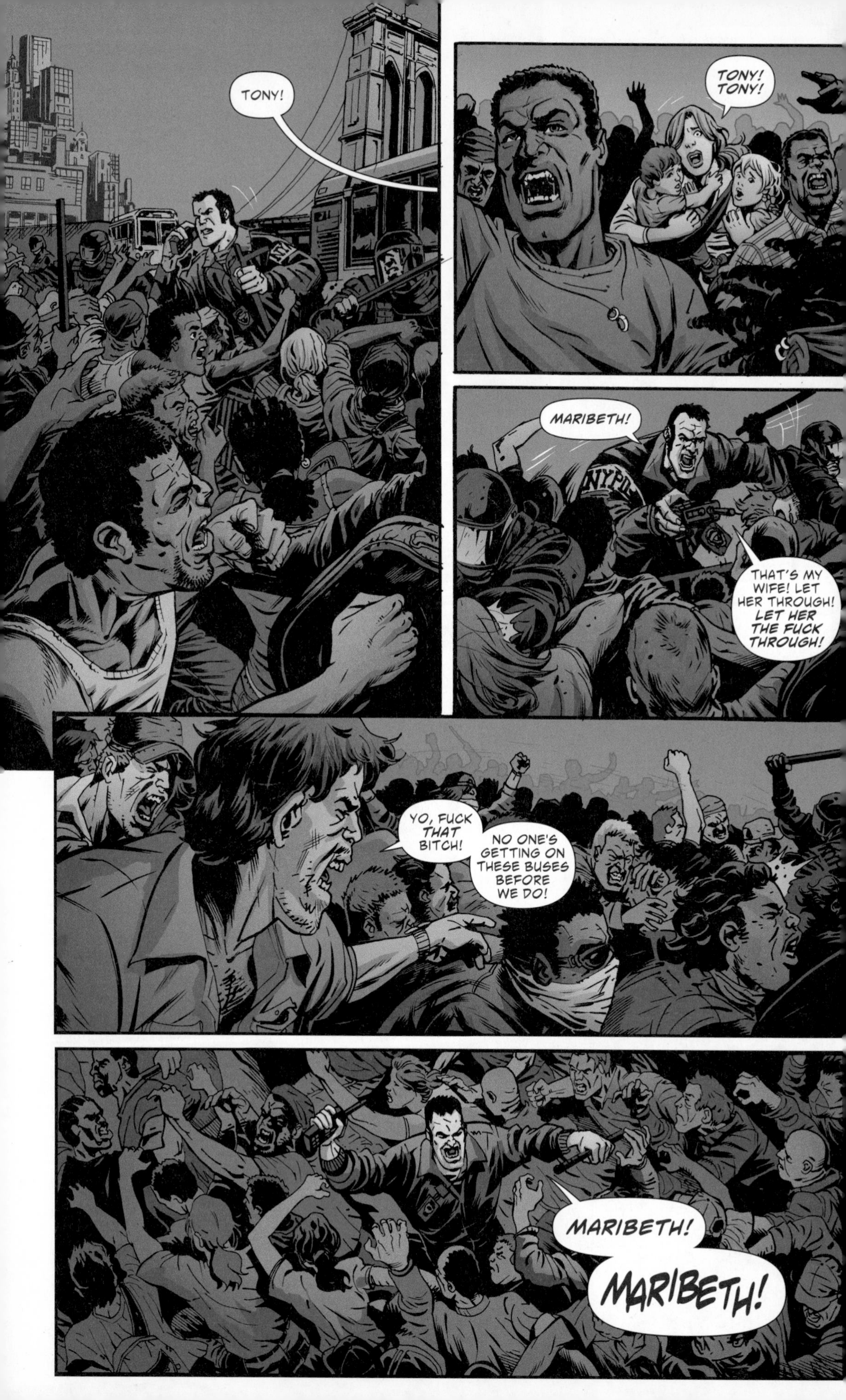
TONY!
TONY! TONY!
MARIBETH!
THAT'S MY WIFE! LET HER THROUGH! LET HER THE FUCK THROUGH!
YO, FUCK THAT BITCH!
NO ONE'S GETTING ON THESE BUSES BEFORE WE DO!
MARIBETH!
MARIBETH!

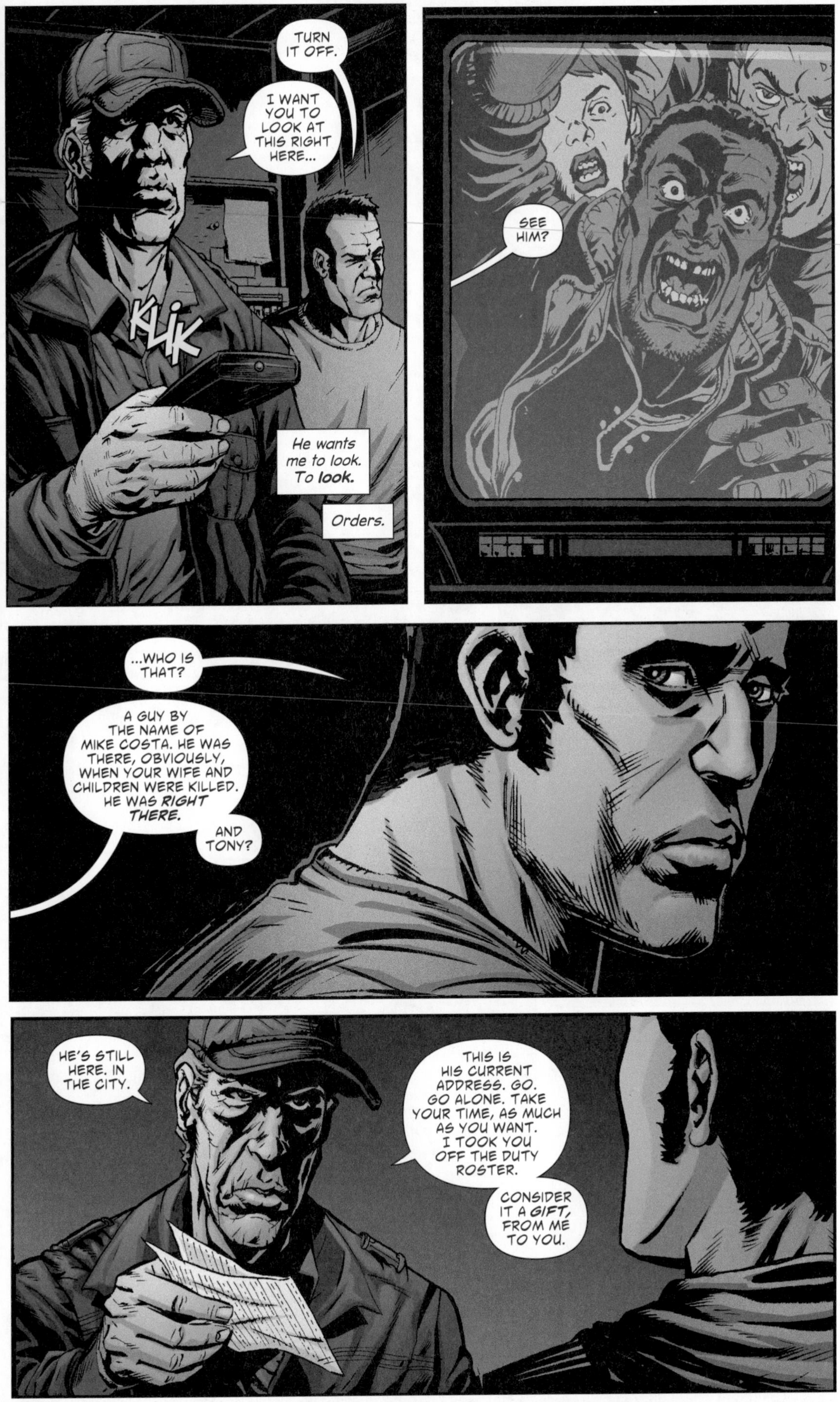

TURN IT OFF.
I WANT YOU TO LOOK AT THIS RIGHT HERE...
KLIK
He wants me to look. To **look.**
Orders.
SEE HIM?
...WHO IS THAT?
A GUY BY THE NAME OF MIKE COSTA. HE WAS THERE, OBVIOUSLY, WHEN YOUR WIFE AND CHILDREN WERE KILLED. HE WAS *RIGHT THERE.*
AND TONY?
HE'S STILL HERE. IN THE CITY.
THIS IS HIS CURRENT ADDRESS. GO. GO ALONE. TAKE YOUR TIME, AS MUCH AS YOU WANT. I TOOK YOU OFF THE DUTY ROSTER.
CONSIDER IT A *GIFT,* FROM ME TO YOU.

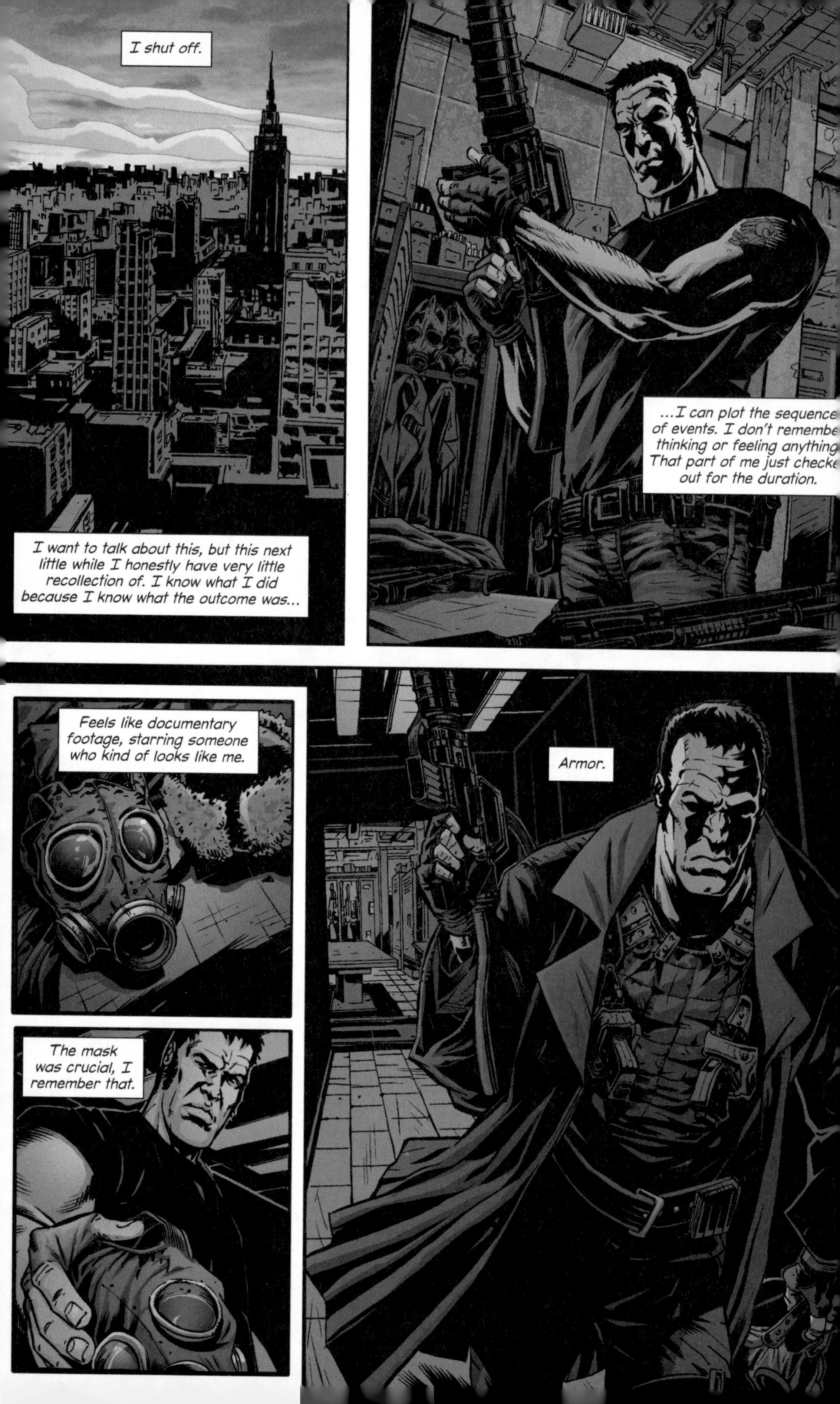
I shut off.
I want to talk about this, but this next little while I honestly have very little recollection of. I know what I did because I know what the outcome was...
...I can plot the sequence of events. I don't remembe thinking or feeling anything That part of me just checke out for the duration.
Feels like documentary footage, starring someone who kind of looks like me.
The mask was crucial, I remember that.
Armor.

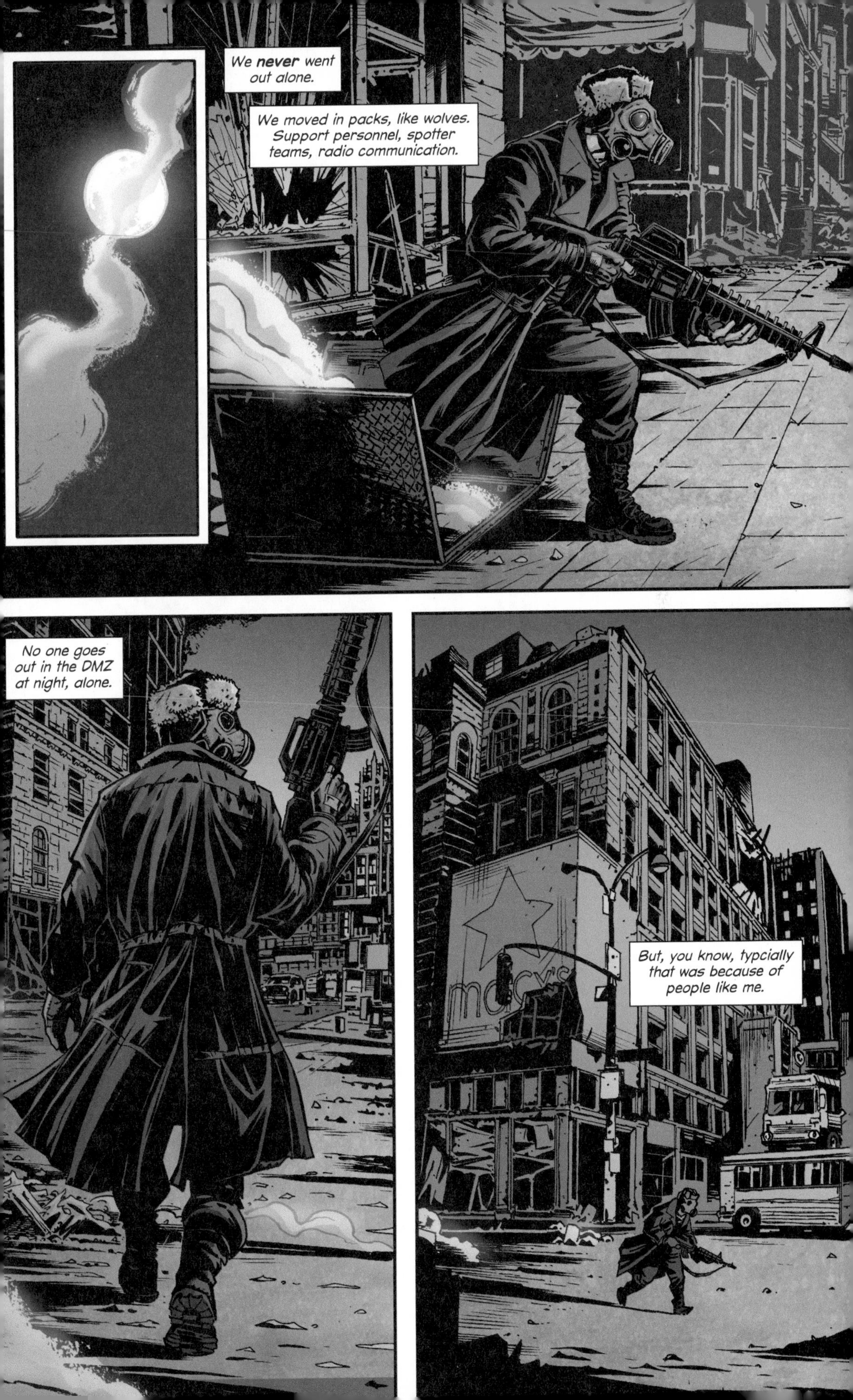
We **never** went out alone.
We moved in packs, like wolves. Support personnel, spotter teams, radio communication.
No one goes out in the DMZ at night, alone.
macy's
But, you know, typcially that was because of people like me.

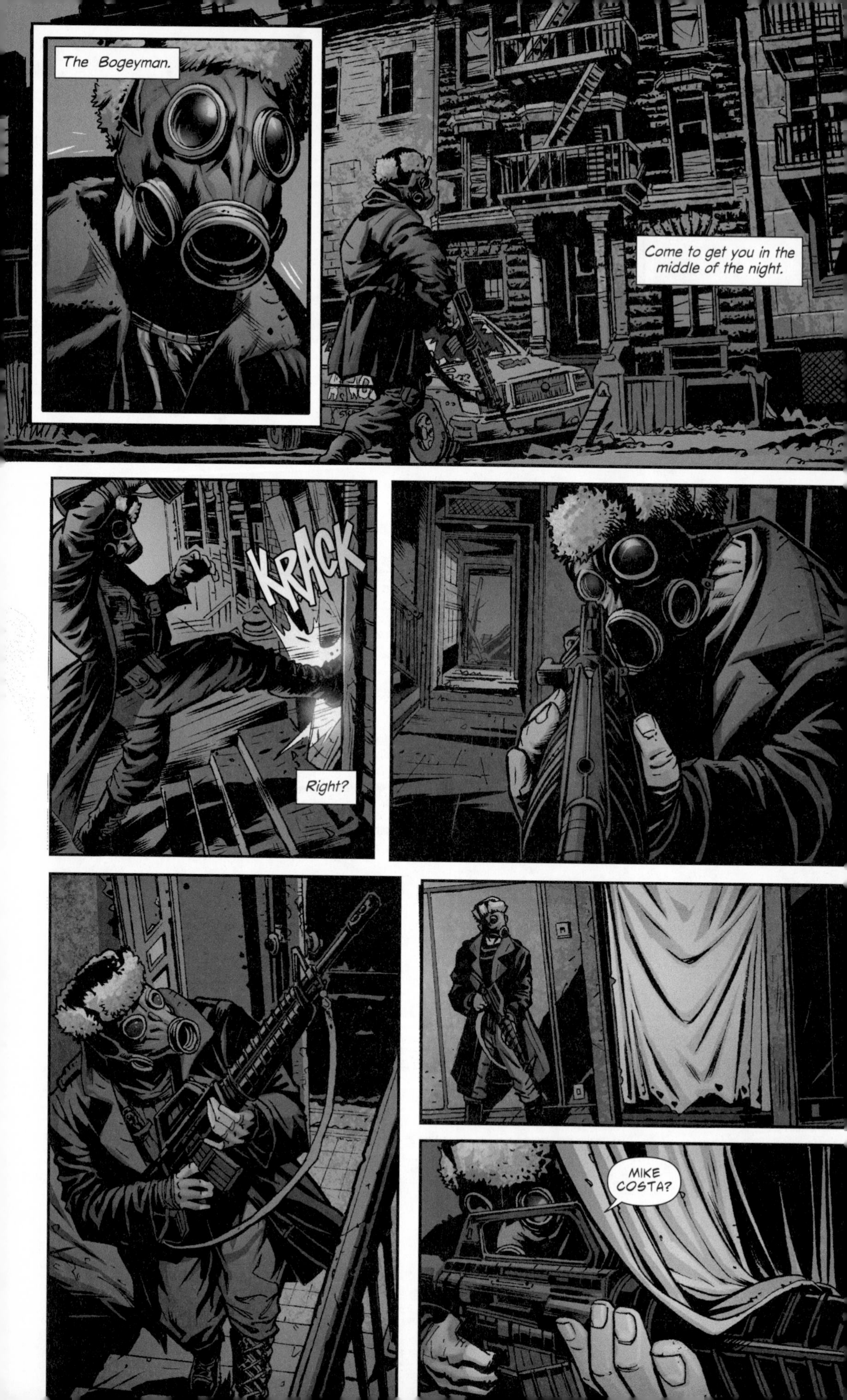
The Bogeyman.
Come to get you in the middle of the night.
KRACK
Right?
MIKE COSTA?

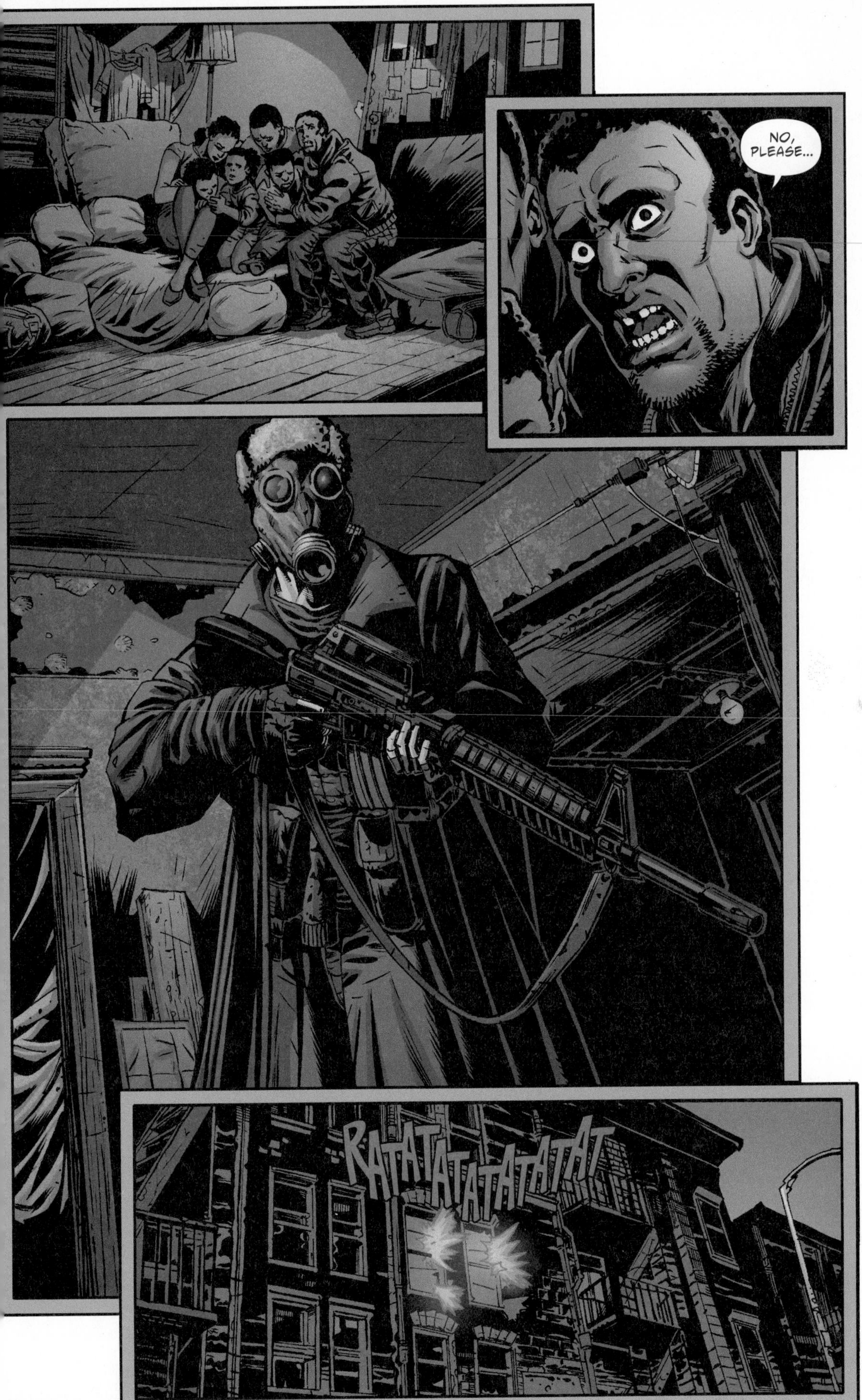
NO, PLEASE...
RATATATATATATAT

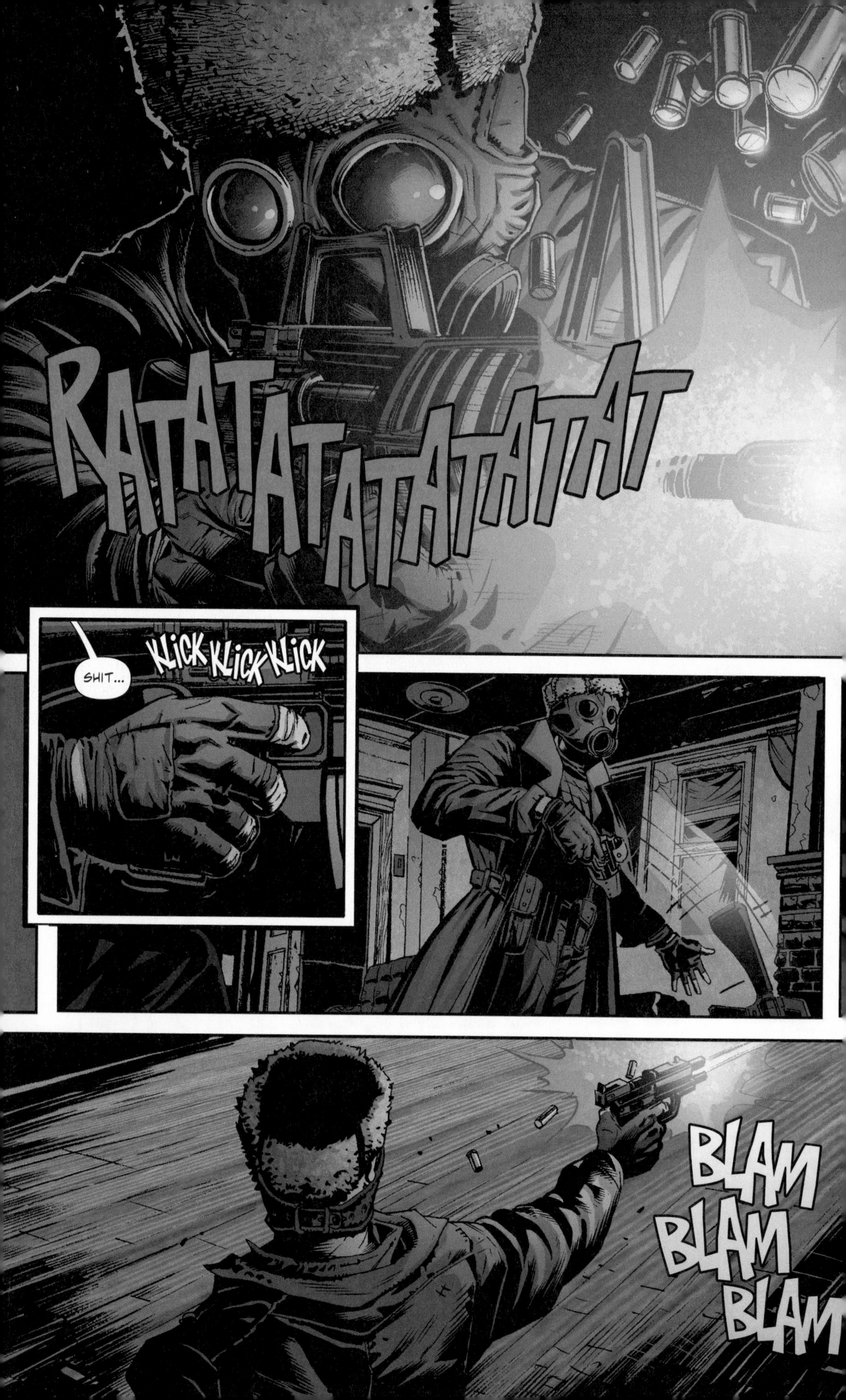
RATATATATATATAT
SHIT...
KLICK KLICK KLICK
BLAM
BLAM
BLAM

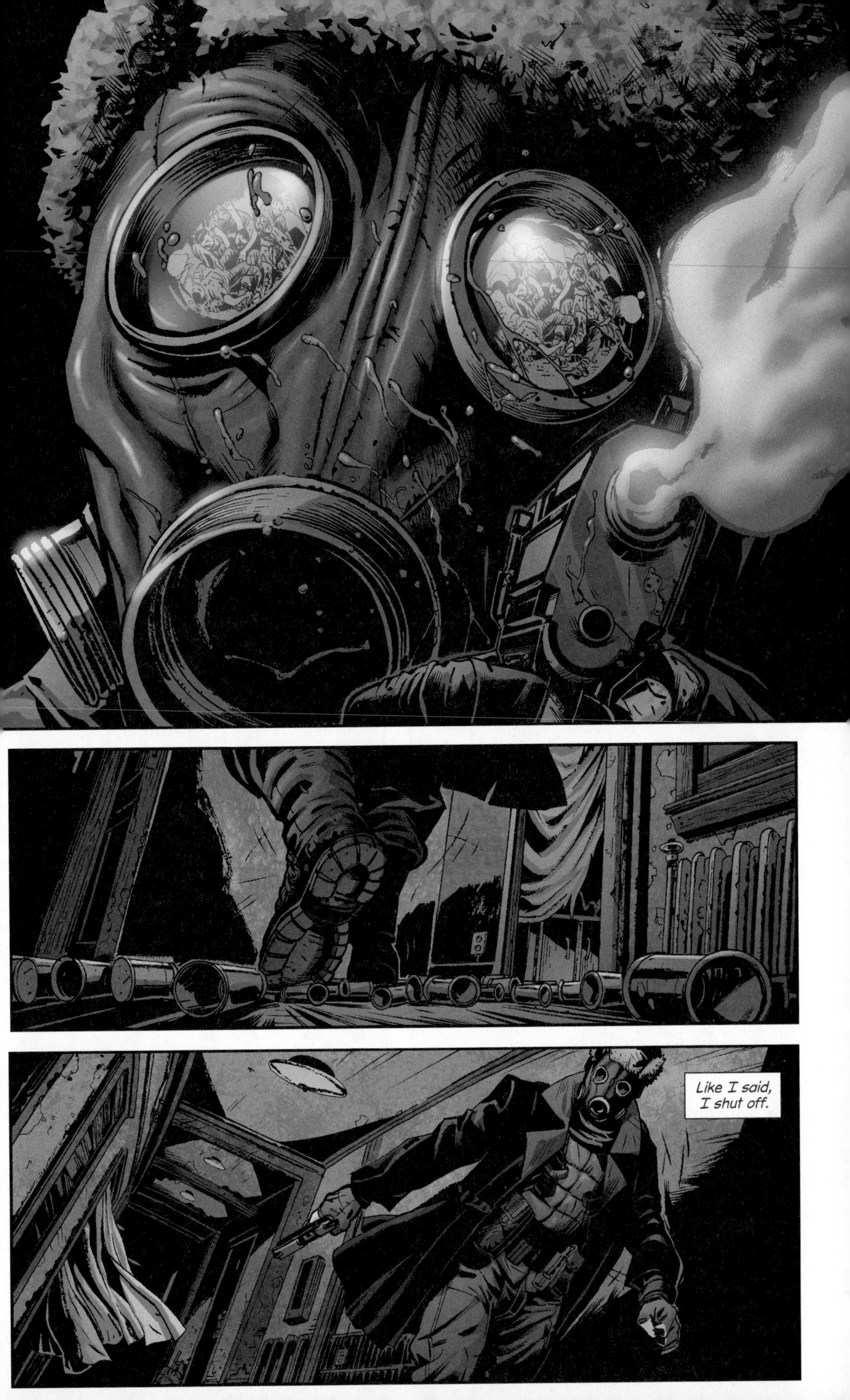
Like I said,
I shut off.

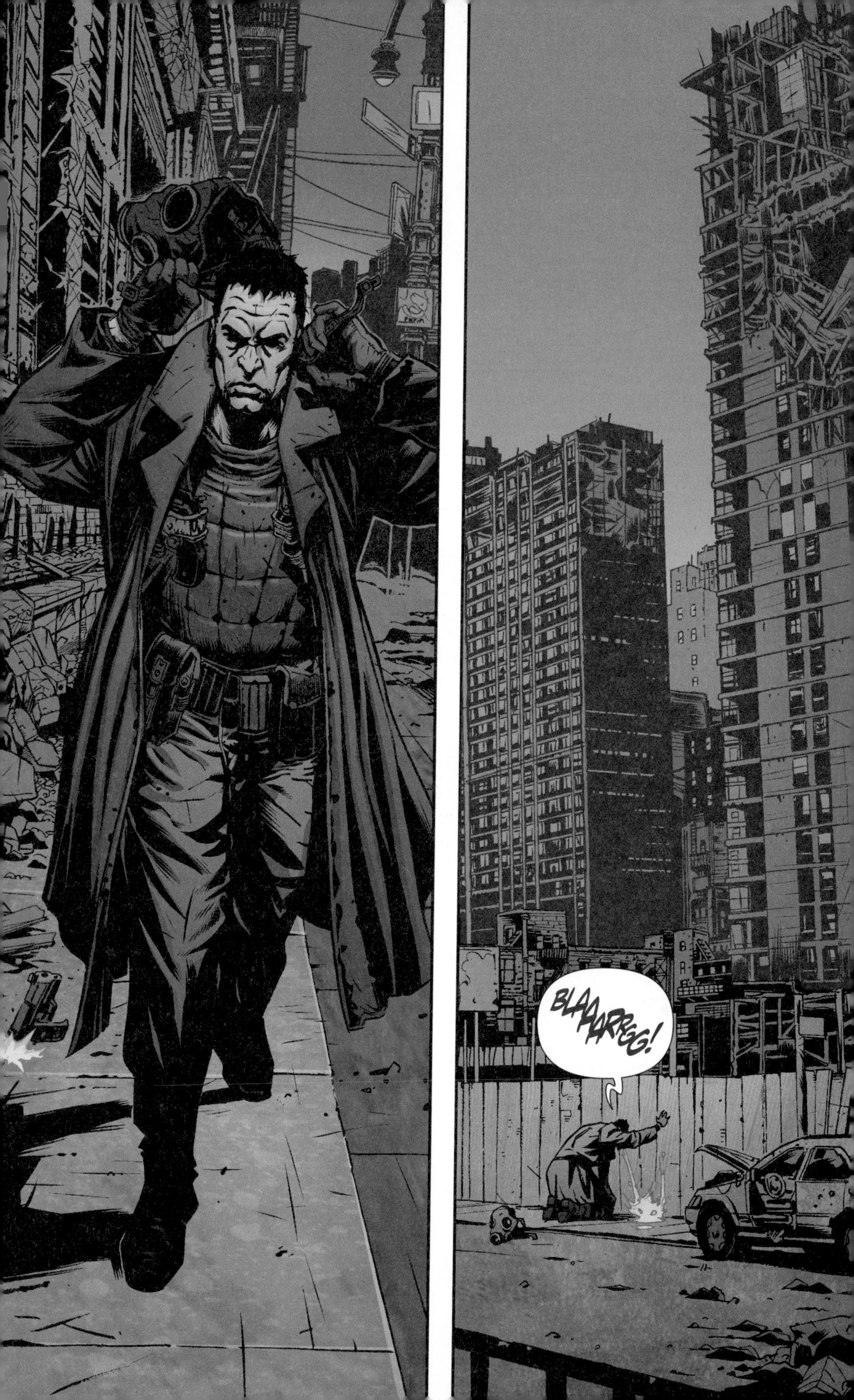
BLAAARRGG!

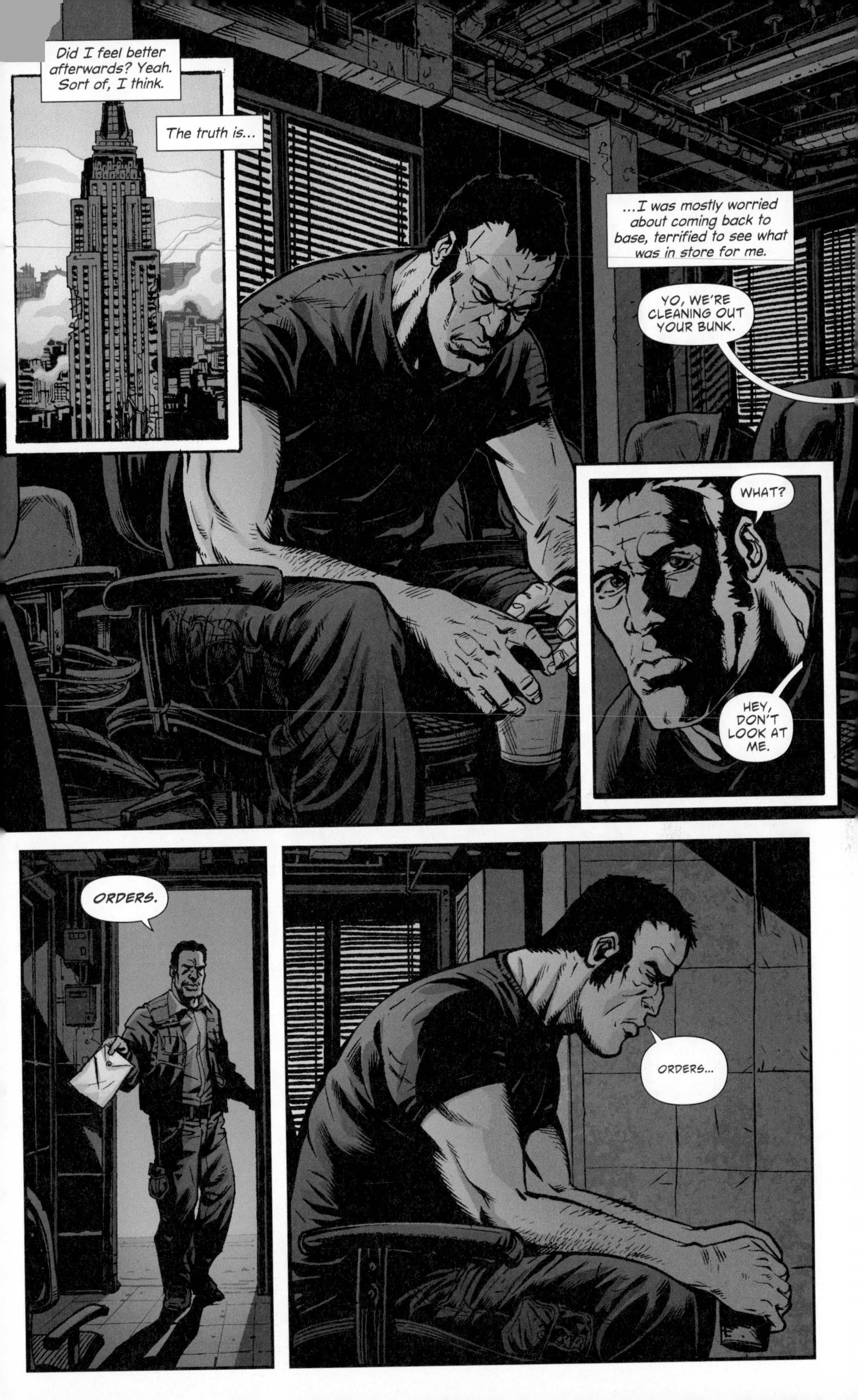
Did I feel better afterwards? Yeah. Sort of, I think.
The truth is...
...I was mostly worried about coming back to base, terrified to see what was in store for me.
YO, WE'RE CLEANING OUT YOUR BUNK.
WHAT?
HEY, DON'T LOOK AT ME.
ORDERS.
ORDERS...

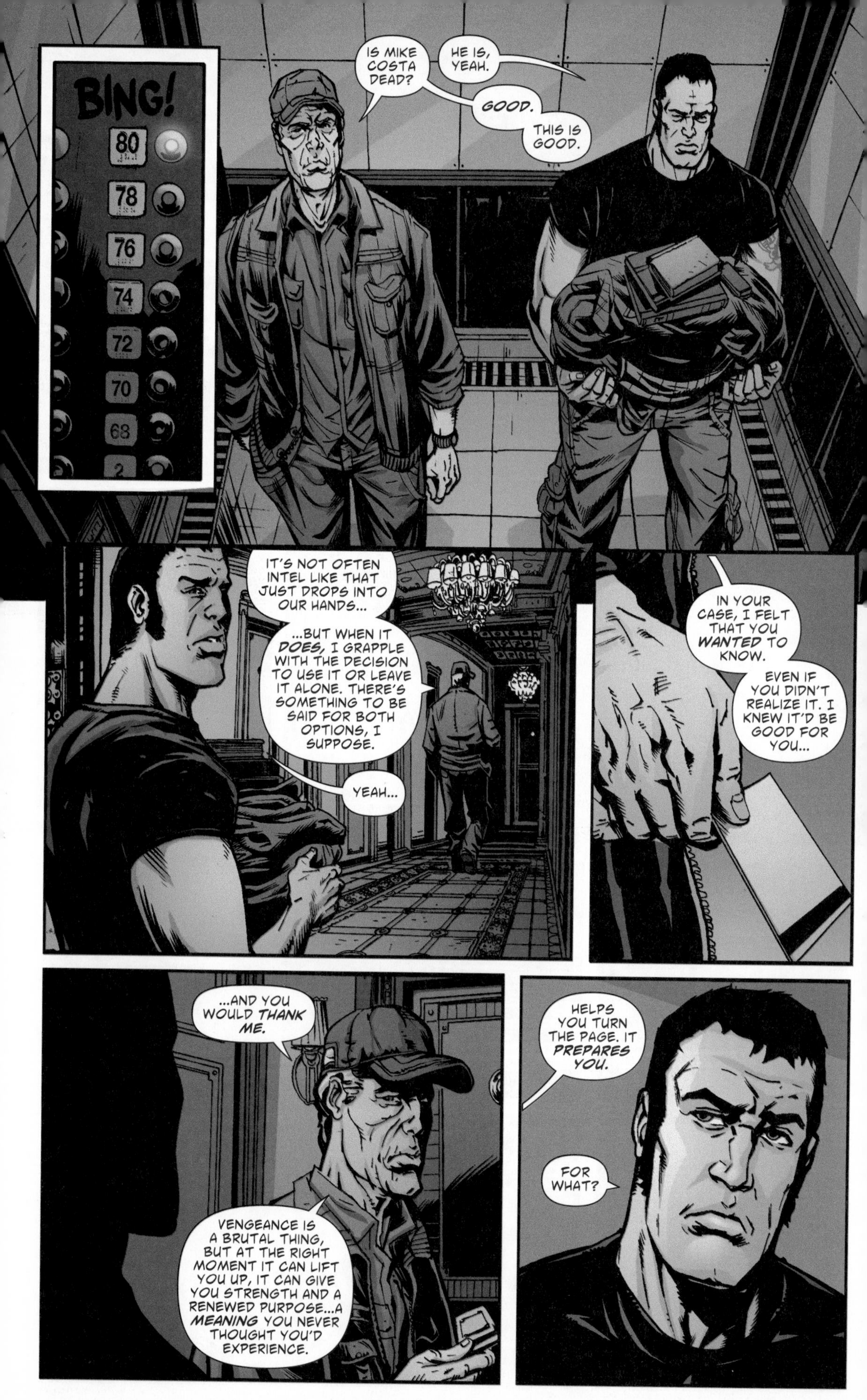
BING!
80
78
76
74
72
70
68
2
IS MIKE COSTA DEAD?
HE IS, YEAH.
GOOD.
THIS IS GOOD.
IT'S NOT OFTEN INTEL LIKE THAT JUST DROPS INTO OUR HANDS...
...BUT WHEN IT DOES, I GRAPPLE WITH THE DECISION TO USE IT OR LEAVE IT ALONE. THERE'S SOMETHING TO BE SAID FOR BOTH OPTIONS, I SUPPOSE.
YEAH...
IN YOUR CASE, I FELT THAT YOU WANTED TO KNOW.
EVEN IF YOU DIDN'T REALIZE IT. I KNEW IT'D BE GOOD FOR YOU...
...AND YOU WOULD THANK ME.
VENGEANCE IS A BRUTAL THING, BUT AT THE RIGHT MOMENT IT CAN LIFT YOU UP, IT CAN GIVE YOU STRENGTH AND A RENEWED PURPOSE...A MEANING YOU NEVER THOUGHT YOU'D EXPERIENCE.
HELPS YOU TURN THE PAGE. IT PREPARES YOU.
FOR WHAT?

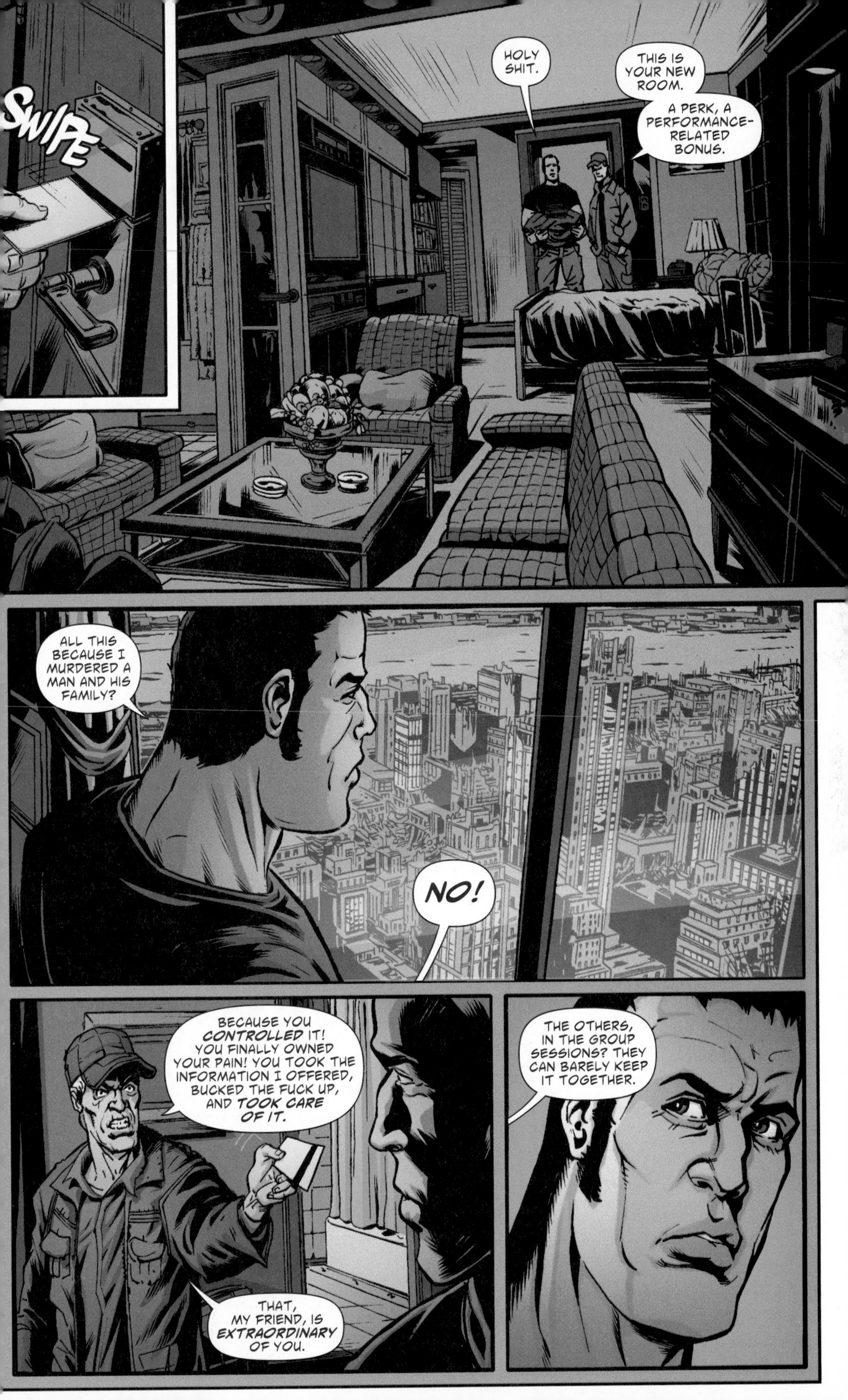
SWIPE
HOLY SHIT.
THIS IS YOUR NEW ROOM.
A PERK, A PERFORMANCE-RELATED BONUS.
ALL THIS BECAUSE I MURDERED A MAN AND HIS FAMILY?
NO!
BECAUSE YOU CONTROLLED IT! YOU FINALLY OWNED YOUR PAIN! YOU TOOK THE INFORMATION I OFFERED, BUCKED THE FUCK UP, AND TOOK CARE OF IT.
THAT, MY FRIEND, IS EXTRAORDINARY OF YOU.
THE OTHERS, IN THE GROUP SESSIONS? THEY CAN BARELY KEEP IT TOGETHER.

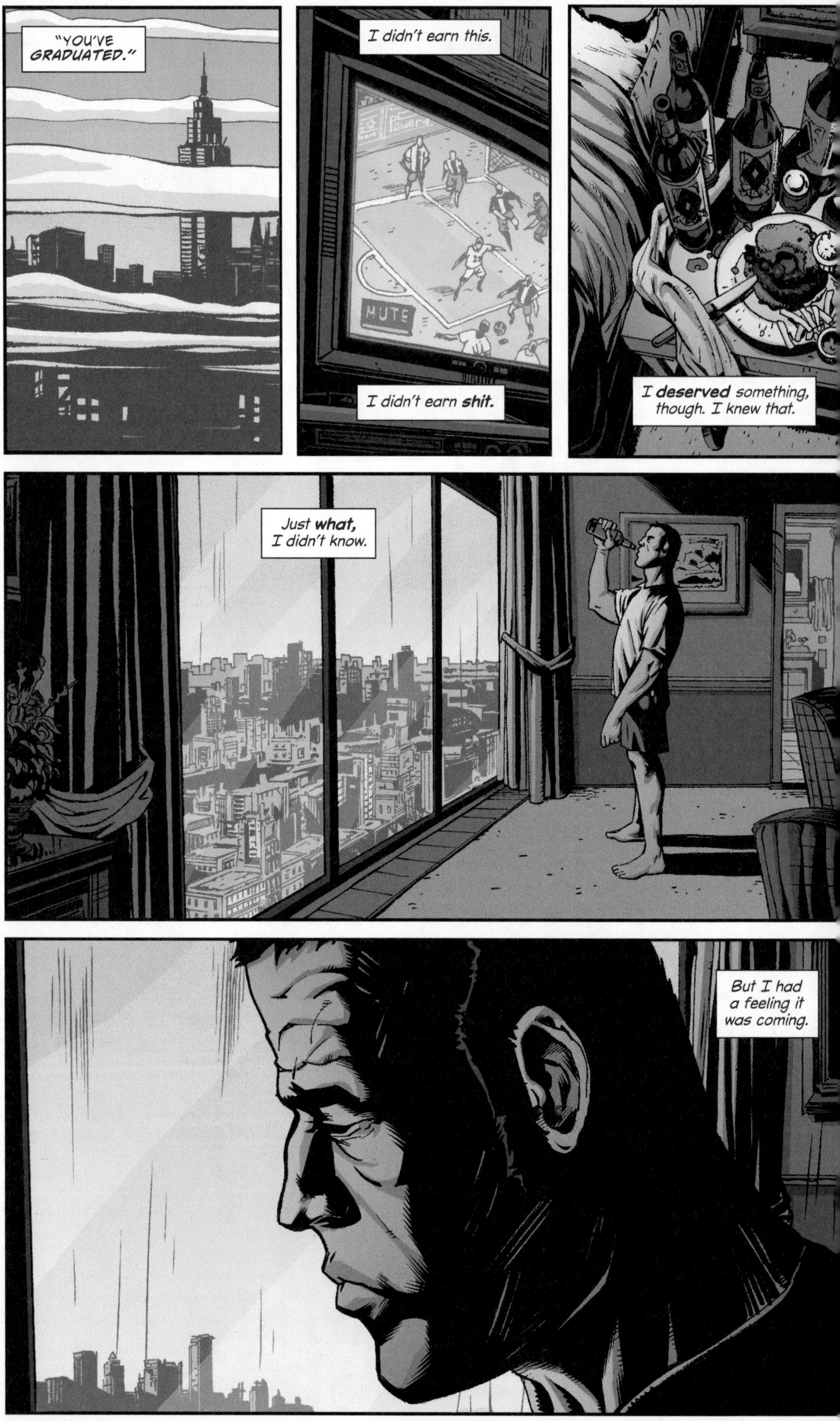
"YOU'VE GRADUATED."
I didn't earn this.
MUTE
I didn't earn **shit.**
I **deserved** something, though. I knew that.
Just **what,** I didn't know.
But I had a feeling it was coming.

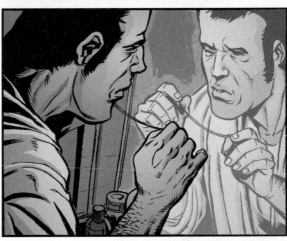

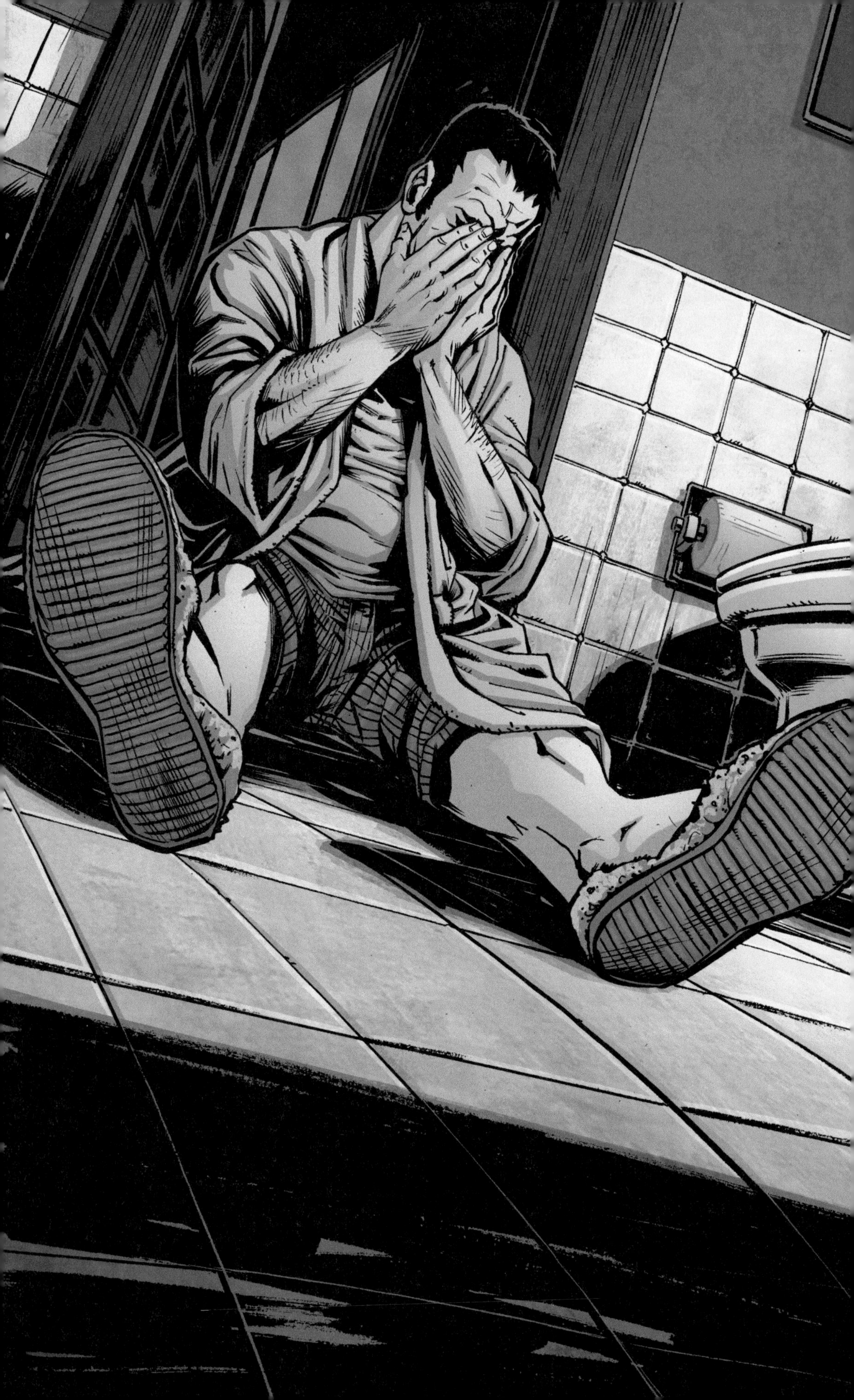

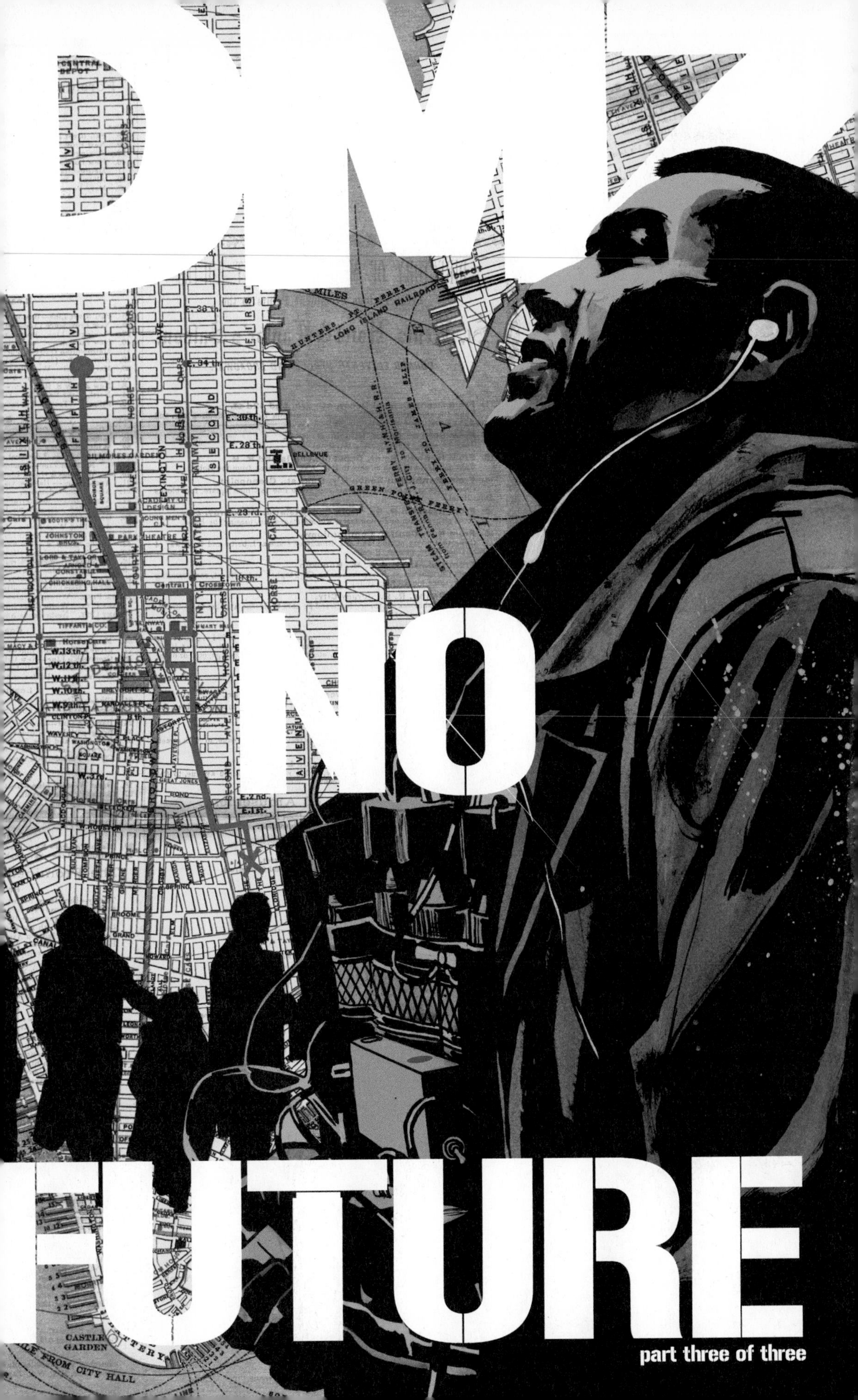
DMZ
NO
FUTURE
part three of three

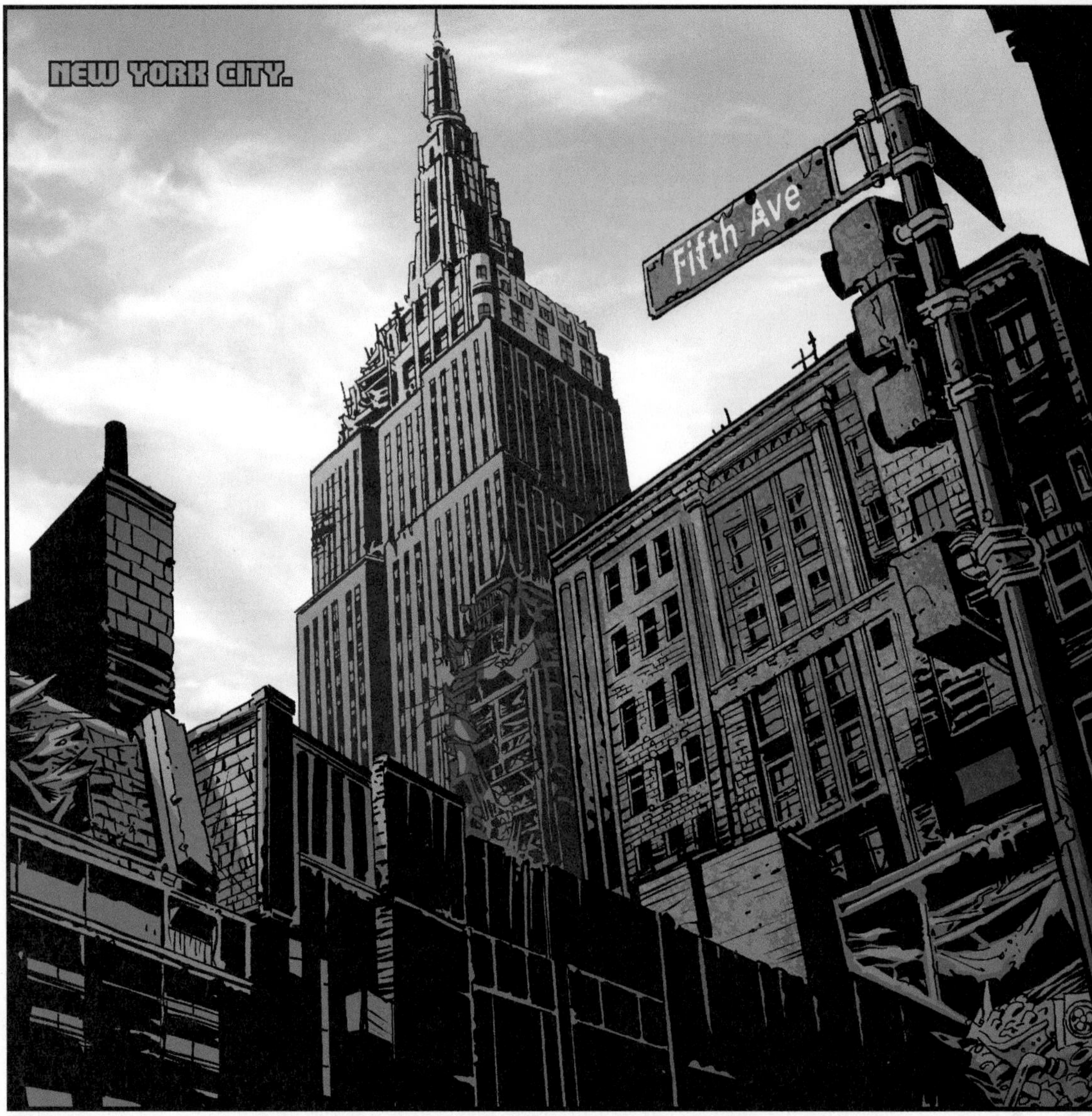
NEW YORK CITY.
Fifth Ave

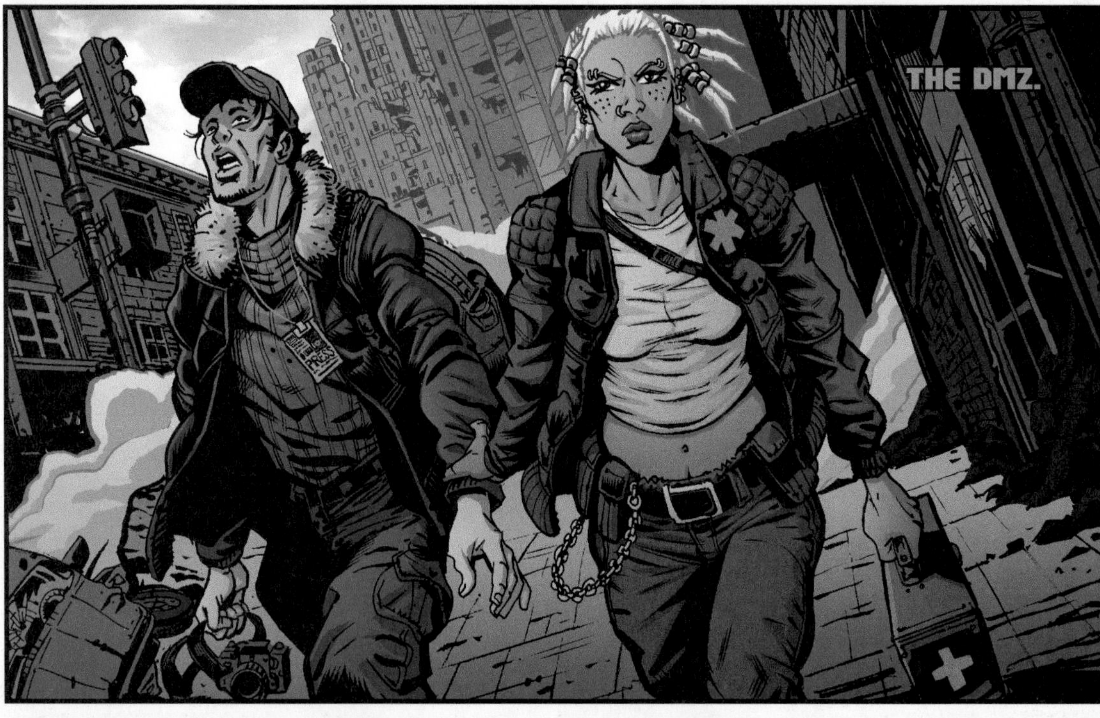
THE DMZ.

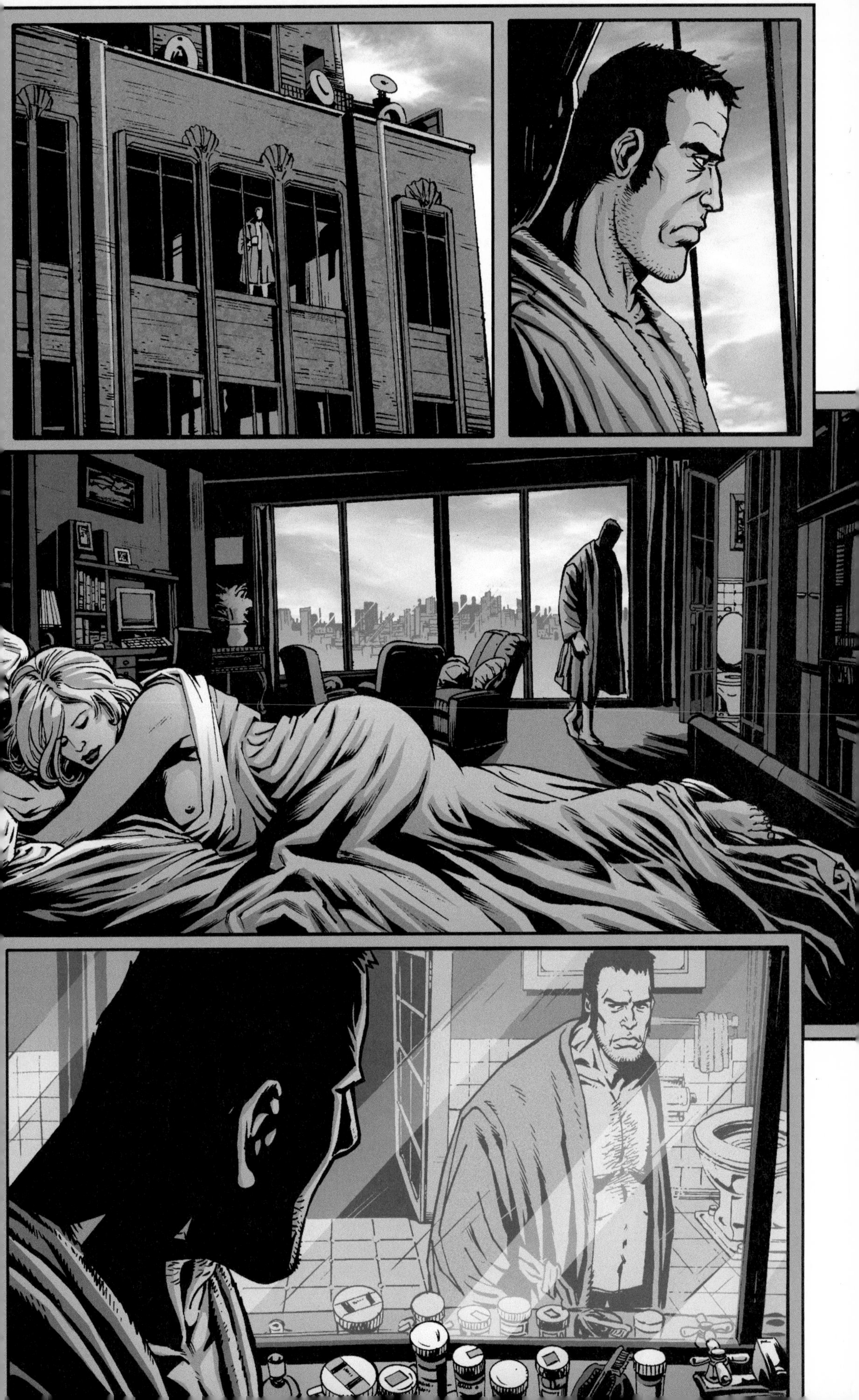

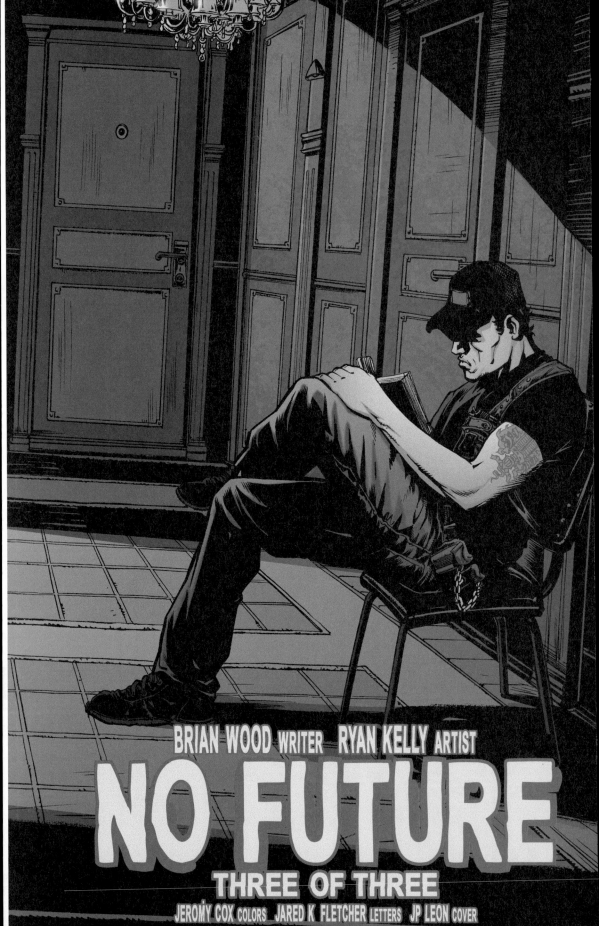

BRIAN WOOD WRITER   RYAN KELLY ARTIST

NO FUTURE

THREE OF THREE

JEROMY COX COLORS   JARED K FLETCHER LETTERS   JP LEON COVER

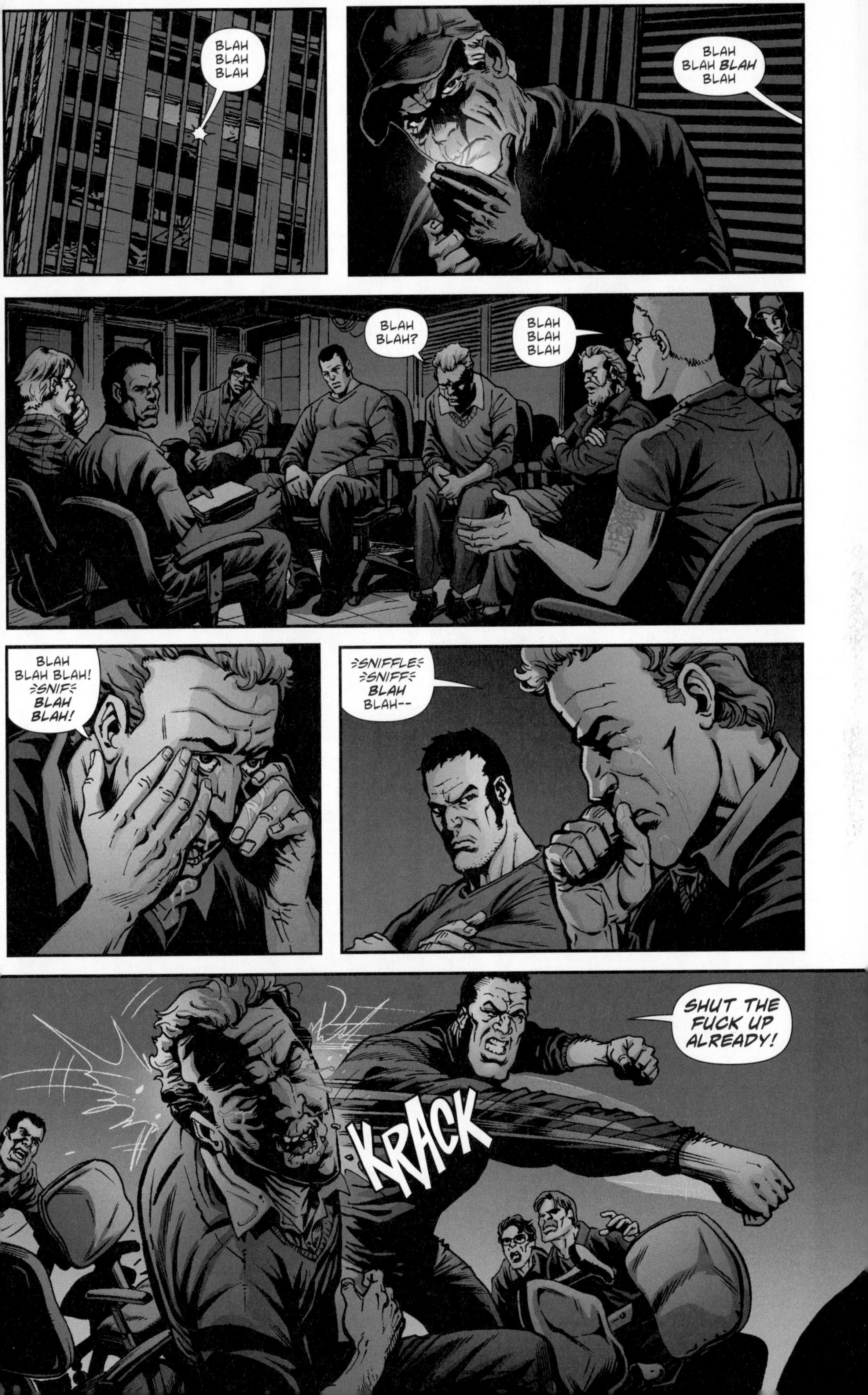

BLAH
BLAH
BLAH
BLAH
BLAH BLAH BLAH
BLAH
BLAH
BLAH?
BLAH
BLAH
BLAH
BLAH
BLAH BLAH!
≈SNIF≈
BLAH
BLAH!
≈SNIFFLE≈
≈SNIFF≈
BLAH
BLAH--
SHUT THE
FUCK UP
ALREADY!
KRACK

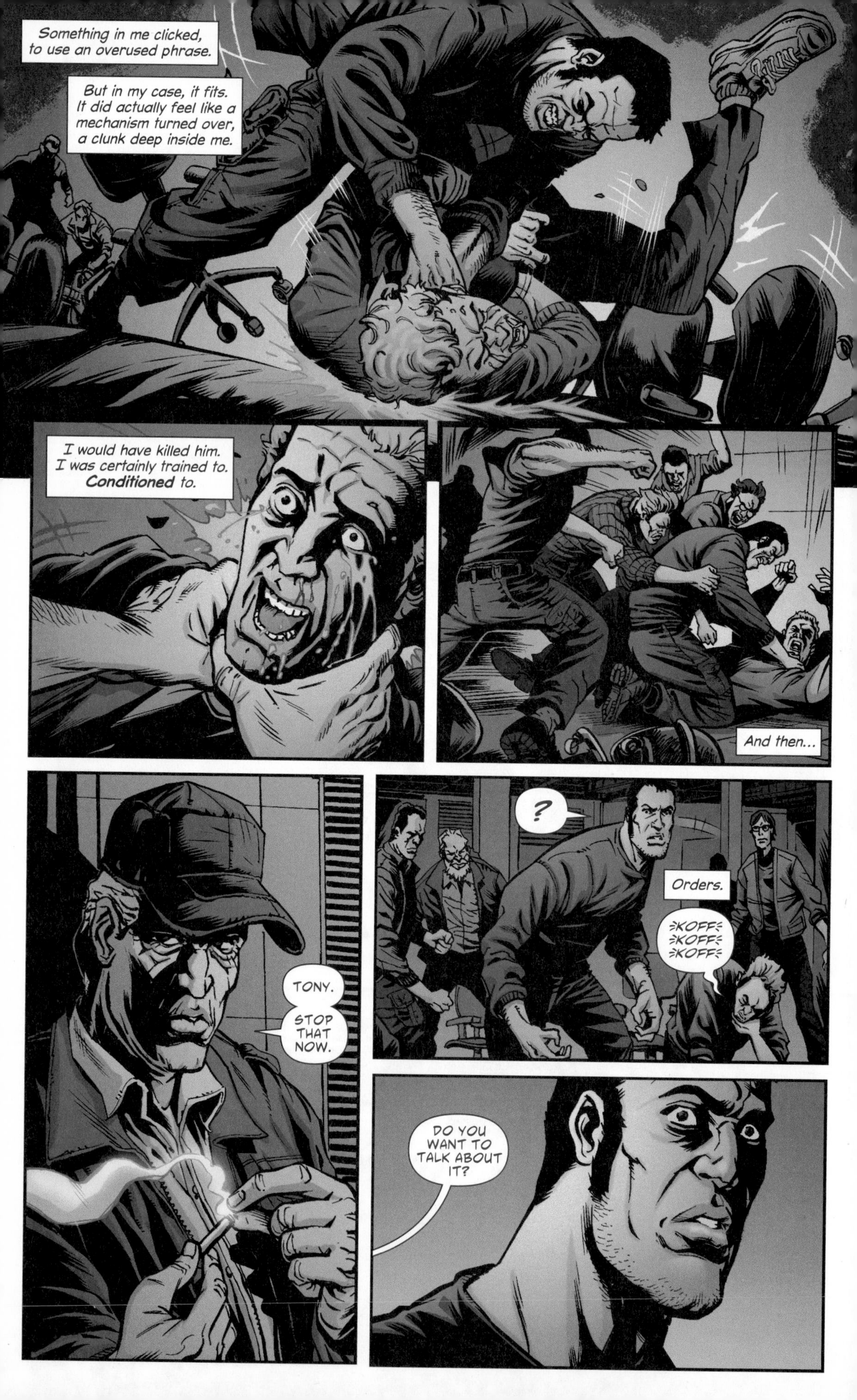
Something in me clicked, to use an overused phrase.
But in my case, it fits. It did actually feel like a mechanism turned over, a clunk deep inside me.
I would have killed him. I was certainly trained to. **Conditioned** to.
And then...
TONY.
STOP THAT NOW.
?
Orders.
KOFF KOFF KOFF
DO YOU WANT TO TALK ABOUT IT?

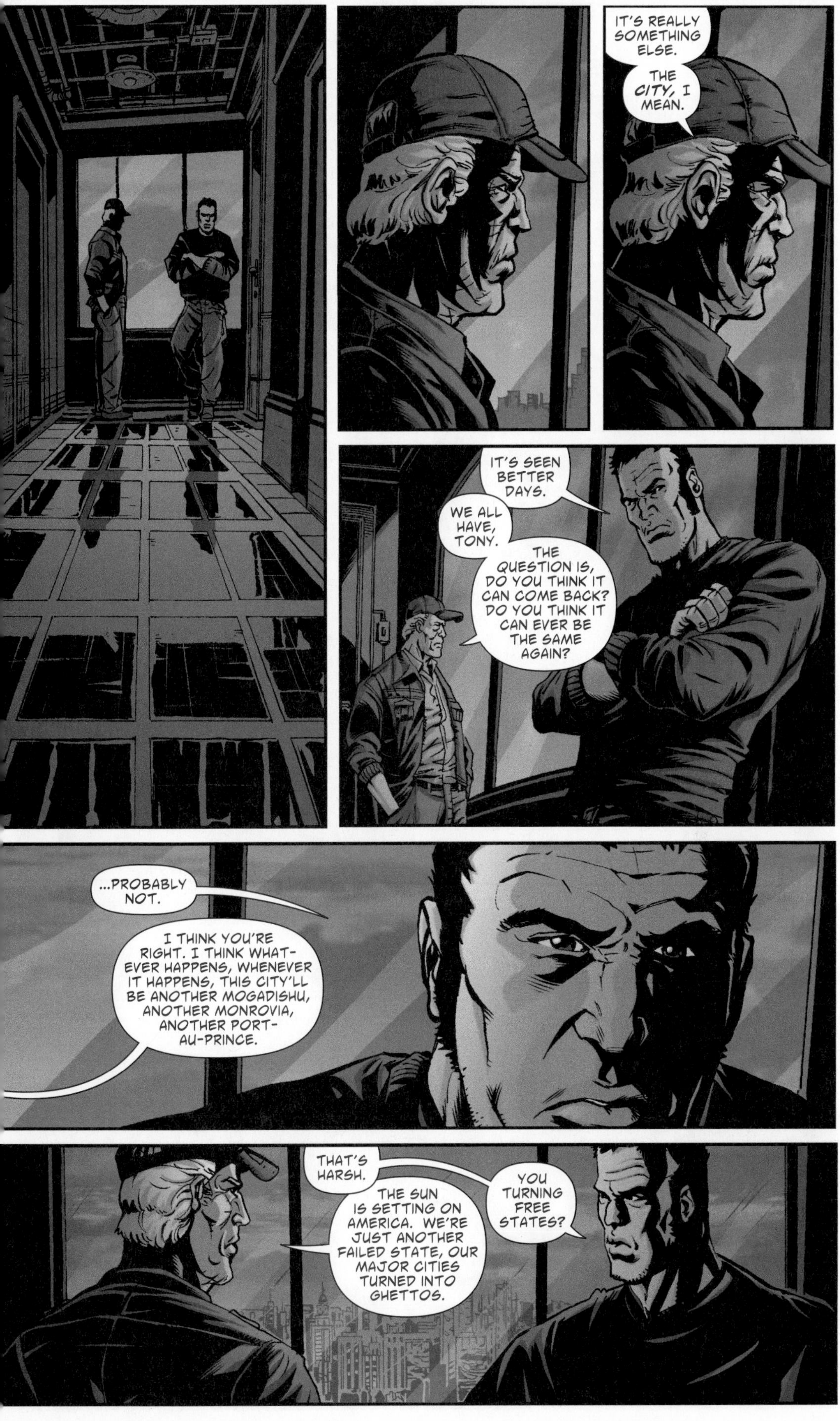
IT'S REALLY SOMETHING ELSE.
THE CITY, I MEAN.
IT'S SEEN BETTER DAYS.
WE ALL HAVE, TONY.
THE QUESTION IS, DO YOU THINK IT CAN COME BACK? DO YOU THINK IT CAN EVER BE THE SAME AGAIN?
...PROBABLY NOT.
I THINK YOU'RE RIGHT. I THINK WHAT-EVER HAPPENS, WHENEVER IT HAPPENS, THIS CITY'LL BE ANOTHER MOGADISHU, ANOTHER MONROVIA, ANOTHER PORT-AU-PRINCE.
THAT'S HARSH.
YOU TURNING FREE STATES?
THE SUN IS SETTING ON AMERICA. WE'RE JUST ANOTHER FAILED STATE, OUR MAJOR CITIES TURNED INTO GHETTOS.

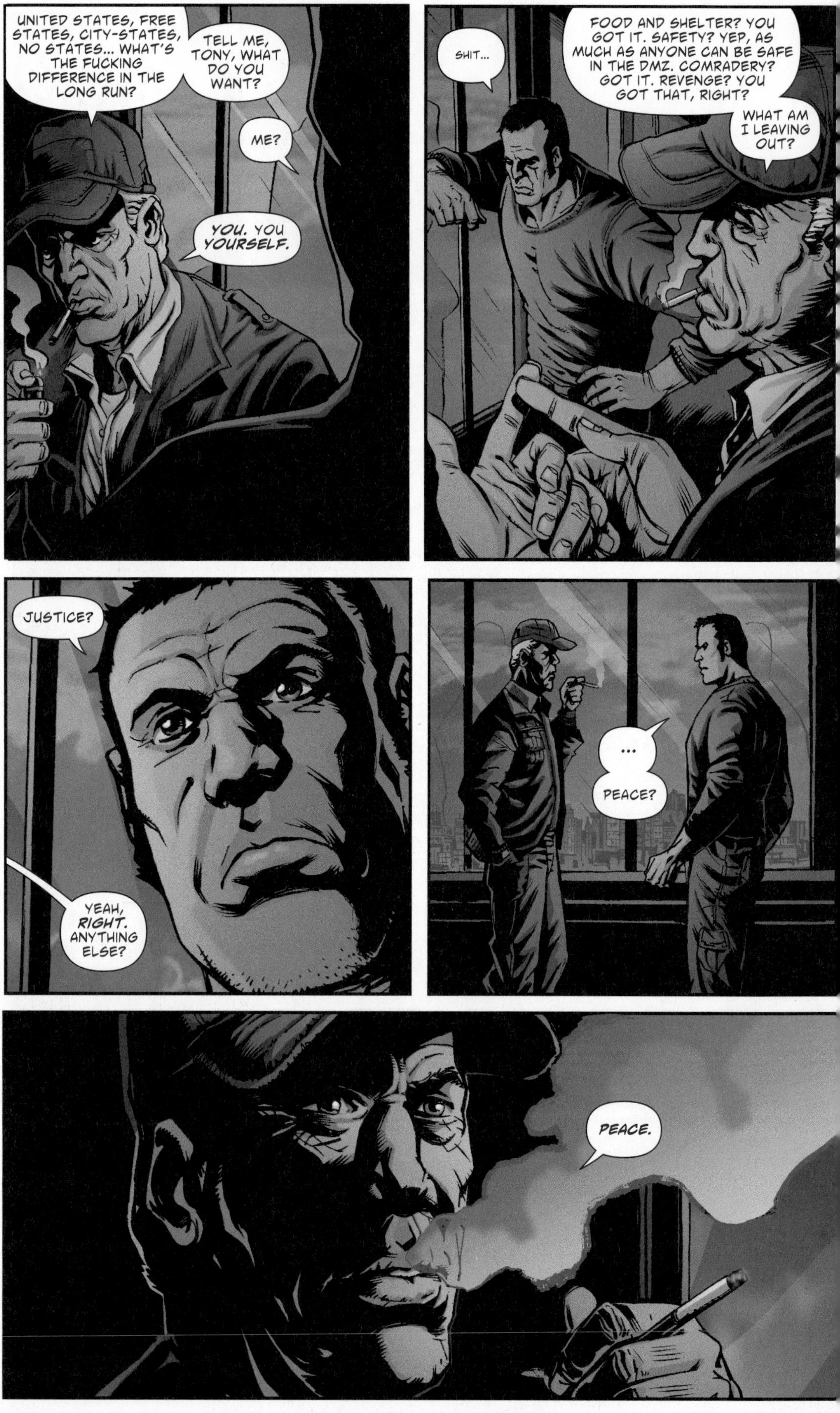
UNITED STATES, FREE STATES, CITY-STATES, NO STATES... WHAT'S THE FUCKING DIFFERENCE IN THE LONG RUN?
TELL ME, TONY, WHAT DO YOU WANT?
ME?
YOU. YOU YOURSELF.
SHIT...
FOOD AND SHELTER? YOU GOT IT. SAFETY? YEP, AS MUCH AS ANYONE CAN BE SAFE IN THE DMZ. COMRADERY? GOT IT. REVENGE? YOU GOT THAT, RIGHT?
WHAT AM I LEAVING OUT?
JUSTICE?
YEAH, RIGHT. ANYTHING ELSE?
...
PEACE?
PEACE.

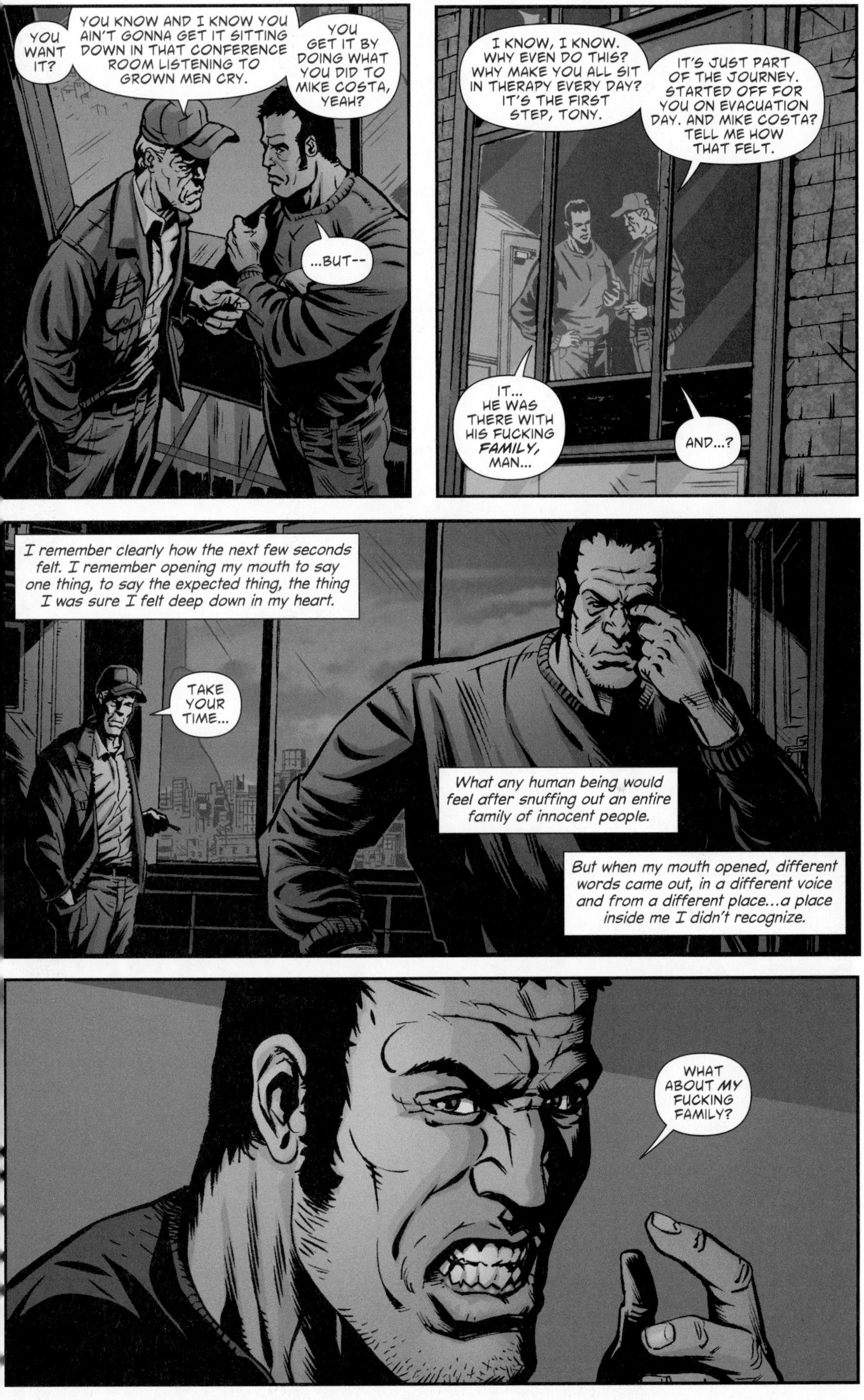
YOU WANT IT?
YOU KNOW AND I KNOW YOU AIN'T GONNA GET IT SITTING DOWN IN THAT CONFERENCE ROOM LISTENING TO GROWN MEN CRY.
YOU GET IT BY DOING WHAT YOU DID TO MIKE COSTA, YEAH?
...BUT--
I KNOW, I KNOW. WHY EVEN DO THIS? WHY MAKE YOU ALL SIT IN THERAPY EVERY DAY? IT'S THE FIRST STEP, TONY.
IT'S JUST PART OF THE JOURNEY. STARTED OFF FOR YOU ON EVACUATION DAY. AND MIKE COSTA? TELL ME HOW THAT FELT.
IT... HE WAS THERE WITH HIS FUCKING *FAMILY,* MAN...
AND...?
I remember clearly how the next few seconds felt. I remember opening my mouth to say one thing, to say the expected thing, the thing I was sure I felt deep down in my heart.
TAKE YOUR TIME...
What any human being would feel after snuffing out an entire family of innocent people.
But when my mouth opened, different words came out, in a different voice and from a different place...a place inside me I didn't recognize.
WHAT ABOUT *MY* FUCKING FAMILY?

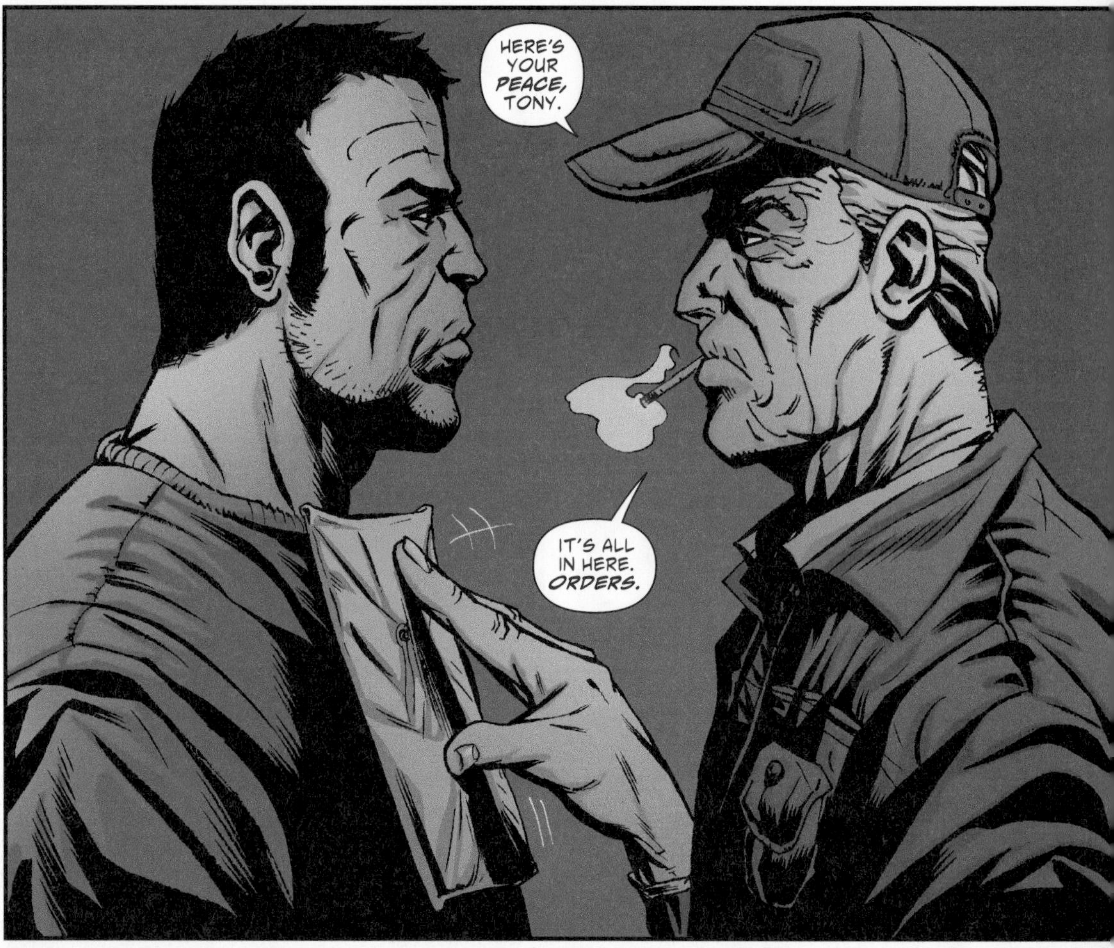
HERE'S YOUR PEACE, TONY.
IT'S ALL IN HERE. ORDERS.

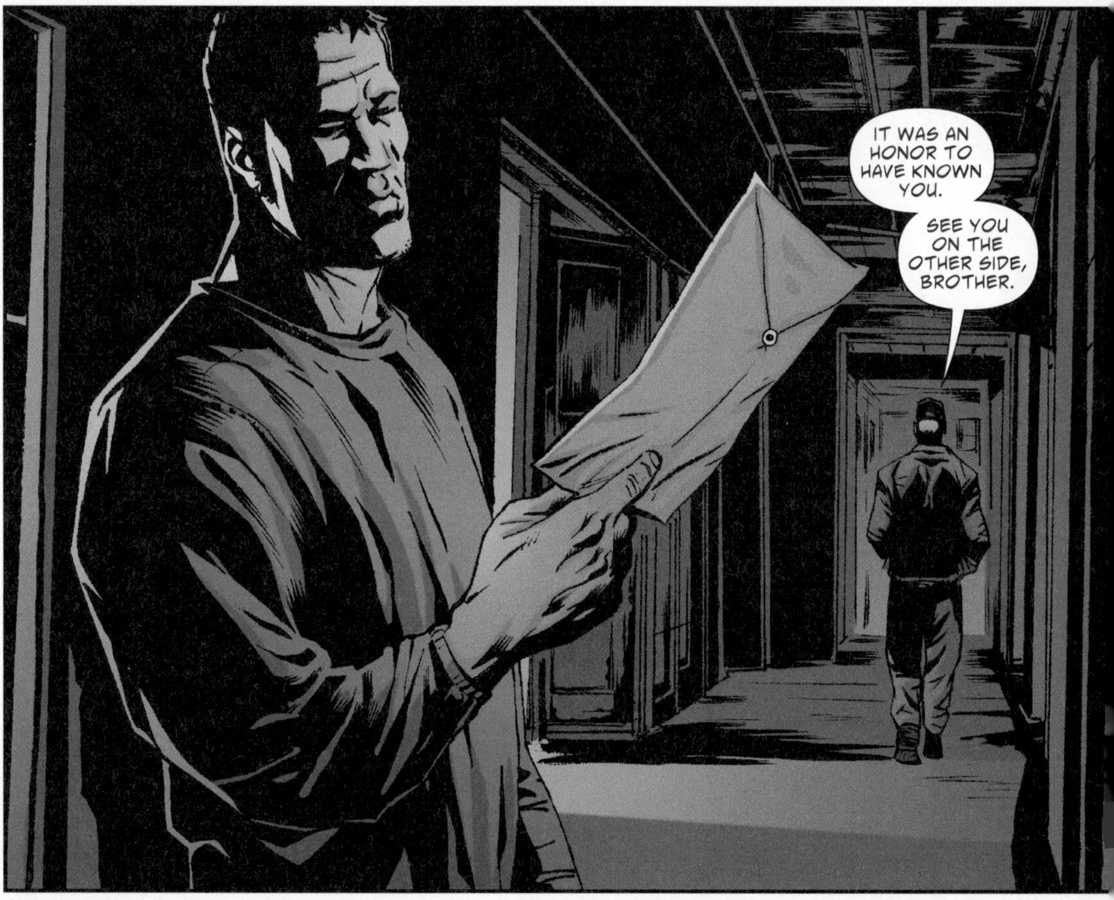
IT WAS AN HONOR TO HAVE KNOWN YOU.
SEE YOU ON THE OTHER SIDE, BROTHER.

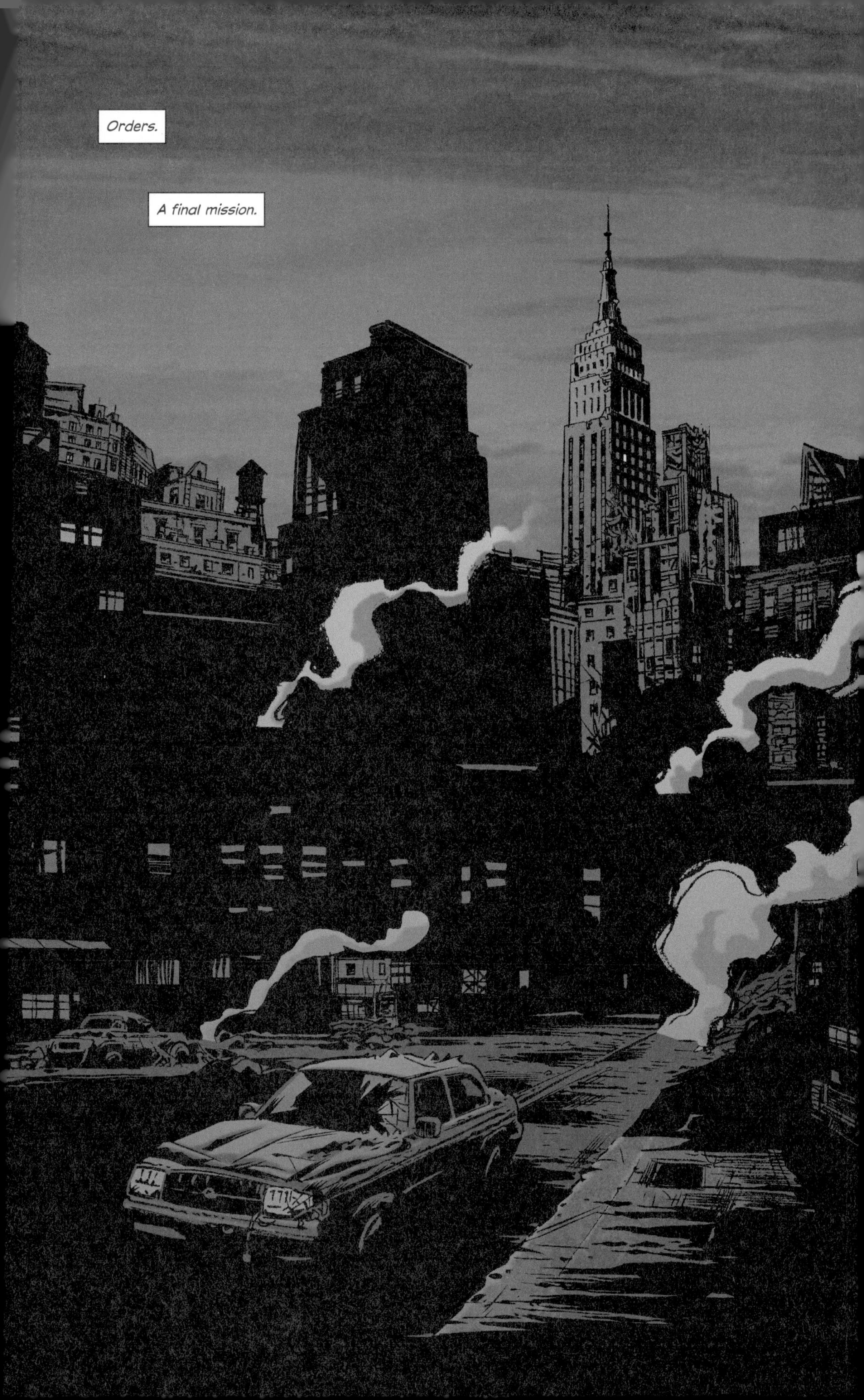
Orders.
A final mission.

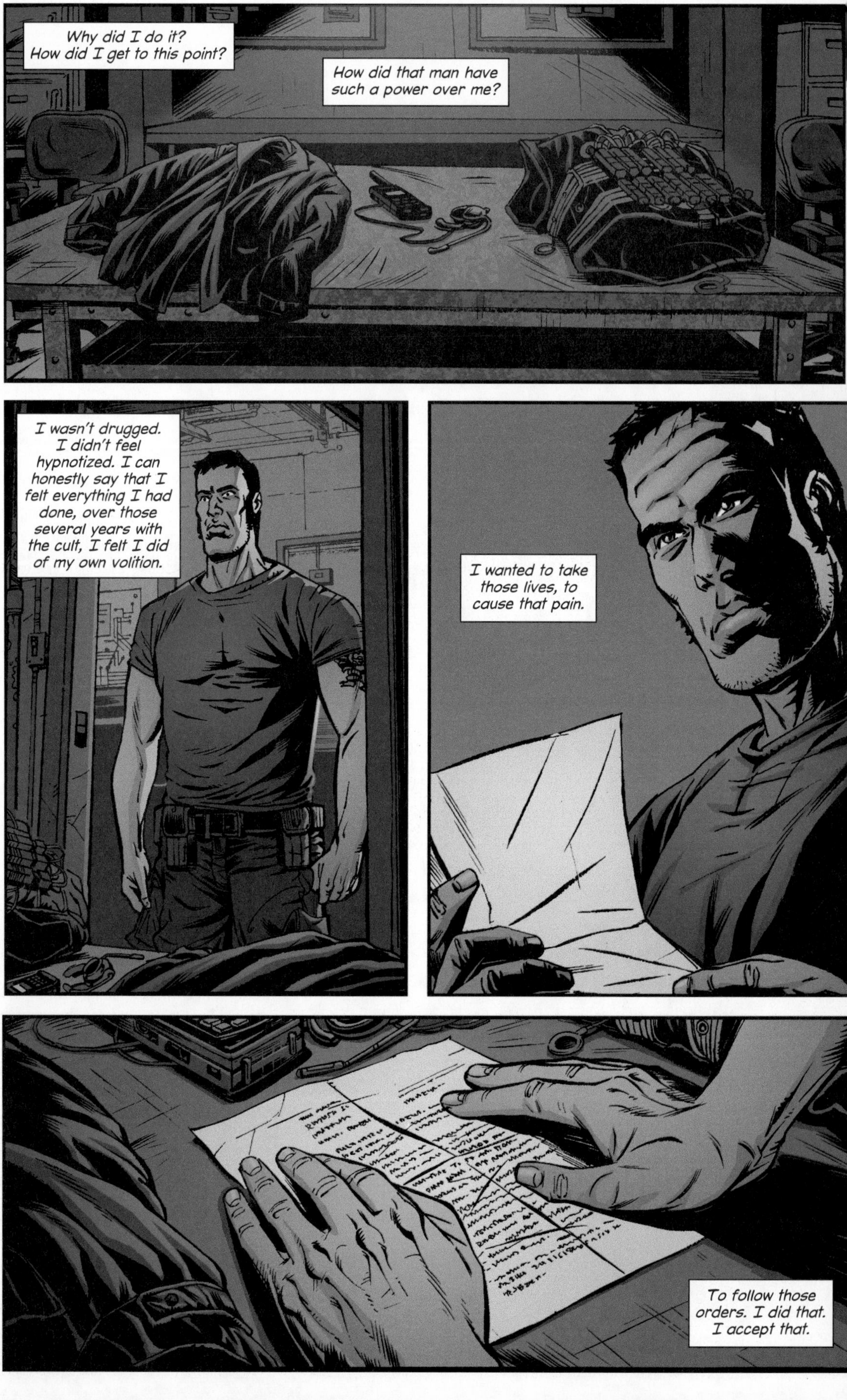

Why did I do it? How did I get to this point?
How did that man have such a power over me?
I wasn't drugged. I didn't feel hypnotized. I can honestly say that I felt everything I had done, over those several years with the cult, I felt I did of my own volition.
I wanted to take those lives, to cause that pain.
To follow those orders. I did that. I accept that.

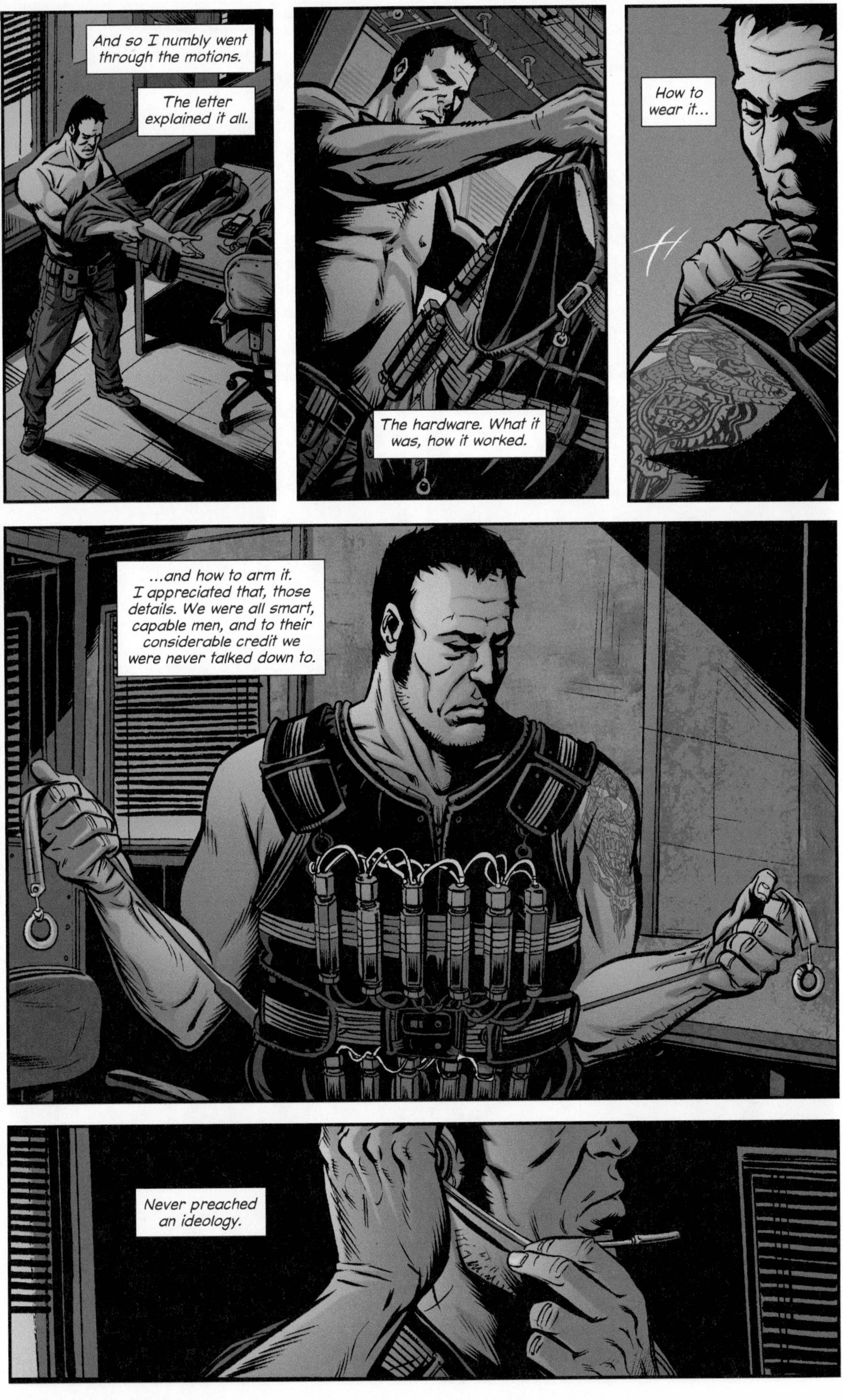
And so I numbly went through the motions.
The letter explained it all.
The hardware. What it was, how it worked.
How to wear it...
...and how to arm it. I appreciated that, those details. We were all smart, capable men, and to their considerable credit we were never talked down to.
Never preached an ideology.

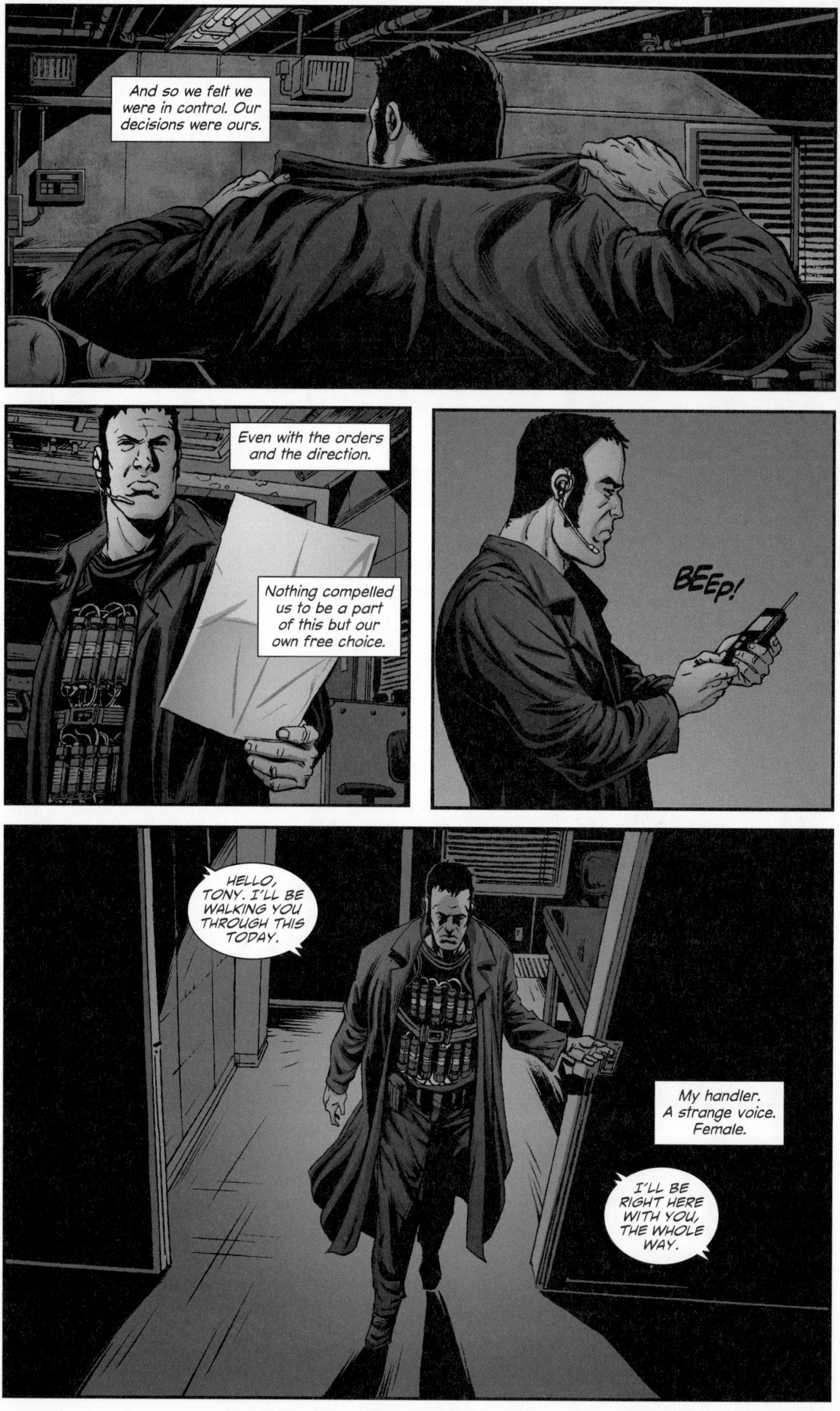
And so we felt we were in control. Our decisions were ours.
Even with the orders and the direction.
Nothing compelled us to be a part of this but our own free choice.
BEEP!
HELLO, TONY. I'LL BE WALKING YOU THROUGH THIS TODAY.
My handler. A strange voice. Female.
I'LL BE RIGHT HERE WITH YOU, THE WHOLE WAY.

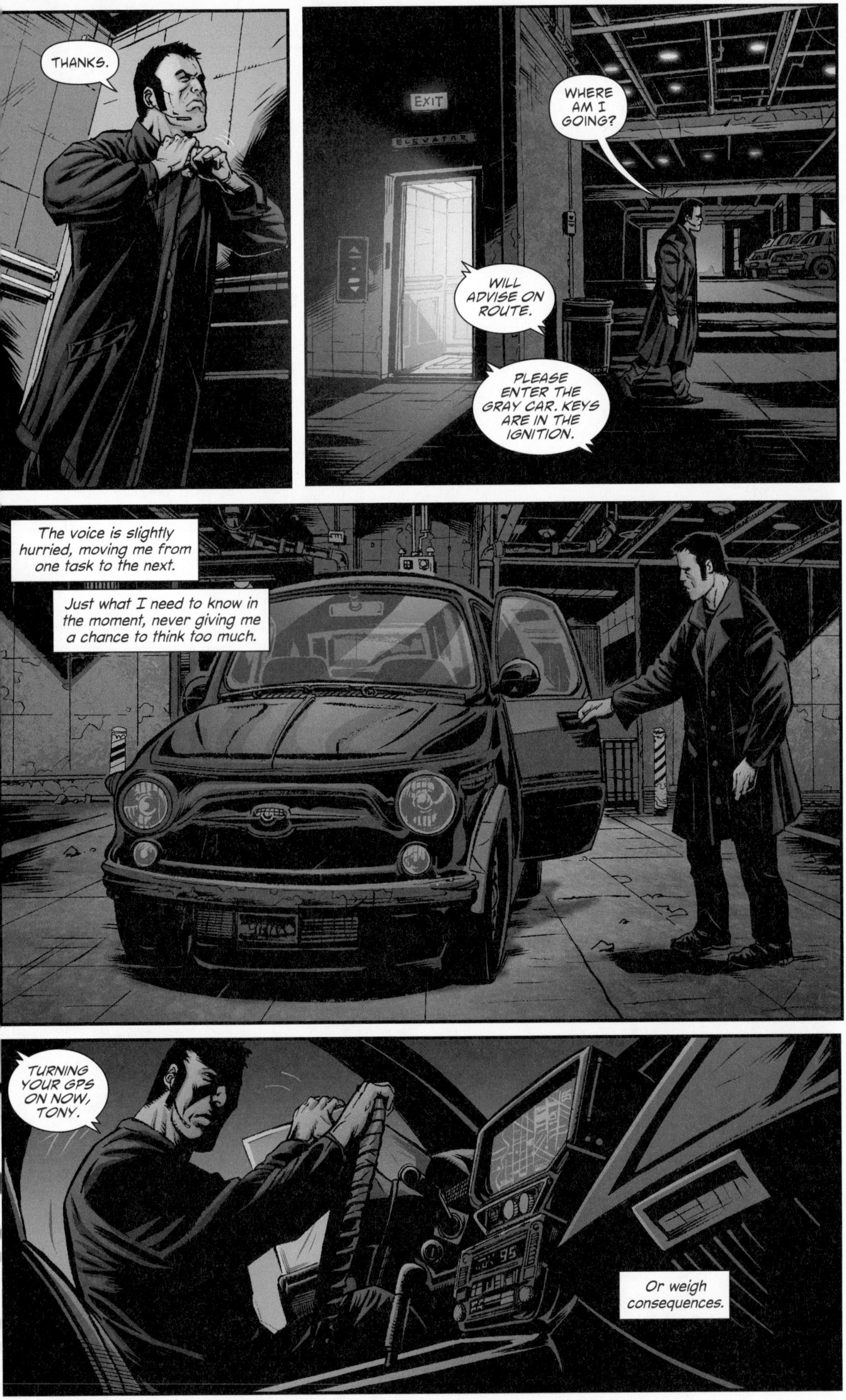
THANKS.
WHERE AM I GOING?
WILL ADVISE ON ROUTE.
PLEASE ENTER THE GRAY CAR. KEYS ARE IN THE IGNITION.
EXIT
The voice is slightly hurried, moving me from one task to the next.
Just what I need to know in the moment, never giving me a chance to think too much.
TURNING YOUR GPS ON NOW, TONY.
Or weigh consequences.

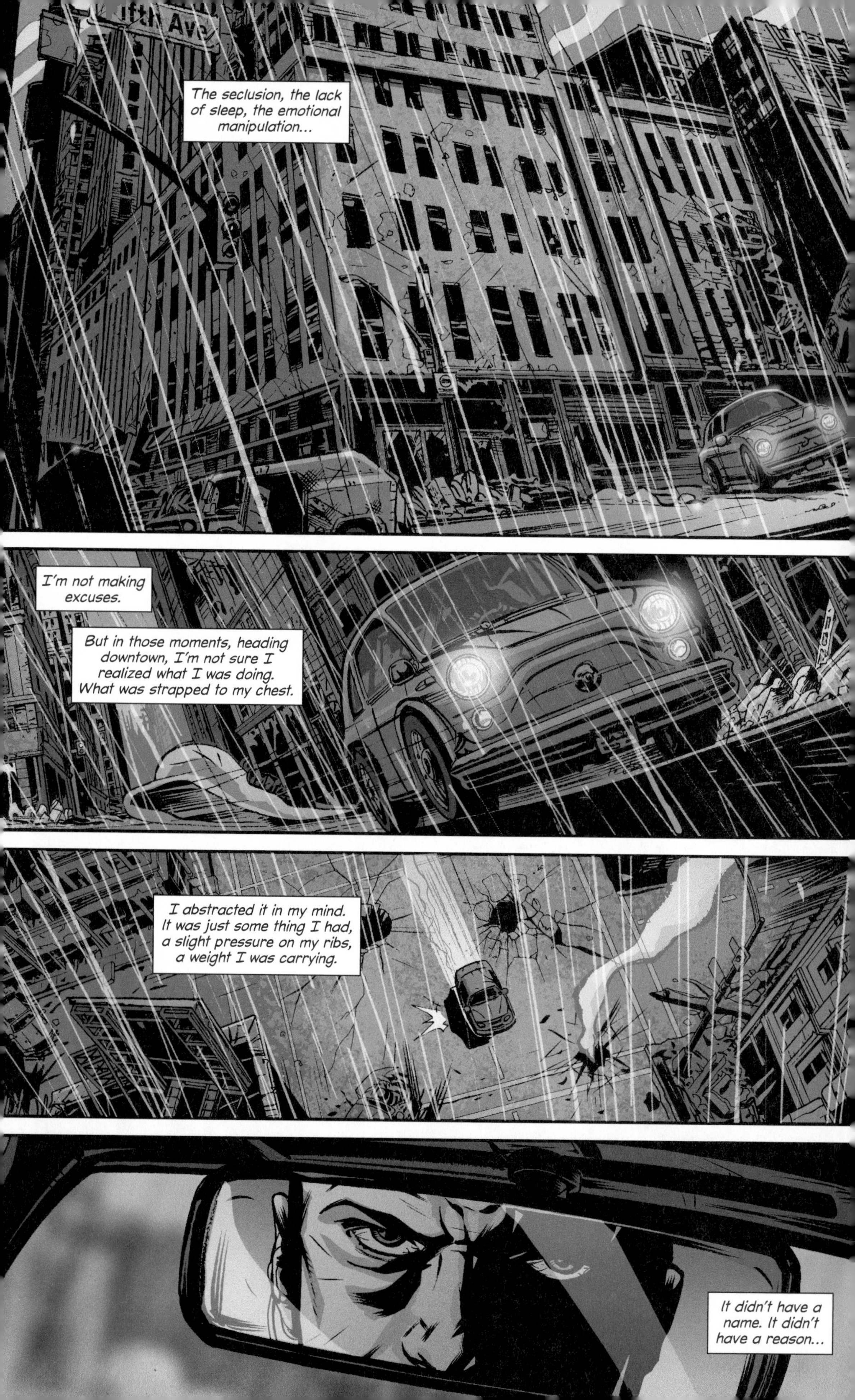
11th Ave
The seclusion, the lack of sleep, the emotional manipulation...
I'm not making excuses.
But in those moments, heading downtown, I'm not sure I realized what I was doing. What was strapped to my chest.
I abstracted it in my mind. It was just some thing I had, a slight pressure on my ribs, a weight I was carrying.
It didn't have a name. It didn't have a reason...

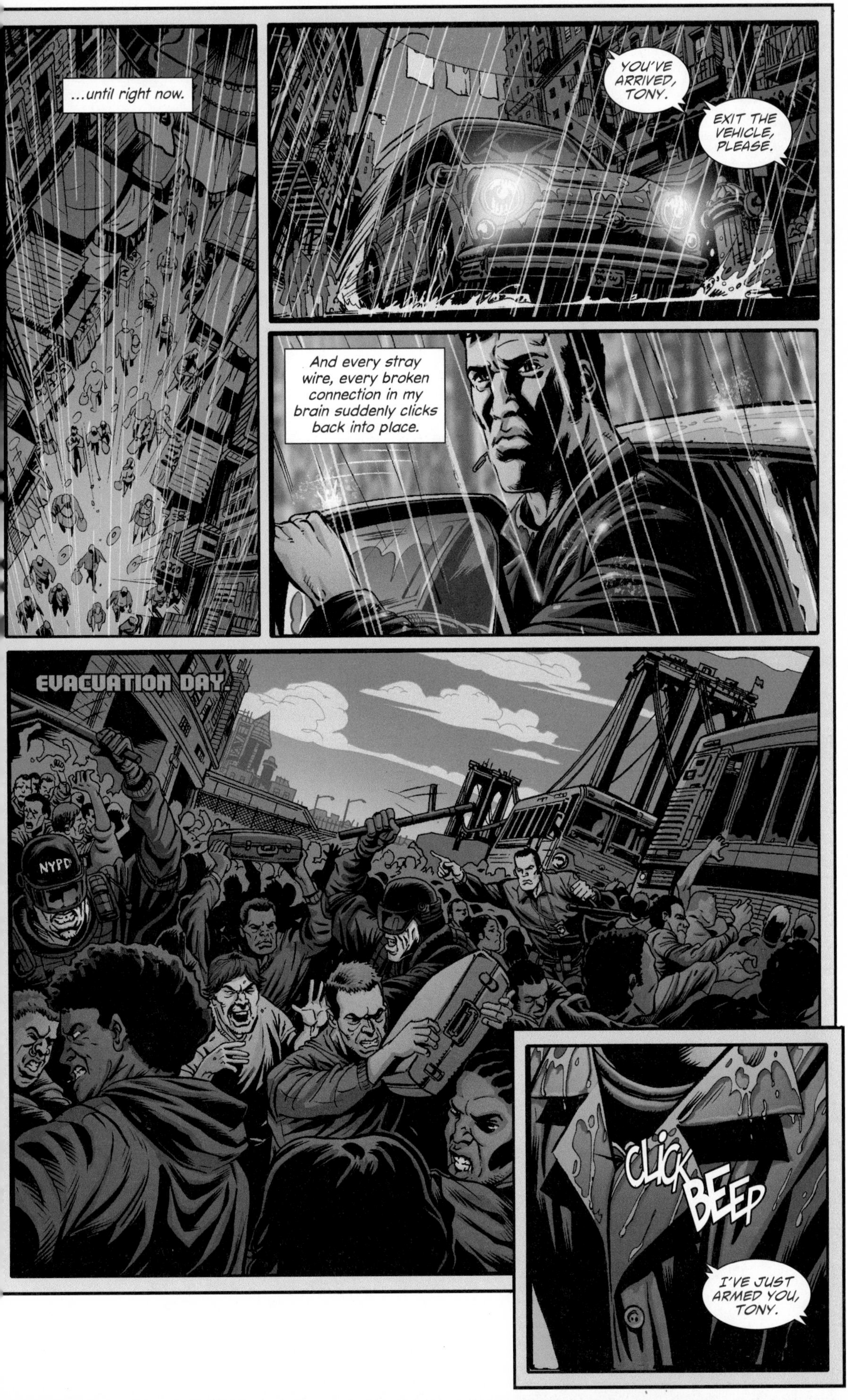
...until right now.
YOU'VE ARRIVED, TONY.
EXIT THE VEHICLE, PLEASE.
And every stray wire, every broken connection in my brain suddenly clicks back into place.
EVACUATION DAY.
NYPD
CLICK
BEEP
I'VE JUST ARMED YOU, TONY.

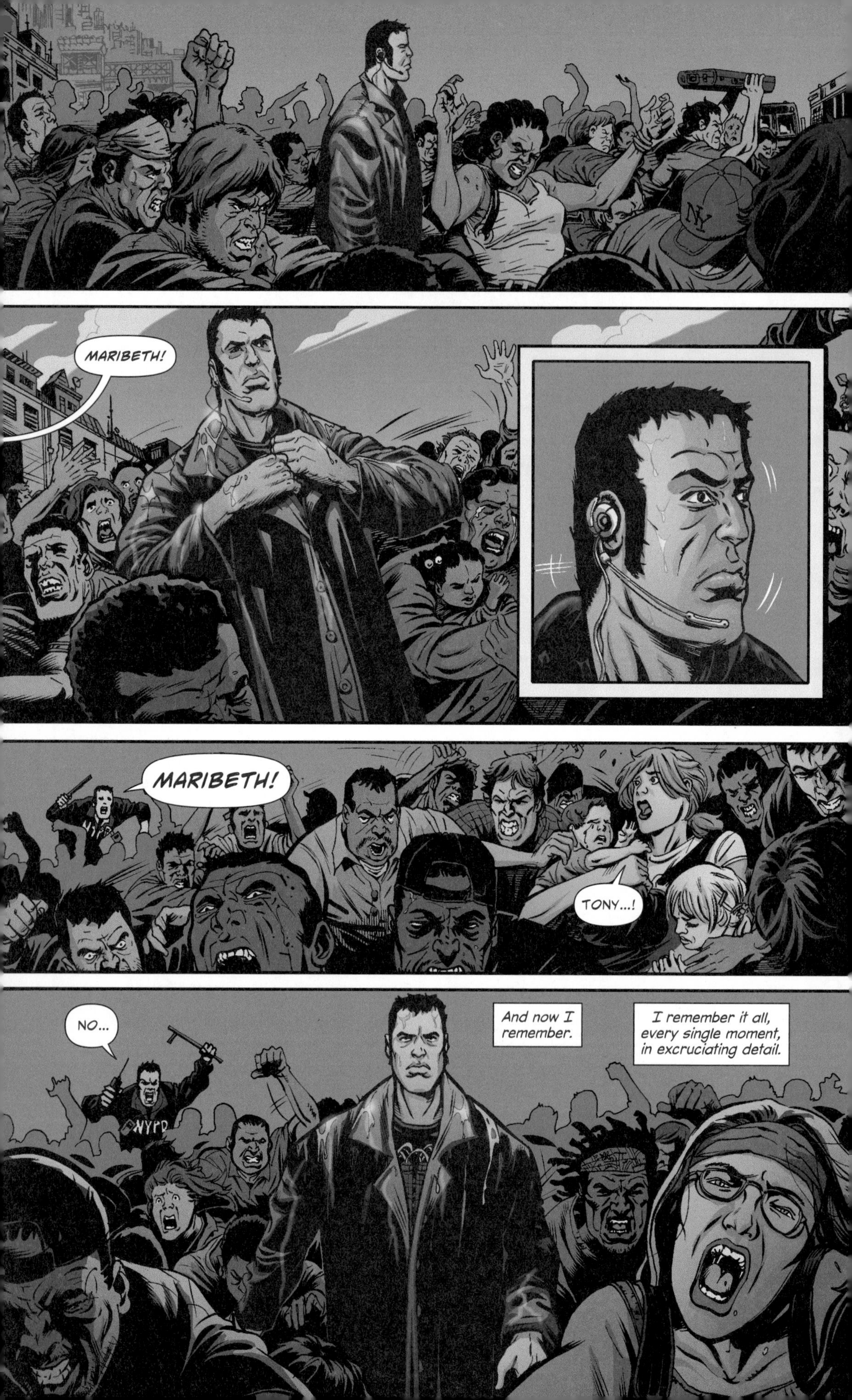
MARIBETH!
MARIBETH!
TONY...!
NO...
And now I remember.
I remember it all, every single moment, in excruciating detail.

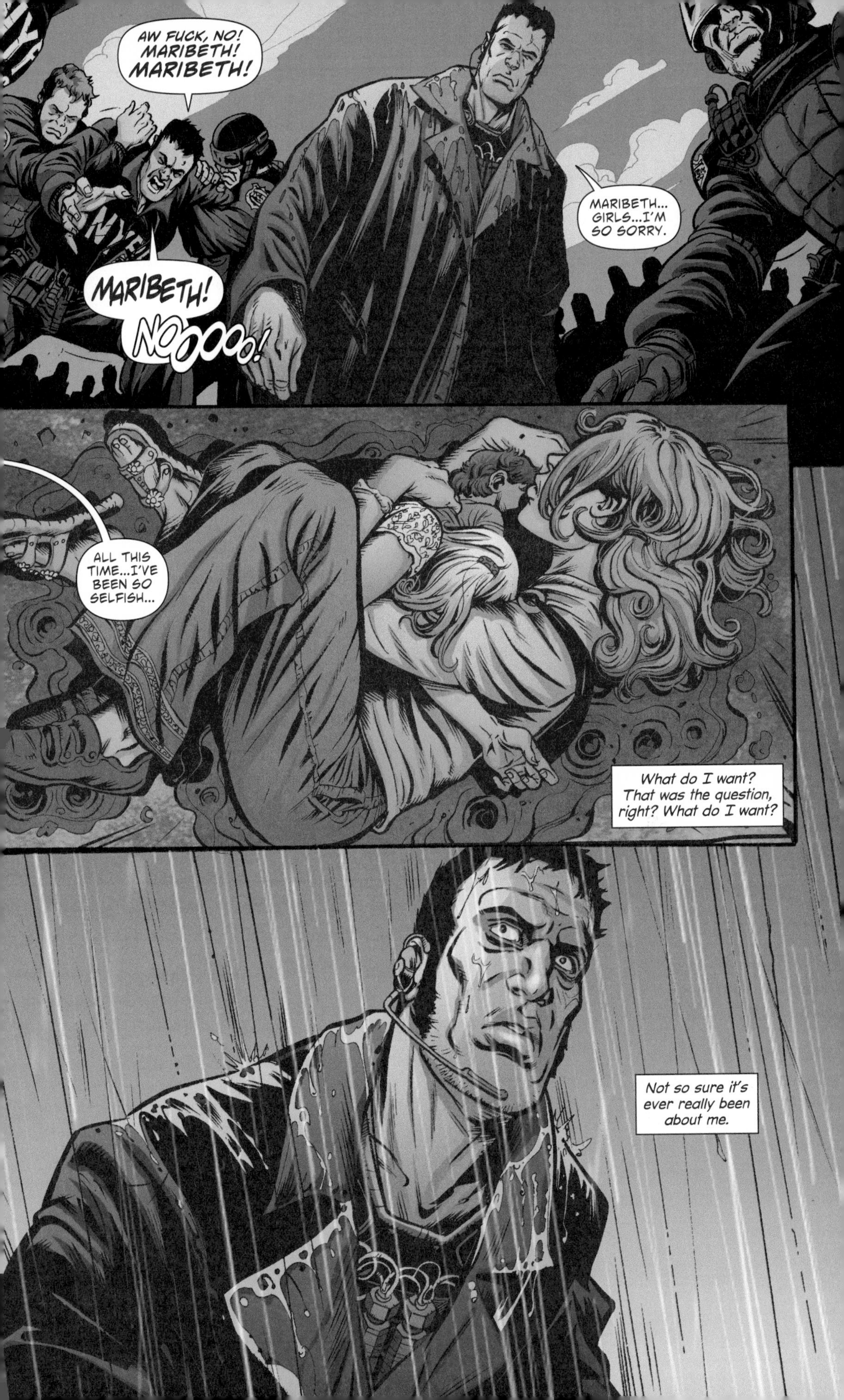
AW FUCK, NO! MARIBETH! MARIBETH!
MARIBETH!
NOOOOOO!
MARIBETH... GIRLS...I'M SO SORRY.
ALL THIS TIME...I'VE BEEN SO SELFISH...
What do I want? That was the question, right? What do I want?
Not so sure it's ever really been about me.

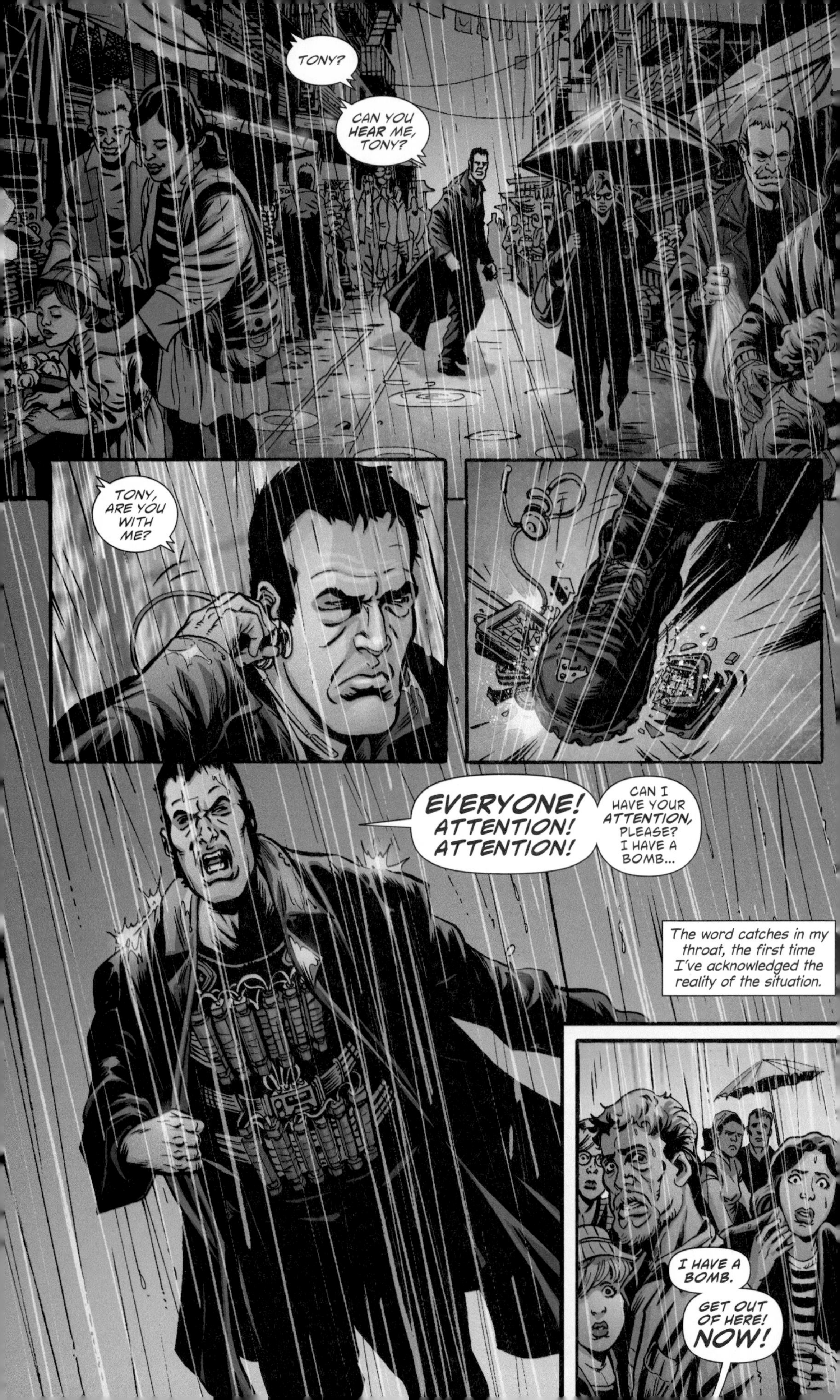
TONY?
CAN YOU HEAR ME, TONY?
TONY, ARE YOU WITH ME?
EVERYONE! ATTENTION! ATTENTION!
CAN I HAVE YOUR ATTENTION, PLEASE? I HAVE A BOMB...
The word catches in my throat, the first time I've acknowledged the reality of the situation.
I HAVE A BOMB.
GET OUT OF HERE! NOW!

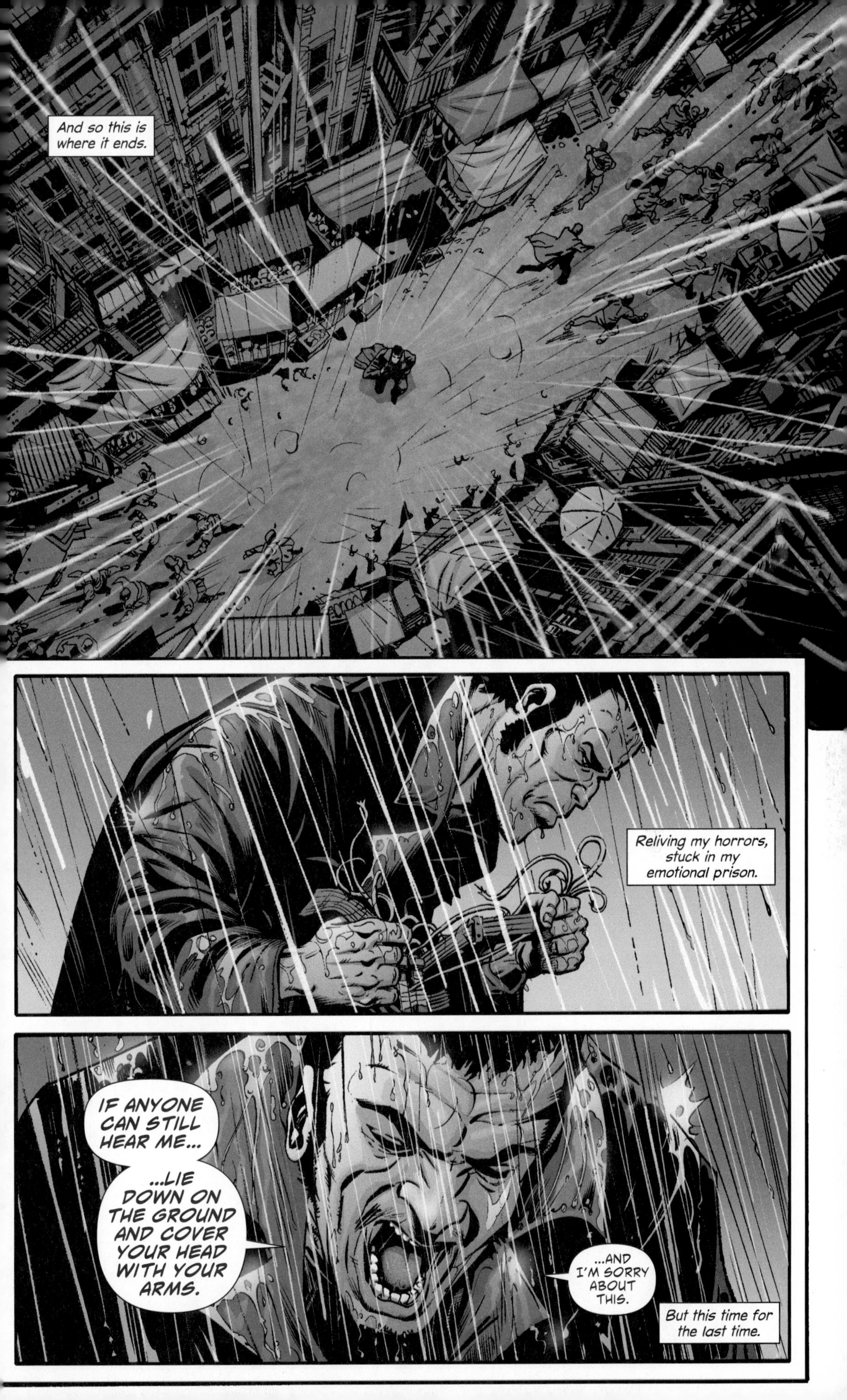
And so this is where it ends.
Reliving my horrors, stuck in my emotional prison.
IF ANYONE CAN STILL HEAR ME...
...LIE DOWN ON THE GROUND AND COVER YOUR HEAD WITH YOUR ARMS.
...AND I'M SORRY ABOUT THIS.
But this time for the last time.

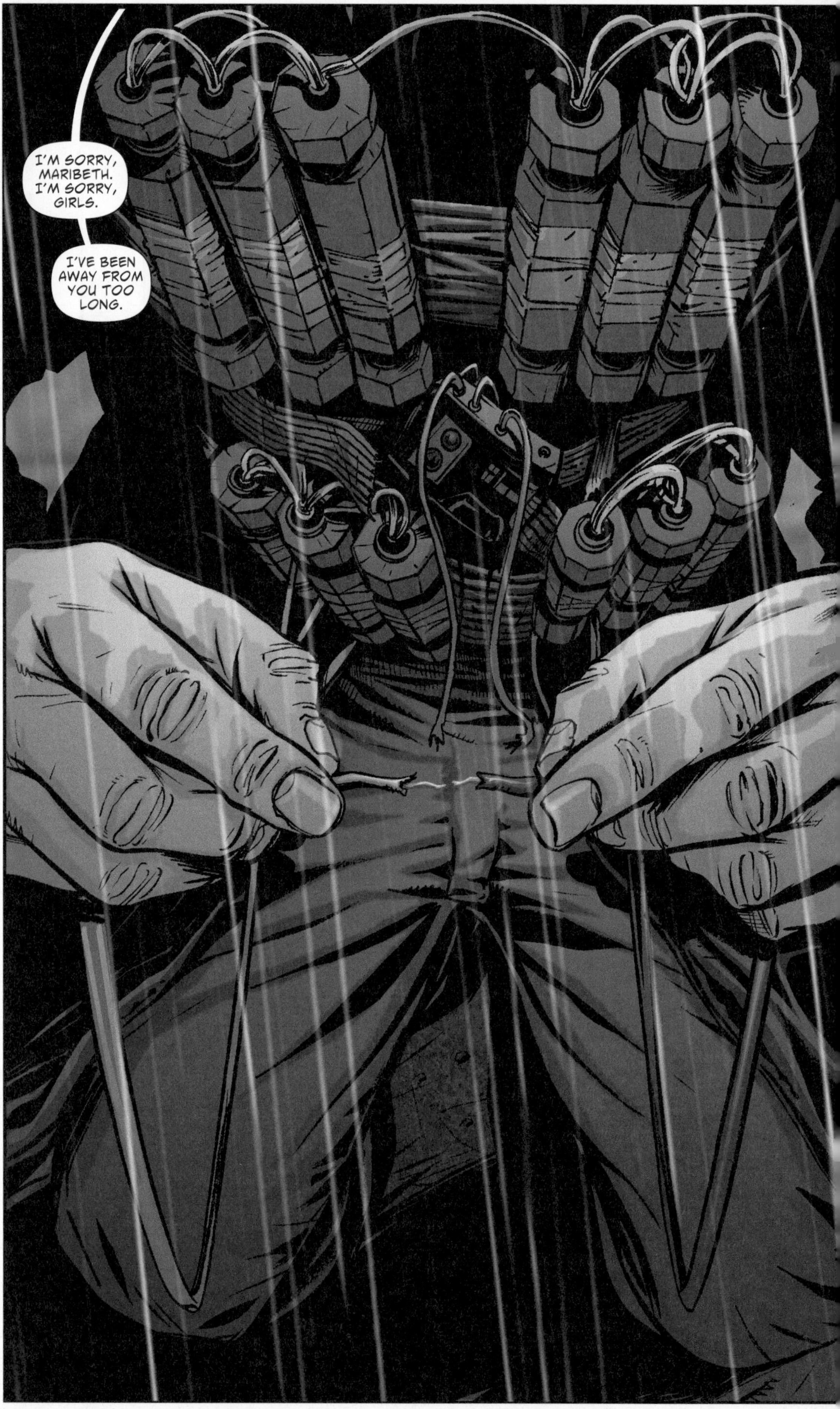
I'M SORRY, MARIBETH. I'M SORRY, GIRLS.
I'VE BEEN AWAY FROM YOU TOO LONG.

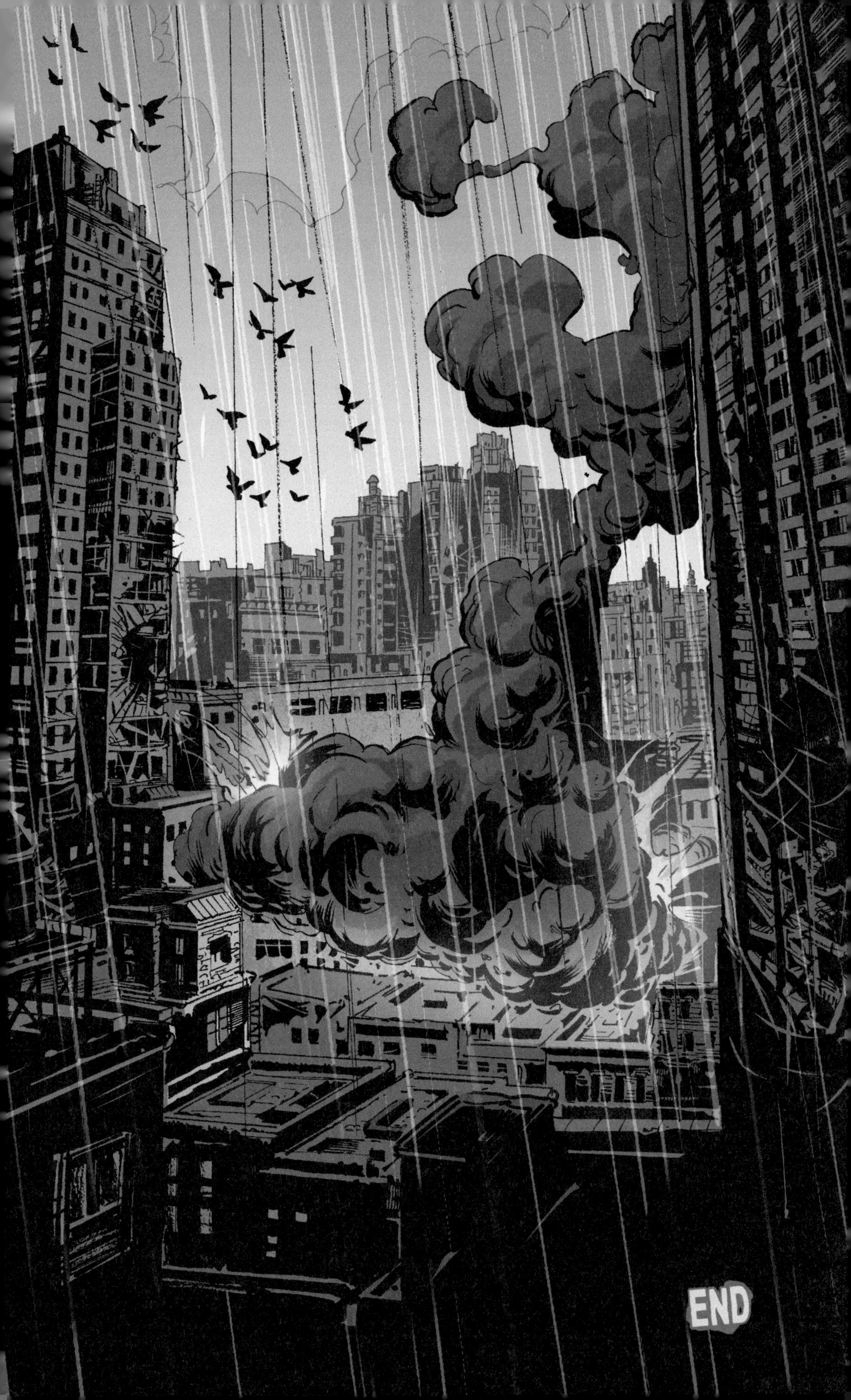
END

BOOK THREE

DMZ BOOK THREE

Justin Giampaoli is an award-winning writer at *Thirteen Minutes* and a contributing writer at *Comics Bulletin*. He created *Live from the DMZ*, the only site featuring extensive interviews and bonus content dedicated to Brian Wood's contemporary classic.

,,,

Brian, did you set out to write a game-changer with this arc? It has that distinct feeling that one era is ending and a new chapter in Matty's life is beginning.

Not originally. I mean, I didn't think Parco would persist past this storyline until probably the second issue, when it began to occur to me what a fantastic villain he could be, how Matty could play off of him, and be corrupted by him. My initial goal was to tell an election story, because what good is a comic about a journalist without an election story, right? At the same time, I had this nagging thing in the back of my head that my editor, Will Dennis, put there, about how Matty needed a friend. He knows a lot of people, but it's rife with tension and suspicion. I wanted to give Matty a real friend, and for a long time that's what Parco was for him.

How heavily did the occupation of Iraq affect your writing? The language being used in this arc is overt; "surge tactics" and a "provisional government," all buzzwords we've heard on CNN.

I've always tried to use those words and phrases, going back all the way to "On the Ground," which was getting some really heavy usage at the time. It just happened that this arc gave me a lot of those opportunities. I'm simultaneously attracted and disgusted by the fact that those phrases, which would've before been unknown outside of war rooms, are now common household things.

Where did the charming and dangerous Parco Delgado originate?

If there was a single inspiration for Parco, it would be Hugo Chávez, with a dash of Che Guevara, and then a bit of Al Sharpton. I was looking for a populist guy that would inspire fanatical devotion from the downtrodden and dispossessed, but still be a part of the system, and still be a political figure. I loved writing the two of them together, Matty and Parco.

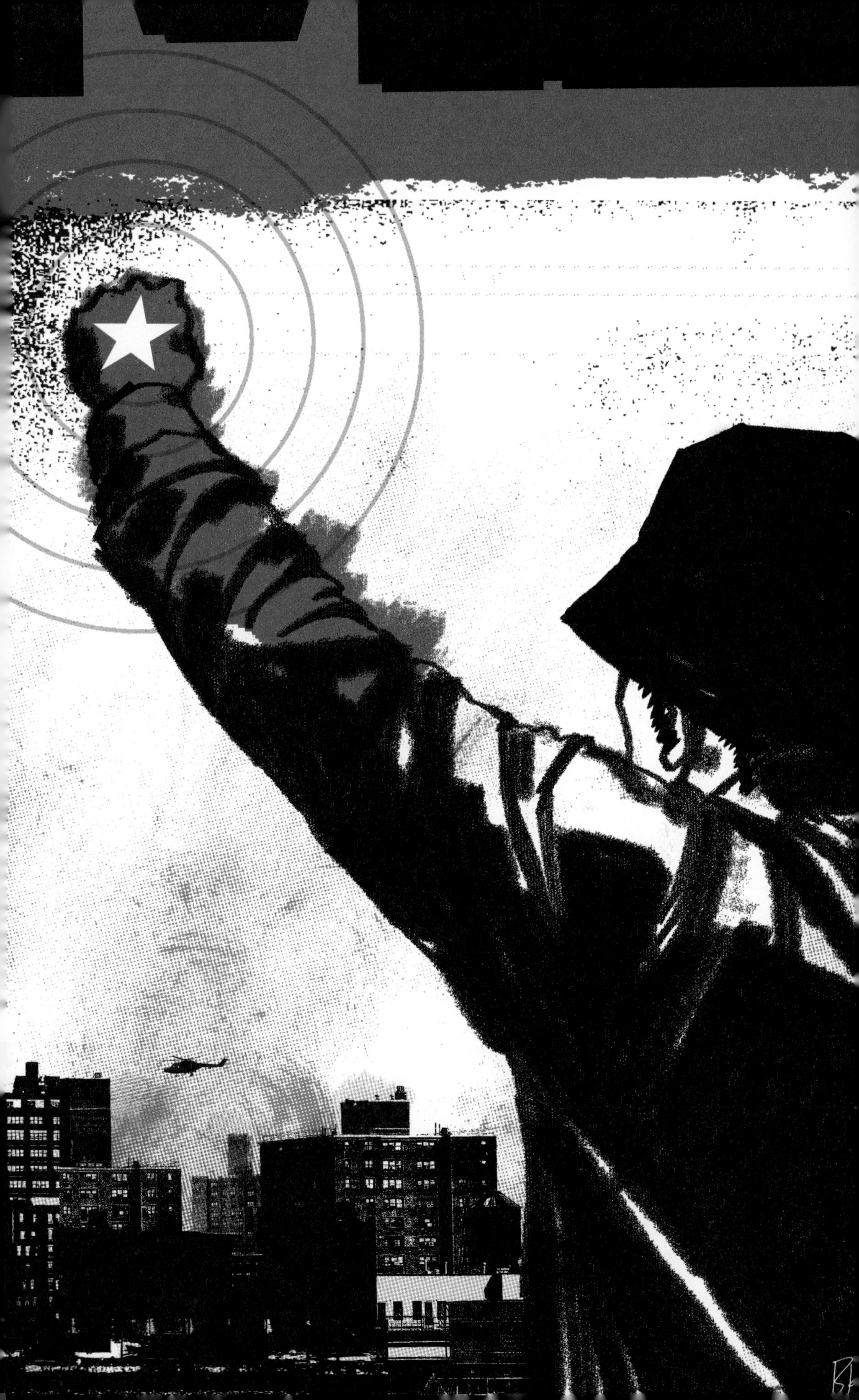

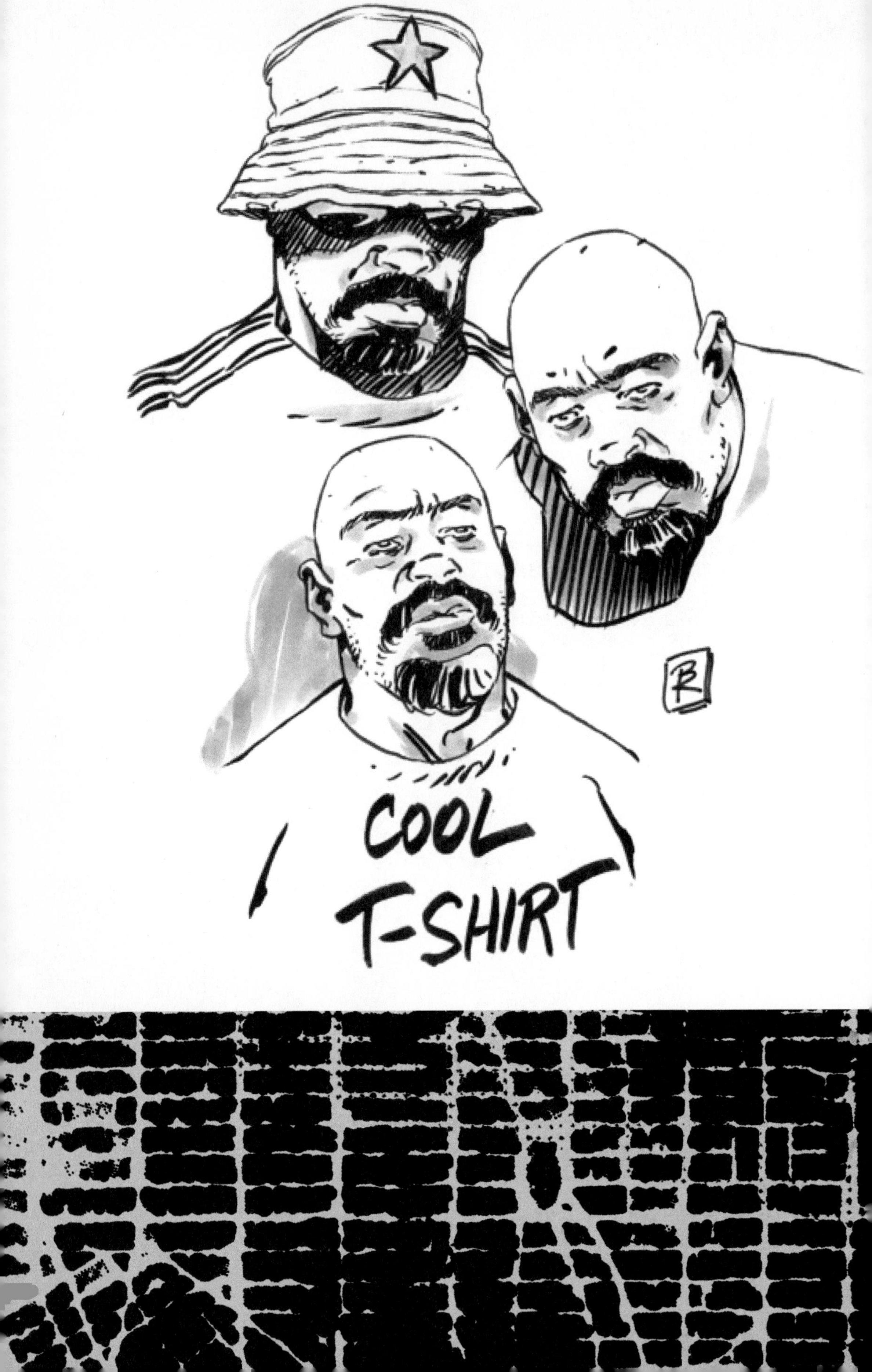
COOL
T-SHIRT

Why does Matty ultimately throw in with Parco and become politically active? Is it just Parco's charm or is something deeper driving Matty?

It's about Matty wanting to belong. It all seemed so obvious to me, that Parco was laying it on thick, and Matty was so charmed, so thrilled that a guy like Parco was bringing him into the inner circle. Matty's NEVER been in the inner circle of anything, and now he was. He belonged. He felt appreciated. He felt wanted and needed, part of something larger than himself. I felt like the readers could have seen the other shoe drop a thousand miles off. But, I didn't care. It was a blast to write.

The other aspect to this is that Matty isn't a journalist. Meaning, he's not one by trade or by training, and even though he acts like one sometimes, he's not bound by any code of ethics other than what his gut, or Zee, dictates. So, why not get involved, cross that line, and toss objectivity out the window? Matty was quickly elevated to a position of power in a political movement that was going to make NYC a new nation on the face of this earth. How could he resist? Matty lacks the tools to resist.

The Delgado Nation: Is there an actual platform of issues here?

The platform was super simple: get the marginalized to exercise their power, and affect change from the inside. *New York for New Yorkers*. Get the troops out. Declare independence. Rebuild. Heal. Even now, I believe that Parco was genuine in his original goals. He didn't have what it took, and no one was about to make it easy for him.

What does the FSA leadership think of Parco Delgado?

Well, we get into that in later arcs, but for the time being, the FSA is absent for the most part. We can probably assume they at least enjoy seeing the establishment squirm every time Parco speaks.

Tell us about Matty's relationship with his mom.

Matty's relationship with his parents is garbage, and not exploring that better is another one of my big regrets. I didn't have the space. But, if Matty's dad is, or was at the start, kind of a neo-con jackass, then Matty's mom is the classic example of what some people refer to as a "limousine liberal." In a very over-the-top turn, I have her living in France. I brought her back specifically to harsh Matty's boner in regard to the Delgado Nation... just when he feels cool and like he's making his own moves, here comes his mother to remind people that his name is actually "Matthew."

Is this arc written in a more decompressed style than most? There's some dramatic tension as we wait for the election results, but not a whole lot actually happens. It feels like we're in the eye of the storm waiting for the other side to make landfall.

That's a good question. It wasn't conscious, but I don't really read my own work after it goes to print, so I don't know. But, yeah, I can see that being the case. For me, this arc was always really about what does Parco + Matty = ?

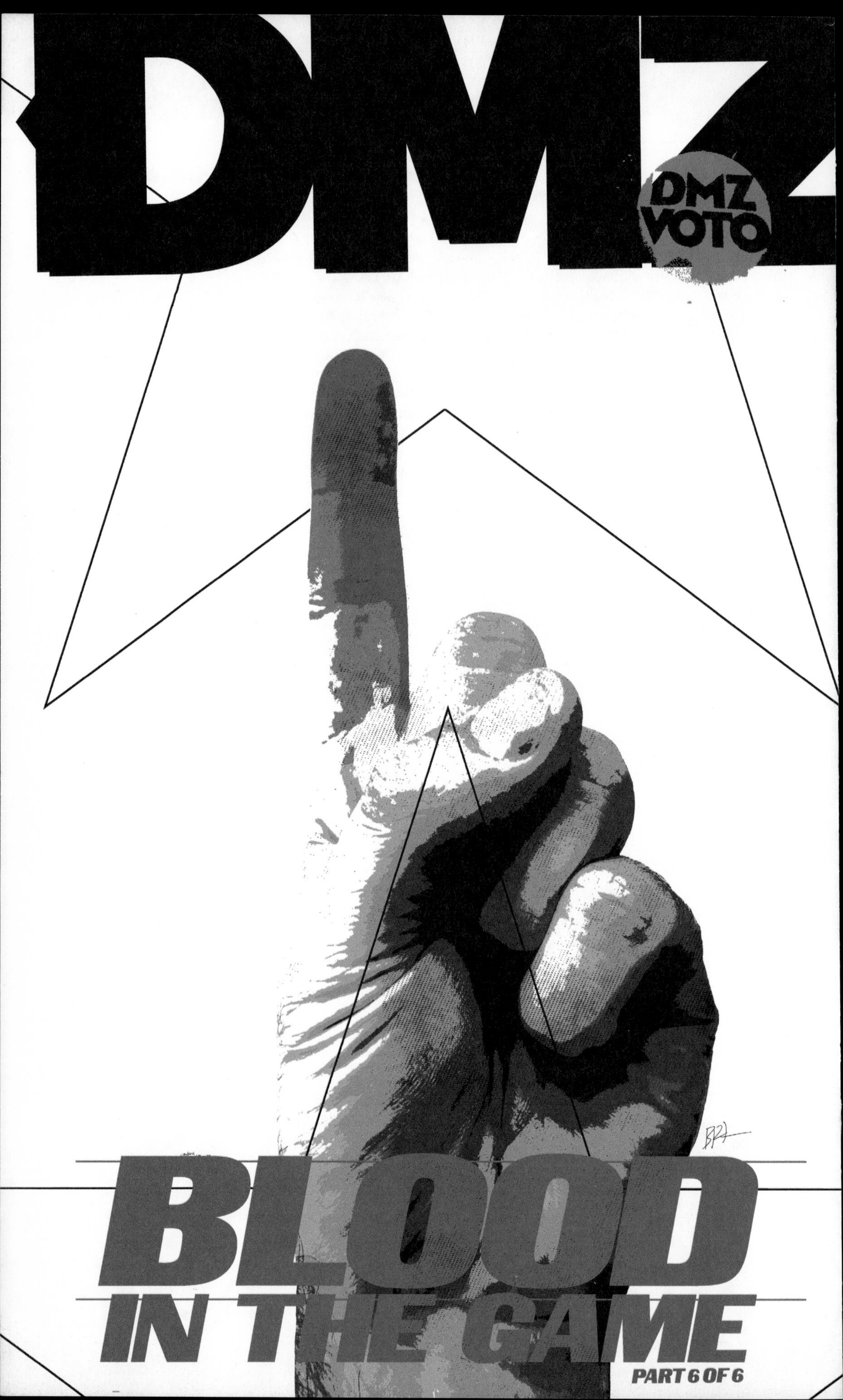
DMZ
DMZ VOTO
BLOOD IN THE GAME
PART 6 OF 6

DELGADO NATION
DMZ VOTO

DMZ
THE ISLAND
1 OF 2

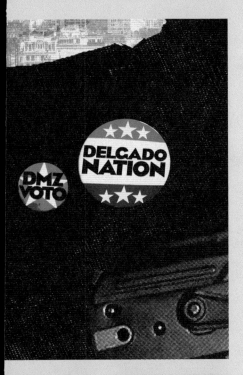

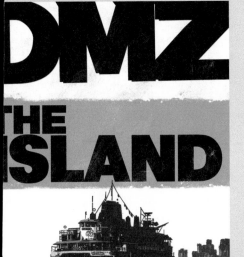

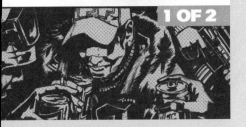

You don't read your own work because you focus on perceived flaws or missed opportunities?

Sure, a large part of it is that fear of finding an error, or some particularly cringe-worthy writing, or something else that I'll forever associate with that volume. But another part of it is the never-ending nature of writing comics, where by the time any one issue hits the stands, my brain is already three to four scripts into the future. Looking back is pointless.

Your covers to this arc have a very industrial, early Socialist propaganda feel. Can you discuss some of your inspiration for these covers?

These were my last six covers on the series, in terms of the monthlies. I was struggling creatively to hit the notes I wanted to, and I was getting more pushback than usual from DC. I think it was the right time to end it, so I appreciate your mentioning them. That first cover, the one with the raised fist, and the cover with the map on it, are two of my all-time favorites. There was no overt direction to them, unlike, say, "The Hidden War," which had a theme of sorts.

I like the very early covers because they have more of your analog DIY style, but there's no doubt the "Blood in the Game" covers are very iconic. The images stick with you.

I will forever wish I'd made "VOTE PARCO" pins in that style.

Issue 35 is the first cover designed by John Paul Leon, who first caught my attention on THE WINTER MEN at WildStorm. Were any other artists considered?

No one else was ever considered. He was my first choice and I'm lucky it worked out. I've actually been a fan of his for so long, I can remember being in art school and taking this prestige format book he did, *Logan: Path of the Warlord*, and just taking it apart at the seams to figure out how he drew like that, and how I could draw like that, too. I still feel that way, actually.

What was the thought process in pairing Kristian Donaldson's art with the happenings in "The Island"?

I don't know to what extent it came across in the end. I take full responsibility if it didn't, but I was going for a slightly crazy, sorta darkly humorous, just-on-the-edge-of-chaos vibe with that story. I think he's a good fit for that; his style is a nice contrast to some of the nastier parts of the story.

I think that vibe comes across. In the documentary "Hearts of Darkness: A Filmmaker's Apocalypse," Francis Ford Coppola makes the point about Duvall's portrayal of Lt. Colonel Kilgore and his unit, that the more they brought in the BBQs and the music and the surfing,

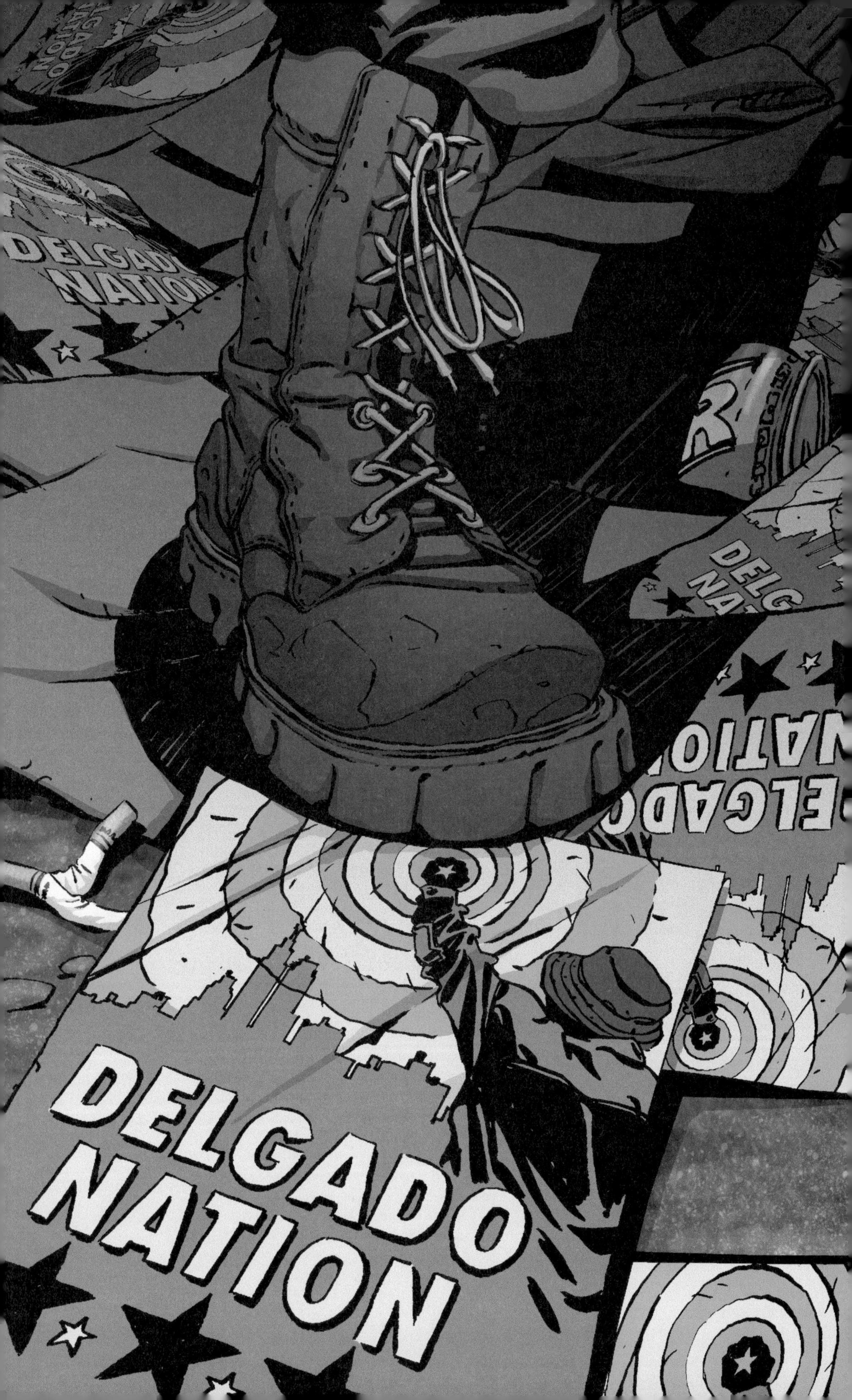
DELGADO NATION

the more they tried to make it like home, the more removed and surreal it actually became. The juxtaposition of those things in Vietnam actually made it more foreign and less like home, totally backfired. "The Island" reminded me of that.

The FSA is everywhere; they've penetrated Trustwell, the U.S. Forces, and they're active in the DMZ. Why do you think you're so drawn to this theme of asymmetrical warfare where nobody knows who's who?

Thank Donald Rumsfeld for popularizing that term, "asymmetrical warfare," by the way. Remember when he used it to define all those suicides that were happening in Guantanamo Bay among the detainee population? I miss that guy like I miss anal fissures.

The FSA is a concept, not a standing army, and it is *everywhere*. That's a terrifying notion if it's something you feel threatened by. Or are told to feel threatened by it, as in the case of our current "War on an Overly Broad Term," a.k.a. "The War On Terror." The idea of an invisible enemy that can take any form, it's a compelling one.

What was the intention behind showing these soldiers from both sides building an unofficial cease-fire agreement?

It's one of those logical assumptions on my part, really. In a civil war with politicians and ideologies driving the conflict, why should we assume that all soldiers will blindly carry out their orders? They literally have everything in common with each other and are all human beings under their uniforms. It's totally logical to assume some independent thought. I wish I had done more with that, actually.

In "War Powers," Matty has been in the DMZ three years at this point, which is about as long as the series had been running. Was a deliberate effort made to tell the story in sync with real time?

Not super accurately, but certainly as a rough guide. You'll really see that on display in the final issue, where the events are marked as "Year Two," etc. in capitalized words, so it's a formalized indicator of Matty's time spent there. Looking back, I sorta wish I had visually indicated the passage of time better with things like seasons, weather and holidays... there's not enough of that in comics. There's not enough weather! Will Dennis and I have talked about that on more than one occasion, but when you're writing in a serialized way, it can easily slip the mind.

We talked at San Diego Comic Con about DMZ being an endurance test for you as a writer. At this point in the series, you're about halfway through, so did you know you were halfway, or were you still worried about where you'd stick the landing, or if you'd be cancelled, etc.?

This may sound a little too pleased with myself, but after the first year or so there was no real worry of cancellation. The DMZ trades sell extraordinarily well. I always worried a little about the sales on the single issues, but who doesn't? Somewhere around the halfway mark, I did make a plan for the rest of the series, specifically to nail down a final issue number. We ended up running a little long... I think my plan was to end at #66. Shelly Bond, another Vertigo editor, suggested I should go to #75 or so, just to beat SANDMAN. But honestly, in that last year with the new regime at DC, and the drastically changed standards for success and failure, I'm not sure DMZ wouldn't have been cancelled if it wasn't already ending.

What did you want to trigger by making Parco's campaign poster resemble Shepard Fairey's "Hope" poster for the Obama campaign?

It was nothing more than a pop-cultural association, although I think I wrote it more as a Che poster than an Obama one. I was deeply sensitive about making overt connections between Obama and Parco. I honestly hate it whenever anyone sees Parco and mentions Obama, because I see the two of them as having almost nothing in common aside from skin color and charm. I guess history is proving me a little bit wrong, since the Obama of today is not the same Obama that existed back when I was first writing this arc.

There's this mangy emaciated dog running around that caught my eye; is this symbolism for Matty having lost his way?

There's this running list in my head of images I see when I think of DMZ, little bits of scenes or elements I remind myself to include. Che Guevara-style posters are one, the plight of household pets in the war zone is another. There's not much more to it than that, just trying to answer a few of those millions of questions: "what would *blank* be like in a war zone?"

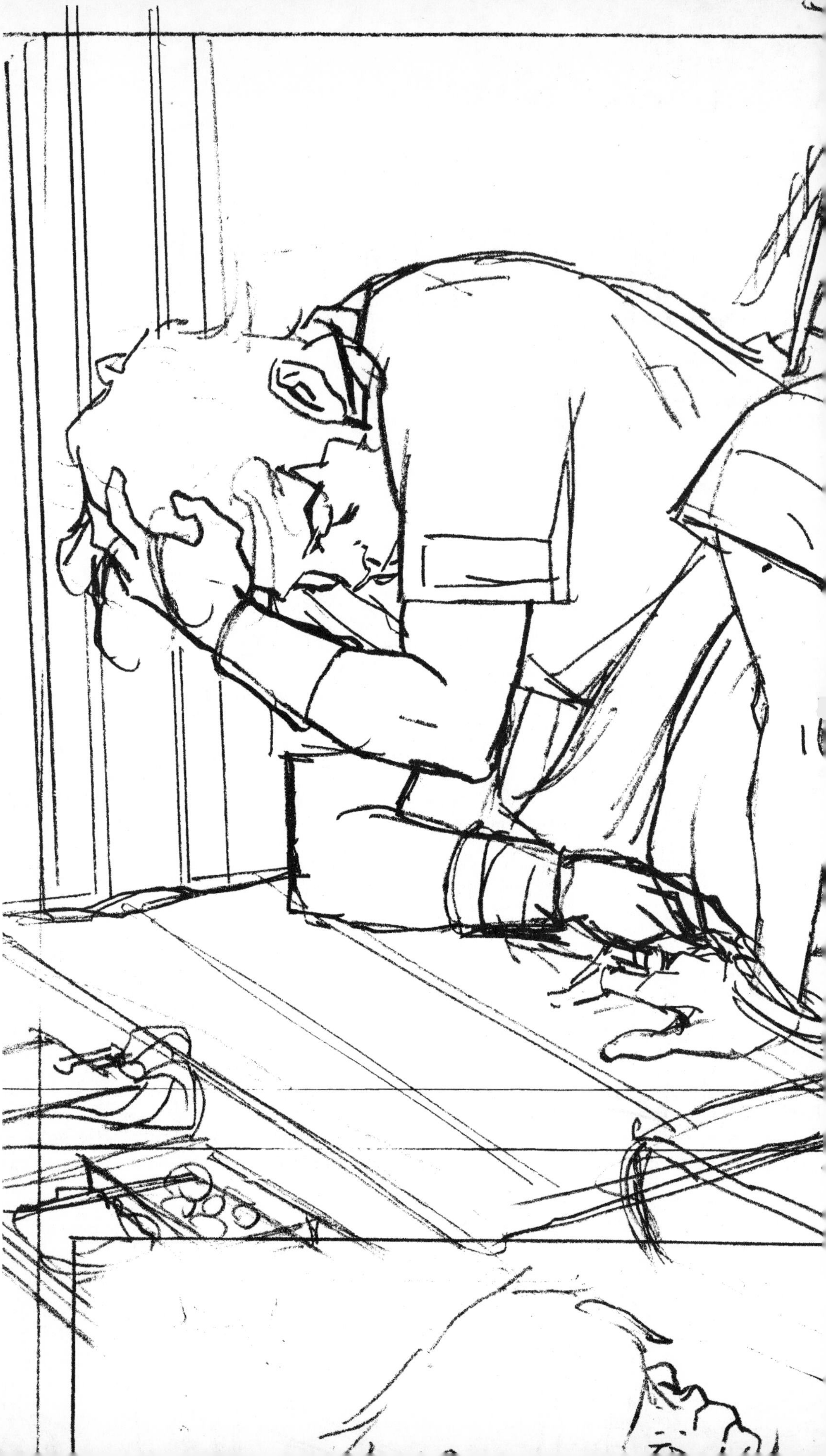

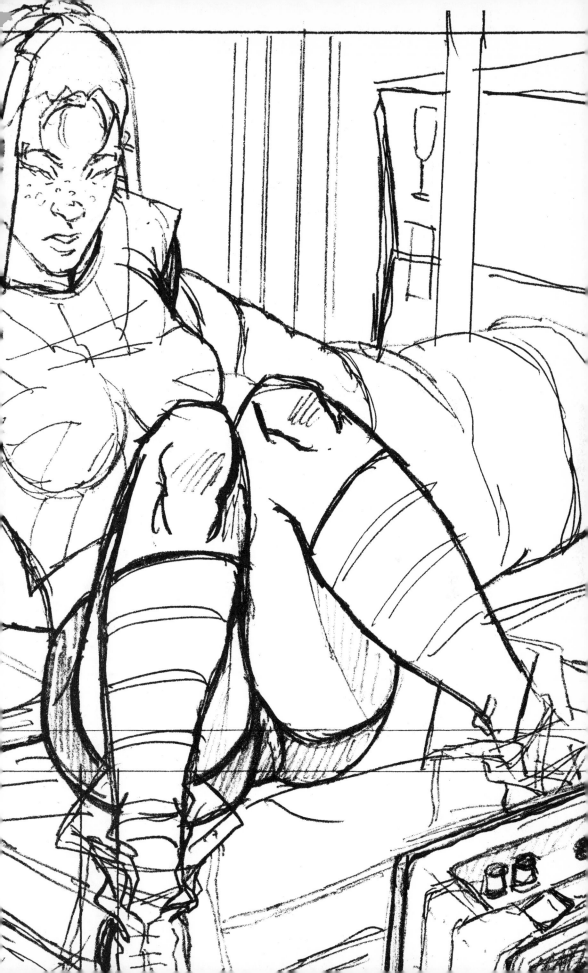

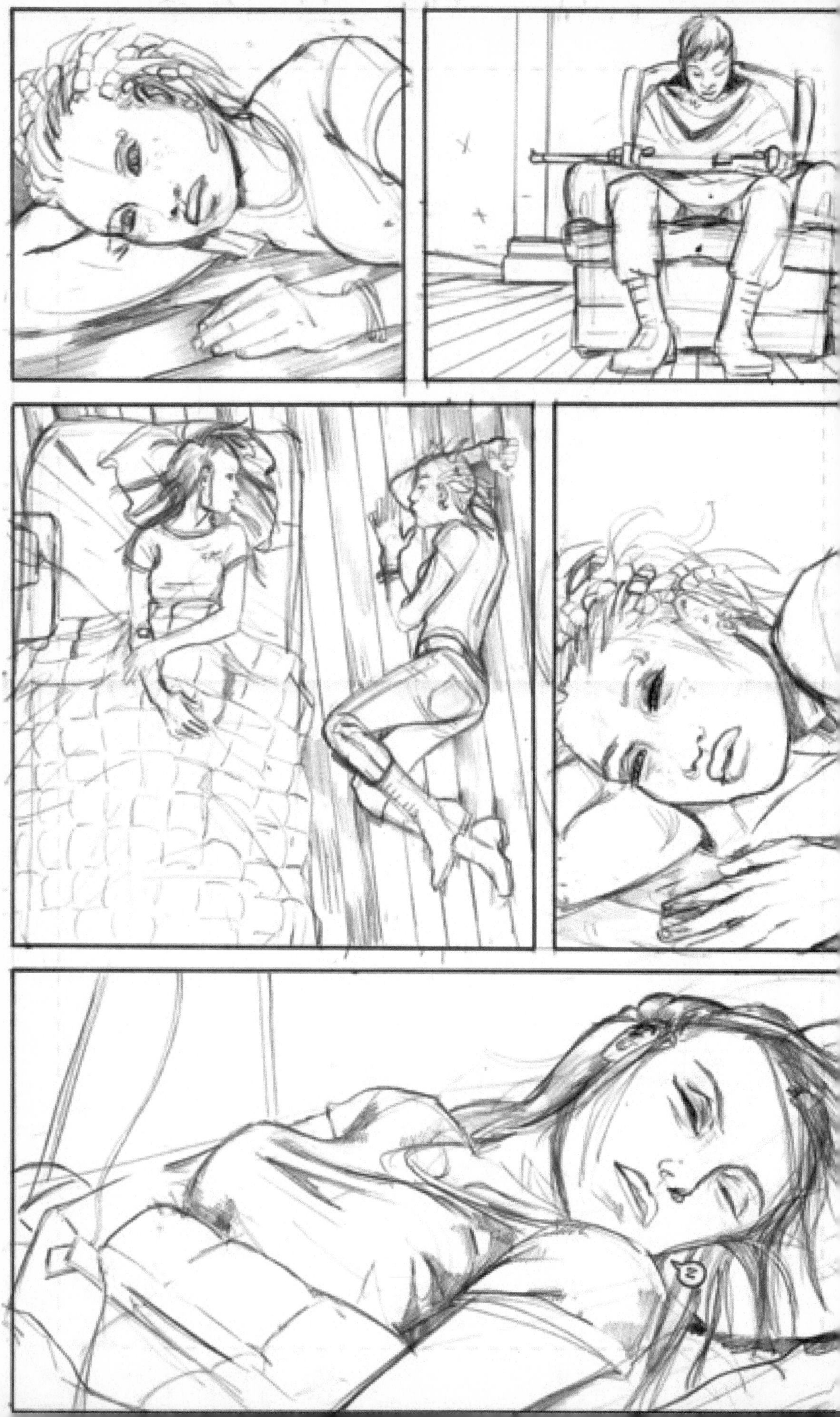

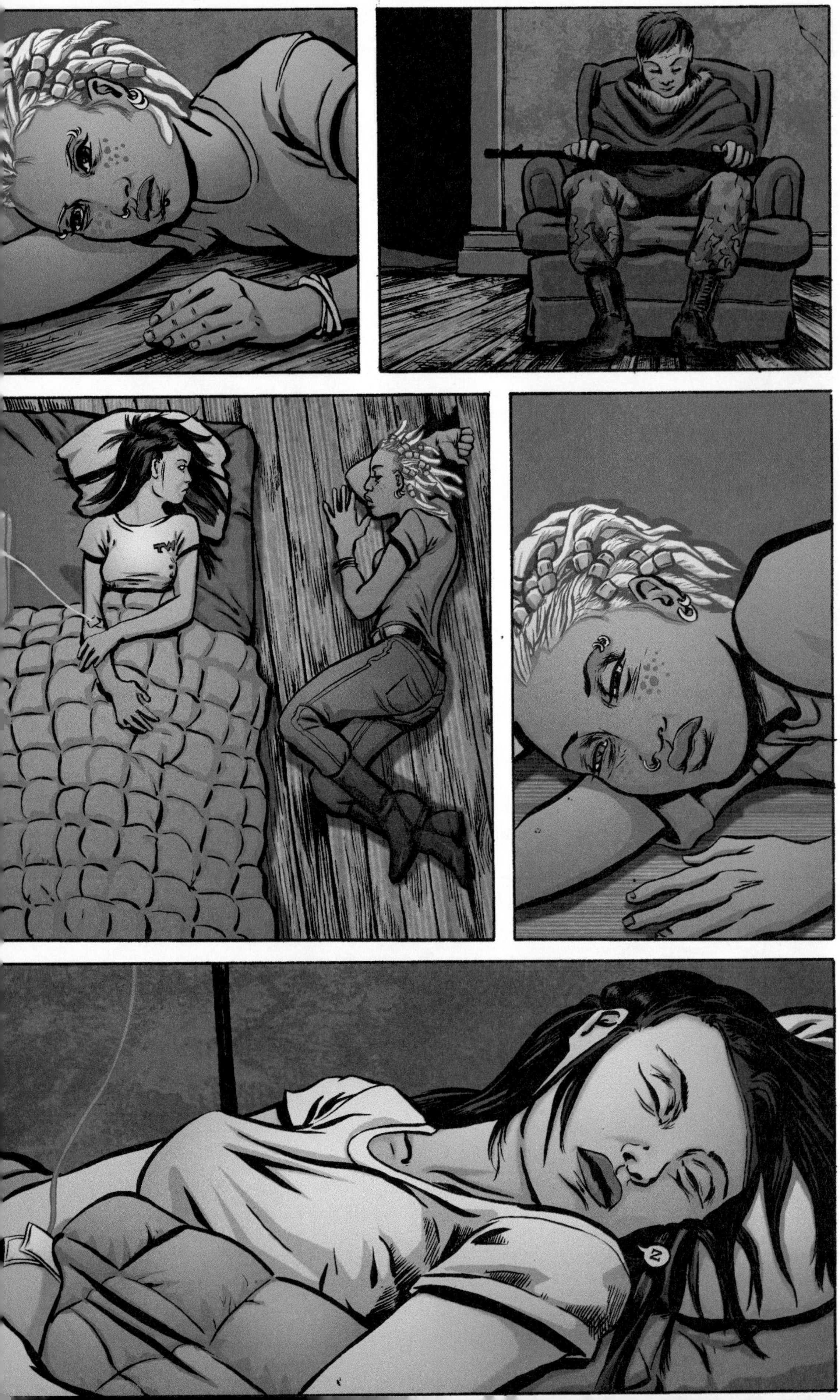

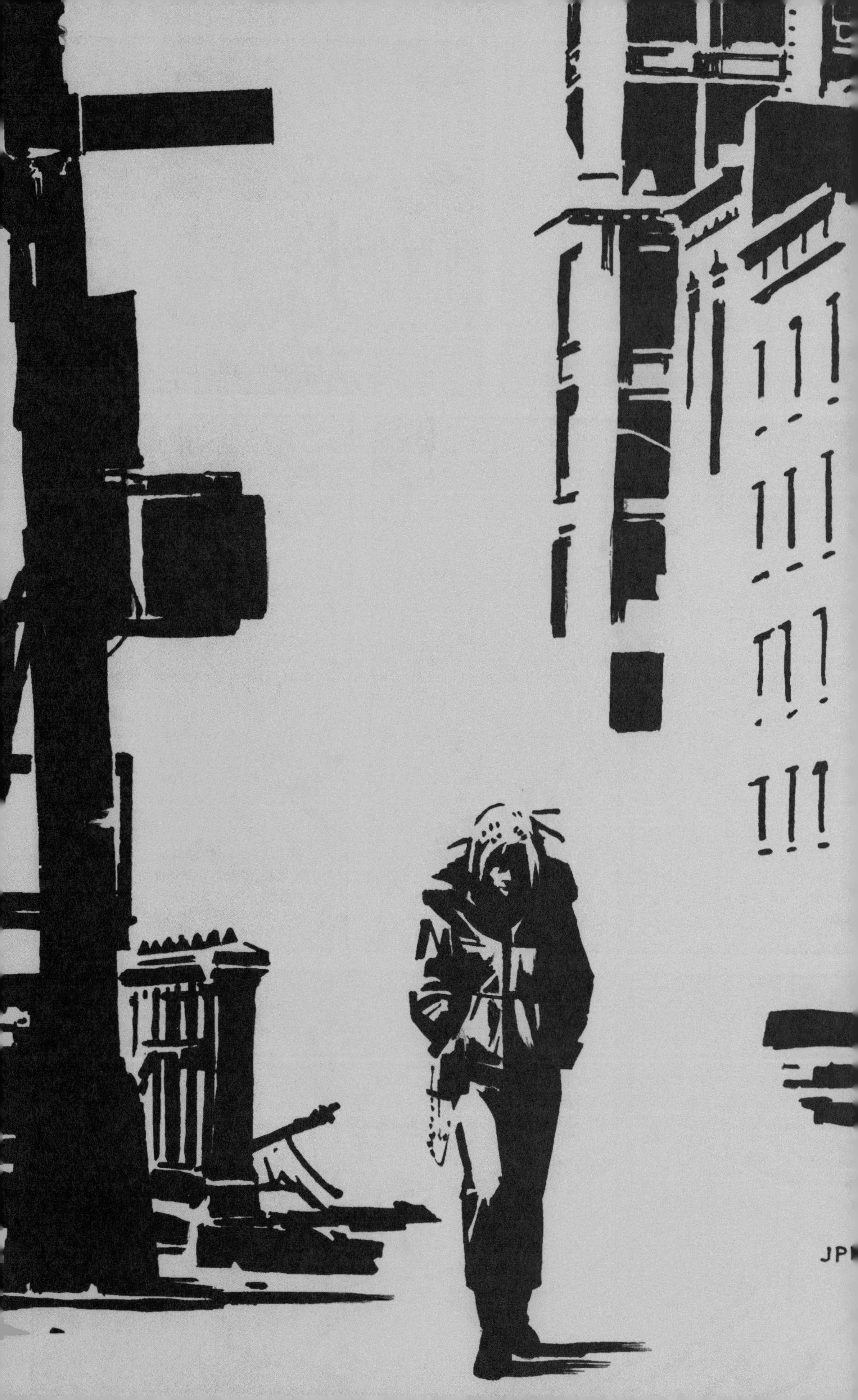

Sometimes I don't think you give yourself enough credit. Maybe these things are happening subconsciously, but I don't feel like everything can be taken at just face value. That dog serves as a nice bit of foreshadowing for "M.I.A." I mean, Matty *becomes* that dog in "M.I.A.," wandering around aimlessly uptown. At one point, he even slurps some ramen noodles out of a dog's water bowl.

Okay, Wilson's Chinatown gold! Where did the idea for this urban legend come from?

I dunno, probably that David O. Russell film *Three Kings*, mixed with a little bit of that one *Die Hard* film set in New York. I'm half serious there. The gold IS there, in this city, and Wilson's the sort of guy who could have made a play for it. And the urban legend nature of it all just reinforces Wilson's mythical status. What's better than the Ghost Protector of Chinatown hoarding a massive treasure?

There's a moment in "War Powers" that really struck me in terms of how Matty's changed. He's not reporting stories, he's fully armed with his own crew, he's rolling in an FSA Humvee with millions in Wilson's gold, and he buys a tactical nuke for Parco Delgado from the Ghosts of Central Park! Where did this person come from? Is power corrupting him?

This is precisely why I cannot over stress Parco's importance to the overall story: it's all because of him. Parco buffed his ego, he propped him up, he was his pal and he enabled him to be this guy. Have you ever had such a charming and charismatic friend that you found yourself doing or acting differently while around him? Matty and Parco are an extreme example, but the DMZ is an extreme place. Deep down, Matty has always just wanted to matter, to belong in the city, to not be the outsider. Parco handed him all of that on a silver platter.

Can you discuss the collaboration with Nikki Cook for the Zee story?

It was a struggle, from the start of this series to the end, to give everything the time and attention it needed. Zee is a good example of that, but she's so important that I felt it was good to spend an issue on her every once in a while. Nikki's a friend, and we'd been trying to work together on something for a while, so this seemed like a good opportunity. With this story in particular, I wanted to take away some of the "goodness" of Zee, show the more fucked-up side of her as opposed to her being some kind of constant force for good. I mean, she's not super fucked up in this issue, but she's pretty dysfunctional, as she should be considering all she's gone through.

2008

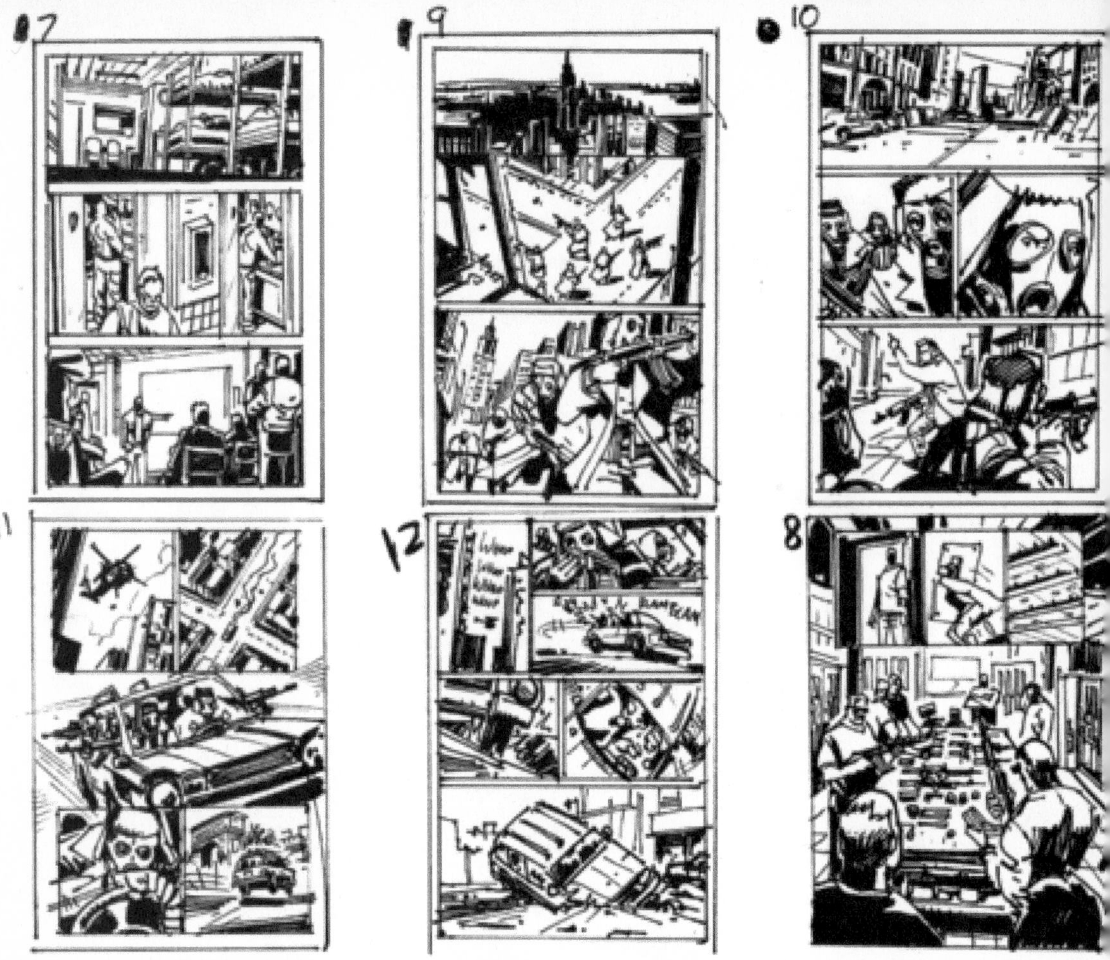
7
9
10
11
12
8

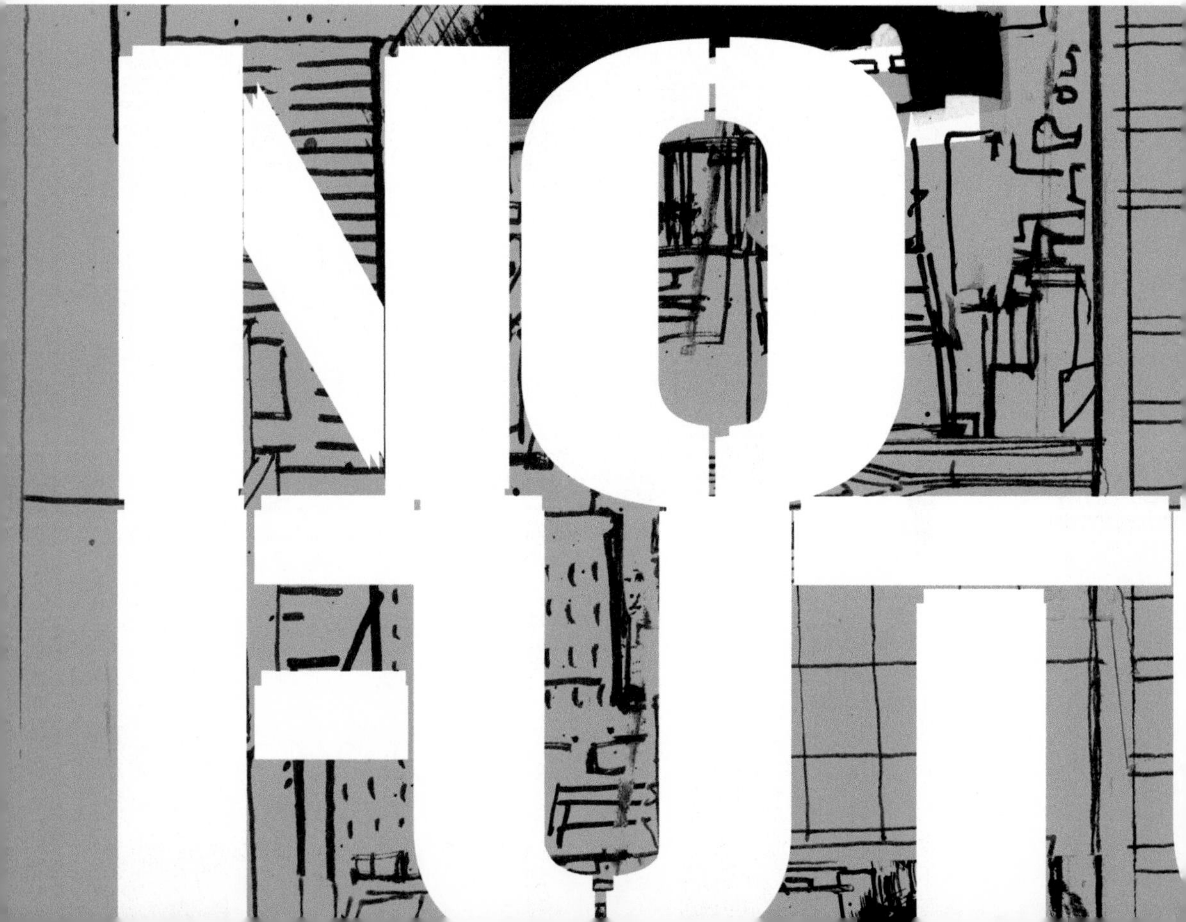
NO

Would Matty make a good citizen of NYC today, in a modern, post-9/11, post-DMZ world?

It's hard to answer this 100 percent truthfully without spoilers for the last issue, but I think Matty, as a normal guy coming to a normal New York, would not find his place. He was lucky, if you can call it luck, to come in under such extraordinary circumstances, and with so many things going for him that made him something of a powerful guy. All of that coming-of-age stuff, figuring himself out, would not make him unique, or cause anyone like Zee to help him out under normal circumstances. He'd probably last six months in the city before becoming so discouraged that he gets on the train back to Long Island.

Is Matthew Roth actually the main character of the series or is it the DMZ itself?

It has to be both. I think about it, and all the different phases the book's gone through, and some are more about the city, and some are more about Matty. It's big enough to be both, I think.

"No Future" is really the first arc where you can substantively prove it. Matty's not even present and it's interesting that structurally DMZ allows a story without its ostensible protagonist. You always hear that places like Gotham City or the Prairie Rose Indian Reservation in SCALPED are really the stars. They're storytelling engines that can churn out anything.

I agree with you about DMZ and the other books you mentioned, but from a practical, or a commercial standpoint, there's always a bit of a downside to that. You take a hit every time you appear to deviate from the "real" story. Most readers get impatient and view something like "No Future" as filler, something that doesn't really count. Both times I did extended runs of character one-shots in DMZ, *that's* when I got reader mail, asking when the "real story" was coming back.

I like the extreme realities that the DMZ imposes upon people. We see this everyman cop become an insurgent, and we see Matty the intern become a real player in the DMZ. How do you approach character development?

As any writer will tell you, I like to put my characters through absolute hell and see what happens. I like tragedies, I think there's real truth and beauty in sad endings, and there's a lot to be said in leaving one or two questions open-ended. I find endless fascination in that point, that moment in a character's life when they're at a crossroads, and they KNOW that whatever they do will irrevocably change their lives. DEMO, for one, is constructed from that single point in time, being on the precipice of change.

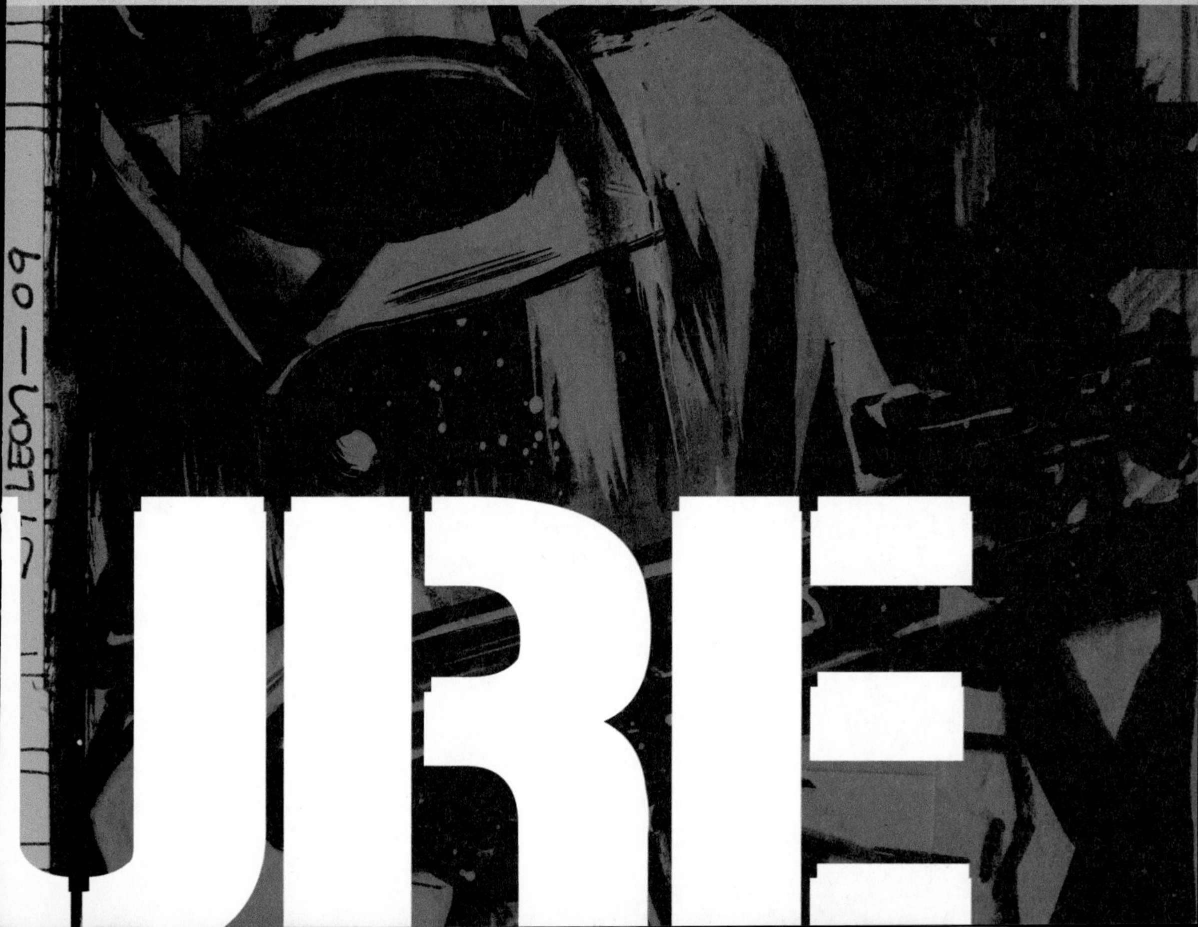
URE

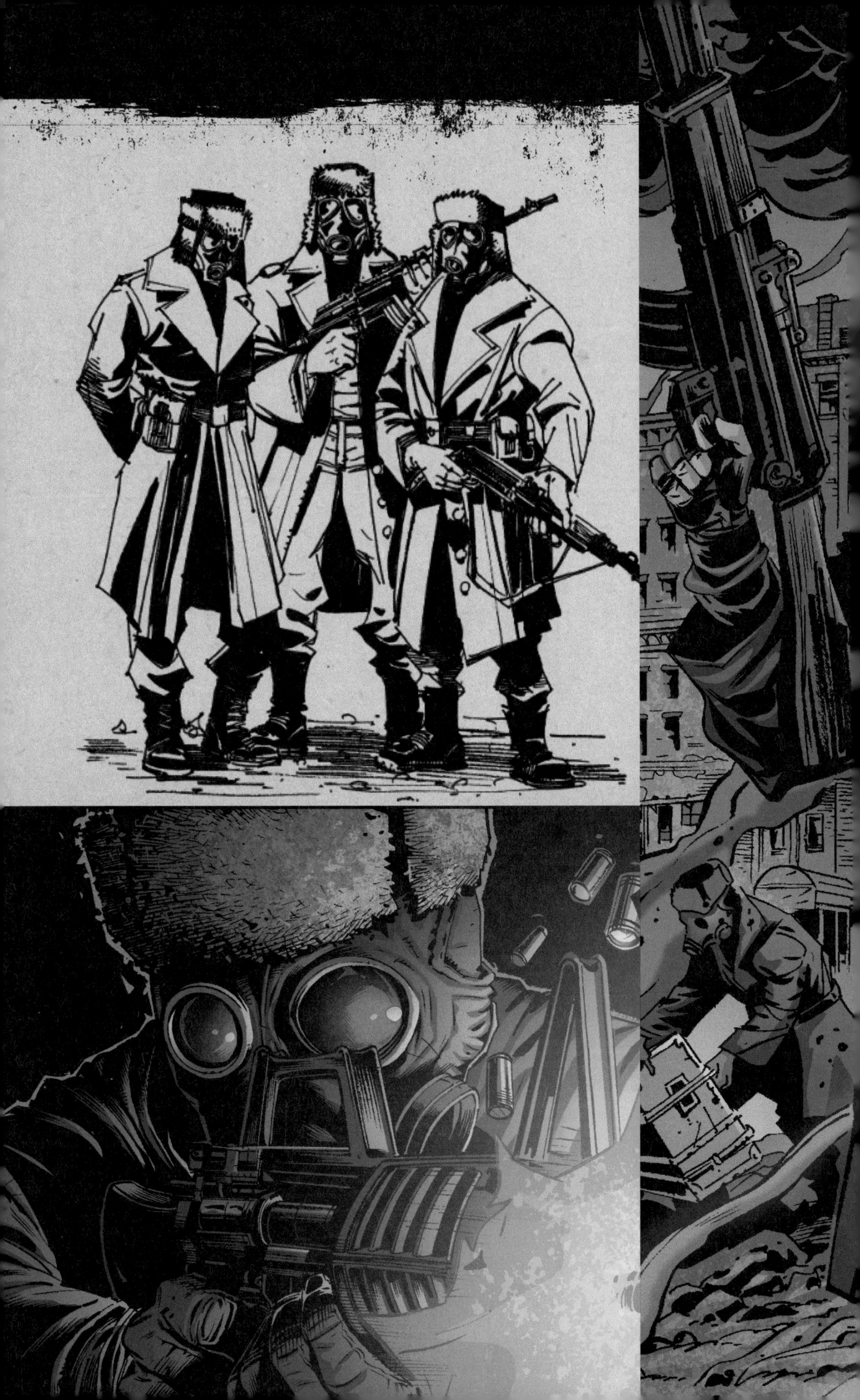

There's a shot of these guys geared up with their gas masks looking like urban shock troops. I'd never seen Ryan Kelly's art so menacing before. Can you discuss your collaboration with him specific to DMZ?

There was no real discussion or mission plan with Ryan. Like all of my collaborators who I've worked with before, there was trust and respect on both sides, so I just gave him scripts and he drew the hell out of them. I think he'd just gotten done with his NORTHLANDERS run, and I wanted to keep working with him. He was under a DC exclusive contract at the time and they needed to put him on something, so it all worked out.

The guys indoctrinating Tony in the "No Future" arc are the Nation of Fearghus, right? What's their story?

That's interesting... but no, that was never my intent. What they are, by profession, are first-responder types, cops, firemen, EMS, etc. who, for a variety of reasons, were caught within the DMZ after the last chance to get out at the start of the war. It's safe to say they're all a bit tweaked in the head.

Okay, I think when they're geared up for patrol they looked like the Nation of Fearghus guys we'd seen previously in the run. This is the same crew that's holed up in the Empire State Building, then, like that last holdout in "The Five Nations of New York"?

Yeah, he's a holdout, afraid to rejoin the world. I agree their gear is visually over-the-top a little... I think, to Ryan, I jokingly referred to their visual as "the Punishers of the DMZ," and that's not too far off the mark. Riccardo had drawn these fur hat dudes into the very first issue of DMZ and I liked it so much. I liked how they looked and wanted to find a place to use them.

The Bowery and Delancey area of the city is easily the most referenced set of streets in the series; is there something more personal behind that geography?

Man, I could probably name ten reasons why that's the case, but I don't think every instance was done so consciously. In terms of practicality, those are wide, open streets that lend themselves well to action sequences and other scenes where we need to move around a bit. And, truth be told, they sort of look the part of a war zone, with lots of run-down buildings and warehouses, although the Bowery has become something of a high-end restaurant row now.

I never lived on those streets, but I spent a lot of time walking them. Delancey terminates at the Williamsburg Bridge to Brooklyn, and Bowery brings us down into Chinatown, both important DMZ locations.

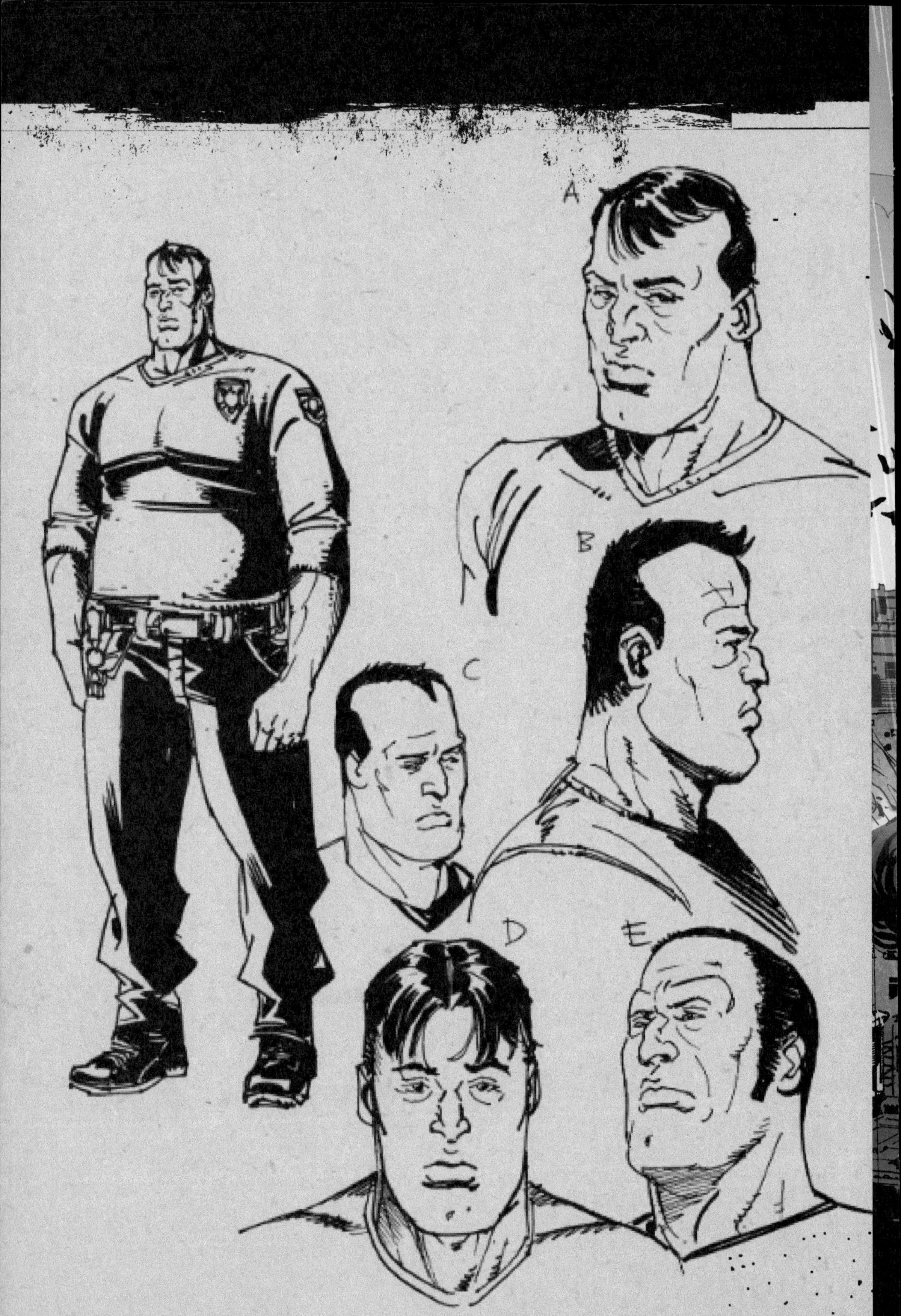
A
B
C
D
E

Lastly — and if there's anything at all to this, it's purely on a subconscious level — in the days after 9/11 when I first got into the city, I came up on Delancey to the stench of war and the sight of soldiers. Maybe my mind's making connections.

In this edition, we learn the other side of the Viktor Ferguson story thread, which is a self-referential loop back to the very first issue. Was this planned from the start or just a happy coincidence you were able to take advantage of?

It was total spur of the moment, right as I was scripting. I saw the opportunity to connect a few events, which is something I think comic book readers are hard-wired to respond to.

There's some poetic commentary on the legacy of the United States in this edition, things like "another failed state" or "the sun is setting on America." Do these statements reflect your own political worries or are they purely character-driven?

I think it's all just more examples of real-world buzzwords that are part and parcel of how I write this book. "Failed States" is a political term that was probably strictly an insider term until fairly recently. I love using them; I love them in an anthropological sense. I love the idea that we, as everyday citizens, know the names of field commanders in Iraq like we know the names of people on *American Idol*.

But sure, I hear on the news about this idea of America fading in terms of cultural importance and financial power. I believe in the concept of ebb and flow, and I think all empires eventually recede. I hope it doesn't happen here, because on the way down, this country, so deeply divided in ideology, will probably rip itself apart.

End Transmission

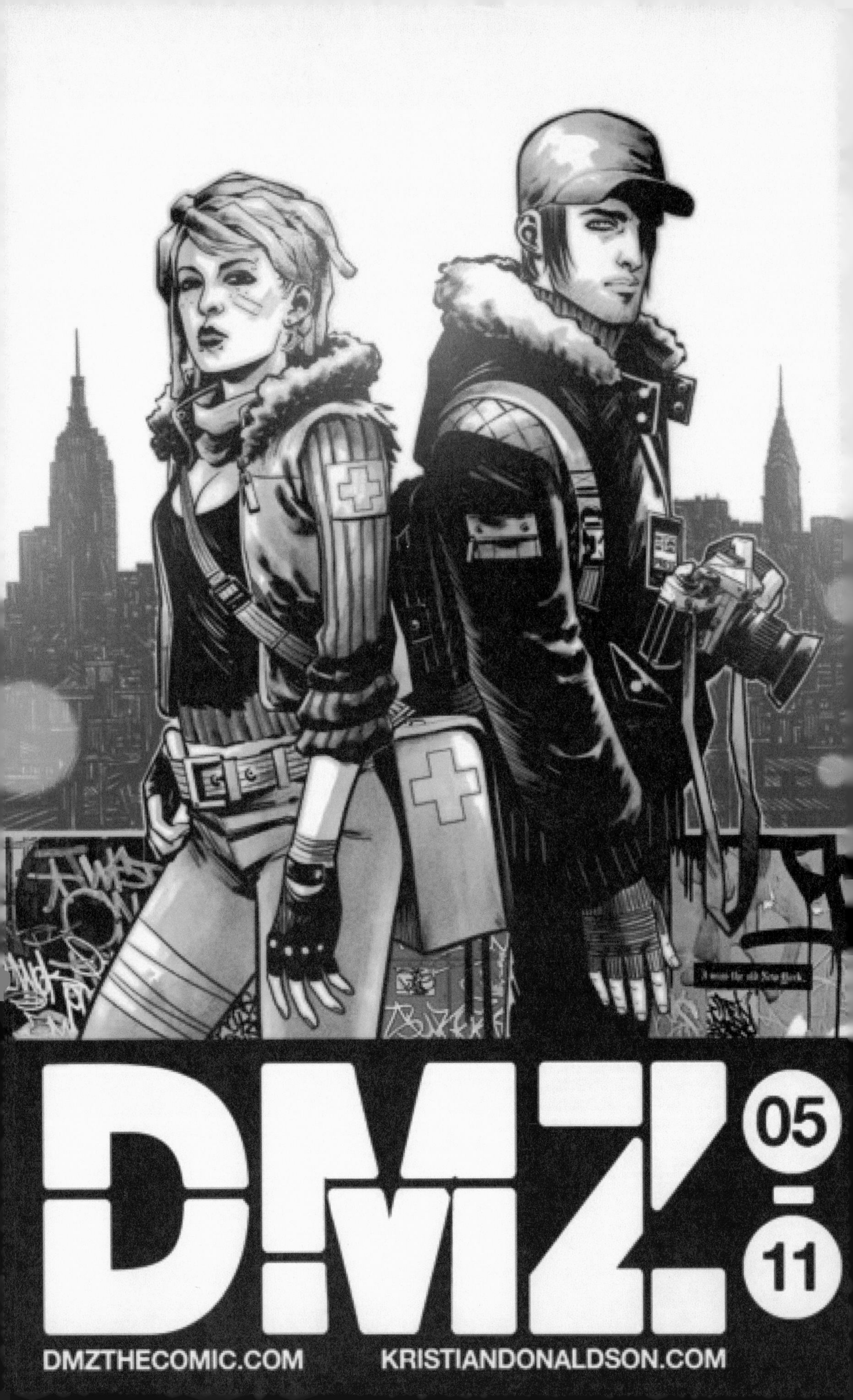
DMZ
05
-
11
DMZTHECOMIC.COM
KRISTIANDONALDSON.COM

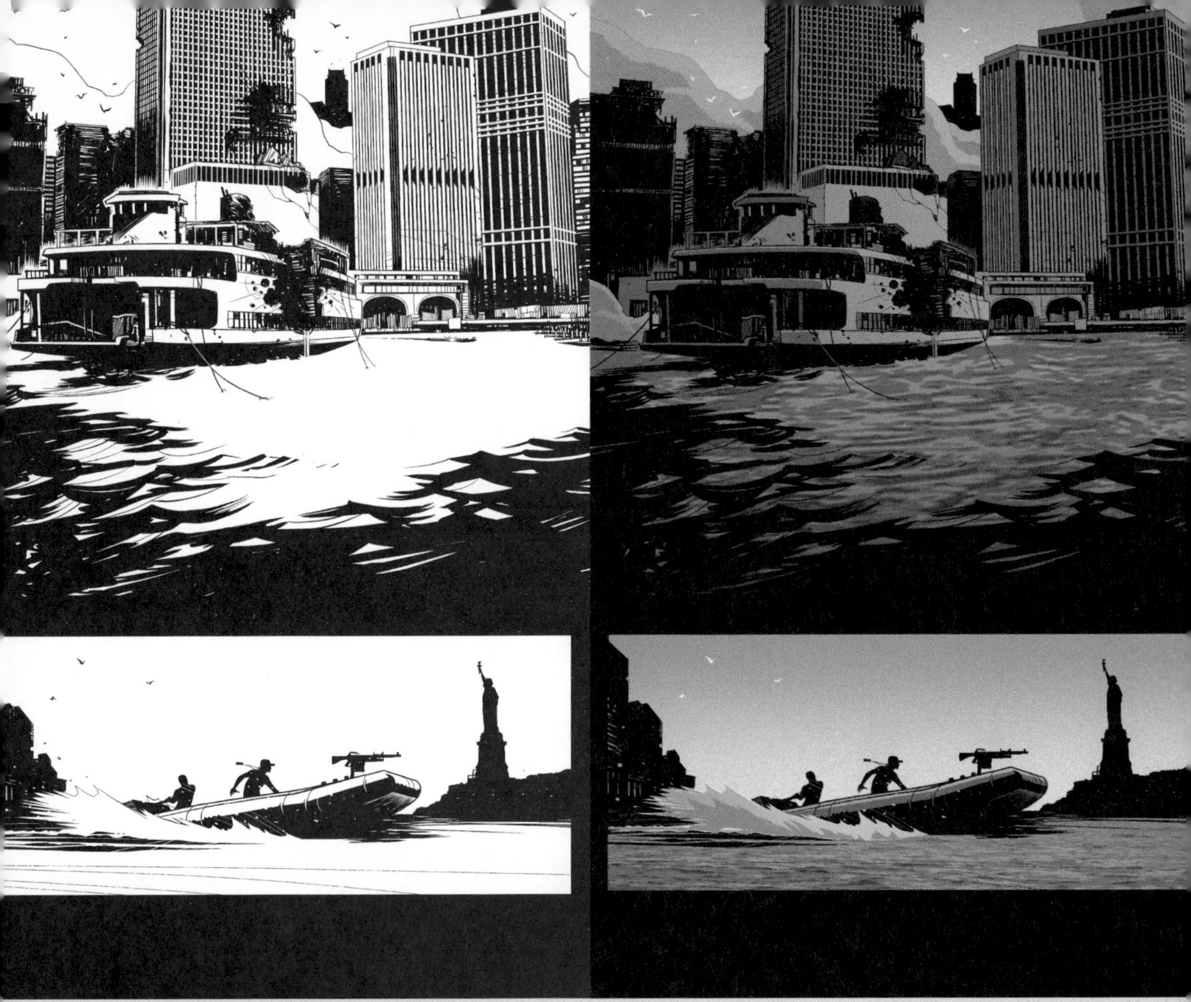

KRISTIAN DONALDSON INTERVIEW

Kristian, first, I want to thank you for creating the original piece for LIVE FROM THE DMZ. It captures everything I like about your style, the penchant for generous background details, vibrant use of colors, strong design sensibility and the general mood you can compose. How would you describe your general aesthetic? I can't really spot any overt influences.

It's a mishmash for sure. I'm not sure where it's going right now, but I'm trying to strike a balance between tight design and messier inking. I like an artistically broad range of books and artists, and try to stay on top of the possibilities being explored, while hopefully not wearing my influences on my sleeve. Stylistically, I dig a lot of European and Japanese stuff, and I think there's a lot of elegance to be gleaned from those sources. I think the bones of it all, storytelling and design, owe to the American side of things.

Do you always ink and color your own work?

It's the default for how I like to operate, but it's not always possible. You can come up with interesting things when you do it all yourself. Not every project calls for the same approach, so I like to recalibrate with each new project. If I were to color a new project right now, it would probably look different from my previous stuff. On my pinups and covers, I actually don't use color the way I used to. Not as bold or arbitrary, I'm questing after some more subtlety now. One of my last big projects, 99 DAYS [Vertigo Crime], I inked and gray-scaled, and it developed its own feel.

I first became aware of your work on *Supermarket*, also written by Brian Wood. How'd you guys end up working together?

I was a fan of *Channel Zero* and *The Couriers*. I sent Brian some work when I was young, like 21 or 22. He was very generous with his time and gave me practice scripts that I used for projects in school. He was very gracious and cool, and I'd just touch base with him from time to time, until 2005, when he asked if I'd like to do *Supermarket*. We did some pitch stuff together and it worked out.

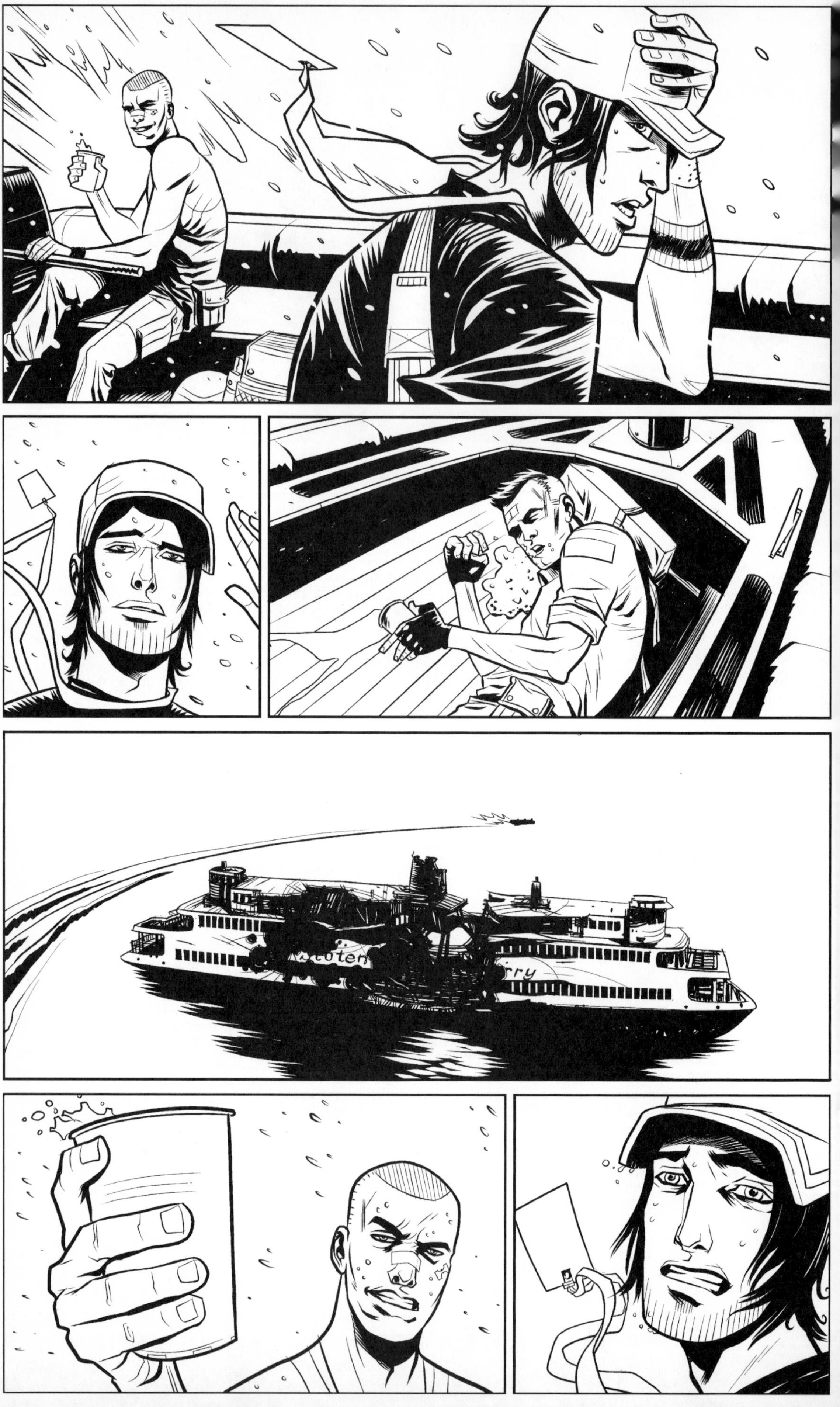

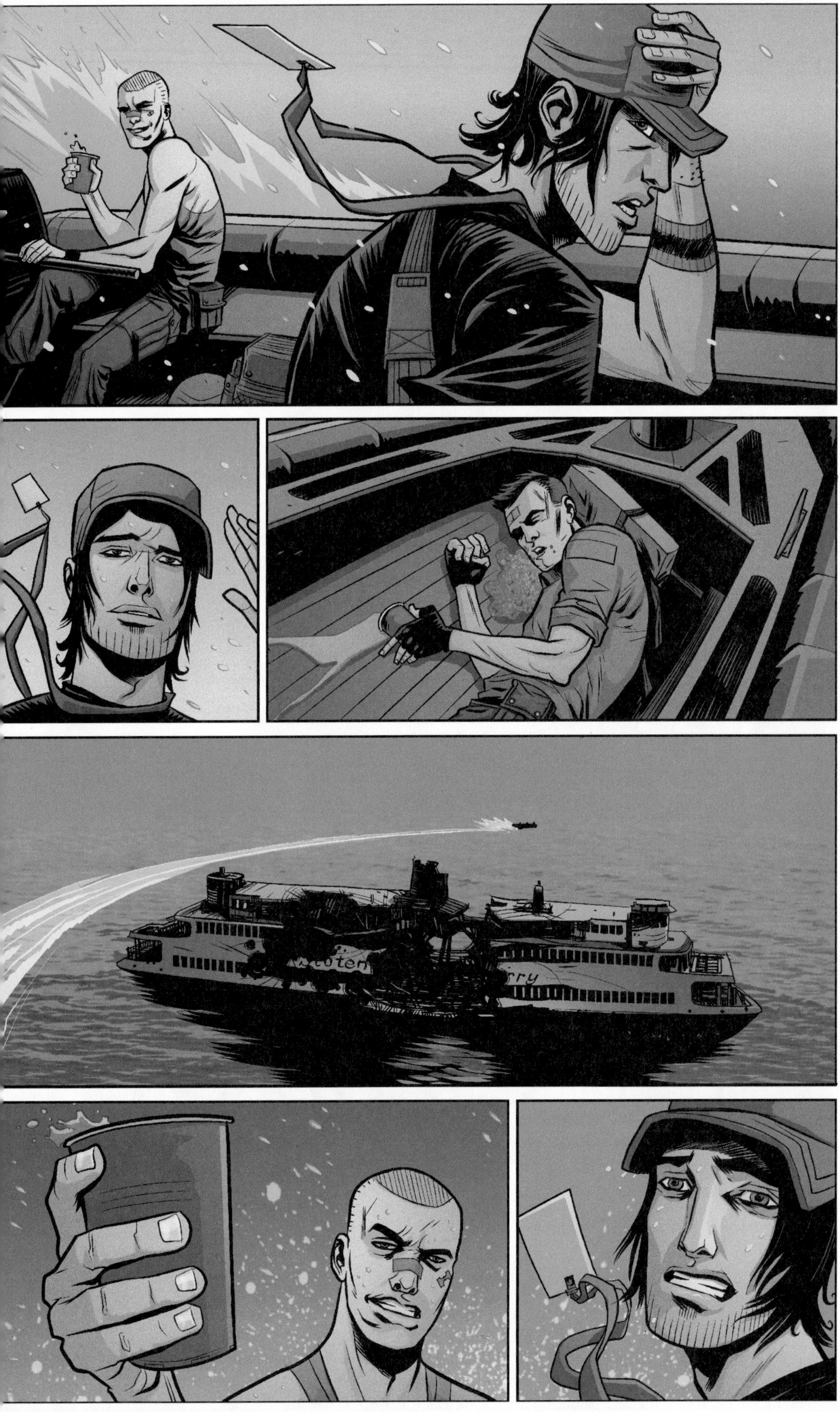

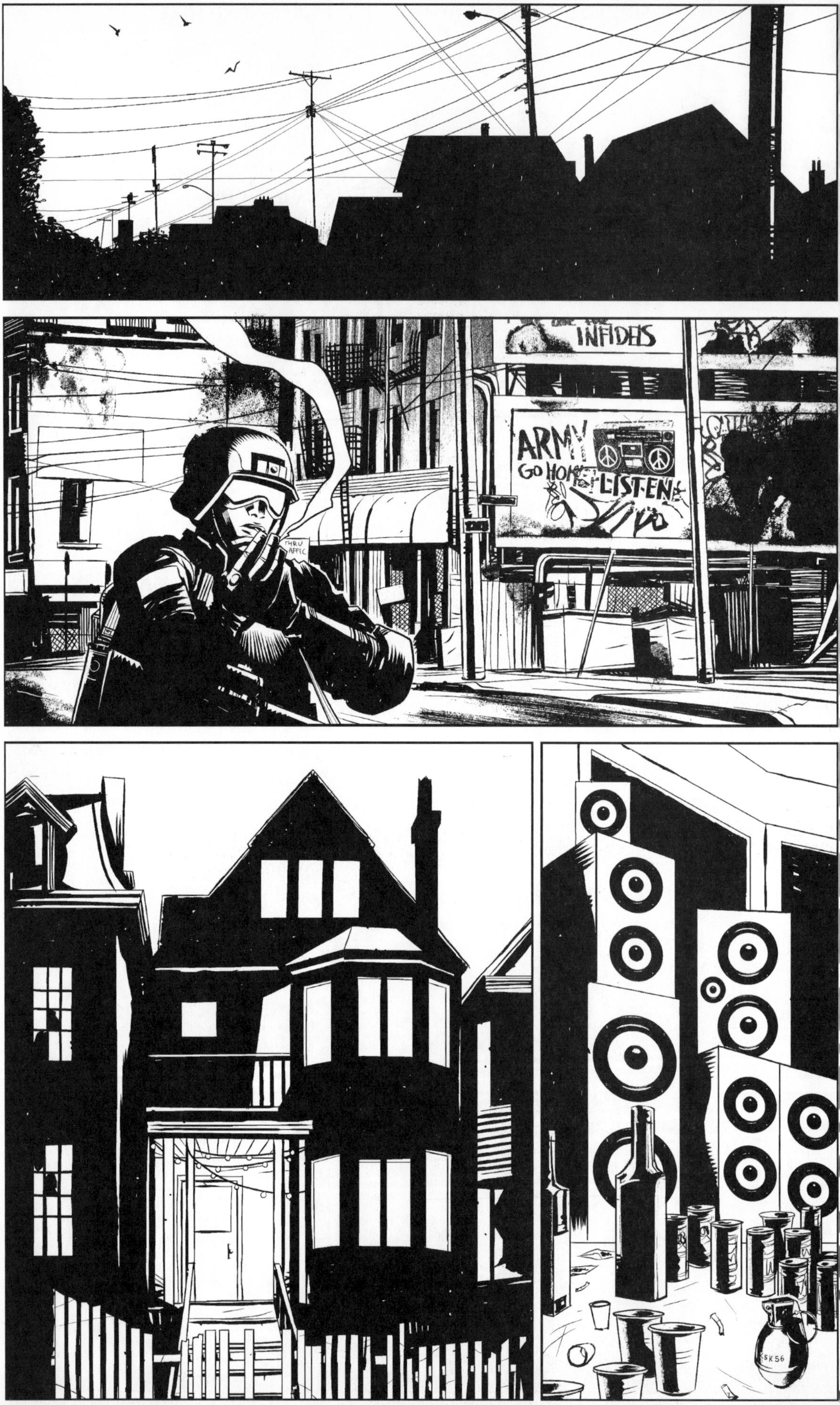
INFIDELS
ARMY GO HOME
LIST-EN
THRU
AFFIC
5K56

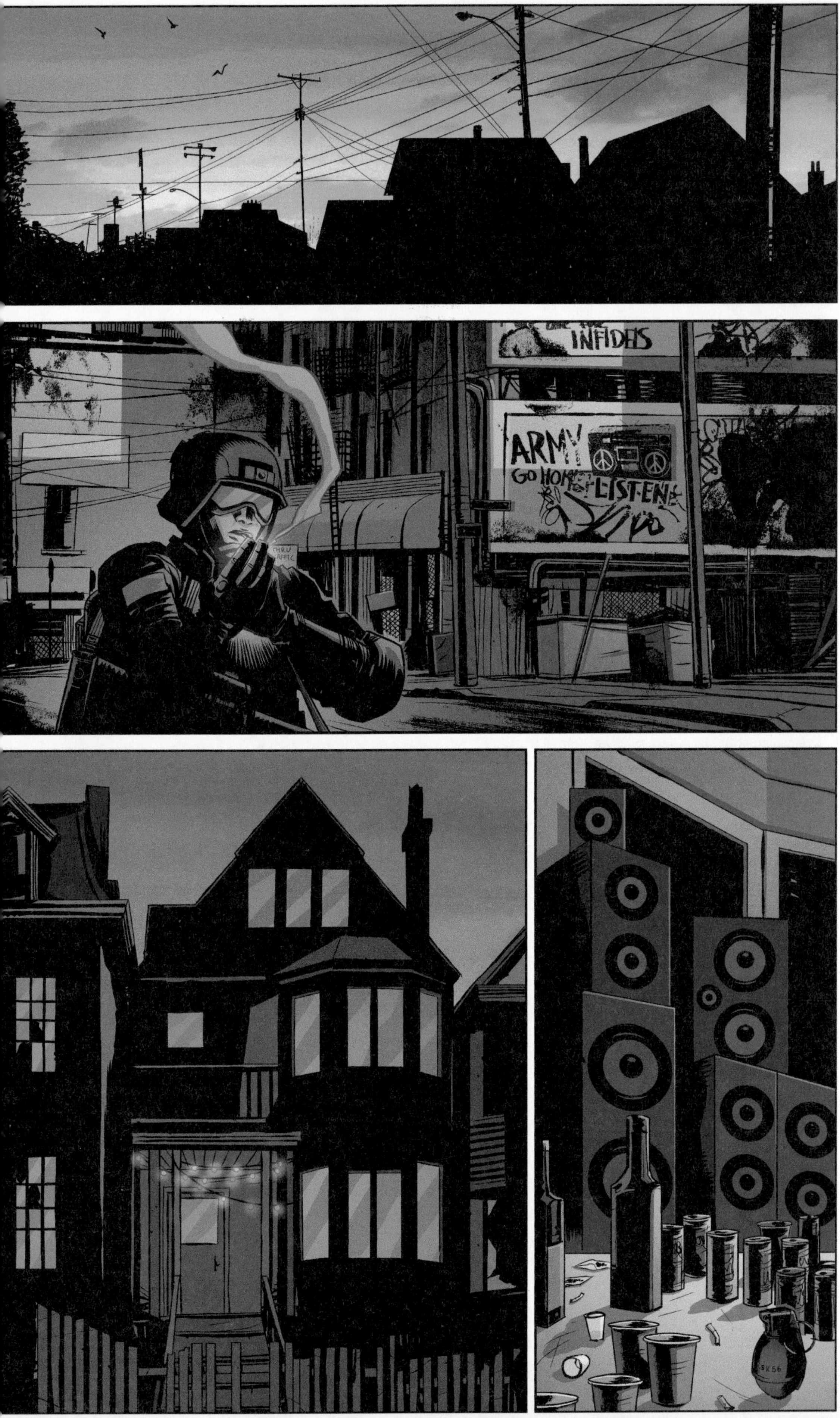
INFIDELS
ARMY
GO HOME!
LIST-EN

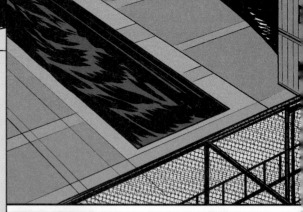

You have the distinction of being the first guest artist on DMZ. On top of that, you told the origin story of Zee, a character very near and dear to Brian. Was that daunting to jump into?

It was great. I was thrilled. It was different from anything else I'd done before, so I was really into it. Zee's a fantastic character, and I liked the idea of showing her backstory. I love design opportunities, and there were plenty to be tackled on my first issue of DMZ.

Is your general approach to DMZ different from other projects? Does the fact that Brian began as an artist change the dynamic?

To your first question, sure, because getting the tone right is really important. I tried to shed some of the "cartoony" qualities that I'd had up to that point. Issues 35 and 36 came about 60 pages into 99 DAYS, so I'd hardened up my style significantly by then. Approaching DMZ has to be specific because it's a realized universe. Drawing it is like taking a trip there. It has to feel familiar, but it's been transformed into a unique place.

The fact that Brian is an artist and designer shows in the way he writes for other artists. The scripts always make sense; it's all stuff you can actually draw. There are no physical contradictions. There isn't an ounce of fat on any of it.

What's Brian like to collaborate with? He admits he's not a big collaborator type, very much an internal thinker. So, tell the truth! What's the dirt?

I enjoy getting the opportunity to work with him. I think his writing pulls a certain quality out of my work. I think he likes the way my art turns out on his scripts. I get a degree of freedom and leeway I don't always get to experience, and I never get bored with the work. I'm the luckiest dude in the world. I'm personally a bit of a lunatic, so maybe it takes opposite ends of the spectrum to unite in the middle!

You worked on Zee's account of the Day 204 Massacre, and the Day 204 posters are particularly iconic.

The posters are Brian. I re-inked over them in my hand, but it's his design. That issue was brutal, there's some really intense stuff in there. Structurally, it was interesting, too, Matty moving from interview to interview, with small flashouts. That was 2007, so I was starting to get more confident in the way I was working my style.

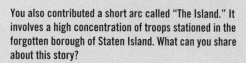

You also contributed a short arc called "The Island." It involves a high concentration of troops stationed in the forgotten borough of Staten Island. What can you share about this story?

The opening where we go from sea, to street, to house party, and through the party... the way that Brian moves Matty through that scene is so awesome. It's subtle, but it's so good, and I'd never drawn a sequence like that before. It's nine pages, and we accompany Matty from crossing to Staten Island at high speed on water, past a bombed-out financial district, to him perched on a roof looking out over a chaotic soldier party where they're fighting for fun, with Christmas lights lighting the yard. C'mon, when am I ever gonna get to draw that again?! There's some stuff in issue 36 I like, specifically the page where the Free States guy is in the cage bumming the light from his former buddy, and the panel where the two sides square off, where the Free States guys have screwdrivers and shit.

You mentioned the Vertigo Crime book 99 DAYS, written by Matteo Casali. What else is next for you, any other work with Brian on the horizon?

In 99 DAYS, Matteo and I crafted a very cinematic noir story, and I'm excited for people to check it out. There's some really dark stuff in there, my stuff got really technical and my style got really tight. Yeah… Brian and I are currently working together on a new project. Details will come later! [Note: This project turned out to be *The Massive* at Dark Horse.]

Why do you think DMZ is such a long-running success?

It's a complete world, and a one-of-a-kind work of fiction in any medium. Brian, Riccardo, John Paul Leon, Jeromy Cox, Will Dennis and Mark Doyle on the editorial side, and everyone else who had a hand in it really brought it. I'm happy to have had some time with DMZ.

End Transmission

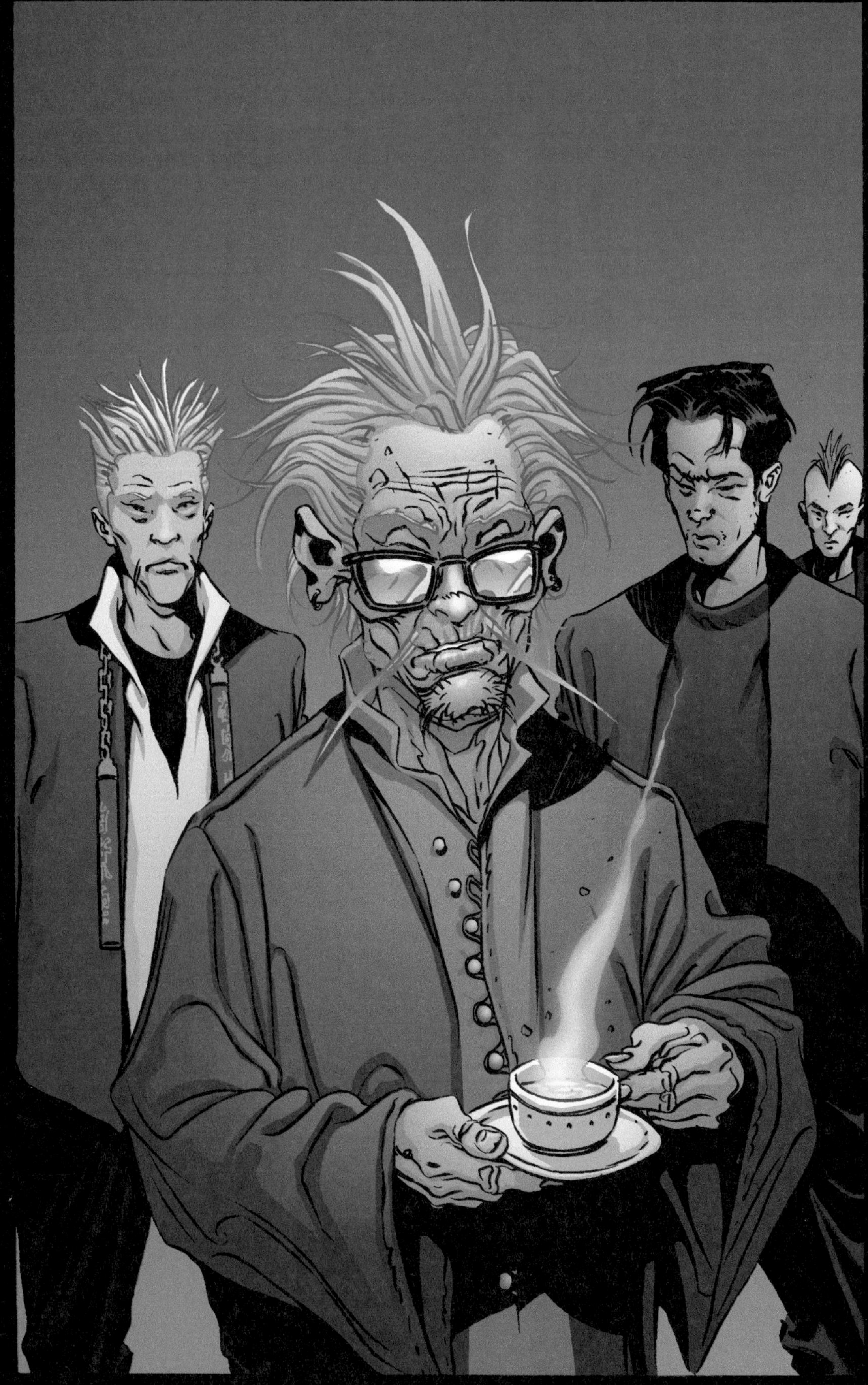

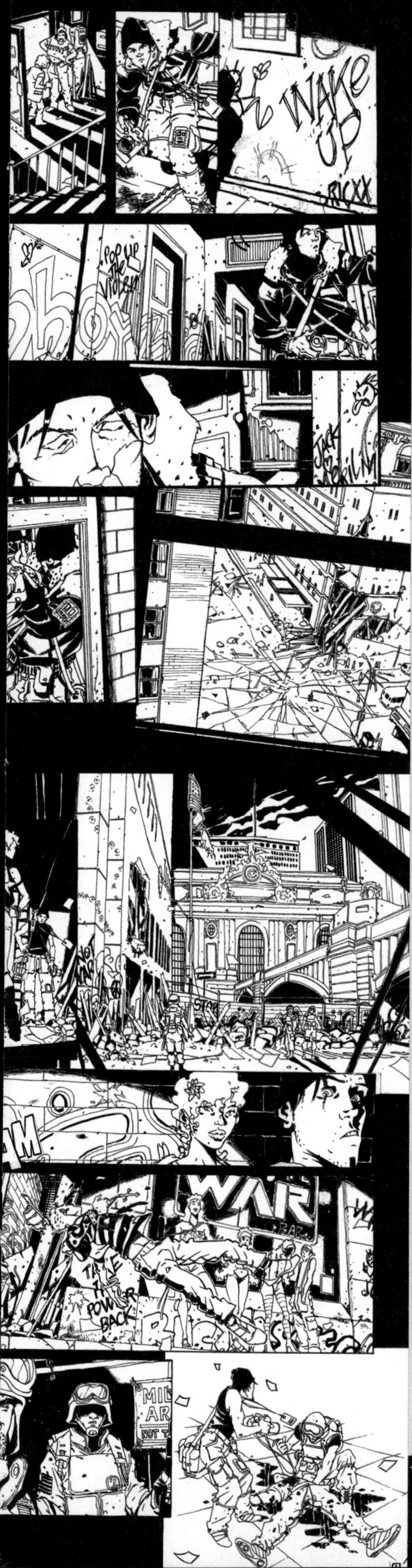
WAKE UP
WAR

RICCARDO BURCHIELLI INTERVIEW

Riccardo, tell us about your background. Did you attend art school or are you self-taught? What other projects have you worked on in Italy?

I actually never attended art school. I'm self-taught, and everything I know I learned from studying the works of the artists I most admired, and spending many long nights awake while drawing. I was hired by DC Comics pretty early in my comics career. Prior to DMZ, I had just drawn three *John Doe* books. This series, published by the historic Eura Editoriale, eventually developed a small cult following and was, up to that point, my only experience as a professional in the comics industry.

What tools do you typically use for illustration? Are you still pencilling analog, or have you transitioned to digital?

I'm still an analog guy. I love to feel the texture of the paper under my fingers and to get my hands dirty with brushes and pencils. I have to admit that in the past couple of years, I've been thinking about going digital, but just to speed up the initial layouts and pencils, because I would never give up the effect of "real" inks and the joy of having stains all over my hands!

Your work was historically in black and white up until DMZ, so how do you feel about other artists coloring your work?

I've always tried not to think about colors. Just to be clear, my pages have been blessed with colors by some of the best professionals in the field and they did some pretty amazing work on my stuff, but if I think about the way I'd like my work to be published if I had my way, it would always be in black and white. Not for a particularly esoteric philosophical reason, it's just the way I'm cut as an artist. I always wanted to draw some black and white pages for DMZ. It usually wasn't possible to have them on the regular series, so I had to wait for the right opportunity to arise, and the short in special issue #50 ["Heart of North Jersey"] was just the right one.

Will Dennis mentioned that you did some unprompted "tryout" pages for DMZ that landed you the job, correct?

Exactly. Will Dennis visited the Napoli Comic-Con in 2003, if memory serves. He was able to review some of my original *John Doe* pages and took a few back with him to New York. It was one year later, and he called me saying he'd love to do something with me, and after some test pages and studies I did, he gave me the opportunity to work on DMZ. I remember they asked me for character sketches first,

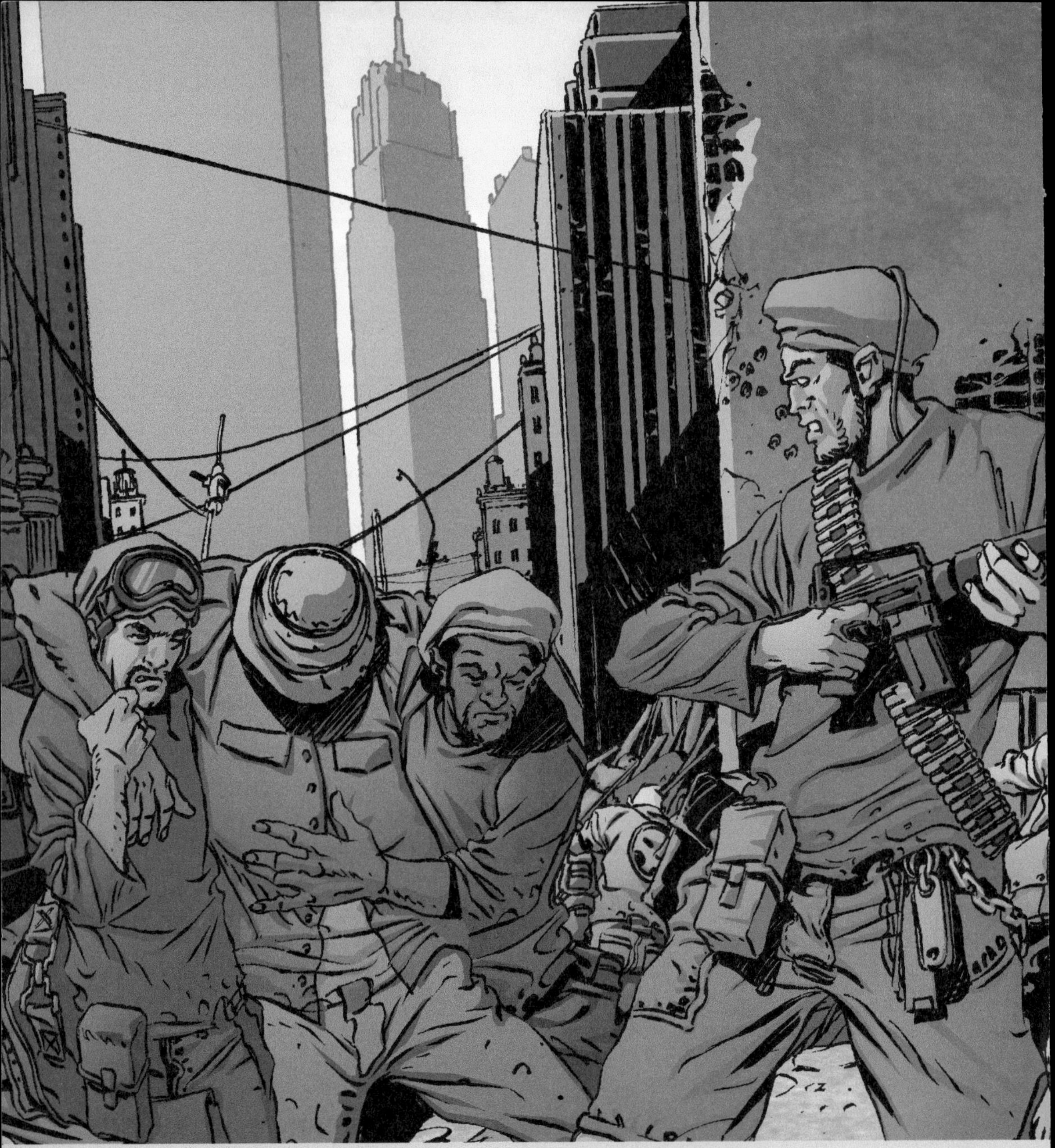

but I was so excited that I just drew two or three full action-packed pages with my interpretation of New York City under siege. I got the gig the same afternoon. It was incredible. I still can't believe it really happened.

What's it like collaborating with Brian?

Working with Brian is fantastic. He's a great, talented writer. He gives the artist a lot of room for their own vision. With DMZ, even if he'd already done most of the basic visuals on paper or in his head, he always gave me all the freedom I needed in order to build the series' unique aesthetic vibe and character designs. We clicked immediately and we're still very good friends. Working with him has been a great experience that shaped me as an artist.

What was your approach to the art? How did you formulate the character designs?

I just love to draw dozens of different characters. I grew up reading Italian comics, but also Spanish and South American ones, which influenced me heavily. The artists working on those books were real masters in character design. I think this trait really resonated with me and became a part of my identity as an artist. In real life, each face tells the story of the individual who wears it. If only we could stop and observe people, I think we would appreciate the great beauty that surrounds us every day. This is really what mesmerizes me watching movies and reading comics. I just try to capture that feeling in my work.

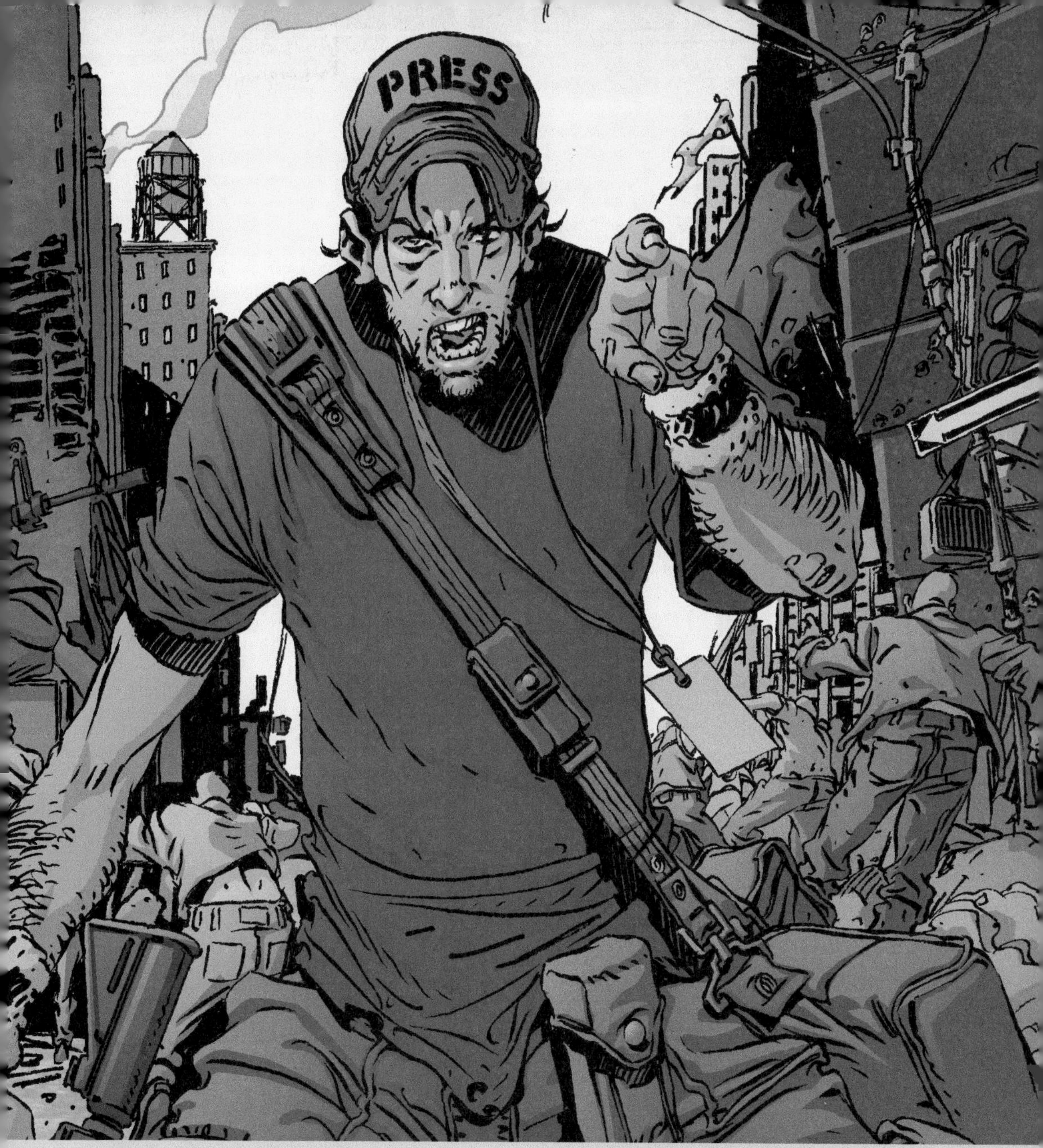
PRESS

Was it intimidating creating imagery of the most famous city in the world? How did you obtain reference photos of New York while living in Italy?

I ransacked books and websites. But I never actually realized what NYC really is before moving there for a brief period. It's a living thing, a huge creature full of thousands of feelings. Sometimes you can almost hear it breathe.

Do you have a favorite panel issue, or moment, something you're particularly proud of, that you'd like to comment on?

It really ties back to the character design topic. One of the moments I'm most proud of is the creation of Wilson. In that particular case, I drew a very raw and quick sketch, because I thought he wouldn't be a recurring character, but just a minor one. Instead, he grew to be one of the most beloved characters in the whole series, thanks to the writing, and the readers' love. Thank God I got him right!

How would you like DMZ to be remembered?

I'd like DMZ to be remembered as the phenomenon that it really was: a bold, raw story, with lots of social commentary on western civilization and the world we live in, one which speaks of a dystopian near-future, which warns us about our present path.

End Transmission

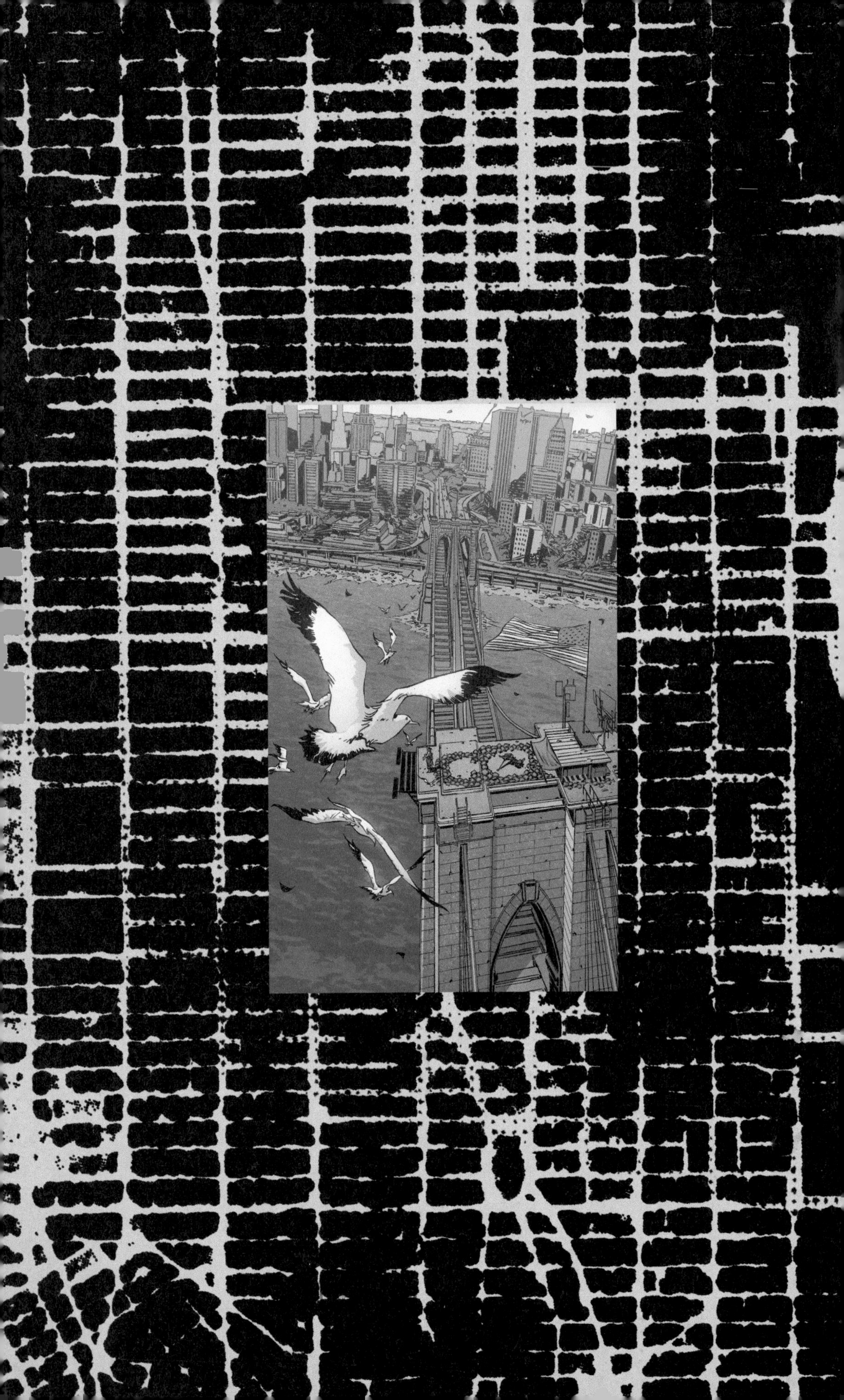